Rules of Play

Rules of Play
Game Design Fundamentals

Katie Salen and Eric Zimmerman

The MIT Press
Cambridge, Massachusetts
London, England

book design and photography | Katie Salen

This book was set in 8.8-point Myriad by Katie Salen and was printed and bound in the United States of America.

Library of Congress Cataloging-in-Publication Data

Salen, Katie.
    Rules of play : game design fundamentals / Katie Salen and Eric Zimmerman.
    p. cm.
    Includes bibliographical references and index.
    ISBN 0-262-24045-9 (hc : alk. paper)
    1. Computer games—Design. 2. Computer games—Programming. I. Zimmerman, Eric. II. Title.
QA76.76.C672S25 2003
794.8'1526—dc21
                                                                 2003045923

10 9 8 7 6 5 4 3 2 1

To those for whom the game is made.
Mr. Triggs, Tom Ockerse, H.F., and Dad; Enid, Gil, Laura, and Zach
In gratefulness and love.

Thank you to the many individuals who gave their time, expertise, support, friendship, and ideas; to the game designers and developers who created the incredible body of work we examined in the course of our study, including Reiner Knizia, James Ernest, Kira Synder, Frank Lantz, and Richard Garfield, who all contributed original work to this volume; to our fearless readers John Sharp, Frank Lantz, Henk van Assen, Ranjit Bhatnagar, Nancy Nowacek, Mark Owens, Peter Lee, and Julian Kücklich; to our own teachers and students who helped inspired clarity and invention; to Doug Sery and the rest of MIT Press; and most of all to our families and friends, who waited patiently for us to join them back in the real world. We could not have done it without you.

Contents

For hundreds of years, the field of game design has drifted along under the radar of culture, producing timeless masterpieces and masterful time-wasters without drawing much attention to itself—without, in fact, behaving like a "field" at all. Suddenly, powered by the big bang of computer technology, game design has become a very big deal and the source of some provocative questions about the future of art and entertainment.

In addressing these questions, the book you are holding raises quite a few of its own. On its surface *Rules of Play* appears to be calm and reasonable, carefully laying out a broad theoretical framework for understanding the field of game design. But beneath this calm surface, the book actually stakes out a controversial position in a dramatic, ongoing discussion about what games are and what they could become.

In fact, from certain angles this book appears to have the burning impatience of a manifesto. What is the nature of this impatience? To some extent it is the frustration of workers who are asked to build a cathedral using only a toothbrush and a staplegun. Games are remarkably complex, both in their internal structure and in the various kinds of player experiences they create. But there exists no integrated set of conceptual tools for thinking about games. Until recently, if you were a game designer interested in the theoretical underpinnings of your field, you would be forced to stitch together a set of perspectives from sociology, anthropology, psychology, and mathematics, each of which brought its blindman's view of the elephant, and none of which considered games as a creative domain.

More recently, within the field itself there has emerged a Babel of competing methodologies. Most of these have a practical focus on the nuts-and-bolts questions of the creative process of game design; few of them have attempted to ground their insights in a general theoretical system. But the impatience that gives this book its undercurrent of urgency is more than a response to the field's underdeveloped level of discourse. Why, after all, does game design need a theoretical framework? There is something more than insight, knowledge, and understanding at stake here.

Remember that the authors of this book are not just academics looking at games from the outside; they are themselves active practitioners. Like many people working in this field, they are driven by the feeling that despite the breathtaking pace of recent technical and commercial advancement, games have remained creatively stunted. On the one hand, there is a sense of boundless potential, the much-discussed possibility that games could succeed film as the defining form of popular

Frank Lantz

FOREWORD

culture for the new century. On the other hand, there is the reality of the game store—endless racks of adolescent power fantasies, witless cartoon characters, and literal-minded sports simulations.

To get a feeling for the sense of potential that fuels this impatience, consider the vast kinds of experiences games can produce—complex networks of desire and pleasure, anxiety and release, wonder and knowledge. Games can inspire the loftiest form of cerebral cognition and engage the most primal physical response, often simultaneously. Games can be pure formal abstractions or wield the richest possible representational techniques. Games are capable of addressing the most profound themes of human existence in a manner unlike any other form of communication—open-ended, procedural, collaborative; they can be infinitely detailed, richly rendered, and yet always responsive to the choices and actions of the player.

But where are the games that explore these diverse possibilities? Instead of the rich spectrum of pleasures games are capable of providing, we seem cursed to suffer an embarrassment of variations on the all-too familiar pleasures of running and jumping, of Hide and Go Seek and Tag, of Easter egg hunts and Cops and Robbers. And what happened to the explosion of formal experimentation during the early days of computer games? For a while it seemed that every other title was a fresh attempt to answer the question "What can you do with a computer?" Compare that with the current crop of computer games, the majority of which seem to be addressing the question "What can you do while controlling an avatar that is moving through a simulated three-dimensional space?"

This, then, is what is at stake: a vast discrepancy between the radical possibilities contained in the medium and the conservative reality of mainstream game development. And this is the way in which *Rules of Play* is more than a conceptual analysis of what games do; it is also an examination of what they *can* do, and by extension what they *should* do.

One of the implications of *Rules of Play's* approach to its subject is that the proper way to understand games is from an aesthetic perspective, in the same way that we address fields such as architecture, literature, or film. This should not be confused with the domain of visual aesthetics, which is simply one facet of a game's creative content. Like film, which uses dramatic storytelling, visual composition, sound design, and the complex dynamic organizational process of editing in the construction of a single work, the field of game design has its own unique aesthetic.

As laid out in the following pages, the real domain of game design is the aesthetics of interactive systems. Even before computers existed, creating games meant designing dynamic systems for players to inhabit. Every game, from Rock-Paper-Scissors to The Sims and beyond is a space of possibility that the players explore. Defining this space is the collaborative work of the game design process.

Rules of Play is perhaps the first serious attempt to lay out an aesthetic approach to the design of interactive systems. At the dawn of the twenty-first century, interactive systems surround us not just as the material reality of our lives but also as a key conceptual model for understanding the world and our place in it, just as mechanical systems did for the Victorians. This is one reason that the importance of this book's project should not be underestimated.

There is a reasonable oppositional perspective to the one I have imputed to the authors of *Rules of Play*. It goes something like this: all of this talk about aesthetics smacks of pretension and self-aggrandizement. Games are recreation, their purpose is to amuse us, and we shouldn't expected them to achieve profound levels of creative expression or relentlessly push creative boundaries. They are simply entertainment.

There isn't much that you can say to this argument except to point out that pop culture has a surprising way of moving back and forth between the trivial and the profound. One person's harmless waste of time might be another's bid for transcendence—and games are certainly one of the best examples of how entertainment can be far from simple. In any event, the argument itself molds the subject of this debate. If enough people believe that games are meant to be mindless fun, then this is what they will become. If enough people believe that games are capable of greater things, then they will inevitably evolve and advance.

We know that games are getting very big, very fast. But it is too early to tell exactly what direction their evolution will take. At this stage the entire field has the unpredictable energy of something enormous, balanced on one thin edge, still vulnerable to the effects of even a slight pressure. Under the guise of examining this curious object, the authors of *Rules of Play* are giving it an energetic shove.

Of course, if you are holding this book then you also have a hand in it yourself.

Which way will you push?

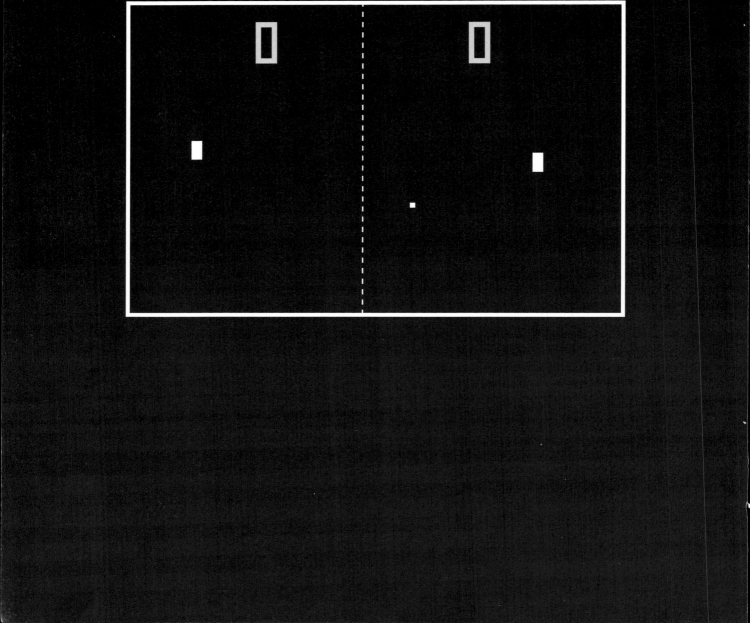

People love pong.

They do. But why?

Really. What's to love? There isn't much to the game: a pair of paddles move two blunt white lines on either side of a black screen, a blocky excuse for a ball bounces between them, and if you miss the ball, your opponent scores a point. The first player to score fifteen points wins. Big deal. Yet despite its almost primitive simplicity, Pong creates meaningful play.

In video game years, Pong is ancient. Originally designed by Ralph Baer for the Magnavox Odyssey home video game system, in 1972 Pong was engineered into an arcade machine and a home console by Nolan Bushnell and Atari. It is no exaggeration to say that Pong was an overnight sensation. The first prototype was released to the public in a bar called Andy Capp's, in Sunnyvale, California, near the Atari headquarters. According to computer game historians, the first night that the glowing TV monitor and cabinet were installed in a corner of the bar, patrons were intrigued but confused. The instructions read only, *Avoid missing ball for high score.* Someone familiar with quarter-operated pinball machines eventually plunked in a coin and watched the ball shoot from side to side as the scores racked up. One of the players finally nudged a paddle, and the ball bounced off with a satisfying "pong" sound. That was enough to tell them what to do, and they began to play. By the end of the first game, both players had learned to volley. By the end of the first night, everyone in the bar had tried a game or two. The next morning, a line had formed outside Andy Capp's: people couldn't wait to play more Pong.[1]

Pong is still alive and well today. You can play Pong via emulators and in Internet banner ads. Clever homages to Pong such as Battle Pong and Text Pong thrive on the web. Pong features prominently in classic gaming flea markets and fan conventions. The game publisher Infogrames released a souped-up, 3D version of Pong a few years ago. Most importantly, the original is still fun to play. When the Super Pong Games IV at gameLab is hooked up to the TV, it never fails to gather a crowd.

All of which brings us back to the question: Why? Why do people love Pong?

Although this is not a book about Pong, or about computer and video games, it is a book about game design. It is crucial for game designers to understand why people play games and why some games are so well-loved. Why do people play Pong? We can think of many reasons:

PREFACE

Pong | Atari

It is simple to play. The one-line instructions and intuitive knob interface makes Pong approachable and easy to understand. There are no hidden features to unlock or special moves to learn.

Every game is unique. Because the ball can travel anywhere on the screen, Pong is an open-ended game with endless possibilities. Pong rewards dedicated play: it is easy to learn, but difficult to master.

It is an elegant representation. Pong is, after all, a depiction of another game: Table Tennis. The abstracted nature of Pong, where your avatar is reduced to a single white line, creates an immediately satisfying physical and perceptual relationship to the game.

It is social. It takes two to play Pong. Through playing the game, you interact with another human being. Pong's social circle also extends beyond two players: it makes a great spectator sport.

It is fun. Simple though it may seem, it is genuinely fun to interact with Pong. Players derive pleasure from the game for many different reasons, from the pleasure of competition and winning to the satisfyingly tactile manipulation of the knob.

It is cool. As a cultural artifact, Pong is a poster child for the hip, low-fi graphics of classic arcade gaming. It evokes nostalgia for afternoons spent in the living-room with friends, huddled around the TV playing video games, eating Cheetos and swigging Mountain Dew.

People love Pong for all of these reasons and more. The interactive, representational, social, and cultural aspects of Pong simultaneously contribute to the experience of play. Games are as complex as any other form of designed culture; fully to appreciate them means understanding them from multiple perspectives.

Pong and the games of its time did something revolutionary. They turned the one-way interactivity of the television on its head, transforming viewers into players, permitting them not just to watch a media image, but to *play* with it. This two-way electronic communication engaged players in hours of meaningful interaction, achieved through the design of a white ball bouncing back and forth on a simple black screen. Although Pong was the product of technical innovation and a unique economic vision, it was also an act of *game design*.

As game designers, have we fully taken into account the implications of this revolutionary act? Do we really understand the medium in which we work or the field of design to which we belong? Can we articulate what it is that generates meaningful play in any game, whether a video game, a board game, a crossword puzzle, or an athletic contest?

The truth? Not yet. Compare game design to other forms of design, such as architecture or graphic design. Because of its status as an emerging discipline, game design hasn't yet crystallized as a field of inquiry. It doesn't have its own section in the library or bookstore. You can't (with a few exceptions) get a degree in it. The culture at large does not yet see games as a noble, or even particularly useful, endeavor. Games are one of the most ancient forms of designed human interactivity, yet from a design perspective, we still don't really know what games are.

Our hope is that this book will inform and inspire those interested in designing games. Its purpose is to help game designers create their own games, their own concepts, their own design strategies and methodologies. The ideas and examples we offer represent one way of looking closely at games, with room for more to come. Pong is just the beginning.

This is why we were compelled to write this book: not to define, once and for all, what game design is, but to provide critical tools for understanding games. Not to claim and colonize the unexplored terrain of game design, but to scout out some of its features so that other game designers can embark on their own expeditions. We hope that this book will be a catalyst, a facilitator, a kick in the ass. Take these concepts and run with them, quickly, meaningfully, with the same kind of joy that the very first players of Pong must have felt.

We're all in this together. Are you ready to play?

Katie Salen and Eric Zimmerman
New York City, May 2003

Notes

1. Scott Cohen, *Zap: The Rise and Fall of Atari* (New York: McGraw-Hill, 1984), p. 17.

About This Book

1

What Is This Book About?

This book is about games, all kinds of games: paper-based strategy games and first person shooters, classical board games and glitzy gambling games; math puzzles and professional sports; austere text adventures and giggly teenage party games. This book links these diverse play activities within a common framework—a framework based in *game design*.

In *The Study of Games,* Brian Sutton-Smith writes, "Each person defines games in his own way—the anthropologists and folklorists in terms of historical origins; the military men, businessmen, and educators in terms of usages; the social scientists in terms of psychological and social functions. There is overwhelming evidence in all this that the meaning of games is, in part, a function of the ideas of those who think about them."[1] What, meaning, then, does the *game designer* bring to the study of games? What does it mean to look at games from a game design perspective?

To answer this question, we first need to clarify what we mean by "game designer." A game designer is a particular kind of designer, much like a graphic designer, industrial designer, or architect. A game designer is not necessarily a programmer, visual designer, or project manager, although sometimes he or she can also play these roles in the creation of a game. A game designer might work alone or as part of a larger team. A game designer might create card games, social games, video games, or any other kind of game. The focus of a game designer is designing *game play,* conceiving and designing rules and structures that result in an experience for players.

Thus game design, as a discipline, requires a focus on games in and of themselves. Rather than placing games in the service of another field such as sociology, literary criticism, or computer science, our aim is to study games within their own disciplinary space. Because game design is an emerging discipline, we often borrow from other areas of knowledge—from mathematics and cognitive science; from semiotics and cultural studies. We may not borrow in the most orthodox manner, but we do so in the service of helping to establish a field of game design proper.

This book is about game *design,* not game *development.* It is not a "how to" book, offering tips and tricks for making successful digital games. It is not a book about digital game programming or choosing development tools; it is not about writing design documents or generating game ideas. And it is definitely not about development team dynamics or about funding, marketing, and distributing games. As a book on game design it is not a general introduction to games, a history of games, or a journalistic account of the people and circumstances that create games. There are plenty of books that cover all of these topics very well.

Instead, *Rules of Play* provides something altogether different. Bridging the theoretical and practical aspects of making games, we look closely at games as designed systems, discovering patterns within their complexity that bring the challenges of game design into full view. As we explore game design as a design practice, we outline not only the concepts behind the creation of meaningful play (a core idea of this book), but also concrete methods for putting these concepts to use in your games. Written with the interests and needs of practicing designers, students, and educators in mind, our approach comes from our own experience of designing games, playing games, and teaching game design.

But the book is not just for game designers. In writing *Rules of Play,* we quickly realized that it has direct application to fields outside game design. The concepts and models, case studies, exercises, and bibliographies can be useful to interactive designers, architects, product designers, and other creators of interactive systems. Similarly, our focus on understanding games in and of themselves can benefit the emerging academic study of games in fields as diverse as sociology, media studies, and cultural policy. Engagement with ideas, like engagement with a game, is all about the play the ideas make possible. Even if you are not a game designer, we think you will find something here that lets you play with your own line of work in a new way.

Establishing a Critical Discourse

One way to describe the project of this book is to say that we are working to establish a critical discourse for game design. We agree with veteran game designer Warren Spector that "It is absolutely vital that we start to build a vocabulary that allows us to examine, with some degree of precision, how games evoke emotional-intellectual responses in players".[2] As a nascent field of inquiry, there are not yet well-developed ways of talking about games and how they function.

What is the point of establishing a critical discourse? Simply put, a critical vocabulary lets us talk to each other. It lets us share ideas and knowledge, and in doing so, expands the borders of our emerging field. Media theorist and game scholar Henry Jenkins identifies four ways that building a critical discourse around games can assist not just game designers, but the field as a whole:

- *Training:* A common language facilitates the education of game designers, letting them explore their medium in more variety and depth.

- *Generational Transfer:* Within the field, a disciplinary vocabulary lets game designers and developers pass on skills and knowledge, rather than solving the same problems over and over in isolation.

- *Audience-building:* In finding a way to speak about them, games can be reviewed, critiqued, and advertised to the public in more sophisticated ways.

- *Buffer Against Criticism:* There are many factions that would seek to censor and regulate the content and contexts for gaming, particularly computer and video games. A critical discourse gives us the vocabulary and understanding to defend against these attacks.[3]

Creating a critical discourse requires that we look at games and the game design process from the ground up, proposing methods for the analysis of games, assessing what makes a great game great, and asking questions about what games are and how they function. The result is a deeper understanding of game design that can lead to genuine innovation in the practice of making games.

Part of creating a critical discourse is defining concepts, but arriving at such a vocabulary is no simple task, for it involves creating definitions for words that often thread their way through multiple and contradictory contexts. One challenge of our project has been formulating a set of definitions for terms such as "game," "design," "interactivity," "system," "play," and "culture," terms that form the foundation of our critical vocabulary. As we explore the largely uncharted terrain of game design, definitions stake out boundaries, the way a set of points define a plane in space.

Practically speaking, defining terms is useful. But an overemphasis on definitions can be dangerous. Held in too orthodox a manner, definitions become a way of shutting down communication and insight. For us, a definition is not a closed or scientific representation of "reality." For a designer, the value of a definition is its ability to serve as a critical tool for understanding and solving design problems. In other words, by including definitions, our intention is not to exclude other definitions that might complement or contradict our own. We wholeheartedly acknowledge that our definitions, concepts, and models leave some things out and work better in some circumstances than others. But this doesn't lessen their overall utility.

It is often along the seams and cracks formed when competing definitions bump up against one another that new ideas are born. Our hope for game design is that it becomes a field as rich as any other, filled with vibrant discussion and dialogue as well as virulent debate and disagreement.

Ways of Looking

A game is a particular way of looking at something, anything.
*—**Clark C. Abt,** Serious Games*

Social theorist Clark C. Abt makes a powerful suggestion. In his claim that a game is a particular way of looking at something, at anything, we find inspiration for our own approach to game design. How can we use games as a way to understand aesthetics, communication, culture, and other areas of our world that seem so intertwined with games? Conversely, how can we use our understanding of these areas to enrich our practice of designing games? Too often, analyses and readings of games simply do not do justice to their complexity. Game designer and theorist Jesper Juul has made the comment that theories about games tend to fall into two camps: *Everything is a game* ("War is a game; politics are a game; life is a game; everything is a game!") or *Games are X* ("Games are an interactive storytelling medium."; "Games are how a child learns about rules.").[4]

If games are not everything, nor just one thing, what are they? Perhaps they are many things. It would be strange for us to say, for example, that poetry *is* storytelling. Although storytelling is one way of understanding poetry, it is just one of many possible perspectives. We could also explore poetry formally, within the context of rhyme and meter, or historically, with an emphasis on printing technologies. Each of these perspectives offers a valid way of looking at poetry—yet utilizing just one of them gives access to only part of the total picture. On the other hand, these frames, and many others, considered together begin to sketch out the heterogeneous and multifaceted cultural phenomena called poetry. In *Rules of Play,* this is exactly what we do with games. Our general strategy is to provide multiple points of view for understanding. In doing so, we hope to avoid the common pitfalls Juul mentions while being true to the complex and polymorphous nature of games.

Is this approach appropriate for design? Absolutely. In his book *Notes on the Synthesis of Form,* architect Christopher Alexander wrestles with the challenges of design, describing a methodology that centers on the inherent complexity of design problems. His argument is based in part on the assumption that clarity in form cannot be achieved until there is first clarity in the designer's mind and actions. Alexander asks us to consider the range of factors affecting the design of a kettle.

> Let us look again at just what kind of difficulty the designer faces. Take, for example, the design of a simple kettle. He has to invent a kettle, which fits the context of its use. It must not be too small. It must not be hard to pick up when it is hot. It must not be easy to let go of by mistake. It must

not be hard to store in the kitchen. It must not be hard to get the water out of. It must pour cleanly. It must not let the water in it cool too quickly. The material it is made out of must not cost too much. It must be able to withstand the temperature of boiling water. It must not be too hard to clean on the outside. It must not be a shape which is too hard to machine. It must not be a shape which is unsuitable for whatever reasonably priced metal it is made of. It must not be too hard to assemble, since this costs man-hours of labor. It must not corrode in steamy kitchens. Its inside must not be too difficult to keep free of scale. It must not be hard to fill with water. It must not be uneconomical to heat small quantities of water in, when it is not full. It must not appeal to such a minority that it cannot be manufactured in an appropriate way because of its small demand. It must not be so tricky to hold that accidents occur when children or invalids try to use it. It must not be able to boil dry and burn out without warning. It must not be unstable on the stove while it is boiling.[5]

Alexander's answer to the challenge of complexity is to organize and classify aspects of the design problem at hand. The patterns that arise as a result of this analysis allow the designer to, as Alexander puts it, "overcome the difficulties of complexity." As the designer systematizes elements of the problem, he or she gives it shape, casting the problem in a whole new light.

Games too, share in this degree of complexity. As products of *human culture,* games fulfill a range of needs, desires, pleasures, and uses. As products of *design culture,* games reflect a host of technological, material, formal, and economic concerns. It would be ineffective (and even silly) to try and view such a complex phenomenon from a single perspective. To do so would be to miss most of the design problem entirely. Our solution? *Game design schemas.*

Game Design Schemas

Most of the chapters of this book are organized under the heading of a game design schema. A *schema* is a way of framing and organizing knowledge. A *game design schema* is a way of understanding games, a conceptual lens that we can apply to the analysis or creation of a game. What are some of the game design schemas we employ in the course of this book? We look at games through the mathematical lens of probability. We look at them as contexts for social interaction. We look at games as storytelling systems. We look at them as sites of cultural resistance. We do so in every case from the point of view of game design.

We organize these varied points of view according to three *primary schemas,* each one containing a cluster of related schemas. Our primary schemas are **RULES, PLAY,** and **CULTURE***:*

- **RULES** contains formal game design schemas that focus on the essential logical and mathematical structures of a game.

- **PLAY** contains experiential, social, and representational game design schemas that foreground the player's participation with the game and with other players.

- **CULTURE** contains contextual game design schemas that investigate the larger cultural contexts within which games are designed and played.

These schemas not only organize ways of looking at games but also, when taken as a whole, offer a general method for the study of game design. Each schema brings certain aspects of games to light, while building on previous schemas to arrive at a multivalent understanding of games. The three primary schemas are neither mutually exclusive nor scientific in nature. We have not created them as a taxonomy, in order to say "*this* is a feature of **RULES,** *not* a feature of **PLAY.**" Rather, they are conceptual design tools to help focus our thinking for particular design problems.

As a framework, **RULES, PLAY, CULTURE** is not merely a model for game design. It also represents a way of understanding any kind of design. Consider the model applied more broadly:

- **RULES** = the organization of the designed system
- **PLAY** = the human experience of that system
- **CULTURE** = the larger contexts engaged with and inhabited by the system

In analyzing or creating a typeface, for example, you might study the formal rules of the system (how the visual weights of the letterforms relate to each other), the play of the system (the kind of reading experience that the typeface engenders), or the cultural aspects of the system (historical references and the contexts where the typeface will be seen). **RULES, PLAY,** and **CULTURE** is a structure that can facilitate critical design thinking in any design field.

Game Design Fundamentals

Rules of Play is a book about fundamentals. As a design practice, game design has its own essential principles, a system of ideas that define what games are and how they work. Innovation in the field can grow only from a deep understanding of these basic concepts. What are these game design fundamentals? They include understanding design, systems, and interactivity, as well as player choice, action, and outcome. They include a study of rule-making and rule-breaking, complexity and emergence, game experience, game representation, and social game interaction. They include the powerful connection between the rules of a game and the play that the rules engender, the pleasures games invoke, the meanings they construct, the ideologies they embody, and the stories they tell.

As fundamental principles, these ideas form a system of building blocks that game designers arrange and rearrange in every game they create. As unlikely as it may sound, Go, Trivial Pursuit, Dance Dance Revolution, and Unreal Tournament all share the same fundamental principles, articulated in radically different ways. The range of game design expression is vast, deep, and largely unexplored. By clarifying these ideas, we can provide a set of strategies that help you fit these fundamentals to your particular design needs.

Rules of Play is a book for practicing game scholars and designers, but it is also very much about teaching and learning. Game design education represents an important counterpoint to game design theory and practice, for in the classroom the fundamentals established in this book can be explored, dissected, critiqued, and reinvented. In developing material for teaching and learning, we had to ask, *What are the principle elements that constitute a game design curriculum? What courses does the curriculum include, what are the objectives of the courses, what is it that students need to know to become game designers?*

These are questions certain to be raised by colleges, universities, and other professional institutions as they develop educational programs in game design. The needs of these programs are diverse: there is a tremendous difference between a graduate game design degree program in a school of fine arts, an undergraduate minor in game design within a comparative media department, and an industry workshop on game design at a professional conference.

No single curriculum can fit all of these contexts. Rather than design a single program, we have instead provided tools to allow faculty to address their own particular circumstances. We developed the bibliography, suggested readings, case studies, commissioned games, and game design exercises with this kind of flexibility in mind. We believe that a variety of curricula that meet the needs of different (and perhaps competing) perspectives will lead to better games, better game designers, and hours and hours of more meaningful play.

Further Readings

At the end of most of the chapters to follow, we include a list of books to suggest further readings. These readings might be used to construct a syllabus for a class, a handout for a workshop, or to round out curiosity on a topic introduced in the chapter. The selected readings reflect our own idiosyncrasies, and are not meant as a definitive canon for game design theory. However, they do represent what we felt were the most relevant sources on the topic.

Each chapter lists only a handful of further readings, but there are other research sources in this book as well. At the end of the book, we include a few more suggested readings that did not fit into any particular chapter. The chapter footnotes and general bibliography also contain many references that are not found in any of the further readings listings. Following are the suggested readings for this chapter.

Further Reading

The Art of Computer Game Design, by Chris Crawford

Chris Crawford is a game designer who started his career at Atari. He wrote *The Art of Computer Game Design* in 1982, at a time when computers were just beginning to appear in people's homes. The book was one of the very first texts dealing with the nature of game design, and although some of the ideas have been dated by advances in the field, it is still an excellent resource for basic game design principles. The book is out of print, but the text is available online at: <http://www.vancouver.wsu.edu/fac/peabody/gamebook/Coverpage.html>

> *Recommended:*
>
> Chapter 1: What Is a Game?
>
> Chapter 3: A Taxonomy of Computer Games
>
> Chapter 5: The Game Design Sequence

Gamasutra, The Art and Science of Making Games <www.gamasutra.com>

Part of the Gama Network, which includes the Game Developers Conference and Game Developer Magazine, *Gamasutra* is one of the very best game design resources around. The site supports news from the game development industry, editorial features on practical game design problems, and post-mortems of commercial games. They recently added a section on education, publishing more academically-oriented writing on games and game design. We visit this site regularly.

Game Studies: The International Journal of Computer Game Research, edited by Espen Aarseth, Markku Eskelinen, Marie-Laure Ryan, Susana Tosca <www.gamestudies.org>

A good resource for new scholarly writing on games, *Game Studies* is a cross-disciplinary, peer-reviewed journal on computer and video games. Edited by an excellent team of academics and researchers with a deep interest in the study of games, the journal focuses on games research from a humanities and ludology perspective. While the material does not necessarily have a game design focus, the articles offer various models and critiques of larger theoretical issues regarding narrative, media, interactivity, and immersion.

IGDA Curriculum Framework: The Study of Games and Game Development, by the International
Game Developers Association, Education Committee

For the last few years, IGDA members Doug Church, Robin Hunicke, Jason Della Roca, Warren Spector,
and Eric Zimmerman have been creating a document that provides a practical framework for a game
design curriculum. The document not only addresses game design, but also related fields as diverse as
visual design, programming, business, and humanities and social science-based game studies. The
Curriculum Framework is intended for educators and students and takes the form of a modular framework that can be applied to a variety of different contexts. Find the current draft of the document at
<http://www.igda.org/>.

"I Have No Words but I Must Design," by Greg Costikyan

Greg Costikyan is a computer and paper game designer who has written many essays on game design.
I Have No Words was originally published in 1994 in the second issue of *Interactive Fantasy*. The article is
found on Costikyan's website at <http://www.costik.com/nowords.html> and is an attempt to formulate a critical vocabulary for game design. Although short, it is an ambitious and influential essay, and
includes a useful definition of games.

"Rules, Play, and Culture: Checkmate!" by Frank Lantz and Eric Zimmerman

This essay, originally published in 1999 in *Merge Magazine*, is the first appearance of the three-part
Rules/Play/Culture model for thinking about games, which the authors developed while teaching game
design together at New York University. Elements of this model were the basis for the overall structure of
this book. As such, the essay offers a brief and useful overview of these core game design topics.

Notes

1. E.M. Avedon, "The Structural Elements of Games," In *The Study of Games,* edited by E.M. Avedon and
   Brian Sutton-Smith (New York: Wiley, 1971), p. 438.

2. RE:PLAY: Game Design + Game Culture. Online conference, 2000. <www.eyebeam.org.replay>

3. "Computer and Video Games Come of Age. A National Conference to Explore the Current State of an
   Entertainment Medium." February 10–11, 2000. Comparative Media Studies Department, MIT. Transcripts. Henry Jenkins.

4. Jesper Juul, Digital Arts and Culture Conference at Brown University, 2001.

5. Christopher Alexander, *Notes on the Synthesis of Form* (Cambridge: Harvard University Press, 1964), p.
   60.

The Design Process

2

*How do you like that. I'm right back into efficacious play, now planfully impro-
vising a route by turning what looked like a mistake into an alternative way to go.*
—**David Sudnow,** *Pilgrim in the Microworld*

Iterative Design

A game design education cannot consist of a purely theoretical approach to games. This
is true of any design field: designers learn best through the process of design, by directly
experiencing the things they make. Therefore, a large part of their training as students of
game design must involve the creation of games. As conceptual as this book might seem,
its intention is not just to spark debate and analysis but to facilitate the design of games.
In this chapter we offer a number of tools for integrating our ideas about games into the
process of making them.

This book does not provide a hands-on guide to game programming, project management, or other aspects of game development. What it does offer is a way of thinking about
the process of designing games. It is a very simple and powerful approach, one that grows
out of more than a decade of experience in teaching and designing games. We call this
approach *iterative design*. We are certainly not the first to use this term or the design
methodology it represents, but our experience has shown that it is an invaluable tool for
any game designer.

Iterative design is a play-based design process. Emphasizing playtesting and prototyping,
iterative design is a method in which design decisions are made based on the experience
of playing a game while it is in development. In an iterative methodology, a rough version
of the game is rapidly prototyped as early in the design process as possible. This prototype
has none of the aesthetic trappings of the final game, but begins to define its fundamental rules and core mechanics. It is not a visual prototype, but an interactive one. This prototype is played, evaluated, adjusted, and played again, allowing the designer or design
team to base decisions on the successive *iterations* or versions of the game. Iterative
design is a cyclic process that alternates between prototyping, playtesting, evaluation,
and refinement.

Why is iterative design so important for game designers? Because it is not possible to fully anticipate play in advance. It is never possible to completely predict the experience of a game. Is the game accomplishing its design goals? Do the players understand what they are supposed to be doing? Are they having *fun?* Do they want to play again? These questions can never be answered by writing a design document or crafting a set of game rules and materials. They can only be answered by way of play. Through the iterative design process, the game designer becomes a game player and the act of play becomes an act of design. Learning to play a game critically, seeing where it excels and where it grinds to a halt, and being able to implement changes that will push the game toward meaningful play are all core game design skills.

We have a straightforward rule of thumb regarding prototyping and playtesting games: a game prototype should be created and playtested, at the absolute latest, 20 percent of the way into a project schedule. If a game is a two-week student assignment, the students should be playing a version of the game two days after it is assigned. If it is a commercial computer game with a 15-month concept-to-gold schedule, a prototype should be up and running three months into development—at the absolute latest.

Early prototypes are not pretty. They might be paper versions of a digital game, a single-player version of a networked experience, hand-scrawled board and pieces for a strategy wargame, or a butt-ugly interactive mock-up with placeholder artwork. Still, the prototype is more than an interactive slideshow—it is a genuinely playable game that begins to address game design challenges of the project as a whole. The online multiplayer game SiSSYFiGHT 2000 was first prototyped on Post-It notes around a conference table, next as a text-only IRC (Internet Relay Chat) game, and then as a skeletal web-based game, which became the basis for the final application. At each stage, the game prototype was rigorously played, evaluated, tweaked, and played again.

Most paper-based game designers follow an iterative design process, but most digital game designers do not. Typically, a commercial computer game is copiously designed in advance, with extensive storyboards and design documents often hundreds of pages long, completed before any actual game production begins. These documents invariably become obsolete as soon as production development starts. Why? Because the play of a game will always surprise its creators, particularly if the game design is unusual or experimental. Even a veteran designer cannot exactly predict what will and will not work before experiencing the game firsthand. Prototype your game early. Play it throughout the entire design process. Have as many other people as you possibly can play your game, and observe them playing. Let yourself be surprised and challenged. Remain flexible. And don't forget to have fun.

Managing game software development or any kind of game development offers its own challenges, and we are not suggesting that iterative design represents a complete development methodology. Our focus is game design, not game development. Iterative design is just one part of a much larger process for moving a game project from concept to completion. But taken on its own, it is an excellent starting point for a rigorous and effective game design process.

Commissions

One of the best ways to understand iterative design is to study the processes of other game designers. How do they come up with ideas for games? How do they implement, playtest, and refine these ideas? How do their games evolve and change during the design process? In order to present possible answers to these questions, we commissioned four game designers to create games specifically for this book. We asked each designer to design a game that could be printed and played as a supplement to the game design principles covered in the text. In addition (as if that weren't enough!), we asked them to keep a log of their design process, as a way to share the bumps, battles, and roadblocks encountered along the way. These design dairies are rich and varied documents that detail the experience of game design itself. Although each designer presents a very different point of view, all of them make rigorous use of an iterative design process.

And in our humble opinion, the commissioned games are all fun to play. Of course, you will have to decide for yourself. The four games and their accompanying design logs appear in different sections of the book, supplementing a particular chapter or set of chapters. The games use different sets of materials, some printed in the book, others you provide, such as dice, game tokens, or a deck of playing cards. Kira Snyder's game uses the book itself as a game material, whereas Richard Garfield's game uses a gameboard that you must photocopy in order to play. Each game includes a synopsis and rule set, but below is a quick overview of each.

Richard Garfield: Sibling Rivalry (page 106)
A board game for two or more players, Sibling Rivalry is a game of conflict between misbehaving siblings. Players roll dice and move along a series of "tracks" on a board, trying their best to behave badly while still avoiding detection and punishment by their parents.

Frank Lantz: Ironclad (page 284)
Ironclad is a two-payer game composed of two "sub-games" played simultaneously on the same board. One is a game of arena combat between opposing teams of massive, armed robots. The other is a game about two logicians attempting to resolve a philo-

sophical debate. Players play in both games each turn, and no one is certain which game is actually being played until one of the sets of victory conditions is met. Ironclad is played on a checkerboard grid, with Go stones and Checkers pieces.

Kira Snyder: Sneak (page 490)

Sneak is a game of social deception, played with four or more players. One player among the group is secretly assigned the status of double agent, known as the Sneak. Information printed within this book provides players with actions to help reveal who among the group is the Sneak. Earn the most points by successfully identifying the Sneak and by fooling other players into guessing incorrectly.

James Ernest: Caribbean Star (page 588)

Played with a deck of ordinary playing cards, Caribbean Star is a battle between two cruise ship magicians who have been accidentally booked on the same ship. The magicians have exactly one week to prove who is the better magician, a feat that is played out as the magicians show off their skills by strategically composing entertaining magic shows out of cards.

To give insight into a more involved game design process, we commissioned one additional essay. Written by the prolific board game designer Reiner Knizia, the essay describes the conceptual and practical process of designing the Lord of the Rings Board Game. This detailed account of his iterative design process appears immediately following this chapter.

Game Design Exercises

In the pages that follow, we offer a number of practical game design exercises, for students and designers, for use in classrooms and professional workshops, for solo or collaborative efforts, for short-term experiments or long-term theses. There are innumerable possibilities for what a game design exercise might be. Rather than provide an extensive list, we offer a series of examples that you can alter to fit the needs of the context in which you are working. The exercises presented here by no means represent a comprehensive catalog of assignments; they are meant to act as jumping off points for the development of your own game design exercises.

Each exercise listed has a particular *design focus,* corresponding to a chapter or set of chapters in this book. The design focus serves two crucial roles. First, it guides students as they work, giving them a concrete way to direct their thinking and design method. Second, a design focus gives instructors a way to evaluate a project during and after the design process, offering a conceptual framework for analyzing a game's successes and failures. In each exercise, the design focus helps identify the design problem as well as potential solutions.

The exercises are divided into three categories: game creation, game modification, and game analysis. Note that many of them make use of concepts and terms that are explained in the associated chapters. Of course, it goes without saying that all of these exercises should make use of an iterative design process. Learning how to design iteratively is the single most important skill that a game design student can learn.

Computers in the Classroom

The phenomenon of games encompasses more than just computer games, and teaching game design does not have to happen through the creation of games on computers. In our many years of teaching game design, most of our classes have not required students to actually program games. Programming is not the equivalent of game design and as soon as students are tasked with creating games on a computer, programming can quickly become their primary activity.

In our classes, students are asked to focus on core game design issues, issues which are not intrinsic to digital technology. In many cases, the students work off of the computer to create board games, card games, physical games, and social games. Even when the course emphasizes the creation of digital games, game design issues take center stage. This is not to say that it is an either-or situation. For example, a paper-based game design could be later implemented within a digital medium.

There are many ways to incorporate computer technology into game design exercises, such as using a commercial game level editor to design game levels, creating an email-based game in which a human moderator processes the outcome of game actions, or by programming games from scratch. Game design can even be used to teach a conceptual approach to programming, one rooted in iteration, object relationships, actions and outcomes. It goes without saying that the curriculum you create should be based on your own skills and interests—just remember to carefully manage the balance between game design fundamentals and media production skills.

Creation

Game creation exercises involve making a game from scratch. Any of the game creation exercises included here might be designed to take place within a single class, over a weekend, during two or three weeks, or over the course of a single semester.

In each exercise the design focus manifests as a set of parameters given to the students in order to limit and focus their design thinking. For example, a group of students creating a game with a design focus on social interaction might be given parameters specifying the number of players (2, 5, or 20) and the kind of social relationships the game creates (such as camaraderie, animosity, or flirtation). Parameters can also address the medium or format of the game being designed. These parameters can be created before class, written on index cards and randomly distributed to teams of students (teams of 2–4 often work best, depending on the context and the assignment). Alternatively, students might select their own parameters. Typically two or three parameters are sufficient to focus student thinking without suffocating them with too many restrictions.

Information Manipulation

*Design Focus: **Games as Systems of Information*** (chapter 17)

Description: Students are given design parameters based on the use of public and private information. Examples include: all game information is public, some game information is private, one player in the game has special private knowledge, the game contains information that is hidden from all players at the start of the game, etc. In order to keep the game focused on formal issues, rather than the invention of game media, the materials are limited to traditional game materials such as a deck of cards or a board and game pieces.

The Exquisite Corpse Game Game

*Design Focus: **Rules on Three Levels*** (chapter 12)

Description: This formal design exercise works best with groups of three. The first person in each group secretly writes down two game rules for a game that could be played in the classroom, each rule on a separate line of a sheet of paper. The top rule is covered up and the second is left visible. The second person looks at the second rule and writes two more, leaving the last rule visible for the third person to write one more rule and a winning condition. The rules are then revealed and the group has to fashion a game out of the total set of rules. The goal of the exercise is to see how rules interact with each other within the system of a game, and to explore the limits of ambiguity and specificity in rules. With more people in each group, students might write only a single rule, to keep the rule-set from becoming too complex.

Sensations of Play

Design Focus: ***Games as the Play of Experience*** (chapter 23)

Description: In this play-based exercise, students are given experiential parameters to limit and focus their game design, including the senses (design a game that emphasizes the experience of touch, taste, or smell), emotions (cause the players to experience anger, fear, or laughter), or one of the typologies of play experience from chapter 23 (design a game around Caillois' concepts of ilinx, alea, agôn, or mimicry). The medium of the game is wide open and could serve as a parameter as well.

Engendering the Metagame

Design Focus: Games as ***Social Play*** (chapter 28)

Description: Students create a game that is specifically designed to foster emergent metagames. For example, the parameters for this exercise might be that the game must last for no more than 60 seconds and is designed to be played in rapid succession. Students would report on and analyze the resulting metagame as part of the overall exercise.

Site-Specific Resistance

Design Focus: ***Games as Cultural Resistance*** (chapter 32)

Description: Players create a game designed for a particular physical context, such as a landmark, subway car, Starbucks café, etc. The game should both reflect and transform the cultural ideology of the chosen context through the play of the game. Students might be limited to games that they can actually implement or they might complete games that are too large in scope to be playtested, such as a game that involves the population of an entire city. If students cannot play their entire game, they should still isolate some aspect of the game play to prototype and test.

Open Source Game Systems

Design Focus: ***Games as Open Culture*** (chapter 31)

Description: Each student or group creates a set of game materials (or game system) that could be used as the basis for a variety of games. They then design the rules of a single game using the game system. Each group is then given the game system of another group and asked to design a game using the new system. Groups then take the game systems they originally created, along with the two sets of game rules, and create a third game that is a synthesis of the two. The focus of this exercise is on designing an open source set of game materials that lend themselves to a diversity of game designs.

In all game creation problems, it is particularly important to emphasize the iterative design process. It is often difficult for students to shift from brainstorming game ideas to implementing their concepts within an actual game prototype. This is one reason why it is important to choose design parameters wisely. The parameters will provide students with limitations that help them focus, allowing them to arrive at a coherent design idea. Make sure that the parameters you do assign embody the design focus of the exercise as a whole. This will help students understand the objective of the assignment and assess their designs as they are creating them.

One common game creation scenario is that a student is placed in a situation where he or she is creating a game from scratch with few or no parameters to guide the work. This happens most often in semester-long or year-long thesis or studio projects. Students tend to be grossly over-ambitious and under-organized in these situations; sometimes a design focus and the inclusion of specific design parameters can help them maintain a more directed design process. Also, unless students are working in a team or want to spend most of their time programming or creating audio and visual assets, they should be designing a non-digital game, or an extremely simplified digital one.

Modification

Modification exercises represent another category of game design problems. Instead of coming up with a game using only a set of parameters, the starting point of a modification exercise is an existing game that is altered through an act of design. The same points made earlier about the importance of a design focus, careful selection of design parameters, and the use of iterative design apply equally here.

Change the Rules

*Design Focus: **Defining Rules**, and **Rules on Three Levels*** (chapters 11, 12)
Description: In this straightforward exercise, players take a game and change some of the rules to see how the changes affect game play. The rule changes should be given a conceptual focus. For example, students might be given simplistic, somewhat unsatisfying games like Tic-Tac-Toe or the card game War with the idea that the rule changes must result in more meaningful play. This exercise can also be used as an opportunity to understand the importance of crafting clear operational rules: each group must write the complete rules for its game variant and watch other groups try to play their games with only the written instructions as a guide.

Destabilization

*Design Focus: **Games as Cybernetic Systems*** (chapter 18)
Description: The starting point for this exercise is a well-balanced game. Using principles of feedback loops, students must change the rules to introduce a positive or negative feedback loop that either keeps the game state overly static or

makes it swing wildly out of control. Each group then hands its "broken" game to another group, who must fix the design problem but keep the first group's rule alteration as part of the game.

A Shift in Scale

*Design Focus: **Games as the Play of Experience** (chapter 23)*

Description: In this game modification exercise, students take an existing game and alter it by changing the game materials. The scale or some other physical attribute of the game should be radically transformed. Because the rules of the game remain the same, the difference between the two versions will lie in the experiential play of each.

Transporting the Core Mechanic

*Design Focus: **Games as the Play of Pleasure** (chapter 24)*

Description: Students begin by analyzing an existing game and identifying its core mechanic. They then extract the concept of the core mechanic and use it to modify a second existing game. A variant on this exercise is to turn it into a game creation problem in which students design a game around the core mechanic they initially identified. In either case, the point of the exercise is to understand the central role of a core mechanic and to see whether or not core mechanics can be successfully transplanted from one game context to another.

New Depictions

*Design Focus: **Games as the Play of Simulation** (chapter 27)*

Description: In this exercise, players take a game that depicts one form of conflict or activity and modify the game so that it depicts another form. The design parameters might be a shuffling of the territory/economy/knowledge distinction (make Chess a conflict over knowledge or Trivial Pursuit a territorial conflict). Another possibility is to modify the games to depict subject matter not normally found in games, such as social or psychological conflict. The games should use techniques of procedural representation to depict their subject matter.

The Rhetoric of the Lottery

*Design Focus: **Games as Cultural Rhetoric,** and **Games as Cultural Resistance** (chapters 30, 32)*

Description: Each student or group is given an existing lottery scratch-off game ticket as a starting point. Through an analysis of the ideological rhetorics implicit in the game, students redesign the graphical and formal elements of the ticket in order to subvert the rhetoric. As part of the design exercise, students might also reconceive the architectural or social context in which the game is played. A third variant asks the students to select a cultural rhetoric that is at odds with a lottery's existing rhetoric (such as selecting Progress in opposition to Fate). The students then redesign the game's system of information to create friction between the two competing ideologies.

Analysis

In addition to creating and modifying games, it is incredibly important that game design students play games, lots and lots of them. Students should play every possible kind of game, digital and non-digital, contemporary and historical, masterpiece and stinker. Game design students play these games in order to cultivate a historical awareness and critical sensibility about the kinds of games that have already been designed, to learn how games function to create experiences, and to discover what does and doesn't work about particular design choices.

Every time students play a game, they should analyze it. The analysis might take the form of an informal discussion, or it might be a formal written essay. Written analyses can range from short, three-page papers to major research theses. Written analyses are particularly useful in sharpening a student's critical thinking, but they must be assigned with a clear conceptual focus or they run the risk of becoming a largely descriptive "movie review" of a student's favorite game. Each schema in this book provides a highly specific framework to direct a student analysis.

Cybernetic Analysis

*Design Focus: **Games as Cybernetic Systems** (chapter 18)*

Description: The emphasis of this analysis is on identifying cybernetic feedback loops within the formal structure of a game. Students must select a game and find at least one feedback loop that contributes to the overall system of the game. Students also should identify the sensor, comparator, and actuator in the loop and whether it is a positive or negative feedback loop. Further questions for analysis include: How does the feedback loop affect the overall game play experience? What would happen if it were taken out of the game? How could the rules be changed to exaggerate the effects of the feedback loop? What is a different feedback loop that might further improve the game?

Narrative Analysis

*Design Focus: **Games as Narrative Play** (chapter 26)*

Description: Students choose a game and study it as a system of narrative representation. They must identify elements of embedded and emergent narrative, as well as discuss the different forms of narrative descriptors used by the game. For example, what role do setting, plot, and character play? What about the visual design, the title of the game, the spatial construction of the game world?

Social Interaction Analysis

Design Focus: **Games as Social Play** (chapter 28)

Description: Using concepts from the schema on social play, students analyze a game. They must identify at least two of the following social play phenomena in their paper and describe how these elements contribute to meaningful play: player roles, player community, core social mechanics, metagaming, forbidden play.

Cultural Environment Analysis

Design Focus: **Games as Cultural Environment** (chapter 33)

Description: For this exercise, students select a game that blurs the boundaries of the magic circle to operate as a cultural environment. The analysis should address the following kinds of questions: What social, architectural, narrative, or other aspects of the game overlap with the world outside the magic circle? How does the blurring of the boundary support meaningful play? In what ways does the formal structure of the game keep the game contained? What cultural rhetorics are reflected or transformed by the play of the game?

Further Reading

The Well-Played Game: A Player's Philosophy, by Bernard DeKoven

As the former director of the New Games Foundation, Bernard DeKoven spent countless hours designing play. In *The Well-Played Game,* DeKoven gives an overview of an ideology of play that focuses on giving players the power to affect their own play experiences by redesigning rules, helping other players, and inventing new games of their own. The book is more of a gentle philosophical text than a game design handbook, but we found it to be tremendously inspiring.

> *Recommended:*
> Chapter 2: Guidelines
> Chapter 3: The Play Community
> Chapter 5: Changing the Game

The New Games Book, by Andrew Fluegelman and Shoshana Tembeck

The bible of the New Games Movement, *The New Games Book* still makes a delightful read. It primarily consists of descriptions of games, organized by number of players and degree of activity. Some of the New Games games are twists on classic designs; others are remarkably original. As a source book for well-designed physical and social games to play and analyze, *The New Games Book* is an invaluable resource. Also included in the book are a handful of essays.

> *Recommended:*
> "Creating the Play Community," Bernard DeKoven
> "Theory of Game Change," Stewart Brand
> *For Examples of Iterative Design:*
> The Player-Referee's Non-Rulebook
> New Volleyball

New Rules for Classic Games, by R. Wayne Schmittberger

New Rules for Classic Games is filled with exactly what the title implies—redesigned versions of games like Monopoly, Chess, Checkers, and Backgammon. Some of the variations change the numbers of players, others adjust the game materials, and some merely fix design flaws in the original games. A fantastic resource for game modification exercises, the final chapter recommended below lists suggestions for designing variants of existing games.

> *Recommended:*
> Chapter 15: Creating Your Own Winning Variations

COMMISSIONED ESSAY

Reiner Knizia

The Design and Testing of the Board Game—
Lord of the Rings

The design of the Lord of the Rings Board Game was a great opportunity but also an extraordinary challenge. Tolkien's powerful epic of more than a thousand pages is loved by millions. This game would reach a large audience, but they would have high and very specific expectations. My brief from the publisher was to design a sophisticated family game of about one hour playing time. Even though I couldn't cover the entire story line, my aim was to stay within the spirit of the book so that the players would experience something similar to the readers of the book. These design goals would have many consequences for the game design.

Design Process

I don't have a fixed design process. Quite the contrary, I believe that starting from the same beginning will frequently lead to the same end. Finding new ways of working often leads to innovative designs. Of course, there are always the basic ingredients of game mechanics, game materials, and the theme or the world. These are good anchor points and in a balanced design these dimensions will blend together nicely and support each other. Furthermore, there are some fundamental design questions about the player's point of view: Who am I? What am I trying to achieve? What are my main choices? How do I win?

In the early design stages I often close my eyes and look into new worlds, new systems, and new materials, searching for exciting game play. I try to develop an understanding of what I want to feel when I play the game: the thrill, the fun, the choices, the challenges. Clearly, for the Lord of the Rings Board Game I needed to develop a deep understanding of Tolkien's world, the underlying themes, and the motivations of the characters. This was not achievable by merely reading the book itself. I also needed to know what excited the fans, and what was at the center of their discussions. Dave Farquhar, a friend and regular playtester, was a great fan of Tolkien. We spent countless hours going through the story page by page, discussing its relevance for the game. Clearly I could not reflect much of the detail of the books. But more important was the feeling of the world. The true focus of the book was not the fighting, but more personal themes—the development of each character's sense of self as they attempt to overcome adversity.

The story starts with the hobbits leaving their home to venture into unknown lands. I decided that each player would represent a hobbit, aided by the good characters and peoples in Middle Earth. Of course their only chance was to cooperate. To do Tolkien's masterpiece justice, the players would have to play together. This structure would make the game design very unusual. But the rules could not simply demand cooperative play: the game system had to intrinsically motivate this type of play. Therefore, I embedded the hobbits' mutual foe, Sauron, into the game system itself. Even the most competitive players would soon realize that the game system threw so many dangers at the players that they would naturally have to support each other to maintain a strong front against their common enemy.

In contrast to a book, a game must be replayable many times, giving fresh excitement each time. As the storyline would already be known to many of the players but not all of them, the game would have to work and play well irrespective of the players' knowledge of Tolkien's world. Another important consideration was the physical appearance of the game and its graphical presentation. *The Lord of the Rings* is full of atmosphere, and has long been a source of inspiration for beautiful illustrations. John Howe, a famous Tolkien artist, was signed up to do the artwork, and I wanted to give him plenty of opportunities to enrich the game and excite the Tolkien fans with powerful visuals. Furthermore, the target retail price and the square box shape would influence the components I could use.

Scripted Game System

Considering the challenge of distilling an epic story into a game, I started to develop a general approach that I call the "scripted game system." Essentially, this is a method of distilling the key parts of a story and presenting them in game form. It enables episodes to be linked together in a storyline that compresses some parts, but expands the key adventures that the players will play in detail.

Applying this approach to the Lord of the Rings Board Game, I imagined a "summary board," showing the overall progress of the players' journey, and a corruption line to visualize the growing power of Sauron. Below would be a number of more detailed and beautifully illustrated "adventure boards" on which the key episodes would be played in sequential order. These boards would reflect the flavor of particular episodes through thematic events and play would take place on activity tracks representing fighting, movement, hiding, or friendship. Each scenario board would have a primary track that provided the main route through the scenario and measured the players' overall progress. Shields, representing victory points, would generally be acquired on the primary track.

In order to avoid players merely concentrating on the main track and moving swiftly through the scenario, valuable life tokens, resources, and allies would appear on the minor tracks. A scenario could be finished in two ways, either by completing the primary track, or because the events had run their course and had overtaken the players —usually with serious consequences. To create more predicaments, players would be required to complete the scenarios with three life tokens (one of each kind), or they were pushed along the corruption line on the summary board toward Sauron.

The corruption line was designed as the primary pressure being applied to the players. Their hobbit figures would start at the "light end," with Sauron beginning at the "dark end." As the game progressed, events would draw the hobbits toward the dark, while Sauron moved toward them. If Sauron met a hobbit, that player would be eliminated from the game and all his resources would be lost. Even worse, if the hobbit who possessed the One Ring was caught by Sauron, the game would end in defeat for all players. Although players could sacrifice time and resources to move back toward the light, Sauron would never retreat. So over the course of the game the players would gradually slip toward the dark, creating a sense of claustrophobia and impending doom— just as in the book.

Tolkien's hobbits were rarely in control of their situation. To reflect, this I introduced a general tile deck with a series of events that affected the players directly, creating a significant time pressure in the individual adventure scenarios. The event deck would simply trigger the next event, but the events themselves would be different in each scenario, reflecting the specific flavor of the episode. Although the players would know which events could happen in each scenario, they would not know how soon they would occur.

The interplay of all of these game systems would create many threats, operating differently each time the game was played, and creating opportunities for discussion and planning. Many tactical choices would present themselves and hopefully lead to a rich interaction between the players. The players, bringing different personalities and playing styles to the table, would have to pull together and truly collaborate. This would create a similar feel to the book—the game would not just re-tell Tolkien's plot, but more importantly it would make the players feel the emotional circumstances of the story.

Playtesting

My primary design technique is to create a game first in my mind and play it there over and over again. This can go on for many weeks. When I feel the need for practical playing experience, I finally build the first prototype and play it with my playtest groups. The decision to enter the prototype stage is critical. Moving too early without a clear concept wastes a lot of time, as it is much simpler to change things in one's mind than in a physical prototype. Moving too late may not reveal design weaknesses early enough and may require a complete redesign.

Once the initial concept is properly elaborated, playtesting becomes the core activity of game development. The fun and excitement of playing cannot be calculated in an abstract fashion: it must be experienced. I prepare each of my playtest sessions in great detail—I plan the exact issues I want to monitor and test. During play, I record relevant data about the game flow. Afterwards, I analyze the results and then make necessary or exploratory changes. This becomes the preparation for the next playtest session, during which I can find out how the changes will affect the game. The revolving process usually continues over many months, sometimes years. With experienced playtesters, we spend much time after each test discussing how it went—what worked and what didn't. Often we make changes on the spot and play again.

The first stage in prototyping the Lord of the Rings Board Game was to prepare just one scenario and to see how the basic system played. It was somewhat natural to choose the intended first scenario, the departure from Bag End and the journey to Bree. The first test usually brings many surprises. It is a reality check in which my mental picture of the game is compared to what happens with real people. The first prototype was soon extended by the next two scenarios, bringing us up to Rivendell.

Initially I anticipated the game would cover eight or ten scenarios, but this was a major miscalculation. Very soon it became apparent that the game was becoming too long; by the end of the first hour, instead of climbing Mount Doom we were only just reaching Rivendell. I realized that I had to focus on the core episodes of Tolkien's story, and as a consequence none of the first three scenarios were realized in the Base Game (though I was later to resurrect the journey to Bree in the first expansion).

I selected four main episodes from the story: Moria, Helm's Deep, Shelob's Lair, and Mount Doom, and created corresponding scenario boards. These scenarios were then linked on the summary board with small episodes in Rivendell and Lothlorien. I played and played the game with my playtest groups over the better part of a year—typically three or four playtest sessions each week with changes between each session. In addition, I gave Dave Farquhar a test copy to use with other testers and generate even more playtest results. Many details were analyzed for each board, including the positions of the hobbits and Sauron on the corruption line, cards and shields held by each player, tiles drawn, and number of turns played.

One of the vital tenets of good playtesting is comprehensively to explore every possible strategy and style of play. A frequent error committed by inexperienced designers is to develop a game for just one test group. Of course, to be successful a game must appeal to many different types of players. It must be robust and exciting on many levels, for casual players as well as for experienced gamers. My basic approach in the Lord of the Rings Board Game was to offer the players plentiful but nevertheless limited resources.

Beginners usually spend these resources freely, proceeding optimistically through the game until the resources become scarce and they succumb to Sauron. With more experience, players realize that spending resources early in the game will have serious consequences later on. Players foresee future threats and pitfalls, and the discussions focus much more on strategy and risk. The more the game proceeds, the more apprehensive you get, and the greater the need for the players to strategically cooperate. Like the book, the game offers a journey of personal growth. In the game, you have the advantage of being able to play over and over again to do better each time.

More Changes

I like my game designs to begin with elaborate concepts and too many features, and then later streamline the game play, only retaining the best parts of the design. I find this process easier than trying to bolt on additional elements later, and overall it has led me to more satisfying game designs.

Apart from identifying the most interesting features and the most intuitive rules, an important focus of the continual playing and replaying was to balance the game. Each game should play out differently, but all games should present roughly the same degree of difficulty. Luck should not make a game too easy, nor too difficult. Each of the adventure boards required balancing the flow of events needed to provide an escalating challenge. If events occurred too early the players would be drained of resources and find themselves unable to go on. Key events encouraged the party to move along different tracks, giving them important choices about how to proceed. The game also had to be balanced for the varying numbers of players. Otherwise, it could become substantially easier the more players took part, because they had more resources among them. Or it might become tougher with more players, as each character had to be looked after.

Two further thematic challenges arose as testing progressed. First, I wanted to bring Gandalf more fully into the game; and second, I wanted to give the shield tokens a purpose other than merely to measure victory points. Often I find it harder to solve a single design problem than to address two at the same time. A single problem allows many possible solutions and—being a perfectionist—it is difficult for me to identify the single "best" solution. When looking at two problems at once, a common solution often appears more readily. In this case I introduced a Gandalf deck containing powerful cards that the players could buy using the shields.

This also illustrates another important game design principle. Solving a specific design issue should not just address the issue in isolation but should ideally contribute to the overall game play. This differentiates a game fix from a game feature, and of course, games should never use fixes. The Gandalf cards are a nice game feature, because they allow the players more tactical choices and help in balancing the game. Players may decide to keep their shields to achieve a higher score, or "invest" them to gain more powerful resources or overcome an obstacle. And of course, different players may prefer different approaches and have to arrive at a consensus.

I had originally conceived the game for three to five players, but as I monitored the results I wondered whether it would play well with just two. I often initially aim for two to four, or three to five players to satisfy the market requirements. When I have a stable design, I then explore whether I can extend the player numbers through minor design changes. Initial test results with the game confirmed that the two-player version was playable, but it was too easy to win. In response, I decided to reduce the number of resource cards given to the two players in Rivendell and Lothlorien.

One side effect of all this testing was that the game was being optimized for experienced players, so new players were finding it too difficult. In setting the final variables, I took this into account. Never forget your target audience! For confidentiality reasons, I normally keep testing within my own groups, but this game was so unusual that I needed to confirm once more how the general public would react to it. So we set up separate test sessions, some with game players and some with non-players. Sometimes the non-player groups did better than the game players! So we knew that we had what we wanted.

The Road Goes Ever On

After eighteen months, the design was finished and delivered to the publisher. But the design process continued. Nine months later, in October 2000, the game was released into the market. One year later, in October 2001, came the first expansion, *Friends & Foes,* with two new scenario boards and an entirely new game element of 30 foes. Exactly one year later, the second expansion, called *Sauron,* let a player take the role of Sauron and actively lead the dark forces against the hobbits. Today, the Lord of the Rings Board Game is available worldwide in 17 languages, with sales of over one million copies.

Reiner Knizia

Reiner Knizia was born in Germany and now lives in the United Kingdom designing award-winning board games and card games. His past lives include being a professor of Mathematics and a Director of Strategic Planning in major German banks. Reiner is one of the most prolific and respected game designers working today, with more than 200 published games and several books on games and design. Games include Lord of the Rings, Taj Mahal, Safari, and Lost Cities.

Unit 1: **Core Concepts**

Meaningful Play
Design
Systems
Interactivity
Defining Games
Defining Digital Games
The Magic Circle
The Primary Schemas: RULES, PLAY, CULTURE

He who hopes to learn the fine art of the game from books will soon learn that only the opening and closing moves of the game admit of exhaustive systematic description; and that the endless variety of moves which develop from the opening defies description; the gap left in the instructions can only be filled in by the zealous study of games fought out by master hands.—**E. M. Avedon,** *The Study of Games*

How does play happen?

How is it that a game board and a pair of dice, or a game program on a hard drive, or a baseball, a bat, and an empty lot somehow ramify into the experience of play—an experience of endless pleasure and variety that defies ordinary description? What are games? What is game design? And how do we design for meaningful play? In this unit, we begin to answer these questions by clarifying several key concepts that inform our study. After first looking closely at the concept of *meaningful play,* we introduce three interrelated ideas—*design, systems,* and *interactivity*—that lead us directly to a definition of *games* and *game design.* These core concepts provide the crucial foundation for any understanding of game design and meaningful play.

Revision 88 / Serial number 840726

West of House
You are standing in an open field west of a white house,
with a boarded front door.
There is a small mailbox here.

>open mailbox
Opening the small mailbox reveals a leaflet.

>take leaflet
Taken.

>read leaflet
"WELCOME TO ZORK!

ZORK is a game of adventure, danger, and low cunning. In
it you will explore some of the most amazing territory
ever seen by mortals. No computer should be without one!"

>█

Unit 1 | Core Concepts

MEANINGFUL PLAY

meaning
designed choice
action
outcome
discernability
integration

3

We have only to watch young dogs to see that all the essentials of human play are present in their merry gambols. They invite one another to play by a certain ceremoniousness of attitude and gesture. They keep to the rule that you shall not bite, or not bite hard, your brother's ear. They pretend to get terribly angry. And—what is most important—in all these doings they plainly experience tremendous fun and enjoyment. Such rompings of young dogs are only one of the simpler forms of animal play. There are other, much more highly developed forms: regular contests and beautiful performances before an admiring public.

*Here we have at once a very important point: even in its simplest forms on the animal level, play is more than a mere physiological phenomenon or a psychological reflex. It goes beyond the confines of purely physical or purely biological activity. It is a significant function—that is to say, there is some sense to it. In play there is something "at play" which transcends the immediate needs of life and imparts meaning to the action. All play means something.—**Johann Huizinga,** Homo Ludens*

Introducing Meaningful Play

Johann Huizinga is one of the greatest scholars of play in the twentieth century. His groundbreaking book, *Homo Ludens,* is a unique investigation of the role of play in human civilization. The title is a play on *Homo Sapiens,* and translates as *Man the Player.* According to Huizinga, play and games, which have been maligned in recent history as trivial and frivolous, are in fact at the very center of what makes us human. "Play is older than culture," as Huizinga puts it, and *Homo Ludens* is a celebration of play that links the visceral, combative nature of contest directly to war, poetry, art, religion, and other essential elements of culture. *Homo Ludens* is, in many ways, an attempt to redefine and elevate the significance of play.

Huizinga's vision of play offers a perfect point of departure for the development of the concept of meaningful play. We begin with a close reading of one section of the opening passage from *Homo Ludens:*

> It [play] is a significant function—that is to say, there is some sense to it. In play there is something "at play" which transcends the immediate needs of life and imparts meaning to the action. All play means something.[1]

Huizinga emphasizes the fact that all play means something, that there is "sense" to play, that it transcends. The idea that "all play means something" is a wonderfully complex statement we can interpret in a variety of ways. In fact, all of the following are possible readings of the text:

- Huizinga says that play is a *significant function.* Does this mean that play is an important (and possibly unrecognized) force in culture—that it is significant in the way that art and literature are? Or does he mean that play *signifies*—that it is a symbolic act of communication?

- He mentions that there is *some sense* to play. Does he mean that play isn't soley chaotic, but is instead an event that can be understood and analyzed if one looks closely enough? Or is he implying that sense itself (the opposite of nonsense) is something intrinsically related to play?

- There's the complex statement: *In play there is something "at play."* Does Huizinga mean that there is always something deeper "at play," which constitutes any instance of play we observe in the real world? Or that in play something is always in motion, never fixed, and in a constant state of transformation?

- This "at play" quality of play *transcends the immediate needs of life.* Does the word "transcend" imply something spiritual? Or does Huizinga simply mean that play creates an artificial space beyond that of ordinary life?

- The same "at play" characteristic of play *imparts meaning to the action.* Does the fact that play is always "at play" relate to the meaning of the action? Or does it imply that play must be understood as one element of a more general system out of which meaning grows?

- The passage concludes with the sentence, *All play means something.* But what does play mean? To who or what is it meaningful? What is the process by which meaning emerges from play?

These are complex and multi-layered questions, lacking definitive answers. In some sense, each of the interpretations posed are implied in Huizinga's statement, and all of them point to key aspects of play and play's participation in the creation of meaning. These important questions, and their possible answers, contain all of the main themes of this book. We will, in the pages that follow, investigate the intricate relationships among game design, play, and meaning.

Meaning and Play

Meaning, meaning, meaning. If you repeat the word enough, you can almost coax it into the realm of pure non-sense. Because asking about the meaning of meaning can quickly turn into a jumbled, meaningless mess, let's frame the connection between play and meaning as simply as we can. In the game of Pong, for example, the meaning of the interaction between player and game is mediated by play, from the play of pixels representing the ball, to the play of the mechanical knobs controlling the digital paddles, to the competitive social force of play between opponents. It is for these reasons, and many others, that game designers should care about the relationship between meaning and play.

Learning to create great game experiences for players—experiences that have meaning and are meaningful—is one of the goals of successful game design, perhaps the most important one. We call this goal the design of *meaningful play,* the core concept of our approach. This concept is so critical to the rest of this chapter that we are going to repeat ourselves: *the goal of successful game design is the creation of meaningful play.* Meaningful play is that concept which can address all of the "unanswerable" questions raised by Huizinga. It is also a concept that raises questions of its own, challenging assumptions we might have about the role of design in shaping play.

One of the difficulties in identifying meaningful play in games is the near-infinite variety of forms that play can take. Here are some examples:

· the intellectual dueling of two players in a well-met game of Chess

· the improvisational, team-based balletics of Basketball

· the dynamic shifting of individual and communal identities in the online role-playing game EverQuest

· the lifestyle-invading game Assassin, played on a college campus

What do all of these examples have in common? Each situates play within the context of a game. Play doesn't just come from the game itself, but from the way that players interact with the game in order to play it. In other words, the board, the pieces, and even the rules of Chess can't alone constitute meaningful play. Meaningful play emerges from the interaction between players and the system of the game, as well as from the context in which the game is played. Understanding this interaction

helps us to see just what is going on when a game is played. One way of framing what players do when they play a game is to say that they are making choices. They are deciding how to move their pieces, how to move their bodies, what cards to play, what options to select, what strategies to take, how to interact with other players. They even have to make the choice whether or not to play!

When a player makes a choice within a game, the action that results from the choice has an outcome. In Chess, if a player moves a piece on the board, this action affects the relationships of all of the other pieces: one piece might be captured, or a king might suddenly find itself in check. In Assassin, if a player stealthily stalks her target and manages to shoot him with a dart gun, the overall game changes as a result of this action: a hit is scored, the victim is out for the rest of the game, and he must give *his* target name to the player that just shot him. In EverQuest, if you engage with and kill a monster, the stats and equipment of your character can change; the larger game-world is affected as well, even if it simply means that for the moment there is one less monster.

Playing a game means making choices and taking actions. All of this activity occurs within a game-system designed to support meaningful kinds of choice-making. Every action taken results in a change affecting the overall system of the game. Another way of stating this point is that an action a player takes in a game results in the creation of new meanings within the system. For example, after you move a piece in Chess, the newly established relationships between Chess pieces gives rise to a new set of meanings—meanings created by the player's action.

Two Kinds of Meaningful Play

We define meaningful play in two separate but related ways. The first sense of meaningful play refers to the way game actions result in game outcomes to create meaning. Framing the concept in this way, we offer the following definition:

Meaningful play **in a game emerges from the relationship between player action and system outcome; it is the process by which a player takes action within the designed system of a game and the system responds to the action. The** *meaning* **of an action in a game resides in the relationship between action and outcome.**

Think about an informal game of "Gross-Out" played during an elementary school recess. One by one, players tell a gross-out story, each tale more disgusting than the last. When a story is finished the group spontaneously and collectively responds, confirming or denying the player's position as master of the playground, until an even grosser story is told.

If we look at Gross-Out from the perspective of meaningful play we see that a player takes an action by telling a story. The *meaning* of the action, as a move in a game, is more than the narrative content of the story. It is also more than the theatrics used to tell the story. The outcome of the storytelling action depends on the other players and their own voting actions. Meaningful play emerges from the collective action of players telling and rating stories. The *meaning* of the story, in the sense of meaningful play, is not just that Hampton told a whopper about his big sister eating a live beetle—it is that Hampton's story has beaten the others and he is now the undisputed Gross-Out king.

This way of understanding meaningful play refers to the way *all* games generate meaning through play. Every game lets players take actions, and assigns outcomes to those actions. We therefore call this definition of meaningful play *descriptive,* because it describes what happens in every game. This is our first understanding of meaningful play.

At the same time, some games create more meaningful play than other games: the design of some games generates truly meaningful experiences for players, whereas other, less successful game designs result in experiences that somehow fall short. Even if meaningful play is a goal that we strive to achieve in our games, sometimes we don't quite get it right. So, in addition to

our descriptive understanding of meaningful play, which describes what happens in all games, we need something that will help us be more selective in determining when meaningful play occurs.

This is the second sense of meaningful play. Instead of being a description of the way games operate, it refers to the goal of successful game design. This sense of meaningful play is *evaluative:* it helps us critically evaluate the relationships between actions and outcomes, and decide whether they are meaningful enough within the designed system of the game:

Meaningful play **occurs when the relationships between actions and outcomes in a game are both** *discernable* **and** *integrated* **into the larger context of the game. Creating meaningful play is the goal of successful game design.**

The word "meaningful" in this sense is less about the semiotic construction of meaning (how meaning is made) and more about the emotional and psychological experience of inhabiting a well-designed system of play. In order to understand why some play in games is more meaningful than others, we need to understand the key terms in the definition: *discernable* and *integrated.*

Discernable

Discernable means that the result of the game action is communicated to the player in a perceivable way. In the following excerpt from *Game Design: Theory and Practice,* Richard Rouse III points out the importance of displaying discernable information to the player within the context of the game world. His example looks explicitly at computer games where there is an obvious need to condense massive amounts of data into a representative form that can be clearly communicated to the player. However, the idea of discernable outcomes applies to all games, digital or otherwise. Rouse writes,

> Consider a strategy game in which the player has a number of units scattered all over a large map. The map is so large that only a small portion of it can fit on the screen at once. If a group of the

player's units happen to be off-screen and are attacked but the player is not made aware of it by the game, the player will become irritated. Consider an RPG where each member of the player's party needs to be fed regularly, but the game does not provide any clear way of communicating how hungry his characters are. Then, if one of the party members suddenly keels over from starvation, the player will become frustrated, and rightly so. Why should the player have to guess at such game-critical information?[2]

If you shoot an asteroid while playing a computer game and the asteroid does not change in any way, you are not going to know if you actually hit it or not. If you do not receive feedback that indicates you are on the right track, the action you took will have very little meaning. On the other hand, if you shoot an asteroid and you hear the sound of impact, or the asteroid shudders violently, or it explodes (or all three!) then the game has effectively communicated the outcome of your action. Similarly, if you move a board game piece on the board but you have absolutely no idea whether your move was good or bad or if it brought you closer to or farther away from winning—in short, if you don't know the meaning of your action—then the result of your action was not discernable. Each of these examples makes clear that when the relationship between an action and the result of that action is not discernable, meaningful play is difficult or impossible to achieve.

Discernability in a game lets the players know *what* happened when they took an action. Without discernability, the player might as well be randomly pressing buttons or throwing down cards. *With* discernability, a game possesses the building blocks of meaningful play.

Integrated

Another component of meaningful play requires that the relationship between action and outcome is *integrated* into the larger context of the game. This means that an action a player takes not only has immediate significance in the game, but

also affects the play experience at a later point in the game. Chess is a deep and meaningful game because the delicate opening moves directly result in the complex trajectories of the middle game—and the middle game grows into the spare and powerful encounters of the end game. Any action taken at one moment will affect possible actions at later moments.

Imagine a multi-event athletic game, such as the Decathlon. At the start of the game, the players run a footrace. What if the rules of the game dictated that winning the footrace had nothing to do with the larger game? Imagine what would happen: the players would walk the race as slowly as possible, trying to conserve energy for the other, more meaningful events. Why should they do anything else? Although one of them will win the footrace, it will have no bearing on the larger game. On the other hand, if the players receive points depending on how well they rank and these points become part of a cumulative score, then the actions and the outcomes of the footrace are well integrated into the game as a whole.

Whereas discernability of game events tells players *what* happened *(I hit the monster)*, integration lets players know *how* it will affect the rest of the game *(If I keep on hitting the monster I will kill it. If I kill enough monsters, I'll gain a level.)*. Every action a player takes is woven into the larger fabric of the overall game experience: this is how the play of a game becomes truly meaningful.

Meaningful play can be realized in a number of ways, depending on the design of a particular game. There is no single formula that works in every case. In the example of the asteroid shooting game, immediate and visceral feedback was needed to make the action discernable. But it might also be the case that in a story-based game, the results of an action taken near the beginning of the game are only understood fully at the very end, when the implications are played out in a very unexpected and dramatic way. Both instances require different approaches to designing meaningful play.

Meaningful play engages several aspects of a game simultaneously, giving rise to layers of meaning that accumulate and shape player experience. Meaningful play can occur on the formal, mathematically strategic level of a single move in Chess. It can occur on a social level, as two players use the game as a forum for meaningful communication. And it can occur on larger stages of culture as well, where championship Chess matches can be used as occasions for Cold War political propaganda, or in contemporary philosophical debates about the relative powers of the human mind and artificial intelligence.

The next three chapters elaborate on the many ways that game designers construct spaces of meaningful play for players. Among the many topics we might select, we cover three core concepts that form several of the fundamental building blocks of game design: *design, systems,* and *interactivity.*

Notes

1. Johann Huizinga, *Homo Ludens: A Study of the Play Element in Culture* (Boston: Beacon Press, 1955), p. 446.

2. Richard Rouse III, *Game Design: Theory and Practice* (Plano, TX: Wordware Publishing, 2001), p. 141.

Meaningful Play SUMMARY

- Meaning, play, and games are intimately related concepts. The goal of successful game design is **meaningful play.**

- There are two ways to define meaningful play: **descriptive** and **evaluative.** The descriptive definition addresses the mechanism by which all games create meaning through play. The evaluative definition helps us understand why some games provide more meaningful play than others.

- The **descriptive** definition of meaningful play: **Meaningful play** in a game emerges from the relationship between player action and system outcome; it is the process by which a player takes action within the designed system of a game and the system responds to the action. The *meaning* of an action in a game resides in the relationship between action and outcome.

- The **evaluative** definition of meaningful play: **Meaningful play** is what occurs when the relationships between actions and outcomes in a game are both **discernable** and **integrated** into the larger context of the game.

- **Discernability** means that a player can perceive the immediate outcome of an action. **Integration** means that the outcome of an action is woven into the game system as a whole.

- The two ways of defining meaningful play are closely related. Designing successful games requires understanding meaningful play in both senses.

DESIGN

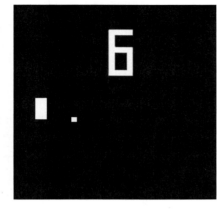

semiotics
system
signs
context
meaning
representation

4

Design is the successive application of constraints until only a unique product is left.
—Donald Norman, *The Design of Everyday Things*

Introducing Design

"Design" is half of "game design." As a concept and as a practice, the idea of design sits at the center of an exploration of games and meaningful play. Yet it is difficult to define. Like the term *game, design* is a concept with many meanings, "Its definition depends on whether design is considered to be an idea, a knowledge, a practice, a process, a product, or even a way-of-being."[1] Lacking a neat consensus, is it possible, or even appropriate, to offer a general definition of design? Where do we go from here?

We could begin by listing familiar kinds of design practice: graphic design, industrial design, architecture, fashion design, textile design, urban planning, information architecture, design planning . . . the list could go on. Each of these practices involves the "design" of something, be it an object (such as a chair or a typeface) or a plan (such as a transportation system or an identity system). What else do these practices share in common? People, of course. Each design practice has a human being at its core. Although this might seem obvious, it an often overlooked basic feature of design. We think it is of particular importance to game designers, for people are at the heart of the games we create.

Some Definitions of Design

Unfortunately, a list of design practices doesn't bring us closer to a general definition of design suited to our study of games. For precedents of such general definitions, we can look to design theory, as a way to map the territory of possible approaches. We have assembled a number of definitions within a comparative list, in order to emphasize their differences.

> "The etymology of design goes back to the Latin *de + signare* and means making something, distinguishing it by a sign, giving it significance, designating its relation to other things, owners, users, or gods. Based on this original meaning, one could say: 'design is making sense (of things).'"[2] This definition places *making* (sense) at the center of design.

> Richard Buchanan argues that "design is concerned with the conception and planning of all of the instances of the artificial or human-made world: signs and images, physical objects, activities and services, and systems or environments." Such a perspective situates design within the *artificial.* [3]

Herbert Simon's definition emphasizes *action,* which is fundamentally related to his theories of management science: "Everyone designs who devises courses of action aimed at changing existing situations into preferred ones."[4]

John Heskett employs a more traditional definition, emphasizing the *visual appearance* of products as things: "design, the conception of visual form."[5]

George Nelson's definition emphasizes design as *communication:* "Every design is in some sense a social communication, and what matters is…the emotional intensity with which the essentials have been explored and expressed."[6]

Donald Schon regards design as a material conversation with the forms, substances, and concepts of a design problem as they are being used. His design approach is *process-driven* and *reflective,* emphasizing the iterative qualities of design. "In a good process of design, this conversation is reflective . . . the designer reflects-in-action on the construction of the problem, the strategies of action, or the model of the phenomena, which have been implicit in his moves."[7]

Designer Emilio Ambasz gives a descriptive but intellectually powerful definition, emphasizing poetic *thought:* "It has always been my deep belief that architecture and design are both myth-making acts."[8]

Design historian Clive Dilnot suggests that design *transforms* by exploring the tension between the existing and the potential. "What design, as a mode of transformative action, allows us to see is how we negotiate the limits of what we understand, at any moment, as the actual. In design, in other words, we begin to see the processes whereby the limits of the actual are continually formed and re-formed."[9]

Design as making; the artificial; action; visual appearance; communication; a reflective process; thought; transformation: each definition offers valid and useful ways of understanding the practice of design by focusing on particular qualities or characteristics. Taken as a whole, the definitions point to a range of concerns affecting designers and help to bring the field of design as a whole into view. But what about game design? Is there a definition that addresses game design's particular territory, the design of meaningful play? In order to answer this question, we must ask another: What is the "design" in *game design* and how is it connected to the concept of meaningful play? As an answer, we offer the following general definition:

Design is the process by which a *designer* creates a *context* to be encountered by a *participant,* from which *meaning* emerges.

Let us look at each part of this definition in relation to game design:

- The *designer* is the individual game designer or the team of people that creates the game. Sometimes, games emerge from folk culture or fan culture, so there may not be an individual designer or design team. In this case, the designer of the game can be considered culture at large.

- The *context* of a game takes the form of spaces, objects, narratives, and behaviors.

- The *participants* of a game are the players. They inhabit, explore, and manipulate these contexts through their play.

- *Meaning* is a concept that we've already begun to explore. In the case of games, meaningful play is the result of players taking actions in the course of play.

This connection between design and meaning returns us to the earlier discussion of meaningful play. Consider a game of Tag. *Without* design we would have a field of players scampering about, randomly touching each other, screaming, and then running in the other direction. *With* design, we have a carefully crafted experience guided by rules, which make certain forms of interaction explicitly meaningful. *With* design a touch becomes meaningful as a "tag" and whoever is "It" becomes the feared terror of the playground. The same is true of com-

puter games as well. As game designer Doug Church puts it, "The design is the game; without it you would have a CD full of data, but no experience."[10]

Design and Meaning

When we ask what something "means," particularly in the context of design, we are trying to locate the value or significance of that instance of design in a way that helps us to make sense of it. Questions such as, "What does the use of a particular color mean on a particular product?" or "What does that image represent?" or "What happens when I click on the magic star?" are all questions of *meaning.* Designers are interested in the concept of meaning for a variety of reasons, not least of which is the fact that meaning is one of the basic principles of human interaction. Our passage through life from one moment to the next requires that we make sense of our surroundings—that we engage with, interpret, and construct meaning. This very human movement toward meaning forms the core of interaction between people, objects, and contexts.

Consider the act of greeting a friend on the street. A wave, a nod, a kiss on the cheek, a pat on the back, a warm hug, a firm handshake, and a gentle punch in the arm are all forms of interaction meaning, "Hello, my friend." As a participant in this scenario, we must make sense of the gesture and respond appropriately. If we fail to make sense of the situation, we have failed to understand the meaning of the interaction. Game designers, in particular, are interested in the concept of meaning because they are involved in the creation of systems of interaction. These systems then give rise to a range of meaning-making activities, from moving a game piece on a board, to waging a bet, to communicating "Hello, my friend" with other online characters in a virtual game world. This question of how users make sense of objects has led some designers, in recent years, to borrow insights and expertise from other fields. In particular, the field of semiotics has been instructive. Semiotics is the study of meaning and the process by which meaning is made. In the next few pages, we will take a slight detour into semiotics, in order to more carefully build our concept of meaningful play.

Semiotics: A Brief Overview

It is…possible to conceive of a science which studies the role of signs as part of life…We shall call it semiology (from the Greek semeîon, "sign"). It would investigate the nature of signs and the laws governing them.— **Ferdinand de Saussure,** *Course in General Linguistics*

Semiotics emerged from the teachings of Ferdinand de Saussure, a Swiss linguist, in the early twentieth century. Originally formulated under the term *semiology,* Saussure's theory of language as a system of signs influenced many later currents of thought, including the anthropology of Claude Levi-Strauss, the philosophy of Jacques Derrida, and the social mythology of Roland Barthes.[11] Each of these writers shared an interest in understanding how products of human culture, from languages to funeral rituals to games, could produce meaning.

In a general sense, semiotics is the study of how meanings are made. The question of what signs represent, or denote, is of central concern to the field. If a high society dinner party was framed as a semiotic system, for example, we would be interested in understanding the meaning of the different elements that make up the dinner party. We could look at the way the table-settings denote a space for eating. We could look at how the presence of fine china or silverware represents the idea of social class, or the representation of status in the arrangement of chairs around the table. We might look at how the event represents concepts such as "elegance," "power," "high-society," or "fine dining," or reference the idea of eating as an activity of survival, sensual pleasure, anxiety, or community. We might even consider what the act of attending the event represents or what it means to those who were not invited. Each of these perspectives contributes to our understanding of the dinner party as a system of meaning, one comprised of signs that refer to things familiar to us from the world "out there." But what do we mean when we say "sign"?

Semiotically speaking, people use *signs* to designate objects or ideas. Because a sign represents something other than itself, we take the *representation* as the *meaning* of the sign. The smell of smoke (sign) represents the concept of "fire," for example, or the tallest piece in Chess denotes the "King." In the game Rock-Paper-Scissors, an outstretched hand means "paper," a fist means "rock," and two fingers spread in a V-shape means "scissors." Our capacity to understand that *signs represent* is at the heart of semiotic study.

Similarly, understanding that signs mean "something to somebody" is at the core of any design practice. A graphic designer, for example, uses typographic signs (letterforms) representing words to design a book; a fashion designer uses silk as a sign representing "beauty" or "femininity" in a new spring line; a game designer uses the classes of Fighter, Wizard, Thief, and Cleric in a fantasy role-playing game to denote four kinds of player-characters within a game. Thus, signs are the most basic unit of semiotic study and can be understood as markers of meaning. As David Chandler notes,

> We do not live among and relate to physical objects and events. We live among and relate to systems of signs with meaning. We don't sit on a complex structure of wood, we sit on a stool. The fact that we refer to it as a STOOL means that it is to be sat on; it is not a coffee table. In our interactions with others we don't use random gestures, we gesture our courtesy, our pleasure, our incomprehension, our disgust. The objects in our environment, the gestures and words we use, derive their meanings from the sign systems to which they belong.[12]

Four Semiotic Concepts

The American philosopher and semiotician Charles S. Peirce defines a sign as "something that stands for something, to somebody, in some respect or capacity."[13] This broad definition recognizes four key ideas that constitute the concept of a sign:

1. A sign represents something other than itself.
2. Signs are interpreted.
3. Meaning results when a sign is interpreted.
4. Context shapes interpretation.

A Sign Represents Something Other Than Itself

A sign represents something other than itself; it "stands for something." The mark of a circle (O) in the game of Tic-Tac-Toe, for instance, represents not only an action by player "O" (as opposed to player "X") but also the capture of a certain square within the game's nine-square grid. Or consider the interaction between two players in a game of Assassin. A tap on the arm might represent "death" or "capture," depending on the rules of the game. In either case, the tap is meaningful to players as something other than a tap.

This concept of a sign representing something other than itself is critical to an understanding of games for several reasons. On one hand, games use signs to denote action and outcome, two components of meaningful play. The marks of an "X" or "O" in Tic-Tac-Toe or the taps on the arms of players in a game of Assassin are actions paired with particular outcomes; these actions gain meaning as part of larger sequences of interaction. These sequences are sometimes referred to as "chains of signifiers," a concept that calls attention to the importance of relations between signs within any sign system.

On the other hand, games use signs to denote the elements of the game world. The universe of Mario, for example, is constructed of a systems of signs representing magic coins, stars, pipes, enemies, hidden platforms, and other elements of the game landscape. The signs that make up the game world collectively represent the world to the player—as sounds, images, interactions, and text. Although the signs certainly make reference to objects that exist in the real world, they gain their symbolic value or meaning from the relationship between signs within the game. We can illustrate the idea of signs deriving meaning from *within* the context of a game with an example drawn from the history of Scrabble.

In late 1993, a campaign was initiated against Hasbro, the company that owns and distributes Scrabble, requesting that the company remove racial and ethnic slurs from *The Official Scrabble Players Dictionary* (OSPD). This rulebook of officially playable or "good" words contained, at that time, words such as

"JEW," "KIKE," "DAGO," and "SPIC." As a result of pressure from the Anti Defamation League and the National Council of Jewish Women, Hasbro announced that fifty to one hundred "offensive" words would be removed from the OSPD. As Stefan Fatsis writes in *Word Freak: Heartbreak, Triumph, Genius, and Obsession in the World of Competitive Scrabble Players,*

> The Scrabble community went ballistic. A handful of players, notably some devout Christians, backed the decision. But a huge majority led by a number of Jewish players, accused Hasbro of censorship. Words are words, and banning them from a dictionary would not make them go away, they argued. Plus, the players tried to explain, the words as played on a board during a game of Scrabble are without meaning. In the limited context of scoring points, the meaning of HONKIE, deemed offensive in the OSPD, is no more relevant than the meaning of any obscure but commonly played word.[14]

Within the context of a game of Scrabble, words are reduced to sequences of letters—they literally do not have meaning as *words*. Rather, the letters are signs that have value as puzzle pieces that must be carefully arranged according to the rules of spelling. Thus, although the sequence of letters H-O-N-K-I-E has meaning as a racial slur *outside* of the context of a game of Scrabble, *within* it the sequence has meaning as a six-letter play worth a number of points on the board. Within Scrabble the chain of signifiers represent words stripped of everything except their syntactical relationships. Outside of Scrabble, however, the words represent racial animosity.

Looking at chains of signifiers within a game means dissecting a game in order to view the system at a micro-level to see how the internal machinery operates. But entire games themselves can also be identified as signs. Viewing them from a macro—rather than micro—perspective allows us to look at games from the outside, seeing them as signs within larger sign systems. The game of Tic-Tac-Toe, for instance, could be seen as a sign representing childhood play, whereas the game of Assassin might stand for college mischief in the 1980s or the film *The 10th Victim,* which inspired the game.

Signs Are Interpreted

Peirce's definition suggests that *signs are interpreted;* they stand for something *to somebody.* It was one of Saussure's fundamental insights that the meanings of signs are arrived at arbitrarily via cultural convention. The idea that the meaning of signs rests not in the signs themselves but in the surrounding system is critical to our study of games. It is people (or players), after all, who bring meaning to signs. As semiotician David Chandler notes,

> There is no necessary reason why a pig should be called a pig. It doesn't look sound or smell any more like the sequence of sounds "p-i-g" than a banana looks, smells, tastes or feels like the sequence of sounds "banana." It is only because we in our language group agree that it is called a "pig" that that sequence of sounds refers to the animal in the real world. You and your circle of friends could agree always to refer to pigs as "squerdlishes" if you wanted. As long as there is general agreement, that's no problem—until you start talking about squerdlishes to people who don't share the same convention.[15]

Chandler's point has resonance when we consider players as active interpreters of a game's sign system. Children playing Tag during recess may change the sign for "home-base" from game to game, or even in the middle of a game, if circumstances allow. A tree in the corner of the playground might be used one day, or a pile of rocks another. Although a home base does have to possess certain functional qualities, such as being a touchable object or place, there is nothing special about the tree or rocks that make them "home base" other than their designation as such by the players of the game. Thus signs are essentially arbitrary, and gain value through a set of agreed upon conventions. Because "there is no simple sign = thing equation between sign systems and reality, it is we who are the active makers of meanings."[16]

Meaning Results When a Sign Is Interpreted

Peirce's definition suggests that meaning results when a sign is interpreted; a sign stands for something, to somebody, *in*

some respect or capacity. Although this may seem like an obvious point it is important to note, for it calls attention to the outcome of the process by which signs gain value within a system. Consider sitting down to eat a bowl of soup at a formal dinner party and finding a pair of chopsticks next to the bowl. One response would be to disregard the chopsticks as a sign for "spoon," and instead ask the waiter for the missing utensil. Within this scenario we are interpreting a set of signs within the sign system representing "soup utensils," of which spoons —and not chopsticks—are part. Within this system, the sign for spoon has value, whereas the sign for chopstick does not.

Another example: If player A in a game of Rock-Paper-Scissors holds up three fingers in the shape of a "W" instead of two in the shape of a "V," she has failed to create a sign that has value, or meaning, within the rock, paper, scissors sign structure of the game. Player B might say, "What is that supposed to be?" in an attempt to infuse the sign with value within the system of the game. If player A responds, "Scissors," then player B has two choices. She can either accept the new sign as representative of "scissors" or she can reject the interpretation. If she accepts the new representation, the players have, in effect, added a new sign to the system; a three-fingered sign that now means "scissors."

Context Shapes Interpretation

Context is a key component to our general definition of design. It also is a key component in the creation of meaning. Design is "the process by which a *designer* creates a *context* to be encountered by a *participant,* from which *meaning* emerges." This definition makes an explicit connection between context and meaning. When we speak of context in language we are referring to the parts of something written or spoken that immediately precede or follow a word or passage that serve to clarify its meaning. The phrase "I am lost," for example, can mean many different things depending on the context in which it is used. If a player of the text adventure game Zork says, "I am trying to install the game and I am lost," we understand that she is having a difficult time making sense of the game's installation instructions. If that same player were to say, "I am in the second chamber and I am lost," we can ascertain that she is actually playing the game, has lost her way, and needs help navigating the fictional game space. In each instance the phrase "I am lost" is given context by the words that follow.

We can also understand context in relation to the idea of *structure,* which in semiotics refers to a set of regulations or guidelines that prescribe how signs, or elements of a system, can be combined. In language, for example, we refer to structure as *grammar.* The grammatical rules of a sentence create a structure that describes how words can and cannot be sequenced. We might refer to these rules as *invisible structure,* as we are not always aware that they are there. In games, this concept of grammar takes the form of game rules, which create a structure for the game, describing how all of the elements of the game interact with one another. Structure (in language or games) operates much like context, and participates in the meaning-making process. By ordering the elements of a system in very particular ways, structure works to create meaning. The communication theorist David Berlo uses the following example to explain how structure supports interpretation:

Structure:

Most smoogles have comcom

We don't know what smoogles and comcom are, but we still know something about them: we know that a smoogle is something countable and can be referred to in the plural, unlike, say, water or milk. We know that smoogles is a noun and not a verb. We know that more than one smoogle is referred to in this sentence. We know that comcom is a noun and that it is a quality or thing which most smoogles are claimed to have. We still don't know what is referred to, but the formal properties of English grammar have already provided us with a lot of information.[17]

Although the structure of any system does provide information that supports interpretation, context ultimately shapes meaning. In the following example, Berlo shows how structure and context work together to aid interpretation:

Context:

My gyxpyx is broken

From the structure of the language you know that gyxpyx is a noun. You know that it's something that it makes sense to refer to as broken.

One of its keys is stuck

Now we're getting a bit closer—a gyxpyx is maybe a typewriter, calculator, or musical instrument; at any rate it's something that has keys.

and I think it could do with a new ribbon, as well

Well, that pretty well clinches it. We're still left with the question of just what the difference is between a typewriter and a gyxpyx or why this person has the odd habit of referring to typewriters as gyxpyxes, but we can be reasonably sure already that a gyxpyx is something typewriter-like.[18]

Berlo goes on to note that the meaning we have for gyxpyx comes partly from the structure. We know it is a noun and we know it can be broken, that it has keys and a ribbon. But structure can only take us so far in our search for meaning; context must often be called upon to complete the quest. Consider the experience of playing a game of Pictionary with friends. Much of the guessing that occurs early in a turn relies on structure to provide clues. A player attempting to draw "Frankenstein" may begin by drawing a head and eyes, as a means of establishing the structure of the human form. This structure helps players to make guesses such as "eyes," "face," or "head," but it soon becomes clear that more information is needed. In response, the player at the drawing board may begin to create a context for the head by drawing a large body with outstretched "zombie" arms, stitch marks denoting surgical scars, and a Tesla coil crackling in the background. Although players might not initially understand what these marks represent (the stitches might just look like squiggly lines), the context created by the other elements of the drawing supply the marks with the meaning they would otherwise lack. Once the players recognize the context "zombie" or "monster," the stitch marks become "scars" and Frankenstein is brought to life.

This relationship between structure, context, and meaning tells us that the act of interpretation relies, in part, on the movement between known and unknown information. Players of Pictionary, for example, will often come across a sign for which they don't have a meaning (stitch marks) within the context of signs for which they do (zombie or monster). The meanings that are known and familiar generate other meanings due to the formal relations between the known and the unknown signs. Keep in mind that the actual elements that constitute structure and context are fluid. The drawing of a head might operate as structure early in the guessing period (if it is the first thing drawn), but when it serves to help identify the squiggles, it becomes part of context.

To design is to create *meaning*. Meaning that can thrill and inspire. Meaning that moves and dances and plays. Meaning that helps people understand the world in new ways. Designers sculpt these experiences of meaning by creating not just one isolated signifier but by constructing whole systems of interlocking parts. As Saussure points out, in language the value of one sign only arises in relation to other signs. In Rock-Paper-Scissors the concept "rock" has identity only in opposition to the concepts "paper" or "scissors." The meaning of a sign does not reside within the sign itself, but from the surrounding system of which it is part. The meaningful play you provide for your players emerges from the designed system of a game—and how that game interacts with larger social and cultural systems. What is it that game designers design? *Systems*. This is the key concept we introduce in the next chapter.

Notes

1. Alain Findeli, "Moholy-Nagy's Design Pedagogy in Chicago, 1937–46." In *The Idea of Design, A Design Issues Reader,* edited by Victor Margolin and Richard Buchanan (Cambridge: MIT Press, 1995), p. 29.

2. Klaus Krippendorff, "On the Essential Contexts of Artifacts or on the Proposition that 'Design is Making Sense (of Things)'." In *The Idea of Design, A Design Issues Reader,* p. 156.

3. Richard Buchanan, "Wicked Problems in Design Thinking." In *The Idea of Design, A Design Issues Reader,* p. 6.

4. Herbert Simon, *The Sciences of the Artificial* (Cambridge: MIT Press, 1968), p. 55.

5. John Heskett, *Industrial Design* (New York: Oxford University Press, 1980), p. 7.

6. Richard Buchanan, "Wicked Problems in Design Thinking." In *The Idea of Design, A Design Issues Reader,* p. 8.

7. Donald A. Schon, *The Reflective Practitioner: How Professionals Think in Action* (New York: Basic Books, 1983), p. 79.

8. Emilio Ambasz, *Emilio Ambasz: The Poetics of the Pragmatic* (New York: Rizzoli International Publications, 1988), p. 24.

9. Clive Dilnot, *The Science of Uncertainty: The Potential Contribution of Design Knowledge,* p. 65–97. Proceedings of the Ohio Conference, Doctoral Education in Design, October 8–11, 1998. Pittsburgh School of Design. Carnegie Mellon University.

10. Doug Church, "Formal Abstract Design Tools." <www.gamasutra.com>, July 16, 1999.

11. Ellen Lupton and J. Abbott Miller, "Laws of the Letter." In *Design, Writing, Research: Writing on Graphic Design* (New York: Princeton Architectural Press, 1996), p. 55.

12. Daniel Chandler, *Semiotics for Beginners.* <www.aber.ac.uk/~dgc/semiotic.html>.

13. *Charles S. Pierce: Selected Writings,* ed. P. O. Wiener (New York: Dover, 1958), p. 37.

14. Stefan Fatsis, *Word Freak: Heartbreak, Triumph, Genius, and Obsession in the World of Competitive Scrabble Players* (Boston: Houghton Mifflin, 2001), p. 149.

15. Daniel Chandler, *Semiotics for Beginners.* <www.aber.ac.uk/~dgc/semiotic.html>.

16. Mick Underwood, CCMS. <http://www.cultsock.ndirect.co.uk/MUHome/cshtml/semiomean/semio1.html>.

17. Ibid.

18. Ibid.

Design SUMMARY

- There are many general definitions of design. Each emphasizes different aspects of the vast range of design practices.

- Our definition of design emphasizes the creation of meaningful experience:

  Design is the process by which a **designer** creates a **context** to be encountered by a **participant,** from which **meaning** emerges.

- **Semiotics** is the study of meaning. It is primarily concerned with the question of how signs represent, or denote.

- People use **signs** to designate objects or ideas. Because a sign represents something other than itself, we take the **representation** as the **meaning** of the sign.

- Charles Pierce identifies four semiotic concepts:
  1. A sign represents something other than itself.
  2. Signs are interpreted.
  3. Meaning results when a sign is interpreted.
  4. Context shapes interpretation.

- **A sign represents something other than itself:** In a game, gestures, objects, behaviors, and other elements act as signs. In the game Assassin, a tap denotes a "kill."

- **Signs are interpreted:** A sign stands for something *to somebody*. Meaning emerges in a game as players take on active roles as interpreters of the game's signs.

- **Meaning results when a sign is interpreted:** A sign stands for something to somebody *in some respect or capacity*. The meaning of a sign emerges from relationships between elements of a system.

- **Context shapes interpretation:** *Context* is the environment of a sign that affects interpretation. The related phenomenon of *structure* also shapes interpretation. Structure is a set of rules or guidelines that prescribe how signs can be combined.

SYSTEMS

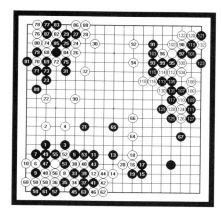

objects
attributes
internal relationships
environment
open systems
closed systems

5

The system is partly a memory of its past, just as in origami, the essence of a bird or a horse is both in the nature and order of the folds made. The question that must be answered when faced with a problem of planning or design of a system, is what exactly is the system? It is therefore necessary to know the nature of the inner structure before plans can be made.—**Wolfgang Jonas,** *"On the Foundations of a 'Science of the Artificial'"*

Introducing Systems

Games are intrinsically systemic: all games can be understood as systems. What do we mean by this? Let's begin our investigations of games and systems by looking at some common understandings of the word "system."

System

1. A group of interacting, interrelated, or interdependent elements forming a complex whole.

2. A functionally related group of elements, especially:

   a. The human body regarded as a functional physiological unit.

   b. An organism as a whole, especially with regard to its vital processes or functions.

   c. A group of physiologically or anatomically complementary organs or parts: the nervous system; the skeletal system.

   d. A group of interacting mechanical or electrical components.

   e. A network of structures and channels, as for communication, travel, or distribution.

3. An organized set of interrelated ideas or principles.

4. A social, economic, or political organizational form.

5. A naturally occurring group of objects or phenomena: the solar system.

6. A set of objects or phenomena grouped together for classification or analysis.

7. A condition of harmonious, orderly interaction.

8. An organized and coordinated method; a procedure.[1]

Some of these definitions focus on the biological or natural idea of the word "system" (2a, 2b, 2c, 5). Others reference mechanical systems (2d) or systems of transportation and communication (2e). Still others focus on the social meanings of the word (4, 7) or on ideas and knowledge (3, 6, 8). Despite differences in emphasis, there is something that all of these definitions of "system" share. Look for it in the very first definition on the list, which describes systems as "a group of interacting, interrelated, or interdependent elements forming a complex whole." This understanding of a system as a set of parts that relate to form a whole contains all of the other special cases of this same concept. When understood in this way—as a set of parts that together form a complex whole—it is clear that games are systems.

In a game of Soccer, for example, the players, the ball, the goal nets, the playing field, are all individual elements. When a game of Soccer begins these elements gain specific relationships to each other within the larger system of the game. Each player, for example, plays in a certain position on one of two teams. Different player positions have roles that interrelate, both within the system that constitutes a single team (goalie vs. forward vs. halfback), and within the system that constitutes the relationship between teams (the goalie guarding the goal while an opposing forward attempts to score). The complex whole formed by all of these relationships within a system comprises the game of Soccer.

As systems, games provide contexts for interaction, which can be spaces, objects, and behaviors that players explore, manipulate, and inhabit. Systems come to us in many forms, from mechanical and mathematical systems to conceptual and cultural ones. One of the challenges of our current discussion is to recognize the many ways that a game can be framed as a system. Chess, for example, could be thought of as a strategic mathematical system. It could also be thought of as a system of social interaction between two players, or a system that abstractly simulates war.

The Elements of a System

A *system* is a set of things that affect one another within an environment to form a larger pattern that is different from any of the individual parts. In his textbook *Theories of Human Communication*, Stephen W. Littlejohn identifies four elements that constitute a system:

- The first is *objects*—the parts, elements, or variables within the system. These may be physical or abstract or both, depending on the nature of the system.

- Second, a system consists of *attributes*—the qualities or properties of the system and its objects.

- Third a system has *internal relationships* among its objects. This characteristic is a crucial aspect [of systems].

- Fourth, systems also possess an *environment*. They do not exist in a vacuum but are affected by their surroundings.[2]

Let us take a detailed look at a particular game, Chess. We will first think about Chess as a strictly strategic and mathematical system. This means considering Chess as a purely formal system of rules. Framed in this way, the four elements of the system of Chess are as follows:

- *Objects:* The objects in Chess are the pieces on the board and the board itself.

- *Attributes:* These are the characteristics the rules give these objects, such as the starting positions of each piece and the specific ways each piece can move and capture.

- *Internal Relationships:* Although the attributes determine the possible movements of the pieces, the internal relationships are the actual positions of the pieces on the board. These spatial relationships on the grid determine strategic relationships: one piece might be threatening another one, or protecting an empty square. Some of the pieces might not even be on the board.

- *Environment:* If we are looking just at the formal system of Chess, then the environment for the interaction of the objects is the play of the game itself. Play provides the context for the formal elements of a game.

But framing the game as a formal system is only one way to think about the system of Chess. We can extend our focus and think of Chess as a system with experiential dimensions as well. This means thinking of Chess not just as a mathematical and logical system, but also as a system of interaction between the players and the game. Changing the way that we frame the game affects how we would define the four components of a system. Framed as an experiential system, the elements of the system of Chess are as follows:

- *Objects:* Because we are looking at Chess as the interaction between players, the objects of the system are actually the two players themselves.

- *Attributes:* The attributes of each player are the pieces he or she controls, as well as the current state of the game.

- *Internal Relationships:* Because the players are the objects, their interaction constitutes the internal relationships of the system. These relationships would include not just their strategic interaction, but their social, psychological, and emotional communication as well.

- *Environment:* Considering Chess as an experiential system, the total environment would have to include not just the board and pieces of the game, but the immediate environment that contained the two players as well. We might term this the *context of play*. Any part of the environment that facilitated play would be included in this context. For example, if it were a play-by-email game of Chess, the context of play would have to include the software environment in which the players send and receive moves. Any context of play would also include players' preconceptions of Chess, such as the fact that they think it is cool or nerdy to play. This web of physical, psychological, and cultural associations delineate—not the experience of the game —but rather the context that surrounds the game, the environment within which the experience of play occurs.

Lastly, we can expand our focus and think about Chess as a cultural system. Here the concern is with how the game fits into culture at large. There are many ways to conceive of games as culture. For example, say that we wanted to look at the game of

Chess as a representation of ideological values associated with a particular time and place. We would want to make connections between the design of the game and larger structures of culture. We would be looking, for example, to identify cultural references made in the design of the game pieces (What is the gendered power relationship between King and Queen implied in their visual design?); references made in the structure and rituals of game play (Was playing Chess polite and gentlemanly or vulgar and cutthroat?); and references made to the people who play (Who are they—intellectuals, military types, or computer geeks?). Framed as a cultural system, the four elements of the system of Chess are as follows:

- *Objects:* The object is the game of Chess itself, considered in its broadest cultural sense.

- *Attributes:* The attributes of the game would be the designed elements of the game, as well as information about how, when, and why the game was made and used.

- *Internal Relationships:* The relationships would be the linkages between the game and culture. We might find, for example, a relationship between the "black and white" sides of the game and the way that race is referenced when the game pieces are represented figuratively.

- *Environment:* The environment of the system extends beyond any individual game of Chess, or even the context of play. The total environment for this cultural framing of Chess is culture itself, in all of its forms.

Note that there are innumerable ways of framing Chess as a cultural system. We could examine the complex historical evolution of the game. Or we could investigate the amateur and professional subcultures (books, websites, competitions, etc.) that surround the game. We could study the culture of Chess variants, in which Chess is redesigned by player-fans, or how Chess is referenced within popular culture, such as the Chess-like game Spock played on the television show *Star Trek*. The list goes on.

Framing Systems

Even though we were talking about the same game each time, as we proceeded from a formal to an experiential to a cultural analysis, our sense of what we considered as part of the system grew. In fact, each analysis integrated the previous system into itself. The hierarchical nature of complex systems makes this integration possible.

> Because of the hierarchical nature of the critical or complex system, with interactions over all scales, we can arbitrarily define what we mean by a unit: In a biological system, one can choose either a single cell, a single individual, such as an ant, the ant's nest, or the ant as a species, as the adaptive unit. In a human social system, one might choose an individual, a family, a company, or a country as the unit. No unit at any level has the right to claim priority status.[3]

In a game system, as in a human social system or biological system, hierarchies and interactions are scalable and embedded, as complexity theorist Per Bak points out in the quote above. Although no single framing has an inherent priority, there are specific relationships among the kinds of framings given here. The formal system constituting the rules of a game are embedded in its system of play. Likewise, the system of play is embedded in the cultural framing of the game. For example, understanding the cultural connotations of the visual design of a game piece still should take into account the game's rules and play: the relative importance of the pieces and how they are actually used in a game. For example, answering a cultural question regarding the politics of racial representation would have to include an understanding of the formal way the core rules of the game reference color. What does it mean that white always moves first?

Similarly, when you are designing a game you are not designing just a set of rules, but a set of rules that will always be experienced as play within a cultural context. As a result, you never have the luxury of completely forgetting about context when you are focusing on experience, or on experience and culture when you're focusing on the game's formal structure. It can be useful at times to limit the number of ways you are framing the game, but it is important to remember that a game's formal, experiential, and cultural qualities always exist as integrated phenomena.

The History of Systems

The formal use of systems as a methodology for study has a rich history, which we can only quickly outline here. Many of the ideas surrounding systems and systems theory come from Ludwig von Bertalanffy's 1928 graduate thesis, in which he describes organisms as living systems. By 1969, von Bertalanffy had formalized his approach in the book *General Systems Theory: Foundations, Development, Applications.* Von Bertalanffy proposed a systems-based approach to looking at radically different kinds of phenomena, from the movement of particles to the cellular structures of organisms to the organization of a society. Von Bertalanffy's book called for a single integrated science of systems that acknowledged the linkages between the way systems operate across radically varying scales. Bertalanffy's systems-based approach contributed to the development of the fields of information theory, game theory, and cybernetics; each of these fields, in turn, contributed to contemporary concepts of computer science.

Although formal systems theory is no longer in common use today, systems-based approaches have given rise to a variety of interdisciplinary fields, including studies of complexity, chaos, and artificial life. Scholars come to these fields from a wide array of disciplines, including mathematics, genetics, physics, biology, sociology, and economics. We will be only be touching on their work here, but if these systems-based investigations interest you, additional references can be found in the suggested readings for chapter 14, *Games as Emergent Systems.*

Open and Closed Systems

There are two types of systems, *open* and *closed*. In fact, the concept of open and closed systems forms the basis of much of our discussion concerning the formal properties of games and their social and cultural dimensions. This concept speaks not only to games themselves, but also to the relationships games have to players and their contexts. What distinguishes the two types of systems? Littlejohn writes, "One of the most common distinctions [in systems theory] is between closed and open systems. A *closed system* has no interchange with its environment. An *open system* receives matter and energy from its environment and passes matter and energy to its environment."[4]

What makes a system open or closed is the relationship between the system and the context, or environment, that surrounds it. The "matter and energy" that passes between a system and its environment can take a number of forms, from pure data (a thermometer measuring temperature and passing the information to the system of a computer program that tries to predict the weather), to human interaction (a person operating and interacting with the system of a car in order to drive down a highway). In both examples the system is open because there is some kind of transfer between the system and its environment. The software system passes temperature information from the outside climate. The car system exchanges input and output with the driver in a variety of ways (speedometer, gas pedal, steering wheel, etc.).

When we frame a game as a system it is useful to recognize whether it is being treated as an open or closed system. If we look at our three framings of Chess, which framings were open and which were closed?

- *Formal system:* As a formal system of rules, Chess is a closed, self-contained system.

- *Cultural system:* As a cultural system, Chess is clearly an open system, as we are essentially considering the way that the game intersects with other contexts such as society, language, history, etc.

- *Experiential system:* As an experiential system of play, things get tricky. Framing Chess as an experiential system could lead to understanding the game as either open or closed. If we only consider the players and their strategic game actions, we could say that once the game starts, the only relevant events are internal to the game. In this sense, the game is a closed system. On the other hand, we could emphasize the emotional and social baggage that players bring into the game, the distractions of the environment, the reputations that are gained or lost after the game is over. In this sense, the play of Chess would be an open system. Framed as play, games can be either open or closed.

In defining and understanding key concepts like design and systems, our aim is to better understand the particular challenges of game design and meaningful play. Game designers do practice design, and they do so by creating *systems.* But other kinds of designers create systems as well—so what is so special about games? The systems that game designers create have many peculiar qualities, but one of the most prominent is that they are interactive, that they require direct participation in the form of play. In the next chapter, we build directly on our understanding of systems and design to tackle this confounding but crucial concept: the enigmatic *interactivity*.

Notes

1. <dictionary.com>.
2. Stephen W. Littlejohn, *Theories of Human Communication,* 3rd edition (Belmont, CA: Wadsworth Publishing Company, 1989), p. 41.
3. Per Bak, "Self-Organized Criticality: A Holistic View of Nature." In *Complexity: Metaphors, Models and Reality,* edited by George A. Cowan, David Pine, and David Meltzer (Cambridge: Perseus Books, 1994), p. 492.
4. Littlejohn, *Theories of Human Communication,* p. 41.

Systems SUMMARY

- A **system** is a set of parts that interrelate to form a complex whole. There are many ways to frame a game as a system: a mathematical system, a social system, a representational system, etc.

- There are four elements that all systems share:

  - **Objects** are the parts, elements, or variables within the system.

  - **Attributes** are the qualities or properties of the system and its objects.

  - **Internal relationships** are the relations among the objects.

  - **Environment** is the context that surrounds the system.

  The way these elements are identified in any individual game depends on the way it is framed as a system. The four elements would be different, for example, if a game were framed as a formal, mathematical system, an experiential system of play, or as a cultural system.

- These three framings of a game as a system, **formal, experiential,** and **cultural,** are embedded in each other. A game as a formal system is always embedded within an experiential system, and a game as a cultural system contains formal and experiential systems.

- Although all three levels (formal, experiential, and cultural) exist simultaneously, it can be useful to focus on just one of them when making an analysis or solving a design problem. It is crucial when designing a game to understand how these three levels interact and interrelate to each other.

- Systems can be **open** or **closed.** An open system has an exchange of some kind with its environment. A closed system is isolated from its environment. Whether or not you consider a game as a closed or open system depends on the way you frame it:

  - **Formal** systems are closed systems.
  - **Experiential** systems can be open or closed systems.
  - **Cultural** systems are open systems.

Unit 1 | Core Concepts

action > outcome
four modes of interactivity
anatomy of a choice
internal event
external event
space of possibility

INTERACTIVITY

The word "interactivity" isn't just about giving players choices; it pretty much completely defines the game medium.—**Warren Spector,** *RE:PLAY: Game Design + Game Culture*

Hotrod joystick | | Volleyball

Introducing Interactivity

Play implies interactivity: to play with a game, a toy, a person, an idea, is to interact with it. More specifically, playing a game means making choices within a game system designed to support actions and outcomes in meaningful ways. Every action results in a change affecting the overall system. This process of action and outcome comes about because players interact with the designed system of the game. Interaction takes place across all levels, from the formal interaction of the game's objects and pieces, to the social interaction of players, to the cultural interaction of the game with contexts beyond its space of play.

In games, it is the explicit interaction of the player that allows the game to advance. From the interactivity of choosing a path to selecting a target for destruction to collecting magic stars, the player has agency to initiate and perform a whole range of explicit actions. In some sense, it is these moments of explicit action that define the tone and texture of a specific game experience. To understand this particular quality of games— the element of interaction—we must more completely grasp the slippery terms "interactive," "interaction," and "interactivity."

Defining Interactivity

Perhaps even more than "design" and "systems," debates over the term "interactivity" have run rampant. Interactivity is one of those words that can mean everything and nothing at once. If everything can indeed be considered interactive, then the concept loses its ability to help us solve design problems. In corralling this runaway word, our aim is to try and understand it in its most general sense, but also to identify those very particular aspects of interactivity that are relevant to games. To this end, we look at several definitions of interactivity. We begin with a general question: What is *"interaction?"* Here are some basic dictionary definitions:

- *interaction:* 1. intermediate action; 2. mutual or reciprocal action or influence;

- *interact:* to act on each other; act reciprocally;

- *interactive:* reciprocally active; acting upon or influencing each other; allowing a two-way flow of information between a device and a user, responding to the user's input.[1]

In the most general terms, interactivity simply describes an active relationship between two things. For our purposes, however, we require a slightly more rigorous definition, one that takes into account the particular nature of games. Instead of asking about interactivity in the abstract, what does it mean to say that something is "interactive?" More specifically, how does interactivity emerge from within a *system?*

Communications theorist Stephen W. Littlejohn defines interactivity this way: "Part and parcel of a system is the notion of 'relationship'…. Interactional systems then, shall be two or more communicants in the process of, or at the level of, defining the nature of their relationship."[2] In other words, something is interactive when there is a reciprocal relationship of some kind between two elements in a system. Conversations, databases, games, and social relationships are all interactive in this sense. Furthermore, relationships between elements in a system are defined through interaction.

Following this definition, digital media theorist and entrepreneur Brenda Laurel brings the concept of *representation* to an understanding of the term: "…something is interactive when people can participate as agents within a representational context. (An agent is 'one who initiates actions.')"[3] Laurel's model emphasizes the interpretive component of interactive experiences, framing an interactive system as a representational space.

In an alternative definition of interactivity, theorist Andy Cameron builds on this interpretive dimension by stressing the idea of *direct intervention.* In his essay "Dissimulations," Cameron writes that

> Interactivity means the ability to intervene in a meaningful way *within the representation itself,* not to *read* it differently. Thus interac-

tivity in music would mean the ability to change the sound, interactivity in painting to change colors, or make marks, interactivity in film…the ability to change the way the movie comes out."[4]

Cameron suggests a connection between interactivity and *explicit action,* a key feature of games and meaningful play. In some sense, it is these moments of explicit action that define the tone and texture of a specific game experience.

A final definition comes from game designer Chris Crawford, who metaphorically defines interactivity in terms of a conversation: "Interactivity: a cyclical process in which two actors alternately listen, think, and speak. The quality of interaction depends on the quality of each of the subtasks (listening, thinking, and speaking)."[5]

While his definition hearkens back to Littlejohn's relational model, Crawford's definition stresses the *iterative quality* of interactivity. He uses the following example for emphasis:

> A conversation, in its simplest form, starts out with two people, Joe and Fred. Joe says something to Fred. At this point, the ball is in Fred's court. He performs three steps in order to hold up his end of the conversation:
>
> *Step One:* Fred listens to what Joe has to say. He expends the energy to pay attention to Joe's words. He gathers in all of Joe's words and assembles them into a coherent whole. This requires an active effort on Fred's part.
>
> *Step Two:* Fred thinks about what Joe said. He considers, contemplates, and cogitates. The wheels turn in his mind as Fred develops his response to Joe's statement.
>
> *Step Three:* Fred expresses his response back to Joe. He forms his thoughts into words and speaks them.
>
> Now the tables are turned; the ball is in Joe's court. Joe must listen to what Fred says; Joe must think about it and develop a reaction; then he must express his reaction to Fred. This process cycles back and forth. Thus, a conversation is an iterative process in which each participant in turn listens, thinks, and speaks.[6]

Each of these definitions provides its own critical way of understanding interactivity: it takes place within a system, it is relational, it allows for direct intervention within a representational context, and it is iterative. Yet none of the definitions describes how and where interactivity can take place, and none of them address the relationship between structure and context, two key elements in the construction of meaning. These questions of the "how," "where," and "by whom" are critical to anyone faced with the challenge of designing interactivity.

In other words, none of these definitions resolve the question of whether or not all media, or even all experiences, are interactive. If interactivity is really so ubiquitous, can it possibly be a useful term for understanding games?

A Multivalent Model of Interactivity

Each of the previous definitions foreground a particular aspect of interaction; in our view, they are all are useful ways of defining interactivity. Rather than try and distill them into a composite definition, we have elected instead to offer a model of interactivity that accommodates each of these definitions. The model presents four modes of interactivity, or four different levels of engagement, that a person might have with an interactive system. Most "interactive" activities incorporate some or all of them simultaneously.

Mode 1: Cognitive interactivity; or interpretive participation
This is the psychological, emotional, and intellectual participation between a person and a system. Example: the complex imaginative interaction between a single player and a graphic adventure game.

Mode 2: Functional interactivity; or utilitarian participation
Included here: functional, structural interactions with the material components of the system (whether real or virtual). For example, that graphic adventure you played: how was the interface? How "sticky" were the buttons? What was the response time? How legible was the text on your high-resolution monitor? All of these elements are part of the total experience of interaction.

Mode 3: Explicit interactivity; or participation with designed choices and procedures
This is "interaction" in the obvious sense of the word: overt participation like clicking the non-linear links of a hyper-text novel, following the rules of a board game, rearranging the clothing on a set of paper dolls, using the joystick to maneuver Ms. Pac-Man. Included here: choices, random events, dynamic simulations, and other procedures programmed into the interactive experience.

Mode 4: Beyond-the-object-interactivity; or participation within the culture of the object
This is interaction outside the experience of a single designed system. The clearest examples come from fan culture, in which participants co-construct communal realities, using designed systems as the raw material. Will Superman come back to life? Does Kirk love Spock?

Some of these modes occur universally in human experience, such as Mode 1, cognitive interactivity. Yet not all of them do. For our purposes, Mode 3, explicit interactivity, comes closest to defining what we mean when we say that games are "interactive." An experience becomes truly interactive in the sense of Cameron's "direct intervention" only when the participant makes choices that have been designed into the actual structure of the experience.

The rest of this chapter focuses primarily on explicit interactivity and how game designers can create the kinds of choices that result in meaningful play. However, even though we will be focusing on Mode 3, it is important to remember that the other three modes of interactivity are also present as players make explicit choices. For example, choosing whether to fold or not in Poker represents a moment of explicit interactivity. But at the same time, the material quality and size of the cards affect the functional interactivity; the fanciful images on the face cards might engender cognitive interactivity; and notions about what it means to be a suave card shark—or perhaps resentment at

being trounced at the Poker table last week—represent forms of cultural participation that lie outside the bounds of the particular game being played.

Interaction, even the explicit interaction of a seemingly straightforward game choice, is never as simple as it appears at first glance. But before we dissect the components of explicit interactive choices, let's pause to consider the role of design itself in creating interactivity.

But Is it "Designed" Interaction?

Interaction comes in many forms. But for the purposes of designing interactivity, it is important to be able to recognize what forms of interactivity designers create. As an example, compare the following two actions: someone dropping an apple on the ground and someone rolling dice on a craps table. Although both are examples of interaction proper, only the second act, the rolling of the dice, is a form of designed interaction.

What about this action has been designed? First, the dice, unlike the apple, are part of a system (a game) in which the interaction between the player and the dice is made meaningful by a set of rules describing their relationship. This relationship, as defined by the rules of Craps, describes the connection between action and outcome—for example, "When the dice are rolled a player counts the number of dots appearing on the face-up sides of the dice." Even this extremely simple rule demonstrates how the act of rolling has meaning within the designed interactive system of the game. Secondly, the interaction is situated within a specific context: a game. Remember that meaningful play is tied not only to the concept of player action and system outcome, but also to a particular context in which the action occurs.

The description of "someone dropping an apple on the ground," on the other hand, does not contain a designed structure or context. What conditions would have to be present to evolve this simple interaction into a designed interaction? The dropping of the apple does meet baseline criteria for interaction: there is a reciprocal relationship between the elements of the system (such as the person's hand, the apple, and the ground). But is it a designed interaction? Is the interactivity situated within a specific context? Do we have any ideas about what dropping an apple might "mean" as a form of interaction between a person and an apple? Do we have a sense of the connection between action and outcome?

No. All we know is that an apple has been dropped. What is missing from this description is an explicitly stated context within which the dropping of the apple occurs. If we change the scenario a little by adding a second player and asking the two participants to toss the apple back and forth, we move toward a situation of designed interaction. If we ask the two apple-tossers to count the number of times in a row they caught the apple before dropping it, we add an even fuller context for the interaction. The simple addition of a rule designating that the players quantify their interaction locates the single act of toss-catch within an overall system. Each element in the system is assigned a meaning: the toss, the catch, and the dropped toss. Even in the simplest of contexts, design creates meaning.

Interaction and Choice

The careful crafting of player experience through a system of interaction is critical to the design of meaningful play. Yet, just what makes an interactive experience "meaningful"? We have argued that in order to create instances of meaningful play, experience has to incorporate not just explicit interactivity, but meaningful *choice*. When a player makes a choice in a game, the system responds in some way. The relationship between the player's choice and the system's response is one way to characterize the depth and quality of interaction. Such a perspective on interactivity supports the descriptive definition of meaningful play presented in chapter 3.

In considering the way that choices are embedded in game activity, we look at the design of choice on two levels: micro and macro. The *micro* level represents the small, moment-to-

moment choices a player is confronted with during a game. The *macro* level of choice represents the way these micro-choices join together like a chain to form a larger trajectory of experience. For example, this distinction marks the difference between tactics and strategy in a game such as Go. The *tactics* of Go concern the tooth-and-nail battles for individual sectors of the board, as individual pieces and small groups expand across territory, bumping up against each other in conflict and capture. The *strategy* of the game is the larger picture, the overall shape of the board that will ultimately determine the winner. The elegance of the design of Go lies in its ability to effortlessly link the micro and the macro, so that every move a player makes works simultaneously on both levels. Micro-interaction and macro-interaction are usually intertwined and there are, of course, numerous shades of gray in-between.

Keep in mind that "choice" does not necessarily imply *obvious* or *rational* choice, as in the selection of an action from a menu. Choice can take many forms, from an intuitive physical action (such as the "twitch" firing of a Time Crisis pistol) to the random throw of a die. Following are a few more examples of designed choices in games.

The choice of whether or not to take a hit in Blackjack. A Blackjack player always has a clear set of choices: the micro-choice of taking or not taking a hit will have the eventual outcome of a win or a loss against the house. On the macro-level, each round affects the total amount of money the player gains or loses over the course of the game. Playing each hand separately, according to its probability of beating the house is like tactics in Go. Counting cards, which links all of a players' hands between rounds, is a more long-term, strategic kind of choice-making.

The choice of what to type into the flashing cursor of a text adventure. This is a more open-ended choice context than the simple hit or pass of Blackjack. The micro-choice of typing in a command gives the player feedback about how the player moves through or changes the world. The choice to type the words "Move North" takes the player to another location in the game where different actions are possible—perhaps actions that will eventually solve the multi-part puzzles that exist on the macro-level of game play. Even when a player tries to take an action that the program cannot parse (such as typing "grab rock" instead of "get rock"), it is meaningful: the outcome of bumping up against the limits of the program's parsing ability serves to further delineate the boundaries of play.

The choice of what play to call in a Football game. This moment of game-choice is often produced collaboratively among a coaching staff, a quarterback, and the rest of the offensive players. There are a large number of possible plays to call, each with variations, and the choice is always made against the backdrop of the larger game: the score, the clock, the field position, the down, the strengths and weaknesses of both teams. The most macro-level of choices address the long-term movement of the ball across the field and the two teams' overall scores. The most micro-level of choices occur once the play is called and the ball is hiked: every offensive player has the moment-to-moment challenge of executing the play as the defensive team does its best to put a stop to it.

As these examples demonstrate, choice-making is a complex, multi-layered process. There is a smooth transition between the micro- and macro-levels of choice-making, which play out in an integrated way for the player. When the outcome of every action is discernable and integrated, choice-making leads to meaningful play. Game designer Doug Church, in his influential online essay "Formal Abstract Design Tools," outlines the way that these levels of choice transition into a complete game experience.

In a fighting game, every controller action is completely consistent and visually represented by the character on-screen. In Tekken, when Eddy Gordo does a cartwheel kick, you know what you're going to get. As the player learns moves, this consistency allows planning—intention—and the reliability of the world's reactions makes for perceived consequence. If I watch someone play, I can see how and why he or she is better than I am, but all players begin the game on equal footing.[7]

As Church points out, the macro-levels of choice-making include not only what to do over the course of a game, but also whether or not you want to play a game, and against whom. If you are beaten in a fighting game that doesn't contain clear and meaningful play, you will never know why you lost and you will most likely not play again. On the other hand, if you know why your opponent is better than you are, your loss is meaningful, as it helps you assess your own abilities, gives you ideas for improvement, and spurs on your overall interaction with the game.

Choice Molecules

[The designers of Spacewar!, the first computer game] identified action as the key ingredient and conceived Spacewar! as a game that could provide a good balance between thinking and doing for its players. They regarded the computer as a machine naturally suited for representing things that you could see, control, and play with. Its interesting potential lay not in its ability to perform calculations but in its capacity to represent action in which humans could participate.—**Brenda Laurel,** *Computers as Theater*

The capacity for games to "represent action in which players participate" forms the basis of our concept of "choice." If we consider that every choice has an outcome, then it follows that this action > outcome unit is the vehicle through which meaning in a game emerges. Although games can generate meaning in many ways (such as through image, text, sound, etc.), to understand the interactive nature of meaningful play, we focus on the kinds of meaning that grow from player interaction. At the heart of interactive meaning is the action > outcome unit, the molecule out of which larger interactive structures are built.

In order to examine this concept more closely we look at the classic arcade game Asteroids, a direct descendent of Spacewar!. In Asteroids, a player uses buttons to maneuver a tiny spaceship on the screen, avoiding moving asteroids and UFOs and destroying them by shooting projectiles. The action > outcome interactive units of Asteroids are manipulated through a series of five player commands, each one of them a button on the arcade game's control panel: rotate left, rotate right, thrust, fire, and hyperspace. Within the scope of an individual game, possible player actions map to the five buttons:

· **Press rotate right button:** spaceship rotates right

· **Press rotate left button:** spaceship rotates left

· **Press thrust button:** spaceship accelerates in the direction it is facing

· **Press fire button:** spaceship fires projectile (up to four on the screen at a time)

· **Press hyperspace button:** spaceship disappears and reappears in a different location (and occasionally perishes as a result)

Action on the screen is affected through the subtle (and not so subtle!) orchestration of these five controls. As the game progresses, each new moment of choice is a response to the situation onscreen, which is the result of a previous string of action > outcome units. The seamless flow that emerges is one of the reasons why Asteroids is so much fun to play. Rarely are players aware of the hundreds of choices they make each minute as they dodge space rocks and do battle with enemy ships— they perceive only their excitement and participation inside the game.

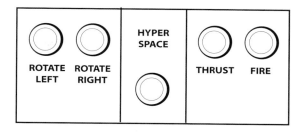

Anatomy of a Choice

Although the concept of choice may appear basic upon first glance, the way that a choice is actually constructed is surprisingly complex. To dissect our action > outcome molecule, we need to ask the following five questions. Together, they outline the *anatomy of a choice:*

1. What happened before the player was given the choice? What is the current state of the pieces on a game board, for example, or the level of a player's health? What set of moves just finished playing out? What is the game status of the other players? This question relates to the both the micro and macro events of a game, and addresses the context in which a choice is made.

2. How is the possibility of choice conveyed to the player? On a game board, the presence of empty squares or a "draw pile" might indicate the possibility of choice, whereas choices in a digital game are often conveyed through the game's controls. In Asteroids, for example, the five buttons on the control panel communicate the opportunity for choice-making to the player.

3. How did the player make the choice? Did the player make a choice by playing a card, pressing a button, moving a mouse, running in the opposite direction, or passing on a turn? The mechanisms a player uses to make a choice vary greatly, but all are forms through which players are given the opportunity to take action.

4. What is the result of the choice? How will it affect future choices? A player taking action within a system will affect the relationships present in that system. This element of the anatomy of a choice speaks to the outcome of a player action, identifying how a single choice impacts larger events within the game world. The outcome of taking a "hit" in Blackjack impacts whether or not the player wants to take another hit, as well as the outcome of the game.

5. How is the result of the choice conveyed to the player? The means by which the results of a choice are represented to a player can assume many guises, and forms of representation are often related to the materiality of the game itself. In a game of Twister, for example, the physical positioning of bodies in space conveys the results of choices; in Missile Command, the result of the choice to "fire" is conveyed by a slowly moving line of pixels, ending in an explosion; in Mousetrap, the mechanical workings (or non-workings) of the mousetrap convey the results of moving a mouse into the trap space. Note that step 5 leads seamlessly back to step 1, because the result of the choice provides the context for the next choice.

These are the five stages of a choice, the five events that transpire every time an action and outcome occur in a game. Each stage is an event that occurs internal or external to the game. *Internal events* are related to the systemic processing of the choice; *external events* are related to the representation of the choice to the player. These two categories make a distinction between the moment of action as handled by the internal game state and the manifestation of that action to the player.

The idea that a game can have an internal event represented externally implies that games are systems that store information. Jesper Juul, in a lecture titled "Play Time, Event Time, Themability," describes this idea by thinking of a game as a state machine:

A game is actually what computer science describes as a state machine. It is a system that can be in different states. It contains input and output functions, as well as definitions of what state and what input will lead to what following state. When you play a game, you are interacting with the state machine that is the game. In a board game, this state is stored in the position of the pieces on the board, in computer games the state is stored as variables, and then represented on the screen.[8]

In Juul's example of a board game, the "internal" state of the game is immediately evident to the players in the way that the pieces are arranged on the board. In the case of a computer game, as Juul points out, the internal variables have to be translated into a representation for the player. The distinction between internal and external events helps us to identify and distinguish the components of a choice. Within the action > outcome molecule, stages 1, 3, and 4 are internal events, and

Anatomy of a choice

1. What happened before the player was given the choice?
(internal event)

↓

2. How is the possibility of choice conveyed to the player?
(external event)

↓

3. How did the player make the choice?
(internal event)

↓

4. What is the result of the choice? How will it affect future choices?
(internal event)

↓

5. How is the result of the choice conveyed to the player?
(external event)

Figure 1

Anatomy of a Choice	Asteroids	Chess
1. What happened before the player was given the choice? (internal event)	Represented by the current positions and trajectories of the game elements.	Represented by the current state of the pieces on the board.
2. How is the possibility of choice conveyed to the player? (external event)	The possible actions are conveyed through the persistent button controls as well as the state of the screen, as it displays the relationships of the game elements.	The possible actions are conveyed through the arrangement of pieces on the board, including the empty squares where they can move.
3. How did the player make the choice? (internal event)	The player makes a choice by pressing one of the 5 buttons.	The players makes a choice by moving a piece.
4. What is the result of the choice? How will it affect future choices? (internal event)	Each button press affects the system in a different way, such as the position or orientation of the player's ship.	Each move affects the overall system, such as capturing a piece or shifting the strategic possibilities of the game.
5. How is the result of the choice conveyed to the player? (external event)	The result of the choice is then represented to player via screen graphics and audio.	The result of the choice is then represented to the player via the new arrangement of pieces on the board.

stages 2 and 5 are external events. These two layers of events form the framework within which the anatomy of a choice must be considered. To see how this all fits together, let us take an even closer look at the way choice is constructed in two of our example games, Asteroids and Chess. *(Figure 1)*

Although all five stages of the action > outcome choice event occurred in both games, there are some significant differences. In Asteroids, the available choices and the taking of an action both involve static physical controls. In Chess, the pieces on the board serve this function, even as they convey the current state of the game. The internal and external states of Chess are identical, but in Asteroids, what appears on the screen is only an outward extension of the internal state of the software. The "anatomy of a choice" structure occurs in every game, although each game will manifest choice in its own way.

This way of understanding choice in a game can be extremely useful in diagnosing game design problems. If your game is failing to deliver meaningful play, it is probably because there is a breakdown somewhere in the action > outcome chain. Here is a sample list of common "failure states" that can often be found in games and the way that they relate to the stages of a choice.

· *Feeling as if decisions are arbitrary.* If you need to play a card from your hand and it always feels like it doesn't matter which card you select, the game probably suffers in stage 4, the effect of the player's choice on the system of the game. The solution is to make sure that player actions have meaningful outcomes in the internal system of the game.

- *Not knowing what to do next.* This can be a common problem in large digital adventure games, where it is not clear how a player can take action to advance the game. The problem is in stage 2, representing choices to the player. These kinds of problems are often solved with additional information display, such as highlights on a map, or an arrow or indicator that helps direct the player.

- *Losing a game without knowing why.* You think that you're about to reach the top of the mountain, when your character dies unexpectedly from overexposure. This frustrating experience can come about because a player has not sufficiently been informed about the current state of the game. The problem might be in stage 5, where the new state of the game resulting from a choice is not represented clearly enough to the player.

- *Not knowing if an action had an outcome.* Although this sounds like something that would never happen, there are many examples of experimental interactivity (such as a gallery-based game with motion sensor inputs) in which the player never receives clear feedback on whether or not an action was taken. In this case, there is a breakdown at stages 3 and 4, when a player is taking an action and receiving feedback on the results.

These examples represent only a small sampling of the kinds of problems that a game's design can have. The anatomy of a choice is not a universal tool for fixing problems, but it can be especially useful in cases where the game is breaking down because of a glitch in the player's choice-making process.

Space of Possibility

We conclude this chapter with an excerpt from David Sudnow's book, *Pilgrim in a Microworld,* a wonderfully detailed personal account of one man's very real obsession with the video game Breakout. Sudnow brings readers into the space of designed interactivity through detailed descriptions of what he experienced—physically, psychologically, emotionally—as he played. There are remarkably few documents that offer such a sensitive and insightful analysis of designed interaction.

> I'd catch myself turning my chair into a more en face position vis-à-vis the TV. An obvious delusion. Maybe I could rest one elbow on the set to help feel the angle of my look and deepen a sense for the scale of things. See it from this side and that, see the invisible backside of things through an imaginary bodily tour of the object. Nonsense. If only I could feel the impact of the ball on the paddle, that would certainly help, would give me a tactile marker, stamping the gesture's places into a palpable little signature so I'd feel each destination being achieved and not just witness the consequences of a correct shot. Nonsense.
>
> Non-sense, just your eyes way up top, to be somehow fixed on things in ways that can't feel them fixing, then this silent smooth little plastic knob down there, neither near nor far away but in an untouchable world without dimensions. And in between all three nodes of the interface there's nothing but a theory of electricity. So fluid, to have to write your signature with precise consistency in size within the strict bounds of a two and three-sevenths of an inch of space, say, while the pen somehow never makes contact with the paper. There's nothing much to hold on to, not enough heft in this knob so your hands can feel the extent of very minor movements, no depth to things you can use to anchor a sense of your own solidity.[9]

As game designers, what can we glean from Sudnow's observations? His analysis suggests that there is a wealth of information to be gained about a game's interactivity by looking at it from the player's point of view. One of our disappointments with current writing on games and interactivity is that much analysis occurs not from the point of view of the player, but from the point of view of an outside spectator. This style of over-the-shoulder journalism fails to recognize that interactivity is something to be experienced, rather than observed. In writing a player-centric account of his encounter with the game, Sudnow calls attention to key concepts for designed interaction. Concepts such as directed choice, player control, amplification of input, system representation, and direct, visible feedback emerge in his poetic meditation on perception, attention, cognition, and the body.

Creating a game means designing a structure that will play out in complex and unpredictable ways, a space of possible action that players explore as they take part in your game. What possible actions might players take in the course of a game of Musical Chairs? They might push, shove, tickle, poke, or fight for their seat once the music stops and the mad scramble for chairs begins. The game designer must carefully craft a system of play in which these actions have meaning in support of the play of the game, and do not distract or interrupt its play.

But game designers do not directly design play. They only design the structures and contexts in which play takes place, indirectly shaping the actions of the players. We call the space of future action implied by a game design the *space of possibility*. It is the space of all possible actions that might take place in a game, the space of all possible meanings which can emerge from a game design. The concept of the space of possibility not only bridges the distance between the designed structure and the player experience, but it also combines the key concepts we have presented so far. The space of possibility is *designed* (it is a constructed space, a context), it generates *meaning* (it is the space of all possible meanings), it is a *system* (it is a space implied by the way elements of the system can relate to each other), and it is *interactive* (it is through the interactive functioning of the system that the space is navigated and explored).

The space of possibility springs forth out of the rules and structures created by the game designer. The space of possibility is

the field of play where your players will explore and cavort, compete and cooperate, as they travel through the experience of playing your game. But like David Sudnow who wishes he could reach out and touch the electronic blip of his Breakout paddle, as a game designer you can never directly craft the possible space of your game. You only can indirectly construct the space of possibility, through the rules you design. Game design is an act of faith—in your rules, in your players, in your game itself. Will your game create meaningful play? You can never know for sure. But understanding key concepts like design, systems, and interactivity can help bring you closer to a meaningful outcome.

Further Reading

Computers as Theater, by Brenda Laurel

Although Laurel is not speaking about games directly, her discussion of a dramatic theory of human-computer activity has many connections to the interactivity of games. The most relevant discussions to game design focus on the mechanics of interaction and the way people interact with machine interfaces.

> *Recommended:*
>
> Chapter 1: The Nature of the Beast
> Chapter 5: Design Principles for Human-Computer Activity

The Design of Everyday Things, by Donald Norman

Norman's book is a must read for any designer involved in the design of interactive systems. His approach has been formalized more recently within the catch-phrase "experience design," which places the user at the center of any designed activity. Although Norman is writing about everyday objects such as telephones and car doors, his observations have direct application to the design of games as interactive systems.

> *Recommended:*
>
> Chapter 1: The Psychopathology of Everyday Things
> Chapter 2: The Psychology of Everyday Actions
> Chapter 3: Knowledge in the Head and in the World

"Designing Interactive Theme Park Rides: Lessons From Disney's Battle for the Buccaneer Gold," by Jesse Schell and Joe Shochet

In this design postmortem of one of Disney's interactive theme park rides, Schell and Shochet discuss the reasons for the ride's success. Their analysis is design-driven, and offers insight into the tools, techniques, and psychology used to create an effective and entertaining interactive experience. Available at <www.gamasutra.com>.

"Formal Abstract Design Tools," by Doug Church

In making one of the most robust arguments for the development of a common vocabulary for games, Doug Church establishes a precedent for critical thinking within the emerging field of game design. "Formal Abstract Design Tools" is written from a game design perspective and explores concrete concepts of interactivity in the design of player experience. Available at <www.gamasutra.com>.

Pilgrim in the Microworld, by David Sudnow

This first-person account of one man's genuine obsession with the Atari 2600 game Breakout offers a clear portrait of the aesthetics of interactive systems. Concepts related to the anatomy of a choice, discernability and integration of player action, pleasure, and core mechanics are discussed in terms of player experience, making it a valuable resource for those intent on understanding just what is happening from moment-to-moment during game play.

> *Recommended:*
>
> Memory
> Interface
> Cathexis
> Eyeball
> Coin

The Art of Interactive Design: A Euphorious and Illuminating Guide to Building Successful Software, by Chris Crawford

The Art of Interactive Design is a non-technical book about the design of interactivity. Crawford uses his experience as a designer of games and interactive systems to discuss how interactivity works. For Crawford, interaction is "a cyclic process in which two actors alternatively listen, think, and speak." This conversational model of interaction is used throughout the text to good effect.

> *Recommended:*
>
> Part I: Chapters 1–6

Notes

1. <dictionary.com>.
2. Stephen W. Littlejohn, *Theories of Human Communication,* 3rd edition (Belmont, CA: Wadsworth Publishing Company, 1989), p. 175.
3. Brenda Laurel, *Computers as Theater* (Reading, MA: Addison-Wesley Publishing Company, 1993), p. 112.
4. Andy Cameron, *Dissimulations: Illusions of Interactivity* (MFJ No. 28: Spring 1995), <http://infotyte.rmit.edu.au/rebecca/html/dissimulations.html>.
5. Chris Crawford, *Understanding Interactivity* (San Francisco: No Starch Press), 2002, p. 6.
6. Ibid; p. 7.
7. Doug Church, "Formal Abstract Design Tools." <www.gamasutra.com>, July 16, 1999.
8. Jesper Juul, Computer Games and Digital Textuality. Conference at IT University of Copenhagen, March 1–2, 2001.
9. David Sudnow, *Pilgrim in a Microworld* (New York: Warner Books, 1983), p. 117.

Interactivity
SUMMARY

- **Interactivity** is closely linked to the concepts of design, systems, and meaningful play. When a player interacts with the designed system of a game, meaningful play emerges.

- There are many valid definitions of interactivity. Cutting across all of them are **four modes of interactivity:**

   Mode 1: Cognitive interactivity; or interpretive participation;
   Mode 2: Functional interactivity; or utilitarian participation;
   Mode 3: Explicit interactivity; or participation with designed choices and procedures;
   Mode 4: Beyond-the-object-interactivity or cultural participation.

- These four modes are not distinct categories but are instead overlapping ways of understanding any moment of interactivity. They usually occur simultaneously in any experience of a designed system.

- Not all interaction is **designed interaction.** When an interaction is designed, it has an internal structure and a context that assign meaning to the actions taken.

- An interactive context presents participants with **choices.** Choices can be **micro-**choices of moment-to-moment interactivity or **macro-**choices, which concern the long-term progress of the game experience.

- The basic unit out of which interactive meaning is made is the **action > outcome** unit. These units are the molecules out of which interactive designers (including game designers) create larger structures of designed interaction.

- Within each action > outcome event is a series of five stages that help construct a choice in a game. These stages are expressed through the following questions:

   1. What happened before the player was given the choice?
   2. How is the possibility of choice conveyed to the player?
   3. How did the player make the choice?
   4. What is the result of the choice? How will it affect future choices?
   5. How is the result of the choice conveyed to the player?

- Each of these stages represents either an **internal event,** in which the system of the game processes and receives the choice, or an **external event,** in which the choice is represented to the player.

- The **space of possibility** of a game is the space of all possible actions and meanings that can emerge in the course of the game. This concept ties together meaning, design, systems, and interactivity.

SPY vs SPY

OF RISK

THE CATTLEMEN WESTERN STRATEGY GAME

the game is nirtz

Made in U.S.A. by Ideal Toy Corporation, Hollis, N.Y. NO. 2300-2-300

IDEA

MILTON THE MONSTER GAM

"Goodbye, Mr. Chips" GAME

Based o
of the s

DOUBLE DRAGON

THE BOARD GAME

2 to 4
Players
Ages
7 to 14

POLE POSITION

Can You Dodge The Mad M
And Rescue The Jungl

JUNGLE HUNT

CA
THE FRE

Unit 1 | Core Concepts

DEFINING GAMES

play
games
designed system
artificial
conflict
rules
quantifiable outcome
games and puzzles
role-playing games

7

The word [game] is used for so many different activities that it is not worth insisting on any proposed definition. All in all, it is a slippery lexicological customer, with many friends and relations in a wide variety of fields.—**David Parlett,** *The Oxford History of Board Games*

What are games? Are they things in the sense of artifacts? Are they behavioral models, or simulations of social situations? Are they vestiges of ancient rituals, or magical rites? It is difficult and even curious when one tries to answer the question "what are games," since it is assumed that games are many things and at the same time specific games are different from one another—but are they?—**E. M. Avedon,** *"The Structural Elements of Games"*

Entering by way of meaningful play, following a path of embedded concepts connecting design to systems to interactivity, we have arrived at the heart of our study: games. It is therefore high time to define just what it is that makes a game a game. Should we even attempt such a definition? Perhaps, as game historian David Parlett warns in the quote that opens this chapter, any attempt to define the word "game" is a foolish endeavor. On the other hand, if one of our goals is to help formalize the field of game design, then it seems crucial to define the object that is so central to the discipline.

Historically, play and games have been studied in a myriad of ways, from economists using game-like simulations to literary theorists studying the "play" of meaning in language and literature. These investigations study games or play in the service of another field. Our intent, on the other hand, is to study play and games within the field of game design. A definition of "game" should help to not only distinguish game design from other design practices, but also bring us closer to an understanding of meaningful play.

Play and Game

As a first step, let us see how *game* relates to the equally complex *play*. We begin with an obvious question: Is there a difference between the words "play" and "game"? Do they refer to the same thing? In English, there is a clear distinction between the two words. But as David Parlett points out in the *The Oxford History of Board Games,* not all languages separate the two concepts. The phrase "to play a game," in both German and French, for example, uses different versions of the same word for both "play" and "game." In French *"on joue á un jeu;* in German, *man spielt ein Spiel."*[1] Although there are many ways to define play and games, we will take advantage of the difference that English affords to consider games and play as two separate ideas with related, but distinct meanings.

It turns out that play and games have a surprisingly complex relationship. Play is both a larger and a smaller term than "game," depending on the way it is framed. In one sense, "play" is a larger term that includes "game" as a subset. In another, the reverse is true: "game" is the bigger term, and includes "play" within it. Consider each of these relationships separately:

Relationship one: Games are a subset of play.
If we think about all of the activities we could call play, from two dogs playfully chasing each other in a grassy field, to a child singing a nursery rhyme, to a community of online role-players, it seems that only some of these forms of play would actually constitute what we might think of as a game. Playing Dodge Ball, for example, is playing a game: players obey a formalized set of rules and compete to win. The activities of playing on a seesaw, or horsing around on a jungle gym, however, are forms of play which do not constitute a game. Most forms of play are looser and less organized than games. However, some forms of play are formalized, and these forms of play can often be considered games. In this sense, it is clear that "game" is a subset of "play." This is a typological approach, one that defines the relationship between play and games according to the forms they take in the world.

Relationship two: Play is a component of games.
In a different sense, games can be thought of as containing play. This entire book is about games, and one component of games is play. The experience of play is but one of many ways of looking at and understanding games. Within the larger phenomenon of games, then, the play of the game represents one aspect of games. Although play is a crucial element of the larger concept of games, "play"

is in fact a subset of "game." Rather than typological, this pairing of the terms represents a more conceptual approach that situates play and games within the field of game design.

This double formulation of play and games may sound contradictory, but it is not simply a terminological sleight-of-hand. The point is that there are important differences between the words "game" and "play." English may be an anomaly in the way that it differentiates between these two terms, but it is an extremely useful distinction. A good definition of game should distinguish it clearly from play in both of the senses described here.

Comparing Definitions

One challenge of understanding the term "game" is that it has so many uses. Consider, for example, many of the ways that the word is utilized in English:

- limp or crippled: a *game* leg

- a hunted animal: *game* hunting season is open

- being skilled, particularly in sports or in romance: having *game;* "he got *game*"

- to partake in gambling: to spend a night *gaming* in Vegas

- social and psychological manipulation: playing head *games*

- a procedure for gaining an end: playing the waiting *game* with a stubborn friend

- a field in which one earns a living: the writing *game* and, of course

- board *games,* card *games,* computer *games,* etc.

For our purposes, only a single subset of all of the possible meanings of "game" is relevant: the category of games proper, a category that includes board games, card games, sports, computer games, and similar activities. Put another way, games are what game designers create. Although this is an important qualification, it does not bring us any closer to a precise understanding of what is and what is not a game.

Luckily, we are not the first to attempt a definition of "game," so we will be taking a close and comparative look at eight definitions that come from a variety of fields. In and among the definitions a handful of thorny issues appear again and again. These issues not only include articulating the unique qualities that make a game a game, but also differentiating games from similar phenomena, such as other forms of play, conflict, and contestation. It is also clear that there is a difference between defining games themselves and defining the act of playing a game.

There is one final point to make regarding the difference between "play" and "game." The definitions of "game" to follow were written in many languages, and when translated to English there is some slippage between "play" and "game." As a result, we look at definitions of play as well as "game" in the course of our investigation. Bear in mind that we are not building a definition of play (that comes in a later chapter), but are using definitions of play to shed light on an understanding of games.

Definition 1: David Parlett

David Parlett is a game historian who has written extensively on card games and board games. Earlier we noted Parlett's skepticism regarding the ability to define the slippery term "game." Yet despite his assertion to the contrary, Parlett does provide a model for understanding games.

Parlett begins by distinguishing between formal and informal games. "An informal game is merely undirected play, or 'playing around,' as when children or puppies play at rough and tumble." He contrasts this kind of activity with a "formal game":

> A formal game has a twofold structure based on ends and means:
>
> *Ends*. It is a contest to achieve an objective. (The Greek for game is agôn, meaning contest.) Only one of the contenders, be they individuals or teams, can achieve it, since achieving it ends the game. To achieve that object is to win. Hence a formal game, by definition, has a winner; and winning is the "end" of the game in both senses of the word, as termination and as object.
>
> *Means*. It has an agreed set of equipment and of procedural "rules" by which the equipment is manipulated to produce a winning situation.[2]

Parlett's distinction between formal and informal games directly addresses a key challenge in arriving at a definition of "game:" how to distinguish games from other forms of play. What Parlett calls an "informal game" of two puppies romping about might more simply be called *play*. His definition of a "formal game" has two main components:

* *Ends:* The fact that a "formal game" is a contest with an endpoint as its goal.

* *Means:* The agreed-upon rules and materials by which one wins the contest.

Both components—the idea of winning and the idea of doing so by means of rules—are key ideas in defining games, and in distinguishing them from other, less "formal" kinds of play.

Definition 2: Clark C. Abt

In his book *Serious Games,* Clark C. Abt proposes the following definition of games:

> Reduced to its formal essence, a game is an *activity* among two or more independent *decision-makers* seeking to achieve their *objectives* in some *limiting context*. A more conventional definition would say that a game is a context with rules among adversaries trying to win objectives.[3]

Abt's definition offers an understanding of games that emphasizes the active role of players in a game. Here are the four key terms he highlights:

* *Activity:* a game is an activity, a process, an event;

* *Decision-makers:* games require players actively making decisions;

* *Objectives:* as with Parlett's definition, games have goals;

* *Limiting context:* there are rules that limit and structure the activity of the game.

Comparing Abt's definition to Parlett's, we have another instance where games are seen to have a goal or objective. Abt refines Parlett's idea of rules-based *means* by implying that rules are intrinsically limiting. But perhaps the most interesting component is Abt's acknowledgment that games are an activity in which players *make decisions*. We know from our discussion of meaningful play that the interactivity present in games is based on players making decisions that have meaningful outcomes.

Does the scope of Abt's definition feel appropriate? A definition of games can fail by being so narrow as to leave things out that are games or by being so broad that it includes things that are not games. Abt writes, in the same volume, that his definition fails on both accounts:

> The trouble with this definition is that not all games are contests among adversaries—in some games the players cooperate to achieve a common goal against an obstructing force or natural situation that is itself not really a player since it does not have objectives.[4]

Abt, of course is correct. With its requirement of two or more independent decision-makers and emphasis on adversarial contest, his definition is too narrow—it leaves out cooperative or solitaire games. And, as he goes on to add, the definition is also too broad:

> Of course, most real-life activities involve independent decision-makers seeking to achieve objectives in some limiting context.... Political and social situations can often also be viewed as games. Every election is a game. International relations are a game. Every personal argument is a game. And almost all business activity is a game. Whether these contests of politics, war, economics, and interpersonal relations are played with resources of power, skill, knowledge, or luck, they always have the common characteristics of reciprocal decisions among independent actors with at least partly conflicting objectives."[5]

War? Elections? Arguments? Games do bear similarity to other forms of human conflict. Although there are some very useful concepts in Abt's definition, we still have a long way to go in demarcating exactly what does and does not constitute a game.

Definition 3: Johann Huizinga

In 1938, Dutch Anthropologist Johann Huizinga published a groundbreaking study of the play element in culture, *Homo Ludens* ("Man the Player"). Among other things, *Homo Ludens* provides a definition of what Huizinga calls "play":

> [Play is] a free activity standing quite consciously outside "ordinary" life as being "not serious," but at the same time absorbing the player intensely and utterly. It is an activity connected with no material interest, and no profit can be gained by it. It proceeds within its own proper boundaries of time and space according to fixed rules and in an orderly manner. It promotes the formation of social groupings, which tend to surround themselves with secrecy and to stress their difference from the common world by disguise or other means.[6]

In this definition, Huizinga asserts that play:

- is outside ordinary life;
- is "not serious";
- is utterly absorbing;
- is not to be associated with material interest or profit;
- takes place in its own boundaries of time and space;
- proceeds according to rules;
- creates social groups that separate themselves from the outside world.

One of strengths of this definition is that Huizinga manages to identify some of the more elusive and abstract qualities of play. The idea that play is both utterly absorbing but also not serious, for example, wonderfully describes the sense of being at play. On the other hand, it is not clear that these experiential qualities will help define a game: just because a poorly designed game fails to be absorbing doesn't mean that it is not a game. Other aspects of his definition, such as his emphasis on play's separation from ordinary life and the fact that play takes place within special boundaries of time and space, point to the intrinsic artificiality of games. Is this feature of artificiality a defining quality of games? We shall see.

Huizinga's definition includes many important ideas, but on the whole it has some problems. Several of the components, such as the fact that play creates social groups, address the effects of play and games rather than games themselves. Other elements, such as the disavowal of material gain from play, are too closely linked to the ideological agenda of *Homo Ludens*. In the end, the inclusive generality of Huizinga's definition is its greatest weakness. It does not, for example, ultimately differentiate between "play" and "game".

Definition 4: Roger Caillois

Expanding on the work of Huizinga during the 1960s, the French sociologist Roger Caillois published *Man, Play, and*

Games, a book that is in many ways a direct response to *Homo Ludens.* Caillois also presents a definition of play, describing it as being:

- *Free:* in which playing is not obligatory; if it were, it would at once lose its attractive and joyous quality as diversion;

- *Separate:* circumscribed within limits of space and time, defined and fixed in advance;

- *Uncertain:* the course of which cannot be determined, nor the result attained beforehand, and some latitude for innovations being left to the player's initiative;

- *Unproductive:* creating neither goods, nor wealth, nor new elements of any kind; and, except for the exchange of property among the players, ending in a situation identical to that prevailing at the beginning of the game;

- *Governed by rules:* under conventions that suspend ordinary laws, and for the moment establish new legislation, which alone counts;

- *Make-believe:* accompanied by a special awareness of a second reality or of a free unreality, as against real life.[7]

Some of these ideas were part of the previous definitions; several are new. Every definition so far includes reference to the fact that play is governed by rules. The ideas that play exists in a separate space and does not create capital are borrowed from Huizinga. But Caillois extends an understanding of play by describing it as free or voluntary, by pointing out that the end of a game is uncertain, and by associating play with a sense of make-believe.

Do all of the elements Caillois lists really describe games? Although they seem to make intuitive sense, it is possible to think of situations where games are not voluntary, uncertain, or make-believe. If you are pressured by your friends into playing a game that you don't want to play, is it still a game? If a Chess master plays against a beginner, is the outcome of the game uncertain for the Chess master? Is there a make-believe element to Tic-Tac-Toe?

A central problem with Caillois' definition is that like Huizinga's definition, it is too broad for our purposes. In *Man, Play, and Games,* Caillois includes under the rubric of play activities such as theater and informal rough-housing. Although these activities might be considered play, we are looking for a definition that more narrowly addresses the particular instance of games.

Definition 5: Bernard Suits

Bernard Suits is a philosopher with a strong interest in games. His playful book *Grasshopper: Games, Life, and Utopia* is a retelling of the Grasshopper and the Ants fable; it is also a deep investigation into the nature of games. Suits offers this definition of games:

> To play a game is to engage in activity directed towards bringing about a specific state of affairs, using only means permitted by rules, where the rules prohibit more efficient in favour of less efficient means, and where such rules are accepted just because they make possible such activity.[8]
>
> —or more succinctly—
>
> I also offer the following simpler and, so to speak, more portable version of the above: playing a game is the voluntary effort to overcome unnecessary obstacles.[9]

Although Suit's definitions sound abstract, he is covering familiar territory. Here are the primary elements from both versions:

- *Activity:* as with Abt, Suits emphasizes the activity of playing a game;

- *Voluntary:* games are freely entered into;

- *A specific state of affairs:* games have a goal;

- *Rules:* as in the previous definitions, Suits identifies rules as a component of games;

- *Inefficiency:* the rules of games limit behavior, making it less efficient;

- *Rules are accepted:* playing a game means accepting the rules.

Other definitions have included many of these elements: the fact that a game is an activity, that it is voluntary, has a goal, and involves rules. However, Suits adds some new ideas to the mix. When he states that "the rules prohibit more efficient in favour of less efficient means…such rules are accepted just because they make possible such activity," he is referring to what he calls the *lusory attitude,* the peculiar state of mind of game players. Part of the lusory attitude is that the rules of a game make play inefficient: if a runner wanted to cross the finish line as efficiently as possible, she might leave the track and cut across the field—but the rules tell her to stay within the white lines. Another component of the lusory attitude is that players accept these rules, taking on the "unnecessary obstacles" of a game simply because they make play possible. Suits is actually pointing to the way that games create *meaning* as players accept these rules, goals, and obstacles in order to play.

As insightful as this definition is, it is important to note that Suits does not ultimately offer a definition of game, but a definition of the act of *playing a game.* In fact, the definitions of Huizinga and Caillois similarly focus on the activity of play rather than on games themselves. However, the next two definitions will bring us closer to the territory of games themselves.

Definition 6: Chris Crawford
Chris Crawford is a pioneering computer game designer who has written extensively about game design, narrative, and interactivity. In his influential book *The Art of Computer Game Design,* Crawford does not offer a succinct definition of games, but he does list four primary qualities that define the category of things we call games: representation, interaction, conflict, and safety. We have pulled together excerpts from the first chapter of his book, where he summarizes these four qualities:

> *Representation:* A game is a closed formal system that subjectively represents a subset of reality. By "closed" I mean that the game is complete and self-sufficient as a structure. The model world created by the game is internally complete; no reference need be made to agents outside of the game. By formal I mean only that the game has explicit rules. A game's a collection of parts which interact with each other, often in complex ways. It is a system. A game creates a subjective and deliberately simplified representation of emotional reality.[10]

> *Interaction:* The most fascinating thing about reality is not that it is, or even that it changes, but *how* it changes, the intricate webwork of cause and effect by which all things are tied together. The only way to properly represent this webwork is to allow the audience to explore its nooks and crannies, to let them generate causes and observe effects. Games provide this interactive element, and it is a crucial factor in their appeal.[11]

> *Conflict:* A third element appearing in all games is conflict. Conflict arises naturally from the interaction in a game. The player is actively pursuing some goal. Obstacles prevent him from easily achieving this goal. Conflict is an intrinsic element of all games. It can be direct or indirect, violent or nonviolent, but it is always present in every game.[12]

> *Safety:* Conflict implies danger; danger means risk of harm; harm is undesirable. Therefore, a game is an artifice for providing the psychological experiences of conflict and danger while excluding their physical realizations. In short, a game is a safe way to experience reality. More accurately, the results of a game are always less harsh than the situations the game models.[13]

We can consider each of these four qualities separately. Crawford's notion of *representation* is reminiscent of the quality of make-believe listed by Caillois. But Crawford takes the concept one step further, linking the game's capacity for representation directly to its rules, and to its status as a *system* of interlocking parts. In fact, Crawford's definition is the first to explicitly call games a system, perhaps because he is the first of these authors writing from a digital game point of view. Tied closely to the systemic nature of games is Crawford's element of *interaction.* His scheme of interactive "cause and effect" parallels the ideas of action and outcome outlined in the previous chapter.

Crawford's definition names *conflict* for the first time. Although Parlett's "contest to achieve an objective" and Abt's "contest among adversaries" imply conflict, Crawford names conflict explicitly, linking it directly to the fact that games have goals. His final characteristic of games, *safety,* echoes the emphasis made in other definitions on the artificiality of games, that they take place in a space and time separate from ordinary life. Although these four characteristics describe games, they are not, strictly speaking, definitional.

Definition 7: Greg Costikyan

Greg Costikyan, a game designer and writer who has authored many articles on games, proposes a definition for the term in his essay, "I Have No Words and I Must Design:"[14]

> A game is a form of art in which participants, termed players, make decisions in order to manage resources through game tokens in the pursuit of a goal.

The key terms in this definition are:

- *Art:* games are identified as a form of culture;

- *Decision-making players:* games require active participation as choices are made;

- *Resource management:* player decisions hinge on manipulating resources;

- *Game tokens:* the means by which players enact their decisions;

- *Goal:* a game has an objective.

Like Crawford, Costikyan is influenced by digital game design and shares an emphasis on the decision-making, interactive quality of game playing. Although his acknowledgement of the goal of a game is something mentioned in other definitions, Costikyan's formulation has a number of unique elements. For example, his is the only definition to leave out the special quality of rules in defining a game. Also notable is a detailed explication of the systemic quality of a game: the way that players manage game resources through game tokens. Costikyan is also the only writer to link games to art, or to any other cultural practice, for that matter. While we also emphasize the fact that games are cultural, Costikyan's decision to associate games with "art" is less useful for our purposes. Labeling games as art embroils them in contemporary debates about games and art, high culture and low culture, and the social status of games. Undoubtedly, this is Costikyan's provocative intention.

Definition 8: Elliot Avedon and Brian Sutton-Smith

Brian Sutton-Smith is perhaps the most prolific and important scholar of play and games in the twentieth century. In *The Study of Games,* which Sutton-Smith co-edited with Elliot Avedon, the authors present an extremely concise and powerful definition of games:

> Games are an exercise of voluntary control systems, in which there is a contest between powers, confined by rules in order to produce a disequilibrial outcome.[15]

The key elements of this definition are:

- *Exercise of control systems:* games involve some form of physical or intellectual activity:

- *Voluntary:* games are freely entered into;

- *Contest between powers:* games embody a conflict between players;

- *Confined by rules:* the limiting nature of rules is emphasized;

- *Disequilibrial outcome:* the outcome of a game is a goal-state which is different than the starting state of the game.

Although none of these elements are wholly original to this definition, the strength of Avedon and Sutton-Smith's formulation is that it is compact, clear, and addresses games themselves, rather than the activity of playing them. Elegantly narrow in scope, their definition clearly demarcates games from less formal play activities. On the other hand, it doesn't contain all of the elements found in other definitions. Perhaps it is time to step back and take stock.

Elements of a game definition	Parlett	Abt	Huizinga	Caillois	Suits	Crawford	Costikyan	Avedon | Sutton-Smith
Proceeds according to rules that limit players	√	√	√	√	√	√		√
Conflict or contest	√					√		√
Goal-oriented/outcome-oriented	√	√			√		√	√
Activity, process, or event		√			√			√
Involves decision-making		√				√	√	
Not serious and Absorbing			√					
Never associated with material gain			√	√				
Artificial/Safe/Outside ordinary life			√	√		√		
Creates special social groups			√					
Voluntary				√	√			√
Uncertain				√				
Make-believe/Representational				√		√		
Inefficient					√			
System of parts/Resources and Tokens						√	√	
A form of art							√	

A Comparison

The chart above summarizes the elements of a game, as described in each of the definitions.

In simplifying complex ideas to a grid of common elements, much of the context and subtlety of the authors' ideas is clearly lost. Each author defines games for particular reasons within specific contexts; for example, with the exception of Chris Crawford and Greg Costikyan, none of the authors are operating from within the field of game design. On the other hand,

this cannibalistic dissection of their approaches to defining games yields some interesting comparative results. All of the authors except Costikyan include rules as a key component. Beyond this there is no clear consensus. Although 10 of the 15 elements are shared by more than one author, apart from rules and goals, there is no majority agreement on any one of them.

It is clear that not all of the elements need to be included in a definition of game. Some elements, such as games being voluntary or inefficient, do not seem to apply to all games. Others, such as the fact that games create social groups, describe the effects of games rather than games themselves. Still other elements, such as the representational or make-believe quality of games, appear in many other media and do not help differentiate games from other kinds of designed experiences.

Our Definition

Cobbling together elements from the previous definitions and whittling away the unnecessary bits leaves us with the following definition:

A *game* is a system in which players engage in an artificial conflict, defined by rules, that results in a quantifiable outcome.

This definition structurally resembles that of Avedon and Sutton-Smith, but contains concepts from many of the other authors as well. Here are the definition's primary ideas:

System: We introduced the concept of a system in chapter 5. Systems are fundamental to our approach to games.

Players: A game is something that one or more participants actively play. Players interact with the system of a game in order to experience the play of the game.

Artificial: Games maintain a boundary from so-called "real life" in both time and space. Although games obviously occur within the real world, artificiality is one of their defining features.

Conflict: All games embody a contest of powers. The contest can take many forms, from cooperation to competition, from solo conflict with a game system to multiplayer social conflict. Conflict is central to games.

Rules: We concur with the authors that rules are a crucial part of games. Rules provide the structure out of which play emerges, by delimiting what the player can and cannot do.

Quantifiable outcome: Games have a quantifiable goal or outcome. At the conclusion of a game, a player has either won or lost or received some kind of numerical score. A quantifiable outcome is what usually distinguishes a game from less formal play activities.

For the rest of this book, this definition is what we mean when we say "game." It applies to all kinds of games, from computer and video games to parlor games and sports. We can also use this definition to define the field of study at the center of this book:

Game design is the process by which a game designer creates a game, to be encountered by a player, from which meaningful play emerges.

Aren't you happy to finally know what it is this book is about?

The Puzzle of Puzzles

This definition of games is intentionally quite narrow. It is not our intent to understand the broad phenomena of play, but instead to clearly demarcate the realm of games and game design. But is the definition *too* narrow? Are there things that are clearly are games but that don't fit this definition? This chapter on defining games concludes by looking at two kinds of game-activities that may or may not fit into the category of games this definition delineates. These "limit cases" will help clarify how this definition can help us investigate game-like phenomena.

First, puzzles. According to puzzle and game designer Scott Kim, puzzles are different from games because puzzles have a correct answer or outcome. Think of a crossword puzzle: the puzzle designer creates the correct answer, and the player's activity consists of trying to reconstruct that answer. This is a very different situation than a game of Poker, for example, in which there is no fixed "right answer" posed by the creator of the game. Instead, in Poker, players make complex decisions at every moment, taking into account the evolving dynamics of the game.

But this does not mean that a puzzle is not a game. Recall our definition:

A *game* is a system in which players engage in an artificial conflict, defined by rules, that results in a quantifiable outcome.

A crossword puzzle contains all of the elements of this definition. It is a system of squares, letters, and clues, in which a player follows rules in order to arrive at an appropriate outcome. Although the conflict is between the player and the system rather than between a set of players, a crossword puzzle is most certainly a game. In fact, all kinds of puzzles are games. They might be considered a special subset of games, but they clearly meet the requirements of the definition.

Sometimes, it is difficult to determine whether or not a game is a puzzle. In his article, "What is a Puzzle?"[16] Kim references game designer Kevin Maroney, who points to Solitaire as a borderline case. If we think about Solitaire as an open-ended activity that can play out in many ways, it is not a puzzle. On the other hand, as Kim states, "in fact it is a kind of puzzle, since any given deck has a definite solution (or sometimes no solution). Shuffling the cards is a way to randomly generate a new puzzle."[17]

We are not going to split hairs. In our opinion, all puzzles are games, although they constitute a special kind of game. Thinking about a game as a puzzle, a game with a correct answer or set of answers, can be a useful way to frame a game. For example, is your 3D adventure game lacking a sense of play? Perhaps it is too puzzle-like, with all of the outcomes predetermined, and you need to ease the overall design away from puzzle territory. Alternately, if your adventure game feels too open-ended, perhaps you can inject some puzzle-like game play into it and better shape the player's sense of accomplishment. The idea of the "puzzle" can be a helpful way to frame game design problems.

Role-Playing Games

The second game "limit case" is role-playing games. Off the computer, these are games such as Dungeons & Dragons, in which players are cast as characters in an imaginary world. Digital role-playing games can be single-player adventures like the classic Ultima games, or multiplayer community worlds like EverQuest. In both cases, the player controls and evolves a character over time within a narrative setting.

Role-playing games (or RPGs) certainly have the trappings of games. A paper-based, tabletop RPG usually involves dice, rulebooks, statistics, and a fair amount of strategic play. Role-playing games clearly embody every component of our definition of game, except one: a quantifiable outcome. As an RPG player, you move through game-stories, following the rules, overcoming obstacles, accomplishing tasks, and generally increasing the abilities of your character. What is usually lacking, however, is a single endpoint to the game. Role-playing games are structured like serial narratives that grow and evolve from session to session. Sometimes they end; sometimes they do not. Even if a character dies, a player can rejoin as a different character. In other words, there is no single goal toward which all players strive during a role-playing game. If a game does end, it does not do so quantifiably, with players winning or losing or receiving a score. Gary Gygax, co-designer of Dungeons & Dragons, would concur: "Advanced Dungeons and Dragons is, as are most role-playing games, open-ended. There is no 'winner,' no final objective, and the campaign grows and changes as it matures."[18] This is true of both digital and non-digital multiplayer RPGs. (Note that single-player digital RPGs are structured differently—usually with an adventure game-style winning outcome.)

From this description, it would appear that multiplayer role-playing games are not, in fact, games. But this seems like a ridiculous conclusion, because RPGs are so closely bound up in the development of games and gaming culture. Our position is this: RPGs can be framed either way—as having or not having a quantifiable outcome. If you look at the game as whole, there may not be a single, overriding quantifiable goal. But if you consider the session-to-session missions that players complete, the personal goals players set for themselves, the levels of power that players attain, then yes, RPGs do have quantifiable outcomes. In this sense, an RPG is a larger system that facilitates game play within it, giving rise to a series of outcomes that build on each other over time. Game designer Greg Costikyan puts it this way: "No victory conditions, true. But certainly [RPGs] have goals; lots of them, you get to pick. Rack up the old experience points. Or fulfill the quest your friendly GM has just inflicted on you. Or rebuild the imperium and stave off civilization's final collapse. Or strive towards spiritual perfection. Whatever."[19]

It is possible, of course, for RPGs to become more game-like. At game conventions, there are often "tournament-style" games, in which players or teams earn points for completing certain actions and accomplishing goals, and a single winner can in fact be declared. Conversely, there are RPGs that de-emphasize power, statistics, and advancement and instead focus on storytelling and narrative. This form of RPG seems very unlike games as we have defined them.

Role-playing games are not the only kind of play activity that exists on the border of our definition. A computer program like Sim City does not have explicit goals, and in that way is more like a toy than a game. However, as its designer Will Wright has often stated, players can turn it into a game by constructing their own goals. Does this make Sim City an informal play activity or a formalized game? It all depends on how it is framed.

Sometimes the answer to the question of whether or not a game is a game rests in the eye of the beholder. Any definition of a phenomena as complex as games is going to encounter instances where the application of the definition is somewhat fuzzy. Rather than seeing these moments as a breakdown of the definition, we view them as valuable opportunities to understand games as a whole. The terrain along the borders of more rigid definitions offers fertile ground for insight and investigation. In these playful and liminal spaces, assumptions are challenged, ideas evolve, and definitions change. It is this kind of transformative play that is at the heart of our model of game design.

Further Reading

Man, Play, and Games, by Roger Caillois

A book that builds directly from the work of Johann Huizinga's *Homo Ludens, Man, Play, and Games* by philosopher Roger Caillois has a similar agenda: to identify and analyze the general phenomenon of play and locate its larger significance within culture. For our purposes, his early chapters on defining and classifying games are the most useful, providing insightful typologies and definitions for understanding play in and out of games.

> *Recommended:*
> I. The Definition of Play
> II. The Classification of Games

Notes

1. David Parlett, *The Oxford History of Board Games* (New York: Oxford University Press, 1999), p. 1.

2. Ibid. p. 3.

3. Clark C. Abt, *Serious Games* (New York: Viking Press, 1970), p. 6.

4. Ibid. p. 7.

5. Ibid. p. 7–9.

6. Johann Huizinga, *Homo Ludens: A Study of the Play Element in Culture* (Boston: Beacon Press, 1955), p. 13.

7. Roger Caillois, *Man, Play, and Games,* Translated from the French by Meyer Barash (Champaign: University of Illinois Press, 2001), p. 9–10.

8. Bernard Suits, *Grasshopper: Games, Life, and Utopia* (Boston: David R. Godine, 1990), p. 34.

9. Ibid. p. 41.

10. Chris Crawford, *The Art of Computer Game Design.* <http://www.van-couver.wsu.edu/fac/peabody/game-book/Coverpage.html>.

11. Ibid.

12. Ibid.

13. Ibid.

14. Greg Costikyan, "I Have No Words and I Must Design." *Interactive Fantasy* #2, 1994 <www.geocities.com/SiliconValley/Bay/2535/nowords.html>.

15. Elliott Avedon and Brian Sutton-Smith, eds, *The Study of Games* (New York: John Wiley & Sons, 1971), p. 405.

16. Scott Kim, "What is a Puzzle?" <www.scottkim.com/articles.html>.

17. Ibid.

18. Gary Gygax, *Advanced Dungeons and Dragons Players Handbook* (Lake Geneva: TRS Hobbies, 1978), p. 7.

19. Costikyan, "I Have No Words and I Must Design." <http://www.geocities.com/SiliconValley/Bay/2535/nowords.html>.

Defining Games SUMMARY

- The words **play** and **games** have a unique relationship in the English language. There are two ways to frame their relationship, both of which are useful:

   1. Games are a subset of play: The category of play represents many kinds of playful activities. Some of these activities are games, but many of them are not. In this sense, games are contained within play.

   2. Play is a subset of games: Games are complex phenomena and there are many ways to frame them and understand them. **RULES, PLAY,** and **CULTURE** are three aspects of the phenomena of games. In this sense, play is contained within games.

- *A game is a system in which players engage in an artificial conflict, defined by rules, that results in a quantifiable outcome.* The key elements of this definition are the fact that a game is a *system, players* interact with the system, a game is an instance of *conflict,* the conflict in games is *artificial, rules* limit player behavior and define the game, and every game has a *quantifiable outcome* or goal.

- A **puzzle** is a special kind of game in which there is a single correct answer or set of correct answers. All puzzles are games.

- Multiplayer **Role-playing games** (RPGs) do not clearly possess a quantifiable outcome. Whether or not they fit the definition of a game depends on how they are framed. As with other open-ended game-like experiences such as Sim City, RPGs have emergent quantifiable goals but usually no single overriding outcome.

Unit 1 | Core Concepts

immediate interactivity
narrow input and ouput
information manipulation
automation
networked communication

8

DEFINING DIGITAL GAMES

*[The video game] is the most complex toy ever built and is vastly more responsive than any other toy ever invented. Compare it, for example, with its contemporary, the doll Chatty Cathy, which has about a dozen different sentences with which to respond when you pull the string. Chatty Cathy does not take into account the variety of your responses; the computer does. Chatty has a dozen responses; the computer has millions.—**Brian Sutton-Smith,** Toys as Culture*

The definition of "game" that we proposed in the previous chapter makes no distinction between digital and non-digital games—the qualities that define a game in one media also define it in another. Most of the thinkers whose definitions we explored were writing before the invention of computer games, let alone before the recent explosion of the video game industry. Yet computer and video games are an important part of the game landscape, as they bring a number of unique qualities and concerns to the practice of game design. Before proceeding any further, in this chapter we take a brief look at the special qualities of digital games.

The Computer Is Not a Computer

Digital and electronic games take a multitude of forms and appear on many different computer platforms. These include games for personal computers or TV-attached game consoles such as the Sony Playstation or Microsoft XBox; handheld game devices such as the Nintendo Game Boy Advance or specialized handhelds that only play one game; games for PDAs or cell phones; and games for arcades or amusement parks. Digital and electronic games can be designed for a single player, for a small group of players, or for a large community. For simplicity's sake, we will refer to all of these game forms as *digital games.*

Digital games are systems, just like every other game discussed so far. The physical medium of the computer is one element that makes up the system of the game, but it does not represent the entire game. The computer hardware and software are merely the materials of which the game is composed. One would not say that a deck of UNO cards is the same thing as the game of UNO. But people often fall into this kind of thinking when it comes to describing digital games. Take a straightforward example of a digital game: the game title Tetris for the Nintendo Game Boy handheld platform. Is the system of the game constituted entirely by the Game Boy console and the Tetris game cartridge? As outlined in **Systems,** the four elements of a system are objects, attributes, relationships, and an environment. The identities assigned to these elements within a game depend on how the game is framed: as a formal system

of rules, as an experiential system of play, or as a contextual system embedded within larger systems of culture.

In order to see how this analysis functions within the present discussion of games and digital technology, we start with the widest frame—culture—and work our way in. If we view Tetris as a system of *cultural context,* the actual hardware and software of the game is a relevant component, but it hardly tells the whole story. In considering Tetris within the context of culture, we would need to include elements such as game fan magazines (*Nintendo Power,* for example), the marketing, manufacturing, and economics of the Game Boy console, the hybrid cultural identity of the game (Tetris' original designer, Russian Alexy Pajitnov and Japanese publisher Nintendo), the demographics of players, and so on. We would need to take each of these components into account. The exact elements to investigate depend on the specific cultural reading undertaken. In any case, culturally speaking the technological facet of Tetris is merely one element among many others.

Now consider the *experiential play* of Tetris: the cognitive and psychological, physical and emotional relationships that emerge between a player and the game. In this case, the elements of the system are constituted by 1) the player and 2) the Game Boy Advance console. The circuit of interaction between player and game runs in a kind of loop as the player plays, responding to the game even as the game responds to the player. In this picture, the digital technology itself is a part of the system, but certainly does not constitute it entirely.

Narrowing the focus to the *formal rules* of Tetris, the mathematical system of the game that exists apart from the player, are we talking just about the technology? Yes and no. The rules are embedded in the hardware and the software, but they are also something separate from the code. For example, the enactment of the rules is contingent on the player. The rules determine, among other things, what happens when a player pushes a button at a certain moment in the game. In this way, the internal logic of the game is not something that can be completely severed from the ways that the game exchanges information with the outside world. Even here, in looking at Tetris as a formal system, considering the technology as an end in itself can be misleading.

What is the point of these multiple framings? A game designer doesn't create technology. A game designer creates an experience. Computer and video game technology can be a part of that experience—it can even be the focal point of that experience—but in order to design meaningful play a designer has to consider the complete picture.

What Can It Do?

The key question for game designers and digital media is not, *What is it?* But instead, *What can it do?* Confronted with a digital platform, a game designer needs to understand how to harness the technology into a designed system that results in meaningful play. This emphasis is not unique to digital games: the materials that constitute a game are always crucial in designing an experience.

What can digital technology do? What are the special qualities of digital media that can support gaming experiences not possible in other game forms? We can list four "traits" of digital media. The qualities are not mutually exclusive—there is some overlap between categories—and they do not constitute a definitive list of traits that appear in every digital game. In fact, these traits appear in non-digital games as well. But they do represent the qualities that appear most robustly in digital games, characteristics that game designers should take advantage of when creating games in a digital medium.

Trait 1: Immediate but Narrow Interactivity

One of the most compelling qualities of digital technology is that it can offer immediate, interactive feedback. Designing systems of actions and outcomes, where the game responds seamlessly to a player's input, is a common element in digital games. Digital technology thus offers real-time game play that shifts and reacts dynamically to player decisions.

A common misconception about digital interactivity is that it offers players a broad and expressive range of interaction—that a computer can mimic any medium and provide any kind of experience. In fact, the kind of interaction that a participant can have with a computer is quite narrow. Interaction with a home computer is generally restricted to mouse and keyboard input, and screen and speaker output. Compare the anemic activities of clicking, dragging, and typing with the range of possible non-computer game interactions: the kinesthetically engaging athletic, perceptual, and strategic interaction of Tennis; the performative theatrical communication of Charades; the ritualized formality of a professional Go match. So although the immediate interactivity of digital games is a powerful element for designers to consider, the medium is rife with limitations.

On the other hand, limitations in games help shape the space of possibility. For example, an arcade fighting game such as Street Fighter II gives a player only six button pushes and eight joystick directions as a means of input, far fewer than a mouse and keyboard. Yet within this limited interactive vocabulary, players can develop highly personal fighting styles and take part in a vast range of different game experiences. The lightning-quick response of the program, paired with the streamlined control input, contribute to the uniquely meaningful play of a well-designed fighting game.

Similar pairings of limited but immediate interactivity appear in non-digital games as well. A sport such as bicycle racing gives players a very restricted set of interactions. At the same time, players receive immediate feedback for each tiny modification of speed, steering, and the position of their bodies on their bicycles. Much of the deep engagement that cyclists experience while racing emerges directly from the narrow but immediate interactivity of the sport.

Trait 2: Information Manipulation

One way of framing digital media is as machines for storing and manipulating information. Games certainly capitalize on this capacity for what Janet Murray, in *Hamlet on the Holodeck* calls the "encyclopedic" quality of digital media.[1]

Digital games can and do make good use of data: they are often filled to bursting with text, images, video, audio, animations, 3D content, and other forms of stored data. In fact, it is fair to say that digital games tax the data-rendering capabilities of computers far more than any other genre of consumer software. High-end personal computers, specially configured for the best display of 3D graphics and audio, are marketed as "gamer" machines.

But graphics and audio are not the only kind of information that a digital game manipulates. Every aspect of a digital game, in fact every aspect of its program—the internal logic, mechanisms for handling player interactivity, memory management—can be regarded as information. Digital games manipulate this information in ways that non-digital games generally cannot. For example, consider the rules of a game. In a typical board game it is necessary for at least one of the players to learn the rules and understand them fully before a game begins. On the other hand, with a digital game it is possible, as designer Karen Sideman has pointed out, to learn the rules of the game as it is being played; to make the discovery of the way that the game operates part of the play of the game.[2]

Digital games are also excellent at hiding information from players and revealing it in very particular ways. Warcraft III, for example, is a real-time strategy game that makes use of a "fog of war" mechanic: the game is played on a large map, and the territory and actions of a player's opponents are initially hidden and only revealed as the player's units explore the game map. Of course, many non-digital games involve information manipulation as well. The simple card game Memory, in which players lay a grid of cards face-down and attempt to pick up pairs of identi-

cal cards by remembering past moves of their opponents, is a game explicitly about the manipulation and gradual discovery of hidden information.

Trait 3: Automated Complex Systems

Perhaps the most pervasive trait of digital games is that they can automate complicated procedures and in so doing, facilitate the play of games that would be too complicated in a non-computerized context. In most non-digital games, players have to move the game forward at every step, by manipulating pieces or behaving according to explicit instructions outlined by the rules. In a digital game, the program can automate these procedures and move the game forward without direct input from a player.

When miniatures wargamers get together to stage their battles with tiny lead figures, they follow complex rules that determine the movement, lines of sight, and combat resolution of their armies. Even though wargamers tend to have a high tolerance for complex sets of rules, there are certainly limits on the degree of complexity that they can endure before the game becomes an exercise in tedium. This is exactly the kind of complexity that computers handle with ease. In fact, wargames created for play on computers generally take into account many more dynamic variables than their non-digital counterparts.

This is not necessarily a good thing. As James Dunnigan, a designer of wargames on and off the computer states, "While computer wargames had many advantages over manual games, they had one major minus for game designers. Computer games did not reveal their internal workings."[3] Dunnigan calls this the "Black Box Syndrome" of computer games:

Another advantage of paper games is that you know why things are happening a certain way in the game. All the rules and probability tables are right there in front of you. Yes, it takes a lot of effort to wade through all of that detail, but you do end up with a good idea of how the inner workings of the game function. A popular benefit of this is the opportunity to change the game's rules and probability tables. Many players do this, and that's how gamers eventually turn into game designers. Computer wargames show you very little of how it does its thing. The computer program just does it, leaving you sometimes muttering about mysterious "black boxes."[4]

Dunnigan feels that a player's appreciation and understanding of the internal game mechanics are a key component of the play of wargames. Because of the automated nature of digital games, computer wargames generally leave the internal machinations out of the picture, diminishing a player's experience of the game.

The kinds of automated complex systems that appear in digital games vary greatly, from the evolving ecosystems of Sim City, to the sophisticated artificial intelligence opponents of Thief, to the complex light-and-shadow rendering routines of Unreal, to the natural language parsing of Zork. It is safe to say that nearly every aspect of digital games is automated in some way.

Once again, however, there are examples of non-digital games that contain complex automated systems. The Japanese pinball-like game of Pachinko involves a complex randomizing system of metal balls falling over pegs. Once the player launches a ball, the automated, complex process of the game system takes over, determining where the ball will land and if it will score points for the player. Becoming skilled at Pachinko entails getting to know the inner workings of a particular game, and knowing how to use subtle control to arrive at the desired result.

Trait 4: Networked Communication

A final trait that many (but not all) digital games possess is that they can facilitate communication between players. There are many forms of digitally mediated communication, from email and text chat to real-time video and audio communication. Two Game Boy consoles connected through a link cable can even be considered a miniature digital game network.

It is clear that all multiplayer games, digital or non-digital, are contexts for communication among players. However, digital games offer the ability to communicate over long distances and to share a range of social spaces with many other participants. For example, the persistent worlds of Ultima Online draw tens of thousands of players, all brought together in the same complex social space.

Although communication input and output are limited by the narrow input and output of digital media, communication in a digital game does not have to be restricted to text. For example, a Quake deathmatch gathers a small number of players together in a single communicative game space. And although text chat is one way that the players interact, their primary form of communication takes place through the split-second decisions they make about their player's movement and weapon attacks. Game play itself is a form of social communication.

As with the other traits of digital games, networked communication, even over long distances, occurs in non-digital games. The postal system has long served as a medium for game play, from play-by-mail games of Chess and Diplomacy to role-playing games that take place entirely through written correspondance. In a wider sense, sports stats and records, whether for the Olympics or for a high school Basketball team, serve a communicative function similar to online high score boards.

Integration

In concluding the discussion of the qualities of digital games, it is important to remember that these four traits are not a roadmap for designing games or a checklist for analyzing them. They simply highlight ways of understanding the capabilities of digital game design. In a Quake deathmatch, for example, we can see all four traits in operation:

- *Immediate but narrow interactivity:* The game controls require deft manipulation of the mouse and keyboard, with instantaneous response from the game system.

- *Manipulation of information:* Like all digital games, Quake manipulates information, from the 3D data defining the deathmatch map to the way that players' movements are present but hidden from each other.

- *Automated complex systems:* The graphics engine, control routines, opponent AI, and all other formal aspects of the game are automated.

- *Networked communication:* The online deathmatches create a forum for rich social interaction between players.

During any actual game experience, the four categories generally overlap and operate simultaneously, together providing the overall experience of play.

Before we end this chapter, let's take a moment to consider a "border-line" case: the board game Stay Alive. In this non-digital game, play takes place on a grid that houses a simple mechanical set of plastic switches. There are two sets of switches, at ninety degrees to each other. Some of the switch positions have holes and some do not. Players place their marbles on the grid and then try to eliminate opponents' marbles by moving the switches in turn.

Stay Alive is not a digital game, but it has some of the properties of a digital game. For example, Stay Alive contains a complex system that functions semi-autonomously from the players. Because there is hidden information about which positions of the sliders have holes and will drop marbles, players interact with the system indirectly, moving sliders on the margins of the system to see how the playfield is affected as a result. Players do not internalize the rules of all of the positions of the sliders; instead, this information is contained in the mechanical construction of the playfield.

Stay Alive

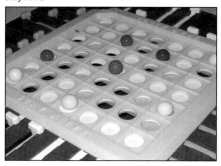

Is Stay Alive a digital game? Of course not. It is not electronic and does not make use of digital technology. However, it clearly demonstrates how many of the elements of digital games are not really unique to the medium. In fact, a deck of cards can hold information as well: if a player shuffles the cards, the player does not need to internalize the order of the cards. Instead, the physical properties of the deck (the fact that it can be shuffled and that the cards can be face-down) lets the cards contain information that is autonomous from the players, such as which card is on the top of a face-down deck.

These examples of game technologies (a deck of cards, Stay Alive, a digital game) provide a sliding scale for the kinds of complexity that game materials can embody. They also help to underscore a larger point: although different game materials allow for different game experiences, the underlying properties of games are ultimately more similar than different. The core challenges of designing meaningful play hold true in any game medium.

Notes

1. Janet Murray, *Hamlet on the Holodeck* (New York: The Free Press, 1997), p.83

2. Karen Sideman, Game Design address, 2000.

3. James F. Dunnigan, *Wargames Handbook: How to Play and Design Commercial and Professional Wargames,* 3d ed. (San Jose: Writers Club Press, 2000), p. xii.

4. Ibid. p.74–5.

Defining Digital Games
SUMMARY

- If a game is framed as a system, it is clear that the game's physical medium is an important element of the game, but does not constitute the entire system. Digital technology should not be emphasized as an end in itself, but instead should be understood as one element in a larger designed system.

- There are four traits that summarize the special qualities of digital games. These traits are also present in non-digital games, but digital games generally embody them more robustly:

  Trait 1: Immediate but narrow interactivity
  Trait 2: Manipulation of information
  Trait 3: Automated complex systems
  Trait 4: Networked communication

- The underlying properties of games and the core challenges of game design hold true regardless of the medium in which a game manifests.

THE MAGIC CIRCLE

play frame
open system
closed system
lusory attitude

9

This is the problem of the way we get into and out of the play or game…what are the codes which govern these entries and exits?—**Brian Sutton-Smith,** *Child's Play*

What does it mean to enter the system of a game? How is it that play begins and ends? What makes up the boundary of a game? As we near the end of our first Unit, we need to address one last set of key concepts. These concepts are embedded in the question raised by Sutton-Smith: "How do we get into and out of the play or game?" At stake is an understanding of the artificiality of games, the way that they create their own time and space separate from ordinary life. The idea that the conflict in games is an *artificial* conflict is part of our very definition of games.

Steve Sniderman, in his excellent essay "The Life of Games," notes that the codes governing entry into a game lack explicit representation. "Players and fans and officials of any game or sport develop an acute awareness of the game's 'frame' or context, but we would be hard pressed to explain in writing, even after careful thought, exactly what the signs are. After all, even an umpire's yelling of 'Play Ball' is not the exact moment the game starts."[1] He goes on to explain that players (and fans) must rely on intuition and their experience with a particular culture to recognize when a game has begun. During a game, he writes, "a human being is constantly noticing if the conditions for playing the game are still being met, continuously monitoring the 'frame,' the circumstances surrounding play, to determine that the game is still in progress, always aware (if only unconsciously) that the other participants are acting as if the game is 'on.'"[2]

The "frame" to which Sniderman alludes has several functions, which we will cover in later chapters. For now, it is sufficient to note that the frame of a game is what communicates that those contained within it are "playing" and that the space of play is separate in some way from that of the real world. Psychologist Michael Apter echoes this idea when he writes,

> In the play-state you experience a *protective frame* which stands between you and the "real" world and its problems, creating an enchanted zone in which, in the end, you are confident that no harm can come. Although this frame is psychological, interestingly it often has a perceptible physical representation: the proscenium arch of the theater, the railings around the park, the boundary line on the cricket pitch, and so on. But such a frame may also be abstract, such as the rules governing the game being played.[3]

In other words, the frame is a concept connected to the question of the "reality" of a game, of the relationship between the artificial world of the game and the "real life" contexts that it intersects. The frame of a game creates the feeling of *safety* that is part of Chris Crawford's definition of a game explored in **Defining Games.** It is responsible not only for the unusual relationship between a game and the outside world, but also for many of the internal mechanisms and experiences of a game in play. We call this frame the *magic circle,* a concept inspired by Johann Huizinga's work on play.

Boundaries

What does it mean to say that games take place within set boundaries established by the act of play? Is this really true? Is there really such a distinct boundary? In fact there is. Compare, for example, the informal play of a toy with the more formal play of a game. A child approaching a doll, for example, can slowly and gradually enter into a play relationship with the doll. The child might look at the doll from across the room and shoot it a playful glance. Later, the child might pick it up and hold it, then put it down and leave it for a time. The child might carelessly drag the doll around the room, sometimes talking to it and acknowledging it, at other times forgetting it is there.

The boundary between the act of playing with the doll and not playing with the doll is fuzzy and permeable. Within this scenario, we can identify concrete play behaviors, such as making the doll move like a puppet. But there are just as many ambiguous behaviors, which might or not be play, such as idly kneading its head while watching TV. There may be a frame between playing and not playing, but its boundaries are indistinct.

Now compare that kind of informal play with the play of a game—two children playing Tic-Tac-Toe. In order to play, the children must gather the proper materials, draw the four lines that make up the grid of the board, and follow the proper rules each turn as they progress through the game. With a toy, it may be difficult to say exactly when the play begins and ends. But with a game, the activity is richly formalized. The game has a beginning, a middle, and a quantifiable outcome at the end. The game takes place in a precisely defined physical and temporal space of play. Either the children are playing Tic-Tac-Toe or they are not. There is no ambiguity concerning their action: they are clearly playing a game.

The same analysis can occur within the context of digital media. Compare, for example, a user's casual interaction with a toy-like screensaver program to their interaction with a computer game such as Tetris. The screensaver allows the user to wiggle the mouse and make patterns on the screen, an activity that we can casually enter into and then discontinue. The entry and exit of the user is informal and unbound by rules that define a beginning, middle, and end. A game of Tetris, on the other hand, provides a formalized boundary regarding play: the game is either in play or it is not. Players of Tetris do not "casually interact" with it; rather, they are playing a game. It is true that a Tetris player could pause a game in progress and resume it later—just as two Tennis players might pause for a drink of water. But in both cases, the players are stepping out of the game space, formally suspending the game before stepping back in to resume play.

As a player steps in and out of a game, he or she is crossing that boundary—or frame—that defines the game in time and space. As noted above, we call the boundary of a game the *magic circle,* a term borrowed from the following passage in Huizinga's book *Homo Ludens:*

> All play moves and has its being within a play-ground marked off beforehand either materially or ideally, deliberately or as a matter of course.... The arena, the card-table, the magic circle, the temple, the stage, the screen, the tennis court, the court of justice, etc., are all in form and function play-grounds, i.e., forbidden spots, isolated, hedged round, hallowed, within which special rules obtain. All are temporary worlds within the ordinary world, dedicated to the performance of an act apart.[4]

Although the magic circle is merely one of the examples in Huizinga's list of "play-grounds," the term is used here as shorthand for the idea of a special place in time and space created by a game. The fact that the magic circle is just that—a circle—is an important feature of this concept. As a closed circle, the space it circumscribes is enclosed and separate from the real world. As a marker of time, the magic circle is like a clock: it simultaneously represents a path with a beginning and end, but one without beginning and end. The magic circle inscribes a space that is repeatable, a space both limited and limitless. In short, a finite space with infinite possibility.

Enter In

In a very basic sense, the magic circle of a game is where the game takes place. To play a game means entering into a magic circle, or perhaps creating one as a game begins. The magic circle of a game might have a physical component, like the board of a board game or the playing field of an athletic contest. But many games have no physical boundaries—arm wrestling, for example, doesn't require much in the way of special spaces or material. The game simply begins when one or more players decide to play.

The term magic circle is appropriate because there is in fact something genuinely magical that happens when a game begins. A fancy Backgammon set sitting all alone might be a pretty decoration on the coffee table. If this is the function that the game is serving—decoration—it doesn't really matter how the game pieces are arranged, if some of them are out of place, or even missing. However, once you sit down with a friend to play a game of Backgammon, the arrangement of the pieces suddenly becomes extremely important. The Backgammon board becomes a special space that facilitates the play of the game. The players' attention is intensely focused on the game, which mediates their interaction through play. While the game is in progress, the players do not casually arrange and rearrange the pieces, but move them according to very particular rules.

Within the magic circle, special meanings accrue and cluster around objects and behaviors. In effect, a new reality is created, defined by the rules of the game and inhabited by its players. Before a game of Chutes and Ladders starts, it's just a board, some plastic pieces, and a die. But once the game begins, everything changes. Suddenly, the materials represent something quite specific. This plastic token is *you*. These rules tell you how to roll the die and move. Suddenly, it matters very much which plastic token reaches the end first.

Consider a group of kids in a suburban front yard, casually talking and hanging out. They decide to play a game of Hide-and-Seek. One of the kids takes a rock and plants it in the middle of yard to represent home base. The group huddles around it, playing "eenie-meenie-miney-moe" to pick the first person to be "It"; then they scatter and hide as "It" covers his eyes and starts to count to twenty. All at once, the relationships among the players have taken on special meanings. Who is "It" and who is not? Who is hidden and who can be seen? Who is captured and who is free? Who will win the game?

What is going on in these examples of Backgammon, Chutes and Ladders, and Hide-and-Seek? As Huizinga eloquently states, within the space of a game "special rules obtain." The magic circle of a game is the boundary of the game space and within this boundary the rules of the game play out and have authority.

Temporary Worlds

What lies at the border of the game? Just how permeable is the boundary between the real world and the artificial world of the game that is circumscribed and delimited by the magic circle? Huizinga calls play-worlds "temporary worlds within the ordinary world." But what does that mean? Does the magic circle enframe a reality completely separated from the real world? Is a game somehow an extension of regular life? Or is a game a just a special case of ordinary reality?

Let us return to the concept of a system. We have already established that games are systems. As systems, games can be understood as being either open or closed. In his definition of systems, Littlejohn informs us that "a *closed system* has no interchange with its environment. An *open system* receives matter and energy from its environment and passes matter and energy to its environment."[5] So what does this have to do with the magic circle? The question at hand has to do with the boundary between the magic circle of a game and the world outside the game. One way of approaching that question is to consider whether that boundary is closed, framing a completely self-contained world inside; or whether it is open, permitting interchange between the game and the world beyond its frame. As Bernard DeKoven notes in *The Well-Played Game,* "Boundaries help separate the game from life. They have a critical function in maintaining the fiction of the game so that the aspects of reality with which we do not choose to play can be left safely outside."[6] Moreover, the answer to the question of whether games are closed or open systems depends on which schema is used to understand them: whether games are framed as **RULES**, as **PLAY**, or as **CULTURE.**

> **RULES:** Games considered as **RULES** are closed systems. Considering games as formal systems means considering them as systems of rules prior to the actual involvement of players.

> **PLAY:** Considered as **PLAY**, games can be either *closed systems* or *open systems.* Framed as the experience of play, it is possible to restrict our focus and look at just those play behaviors that are intrinsic to the game, ignoring all others. At the same time, players bring a great deal in from the outside world: their expectations, their likes and dislikes, social relationships, and so on. In this sense, it is impossible to ignore the fact that games are open, a reflection of the players who play them.

CULTURE: Considered as **CULTURE**, games are extremely open systems. In this case, the internal functioning of the game is not emphasized; instead, as a cultural system the focus is on the way that the game exchanges meaning with culture at large. In considering the cultural aspects of professional Football—political debates over Native American team mascots, for example—the system of the game is opened up to expose the way that it interfaces with society as a whole.

Is it a contradiction to say that games can be open and closed systems at the same time? Not really. As with many complex phenomena, the qualities of the object under study depend on the methodology of the study itself. The answer to the question of whether games are closed or open systems, whether they are truly artificial or not, depends on the schema used to analyze them. We return to this important question many times over the course of this book.

The Lusory Attitude

So far in the discussion of the magic circle we have outlined the ways that the interior space of a game relates to the real world spaces outside it, how the magic circle frames a distinct space of meaning that is separate from, but still references, the real world. What we have not yet considered is what the magic circle represents from the player's point of view. Because a game demands formalized interaction, it is often a real commitment to decide to play a game. If a player chooses to sit down and play Monopoly, for example, he cannot simply quit playing in the middle without disrupting the game and upsetting the other players. On the other hand, if he ignores this impulse and remains in the game to the bitter end, he might end up a sore loser. Yet, these kinds of obstacles obviously don't keep most people from playing games. What does it mean to decide to play a game? If the magic circle creates an alternate reality, what psychological attitude is required of a player entering into the play of a game?

In **Defining Games** we looked at the definition of games Bernard Suits gives in his book *Grasshopper: Games, Life, and Utopia*. One of the unique components of Suits' definition is that he sees games as inherently inefficient. He uses the example of a boxer to explain this concept. If the goal of a boxing match is to make the other fighter stay down for a count of 10, the easiest way to accomplish this goal would be to take a gun and shoot the other boxer in the head. This, of course, is not the way that the game of Boxing is played. Instead, as Suits points out, boxers put on padded gloves and only strike their opponents in very limited and stylized ways. Similarly, Suits discusses the game of Golf:

> Suppose I make it my purpose to get a small round object into a hole in the ground as efficiently as possible. Placing it in the hole with my hand would be a natural means to adopt. But surely I would not take a stick with a piece of metal on one end of it, walk three or four hundred yards away from the hole, and then attempt to propel the ball into the hole with the stick. That would not be technically intelligent. But such an undertaking is an extremely popular game, and the foregoing way of describing it evidently shows how games differ from technical activities.[7]

What the boxer and the golfer have in common, according to Suits, is a shared attitude toward the act of game-playing, an openness to the possibility of taking such indirect means to accomplish a goal. "In anything but a game the gratuitous introduction of unnecessary obstacles to the achievement of an end is regarded as a decidedly irrational thing to do, whereas in games it appears to be an absolutely essential thing to do."[8] Suits calls this state of mind the *lusory attitude*, a term we introduced under his definition of a game. The lusory attitude allows players to "adopt rules which require one to employ worse rather than better means for reaching an end."[9] Trying to propel a miniature ball with a metal stick into a tiny hole across great distances certainly requires something by way of attitude!

The word "ludo" means *play* in Latin, and the root of "lusory" is the same root as "ludens" in "Homo Ludens." The lusory attitude is an extremely useful concept as it describes the attitude that is required of game players for them to enter into a game. To play a game is in many ways an act of "faith" that invests the game with its special meaning—without willing players, the game is a formal system waiting to be inhabited, like a piece of sheet music waiting to be played. This notion can be extended to say that a game is a kind of social contract. To decide to play a game is to create—out of thin air—an arbitrary authority that serves to guide and direct the play of the game. The moment of that decision can be quite magical. Picture a cluster of boys meeting on the street to show each other their marble collections. There is joking, some eye rolling, and then a challenge rings out. One of the boys chalks a circle on the sidewalk and each one of them puts a marble inside. They are suddenly playing a game, a game that guides and directs their actions, that serves as the arbiter of what they can and cannot do. The boys take the game very seriously, as they are playing for keeps.

Their goal is to win the game and take marbles from their opponents. If that is all they wanted to do, they could just grab each other's marble collections and run. Instead, they play a game. Through a long and dramatic process, they end up either losing their marbles or winning some from others. If all that the boys wanted to do was increase the number of marbles in their collection, the game might seem absurd. But the lusory attitude implies more than a mere acceptance of the limitations prescribed by the rules of the game—it also means accepting the rules because the play of the game is an end in itself. In effect, the lusory attitude ensures that the player accepts the game rules "just so that the activity made possible by such an acceptance can occur."[10] Our marble players would take their game seriously even if they weren't playing for keeps.

There is a pleasure in this inefficiency. When you fire a missile in Missile Command, it doesn't simply zap to the spot underneath the crosshairs. Instead, it slowly climbs up from the bottom of the screen. To knock down a set of bowling pins, you don't carry the bowling ball down the lane; instead you stand a good distance away and let it roll. From somewhere in the gap between action and outcome, in the friction between frustrated desire and the seductive goal of a game, bubbles up the unique enjoyment of game play. Players take on the lusory attitude for the pleasure of play itself.

The magic circle can define a powerful space, investing its authority in the actions of players and creating new and complex meanings that are only possible in the space of play. But it is also remarkably fragile as well, requiring constant maintenance to keep it intact. Over the course of the following chapters we explore the design structures that serve to create and support the magic circle, as well as qualities of a game's design that affect the lusory attitude and the possibility of meaningful play.

Having now passed through definitions of design, systems, interactivity, and games, the way has been paved for our entrance into the magic circle. Passing through its open and closed boundaries, we find ourselves in its center. What we find there, at the very heart of games, is **RULES**, the space of games framed as formal systems.

Further Reading

Grasshopper: Games, Life, Utopia, by Bernard Suits

A retelling of Aesop's fable of the Grasshopper and the Ants, *Grasshopper* is an engaging and insightful book that addresses some of the philosophical paradoxes raised by games. Cheating, rule-following, and the reality of games versus the real world are among the topics Suits addresses. It is from this book that we derive our concept of the lusory attitude, an important game design concept.

Recommended:

Chapter 3: Construction of a Definition
Chapter 4: Triflers, Cheats, and Spoilsports

Homo Ludens, by Johann Huizinga

Perhaps the most influential theoretical work on play in the twentieth century, in *Homo Ludens* (Man the Player), Dutch philosopher and historian Huizinga explores the relationship between games, play, and culture. His point of view is certainly not that of design; however, Huizinga's work directly influenced many of the other authors we reference here, such as Roger Caillois and Brian Sutton-Smith. In the chapter recommended below, Huizinga establishes his essential definition of play.

> *Recommended:*
>
> Chapter 1: Nature and Significance of Play as a Cultural Phenomenon

Notes

1. Steven Sniderman, "The Life of Games" p. 2. <www.gamepuzzles.com/tlog/tlog2.htm>.
2. Ibid. p. 2.
3. Michael J. Apter, "A Structural-Phenomenology of Play," in *Adult Play: A Reversal Theory Approach,* edited by J. H. Kerr and Michael J. Apter (Amsterdam: Swets and Zeitlinger, 1991), p. 15.
4. Johann, Huizinga, *Homo Ludens: A Study of the Play Element in Culture* (Boston: Beacon Press, 1955), p. 10.
5. Stephen W. Littlejohn, *Theories of Human Communication,* 3rd edition (Belmont, CA: Wadsworth Publishing Company, 1989), p. 41.
6. Bernard DeKoven, *The Well-Played Game* (New York: Doubleday, 1978), p. 38.
7. Bernard Suits, *Grasshopper: Games, Life, and Utopia* (Boston: David R. Godine, 1990), p. 23.
8. Ibid. p. 38–9.
9. Ibid. p. 38–9.
10. Ibid. p. 40.

The Magic Circle SUMMARY

- Every game exists within a **frame:** a specially demarcated time and space. The frame communicates to players, consciously or unconsciously, that a game is being played.

- The **magic circle** of a game is the space within which a game takes place. Whereas more informal forms of play do not have a distinct boundary, the formalized nature of games makes the magic circle explicit.

- Within the magic circle, the game's rules create a special set of **meanings** for the players of a game. These meanings guide the play of the game.

- As a system, a game can be considered to have an **open** or **closed** relationship to its context. Considered as **RULES**, a game is closed. Considered as **PLAY**, a game is both open and closed. Considered as **CULTURE**, a game is open.

- The **lusory attitude** is the state of mind required to enter into the play of a game. To play a game, a group of players accepts the limitations of the rules because of the pleasure a game can afford.

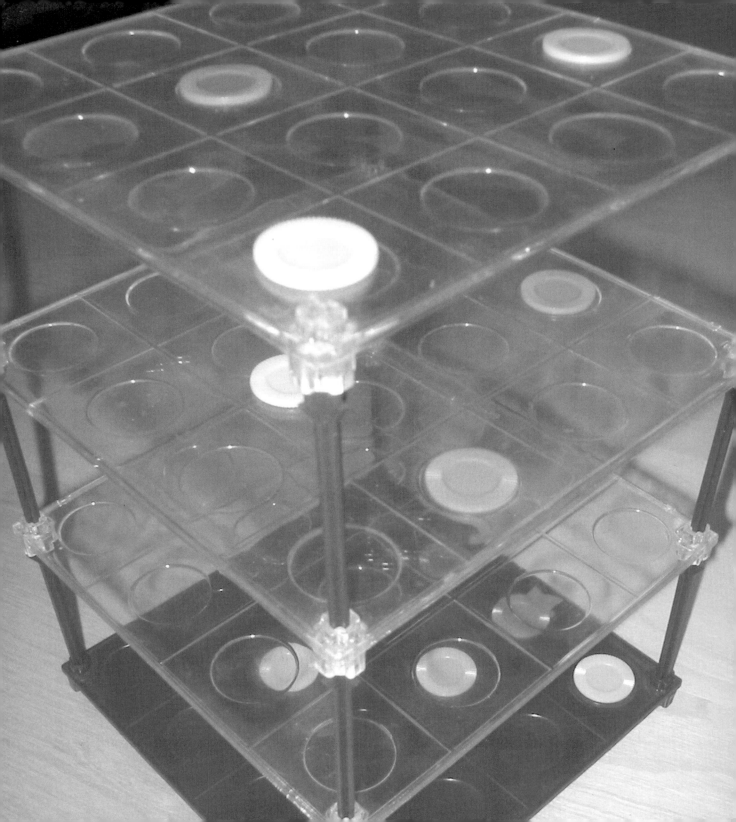

schema
RULES
PLAY
CULTURE

10

THE PRIMARY SCHEMAS

In sum, there are the rhetorics of the larger culture that have their own socializing influence, there is the game-relevant rhetoric of the group that plays the game…and then, within both of these, there is the game itself.—**Brian Sutton-Smith,** *The Ambiguity of Play*

A Conceptual Framework

This chapter represents a turning point: in a certain sense, everything so far has been preparatory work. The concepts of design, systems, and interactivity have shaped our understanding of the design of meaningful play and helped to order a definition of *game*. It is clear—at least for the purposes of this book—what constitutes a game. But the study of games and game design requires more than a set of definitions; it requires a robust conceptual framework. The role of a framework is to organize how games are studied. For example, a study of games might be organized by topic, or by chronology; by type of game or technological platform. In each case, the framework would guide how games are explored and explained.

The framework guiding the study of game design in this book is not topical or historical, and does not separate games by type or platform. Instead, it is based on the idea of *game design schemas,* which conceptually frame games from distinct perspectives. A game design schema is a way of understanding games, a lens that we can apply to the analysis or creation of any game. The variety of schema that could be selected is vast, as there are many, many ways of looking at games. For our purposes, we selected three primary schemas: **RULES, PLAY,** and **CULTURE.**

- **RULES** is a *formal* primary schema, and focuses on the intrinsic mathematical structures of games.

- **PLAY** is an *experiential* primary schema, and emphasizes the player's interaction with the game and other players.

- **CULTURE** is a *contextual* primary schema, and highlights the cultural contexts into which any game is embedded.

This three-part structure is the conceptual architecture supporting even more detailed schemas. Contained within **RULES, PLAY,** and **CULTURE** are a set of specialized schemas, which frame games in very particular ways. For example, contained within **RULES** are the schemas *Games as Information Systems* and *Games as Systems of Uncertainty,* among others. Each of these more specialized schema are formal in scope (looking at

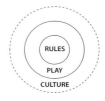

Primary Schemas

games as formal, mathematical systems) but each looks at games with a different formal emphasis. The three primary schemas **RULES, PLAY,** and **CULTURE** each also contain smaller embedded schemas.

The end result is a system that frames and reframes games from a series of overlapping perspectives. The use of schemas not only offers a general framework for uncovering the richness of games, but also, when taken as a whole, offers a general method for any design study. As we mentioned in the opening chapter, the framework of **RULES, PLAY,** and **CULTURE** can help facilitate critical design thinking in any design field.

What Is a Schema?

Schemas are the building blocks of our **RULES, PLAY, CULTURE** framework. But what is a schema, really, and why is it a concept appropriate to the study of games? In his essay, "The Schema,"[1] Ben Martin traces the history of the concept back to Plato and Aristotle. According to Martin, Plato used the word schema to mean "important rather than exhaustive information."[1] This property, *summarization,* is the primary characteristic of a schema: "A schema acts as a reduced description of important aspects of an object or event."[2] Martin then traces the concept to Kant's formulation that "knowledge can only come to us through schemata," that schemas are the frameworks that construct our knowledge about the world.[3] In more contemporary times, the concept of schema falls under the domain of psychology and cognitive science, through the work of psychologists Frederic Bartlett and Piaget, as well as cognitive theorists such as Marvin Minksy. For these thinkers, *schema* refers to the way that the mind acquires, represents, and transforms knowledge. The use of the concept of schema as a way of organizing the study of game design draws directly on this tradition, even as it appropriates and transforms the concept.

David Rumelhart and Andrew Ortony, in their essay "The Representation of Knowledge in Memory"[5] undertake a detailed theory of schema that draws on the disciplines of both cognitive psychology and computer science. Rumelhart and Ortony point out four qualities of schemas:

> *Schemas have variables.* Schemas provide a framework into which new information from the environment is integrated.

> *Schemas can embed.* In other words, the schema that constitutes a framework for understanding the concept *airplane* may contain a schema for representing information about wings or even about the process of traveling.

> *Schemas represent knowledge at many levels of abstraction.* For example, schemas can represent information about objects in the environment, but they can also represent information about the way objects interact or the nature and structure of events.

> *Schemas represent knowledge rather than definitions.* Schemas are essentially "encyclopedic" rather than "definitional."[5]

All four of these qualities are important for our use of schema. The first quality, that schema are a framework for understanding information, is the primary sense in which we use the term. Game design schemas provide frameworks for understanding the formal, experiential, and cultural aspects of games. The second and third qualities of schema, that they can be embedded in each other and that they can represent knowledge at different levels of abstraction, are also key. These qualities refer to the flexibility of schema as critical design tools. Rather than isolated frameworks, schema are linked together through common concerns. The schema *Games as Social Play* is embedded within the larger primary schema of **PLAY**, for example, as are the schemas *Games as Narrative Play* and *Games as the Play of Pleasure.*

Last, the idea that schema represent knowledge, rather than definitions, is critical. Although we offer many definitions of concepts in the following pages, we never define schemas themselves in absolute terms. As lenses or general frameworks for understanding games and the practice of game design, schemas are useful because they allow us to sort through the complex phenomena of games in a loose and intuitive fashion, highlighting particular features of games. Schemas are not defined concepts—they are ways of thinking that allow us to assimilate the knowledge of a game. In this sense, schemas act as a counterpoint to the more clearly defined concepts that we construct throughout this book.

RULES: Formal Schemas

Games have rules. This is perhaps the most prominent feature of games, one that distinguishes them from other forms of media, art, and entertainment. In comparing the many definitions of "game" in the previous chapter, the idea that games were ordered and structured by rules was the most common definitional element we found. It is therefore critical that our framework includes rules as a primary focus. The schemas that fall under the rubric of **RULES** are *formal schemas*. They include, among others, looking at games as systems of public and private information, as systems of conflict, and as Game Theory systems. How are all of these ways of looking at games formal? More specifically, to what does the word "formal" refer?

There are at least two senses in which the **RULES** schemas offer a "formal" way of looking at games. First, the term *formal* is used in the sense of "form": rules constitute the inner *form* or organization of games. In other words, rules are the inner, essential structures that constitute the real-world objects known as games. For example, consider two games of Go that differ in a variety of ways. They might differ in terms of:

- *Material:* one version is played with stones on a wooden board; the other is played on a computer.

- *Motivation:* in one a friend teaches the game to a friend; in the other, two masters compete for a prize.

- *Outcome:* in one game white wins easily; the other game is a very close match with black pulling ahead at the end.

- *Time and space:* one game is played in ancient China; the other is played in contemporary France.

The list could go on. The point is that although these games of Go would be radically different as game play experiences, all would be identified as the game of "Go." Despite their differences, the games share one thing in common: the rules of Go. These "rules of play" unite all of the games of Go that have ever been or will ever be played. It is in this sense that the rules of Go constitute the formal identity of the game of Go.

A second sense in which the word *formal* is used has to do with the concept of "formalization," the idea that there is something methodical and precise about looking at games as **RULES.** The schemas clustered under **PLAY** and **CULTURE** tend to be fuzzy and more difficult to quantify; it is in **RULES** that the schemas are most analytical. In addition, most of the formal schemas employed contain a mathematical component. Looking at games as **RULES** means looking at games as formal systems, both in the sense that the rules are inner structures that constitute the games and also in the sense that the **RULES** schemas are analytic tools that mathematically dissect games.

PLAY: Experiential Schemas

Although all games have rules, it is certainly also true that the very concept of games is closely intertwined with the idea of play. Play is, in fact, what we do with games. We play Chess, we play Baseball, and we play Tekken. Although other things are played as well (the radio, the trumpet, or a role in a theater production), play has a very special relationship to games and game design.

The game design schemas clustered under the heading of **PLAY** are quite different from those grouped under **RULES.** Rather than being focused on the formal qualities of the game object itself, **PLAY** schemas are *experiential schemas,* directly focused on the actual experience of the game players. This is a radical shift in point of view from **RULES,** a shift that opens up many new ways of looking at games. But why is this the case? What does **PLAY** offer that **RULES** does not?

It is simple, really. The play of a game is something that only exists as an experience. It is possible to consider the logic of a rule system, to consider the game formally, without understanding how that rule-system will be experienced. However, in framing games as **PLAY,** we must consider not only the rules, but also the rule-system as a context designed to deliver a particular experience of play for the game's participants. That experience might be a social experience, or a narrative experience, or an experience of pleasure. Looking at games as experiential systems means looking at them as participation, as observation, as a mental state, as bodily sensation, as emotion, as something *lived.* In **PLAY,** the experiential dimensions of games are made explicit.

CULTURE: Contextual Schemas

Even though the realm of play may seem expansive and varied compared to the analytic world of rules, play is, in some sense, bounded too. Games take place in definite locales of time and space. It is when we explore games within the realm of culture that the overlap between the game world and the world at large comes to light. When we consider games as **PLAY,** we confine the analysis to the space defined by the actual game itself. In **PLAY,** we emphasize the human experience of the game, but without straying too far outside the boundaries of the game. Once we begin to look beyond the internal, intrinsic qualities of games toward the qualities brought to the game from external contexts, the focus extends deep into the territory of **CULTURE.**

The schemas presented under **CULTURE** are contextual schemas. They focus on the cultural dimensions of games, game design, and play. In considering games from a cultural point of view, our goal is to understand how the design of a game, as the design of meaningful play, engages shared systems of value and meaning. While taking into account both the formal and experiential qualities of games, these schemas look at the effects of culture on games, and the effects of games on culture. From ideas of rhetoric and representation to the leaking of the artificial world of a game into the real world, these schemas highlight the variable boundaries between games and the contexts in which they are played and produced.

The role of context is critical to the study of games because a context is the environment of the game system. It is the space that surrounds and exists outside the system. In creating the outer boundary of the system, the context also helps define the system itself. Furthermore, if the system is an open system, it interacts with its environment, changing its context even as it is changed itself.

With this outline of our three Primary Schemas, we end Unit 1 of *Rules of Play*. In the chapters to come, we flesh out this skeletal structure, building on our fundamental key concepts to bring game design and meaningful play fully to life.

Notes

1. George Cowen and David Pines, *Complexity: Metaphors, Models and Reality* (Santa Fe: Addison Wesley Longman, 1994), p. 263–277.
2. Ibid. p. 265.
3. Ibid. p. 268.
4. David Rumelhart and Andrew Ortony, "The Representation of Knowledge in Memory." In *Schooling and the Acquisition of Knowledge*, edited by Richard Anderson, Rand Spiro, and William Montague (Hillsdale, NJ: Lawrence Earlbarm, 1997), p. 99–135.
5. Ben Martin, "The Schema." In *Complexity: Metaphors, Models and Reality*, edited by George Cowen and David Pines (Santa Fe: Addison Wesley Longman, 1994), p. 272–273.

The Primary Schemas: Rules, Play, Culture — SUMMARY

· The conceptual framework for this book provides three ways to frame or understand games: **RULES, PLAY,** and **CULTURE.** Each of these primary schemas contains a number of more specialized schemas.

· **RULES** contains **formal** game design schemas
· **PLAY** contains **experiential** game design schemas
· **CULTURE** contains **contextual** game design schemas

· A **schema** is a way of organizing and framing knowledge. Schemas have the following characteristics:

· **Schemas have variables:** they provide a framework that can integrate new information.
· **Schemas can embed:** they can contain other schemas inside of themselves.
· **Schemas represent knowledge at many levels of abstraction:** they allow many points of view of the same object.
· **Schemas represent knowledge rather than definitions:** they are essentially "encyclopedic" rather than "definitional."

· Rule-based or formal schemas focus on the logical and mathematical structures of games. The word "formal" refers both to the inner form of games as well as to formalization of the knowledge about the game.

· Play-based or experiential schemas focus on human experience and interaction in its many dimensions.

· Cultural or contextual schemas focus on the relationship between a game and the cultural contexts in which it is embedded.

Sibling Rivalry
A game for 2 or more players

Overview

Players are siblings trying to bother one another. If they go too overboard, a parent will step in and punish them. As players score points, they advance on the score track. The object of the game is to be the first player to cross the finish line on the score track.

Rules

Equipment, and Starting the Game

Sibling Rivalry has a playboard, with two parts: the challenge board and the score track. The challenge board is made up of a grid of five challenge tracks numbered with dice, 2–6. The score track is the track with a start and finish, marked with little devils and little angels in some of the squares. Each player has two matching pawns (for example, two dimes.) One pawn progresses from start to finish on the score track, as a player successfully torments their siblings; the other pawn makes challenges on the challenge board. The first pawn will be the challenge pawn; the second the scoring pawn. You also need five dice to play. Select a player to go first.

On Your Turn

At the start of your turn, if your challenge pawn is on the challenge track, remove it and score the number of points in that square by advancing your scoring pawn. *Example: If your challenge pawn was 4 squares along the number two challenge track, on the square labeled "steady stare," you score 3 points.* Of course, on the first turn you won't have any pawns on any track.

During your turn, you roll the five dice and advance your challenge pawn along one of the tracks, one square for each of the track's number you roll. *Example: you roll 2,3,5,6—if you are advancing along the number two track you can advance your challenge pawn 2 squares. If you are advancing on the number three track, you can advance your pawn one square. If you are advancing on the number four track, you cannot advance your pawn at all.* All the 1s you roll are set aside and you may choose to roll again or stop. If you roll again, roll all the dice but your 1s. Continue the process of re-rolling, advancing your scoring pawn, setting the 1s aside until either you choose to stop or you accumulate three (or more) 1s.

You are restricted on which tracks you can advance. When the challenge board is clear you must advance on the number two track. If the board has challenge pawns on it, you can advance in any track with a pawn in it, in an attempt to outdo your sibling, or escalate one track higher. *Example: There is a pawn on the number three track, and a pawn on the number four track. You can advance your challenge pawn in tracks number three, four, or escalate to track number five.*

You may change the track you are advancing during the course of your turn. After advancing along a track you may remove your pawn after a roll and begin advancing along another track. *Example: The board has a challenge pawn in the number four track in the third square, marked "chin." You can only choose to advance your pawn on the number four track, challenging your sibling's tickle, or escalate to the number five track. You roll 1, 2, 4, 6, 6, and advance your challenge pawn one square along the number four track. You then re-roll four dice (you are not allowed to re-roll the dice that rolled the 1), and you roll 1, 5, 5, 5. You may choose to remove your challenge pawn from the number four track and advance 3 along the number five track.*

Ending Your Turn

If you accumulated three (or more) 1s, Mom or Dad has caught you in the act and you move backwards on the score track one square for each 1 you ended your turn with. You also remove your challenge pawn.

If you choose to end your turn and have the only pawn on your challenge track, you leave it there and hope that it is still there at the start of your next turn, so you can score the points for that square.

If you choose to end your turn and are the most advanced pawn along the track you were challenging, remove the other pawn and leave yours there. You may score your pawn if you are still there at the start of your next turn.

If you choose to end your turn and you were tied with or behind another pawn in the track you chose, remove your challenge pawn, because you have not outdone your sibling.

If you manage to advance a challenge pawn to the last square on a track, remove all pawns in that track, score the square, and take another turn.

Scoring

When you advance your scoring pawn:

If you land on another player's pawn move backwards until you are on a free space (or slide off the scoring chart entirely!).

If your scoring pawn isn't on the board yet, ignore backwards movement. Similarly, if you must move your pawn backwards and reach the end of the track, remove your scoring pawn and ignore the excess backward movement.

If your pawn is on "Little Angel," you have somehow gotten into your parent's good graces. It takes four 1s to catch you!

If your pawn is on "Little Devil," your parents have developed a heightened suspicion of you. It takes only two 1s to catch you.

If you advance your scoring pawn past the finish, you have won the game!

FINAL GAME BOARD

Stop looking at me! **6 & SCORE!**	Stop making faces! **7 & SCORE!**	Hahahahaha! **8 & SCORE!**	Oww! Quit it! **9 & SCORE!**	MOM! Is it true? **10 & SCORE!**
Narrow Gaze 5	Eyelids Back 6	Pin and Use Head 7	Machine Gun Jabs 8	You were adopted 9
Smirk 4	Bug Eyes 5	Under Arm 6	Charley Horse 7	I saw bugs crawling in your nose while you slept 8
Steady Stare 3	Moron Face 4	Sides 5	Hair Pull 6	I spat in that 7
Direct Look 2	Pig Nose 3	Chin 4	Pinch 5	Weird… I got the looks AND the brains 6
Sidelong Glance 2	Tongue Out 3	Foot 4	Prod 5	Your underwear is showing 6
Looking Near 2	Kissyface 3	Pretend Tickle 4	Pretend Punch 5	Duhhh! 6

Look	**Faces**	**Tickles**	**Ouchies**	**Teases**

SCORING TRACK

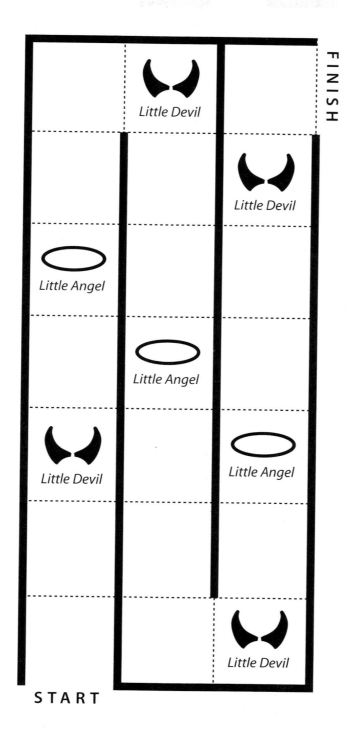

START

FINISH

Sibling Rivalry

Stage 1: General Constraints

The first thing I did was consider the constraints of the project, which included the audience and equipment. The audience I understood to be adults but not necessarily game players. As a result, I was leaning toward a light game, but not one without strategy. In terms of equipment, I had some pages in a book. There was the offer to include die cut counters, but I knew that is a pain both for the publisher and the book owner, so I rejected that option. I decided to limit myself to the use of game materials that people commonly have available (dice, counters, standard decks of cards, writing paper, and so forth). I would use the pages for rules and perhaps a simple board, which could either be copied or perhaps played with inside the book.

Stage 2: Concept

I am constantly toying with game design concepts and game motifs, using them to make little games for my own enjoyment and growth. I only attempt to publish a very small percentage of these games. This means that typically I have a lot of ideas to draw on when I am given a commissioned project.

Motif: One idea I had been mulling over was a game of Sibling Rivalry, with kids trying to bother one another, while not getting caught (or while getting someone else in trouble). I had been thinking of it as a card game with a specialized deck, or a board game with an elaborate board that included all sorts of environments in which the kids might bother each other (back of the car, in front of the TV, at school.) In order to use this motif, I would have to cut back on use of this specialized equipment. I found the flavor fun though, and appropriate for a project like this, so I toyed with ways to address these changes.

Mechanics: I have been interested in press-your-luck mechanics for a while, and have designed a few games based on them. These games are characterized by the choice to keep going or bank your profit. The classic press-your-luck game is Can't Stop, by Sid Sackson. Another example is Six Man Zonk, which was marketed as Cosmic Wimpout. I have used the core mechanic in several of my own games, my favorite being a game I call Gonzo. In Gonzo, players roll five dice, count a particular result—say, 4s—and set aside the 1s, and choose whether to re-roll or bank. If the player ever accumulated three 1s, they lost their turn. I like this mechanic because it always feels like you can get lucky and come back.

Once I had both these concepts in my head—the motif of sibling rivalry, and the game mechanic of Gonzo—I realized I had a combination that probably worked. The idea of my trying to do more and more outrageous things to my sibling while risking getting caught (three 1s), was an appealing idea for a game.

Stage 3: First Prototype

The earliest version I playtested was called "But She Started It!" designed specifically for two players. I tried to make it so that someone "started it"; the player who got caught by mom or dad was in trouble. If the player who got caught wasn't the player who started it, then the victory was especially sweet (that is, worth a lot of points). The game had no board, and players alternated rolling five dice until someone rolled a 2, which indicated that they had "started it." This original design was very similar to the final version, except there was no scoring track, players scored many more points (four 3s were worth 12 points, not the final game's 4 points), and there was a bonus for "starting it" and not getting caught.

It was quickly apparent that "starting it," though a neat game mechanic in principle, required too many rules: it made the game far more complex for only a little play value. Keeping track of points was also a pain, involving a lot of addition and subtraction. This observation led to the construction of a board, which served both to keep track of the score and the current challenge.

Stage 4: Evolution

There were many elements that evolved along somewhat independent tracks:

Evolution of Challenge Board

I've included the design of an early board for reference. Once a board is added to a game, some things become more natural than others. For example, it became natural to give points from the challenge board, because players could write the points on the board. This method was less obvious than "the total number of pips" that I was using before. For a while, I didn't want the challenge tracks to be finite, but obviously they had to be finite: physically if not logically. So the question arose, how big a challenge track is there and what happens when a player reaches the top? Eventually I settled on seven squares (down from an initial ten). With ten squares, if people hardly ever reach the top, then the board is needlessly crowded. Typically, with seven squares someone would reach the top during the course of a game, but not always, so it seemed like a good length. Originally I had a kind of lame rule that when you reached the top you could beat another player at the top. This rule was analogous to the original game in

GAME BOARD PROTOTYPE

				☆		

72	66	60	54	48
60	55	50	45	40
48	44	40	36	32
35	33	30	27	24
24	22	20	18	16

36	30	24	18	12
30	25	20	15	10
24	20	16	12	8
18	15	12	9	6
12	10	8	6	4

| LOOK | MAKE FACE | POKE | TICKLE | TEASE |

which you could always beat the previous player if you got lucky enough. The rule kept the game as close as possible to the original boardless version. With the use of a board I believed that the natural rule was to reward the player who made it to the end with a bonus: an immediate victory plus an additional turn seemed to be a pretty good idea. In particular, this rule makes it so that a player can win on any turn if they are lucky enough, which has a wild feel to it.

Evolution of Scoring Track

The scoring track shrank in size throughout development process, which not only made the scoring more simple, it also allowed the score track to acquire a special play function. For example, the rule that a player must slide backward when the player lands on another player's pawn is a real irritation when the track is 100+ squares long. Sliding back is so minor an idea, and it happens so seldom that it really isn't worth the space the rule takes up. As the board shrank, however, this rule became interesting, in that it would often modify how conservatively a player would play on the challenge board. Similarly, on the smaller track the Little Angel and Little Devil squares affected strategy and play on the challenge board in an interesting way. On the long track it would just be too annoying and difficult to aim for a particular square.

Evolution of Scoring

The system of scoring started out quite cumbersome: a player would have to add the total of all the pips rolled and add or subtract that from their current score. I really wanted to make the scoring simple, so I tried using the opposite extreme: one point received for winning a round, regardless of what number was rolled. As expected, this system was simpler—but also a bit dry. Players were motivated to press their luck, as the higher the number they rolled the less chance they had of being beaten—and losing their point. In the end I settled on a solution somewhere in between, with fixed points for the first three ranks, and points ramping up slowly after that.

Evolution of Number of Players

My philosophy was that as a two-player game, maybe it could be adapted naturally to accommodate three or more players. Playtesting showed that at these numbers the game worked surprisingly well. I am not even sure if there were ever changes made to the game to accommodate groups of more than two players—just changes made to the way I generalized the rules. For example, with two players, I thought that when one player was caught by Mom or Dad, the round would end. With more than two players, it worked best if just the player that was caught was punished and the round continued, until the challenge board was clear.

Evolution of Play Ergonomics

Play ergonomics is how I view the mechanical process of playing: what is awkward, what is too complex, which manipulations take too much time or spawn too many mistakes. An example of a change to the play ergonomics is advancing your pawn along the challenge track during the course of a turn, and removing it if you haven't passed your opponent's pawn. Originally, you only placed the pawn on the board if you beat the other player's pawn, so we could make the rule that a challenge track only ever has one pawn on it. This change didn't affect the game in any way other than allowing players not to mentally keep a tally of their turn's result. It is a very natural outcome but it didn't actually occur to me until about halfway through development, when some players started doing it as a matter of course.

Richard Garfield

Richard Garfield was designing and tinkering with games and game design as a kid, a hobby that stuck with him through his schooling and early career. He earned a doctorate in Mathematics from the University of Pennsylvania, intending to live the life of an academic mathematician. Richard's first published game, Magic: The Gathering, was a game that allowed players to choose their own cards, in effect sharing the role of game designer with the players. The phenomenal success of Magic allowed him to become a full-time game designer. Now he studies and designs games ranging from party games to the trading card game, a genre of paper game that he created.

Unit 2: **RULES**

Defining Rules
Rules on Three Levels
The Rules of Digital Games
Games as Emergent Systems
Games as Systems of Uncertainty
Games as Information Theory Systems
Games as Systems of Information
Games as Cybernetic Systems
Games as Game Theory Systems
Games as Systems of Conflict
Breaking the Rules

*It seems to be the case that the lines drawn in games are not really arbitrary at all. For both **that** the lines are drawn and also **where** they are drawn have important consequences not only for the type, but also for the quality, of the game to be played. It might be said that drawing such lines skillfully (and therefore not arbitrarily) is the very essence of the gamewright's craft. The gamewright must avoid two extremes. If he draws his lines too loosely the game will be dull because winning will be too easy. As looseness is increased to the point of utter laxity the game simply falls apart, since there are then no rules proscribing available means…. On the other hand, rules are lines that can be drawn too tightly, so that the game becomes too difficult. And if a line is drawn very tightly indeed the game is squeezed out of existence.—**Bernard Suits,** Grasshopper: Games, Life, and Utopia*

To play a game is to follow its rules.

Rules are one of the essential qualities of games: every game has a set of rules. Conversely, every set of rules defines a game. Rules are the formal structure of a game, the fixed set of abstract guidelines describing how a game system functions. What are rules? How do they function? And what is their relevance for game design? In this unit on **RULES**, we address these questions and many more regarding the formal structures of games.

Unit 2: **Rules**

DEFINING RULES

formal structures
artificial
limits
unambiguous
fixed
binding
repeatable

11

*The rules of chess, of course, state how the pieces may be moved; they distinguish between legal and illegal moves. Since the knight, for example, is permitted to move only in a highly restricted manner, it is clear the **permitted** means for moving the knight are of less scope than the **possible** means for moving him.—**Bernard Suits,** Grasshopper: Games, Life, and Utopia*

What are game rules? Let's begin with a simple example, one of the most minimal games we can find: Tic-Tac-Toe. The game of Tic-Tac-Toe is defined by the following set of rules:

1. Play occurs on a 3 by 3 grid of 9 empty squares.

2. Two players take turns marking empty squares, the first player marking Xs and the second player marking Os.

3. If one player places three of the same marks in a row, that player wins.

4. If the spaces are all filled and there is no winner, the game ends in a draw.

These four rules completely describe the formal system of Tic-Tac-Toe. They don't describe the experience of playing the game, they don't describe the history and culture of the game, but they do constitute the rules of the game. These four rules are all you need to begin playing a game of Tic-Tac-Toe.

Astonishingly enough, these simple rules have generated millions and millions of hours of game play. Armed with these rules, any two Tic-Tac-Toe players can be assured that when they begin play, they will both be playing the exact same game. Whether played in front of a computer terminal or scratched in the sand of a beach, every game of Tic-Tac-Toe shares the same basic formal identity. In this sense, rules are the deep structure of a game from which all real-world instances of the game's play are derived.

A Deck of Cards

In exploring games as formal systems it is important to determine exactly what are and are not rules. Rules are the logical underbelly beneath the experiential surface of any game. But because games are innately structural, it can be tricky to distinguish which structures in a game are part of the rules and which are not. For example, what elements of the game of Poker constitute the rules of Poker? Some structures are unambiguously part of the rules. The guidelines that dictate how

many cards to deal to each player, how to bet, and the value of different combinations of cards all clearly seem to be part of the game rules.

Any complete set of rules of Poker will also reference a deck of standard playing cards. This deck of cards is part of the rules, because the particular mathematical qualities of the deck (the exact number of cards, the fact that each card is defined by a number and a suit, etc.) are a crucial part of the game. Most variants of Poker, for example, specify whether or not Jokers are to be used. The constitution of a deck of playing cards is always part of the rules of Poker, even though this element of the rules usually goes unstated. The relationship between stated and unstated rules will come up again in later chapters. For now, it is enough to know that the rules of Poker contain—or at least imply—the precise structure of a deck of playing cards.

What if the deck of cards was altered by changing its four suits? Would we still be playing the same game? Perhaps Spades becomes Death, Hearts becomes Love, Clubs becomes War, and Diamonds becomes Sex. The change might entail a graphical alteration to the suits as they appear on the cards or the name by which players refer to the cards. (*"I've got an eight of War."*) This seems like a radical change to make to a deck of cards. But on a formal level, nothing has changed at all: the game remains the same. Players could, with this deck, still play a game of Poker, as long as the deck was composed of four suits in a rank order and 13 numbers. Some aspects of certain Poker variants, such as playing with Red Queens as wild cards, might require a translation to the new deck, but as long as the game's formal structure remained intact, designating the Queens of Love and Sex as wild cards is the same as making the Red Queens wild in a regular deck. Of course it goes without saying that the *experience* of playing Poker with such a deck would be different than the experience a player would have with a standard deck. But the formal system of a game, the game considered as a set of rules, is *not* the experience of the game. Therefore, when looking at games from the point of view of rules, we are less concerned with player experience than with the rules constituting the experience. Although this distinction creates an artificial separation between the structure of a game and players' experience of the structure, the separation allows us to look at games as formal systems.

Formally speaking, as long as a deck of cards has the proper mathematical qualities, it can be used to play Poker. In fact, as long as the game "cards" have the right kind of 4 x 13 information and can be randomized (shuffled), distributed (dealt), and properly kept hidden when necessary (in a hand), they would not have to be cards at all. They could be, for example, carefully marked Popsicle sticks. It would be possible to play a game of "Poker" that would not resemble Poker on the surface, and might not be recognized as Poker by observers, but would still possess the formal structure of Poker.

How is this possible? When we talk about the rules of a game—the formal identity of a game—we are not referring to aesthetic qualities (such as the names of the suits) or representational identity (such as its ability to be recognized by an observer). We

Rules and Strategy

One note of clarification about the difference between the rules of a game and rules of strategy: rules as we understand them here as the formal structure of a game are not the same thing as strategies for play, even though the two might seem similar.

While playing Tic-Tac-Toe, you might devise a "rule of thumb" to assist your play. For example, if your opponent is about to win, you need to place a mark that will block your opponent. This kind of strategic "rule" is an important aspect of games (for example, you might use rules like this to program a computer opponent for a Tic-Tac-Toe game), but these rules of strategy are not part of the formal rules of the game. The actual game rules are the core formal system that constitutes how a game functions. Rules that help players perform better are not a part of this formal system.

are limiting the focus to the set of rules, or formal structures that constitute the game. Looking purely at the rules of a game means repressing many other fascinating qualities of game play and game culture. This is not an easy thing to do. But as we will see, the rules of games are among their most unique features and deserve careful study—analytic study that can be of great benefit in solving game design problems.

Other Kinds of Rules

Often, when we investigate a particular quality of games, we compare them to other forms of culture. Comparison helps situate games within a broader context and also highlights the qualities of games that make them unique. One of our primary intentions is to understand what makes games distinctive and what makes game design unique as a field. But that does not mean that the only kind of comparisons to make are the ones that set games apart from everything else.

Case in point: in trying to figure out exactly what game rules are, it is helpful to ask, *Are rules unique to games?* The answer is both yes and no. There are certainly "rules and regulations" in many kinds of activities. For example, conventions of etiquette are behavioral rules; so are laws of a state or the international "rules" of war. A sign to "keep off the grass" communicates a rule, and so does a memo about a school policy that forbids cheating on tests. Some might define science by saying that it uncovers hidden rules of nature, that molecules, for example, obey certain rules when they combine. If rules are guidelines that guide and direct behavior, there are many contexts in which people or phenomena do seem to "follow the rules."

The word "rules," like the words "play" and "game," can be used in many different ways. For the purposes of game design, it is important to consider in what ways games make use of rules. Perhaps a better question than "Are rules unique to games?" is, "What is unique about the rules found in games?"

Games are artificial systems, separate in some way from ordinary life. The authority of game rules only holds sway within the limited context of the game. The laws of a state, on the other hand, permeate the lived experience of its citizens in a much less limited way. It is true that laws are a social construct, as are game rules. However, from a formal point of view, the artificiality of games keeps their rules from having an impact outside the magic circle of the game. As game designer and philosopher Bernard DeKoven states, "I consider a game to be something that provides us with a common goal, the achievement of which has no bearing on anything that is outside the game."3

Qualities of Rules

The rules of a game are absolutely binding and allow no doubt.—**Johann Huizinga,** *Homo Ludens*

Rules are what differentiate games from other kinds of play. Probably the most basic definition of a game is that it is organized play, that is to say rule-based. If you don't have rules you have free play, not a game. Why are rules so important to games? Rules impose limits—they force us to take specific paths to reach goals and ensure that all players take the same paths. They put us inside the game world by letting us know what is in and out of bounds.—**Marc Prensky,** *Digital Game-Based Learning*

What are game rules like? What sets them apart from other kinds of rules? How do they function in a game? Consider the following list of rule characteristics:

- **Rules limit player action.** The chief way that rules operate is to limit the activities of players. If you are playing the dice game Yatzee, think of all of the things you could do with the dice in that game: you could light them on fire, eat them, juggle them, or make jewelry out of them. But you do not do any of these things. When you play a game of Yatzee, you follow the rules and do something incredibly

narrow and specific. When it is your turn, you roll the dice and interpret their numerical results in particular ways. Rules are "sets of instructions," and following those instructions means doing what the rules require and not doing something else instead.

- **Rules are explicit and unambiguous.** Rules are complete and lack any ambiguity. For example, if you were going to play a board game and it wasn't clear what to do when you landed on a particular space, that ambiguity would have to be cleared up in order to play. Similarly, rules have to be totally explicit in what they convey. If you were playing baseball in an abandoned lot and a tree was being used as second base, ambiguities regarding what counted as second base could lead to a collapse of the game. What can you touch and still be on second base? The roots? The branches? Or just the tree trunk?

- **Rules are shared by all players.** In a game with many players all players share the same set of rules. If one player is operating under a set of rules different than the others, the game can break down. Take the abandoned lot baseball game example. If one player thinks that touching a branch of the tree is legally touching second base, but another player thinks that only the trunk is the base and tags the runner when he is holding onto a branch of the tree, is the player "out"? When the disagreement is raised, the game grinds to a halt. For the situation to be resolved, allowing the game to continue, all players must come to a common understanding of the rules and their application within play. It is not enough that rules are explicitly and unambiguously stated: the interpretation of the rules must also be shared.

- **Rules are fixed.** The rules of a game are fixed and do not change as a game is played. If two players are playing a game of Chess and one of them suddenly announces a new rule that one of her own pawns is invulnerable, the other player would most likely protest this sudden rule improvisation. There are many games in which changing the rules is part of the game in some way; however, the way rules can be modified is always highly regulated. In professional sports, for example, changes to rules must pass through a legislative process by governing organizations. Even in games in which the rules are changed during play itself, such as the whimsical card game Flux (in which playing a card can change the overall game's goals and rules), the ways the rules change are quite limited and are themselves determined by other, more fundamental rules.

· **Rules are binding.** Rules are meant to be followed. Part of the "magic" of the magic circle is that the rules contain their own authority. The reason why the rules of a game can remain fixed and shared is because they are ultimately binding. In some games, the authority of the rules is manifest in the persona of the referee. Like the rules themselves, the referee has an authority beyond that of an ordinary player. If players did not feel that rules were binding, they would feel free to cheat or to leave the game as a "spoil sport."

· **Rules are repeatable.** Rules are repeatable from game to game and are portable between sets of different players. In a Magic: The Gathering tournament, all the players in the tournament follow the same rules when they square off against each other. Outside of the limited context of an individual tournament, the game rules are equally repeatable and portable. Although games often have "home rules," such as the many different versions of rules for the "Free Parking" space in Monopoly, these rule variants are just local variants on largely consistent rule sets. In any case, players must resolve ambiguities between sets of "home rules" in order to play a game.

These qualities of rules are in operation whenever one plays a game. If any of these qualities are not in effect, the game system may break down, making play impossible. If rules are ambiguous, players must resolve the ambiguities before play begins. If rules are not binding, players won't respect their authority and might cheat.

The characteristics on this list constitute the qualities of rules. Describing rules in this way is quite a classical way of understanding games. It is possible, for example, to design a game in which players do not share the same rule set, and resolving this discrepancy is what the game is all about. Or perhaps you want to play a "practice game" with someone, and you won't be obeying all of the rules in order to learn how to play the game. Clearly, the authority of rules is not always strictly obeyed: cheating does happen. As we examine the rules of games from many different angles, some of these qualities may be called into question. But from a strictly formal point of view, these are the general characteristics of all game rules.

Rules in Context

If you think all of this talk about fixed and authoritative rules makes games seem a bit constraining, you are right. Out of all of the possible forms of play, from casual Frisbee-tossing to playful lovemaking, there is something slightly stuffy about games. A completely open-ended game, where rules are constantly invented (such as the example of invulnerable pawns above) is probably not a game by our definition. Although game play can be freewheeling and highly spontaneous, there are other forms of play more improvisational than the play typically found in games. But there is a special kind of lucidity and intelligibility about games. "Real life" is full of ambiguities and partially known information, but that is one of the reasons why games as designed systems are artificial and distinct from daily existence. In ordinary life it is rare to inhabit a context with such a high degree of artificial clarity. These peculiar characteristics of games give rise to the wonderfully unique qualities of game experience. But experience comes into play in later chapters: let us return to rules.

From a formal, rules-based point of view, what does it mean to take part in a game? To play a particular game, players voluntarily submit to the game; they limit their behaviors to the specific restrictions imposed by the game rules. Once play begins, players are enclosed within the artificial context of a game—its magic circle—and must adhere to the rules in order to participate. If you are playing Candyland, who cares which plastic piece reaches the final space first? The other players do, of course. They are the ones who, like yourself, have stepped into the game's magic circle, a shared space of play created by the rules.

There is a vast gap between the rules of Candyland and the experience of the game in play. In the rest of the chapters within **RULES**, we begin to cross that gap by looking at how sets of rules become systems of play. A number of different game design schemas will assist in this task, as we consider games as systems of emergence, uncertainty, information, feedback, decision making, and conflict. We even consider games as systems of rules to be broken. But before leaping into these schemas, it is necessary to understand rules in and of themselves, as formal systems. In the next two chapters, we build a more concrete foundation for understanding exactly what rules are, including the rules of digital games.

- **Rules** constitute the inner, formal structure of games. All games have rules, and rules are one of the defining qualities of games.

- Rules are not the experience of play. It is possible to make experiential changes to a game (such as changing the names of the four suits in a deck of cards) without changing the rules or formal structures of a game.

- Game rules as considered under the Primary Schema of **RULES** are different than rules of strategy. Strategic "rules of thumb" help players to play a game, but do not define the formal identity of a game.

- Game rules are different than the rules of etiquette, law, war, or other social rules. Games are intrinsically artificial and separate from "real-world" contexts, whereas these other forms of rules are not separate from ordinary life.

- Following are the general characteristics that all game rules share:

  - **Rules limit player action**

  - **Rules are explicit and unambiguous**

  - **Rules are shared by all players**

  - **Rules are fixed**

  - **Rules are binding**

  - **Rules are repeatable**

Although some games question and violate these characteristics, these are the common traits of game rules considered from a strictly formal point of view.

RULES ON THREE LEVELS

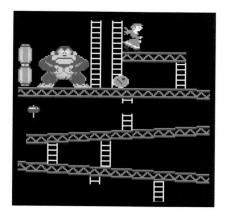

constituative rules
operational rules
implicit rules
formal identity
specificity
elegant rules

12

The *"casual" game of tennis that my buddies and I play is really based on an enormously complex set of "rules"—assumptions, traditions, and conventions—that govern our behavior on the court (whether we are consciously aware of it or not).—* **Stephen Sniderman,** *"Unwritten Rules"*

Consider the game of Chess. Typically it's played with a collection of Chess pieces on a chessboard consisting of black and white squares. We can all agree, I think, that these are indeed real-world objects. Moreover, the game involves a set of rules specifying how the pieces can move, what constitutes a legal position on the board, how one piece captures another and so forth. This is the real-world version of the game of Chess. But there is another version, one existing purely in the world of symbols and syntax (i.e., formal systems), and this version mirrors exactly the real-world game we normally see...the game of Chess is really a relationship between one set of abstract symbols (the black and white pieces) and another set of abstract symbols (the squares on the board). In short, there is nothing crucial about the material embodiment of these symbols insofar as the essentials of the game are concerned.— **John L. Casti,** *Complexification*

Tic-Tac-What?

So far we have discussed rules in a relatively straightforward way. For example, we looked at the rules of Tic-Tac-Toe as they might appear in an instructions manual and argued that these rules fully constitute the rules of the game, the complete formal structure of Tic-Tac-Toe. Here are those rules one more time:

1. Play occurs on a 3 by 3 grid of 9 empty squares.

2. Two players alternate marking empty squares, the first player marking Xs and the second player marking Os.

3. If one player places three of the same marks in a row, that player wins.

4. If the spaces are all filled and there is no winner, the game ends in a draw.

Do these four rules constitute the complete formal system of Tic-Tac-Toe? Although these rules do describe to players what they need to know in order to play, there are aspects of the formal system of Tic-Tac-Toe that are not included here. Specifically, there are two kinds of formal structures that these four rules do not completely cover: the underlying mathematical structures of the game and the implied rules of game etiquette.

Under the Hood

Let us explore these two kinds of formal structures one at a time. First, there is the foundational formal structure that lies "under the hood" of the rules of Tic-Tac-Toe. Does such a structure exist? Is it different than the stated rules of play? There is, in fact, a core mathematical logic that is part of every game but that is not necessarily expressed directly in the stated rules of the game that a player must learn. To understand this point, take a look at a game thought experiment by Marc LeBlanc. The game is called 3-to-15.[1]

Rules for 3-to-15:

1. Two players alternate turns.

2. On your turn, pick a number from 1 to 9.

3. You may not pick a number that has already been picked by either player. If you have a set of exactly 3 numbers that sum to 15, you win.

What does this game have to do with Tic-Tac-Toe? At first glance, 3-to-15 doesn't seem anything like Tic-Tac-Toe. Instead of making Xs and Os, players are picking numbers. There is not even mention of a grid. However, the "punch line" of the game is that 3-to-15 is in fact a kind of Tic-Tac-Toe. If you think you have it figured out, look at the diagram across the page.

3-to-15 is a "magic square" puzzle, in which the numbers in any horizontal, vertical, or diagonal row add up to 15. By picking numbers from the magic square in the fashion proscribed by the rules, players are actually playing a game of Tic-Tac-Toe. Or are they? What do the two games have in common? The underlying rules found in both Tic-Tac-Toe *and* 3-to-15 look something like this:

·   Two players alternate making a unique selection from a grid array of 3 by 3 units.

·   The first player to select three units in a horizontal, vertical, or diagonal row is the winner.

·   If no player can make a selection and there is no winner, then the game ends in a draw.

These "rules" resemble both the rules of Tic-Tac-Toe and 3-to-15, with some significant differences. For example, the rules don't mention how the player makes a selection from the array of choices, or how to record a player's action. The rules above are a kind of abstraction of both games.

Questions remain: is 3-to-15 a variant of Tic-Tac-Toe or a different game entirely? If it is a different game, what does it share with Tic-Tac-Toe? What does all of this say about the "rules" of

The Punch Line

2	9	4
7	5	3
6	1	8

Tic-Tac-Toe? We answer these questions later in this chapter. For the time being, just note that there are in fact formal aspects of games such as Tic-Tac-Toe that lie underneath the stated "rules of play."

Being a Good Sport

If there are aspects of the formal systems of games that underlie the rules as they are expressed to players, there are also aspects of a game that lie beyond or outside the stated rules. These rules are rules of behavior that are implied but usually not explicitly stated in a game. Take a look again at the four "rules" of Tic-Tac-Toe.

1. Play occurs on a 3 by 3 grid of 9 empty squares.

2. Two players alternate marking empty squares, the first player marking Xs and the second player marking Os.

3. If one player places three of the same marks in a row, that player wins.

4. If the spaces are all filled and there is no winner, the game ends in a draw.

Does that really cover every possible rule of Tic-Tac-Toe behavior? Not really. There are other rules that players observe as well. In his essay "Life of Games," Stephen Sniderman points out one of these rules: the implied time limit between turns in Tic-Tac-Toe:

Is there a time limit between moves? Normally, we both "understand" that there is, and we both "know" that our moves should be made within a "reasonable" time, say 20 seconds. If one of us takes longer, the other starts to fidget or act bored, maybe even make not-so-subtle comments, and eventually threatens to quit. Without having stated it, we have accepted a tacit time limit. And because we haven't stated it, it is fairly flexible and very functional.

Suppose it is my turn and, no matter what I do, you will win on your next move. Couldn't I prevent that from happening, within the rules stated, by simply refusing to play? Nothing in the rules forces me to move within a particular amount of time, so I simply do not make my next move. Haven't I followed the rules and avoided losing? And yet, if you've ever played a game, you know that this strategy is almost never employed and would be completely unacceptable. Anybody who seriously resorted to such a tactic would be considered childish or unsportsmanlike or socially undesirable and would probably not be asked to play in the future. This behavior seems to violate some fundamental but rarely stated principle of the game without any of us ever having to discuss it.[2]

There are plenty of other "unwritten rules" besides the self-imposed time limit on turns. For example, it is generally agreed that players will play Tic-Tac-Toe in a way that allows them to easily make Xs and Os. This is why most games take place by marking a piece of paper instead of picking blades of grass out of a large section of land, or making chalk marks on the asphalt of a dangerously busy superhighway—the conditions of play in these cases would make for a nearly impossible game. Other unwritten rules assume that players will not tickle each other, hide the gameboard, or take other actions that prevent their opponents from taking a turn. These rules are implicit in some way in the four stated "rules." But if every possible implicit rule had to be listed, the list would be infinite.

Three Kinds of Rules

As the example of Tic-Tac-Toe demonstrates, in order to fully understand the formal operation of a game, we need to complexify our understanding of game rules. We propose a three-part system for understanding what game rules are and how they operate.

Operational Rules

Operational rules are the "rules of play" of a game. They are what we normally think of as rules: the guidelines players require in order to play. The operational rules are usually synonymous with the written-out "rules" that accompany board games and other non-digital games. The operational rules of Tic-Tac-Toe are the four rules we initially presented.

Constituative Rules

The constituative rules of a game are the underlying formal structures that exist "below the surface" of the rules presented to players. These formal structures are logical and mathematical. In the case of Tic-Tac-Toe, the constituative rules are the underlying mathematical logic that Tic-Tac-Toe shares with the game 3-to-15.

Implicit Rules

Implicit rules are the "unwritten rules" of a game. These rules concern etiquette, good sportsmanship, and other implied rules of proper game behavior. The number of implicit rules of Tic-Tac-Toe is vast and cannot be completely listed. The implicit rules of Tic-Tac-Toe are similar to the implicit rules of other turn-based games such as Chess. However, implicit rules can change from game to game and from context to context. For example, you might let a young child "take back" a foolish move in a game of Chess, but you probably wouldn't let your opponent do the same in a hotly contested grudge match.

The Rules of Chutes and Ladders

So much for the simplicity of rules. Now that we have taken a closer look at the formal structure of Tic-Tac-Toe, it is clear that the phenomenon of game rules is more complex than it initially appeared. Let us continue our investigation of three kinds of rules by turning to the board game Chutes and Ladders. The printed rules of the game read as follows:

How to Play:

1. Everyone spins the spinner. The player with the highest number goes first. Play proceeds to the left.

2. *What to Do on Your Turn:* On your turn, spin the spinner and move your pawn, square by square, the number shown on the spinner. For example, on your first turn, if you spin a 5, move to #5 on the board. Once you move your pawn, your turn is over.

3. Two or more pawns may be on the same space at the same time.

4. *Going Up or Down a Chute or Ladder:* Any time a pawn ends its move on a picture square at the bottom of a ladder, that pawn must climb up to the picture square at the top of the ladder.... *Chutes:* Any time a pawn ends its move on a picture square at the top of a chute, that pawn must slide down the chute to the picture square at the bottom of the chute.

5. If your pawn ends its turn on any of the following spaces, your turn is over:

· a square with no picture

· a square with no picture and just an arrow

· a square that a ladder or chute just passes through

· a picture square at the top of the ladder

· a picture square at the bottom of a chute

Winning the Game:

The first player to reach the Blue Ribbon square #100 wins the game. You can get there two ways:

1. Land there by exact count. If your spin would take you past square #100, don't move. Try again on your next turn.

2. Climb there by ending your move on ladder square #803.

Chutes and Ladders

Although these aren't the complete printed rules that accompany the game (the official rules include a narrative introduction and a Setup section), they give us the information that we need for our formal analysis. How do these printed rules relate to the operational, constitutive, and implicit rules of the game?

Chutes and Ladders: Operational Rules

Like most rules that are written out as instructions for players, the printed rules of Chutes and Ladders consist primarily of operational rules. The operational rules are explicit instructions that guide the behavior of players. How to Play rule number two, for example, tells players: "On your turn, spin the spinner and move your pawn, square by square, the number shown on the spinner."

This is an overt instruction that engages directly with the materials of the game. Because the physical materials of a board game allow players to interact with the game system, it is important for the operational rules to delineate precisely how a player is to manipulate and interpret the objects of a game. The rule mentions the spinner, pawn, and squares of the board, outlining in a single statement the core mechanism of play.

Chutes and Ladders: Constitutive Rules

The primary concern of the operational rules of a game is guiding the behavior of players. In contrast, the constitutive rules of a game—the underlying mathematical structure—exist independently from the player. Whereas operational rules are concrete and describe specific actions that players will take, the constitutive rules are abstract. Constitutive rules are sets of logical relationships that are not necessarily embodied in a material form or in a set of behavioral guidelines for the player. Constitutive rules literally have their own logic, which does not explicitly state how a player will make use of them.

What are the constitutive rules of Chutes and Ladders? They might look something like this:

1. Players all begin with a value of zero.

2. Players alternate turns adding a random number of 1–6 to their current value.

3. The first player to reach a value of exactly 100 wins (if adding the random number to a player's total would make the total exceed 100, do not add the random number this turn).

4. When a player's total exactly reaches certain numbers, the total changes. For example, if a player reaches exactly 9, her total becomes 31. If a player reaches exactly 49, her total becomes 11. (This rule covers the "chutes" and "ladders" of the game. For a true set of constitutive rules, this rule would have to be expanded to include all of the possible "chute" and "ladder" number adjustments for the particular edition of the game.)

Notice that in these rules, there is no mention of a spinner, a board, or pawns. There is no mention of how players are supposed to generate random numbers or to keep track of their numbers during the game. These mechanisms, which involve particular materials and behaviors, are part of the operational rules of the game.

How do the constitutive rules relate to the operational rules? Is there a one-to-one relationship? As a thought experiment, we could use these same four constitutive rules to invent new sets of operational rules that differ from the standard Chutes and Ladders game. Say that we wanted to change only the way that players generated the random number on their turn and the way that they kept track of their progress. Here are a few of the many different ways we could redesign the game:

- *Die and Scoresheet.* Players keep track of their total by writing numbers on a scoresheet and roll a die to generate a random number.

- *Cards and Chips.* Players keep track of their total by taking chips from a central pool and they pick from a set of six shuffled cards to generate a random number.

- *Spinner and Pegs.* Players move pegs along a linear track, using pawns to keep their place. Players use a spinner to generate a random number.

Each of these three games would have its own set of operational rules, which would vaguely resemble the original rules of Chutes and Ladders, but the rules would have to be adjusted to take into account the new materials and behaviors we introduced. For each game, we would have to provide an informational sheet for players to track all of the forward and backward jumps, which in the original game take the form of "chutes" and "ladders" graphically depicted on the board.

These three games all require players to behave differently. Each one creates a different experience for players: rolling a die is a different action than drawing a card. Despite these differences, they all still share the same set of underlying constitutive rules. There is not, therefore, an intrinsic relationship between a game's operational and constitutive rules. The same set of constitutive rules can be expressed in many different operational forms.

Chutes and Ladders: Implicit Rules

Let us turn to our third kind of rules, the implicit rules of a game. There are many implicit rules of Chutes and Ladders. For example, the implicit rule we pointed out in Tic-Tac-Toe relating to the time players should take between turns also applies here. But there are other implicit rules of Chutes and Ladders too. Some of them are even included in the printed game rules. Below is the Setup section from the game's rule booklet:

1. Position the gameboard so that all the players can easily move their pawns from square to square.

2. *All About the Squares:* Take a peek at the gameboard. The squares are numbered from 1 to 100. Players' pawns will move back and

forth across the board, following the numbers upward—starting at square #1 and moving right toward square #10, then up to square #11 and left toward square #20, etc. Of course, you can also move by climbing ladders and unfortunately fall down, too, by sliding down chutes. More about that later.

3. Everyone chooses a pawn to play. Any extra pawns are out of play. Chosen pawns are placed off the board near square #1. Now get ready for the fun![4]

Although these rules might seem obvious, they help illustrate some of the implicit rules of Chutes and Ladders. Setup rule number 1 is a classic example of an implicit rule, here made explicit in the printed text. The gameboard must be positioned so that everyone can access it—in other words, it is necessary that everyone be able to physically and logistically enact the operational rules. The Setup rule that instructs players to put extra pawns out of play (leaving them outside the game) is another rule that is usually implicit, but happens to be written out here.

In the case of these two rules, a normally implicit rule is made an explicitly stated, operational rule through its listing in the rules that come with the game. For Chutes and Ladders' audience of young players, the game designers seemed to think that it was necessary in these cases to spell out what is usually implicit. And because the potential number of implicit rules is infinite, there are many other implicit rules that might be stated as well. Which ones should you include when you are writing instructions, manuals, or help sections for a game? It all depends on your audience and the kind of experience you want the participants to have. Ultimately, sets of rules and instructions need to be designed, analyzed, tested, and revised just as other aspects of a game.

For the purposes of our formal analysis, what does it mean to call these written rules "implicit rules"? If a rule is explicitly written out, how can it possibly be implicit? The boundary between operational and implicit rules can be quite fuzzy. Often, a "rule of play" can shift from implicit to operational, depending on the context. To return to our earlier example of the abandoned lot baseball game, the rule about the tree trunk (and not the branches or roots) being second base could be an implicit rule for a group of kids that have a lot of common experience playing baseball in places where trees are used as bases. However, a newer player might need this implicit rule spelled out, at which point it would become an explicit, operational rule.

The value of this three-part rules model is not in being able to definitively decide whether any given rule is constitutive, operational, or implicit. There will always be some games and game contexts that don't neatly fit into our model. Like all of the concepts in this book, these three ways of understanding rules is not presented as a definitive explanatory typology: it is offered as a framework for identifying, analyzing, and solving design problems as they arise in your game.

The Identity of a Game

Every game has its rules," says Huizinga in Homo Ludens. But we may go further, and say, "Every game is its rules," for they are what define it.—David Parlett, The Oxford History of Board Games

By now we have a grasp on the constituative, operational, and implicit rules of Chutes and Ladders. Here is a question: which of these sets of rules are *really* the rules of Chutes and Ladders? Which set of rules are the true rules of the game? The answer is not obvious. In looking at Chutes and Ladders, we identified the constituative rules, but these rules can also be used to make other games, such as the Die and Scoresheet game. The operational rules seem unique to Chutes and Ladders, but aren't they only an expression of the more fundamental constituative rules? The implicit rules do not seem unique to Chutes and Ladders at all (they are shared with other board games), but at the same time, some of the implicit rules are written out in the instructions that come with the game. And what about game elements that aren't part of the rules: the name of the

game, the visual design of the materials, the mini-narratives of punishment and reward that happen on the board, the history of the game's development, the demographic profile of its players? Do any of these attributes of Chutes and Ladders have a bearing on the game's formal identity?

We start with the last question first. We can define a game in many ways. In the chapters concerning **RULES,** however, the focus is not on the visual design, narrative content, cultural history, or social use of games. Instead, it is on game rules: the formal structures of a game. When it comes to deciding which rules are the "real" rules of the game, we can eliminate all of these non-rule aspects of Chutes and Ladders. Instead, we must look only at the three kinds of rules and decide, from a formal point of view, what constitutes the actual "rules" of Chutes and Ladders. What set of rules gives Chutes and Ladders its unique formal identity?

We can immediately eliminate implicit rules as a possible answer. Although the implicit rules of Chutes and Ladders are crucial to understanding how the game functions, by and large the implicit rules of the game are similar to the implicit rules of other games. Even if we were somehow able to list all of the game's implicit rules, it would not get us any closer to locating the unique formal identity of Chutes and Ladders.

This leaves the other two categories: operational and constituative rules. It turns out that these two kinds of rules are both important in determining a game's uniqueness. The "true and unique identity" of the formal system of Chutes and Ladders (or any game) emerges from the interaction between these two sets of rules. At first glance, it might seem like the constituative rules of a game are the "core" or "essence" of the game rules and the operational rules merely describe ways of accessing the constituative rules. In fact, this is not the case. The constituative and operational rules of a game work in concert to generate the formal "meaning" of a game. There is no "essence" of a game wrapped up in its logical, constituative core.

Are we sure about this? Think back to the variations on Chutes and Ladders that shared the same constitutive rules. Those other game variations just did not feel like Chutes and Ladders—because they were *not* Chutes and Ladders. As much as the formal identity of a game is tied to its constitutive logic, the material way that players experience that logic, as proscribed by the operational rules, is equally important. The fact that players are rolling a die and moving pieces on a board is as much a part of Chutes and Ladders as the mathematical logic that those behaviors express.

If the gameboard and other materials are important, are they not part of the formal identity of the game? What happens if we remove the cute illustrations of boys and girls? What if we replace the illustrations of chutes and ladders with abstract arrows that point at the space where the player is supposed to go? Would the game still be Chutes and Ladders? From an experiential, play-based point of view, no. Removing these elements from the game changes the players' experience—players taking part in the game might not even recognize it as a "stripped down" version of Chutes and Ladders. However, even though the players might not realize it, from a formal point of view, they would be playing Chutes and Ladders. Formally, even with all of the illustrative graphics taken out, the rules of the game would remain the same. When it comes to defining the formal identity of a game, only the rules matter.

Specificity of Rules

Let us take another look at the complex intersection of constitutive and operational rules. Is it really true that for any given game, there exists a single set of constitutive rules? Or are there many sets of constitutive rules we might apply to the same game? What if the constitutive rules of Chutes and Ladders were simplified in the following manner:

1. Players all begin with a value of zero.

2. Players alternate turns generating a number and adding it to their value.

3. The first player to reach a value of 100 wins.

Or simplified even further:

1. Players begin with a value of zero.

2. The first player to reach a value of 100 wins.

Or even further:

1. The first player to satisfy the victory conditions is the winner.

What is going on with these successive simplifications of the constitutive rules? With each stylization, we not only move farther away from Chutes and Ladders, but we also move farther away from a set of constitutive rules that could be contained within a particular set of operational rules.

Because the operational and constitutive rules together create the formal identity of a game, they must embody the qualities of rules we identified in the previous chapter: explicit and unambiguous, as well as shared, fixed, binding, and repeatable. The vague sets of constitutive rules listed above don't meet these criteria: they are simply too general. A similar set of ambiguous operational rules could be created for Chutes and Ladders, such as by telling players to move on the board but not specifying exactly how they are supposed to move. As we know from earlier examples, ambiguity in operational rules leads to disagreements, which must be resolved before play can continue.

The specificity of the rules for any game allows us to identify the game, by saying that it is defined by *this* set of rules and not *that* set of rules. There is no absolute measure for the moment when the identity of one game ends and another begins. But the identity of the game is usually self-evident. So if identity is self-evident, why are we going through such trouble to pin it down? Because the formal identity of a game emerges from the intersection of its constitutive and operational rules, understanding how it operates will help us understand how rules construct a game.

The operational rules are not merely an expression of the constitutive rules of a game. The relationship is more of a two-way street. Operational rules are concrete, real-world rules. Constitutive rules are abstract, logical rules. They are very different, but every game ties them together tightly by virtue of its unique identity. What is the relationship between these two kinds of rules? Mathematician John Casti sheds some light on the problem:

> Given a particular kind of mathematical structure, we have to make up a dictionary to translate (i.e., interpret) the abstract symbols and rules of the formal system into the objects of that structure. By this dictionary-construction step, we attach a meaning to the abstract, purely syntactic structure of the symbols and strings of the formal system. Thereafter, all of the theorems of the formal system can be interpreted as true statements about the associated real-world objects.[5]

Casti is not talking about games (he is discussing the relationships between purely formal systems such as math and the objects that those formal systems name and manipulate). But his thinking is relevant here. In the kinds of systems he describes, there is interpretation between the two levels of a structure, an interpretation that produces meaning as translation occurs between the levels. This same process occurs across all three levels of a game's rules. The formal meaning of a game is dependent on the intertwined constitutive, operational, and implicit rules. How we make sense of a game relies on their interaction, as one form of rules allows for the expression of the others. The significance of rules as a system of expression arises out of the interdependence of its parts. Within the magic circle of a game, formal structures acquire meaning by virtue of these interrelationships.

Designing Elegant Rules

It is curious to realize that when players move pawns or tokens along a track (as in Chutes and Ladders) their action is really just a different way of keeping score. Conversely, any game in which players display or record a numerical score could also be realized as a race game, with representations of the players moving along a track. Why should a game choose one operational form over another? Why should Chutes and Ladders be played on a board if it could also be played in other ways? Can we use the framework of game rules to help make these kinds of design decisions?

As a game designer you generally want players focused on the experience of play, rather than on making sense of the rules. One important aspect of designing rules is creating experiences where elegant rule design maintains proper player focus.

Rules in the Design Process

What do rules have to do with design? Are we advocating that game designers create their games by thinking explicitly in terms of constitutive, operational, and implicit rules?

First of all, there is no magic formula for designing meaningful play. There are as many approaches to creating games as there are game designers. As a game designer, you might be driven by a desire to explore storytelling, visual aesthetics, social interaction, new technologies—or even new kinds of formal rules.

Despite all of these possible approaches, there is something intrinsically structural about games. Even if you are not focused on rules as the creative inspiration for your game design process, you are still going to have to create a set of rules in order to design your game. This means that looking at games formally—as a system of rules—will ultimately be an important part of knowing how your game works. Understanding the formal qualities of games is just as important as understanding their experiential and cultural aspects.

More than a procedure for designing games, the three kinds of rules provide a framework for understanding how rules operate. As a game designer, the systems you're building through the iterative process of game design will have rules as one of their raw materials. Designing and re-designing game systems means, on some level, tinkering with rules. Understanding how rules operate makes it much easier to design meaningful play.

In Chutes and Ladders, there are many reasons why the game takes place on a board, with players moving pawns, instead of, for example, players keeping score on a piece of paper. One reason is the game's audience. Children use the squares to help them count. Instead of adding 6 to 57 on a sheet of paper, they can simply count up six squares to arrive at their new location on the board.

More importantly, however, the board takes care of that pesky constituative rule number four, the rule that embodies "climbing" and "sliding." If the players are keeping score on paper, all of the jumps up and down have to be recorded on a separate sheet for reference. The elegance of the gameboard is that it combines these two operational functions, at once the marker for progress as well as the reference for climbing and sliding. This makes for a successful game experience. Meaningful play emerges from a tight coupling of action and outcome: a *discernable* and *integrated* outcome. The use of a gameboard in the process of generating a random number, recording progress, and seeing whether or not your token climbs or slides, helps emphasize the meaning of the game in a number of ways:

· The board contains all aspects of the game information—progress toward the end space as well as climbing and sliding—at once.

· The representations of the players (their tokens) are all in the same "space," making comparison of relative positions immediate and intuitive.

· Players can clearly see the consequences of their actions, whether it is moving normally during a turn, climbing, or sliding.

It is easy to take the elegance of a game such as Chutes and Ladders for granted. Compare it with a game in which the operational rules make the game *more* difficult to play. Remember Marc LeBlanc's Tic-Tac-Toe variant 3-to-15? The problem with 3-to-15 is that by picking numbers instead of making marks, players cannot see the implications of their actions. Unless players are able to keep a crystal-clear picture of the magic square puzzle in their heads (as well as remember all of the past moves of the game), they will not be able to use the kind of strategies we normally think about when playing Tic-Tac-Toe. 3-to-15 becomes a game about memory and math, instead of the very simple territorial conflict that is Tic-Tac-Toe. If memory and math were what the designer intended to emphasize, then fine. But if your intention is to have players strategically plot their moves on a grid as they play, the operational rules of Tic-Tac-Toe are far superior to those of 3-to-15.

The idea of elegance through clarity works for Chutes and Ladders given its audience of young children, their limited attention and math skills, and the way that the operational rules of the game create an overall experience. However, it is easy to think of games in which the same kind of clarity of information could destroy the game. Imagine, for example, a game of Assassin in which all of the players know everything about each other, such as where they live and who has been assigned to which targets. Assassin is a game that requires secrecy, confusion, and hidden information. Having too much information destroys these elements, making clarity of information an undesirable quality of game play. However, the ways that players learn the game itself—how to enter the system of secrecy, confusion, and hidden information—has to be clear. Rules themselves must ultimately be unambiguous.

When a game creates ambiguity, it is always within some larger frame that is clearly articulated and shared by all players. Creating that clear ruleset and tying it to the actions and outcomes of genuinely meaningful play is one way of understanding the entire process of game design. Understanding how constituative, operational, and implicit rules work together in your game is a key element of this process.

Further Reading

"The Life of Games," by Stephen Sniderman

In this online essay, Sniderman takes a philosophical look at the "unwritten" rules of games. This is the essay from which we derive our understanding of implicit rules, and in it Sniderman makes a number of strong connections between game play, etiquette, and larger notions of cultural behavior. It can be found online at:

<www.gamepuzzles.com/tlog/tlog2.htm>.

Notes

1. Marc LeBlanc, Game Developers Conference 2000.
2. Stephen Sniderman, "The Life of Games." <www.gamepuzzles.com/tlog/tlog2.htm>.
3. Milton Bradley, Chutes and Ladders.
4. Ibid.
5. John Casti, *Complexification: Explaining a Paradoxical World Through the Science of Surprise* (New York: HarperCollins Publishers, 1994), p. 123.

SUMMARY

- The rules of any game exist on three related levels: constitutive rules, operational rules, and implicit rules.

  - **Constitutive rules** are the abstract, core mathematical rules of a game. Although they contain the essential game logic, they do not explicitly indicate how players should enact these rules.

  - **Operational rules** are the "rules of play" that players follow when they are playing a game. Operational rules direct the players' behavior and are usually the kinds of rules printed out in instructions and rulebooks for games.

  - **Implicit rules** are the "unwritten rules" of etiquette and behavior that usually go unstated when a game is played. Similar implicit rules apply to many different games.

- The operational rules for any particular game build directly on that game's constitutive rules. However, any given set of constitutive rules can be expressed in many different operational forms.

- There is a fuzzy boundary between operational and implicit rules. For example, sometimes a game designer may make certain implicit rules explicit by including them in the printed rules of a game.

- The **formal identity** of a game allows us to distinguish a game as formally unique and distinct from other games. This identity emerges from the relationship between the game's constitutive rules and operational rules.

- Key in establishing the formal identity of a game is the **specificity** of the rules. The exact and unambiguous nature of the constitutive and operational rules allow a game to be **this** game and not **that** game.

- There is a **translation** that occurs among the constitutive, operational, and implicit rules of a game. The magic circle is the context for this translation. The formal meaning of a game emerges through a process that bridges all three levels of rules in a game.

- **Elegant rules** allow players to focus on the experience of play rather than on the logic of the rules. Designing meaningful play involves building discernable and integrated relationships between action and outcome into all levels of the rules of a game.

Unit 2: **Rules**

THE RULES OF DIGITAL GAMES

rules and code
internal events
external events
software layers

13

All new media objects, whether created from scratch on computers or converted from analog media sources, are composed of digital code; they are numerical representations.... A new media object can be described formally (mathematically).
—**Lev Manovich,** *The Language of New Media*

So far in this unit, we have drawn most of the examples from the rules of non-digital games. Even though we have an agenda to look at games across digital and non-digital media to understand what is common to all of them, that doesn't mean that there aren't some important distinctions to make. It is, in fact, on a formal level that some of the most pronounced differences between digital and non-digital games occur.

In *Defining Games,* we examined the particular qualities of digital games. In this section, we take a separate look at the formal systems of digital games to see how our three-part model of rules apply.

Rules as a Whole

If all games have rules, then it makes sense that digital games have rules too. What are the rules of a digital game? One answer is that the rules of a digital game are the same thing as the programming code that makes up the game. At first glance, this point of view seems to make sense. Program code is highly structural, like the rules of a game, and like rules, the code does seem to determine what a player can and cannot do in the context of a game.

As an example, take a Tic-Tac-Toe game that you play on a computer. On some level, the rules of this digital version of Tic-Tac-Toe have to be similar to the rules of the non-computer version of the game. Both games operate in the same general fashion, allowing players to alternate turns placing an X or an O in an empty square. At the same time, there are many other tasks that the code performs in the computer version of the game. The code has to manage the program's inputs and outputs (screen and mouse); the code has to interface with the operating system and memory of the computer. Are these sections of the code part of the rules as well?

The answer is no. The code of a computer game is not the exact same thing as its rules. The computer code is part of the medium that embodies the game, just like the written-out rules of Chutes and Ladders are embodied in the medium of printed ink on paper. But as with the rules of a non-digital game, in which aspects of the rules can be hidden "under the hood" on the constitutive level, or pass unspoken on the implicit level, the rules of a digital game take a number of different forms. This means that although there is some overlap between the code of a game program and the rules of the game that the program makes possible, there is not a one-to-one correspondence between them.

So What *Are* the Rules?

A quick review of the qualities of game rules will be helpful. From *Defining Rules,* we know that rules:

- limit player action
- are explicit and unambiguous
- are shared by all players
- are fixed
- are binding
- are repeatable

Many of these qualities seem to be intrinsic qualities of the computer. For example, the idea that computer code is *explicit* and *unambiguous* is true. Code is quite precise: a colon turned into a semicolon, or a zero into a one, can render a program inoperable. Computer code is also *shared* and *repeatable:* all players who buy a game in a store generally buy the same code, minus manufacturing defects. Players certainly won't all have the same game experience, but from a formal point of view, the rules each player will follow are the same.

The idea that rules are *binding,* as well as *fixed* is as true for digital games as it is for non-digital ones. In a classical sense, the rules of the game don't change while the game is being played. Of course, there are plenty of cases of hacking, cheats, and Easter eggs in games, but these interventions only serve to highlight the fact that as a whole, the rules of digital games are indeed fixed and binding.

What characteristics help identify the special qualities of the rules of digital games? The first characteristic of rules, that they *limit player action,* is extremely useful. Rules serve to restrict and stylize players' actions. It makes sense that the rules of a digital game are those aspects directly related to shaping player behavior. How does the player of a digital game take action? How does the game respond when a player makes a choice? What kind of context does the game provide for the player to make decisions? The elements of the game code that address these concerns help construct the rules of a digital game—the rules constitute the structural system that allows choice-making to occur. The parts of the code that manage the use of memory storage, for instance, do not directly involve the player and are not part of the core "rules of the game."

For example, when you are playing Tetris on a PC, the relationship between an action on the keyboard to move or rotate your current piece and the reaction from the computer is part of the rules of the game: the rules define the possible action that a player can take and the outcome that the action elicits from the game system. There are other rules to Tetris as well: the rules for eliminating lines of blocks, the rules for scoring, the rules for losing, the rules that determine the pacing and acceleration of the game. All of these help determine the structure of the game and all are part of its formal system.

The Rules of Tetris

With this in mind, we can list the "rules" of Tetris. Because Tetris varies from platform to platform, we will keep the rules somewhat general (these rules are based on the Game Boy Color version of the game). To keep things simple, we limit ourselves to the basic single-player version of the game ("Marathon"), leaving out elements such as difficulty level and audio selection.

- Play takes place on a grid of 19 by 10 squares.

- Blocks in one of five configurations appear at the top center of the screen. These configurations are made up out of four grid squares and consist of the following pieces:

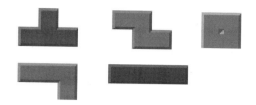

- Blocks appear at the top center of the screen and fall square by square to the bottom of the screen at a set rate that increases over time.

- The player can move the currently falling block left and right one grid square by tapping left and right on the directional pad. If the player presses and holds left or right on the directional pad, after a set pause the block will move quickly in that direction at a set rapid rate.

- Blocks cannot be moved off the left or right borders of the grid.

- The up-direction on the directional pad has no effect.

- The player can rotate the currently falling block using the A or B button. The A button rotates the block 90 degrees clockwise and the B button rotates the block 90 degrees counterclockwise. The block rotates on its center axis.

- When a portion of a block hits the bottom of the grid or another block, the descending block stops falling.

- If, when a block stops falling, one or more rows of the grid are completely filled in with blocks, those rows of block sections disappear. Any sections of blocks that are above the row or rows that disappeared fall downward until they hit the bottom of the grid or another block section.

- As soon as the descending block stops moving (or if rows disappeared, as soon as the upper rows finish falling down), a new randomly selected block appears at the top center of the screen.

- If blocks accumulate on the grid so that the next descending block cannot completely enter onto the grid, the game is over.

- The player receives points for each row that disappeared, according to a scheme in which removing more rows at once (up to four) gives more points than removing fewer rows. The exact points for removing rows depends on the difficulty level selected by the player. Also, when a player uses the down-control to accelerate a block's descent, a player receives one point per grid square that the block descended in this way.

There are a few precise details that we left out for brevity's sake (such as scoring, timing, speed, the exact procedure by which blocks rotate, and so on) but in general, these are the rules by which the game operates. Do the rules seem simpler or more complicated than you expected?

Some aspects of the structure that may seem remote from player action, such as the fact that the game of Tetris randomly determines which kind of block a player is going to receive next, are listed as part of the formal structure of a game. The randomizing of the block type is similar to the way that a random die roll could be called for at a particular moment in a board game, and is clearly part of the rules. To understand how this aspect of Tetris is part of the designed formal structure, imagine other formal schemes for selecting a piece in Tetris, such as cycling through all five shapes in a regular order, giving a player a single kind of shape for an entire game, letting a player pick which of the five shapes to use next, and so on. The decision to randomly give the player a block as opposed to other possible schemes certainly has an affect on the formal structure of how the game proceeds; it is therefore part of the rules. We could use a similar process with each of the rules listed above, considering how changes to the rules would impact the functioning of the game.

Rules and Not Rules

Most or all of the program code that makes up a digital game directly or indirectly affects the experience of the game. But as we have mentioned, that doesn't mean that the code is self-identical to the rules. As with non-digital games, aspects of the program that are not involved in the formal dynamic structure of the game, such as visual and audio aesthetics, are not part of the game rules. In the rules of Tetris listed above, there is no mention of the patterns on the bricks or the sounds that accompany game events. This is one reason why digital games are often prototyped with "placeholder" graphics and audio—elements that do not communicate the intended look and feel of the final game, but instead serve only to visualize the system as is necessary to test its base interactive functioning. This is the same kind of process as prototyping new card games on hastily scrawled index cards.

It is sometimes difficult to determine whether we should consider certain elements of the code to belong to the rules. For example, the code that makes the surface of a pool reflective in a 3D game is not part of the game rules: it is merely part of the code that handles the visual representation of aspects of the experience. This doesn't mean that the reflective water doesn't affect the game experience, just that it is not part of the game rules. On the other hand, if the water's reflectivity is a vital clue that lets players know that the pool is a magical pool with special game properties, then the code that determines the presence or absence of reflectivity would in fact be part of the rules of the game.

The Game Boy *Game and Watch Gallery* game series provides a useful example. These games are based on the Nintendo Game and Watch LCD games from the early 1980s. In the Game Boy versions of these games, players choose from two different play modes: "Classic" and "Modern." The Classic version of each game is a reproduction of the original LCD graphics and sound. The Modern version of each game makes use of more contemporary sprite-based graphics and Game Boy sounds, adding richer

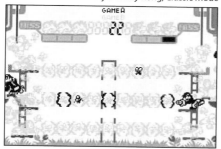

Game and Watch Gallery Donkey Kong, Classic mode

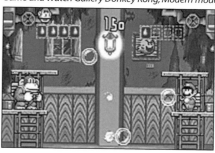

Game and Watch Gallery Donkey Kong, Modern mode

background elements, character animations, music, and sound effects. Although the versions look and sound very different, the player controls and game structure of the two versions are identical. The two versions share the same game rules, which regulate the game logic, player action and outcome, scoring system, structural arrangement of the game space, and so on. The graphics and audio are not intrinsic to these formal qualities of the games and therefore can be changed while keeping the formal structure the same.

On the other hand, if visual representation has an impact on the formal structure of the game, it is part of the rules. In a 2D arcade game where you are trying to avoid touching enemies and obstacles, such as Berzerk, the size of your character's sprite is definitely a part of the game rules: the larger you are, the more difficult it is to avoid hazards. However, the visual identity of your sprite, such as its color, is not part of the rules (unless it becomes invisible or difficult to see). Similarly, the particular visual design of a Chess piece is not part of the formal system of a game, except for the fact that each piece has to be able to unambiguously occupy a single grid square, be able to be moved by players, and each type of piece needs to be easily distinguished from the others.

A subtler example regarding visual code and rules appears in the digital game Thief. In this game, the aspects of the game code that allow computer opponents to creep about in shadows

and be hidden from a player at a distance are part of the game rules. The game play of Thief involves stealthy movement and a good deal of hiding so that you don't alert the computer-controlled agents to your presence. For this reason, the rules that determine how much information you see and the way that characters can be concealed in shadow are part of the game rules. The rules regarding visual representation help distinguish between private information (information hidden from the player) and public information (information known to the player). This information has a direct impact on a player's strategic choice-making and is therefore part of the formal structure of the game. Sometimes, aspects of a game that are normally not considered part of the rules (such as the visual component) can in fact be key parts of the formal structure.

Wheels Within Wheels

If the rules of a digital game are those aspects of the program that have to do with the behavior of the player, where do the rules end? For example, interacting with the game of Tetris to move and rotate falling blocks is interacting with the game. But what about the options screen where the player selects the difficulty level and music for the game? What about the "game over" screen that the player has to move through when a game is finished? What about the main menu screen that a player sees when the game is turned on? The player is interacting with these aspects of the program, too. Is the code that governs the player's interaction with these portions of the program also part of the game rules? Possibly. It depends on how the interaction is framed, just as with non-digital games. Are the unused pawns and the game box of Chutes and Ladders something that the printed rules need to address? Normally not, but as indicated earlier, the written-out rules of Chutes and Ladders make the interaction with these game elements explicit.

In order to more precisely clarify the kinds of lines that we might draw in framing the rules of a digital game, we return to our three-part model of constitutive, operational, and implicit game rules.

> The operation of computer machinery can be described at a number of levels. The "lowest" of these is the electronics of hardware… Descriptions are causal and physical: electrons, currents, voltages. The second level is digital logic. The hardware electronics are designed to represent logical or mathematical operations, such as "AND" or the addition of binary digits or "bits"…. Descriptions are logical, not physical, but they are still tied to the hardware itself, whose structure determines how each operation affects its successor. At a third level lies the "machine language" of the programs that "run" on a particular machine. Machine language consists of the binary representation of program instructions—the language the machine itself "speaks."[1]

One of the trickiest aspects to understanding rules as they apply to digital games is that digital games are structurally very complex. As theorist Paul Edwards points out, computer software operates in a multi-layer fashion, where machine language code interacts with lower-level binary information, which ultimately is derived from electronic signals. The hierarchy could continue upwards as well: machine-level code interacts with a higher-level operating system (such as Windows XP or Mac OS X), which in turn interacts with actual program applications and files. These layers of software and the way that they function to produce an experience for a player vary from platform to platform, program to program, and game to game.

| applications and files |
| operating system |
| machine language code |
| binary information |
| electronic signals |

Although there are some similarities between the framework of constitutive, operational, and implicit rules and the layers of software code by which computer devices operate, we hesitate to apply the three-part model of rules directly to the actual functioning of a computer program. Our model is not meant to directly facilitate technical production of a game program, but to offer a conceptual framework to shape game design thinking. With that said, how might we juxtapose digital games and the three categories of rules?

Constitutive

The constitutive rules of a digital game are remarkably similar to those of a non-digital game. For example, take another look at the constitutive rules of Tic-Tac-Toe:

> 1. Two players alternate making a unique selection from a grid array of 3 by 3 units.
>
> 2. The first player to select three units in a horizontal, vertical, or diagonal row is the winner.
>
> 3. If no player can make a selection and there is no winner, then the game ends in a draw.

These rules would have to be the foundation of a digital game of Tic-Tac-Toe as well. Note that the actions the players take, the way that these actions are represented to the players, and even whether one or both players are human or program-controlled, are not specified. Constituitive rules are concerned only with the internal functioning of the game logic. To use the terms that we established in *Interactivity,* constituitive rules are concerned with internal events (events related to the processing of a choice) and not with external events (events relating to the representation of a choice).

Operational

The operational rules of a digital game are those rules that relate directly to a player's behavior and interaction with the game. Because operational rules directly engage with the materials of the game interaction, the operational rules of a digital game include the use of input devices such as the mouse and keyboard or a game controller. Just as with non-digital games, there are many different sets of operational rules that could be formulated from any given set of constituitive rules. Below is one set of operational rules for a digital Tic-Tac-Toe game, designed for two human players on a computer:

1. A game begins with an empty 3 by 3 grid on the screen.

2. The screen displays an X or an O to one side of the grid to indicate which player will move next. The first player is always X.

3. Players alternate turns, using the mouse to click on an empty square of the grid. When a player clicks on an empty square, the current symbol will be displayed in that square. At the same time, a sound effect of a voice saying "X" or "O" will play (the sound will correspond to the current symbol). Also at that time, the symbol indicating which player is currently taking a turn will flash on and off twice and then switch to the other symbol.

4. If a player attempts to click anywhere else on the screen besides an empty square, there is no effect.

5. If a player places an X or O and thereby creates three symbols in a horizontal, vertical, or diagonal row, the three symbols that are in a row will begin flashing. At the same time, a sound effect of a voice saying "X wins" or "O wins" will play, depending on which symbol won the game. If a player places a symbol and there is no winner and no empty squares, a sound effect of a voice saying "draw" will play.

6. After a win or a draw, if the player clicks anywhere on the screen, the game will reset back to the beginning with an empty 3 by 3 grid.

Note that in describing the operational rules of the game, we only went into detail about the external or representational events that impact player interactivity and formal game events. We did not include the aesthetic, experiential components of the game that did not relate to the rules. We did not describe, for example, the typeface of the "X" and "O" or the personality of the voice-over. But because the voice audio communicates a formal game event to the player, it is part of the operational rules. Is the inclusion of the voice cues absolutely necessary? Probably not. But what is and what is not an "official rule" of a game is a design decision. As a game designer, it is up to you to frame the game's rules in a way that is appropriate and useful.

There are obviously many other ways to construct the operational rules of Tic-Tac-Toe on a computer. In our example, a sound paired with flashing symbols indicates winning. But should a visual element also appear that lets the players know who won? Should a text message be used to more clearly indicate which player is currently taking a turn? What about getting into and out of the game? The version listed above has no exit or quit function, so presumably it is designed for a computer context where a player would exit the program by closing the program window or by using a standard "quit" key command. Are these the best design decisions for the game? Playtesting and careful consideration of your audience will help answer these questions.

Implicit

Many implicit rules are common to digital and non-digital games. If you are playing Tic-Tac-Toe with your friend on a computer, the same implicit rule about taking a "reasonable" amount of time on your turn still applies. In addition, there are implicit rules that are unique to digital games, most of them similar across games designed for the same technological platform. Below are a few examples of implicit rules of the digital Tic-Tac-Toe game:

> 1. When you move the mouse, the cursor on the screen corresponds to the mouse movement.

> 2. The Tic-Tac-Toe game program can be started, stopped, copied, deleted, renamed, etc., like other program files.

> 3. Playing the game will not affect your computer in any permanent way.

Although these implicit rules may seem like obvious assumptions, it is the nature of implicit rules that they are usually taken for granted. But it might be interesting to design a game that surprised players by "playing" with the implicit rules of computer interaction. For example, what if during a game the cursor did not correspond directly to mouse movement? Or what if when you typed in chat to another player in an online multiplayer game, the text that appeared on the other player's screen did not correspond exactly to what you typed? Questioning implicit rules can be a powerful source for design ideas.

Why Rules?

Understanding the rules of a digital game is a tricky business, compounded by the complexities of software operation. In a non-digital game, the rules of a game are generally something that is concretely manifest in an instruction book or in the structure of the game materials. But with a digital game, the rules are buried in layers of program code and are often difficult to identify.

Why is it important to go through the trouble of understanding the rules of digital games? We should emphasize that we do not expect anyone to list every rule of a digital game as it is being designed. It is ultimately not important to be able to distinguish exactly what is and is not a rule of a particular game, or to which of our three categories a rule belongs. It is possible to frame the same formal system in many ways with different results.

As a game designer, it is extremely important to be able to identify the formal structure of any game you are designing. If you can't identify the core rules of a digital game you are hoping to create, you are out of touch with your own design. On the other hand, if you can plot out the rules of a game, as we did with Tetris, you are close to being able to describe specifications for a programmable prototype. Once a version of the game begins to take shape, your knowledge of the rule structure will allow you to more easily modify the rules as you refine the player experience.

The goal of this book is to offer useful frameworks for understanding how games function. Up to this point the discussion of rules has created a general understanding of the formal nature of games. In the next several chapters, we provide formal schemas that present even more specific tools for understanding elements of game design.

Notes

1. Paul N. Edwards, *The Closed World* (Cambridge: MIT Press, 1996), p. 246.

The Rules of Digital Games SUMMARY

- The rules of a digital game are related to the program code, but they are not the same thing as the program code. Rules are abstract tools for thinking about the formal structure of a game and are not necessarily literally manifest in code.

- In a general sense, the rules of a digital game are the same as the rules of a non-digital game: they are directly concerned with the **actions** players take and the **outcome** of those actions. Therefore, the aspects of a game program that structure and take in player input and determine the game's output are those aspects that constitute the game's rules.

- The internal functioning of formal game logic (such as the way a program selects the next block to appear in Tetris) is also part of the rules of a digital game.

- The specific manifestations of the visuals and audio in a digital game are usually not part of the formal structure of the game. However, there are cases where these elements impact the formal structure of a game and should be considered part of the rules.

- The **constitutive rules** of digital and non-digital games are quite similar. The constitutive rules of a digital game serve as the core logic of the game and are usually contained directly in the code in some fashion. The constitutive rules of a digital game handle the game's **internal events.**

- The **operational rules** of digital games are not only concerned with the internal events, but also the **external events** of a game—player input and game output, expressing choices and outcomes to the player. As with non-digital games, there is a fuzzy line between the operational and implicit rules of digital games.

- Digital games share many **implicit rules** with non-digital games. In addition, they have their own kinds of implicit rules, which include the unstated assumptions of the game's platform. Playing with these implicit rules can be the source of innovative design ideas.

- Because game programs are multi-layered, complex objects, determining exactly which aspects of a game program belong to each type of rules is not always clear. However, the value of the three-part rules framework is not for game development or program design, but instead to understand better the abstract formal system of a game and how it functions to produce meaningful play.

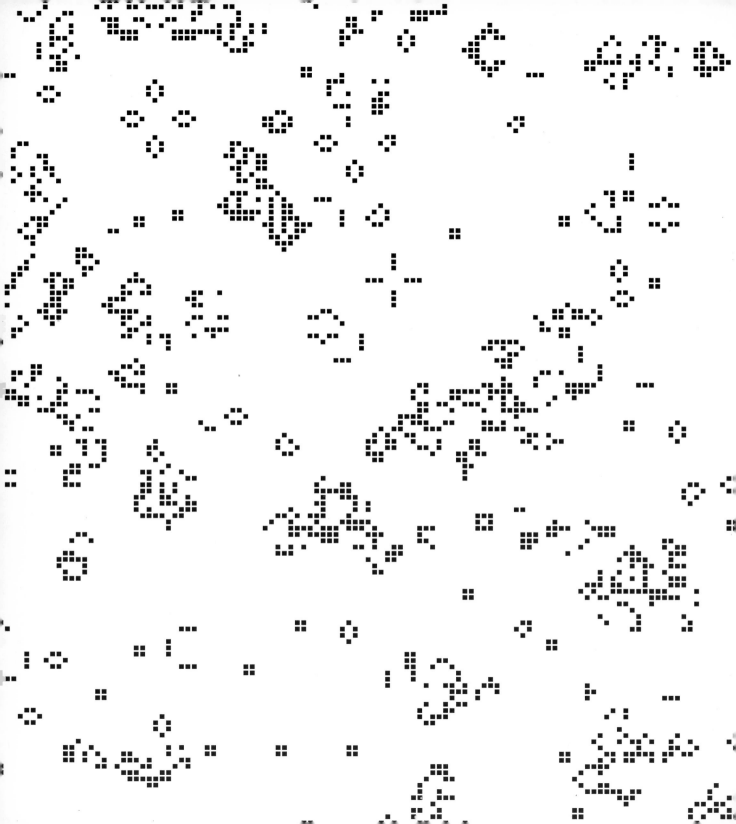

systems
complexity
emergence
bottom-up
engines
second-order design

14

GAMES AS EMERGENT SYSTEMS

*Imagine a billiard table populated by semi-intelligent, motorized billiard balls that have been programmed to explore the space of the table and alter their movement patterns based on specific interactions with other balls. For the most part, the table is in permanent motion, with balls colliding constantly, switching directions and speed every second.... Such a system would define the most elemental form of complex behavior: a system with multiple agents dynamically interacting in multiple ways, following local rules and oblivious to any higher-level instructions. But it wouldn't truly be considered **emergent** until those local interactions resulted in some kind of discernable macro behavior. Say the local rules of behavior followed by the balls ended up dividing the table into two clusters of even-numbered and odd-numbered balls. That would mark the beginnings of emergence, a higher-level pattern arising out of parallel complex interactions between local agents. The balls aren't programmed explicitly to cluster in two groups; they're programmed to follow much more random rules: swerve left when they collide with a solid-colored; accelerate after contact with the three ball; stop dead in their tracks when they hit the eight ball; and so on. Yet out of those low-level routines, a coherent shape emerges.—**Steven Johnson,** Emergence*

Introducing Emergent Systems

Welcome to the first game design schema, *Games as Emergent Systems.* The preceding chapters have defined some of the core concepts relating to games, design, and rules. This chapter offers something a bit different. A schema is a conceptual framework that focuses on a particular aspect of game design. Any particular schema will highlight certain aspects of games and de-emphasize other aspects. Although a given game design schema can be applied to any game, some schemas are more useful for solving certain design problems and less useful for others. The purpose of a game design schema is to facilitate the design of meaningful play.

The schema *Games as Emergent Systems* builds directly on the discussion of systems in chapter 4. As a system, a game is a set of parts that interrelate to form a whole. Being able to identify and analyze each part of a system, its attributes, and its relations to other parts of the system assists in understanding how a game system adds up to a larger experience of play. In this schema, we deepen our appreciation of games as systems by looking at them in terms of *complexity* and *emergence*. As Steven Johnson illustrates in the quote that opens this chapter, emergence arises out of complexity. It is the phenomenon of unplanned patterns appearing from within a system. Emergence is a crucial aspect of games, linking their intrinsically systemic nature to the space of possibility and meaningful play.

Complexity

As a preliminary step to understanding emergence and systems, we begin with the concept of *complexity*. Growing out of classical systems theory, the study of complexity has become its own interdisciplinary field. Researchers in complexity study many different kinds of systems, from computational systems of pure information to biological systems such as cells and organisms to natural ecosystems and human society. The study of complex systems tends to look at systems that are "self-organizing, replicating, learning, and adaptive."[1] In our own brief investigation of complexity, we will admittedly just skim the surface of this fascinating field, perhaps in quite an unconventional way.

Let us begin by clarifying the term "complexity." In his book *Grammatical Man,* Jeremy Campbell weaves together many elements of systems theory to look at relationships between information, language, and DNA. He has this to say about complexity:

> In living organisms, and even in machines, there exists a "complexity barrier." Beyond this barrier, where systems are of a very high complexity, entirely new principles come into play.
>
> Complexity is not just a matter of a system having a lot of parts which are related to one another in nonsimple ways. Instead, it turns out to be a special property in its own right, and it makes complex systems different in kind from simple ones, enabling them to do things and be things we might not have expected. [2]

Campbell doesn't offer a precise definition of complexity, but the passage above does present a useful picture of the concept. Complexity is a property of a system, and according to Campbell, not all systems are complex: only some of them reach what he calls a "complexity barrier." In a complex system, the internal relationships between elements of the system become intricately compounded and extraordinarily complex.

Although mathematical models for precisely defining the "complexity barrier" do exist, for our purposes the difference between a simple system and a complex system is more conceptual than numerical. A simple system such as a wooden table does have parts (four legs and a tabletop) that interrelate to form a whole, and the whole is more than the sum of the parts, since a complete table can serve functions that the isolated pieces cannot. But it is clearly a simple system, as the relationships between parts are fixed and entirely predictable.

The table, as a system, is much simpler than even the most elementary game. In Tic-Tac-Toe, the relationships among the parts, the unpredictability of the player's actions, the dynamic shifting of the system over time, the uncertain outcome, all contribute to the complexity of the game, a kind of complexity that is fundamentally different than that demonstrated by a table. As Campbell points out, this complexity is "a special property in its own right," and in the case of games, their special kind of complexity leads to meaningful play. If complexity is not present in a game, meaningful play cannot occur.

Messengers and Buildings

To separate our discussion of complexity from an analysis of games, let's look at an example of a system that is not a game. Our sample system is a communications network, a fictional city where a messenger has to deliver messages between buildings. In the most straightforward version of this system, there are only two buildings. Each building generates messages that are addressed to the other building; the messenger has to run between them.

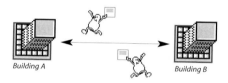

Building A   Building B

On the whole, this is not a complex system. Although the movement of the messenger and the changing states of the buildings makes it is more complicated than our example of a table, the behavior of the system is set in a fixed, predictable pattern. The messenger will oscillate back and forth between the two buildings. Even if the two buildings generate messages at random intervals, so that the messenger never knows when and where the next message will appear, this does not add substantial new states for the system as a whole.

What happens if we add new elements and relationships that push the system toward a higher degree of complexity? Imagine that there are now 10 messengers trying to deliver messages between 50 buildings, randomly positioned on a grid. The different distances between the buildings determine how long the messengers travel. This is important, because we are trying to maximize efficiency: if a message goes undelivered for too

long, the communication system has failed to function properly. With the addition of these elements, the system suddenly increases substantially in complexity.

To appreciate the added complexity, consider writing a computer program to manage the behavior of the messengers. In the two-building system, the program would be very simple, merely shuttling the single messenger between the two buildings. But with 10 messengers and 50 buildings, it becomes a more complex task. If a messenger delivers her last message at a building and there isn't a new message to pick up, where does she go next? This decision should be based partially on which buildings are closest to the messenger, but it should also take into account which buildings other messengers have recently visited; buildings that haven't been visited recently are most likely to have an undelivered message.

Or consider what should happen when a messenger picks up several pieces of mail that need to go to buildings in different parts of the city. What is the logic that determines how to deliver the messages? What if the messengers have the ability to "meet" in-between buildings so that they can swap messages to work more efficiently? How, when, and where will the messengers rendezvous? Consolidating deliveries to the same building by swapping messages may make the system more efficient, but if messengers meet too often, the overall efficiency of the system might go down. The functioning of the communication system is no longer a simple, predictable oscillation between two states. It has achieved a fundamentally new degree of complex, compounded interrelationships.

And if that scenario isn't complex enough, we could add additional variables. For instance, what if some buildings have special relationships with other buildings (a lot of mail passes between the two of them) and that these relationships change over time? Or perhaps the messengers aren't delivering mail between "buildings," but instead they are delivering to "companies." The companies keep changing their building address, so that their physical locations in the grid of the city constantly shift. Or perhaps messengers never have a bird's-eye view of the entire city, but only gain information about the layout and behavior of the city from their own experience and by sharing information with other messengers.

Writing a computer program to simulate all of this would be more challenging than our first scenario. In fact, the sample system highlights some of the problems of information transmission and social behavior modeled in complexity research. What makes our communication system complex? The many dynamic and contingent interrelationships among the parts push the system across the "complexity barrier" Campbell describes. The initial version of the system, with two buildings and one messenger, was primitive and mechanistic by comparison. But the more complex versions of our city resemble an ecosystem filled with intelligent agents. We articulate this conceptual distinction between a simple and a complex system further in the examples that follow.

Simple Complexity

In the case of the messenger city, the system eventually became complex because we loaded lots of complex relationships and contingencies into it. But sometimes complexity can arise quite suddenly and unexpectedly from a handful of simple elements. Here is an example that comes to us from programmer and mathematician John Casti, concerning planetary physics:

> It's known that the behavior of two planetary bodies orbiting each other can be written down completely in closed form. Nevertheless, it turns out to be impossible to combine the solutions of three two-body problems to determine whether a three-body system is stable. Thus, the essence of the Three-Body Problem resides somehow in the linkages between all three bodies.... So here is a case in which complicated behavior arises as a result of the interactions between relatively simple subsystems.[3]

Casti is referring to the fact that in the study of planetary motion, systems with two planetary bodies (such as a star and a single planet orbiting it) can be mathematically articulated to precisely predict the motion of the two bodies in space. But once a third element is added to the system, gravity from each planetary body affects the other two, drastically complicating the mathematical factors determining their relative motion.

The addition of a third planetary body into this system changes everything: the system crosses Campbell's "complexity barrier" to become a genuinely complex system. The relationships among the elements in the system become intertwined in such a complex fashion that the resulting dynamics have yet to be mathematically resolved. What is striking about this example is the low number of elements the system contains. Two planetary bodies have a simple relationship; the addition of just one more element into the system introduces complexity of a completely different order.

There are many examples of seemingly simple systems that in reality are staggeringly complex. A conversation, for example, might only have two people interacting with each other. When all of the cognitive, social, perceptual, linguistic, and contextual factors are taken into account, however, it is clear that even a simple conversation is an exceedingly complex process.

What Complexity Is Not

What is complexity? Certainly ordered systems where every point in time and space looks like every other point are not complex. Also, it does not make sense to talk about complexity when the system is random, and each point in space is complete, uncorrelated with any other point.—**Per Bak,** *How Nature Works*

One way of exploring the concept of complexity is to examine what complexity is not. According to physicist Per Bak, a complex system can't be too orderly, where the system has the same behavior from moment to moment. At the same time, a system can't be completely chaotic, where each moment of the system's operation only randomly corresponds to the next moment. When Bak refers to the points in time and space of a system, he is talking about the way that the system is organized over time. Looking at how the relationships in the system change from moment to moment can help determine whether the system is exhibiting complex behavior.

For example, imagine the non-complex cases as a television screen. A television that is not receiving power or a signal of any kind would have a completely black screen. Every pixel would be identically black from moment to moment ("every point in time and space looks like every other point"). On the other hand, a screen that is full of random static would be completely chaotic, with the color of a dot at one moment having nothing to do with the color of that dot at the next moment, or the color of any other dots ("each point…uncorrelated with any other point").

In contrast, imagine a diagrammatic display of the messenger communication system. The screen would display some static elements (the buildings), but the messengers would move from point to point on the screen as they navigate between the buildings, picking up and dropping off mail, and meeting between buildings to swap messages. Unlike a completely fixed or completely random set of points, the display would have a logic and rhythm, as the messengers moved in patterns through the space. The unpredictable but patterned visualization of these complex behavioral sequences would be a reflection of the genuinely complex system underneath.

Four Kinds of Systems

Before moving into a discussion of complexity and games, let us take stock. We have looked at several examples of systems, some of them complex and some of them not. How do these differing degrees of complexity relate to each other? Christopher Langton, pioneering mathematician of artificial life, provides four ways of understanding the level of complexity of a system.[4]

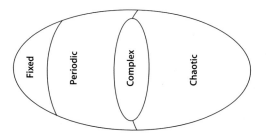

Each category in the chart refers to a different degree of complexity that can appear in a system.

- On the far left are *fixed* systems that remain unchanging. The relationships between their elements are always the same. The black, unchanging TV screen is a good image for this kind of system.

- To the right of fixed systems in the chart are *periodic* ones. Periodic systems are simple systems that repeat the same patterns endlessly. The simple two-building version of the messenger system, where a single messenger oscillates back and forth, is a periodic system.

- On the far right of the chart are *chaotic* systems. In a chaotic system, the elements are constantly in motion, but their states and relationships are random, like a TV screen full of static.

- The final category is the one that interests us the most: *complex* systems. These systems are more complicated and unpredictable than a periodic system, but not so full of dynamic relationships that they end up as a chaotic haze of static.

Considering all of the possible kinds of systems that might exist, *complex* systems inhabit a narrow band. The conditions that allow a complex system to exist are something like the conditions that allow a planet to support life: among all of the planets that exist in the universe, only a small subset have the right combination of temperature, atmosphere, and chemical composition to allow life to emerge. What are the special conditions that allow systems to become complex, especially in the case of games?

Two Horrible Games

At last our discussion of complexity brings us into the realm of game design. We know that games are systems, but what would it take to make a game a *complex* system? Earlier, we looked at systems that *weren't* complex, to help identify characteristics of complex systems. We use a similar strategy next, inventing a couple of games that don't manage to achieve complexity. As games, they are pretty horrible, but like all bad games, they can teach us something. The first game is called Heads or Tails:

> *Heads or Tails,* a game for two players: One player flips a penny out of sight of the other player. The other player guesses whether or not the penny landed on heads or tails. If the guesser is correct, the guesser wins. Otherwise, the player that flipped the penny wins.

This game definitely doesn't sound like much fun. Imagine playing it just one time: as the coin-flipping player, you flip the coin, wait for the answer, and then find out if you won or lost. Even if you played the game over and over, it would still be an exercise in flipping and guessing. The game seems too simple to ever become genuinely complex. The second example of a horrible game isn't nearly as simple, but it too fails to achieve complexity:

> *The Grid,* a game for two players: Play takes place on a grid of 100 squares by 100 squares. Each player has ten identical game pieces, placed randomly on the board at the beginning of the game. A piece occupies one square on a grid, although the pieces stack, so any number of pieces from either player can occupy a single grid square. Players take turns moving all 10 of their pieces once each turn. Moving a piece means moving it 1–1000 spaces in any combination of horizontal, vertical, or diagonal movements. Pieces do not affect each other in any way.

This game also doesn't sound like much fun. The players would take turns, laboriously pushing their pieces around the board, but because players cannot affect each other, the game would go on forever and no one would win. Players might create patterns of pieces on the board, but ultimately those patterns would be meaningless in terms of making progress toward winning the game. Like static, the pieces would be constantly in motion, but they would never form coherent strategic patterns where the points had any meaningful relationship to each other (as Bak put it, the pieces would be "uncorrelated points").

Both Heads and Tails and The Grid lack complexity. They are also very different games. What do they have in common that keeps them from attaining complexity? To answer this question, we return to our core concept of meaningful play.

Meaningful play **in a game emerges from the relationship between player action and system outcome; it is the process by which a**

player takes action within the designed system of a game and the system responds to the action. The *meaning* of an action resides in the relationship between action and outcome.

Thinking about the two games in the context of meaningful play, it is clear that neither one was forging meaningful relationships between player action and system outcome—between the decisions that the player was making and the results of those decisions in the game. In the case of Heads and Tails, the game consists of a single random event that determines the outcome of the game and over which the players have no control. The second game, The Grid, lacks meaningful play in a different way: unlike Heads and Tails, there is no randomness at all and the players make many decisions every turn as they move their pieces. But because there is no way for those decisions to have meaningful game outcomes, The Grid also ultimately lacks meaningful play.

If both of these games lack complexity, and they both lack meaningful play, does that mean that meaningful play and complexity are the same thing? Not at all. Meaningful play and complexity address two different aspects of games. Meaningful play concerns the relationship between decision and outcome, and complexity concerns the way that parts relate to each other in a system. Despite this distinction, the two concepts are closely related. In games where meaningful play does exist, some aspect of the game system will be complex. The complexity might come in the form of formal strategic intricacy, complex social relationships, a rich narrative structure, the psychological complexity of betting real-world money, or in other ways, but complexity is a prerequisite of meaningful play. Without complexity, the space of possibility of a game is not large enough to support meaningful play.

What would it take to turn Heads and Tails into a game that did support meaningful play? We can make a simple adjustment to the system of rules and see how it changes things:

Heads and Tails: The Decision Variant. Instead of randomly flipping the penny, the flipper gets to decide which side is facing up. The other player guesses which side the flipper selected. If the guesser is correct, the guesser wins. Otherwise, the player that flipped the penny wins.

In this version of Heads and Tails, the guesser is trying to determine the other player's decision instead of trying to guess the outcome of a random event. Does this bring meaningful play into the game? Does it make the game more complex? Well, it does make the game less of a random event: one player is trying to "psyche out" the other player and guess at his intentions. But despite this fact, playing the Decision Variant just one time would not push the game into the realm of complexity. Why not? The game still feels arbitrary. Even though the flipper can determine which side of the penny faces up, the overall outcome of the game feels random. Arbitrary play, in which actions seem unrelated to each other, is the opposite of meaningful play. Another important factor is that the game does not last long enough to have any kind of trajectory or larger context into which the player's decisions are *integrated.* Considering a single game, players would iterate the rules just once and then the game would be over, without any opportunity for their decisions to affect future outcomes in a meaningful way.

Whether the flip is random or predetermined, a single game of Heads and Tails lacks complexity because it lacks meaningful play. As we pointed out, meaningful play and complexity are not the same thing: they refer to different aspects of games. But complexity is a necessary prerequisite of meaningful play. Below are a few additional variations to Heads and Tails that underscore this point. Each version of the game makes a few rules modifications that affect the integration of player action and system outcome. Although each variation only adds a few new rules, each one pushes the operation of the game system beyond the complexity barrier and into meaningful play.

The Talking Variant. In this version of the game, the flipper decides which side of the coin is up. But before the guesser guesses, the two players have ten minutes to discuss the decision the flipper made. The flipper might lie about which side is up, tell the truth, or try some complex double-psychology tactic. The guesser wins if the guess is correct and the flipper wins if the guess is incorrect.

Why it is more meaningful: In the Talking Variant, the rich social interaction that ensues elevates the game into the realm of meaningful play. The flipper has to select a strategy of deception, which the guesser tries to defeat. The final guess that the guesser makes is an integrated part of the entire conversation leading up to the decision.

The Repeating Guess Variant. In this variant, the flipper still decides which side of the coin is up. No discussion is allowed, but the players play the game 21 times. Each time the guesser guesses right, he or she gets a point. Each time the guesser guesses wrong, the flipper gets a point. At the end of the game, the player with the most points wins.

Why it is more meaningful: The Repeating Guess is very similar to the Decision Variant. The difference is that because the game is played many times, there is a chance for patterns to emerge. As with Rock-Paper-Scissors, the two players are trying to outguess each other and detect patterns in the other's behavior. Each choice is integrated into past decisions made by both players.

The Increasing Risk Variant: In this game, players alternate the roles of guesser and flipper. Each turn, the current guesser tries to guess the result of a random flip. If the guesser is correct, the guesser earns 1 point and may choose to have the coin flipped to guess again. If the guesser is correct a second time, the points earned double (from 1 to 2). As long as the guesser is correct about the flip, the guesser can continue to guess and try to double the points earned that turn, from 1 to 2 to 4 to 8, etc. But a single wrong guess eliminates all of the points earned that turn and the two players switch roles. The first player to 25 points wins.

Why it is more meaningful: Even though this game still uses a random coin flip, the players make meaningful "press your luck" kinds of choices that can reward or punish risk. Every game action is integrated into the decisions of a particular turn, as well as the game as a whole. For example, if your opponent is about to win, you might be forced to take more risks.

Each Heads and Tails game variant offers meaningful play by providing additional relationships between decision and outcome and integrating these moments of interactivity into a larger game structure. The original Heads and Tails was a simple exercise in probability. But it is impossible to predict how one of the variations might play out. What would the conversation be like in the Talking Variant? What patterns would arise in the Repeating Guess Variant? How much would players be willing to risk in the Increasing Risk Variant? The game experiences that would emerge from within these variations would be surprisingly complex, more so than their very simple sets of rules might lead you to believe. This phenomenon—systems generating complex and unpredictable patterns of behavior from simple rules—is called emergence.

Emergence
A modest number of rules applied again and again to a limited collection of objects leads to variety, novelty, and surprise. One can describe all the rules, but not necessarily all the products of the rules—not the set of all whole numbers, not every sentence in a language, not all the organisms which may arise from evolution.— ***Jeremy Campbell,*** *Grammatical Man*

Emergence is a crucial facet of understanding how the system of a game becomes meaningful for players. In the quote above, Jeremy Campbell describes how emergence arises from complexity. Campbell's first sentence points to the key features of emergence: that a simple set of rules applied to a limited set of objects in a system leads to unpredictable results. This is precisely what happens in the three Heads and Tails variants. The number of different ways that the Talking Variant might play out is virtually infinite. But the game itself is so simple! This is the key to emergence in games: complex possibilities are the result of a simple set of rules.

Most games share these features. The rules of Pong are relatively simple, but if you imagine all of the ways that a game can play out, from a quick-win match where one player dominates, to an extended, dramatic finish, it is clear that the system of Pong demonstrates emergence. Even a game with a much more complicated ruleset, such as Warcraft II, contains emergence. Although the game seems very complex compared to Pong, in essence Warcraft II only has a few dozen different kinds of elements, and the ways that they can interact are quite limited. If two enemy units meet, they won't strike up a conversation or start to dance together—they will either fight or not fight. Despite the complexity of the code, there is still arguably a "modest number of rules" applied to a "limited collection of objects". The system of the game, when it plays out, results in unpredictable patterns of emergence.

In including such a wide range of game phenomena under the heading of emergence, we are admittedly diverging from orthodox complexity theory. Theorists of emergence often make a distinction between "weak" and "strong" emergence—for example, unless the Pong ball was an autonomous, adaptive agent that learned to avoid or follow the paddles, the game would not be considered a case of "strong" emergence. For our purposes, however, we collapse these distinctions to consider emergence in a more general sense. Emergence can come about through complex programmed mechanisms that simulate adaptive agents and systems, but it can also happen on an experiential level, where extremely simple rules give rise to complex social or psychological relationships among players.

Parts and the Whole

Regardless of how we frame it, all of these instances of emergence share certain characteristics:

Emergence is above all a product of coupled, context-dependent interactions. Technically these interactions, and the resulting system, are *nonlinear*: The behavior of the overall system *cannot* be obtained by *summing* the behaviors of its constituent parts. We can no more truly understand strategies in a board game by compiling statistics of the movements of its pieces than we can understand the behavior of an ant colony in terms of averages. Under these conditions, the whole is indeed more than the sum of its parts.[5]

This selection from computer scientist John Holland contains an extremely rich cluster of ideas about emergence. Because Holland moves from the specific to the general, we are going to interpret the text line by line, working from the final statement back to the beginning. In the last sentence Holland tells us that when emergence is in operation, "the whole is indeed more than the sum of its parts." This fits into our general understanding of systems, in which the parts interrelate to form a whole. In an emergent system, there is a special relationship between the parts and the whole. Because an emergent system will play out in unpredictable ways, the whole of the game is more than the sum of the parts.

What does Holland mean by this? Look one sentence earlier: *"We can no more truly understand strategies in a board game by compiling statistics of the movements of its pieces than we can understand the behavior of an ant colony in terms of averages."* Holland uses board games and an ant colony as examples of emergence, pointing out that these systems cannot be understood merely by taking averages of the behavior of independent objects in the system. This notion is very close to one of the ideas that Campbell mentioned, that "One can describe all the rules, but not necessarily all the products of the rules—not the set of all whole numbers, not every sentence in a language, not all the organisms which may arise from evolution." Campbell is pointing out that in an emergent system, we might know all of the initial rules, but we cannot describe all of the ways that the rules will play out when they are set into motion. He provides the diverse examples of math, language, and evolution. In the case of language, for example, we cannot describe every statement that might be uttered in a language even though we might know all of the words in that language along with the rules of grammar that organize them.

Campbell and Holland are both saying the same thing: what makes a system emergent is that there is a special disconnect between the rules of the system and the ways those rules play out. Although the rules might be concise and knowable, the behavior of those rules set into motion in the system creates patterns and results not contained within the rules themselves, results that contain "variety, novelty, and surprise." The rules of grammar might tell us how to organize words into sentences, but they can't account for *Huckleberry Finn,* The U.S. Constitution, and the lyrics to Britney Spears'"Oops! I Did It Again." The grammatical rules, set into motion through the use of language, exceed the complexity barrier to produce emergent results, which could never have been predicted by a mere consideration of the rules by themselves.

This is what Holland means by *"The behavior of the overall system* **cannot** *be obtained by* **summing** *the behaviors of its constituent parts."* Merely consolidating all of the rules together in a list can't account for the diverse variety in the behavior of an emergent system. When he mentions that, *"Technically these interactions, and the resulting system, are* **nonlinear,"** he means nonlinear in the mathematical sense. He is saying that the ways that the objects in the system interact to produce complexity are not just additive, but increase geometrically. This is the kind of complexity seen in the example of the three-planet system. Adding a third planet to the equation did not just increase the complexity of the system by a third: it added orders of magnitude of new complexity.

Object Interactions

We have now arrived at the first line of Holland's quote: *"Emergence is above all a product of coupled, context-dependent interactions."* So far we have looked at the general kinds of

emergence that can come out of a system. But what is it about a system that allows it to cross the complexity barrier and become truly emergent? The key is in the terms "coupled" and "context-dependent." When Holland says that emergence is a product of these two forms of interaction, he means interactions between objects within a system.

Recall from *Systems* Littlejohn's four elements of a system: *objects, attributes, internal relationships,* and *environment.* When the rules of an emergent system are set into motion, the internal relationships between the objects begin to transform the attributes of the elements. These transformations then affect change in the objects' internal relationships, further altering their attributes, resulting in loops and patterns of behavior. Thus, the interactions of a complex system are *coupled,* meaning that the elements of the system are linked recursively. Like ants in a colony, the objects in the system act together to perform in ways that single objects cannot. Because the objects are linked to each other, one change in the system creates another change, which creates another change, giving rise to patterns over the space of the system. These interactions are *context-dependent,* which means that the changes that occur are not the same every time. Instead, the exact nature of the transformations depends on what else is happening in the system at any given moment. Coupled interactions help produce global patterns across a system; context-dependent interactions ensure that the exact arrangement of these patterns are dynamically changing over time.

In the messenger communication system example, the objects (messengers and buildings) have attributes and also have relationships to each other. If a messenger picks up mail from a building, the attributes of the building (Does it have undelivered mail or not?) and the attributes of the messenger (Does the messenger have mail to deliver? What is the next destination?) change as a result. As the system runs, the objects of the system interact with each other in ways determined by the rules of the system. If the system were truly emergent, unexpected patterns would arise in the behaviors of the objects, behaviors not contained in the rules themselves. For example, imagine that we decided to color blue any building that didn't have any messages waiting to be picked up. It could be that patterns of blue buildings would cycle regularly lengthwise across the system. These patterns are not part of any of the system's rules but are patterns that nevertheless arise out of the system as it functions. This is precisely the kind of emergent pattern that Steven Johnson described in his fanciful example of motorized billiard balls in the quote at the beginning of this chapter. In both cases, the coupled, context-dependent interactions among elements of the system are responsible for the emergent phenomena.

Life, the Game

In the field of complexity theory, perhaps the most well-known examples come from the mathematical study of cellular automata. Cellular automata are grid-based systems that vaguely resemble game boards. At any moment, a grid square can either be occupied or unoccupied. A set of rules dictates how the cells behave and how their states change over time. The name "cellular automata" comes from the grid of squares, called "cells," and the fact that once the system is set into motion, the rules move the system forward so that it runs "autonomously," without further input from the outside.

Not all cellular automata systems automatically create emergence. It all depends on the rules that govern the behavior of the cells. For example, if we wanted to replicate a blank TV screen in a cellular automata grid, we could create the following rules:

1. To begin, all of the cells are unoccupied.

2. The state of the cells does not change.

These rules would result in the fixed system of a blank, empty field. If we wanted to replicate a cellular automata system that would result in pure chaos, we could create the following rules:

1. To begin, half of the cells are occupied and half are unoccupied, determined randomly.

2. Every thirtieth of a second, a new set of half of the cells is occupied, randomly determined.

These rules would result in the ever-changing but patternless sheen of dots that make up television static.

Cellular automata were systems originally developed by the mathematicians John Von Neumann and Stanislaw Ulam in the 1930s and 1940s. But the most famous application comes from John Conway. His cellular automata system, The Game of Life, or more simply, Life, was popularized when Martin Gardener published it as a puzzle in *Scientific American* in 1970.

There are many fascinating ways to look at The Game of Life. What interests us about Life is not that it is an early form of artificial life, or even that it is called a game (it isn't a game by our definition), but instead that it is a wonderful example of the principles of emergence and complexity. Life takes place on an infinite grid; the cells of the grid are governed by a simple set of rules, summarized here by Steven Levy in *Artificial Life*:

> Life occurs on a virtual checkerboard. The squares are called cells. They are in one of two states: alive or dead. Each cell has eight possible neighbors, the cells which touch its sides or its corners.
>
> If a cell on the checkerboard is alive, it will survive in the next time step (or generation) if there are either two or three neighbors also alive. It will die of overcrowding if there are more than three live neighbors, and it will die of exposure if there are fewer than two.
>
> If a cell on the checkerboard is dead, it will remain dead in the next generation unless exactly three of its eight neighbors are alive. In that case, the cell will be "born" in the next generation.[6]

Although Conway's Life was not originally created on a computer, it is commonly manifest today as computer software. Life always begins with some of the cells full and some empty, either in predetermined or random patterns. When the program is run, the grid is updated in steps, each step iterating the rules according to the current configuration on the grid. Visually, Life manifests as a set of dynamic, shifting geometric patterns as grid cells die and come to life.

The Game of Life: The Glider

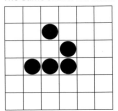 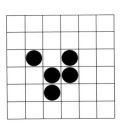 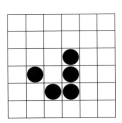 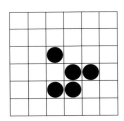 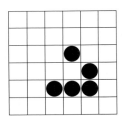

Some triplet histories in the Game of Life

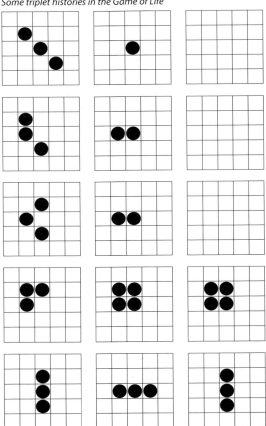

The startling thing about Life is that from these extremely simple rules, strikingly unexpected patterns result. Some shapes die out quickly and disappear from the grid. Others reach stable and fixed patterns, or oscillate forever between two states. Still others move steadily across the grid (like the famous "glider" shape), and yet others exhibit even more complex behavior (such as the "glider gun," which produces a new glider every 30 generations).

By combining these different patterns and unexpected behaviors, fans of Life have made everything from rich visual patterns to functional calculators and other "virtual machines" that operate using the cells on the grid. Life is a complex system that exhibits emergent behavior from a simple set of rules. Using Life as a case study, it becomes clear why emergence is formed from coupled and context-dependent interactions between the elements of a system:

Coupled: In Life, the interaction between any two objects is not an isolated relationship. Instead, the relationships depend on a set of coupled relationships. Whether or not a cell is alive or dead in Life is dependent on the positions of the adjacent cells; the life and death of *those* cells are also dependent on all of *their* adjacent cells. These linked relationships create interlocking forms that multiply across the space as a whole, giving rise to surprising patterns.

Context-dependent: Over time, as the context of an object in a system changes, its relationships to other objects change, giving rise to global transformations in the system. In the case of Life, the context of any given cell is its eight neighbors. At each time step, this context shifts, propagating dynamic behavior across the system. Just as coupled interactions reverberate across the space of the grid, context-dependent interactions ripple out over time as the space of the system transforms and creates new contexts for the system objects.

Bottom-Up Behaviors

The striking thing about The Game of Life is that its coupled and context-dependent interactions emerge from a very simple set of rules. Look at how simply we can summarize the behavior of the cells:

- A living cell will be alive in the next generation if two or three of its neighbors are alive.

- A dead cell will be alive in the next generation if three of its neighbors are alive.

- Otherwise, a cell will be dead.

The fact that these simple rules can produce everything from glider guns to working calculators is astonishing. Glider guns are nowhere described in the three rules listed above. But paradoxically, they do exist in the space of possibility defined by the three rules. All of the possible patterns of cells, all of the virtual machines that have ever been built on the Life grid, all of the many forms of "life" that have been discovered in The Game of Life exist somehow, embedded within those three rules.

Life demonstrates how, within emergent systems, simple local interactions lead to larger, more complex patterns. Complexity theorists often use the phrase *bottom-up* to summarize this phenomenon. Theorist Steven Johnson describes the bottom-up processes in systems such as ant colonies, urban spaces, and adaptive software:

What features do all these systems share?... They are bottom-up systems, not top-down. They get their smarts from below.... In these systems, agents residing on one scale start producing behavior that lies one scale above them: ants create colonies; urbanites create neighborhoods; simple pattern-recognition software learns how to recommend new books. The movement from low-level rules to higher-level sophistication is what we call emergence.[7]

In addition to the kinds of systems Johnson describes, there is another important class of system where bottom-up emergence occurs: games. Games generate complex emergent behavior, as the formal structures of rules facilitate the unpredictable experience of play. Like the possibility of glider guns contained in the rules of Life, all of the Baseball games that have ever been played, all of the strategies for winning, all of the team and player statistics that the game has produced, are somewhere contained within the rules of Baseball.

Bottom-up emergence is intrinsic to games and is not limited to the formal complexities of a game. Emergence occurs in different ways on the level of rules, play, or culture in any game. We are focusing in this chapter on the formal properties of emergence, but in a sense the rest of this book continues the trajectory we begin here, examining the many ways that meaningful play can emerge from a game.

Emergence in Games

Many studies of emergence look at systems such as The Game of Life, which are autonomous and do not require active human participation in order to function. But Life is not really a game. Not only does it lack a quantifiable goal, but it is not a system of conflict in which one or more players participate. It is true that a user can set up the initial set of cells, which are either on or off. But once the game begins, Life runs all by itself. The behavior of Life, once the program is in motion, is divorced from human interaction.

Games are not like this at all. Games require players, and those players make decisions that move the game forward. The concept of meaningful play, for example, is premised on the idea that there are perceivable relationships between player action and game outcome. The participatory nature of games makes them tricky systems to examine, because unlike the "game" of Life, a true game will always include one or more players inside the system making decisions. In games, emergence arises through the interaction of the formal game system and decisions made by players. A wonderful example of this kind of emergence is bluffing in Poker. The strategy of bluffing—pretending to have a better hand than you actually do—is a key component of the game. But it is not explicitly described in the game rules. Bluffing is simply an emergent behavior that occurs in the game, facilitated by the betting procedure, the fact that players' hands are hidden, and the desire for players to win the conflict of the game. Bluffing is like the glider guns in The Game of Life, present in the space of possibility, though never explicitly stated in the rules.

Even the simplest of games can generate vast and unexpected behaviors. John Holland makes this clear in a discussion of board games:

> Board games are a simple example of the emergence of great complexity from simple rules or laws. Even in traditional 3-by-3 Tic-Tac-Toe, the number of distinct legal configurations exceeds 50,000 and the ways of winning are not immediately obvious. The play of 4-by-4-by-4, three-dimensional Tic-Tac-Toe, offers surprises enough to challenge an adult. Chess and Go have enough emergent properties that they continue to intrigue us and offer new discoveries after centuries of study. And it is not just the sheer number of possibilities. There are lines of play and regularities that continue to emerge after years of study, enough so that a master of this century would handily beat a master of the previous century.[8]

Even simple rule sets can create tremendous amounts of emergent complexity. The way that this complexity manifests does not always intuitively follow from the rules. For example, compare two of the games that Holland mentions, Chess and Go. They are among the world's most ancient and sophisticated games, and they are similar in many respects. Both are two-player, turn-based strategy games played with pieces on a gameboard grid. Which game is more complex—at least from a formal, mathematical point of view? Looking at the rules, Chess would appear to be the more complex game. In Chess, there are six different pieces, each with unique ways of moving about the board. There are also numerous "special" rules, such as a pawn's opening move, queening a pawn, and castling a king. In contrast, Go has much simpler rules. There is only one kind of piece, and once placed on the board, a piece does not move on the grid.

Despite Go's simpler set of rules, however, it is a mathematically more complex game. One demonstration of this is the development of artificial intelligence computer programs to play the games. Programming software opponents for both Go and Chess are long-standing computer science problems that have received attention around the world from both academics and commercial game developers over the last few decades. Although the focus of Go research has been in Asia, where the game is more common, the amount of attention given to programming AI for the two games is roughly equivalent. A few years ago, when Gary Kasparov lost to IBM's Deep Blue in Speed Chess, computers arguably exceeded human mastery of Chess. But a Go program has yet to be written that can challenge an advanced player of the game.

Why the discrepancy? Go demonstrates a higher degree of emergent complexity, arising out of the coupled interactions between game pieces. Like a cellular autonoma, each piece in Go forms relationships with neighboring pieces and empty spaces. When these simple relationships are multiplied across the grid of the gameboard (which is larger than a Chess grid), the linked interrelationships of the pieces adds up to a degree of complexity that exceeds Chess in raw numerical possibilities.

The point of this comparison is not to identify which game is a superior game. Chess and Go are both noble pastimes for game players, and playing either one well is a demanding intellectual pursuit. The lesson here is that more complex rules do not necessarily equal more complexity in the system. Paradoxically enough, the simpler rules of Go generate a higher degree of emergent complexity.

Designing Surprise

How do the concepts of complexity and emergence relate to game design? It is clear that games are systems and that complexity and emergence affect meaningful play. But how do emergence and complexity impact the process of design? How can understanding games as complex systems assist in making games?

Complexity is intrinsically linked to meaningful play. Playing a game is synonymous with exploring a game's space of possibility. If a system is fixed, periodic, or chaotic, it does not provide a space of possibility large or flexible enough for players to inhabit and explore through meaningful play. On the other hand, if a system is emergent, exploring possible relationships among game elements is continually engaging. Players will play a game again and again if something about the experience continues to engage them with "variety, novelty, and surprise." In the business of online content development, it is well-known that a good game is the "stickiest" kind of content available. A fan of an animated web series might watch the latest episode two or three times, but someone addicted to a game will play it dozens, hundreds, or thousands of times. The infinite possibility that arises out of an emergent system is a key design strategy to encourage repeat play. A successfully emergent game system will continue to offer new experiences, as players explore the permutations of the system's behavior.

Peter Molyneaux's Populous: The Beginning offers a great example of game emergence. Game designers Rollings and Morris vividly illustrate how a complex game system unexpectedly creates new play possibilities:

> In Populous: The Beginning, when enemy warriors run up to one of your preacher characters, they will stop at a short distance as the preacher starts chanting. For a while, they sit listening. If the process is not interrupted, they will then convert to the preacher's side.
>
> That's one rule. Another is that if enemy warriors have started fighting, a preacher cannot convert them.
>
> What this means in practice is that you can leave your preachers in a perimeter defense around your settlement. The first wave of enemy warriors will be converted. This is automatic, and the player is free to get on with other things. But now consider the second wave of enemy warriors. They come running up, and the first thing they encounter is not the preacher's conversion radius but the attack radius of the last lot of warriors to be converted. A fight breaks out between the groups of warriors, and the preachers cannot intervene to convert the second wave.
>
> The feature that emerges is that you cannot leave your defenses unmanaged. From time to time, you need to scroll around your settlement and move newly converted warriors behind the preachers.
>
> I have no idea whether this was what the designer intended or not. Very possibly it was. However, it is a good example of emergence because it is not immediately obvious that those two rules would give rise to this feature.[9]

According to Rollings and Morris, emergence in Populous occurs on two levels: within the local context of interaction between game units, as well as on the larger level of player behavior. The local interactions between player-controlled preachers and interloping enemy warriors produced context-dependent results. The first interaction between these game elements—with no converted warriors present—converts the enemy warriors. But if a second wave of enemy warriors appears, the altered context containing converted warriors creates a new situation entirely, in which a battle ensues. The rules determining the behavior of these units are relatively simple: preachers convert enemy warriors within a certain radius. But because warriors have their own simple behaviors (they fight enemy warriors and are immune to conversion while fighting), the intersection of these simple rules produces emergent behaviors, which change according to the context in which they are placed.

Emergence occurs on a second level as well: the player's larger behavior within the game. As Rollings and Morris point out, a player needs periodically to "scroll around [his] settlement and move newly converted warriors behind the preachers," managing these emergent relationships throughout the play of a game. The effect of the preacher/warrior interaction ripples outwards, growing from merely local behavior to become incorporated into the larger fabric of the overall play.

One lesson to learn from this example is the specificity with which relationships between elements need to be designed. The emergent behaviors Rollings and Morris observed were only possible because of exactingly particular attributes of the preacher and warrior units. What is the radius within which the preachers can convert enemy warriors? How long does conversion take? What is the range at which enemy warriors can notice preachers, and vice-versa? How fast do the enemy warriors travel? When are they immune to conversion? The attributes of the game units are in a careful balance. If enemy warriors travel too quickly, or if the conversion process takes too long, then enemy warriors might reach the preacher and slay the unit before there is time for the preacher to convert them. If fighting warriors were not immune to conversion, then the second wave of enemy warriors would be converted, thus reducing the player's need to monitor the settlement's preachers. It was only through careful attention to game rules in the design of Populous that these behaviors emerged.

Engine Tuning

Arriving at sets of game rules that produce successfully emergent behavior involves a difficult and often time-consuming design process. It can only be completed through the kind of iterative design outlined in chapter 2. The rules for The Game of Life seem simple and elegant, but it took John Conway two years of testing and refinement to arrive at their final form.

In the example from Populous: The Beginning, emergent behaviors were the result of what game designer Marc LeBlanc calls *game tuning*: iterative tweaking, testing, and refinement of game rules in order to create a rich play experience. Game tuning was also used in the design process for the PC game Gearheads. In that game, one or two players send wind-up toys across a playfield, trying to get as many toys as possible across to the other end of the screen. The longer a player waits to release a toy, the more energy it has and the further it will travel. Once a toy is released, a player has no control over it, so either player can use it to score. Some of the toys are slow, heavy, pushing toys like Big Al the wind-up bulldozer, or quick and light toys like Ziggy the mechanical cockroach. Some toys destroy other toys, like the Walking Time Bomb; still others can change their direction of movement, like Deadhead, a chattering skull that scares toys and reverses the direction they are facing. Each of the game's twelve toys has special abilities, and the interactions between the toys as they move across the playfield is a key aspect of the game's design.

Very early in the design process, a playable prototype was created that allowed the designers to create new kinds of toys and tune their attributes. Inside the game application were pull-down menus with grids of statistics for each toy. As the attributes of each type of toy were altered, the changes immediately took effect in the game, so that even in the middle of a game the designers could easily make adjustments and see how the changes affected the overall game play. The iterative playtesting that took place throughout the 18-month development process helped create a balanced game.

During development, the designers discovered emergent combinations of toys. They found that although toys could be used as individual game units, the real richness of Gearheads arose from using toys in concert with each other. Often the toy combinations they discovered were highly surprising. Designers Frank Lantz and Eric Zimmerman coined the term *engine* to describe these toy combinations: like a mechanical engine, toy combinations were a set of interlocking parts that worked together to achieve a larger effect. We list a few examples of the many engines discovered in the system below:

Punching Roaches. Although Ziggy the wind-up cockroach is the fastest toy in the game, his movement is erratic; when he bumps into another toy, he flips onto his back (a second encounter with a toy will flip him onto his feet again). Another toy, Kanga, is a punching kangaroo character that punches forward any toy it encounters. One simple engine is to release many Ziggys quickly onto the board, most of which end up on their backs. One or two Kanga toys released afterwards punch the light Ziggys, shooting them across the opposite side of the screen to score points.

Bomb Shield. Two of the more destructive toys in the game are Disasteroid and the Walking Time Bomb. Disasteroid, a very slow-moving giant robot, shoots its forward-facing lasers at any toy it encounters, eliminating it. The Walking Time Bomb is a strong and medium-fast toy, but when it runs out of energy it explodes, eliminating all nearby toys—except for Disasteroid, which is the only one that the bomb can't destroy. One engine that uses these toys in combination is to release a Disasteroid, followed immediately behind by a Walking Time Bomb. Pushing from behind, the bomb speeds up the normally slow Disasteroid, which laser-blasts any toys that stand in its way, clearing a path for both toys to score. Even if the Walking Time Bomb explodes before the pair can reach the far side of the screen, Disasteroid still survives the blast and can possibly score on its own.

Perpetual Motion. A more complex engine makes use of the toys Handy and Crush Kringle. Crush Kringle is a professional wrestling Santa Claus toy that moves steadily across the playfield, periodically pausing to stomp the ground. When he stomps, all nearby toys switch directions from left to right. Handy is a walking white glove, and its special ability is that when it encounters a toy on the playfield, it winds it back up, replenishing its energy. Although Crush Kringle is a powerful toy, it is very slow, which means that the player has to spend a long time winding it. However, a game engine provides a shortcut around this limitation. First, players release a very lightly wound Crush Kringle, followed by a Handy, followed by another lightly wound Crush Kringle, all on the same row of the playfield. The faster Handy bumps into the first Crush Kringle, replenishing its energy. The Crush Kringle then stomps, reversing the direction of the Handy, which runs backwards into the second Crush Kringle, which it then winds up as well. The second Crush Kringle toy eventually stomps, sending the Handy back to the first toy. In this way, the trio of toys make their way across the playfield, the Handy toy running back and forth between the two Crush Kringles.

The toy-combination engines were not something designed directly into the rules of Gearheads. They were emergent patterns of play that arose out of the more simple set of attributes that defined each individual toy. In some cases, the toy attributes were refined in order to make a particular engine possible—but most of the time, engines were discovered as the game was played and developed.

As with the example from Populous: The Beginning, emergence in Gearheads manifests on many levels at once. The unexpected local interactions between toys creates larger patterns on the playfield. The player's own decision-making process is also a pattern that emerges as a result of the toy combinations, as players adjust their behavior to take advantage of emergent combinations. Players are encouraged to think in terms of emergence by selecting a limited number of toys before a match starts: experienced players include an engine or two in the four or five toy types they pick for a game. Another way that these engines entered into game development was the AI programming. In designing the computer opponent, engine-based heuristics were included, so that the program was aware of advantageous toy combinations and often used engines against the player. Some Gearheads players learn about certain engines simply by observing the behavior of the AI.

Second-Order Design

Engines such as these occur in non-digital games as well. A card game such as Magic: The Gathering, with its thousands of different cards types, is a hothouse of emergence, designed specifically to facilitate the creation of card-combination engines by its players. In Magic: The Gathering or in Gearheads, the use of game elements in combination with one another facilitates a rich space of possibility. The toys of Gearheads or the cards of Magic are the simple elements of a language. By using them in different combinations, the player makes his or her own meanings through the play of the game. Unit combinations and engines are not the only way to create emergent effects in a game; if your game does contain a number of different kinds of objects, design them to work in combination with each other, so that the breadth of your space of possibility can increase exponentially.

Designing an emergent game system that generates meaningful complexity from a simple set of rules is challenging. Why is it so difficult? As a game designer, you are never directly designing the behavior of your players. Instead, you are only designing the rules of the system. Because games are emergent, it is not always possible to anticipate how the rules will play out. As a game designer, you are tackling a second-order design prob-

lem. The goal of successful game design is meaningful play, but play is something that emerges from the functioning of the rules. As a game designer, you can never directly design play. You can only design the rules that give rise to it. Game designers create experience, but only indirectly.

In a complex emergent system, every element gains its identity by virtue of its possible relationships with other elements. When one element changes, the rest of the relationships are all affected in turn. Key to the iterative process is the ability to think of games as systems, to analyze the way that they function, to know when, why, and how a game system fails to generate meaningful play. Every rule adjustment results in a change to the play of the game, and you will never be able to test out every possible rule variation, or even a tiny fraction of them. That is why anticipating how changes to the formal structure of a game affect its play is one of the core skills that game designers must develop. Over time, game designers acquire a structural "sixth sense" of what will and will not work in a game, of how changes to one part of the system are likely to play out in the experience as a whole. At the same time, one cannot anticipate every effect. One of the great pleasures of being a game designer is seeing your game played in ways that you never anticipated, seeing players explore nooks and crannies of the space of possibility that you never knew existed. Understanding how emergence works and creating a design that encourages emergence is one way your games can bring you this pleasure.

Although a rules-based approach is not the only way to understand games, it is an indispensable part of a game designer's conceptual toolset. By defining rules and framing games as emergent systems, we have laid the groundwork for thinking about games in structural terms. The game design schemas that follow all offer more specific ways of thinking about and designing games as formal systems.

Further Reading

Complexification, by John Casti

This book on the science of complexity written by mathematician John Casti is a non-technical but nevertheless sophisticated approach to the topic. The wide-ranging subject matter, including everything from fractals and emergence to strange attractors and the Turing Test offers a strong introduction to the study of complex systems.

> *Recommended:*
> Chapter 1: The Simple and the Complex
> Chapter 6: The Emergent

Emergence: From Chaos to Order, by John Holland

Known as the "father of genetic algorithms," John Holland is a mathematician and computer scientist. Although the later chapters become somewhat technical, the earlier ones provide a solid introduction to game theory and cellular autonoma. Many of the problems presented in the book relate specifically to game rules and game AI.

> *Recommended:*
> Chapter 2: Games and Numbers
> Chapter 3: Maps, Game Theory, and Computer-Based Modeling

Emergence, by Stephen Johnson

A popular introduction to emergent systems and complexity, in *Emergence*, digital culture maven Stephen Johnson reports on a variety of emergent phenomena, from ant colonies to urban planning to computer games.

> *Recommended:*
> Chapter 1: The Myth of the Ant Queen
> Chapter 5: Control Artist

Grammatical Man, by Jeremy Campbell

Grammatical Man is a wide-ranging, journalistic account of the development of complexity theory, systems theory, information theory, game theory, genetics, and related developments in science and engineering. As a general introduction to the way that these diverse fields integrate, it is a valuable resource.

> *Recommended:*
> Part One: Establishing the Theory of Information
> Part Two: Nature as an Information Process

Turtles, Termites, and Traffic Jams, by Mitchel Resnick

A student of Seymour Papert, Mitchel Resnick is a faculty member at the MIT Media Lab, and his research group is responsible for, among other things, LEGO Mindstorms. *Turtles, Termites, and Traffic Jams* is a highly accessible book about decentralized systems. The volume includes both a general introduction to the subject as well as detailed accounts of Resnick's own work in the field with StarLogo.

> *Recommended:*
> Chapter 1: Foundations

Notes

1. Jeremy Campbell, *Grammatical Man: Information, Entropy, Language, and Life* (New York: Simon & Schuster, 1982), p. 105.

2. Ibid, p. 102.

3. John Casti, *Complexification: Explaining a Paradoxical World Through the Science of Surprise* (New York: HarperCollins Publishers, 1994), p. 40–41.

4. Christopher Langton, *Artificial Life: An Overview* (Cambridge: MIT Press, 1995), p. 112.

5. John Holland, *Emergence* (Reading, PA: Helix Books, 1998), p. 121–122.

6. Langton, *Artificial Life,* p. 52.

7. Steven Johnson, *Emergence: The Connected Lives of Ants, Brains, Cities, and Software* (New York: Scribner, 2001), p. 18.

8. Holland, *Emergence,* p. 22–23.

9. Andrew Rollings and Dave Morris, *Game Architecture and Design* (Scottsdale: Coriolis Group, 1999), p. 26.

Games as Emergent Systems
SUMMARY

- Systems can reach a level of complexity where a "complexity barrier" is crossed. The systems that cross this barrier are **complex systems** and exhibit special behaviors.

- Christopher Langton identifies four categories of systems that represent types of complexity:

  - **Fixed systems** remain the same forever, the relationships between their elements never changing.

  - **Periodic systems** are simple systems that repeat the same patterns endlessly.

  - **Complex systems** lie between periodic and chaotic systems, exhibiting patterns of behavior more complex than the repetition of periodic systems.

  - **Chaotic systems** behave in a completely random fashion.

- Complex systems can be the result of many complex interrelated elements. However, sometimes a complex system can contain just a few elements that relate to each other in very intricate ways.

- When a game lacks complexity, it also lacks meaningful play. When meaningful play is present in a game, some aspect of the game has achieved complexity. Complexity ensures that the space of possibility of a game is large enough to support meaningful play.

- Systems that are **emergent systems** generate unpredictable patterns of complexity from a limited set of rules. In an emergent system, the whole is greater than the sum of the parts. For example, the limited set of the rules of grammar cannot account for all of the possible statements that might be made in a language.

- In an emergent system, the interactions between objects in the system are **coupled** and **context-dependent.** Coupled interactions affect the overall space and pattern of a system as each interaction links to others, which in turn link to others. Context-dependent interactions change from moment to moment depending on what is happening in other parts of the system, creating patterns that change dynamically over time.

- **Bottom-up** behavior in an emergent system refers to the ways that emergent behaviors arise from the local rules of a system to spread up through the system, creating global patterns. For example, The Game of Life is a bottom-up system that produces phenomena such as glider guns, which are not explicitly described in the rules of the system, but which are patterns produced by the bottom-up functioning of its simple rules.

· Emergence in games results from the formal system of the game put to use by players. Bluffing in Poker, for example, is not explicitly stated in the rules of the game, but it is a pattern of player behavior that emerges from the game.

· The way that emergence arises in a game cannot always be intuited from the rules. Go has much simpler rules than Chess, but due to emergence, it is a game with a higher number of mathematical permutations.

· If a game is emergent, it has a space of possibility large enough to reward players for exploring all of the possible ways to play the game. For example, in games with different kinds of units or objects, players can create **engines** by using units in unexpected combinations. Designing a game that can support these kinds of engines generates rich emergence and increases the game's space of possibility.

· **Game design is a second-order design problem.** A game designer designs the rules of the game directly but designs the player's experience only indirectly. A system-based understanding of how games function can greatly improve a game designer's ability to anticipate how changes in a game's rule-structure will ramify into a play experience.

Unit 2: **Rules**

GAMES AS SYSTEMS OF UNCERTAINTY

probability
certainty vs. uncertainty
risk
macro- and micro- uncertainty
randomness

15

It is true that every aspect of the role of dice may be suspect: the dice themselves, the form and texture of the surface, the person throwing them. If we push the analysis to its extreme, we may even wonder what chance has to do with it at all. Neither the course of the dice nor their rebounds rely on chance; they are governed by the strict determinism of rational mechanics. Billiards is based on the same principles, and it has never been considered a game of chance. So in the final analysis, chance lies in the clumsiness, the inexperience, or the naiveté of the thrower—or in the eye of the observer....

*As for billiards, it can easily be transformed into a game of chance by simply tilting the table, outfitting it with studs that would cause the balls to rebound and swerve, and by placing the six pockets at the bottom of the table, or at other points, so that the ball would necessarily fall into one of them. Since we're not trying to favor skill, there would be a mechanical trigger and the ball would be shot up the slope by a spring that the player would pull with more or less force. This game of mechanical billiards is no less random than traditional dice.—**Ivar Ekeland,** The Broken Dice*

Introducing Uncertainty

*Imagine how incomplete you would feel if, before the game, you were already declared the winner. Imagine how purposeless the game would feel.—**Bernard DeKoven**, The Well-Played Game*

Uncertainty is a central feature of every game. That's right: every single game. As game designer and philosopher Bernard DeKoven points out, uncertainty about the outcome of a game is a necessary ingredient in giving a game a feeling of purpose. Uncertainty, in other words, is a key component of meaningful play.

In this chapter, we explore games as *Systems of Uncertainty.* Games express uncertainty on two levels: on a macro-level relating to the overall outcome of a game, and on a micro-level relating to specific operations of chance within the designed system. Although all games possess uncertainty on a macro-level, not all games formally possess elements of uncertainty on a micro-level. As we will see, a player's experience of uncertainty is not always congruent with the actual amount of mathematical chance in a game. Exploring these relationships, linking macro- and micro-uncertainty to each other, and understanding how both of them impact the design of meaningful play, is our primary focus in this schema.

Does every game really possess uncertainty? The word *uncertainty* brings to mind ideas of chance and randomness. But a game does not have to have a die roll or random algorithm to contain an element of uncertainty. If you are playing a multiplayer session of Halo against players of roughly equivalent ability, the outcome of the game is uncertain, even though the game is a game of skill, not chance. When we say that uncertainty is a central feature of every game, we are echoing DeKoven in the quote above: it is crucial in a game that players don't know exactly how it will play out. Think about it: if you knew who was going to win a game before it started, would you even bother to play? There is a reason why televised sports are almost always aired live: robbed of the drama of uncertain outcome, they fail to hold our interest.

One way to understand why games need uncertainty is that if the outcome of a game is predetermined, the experience cannot provide meaningful play. If a game has no uncertainty—if the outcome of the game is completely predetermined—then any choices a player makes are meaningless, because they do not impact the way that the game plays out. Meaningful play arises from meaningful choices. If a player's choices have no meaning in the game, there really is no reason to play.

There is an intrinsic connection between uncertainty and meaningful play. Uncertainty is usually thought of as something that disempowers players by removing a sense of choice and agency, yet paradoxically, it is the uncertain outcome of a game that allows players to feel like their decisions have an impact on the game. Meaningful play, as we know, emerges from these kinds of decision-outcome relationships.

Throughout a game system, this larger notion of an uncertain outcome is linked to the micro-level of uncertainty within a game. The specific mechanisms of uncertainty that incorporate randomness and chance, whether through the spin of a Roulette wheel or the generation of a random number in a game program, are just as important as the larger feeling of uncertainty linked to a game's outcome. From the interaction between these two levels, the meaningful play of uncertainty arises.

Certainty, Uncertainty, and Risk

*The essence of the phenomenon of gambling is decision making. The act of making a decision consists of selecting one course of action, or strategy, from among the set of admissible strategies. A particular decision might indicate the card to be played, a horse to be backed, the fraction of a fortune to be hazarded over a given interval of play…. Decisions can be categorized according to the specific relationship between action and outcome.—**Richard Epstein**, The Theory of Gambling and Statistical Logic*

In *The Theory of Gambling and Statistical Logic,* mathematician Richard Epstein investigates the mathematics of uncertainty in gambling. His research, however, can be applied to all kinds of games. In his emphasis on decision making and the relationship between action and outcome, Epstein echoes some of our own core ideas.

In his book, Epstein identifies three types of decision-outcome relationships, leading to three degrees of uncertainty: *uncertainty, risk,* and *certainty.* Each category corresponds to a different kind of decision-outcome relationship and game experience. A game that is completely *certain* is hardly a game at all, and certainly not much fun to play. It is like flipping a two-headed coin: there is no doubt what the end result will be. Sometimes, certainty is contextual. A game of Tic-Tac-Toe between two people that are completely familiar with the logic of the game play has a *certain* outcome: the game will always end in a draw. Although the specific decisions of the players aren't certain, the overall result of the game will be. In a game that is completely certain, meaningful play is impossible.

Epstein's other two categories describe what we normally think of as uncertainty in games. Risk refers to a situation in which there is some uncertainty but the game's players know the nature of the uncertainty in advance. For example, playing a game of Roulette involves placing bets on the possible outcome of a spin and then spinning the roulette wheel to get a random result. There is some uncertainty in the spin of the wheel, but the percentage chance for a particular result occurring and the resulting loss or gain on the bet can be calculated precisely. Of the thirty-one numbers on the Roulette wheel, 15 are red, 15 are black and one of them (the zero) is neither red nor black. If you bet on red, you have 15 out of 31 chances (or 48.39%) to win and double your bet. In other words, in a game of pure *risk,* you can be completely certain about the degree of uncertainty in the outcome of the game.

Epstein's category of *uncertainty* describes a situation in which players have no idea about the outcome of the game. For example, imagine that you are a moderately skilled Chess player and you go to an online game site to play a game of Chess with an opponent that you select at random. You have no idea who you are going to play against. It might be a Chess master, who will most likely beat you, or it might be someone learning to play for the first time, who you will most likely beat. There is no way for you to predict the outcome of the game. If, in contrast, you are playing a friend that you have played many times before and you know that you usually win three out of four games, you have a good sense of the outcome. But without knowing your opponent, you can't make that kind of guess.

Although games of pure certainty are extremely rare (and not much fun to boot), games of pure risk and games of pure uncertainty are also quite rare. Most games possess some combination of risk and uncertainty. Even though you know something about the general chances of winning against your friend, you certainly don't have absolute mathematical certainty about your chances of winning. And although you know the exact risk each time you make a bet on the Roulette wheel, your overall loss or winnings over an evening of play is much more uncertain.

The Feeling of Randomness

Roulette and Chess point to a very important aspect of uncertainty. Often, the degree of chance in a game has less to do with the actual mathematics of the game system and more to do with how the player's experience of the game is framed. When we look at only a single round of Roulette, the game is an experience of pure risk. But when we frame it as the gain and loss of money over many rounds, the overall outcome is more uncertain. Similarly, it is possible to produce a feeling of uncertainty in games that do not formally possess an element of chance. Below are two examples:

> **Chinese Checkers.** When four, five, or six players play this game, it can feel quite random. As the game unfolds and players move their pieces, the center of the board becomes crowded with a seemingly random arrangement of pieces. This is true even though every single move on the board is the result of a player making a strategic choice about where to play next.

If you closed your eyes and opened them only when it is your turn to move, it might seem like the board is merely reshuffling itself, particularly in the middle period of the game, when the center area is most crowded. This feeling of randomness is only an illusion, however, as there is no formal chance mechanism in the game. Perfectly logical players (who only exist in hypothetical examples) wouldn't feel any randomness: they could look at the board and immediately trace every move back to a series of strategic decisions.

However, for human players, this feeling of randomness is an important part of what makes the game fun to play. Although it is not true of every game, in the case of Chinese Checkers, the feeling of randomness creates a sense of open-ended possibility and players are rewarded for taking advantage of chance configurations on the board. The rule that lets players move their pieces by jumping multiple times over other pieces is designed to emphasize the seemingly random arrangement of the board. Seeing a pattern emerge out the chaos that allows you to jump a piece back and forth all the way across the entire length of the gameboard is a moment of wonderfully meaningful play.

SiSSYFiGHT 2000. In a multiplayer game that emphasizes social interaction, there can be a similar illusion of randomness. In SiSSYFiGHT 2000, because there are many players with their own agendas and strategies, game play often seems random. However, as with Chinese Checkers, there are no genuinely random elements to the game: logic, not chance determines the outcomes of player decisions.

However, the unpredictable combination of events that occurs each round is part of the game's fun. Two players might by chance both attack a third player, creating the impression that they are allies working in concert. Are they actually working together? If not, will the chance event cause them to form an alliance for future rounds? And did anyone else notice? The complexity of possibilities leads to a high degree of uncertainty.

Eliminating this feeling of randomness would require not only perfectly rational players, but players with special psychic powers that allowed them to look into the minds of other players and understand completely the strategies, rivalries, emotions, and other factors that led to their decisions. But who would want to play? Stripped to its logical core in this way, SiSSYFiGHT 2000 would obviously lose much of its appeal.

Both games produce an experience of randomness, even though neither game contains chance-based mechanisms as part of the rule system. This "feeling of randomness" is somewhat paradoxical and mysterious. Does a game of Chess have a feeling of randomness that emerges out of the complexity of relationships between the pieces? Perhaps. But it probably has less of a feeling of randomness than a game of Chinese Checkers, and it most definitely has less of a feeling of randomness than a game of Pick-Up Sticks.

The key point is that the feeling of randomness is more important than randomness itself. How much randomness should you put into your game? There is no magic formula regarding the degree of "feeling of randomness" or the degree of actual randomness in a game. However, the presence or absence of randomness does tend to move a game in one direction or another. A game that doesn't have any feeling of randomness is likely to feel very dry, and generally more intensely competitive than a game that does have an element of randomness. On the other hand, a game that is completely random can feel chaotic and unstructured. In both cases, the goal is to give players meaningful choices within the larger game system. A nonrandom, competitive game can be meaningful as long as the players have a fair opportunity to best their opponents. A completely random game can also be meaningful, if the players are making interesting choices as they explore the game's system, pushing their luck and taking risks.

Probability in Games

The focus of this chapter so far has been on the macro-level of uncertainty inherent in all games. Now we turn to a more specific examination of the micro-operations of chance. The study of mathematical uncertainty is called *probability*. According to Richard Epstein, "The word 'probability' stems from the Latin *probabilis*, meaning 'truth-resembling'; thus the word itself literally invites semantic misinterpretation."[1] What Epstein means by "semantic misinterpretation" is that if something is "truth-resembling," then it isn't actually truthful; at the same time, the truth is exactly what the something does resemble.

It is appropriate that probability would have at its etymological roots such a paradoxical meaning. We have seen that macro-uncertainty has its own paradoxes, such as a feeling of randomness when formal randomness does not exist. The micro-study of uncertainty—exhibited in the form of probability—has its own paradoxes as well. For example, the role that probability can play in a game is twofold. On the one hand, chance elements in a game introduce randomness and chaos, leading to uncertainty. On the other hand, a thorough study of the mathematics of probability reduces wild unknowns to known risk values, increasing the overall certainty of a game.

Appropriately enough, the mathematical study of probability has its origin in games. In the Seventeenth Century, a French nobleman, the Chevalier de Méré (who in contemporary society might be considered a professional gambler), brought a problem to his friend Blaise Pascal, the mathematician. De Méré wanted to know a logical way to divide the stakes in a dice game when the game had to be terminated before it was completed. In working out the solution to this problem, Pascal developed a new branch of mathematics, the *theory of probability*. De Méré's problem amounted to determining the probability that each player had of winning the game, at a given stage in the game.[2]

The study of probability has evolved into an important field of mathematics that goes far beyond simple percentages and betting odds. In fact, for the mathematically inclined, Epstein's book offers a wonderful overview of the field. However, for the purposes of this volume, we will keep the math extremely simple and straightforward.

Dice Probability

Another book that explores probability in games in a completely different manner is *Dice Games Properly Explained*, by game designer Reiner Knizia. In addition to providing an extensive library of dice games, the book contains a chapter that offers a non-technical model of dice mathematics as a foundation for understanding probability. Depending on your experience with and love for mathematics, the following sections might seem ridiculously facile or excruciatingly dry. But it is important in this schema to establish a few basic concepts for understanding what probability in games is all about.

As the first example of probability, consider a single, standard die which has six sides, each side displaying a number from one to six. Knizia calls the numbers one to six the *basic outcomes* of throwing a die. Each time you throw a die, each basic outcome has a 1/6 or 16.67 percent chance of appearing. If you add up all of the chances of basic outcomes, they total to 1 or 100 percent.

Knizia lists three qualities of any basic outcome on a die:

- All basic outcomes are equally likely.

- The process always produces one of the basic outcomes.

- The probabilities of all basic outcomes add up to 1.[3]

A *combined outcome* is a result that puts together more than one basic outcome. To determine a combined outcome, add the basic outcomes. For example, rolling an even number on a single die means rolling a 2, 4, or 6. These three basic outcomes add up to 3/6, so the combined outcome of rolling an even number is 50 percent. Knizia calls rolling a combined outcome an "event" and concludes that, "the probability of any event is calculated by adding up the number of the desired basic outcomes and dividing by the number of all possible basic outcomes."[4]

If you roll more than one die, determining outcomes becomes more complex. With two dice, Knizia notates the basic outcomes in the form of 3~4, where the first number is the number rolled on the first die and the second number is the number rolled on the second die. A chart of all of the possibilities of basic outcomes for two dice are shown in *Table 1*.

Note that symmetrical outcomes such as 2~5 and 5~2 both appear on the chart, as they represent different possible basic outcomes. There are 36 basic outcomes with two dice, so the chance of any one outcome appearing is 1/36. When two dice are thrown in a game, instead of the individual results on each die, the game uses the combined total of both dice. We can determine the chance of rolling a combined outcome equal to a particular number in the same way as with a single die: by adding up the basic outcomes. To determine the chance of rolling a 5, count the basic outcomes that add up to 5: 1~4, 2~3, 3~2, 4~1. This is four basic outcomes, and 4/36 = 1/9 or 11.11 percent.

1~1	2~1	3~1	4~1	5~1	6~1
1~2	2~2	3~2	4~2	5~2	6~2
1~3	2~3	3~3	4~3	5~3	6~3
1~4	2~4	3~4	4~4	5~4	6~4
1~5	2~5	3~5	4~5	5~5	6~5
1~6	2~6	3~6	4~6	5~6	6~6

Table 1

What is the chance of rolling doubles? There are six basic outcomes that are doubles: 1~1, 2~2, 3~3, 4~4, 5~5, 6~6. This is six outcomes, and 6/36 = 1/6 or 16.67 percent.

Putting all of the two-die outcomes on one chart, we get the figures in *Table 2*. Notice the radically unequal distribution of probabilities for rolling the highest and lowest numbers, as opposed to rolling numbers in the middle of the range.

Total	2	3	4	5	6	7	8	9	10	11	12
Outcomes	1~1	1~2	1~3	1~4	1~5	1~6	2~6	3~6	4~6	5~6	6~6
		2~1	2~2	2~3	2~4	2~5	3~5	4~5	5~5	6~5	
			3~1	3~2	3~3	3~4	4~4	5~4	6~4		
				4~1	4~2	4~3	5~3	6~3			
					5~1	5~2	6~2				
						6~1					
Favorable	1	2	3	4	5	6	5	4	3	2	1
Probability	1/36	2/36	3/36	4/36	5/36	6/36	5/36	4/36	3/36	2/36	1/36
		1/18	1/12	1/9		1/6		1/9	1/12	1/18	
Percentage	2.78	5.56	8.33	11.11	13.89	16.67	13.89	11.11	8.33	5.56	2.78

Table 2

We can apply the same basic principles Knizia articulates to a wide variety of game design situations. For example, if your game requires players to flip a coin, you can determine the two basic outcomes as heads and tails, with a 50 percent chance of achieving each outcome. Or you might be designing a computer simulation game that uses lots of random numbers to determine the frequency of events, or a special deck of cards with a particular chance of certain cards appearing each turn. In any of these cases, the general principles remain the same. If players are flipping three coins, how likely is it that they will all come up heads? What is the chance of having a hand of five cards that are all the same?

If you are designing a game that involves dice-rolling, card-shuffling, or other forms of random number generation, it is important that you understand the basic principles of the probabilities involved. However, mathematical principles alone won't lead you to design meaningful play. The key, as with other aspects of games, is in understanding how probability relates to player decisions and outcomes. For example, in designing a board game such as Monopoly, in which players' pieces circle the board on a track, how will you determine the number of spaces on the board? In Monopoly, the board has forty spaces. Because the average combined outcome of a two-die roll is 7, it takes on average six throws to get around the board. This means that by about turn seven, some of the players will likely have already started their second loop, and will begin to land on each other's properties. If you are creating a game with a similar structure, design the board and the use of dice to achieve a pacing of events appropriate for your game.

Chance and Game Play

There is a curious relationship between chance and game play. One way of framing chance, especially a game of pure chance, is that players completely give up control and have to passively accept the results of the game as they occur. As anthropologist Roger Caillois writes in his book *Man, Play, and Games*, chance "signifies and reveals the favor of destiny. The player is entirely passive: he does not deploy his resources, skill, muscles, intelligence. All he need do is await, in hope and trembling, the cast of the die."[5]

With all due respect to Caillois, we wholeheartedly disagree. What Caillois describes may in fact be an accurate depiction of the emotions of some players during a game of chance, but there are plenty of chance-based games that do offer player decision and meaningful play. Even in a game of pure chance, a well-designed game continually offers players moments of choice. Meaningful play requires that at some level a player has an active and engaged relationship to the game and is making choices with meaningful outcomes. A player that does nothing but "await, in hope and trembling, the cast of the die" cannot be engaged in meaningful play.

Let us look again at a game with which we are all too familiar, Chutes and Ladders. Formally, it is a game of pure chance. On your turn, you roll the die, move your token appropriately, and then pass the die to the next player. Players do not make any strategic decisions in the course of play. However, Chutes and Ladders can be a fun game. Even without considering the social, narrative, and cultural forms of pleasure the game might provide, there are any number of ways that Chutes and Ladders provides pleasure through formal aspects of its game play:

- The mechanistic pleasure of inhabiting a game system and helping that system move forward by rolling dice, counting spaces, and moving your token.

- The uncertainty of knowing who will win and the struggle to finish first.

- The chutes and ladders themselves, which reinforce both of the previous pleasures. On the one hand, with the erratic swoops of movement they produce, the chutes and ladders make the mechanistic system itself richer and more fun to inhabit. They also allow for unexpected reversals of fortune, increasing the dramatic potential of who will finish first.

Although it is true that almost any game will possess the first two qualities, it is always challenging to harness these two pleasures in the service of meaningful play. In Chutes and Ladders, it is the chutes and ladders themselves that serve as the central feature in the formal game structure to provide interest. Imagine the game without the chutes and ladders: rolling a die, moving a token, and getting to the last space first. As a game, it would be a completely flat experience. The chutes and ladders create a structure that results in more meaningful play, even without any real choices to make.

How does this happen? Consider the formal flow of the game play. Without the ups and downs of the ladders and the chutes, players' scores would slowly accumulate at a roughly equivalent rate. A player might pull ahead or fall behind, but the pattern of the game would remain fairly flat, with each player moving ahead from one to six spaces each turn. In fact, if a player does move substantially ahead or behind of the rest of the players, he or she is on average more likely to stay there, further reducing dramatic uncertainty. The chutes and ladders provide changes of position greater than the die roll's relatively modest adjustment of 1–6. These leaps disrupt the otherwise flattened chances of winning.

A second and very different example of pure chance games are lottery-based games. The basic game play of a lottery game is incredibly simple: pick a number or series of numbers and then wait to see if your number or numbers were picked. Again, at first glance, it is difficult to imagine how such a simple game could be so compelling. Yet even though a lottery is a game of pure chance, there are many moments at which players make choices: selecting the kind of lottery game to play, selecting a number or set of numbers, selecting the number of times to enter a given lottery, and even (for regular players) selecting a pattern of play over time. Many lottery games offer additional choices, such as a selection of "scratch-off" spaces on a lottery card. Each moment of choice is an event with the potential for meaningful play. Lottery players often use elaborate systems to help them select numbers, based on past winning numbers, their birthdays, random hunches, or other numerological speculations. The simple choice of what number to play becomes infused with meaning as players explore the space of possible options. Of course, the chance to win money is undeniably an essential part of the appeal of lottery games. However, it is not the only aspect of the game that makes its play meaningful. The opportunities for players to decide how to navigate the system of chance are the decisions that let players rail against pure fate, keep hope alive for winning, and help give the game its meaning.

The lesson learned from successful games of pure chance such as Chutes and Ladders or a lottery game is that meaningful play can occur in systems in which there are no actual strategic decisions to make. In games of pure chance, the players' relation to the game system needs to be carefully designed. At every moment that they come into contact with the system, the possibilities for meaningful play should be teased out and emphasized.

Case Study One: Thunderstorm

Although *Dice Games Properly Explained* has an entire chapter on dice probability theory, most of the book offers descriptions and analyses of more than one hundred dice games. The games range from simple children's games to complex betting and bluffing games. Some of them are of Knizia's own design, but most of them are traditional games. Following are two simple game examples from *Dice games Properly Explained* that clearly illustrate the successful integration of chance into game play.

Thunderstorm

This is a popular family game in Germany, there called Gewitter. Hit the required target number, or watch the thunderstorm move close, until lightning finally strikes. Any numbers of players can participate, best with four to eight. You need six dice and a notepad.

Object. The aim of the game is to produce at least one 1 on each turn to become the last remaining player in the game.

Play. One player begins, then play progresses clockwise. The first player throws all six dice. Later players may have fewer dice available, even only one.

· If your throw contains at least one 1, you are fine. Set aside all 1s and pass the remaining dice to the next player. If you roll nothing but 1s, recover all six dice and pass them to the next player.

· If your throw does not contain any 1s, you fail and pass the dice to the next player.

In the course of the game, a six-line house is drawn for each player. Each time you fail, a line is added to your house. When your house is complete and you fail again, your house is struck by lightning and you are out of the game.

The game continues until only one player remains. This player wins.[6]

Thunderstorm, like Chutes and Ladders, is a game of pure chance. The player makes no strategic or tactical decisions. However, it is an engaging game because the design choreographs meaningful choice and outcome on many levels. There is a wonderful translation of information from the die rolls to the drawing of the house. The diagrams offer a clear comparative record that displays the relative positions of the players in the game.

Even though Thunderstorm is a game of pure chance, the kind of chance that a player faces changes from turn to turn. If you are rolling six dice, you have a relatively safe roll and are quite likely to roll a 1. On the other hand, if the previous player hands you just a single die, your chances of rolling a 1 are much lower. Initially, players are making relatively safe rolls, rolling many dice at once. Occasionally a player will get unlucky and miss rolling a 1, but chances are better than 50 percent that for the first few rolls with four, five, or six dice, they will roll a 1. As 1s appear and these dice are stripped away from the group of rolling dice, the tension mounts and the game accelerates as the chance for rolling a 1 decreases. A single die might be passed for quite some time without anyone rolling a 1. Then suddenly someone rolls a 1, avoids drawing a line on his or her house, and the next player begins the pattern again by rolling all six dice.

As a player, you feel two ways about this progression. It is great to see the other players rolling a single die, not rolling 1s, and adding a line to their houses. On the other hand, as the die approaches you around the circle of players, you would love for another player to roll a 1 because it means that the next player rolls all six dice, making it likely that you will have more dice to roll on your turn. This formal structure of uncertainty results in a game with a compelling dramatic rhythm, which takes place in a number of overlapping cycles:

· Every turn a player throws the dice, establishing a regular pace to the game.

· On top of this rhythm, the reduction of the number of dice from six to one and then back to six again sets up a cycle that lasts for many turns and repeats itself a number of times within a single game.

· Each player also sets up a linear progression of house-building. Although the elements of this construction occur in the same sequence for all players, it happens at a different pace for each player.

- The fourth cycle happens near the end, as players begin to drop out of the game and the circle closes until there is only one house left standing, the house belonging to the winner.

The overall result is an exciting game with a sense of dramatic inevitability—the destruction of all of the houses but one becomes a dreadful certainty. What is striking about Thunderstorm (no pun intended) is that all of this complexity arises out of a simple game of pure chance—and no betting. Thunderstorm is an example of a game that provides players with a rich chance-based system that generates surprisingly meaningful play.

Case Study Two: Pig

The game of Pig differs from Thunderstorm in that it offers choice within the context of a game of chance. Like Thunderstorm, Pig demonstrates how meaningful play can be designed into a system with a great deal of uncertainty. The description from *Dice Games Properly Explained* is as follows:

Pig

This is an amusing family game based on a very simple idea. You throw one die and keep adding to your total. If you do not stop before you roll a 1, everything is lost…. Any number of players can play, best is for three to five. You need one die and a notepad.

Object. The aim of the game is to avoid rolling 1s and to be the first player who reaches 100 points or more.

Play. One player begins, then play progresses clockwise. On your turn, throw the die:

- If you roll a 1, you lose your turn and do not score.

- If you roll any other number, you receive the corresponding points.

As long as you receive points you can throw again, and again. Announce your accumulated points so that everybody can easily follow your turn. You may throw as often as you wish. Your turn ends in one of two ways:

- If you decide to finish your turn before you roll a 1, score your accumulated points on the notepad. These points are now safe for the rest of the game.

- If you roll a 1, you lose your turn and your accumulated points.

Record all scores on the notepad and keep running totals for each player. The first player to reach 100 points or more is the winner.[7]

The first thing to note about Pig is how it creates interesting game choices from a very simple structure. A core component of the game—to avoid rolling 1s—is actually an inverse of the formal demands of Thunderstorm, where the players attempt to roll 1s. In Pig, the player has to balance the desire to keep on rolling and accumulate a higher score with the risk of rolling a 1, which becomes more and more likely each time the player chooses to roll again.

We can analyze the game mathematically. From a probability point of view, one out of the six basic outcomes spells disaster for the player: rolling a 1. This means there is a 5/6 or 83.33 percent chance of rolling safely each time you roll—or conversely, a 1/6 or 16.66 percent chance of rolling a 1. However, even though the chances are the same for every roll considered in isolation, the more that you decide to roll, the more likely it is that you will eventually roll a 1. If you decide in advance that you are going to roll twice, the chances of rolling a 1 on your turn is the combined outcome of a 2-die roll. In the 36 possible 2-die rolls, there are 11 ways you can roll a 1 (1~1, 1~2, 1~3, 1~4, 1~5, 1~6, 2~1, 3~1, 4~1, 5~1, 6~1). This adds up to 11/36 or 30.56 percent chance to roll a 1 in two rolls.

Each time you roll again, your overall chance of rolling a 1 increases, and as soon as you roll a 1, your entire accumulated points for that turn are erased. The drama of the decision to roll or not to roll is that each time you roll the die, you increase your chances of getting more points, as well as increasing your chances to fail. But because you have control over your decision to roll more than once, you know the degree of *risk*. Knizia

Table 3

Number of throws	1	2	3	4	5	6	7	8	9	10	11
Probability of Survival	83%	69%	58%	48%	40%	33%	28%	23%	19%	16%	13%
Average Total Points	4	8	12	16	20	24	28	32	36	40	44

plots out the chances of rolling a 1 with successive rolls in the table above . He also calculates the average points you are likely to earn with a certain number of rolls, using 4 as the average number of points per roll (as your possible earnings are 2, 3, 4, 5 or 6). See *Table 3*.

Knizia suggests that the best Pig strategy is to stop rolling once you have 20 points or more. However, he also acknowledges that a good player takes into account the progress of the other players as well. There are two sides to the formal strategy of playing Pig. On the one hand, there is the aspect of a single player playing against chance, trying to maximize points earned each turn. But this moment-to-moment decision-making process also takes place within the larger context of the other players' scores. In other words, if you are falling behind, you may want to press your luck to try and catch up; but if you fail, you will have to risk even more to regain ground. If you are in the lead, perhaps you should play more conservatively. But then it might be easier for other players to catch up to you.

Pig is an elegant game design because the player's simple choice to roll or not to roll is a decision that sits at the nexus of many intersecting vectors of game play meaning. The result is a game that is astonishingly simple, strategically deep, and increasingly dramatic. Pig is a great example of how pure chance can be harnessed through simple choices and transformed into meaningful play. Can you say that the decisions in your game are as meaningful the decision to roll in Pig?

Breakdowns in Uncertainty

Luck is very much fate's last hope. It is the play of the last chance. It is the play of everyman…. In this sense it is useful to think of games of chance not only as models of the irrevocability of fate but also as fate fantasized. —**Brian Sutton-Smith**, *The Ambiguity of Play*

That ends our brief introductory investigation into the classical operations of probability. But before departing from this subject altogether, we would like to discuss a few ways that probability fails to operate in exactly the way that we think it should. As the "feeling of randomness" we discussed earlier demonstrates, the actual operation of probability does not always match up with the way that players experience or interpret it. For the design of meaningful play, understanding the player's point of view is paramount. The next few sections touch on three problematic contexts for probability: randomness on a computer, strategic manipulation of chance processes, and commonly held fallacies about uncertainty.

Breakdown 1: Computer Randomness

If you are designing digital games, it is important to have a sense of how computer programs generate random numbers. Digital games make extensive use of random algorithms, whether to determine which player goes first, to generate the background texture of a game level, or to randomize the behavior of an in-game agent. Ironically, computers cannot produce random numbers. They can execute algorithms that result in random-seeming results, but they are not capable of producing pure randomness. Why is this so? John Casti offers an explanation:

Back in the early days of computers, one of the more popular methods of generating a sequence of random numbers was to employ the following scheme:

1. Choose a starting number between 0 and 1.

2. Multiply the starting number by 4 ("stretch" it).

3. Subtract 4 times the square of the starting number from the quantity obtained in step 2 ("fold" the interval back on itself in order to keep the final result in the same range).

Given a starting number between 0 and 1, we can use the procedure—often termed the *logistic rule*—to generate a sequence of numbers that to all appearance is completely random. For example, in such a sequence each of the ten digits 0 through 9 appears with equal frequency and the statistical correlation between groups of digits is zero. Note, however, that the members of this sequence are specified in a completely deterministic way by the starting number. So the sequence is certainly not random in the everyday sense of being unpredictable; once we know the starting number and the rule for calculating an element of the sequence from its predecessor, we can predict with complete confidence what every element in the sequence will be.[8]

Although Casti uses a historical example, the ways that computer programs generate random numbers today are not fundamentally different. Computers can never compute purely random numbers, because the numbers they provide are always the result of algorithms. A computer program can "flip a coin" internally to determine whether a computer-controlled character will turn left or right with equal probability, but the program is iterating a deterministic formula that only superficially resembles the operation of a random coin flip. The generation of random numbers is a well-heeled problem in computer science. We won't go into detail about it here, except to point out that it remains a challenging dilemma. Still, for most game design purposes, the randomness that computers can generate is sufficiently random.

Usually, an intimate understanding of how computers compute random numbers is not part of what a game designer needs to know. But you should *never* forget that random functions are not infallible. Eric was once working on a game prototype about swarming microbe-like creatures in a fluid environment (the game was never published). The microbes would grow, give birth, and die, flocking together to seek out food in their environment. Although they exhibited complex behavior, it was more or less clear why the microbes were doing what they were doing. However, one aspect of the game was puzzling. The microbes always tended to seek out the upper left corner of their 2D environment. The designers first thought they had stumbled upon a genuinely emergent behavioral pattern, but couldn't for the life of them figure out what was causing it. Did it have to do with the way the food multiplied? Or the way a player was handling the mouse? At the same time, the inevitable and universal drift of the microbes was ruining the game play by making the overall behavior too predictable.

Eventually, they discovered that the emergent behavior was coming from an error in a randomizing function. Each timed step, a microbe would move in one of sixteen directions. Even though they could sense their immediate surroundings and moved accordingly (towards food and away from danger), the program always weighted their decision with a random input. The problem was that because of a programming oversight, the program began counting in the upper left corner, and then counted that corner again at the end, giving the randomizer twice as much chance of picking the upper left than any other position. Even though the degree of additional chance this error added was very small, because of the complexity of the system, the emergent effects were quite strong. Once the randomizer was fixed, the corner drift ceased. The lesson? Even if you are not a computer programmer, understand how randomness operates in your game's program.

Breakdown 2: Strategizing Chance

The second example of the unexpected nature of chance is when the use of chance becomes strategic, when players manipulate uncertainty itself during a game. Will your players really take randomness at face value, or will they scheme to turn chance into strategy? In "Strategies in Counting Out," an essay in *The Study of Games,* folklorist Kenneth Goldstein looks at the ways that children aged four to fourteen in northwest Philadelphia in 1967 secretly and expertly manipulated the operation of chance. His study focuses on "counting-out," operations such as "eenie-meenie-miney-moe" that kids use to determine who will be "It" in a traditional neighborhood game like Kick the Can.

Counting Out is not usually considered a game: it is a procedure that helps determine roles in a future game. However, by our definition, we can consider it as a simple game of chance. In Counting Out, a player appoints himself or herself the counter; the goal of the game is to avoid being selected as "It." The quantifiable outcome requires that one player is selected as the loser. The premise of counting-out procedures is that they are patterns of counting that randomly select a player. This is, in fact, the way that the children in the study described the act of counting-out to Goldstein when he interviewed them. However, his essay's conclusion is that despite the fact that the children described Counting Out as a purely chance operation, they used complex and subtle strategic methods to achieve the results they desired.

Following are the six general methods of manipulation that Goldstein observed in use. Many of them represent techniques that would require sophisticated mathematical skills to operate in a group with changing numbers of participants.[9]

> *Specific Rhyme Repertory:* This straightforward strategy requires the counter to select a rhyme of a specific length that will achieve the desired result.

Extension of Rhyme: The counting-out rhymes are modular and extendable, and if the rhyme is about to end on someone that the counter does not want to be selected, the counter can spontaneously add an additional phrase or rhyme of the proper length to achieve a different result.

Skipping Regular Counts: The counter simply skips himself or herself when going around the circle, if the counter is about to be selected. Although this was the most popular technique employed, it was also the most obvious, and the one most frowned upon.

Stopping or Continuing: Because most rhymes do not specify whether the selected player is "It" or whether the selected player is "counted out" and is safe from becoming "It," the counter can decide the significance of the selection after the first player has been picked.

Changing Positions: This mathematically intensive strategy entails the counter subtly switching to a new spot in the circle in order to be selected as the next player counted "out."

Respite by Calling Out: In this blatant strategy of avoidance, a player will simply call "safe" or "free" and be exempt from counting in the current round. The groups that allowed this technique did place restrictions on it, such as having only one player be able to call "safe" per counting round.

The paradox of Counting Out is that even though players describe it as a game of chance, it is a game with a rich strategic component, in which experienced players can achieve the results they desire. The point of this example, as with the operation of chance in software, is to demonstrate that sometimes the differences between randomness and non-randomness are more subtle than they appear. When you are designing a game, pay close attention to the procedures used to determine randomness and make sure that they operate in the manner that you intend. Of course, the bigger issues to which this example points is that when you design a game, that game is always going to be used in a particular context by particular players. In our schemas on *Breaking the Rules* and *Games as Social Play,* and in many of the chapters within the primary schema **CULTURE,** we explore in more detail some of the experiential and contextual issues raised by this complex example.

Breakdown 3: Probability Fallacies

A third example regarding the problems of probability does not concern computer software or strategy and chance, but the ways that players conceptualize and understand randomness itself. You may have created a game that contains very specific kinds of probabilities, and you may even communicate these to players. But this in no way means that your players will accurately understand the way that chance operates in your game.

Game players will rarely have the same grasp of the random functions of your game system that you do. Game players and the public tend to suffer from a number of fallacies and misunderstandings when it comes to the operations of chance. The following list is a paraphrased sampling from Epstein's longer list of fallacies in *The Theory of Gambling and Statistical Logic.*[10]

- *Overvaluing the long shot.* Game players have a tendency to overvalue "long-shot" bets that have a low probability of achieving a high gain, in contrast to "safe" bets that have a higher probability of achieving a low gain.

- *The tendency to think of successive chance events as additive.* For example, the chance of rolling a 1 on one die is 1/6 or 16.67 percent. The chance of rolling a 1 with two dice is not 2/6 or 33.33 percent, as you might think at first glance. As we know from probability theory, the chances are 11/36 or 30.56 percent. This difference might seem small in this example, but with successive iterations, the differences between the actual probability and the presumed one can be quite large.

- *The Monte Carlo Syndrome.* This refers to the tendency to think that after a run of failures, a success is likely, and vice versa. In other words, if the Roulette wheel has just landed on a black number, it is *not* more likely that the next number will be red.

- *Overemphasis on good outcomes.* Given a very unlikely negative outcome and a very unlikely positive outcome, people tend to overemphasize the good one. Epstein uses the example of winning the lottery and being killed in a car accident in the next year. Both have about the same chance of occurring (1 in 10,000), even though most believe that the lottery win is more likely.

- *Lightning striking twice.* Related to the previous fallacy, people tend to believe that highly unlikely negative events will not repeat themselves (such as getting struck twice by lighting), but that highly unlikely positive events will happen again (such as winning the top jackpot on a slot machine). In fact, the chance of a random event occurring is not related to the frequency of past occurrences.

- *Luck.* From a purely mathematical point of view, there is no such thing as luck. People aren't lucky, dice aren't lucky, charms aren't lucky, calendar dates aren't lucky. However, widespread belief in luck persists, even among experienced game players.

Each of these fallacies has important implications for game design. For example, think about the long shot fallacy. If your game allows players a choice between a long shot and safe bet, you should expect most players to take the long shot and balance your formal system accordingly. Overemphasis on good outcomes and the lightning striking twice fallacies can help keep players optimistic in a game with a large chance element. Even if a player has seen a lot of bad luck, these fallacies keep hope for a turnaround alive.

The larger lesson is that when you design a game with a random element, it is important to understand not just the probabilistic mechanisms of chance, but also the way that players will interpret or misinterpret these mechanisms. All three "breakdowns" of chance highlight common pitfalls to avoid in game design. On the other hand, any of these hiccups in the strictly formal operation of chance could be used positively, as the starting point for a game design:

· It may be true that a computer cannot generate true randomness. Why not make a digital game in which the operation of randomness is *intentionally* out of balance? Perhaps what seems to be a randomly generated string of numbers is really a secret code that needs to be deciphered. Or in certain locations of the game-world, the player can shift the operation of chance to his or her advantage.

· It may be true that chance operations become strategic elements in the hands of competitive players. You might design a game in which players can legally construct or modify the "random" component of a game, such as spending game money to affect the outcome of a die roll or giving players the ability to strategically stack a deck of cards.

· It may be true that players suffer from probability fallacies. Design a game around one of them. Build a game around luck, in which players pick lucky and unlucky numbers for themselves, rolling dice and trying to avoid unlucky numbers and score the lucky ones.

Any "rule" of game design that you might think of can be broken, and as we will discover in **Breaking the Rules,** broken design rules can often lead to innovative game design ideas.

Meaningful Chance

But [chance in a game] is never sure. That's what makes the game interesting. Not only is there a possibility that, despite the odds against us, the chance we take will pay off. There is also the further possibility that, despite the apparent confidence of the players, this hand, which seems to be of markedly unimpressive value, might be, in fact, the best of all. My two kings might win the game for me. That's what confidence games are all about. They provide the opportunity and reward for your display of self as well as for your ability to play well with chance—they call for control over yourself as well as control over the game.—Bernard DeKoven, The Well-Played Game

In thinking about games as systems of uncertainty, we have looked at the micro-level of chance operation as well as the macro-level of the uncertainty of the game as a whole. One important insight we can apply to both of these levels is that the purely mathematical functioning of uncertainty is insufficient to understand the richness of chance within the mechanisms of a game.

As DeKoven observes, it is true that a player interacts with the system of a game, taking risks, placing bets, and calculating the odds. At the same time, that system is also playing with the player, making demands, rewarding and punishing, and asking for leaps of faith. In thinking about games as formal systems, we cannot ultimately divorce the formal system of a game from the ways that players manipulate and inhabit the system. This is as true for the operation of chance as it was for the emergence of complexity. Uncertainty is in the eye of the beholder, or perhaps, in the play of the player.

Further Reading

The Broken Dice and Other Mathematical Games of Chance, by Ivar
Ekeland

Part philosophy, part mathematics, and part folklore, *The Broken Dice* is an
idiosyncratic book that explores philosophical questions of chance and
fate from multiple points of view. Particularly relevant is Ekeland's analysis of the impossibility of generating random numbers on a computer.

> *Recommended:*
>
> Chapter 1: Chance
>
> Chapter 2: Fate
>
> Chapter 5: Risk

Dice Games Properly Explained, by Reiner Knizia

This book by board game designer Knizia packs in descriptions and
analysis of more than a hundred dice games, some of which are original
designs by the author. It also contains a chapter on probability theory
applied to dice—a great non-technical introduction to the subject. The
dice games range from the purely random to the intensely strategic and
are a good source for classroom games.

> *Recommended:*
>
> Chapter 3: The Theory of Dice

The Jungles of Randomness: A Mathematical Safari, by Ivars Peterson

Ivars Peterson writes popular books about mathematics, and in this playful work he tackles the thorny dilemmas of randomness and probability.
He makes common references to games throughout, and the chapter
recommended below includes a spectacular analysis of the layout of the
Chutes and Ladders gameboard.

> *Recommended:*
>
> Chapter 1: The Die is Cast

Notes

1. Richard Epstein, *The Theory of Gambling and Statistical Logic* (San Diego: Academic Press, 1995), p. 43.
2. Elliott Avedon and Brian Sutton-Smith, *The Study of Games* (New York: John Wiley & Sons, 1971), p. 383.
3. Reiner Knizia, *Dice Games Properly Explained* (Tadworth, Surrey: Right Way Books, 1992), p. 62.
4. Ibid. p. 63.
5. Roger Caillois, *Man, Play, and Games* (London: Thames and Hudson, 1962), p. 17.
6. Knizia, *Dice Games Properly Explained,* p. 26–27.
7. Ibid. p. 128–29.
8. John L. Casti, *Complexification: Explaining a Paradoxical World Through the Science of Surprise* (New York: HarperCollins, 1994), p. 93.
9. Kenneth Goldstein, "Strategies in Counting Out" In *The Study of Games,* edited by Elliott Avedon and Brian Sutton-Smith (New York: John Wiley & Sons, 1971), p. 172–177.
10. Epstein, *The Theory of Gambling and Statistical Logic,* p. 393–394.

Games as Systems of Uncertainty

SUMMARY

- **Uncertainty** is a key component of every game. If a game is completely predetermined, the player's actions will not have an impact on the outcome of the game and meaningful play will be impossible.

- There are two levels at which uncertainty operates in a game. On the micro-level are the actual operations of chance that occur at isolated moments in the system of a game. On the macro-level are larger questions of uncertainty, which relate to the ultimate outcome of the game.

- The relationship between a game decision and a game outcome can have three degrees of uncertainty. A **certain** outcome is completely predetermined. A **risk** is an outcome with a known probability of happening. An **uncertain** outcome is completely unknown to the player. It is rare to find a game of pure certainty, risk, or uncertainty. Most games combine some degree of risk and uncertainty.

- It is possible for a game to possess a **"feeling of randomness"** even if no actual random mechanisms are present in the game system. This feeling can stem from strategic or social complexities that cannot be predicted in advance.

- A game that has very little feeling of randomness can become too dry or competitive. A game that has too much of a feeling of randomness can become overly chaotic, leaving the players feeling powerless. There is no magic formula for how much randomness should be present in a game. In all cases, the key is to create meaningful play that takes unique advantage of the game structure.

- When designing a game with chance elements, it is vitally important to understand the basic mathematics of **probability** and how they will impact the system you are designing.

- Even games of pure chance can provide meaningful game play as long as players are given meaningful opportunities to take action within the game system.

- There are many surprising ways that the operation of uncertainty can "break down" in the system of a game:

    - Because computer programs cannot generate true randomness, game designers should be skeptical about the random number-generating algorithms in a game.

    - Players can sometimes take a random component of a game and turn it into a strategic activity.

    - There are many commonly held fallacies about chance.

9	10	11	12	13	14	15
24	25	26	27	28	29	30
39	40	41	42	43	44	45
54	55	56	57	58	59	60
69	70	71	72	73	74	75

Unit 2: **Rules**

GAMES AS
INFORMATION THEORY SYSTEMS

information theory
information
uncertainty
noise
redundancy
freedom

16

Biologists as well as philosophers have suggested that the universe, and the living forms it contains, are based on chance, but not on accident. To put it another way, forces of chance and of antichance coexist in a complementary relationship. The random element is called entropy, the agent of chaos, which tends to mix up the unmixed, to destroy meaning. The nonrandom element is information, which exploits the uncertainty inherent in the entropy principle to generate new structures, to inform the world in novel ways.—**Jeremy Campbell,** *Grammatical Man*

Introducing "Information"

Many of the terms and concepts tackled in this book are challenging to discuss, not just because they represent complex ideas, but also because they are used in many different contexts in many different ways. The term "information" is a particularly feisty one to pin down. We live in the information age. We receive safety information in our airplane seat pockets. We get degrees in information science. We read statistical information about sports and the weather in the newspaper. We send and receive information over telephone lines and Internet cables. We suffer from information overload.

Although it is not our goal to arrive at an ultimate definition for the term "information," within the following two schemas we look closely at two different ways of understanding information, as it relates formally to games. *Games as Information Theory Systems* is the first of two "information" schemas. In it, we frame games within the context of information theory, a close cousin of systems theory.

Information theory studies the movement of information in a system—in our case, game systems. How does information flow within a game? How are choices made meaningful through the input and output of information? How do redundancy and uncertainty affect meaningful play from a formal perspective? What are the qualities of a game as a communication system? Each of these inquiries raises yet more questions about the nature of information in games, questions that we will explore over the course of this schema and the next one.

Information Theory

The field of information theory arose after WWII in tangent with the emerging telecommunications industry. Originally intended as the study of signal transmission, information theory is an interdisciplinary set of concepts and methodologies that cuts across mathematics, physics, and engineering. Since its formalization in the classic 1949 text by Claude Shannon and Warren Weaver, *The Mathematical Theory of Communication,*

information theory has grown beyond its origins in electronics and cryptography to find applications in behavioral and social sciences, as well as in some strands of contemporary critical theory.[1]

Information theory quantitatively studies information flow: how senders send information and how receivers receive it. It is closely linked with systems theory in that information theory studies the mechanics by which systems function—how, for example, the parts of a system communicate with each other. Game systems almost always involve communication among players and interaction among system elements; information theory can be a valuable way to understand these processes.

Before going any further, it is crucial to understand what information theory means by the word "information." Information theory does not use the word in the same way it is used in casual conversation. When you say, for example, that you need more "information" about a car before you purchase it, you are using the word to mean *knowledge*. You need more data about the car in order to better understand it. This is, in some ways, the opposite of how the word is used in information theory. Consider Warren Weaver's description of the way in which information theory understands "information:"

> The word *information*, in this theory, is used in a special sense that must not be confused with its ordinary usage. In particular, *information* must not be confused with meaning. In fact, two messages, one of which is heavily loaded with meaning and the other of which is pure nonsense, can be exactly equivalent, from the present viewpoint, as regards information.[2]

Unlike a knowledge-based understanding of the word, in information theory, "information" is divorced from meaning. But what does this mean exactly? Let's look at another description of "information" that comes from communications theorist Stephen W. Littlejohn:

> Information is the measure of uncertainty in a situation. When a situation is completely predictable, no information is present…. As used by the information theorist, the concept of information does not refer to a message, facts, or meaning. It is a concept bound only to the quantification of stimuli or signals in a situation.[3]

According to Littlejohn, "information" is a way of understanding the mathematical content of a signal: the "quantification of stimuli or signals." With its foundation in formal, quantitative thinking, it should be clear that information theory has a greater affinity to rules than to play or culture. Information theory proceeds from two important premises, both of which are evident in the quotes from Weaver and Littlejohn:

> **Meaning is irrelevant to information.** Information has nothing to do with the content or meaning of a message. As Weaver points out, two strings of letters, one of which makes coherent sense and the other of which is nonsense, could contain the same amount of information.

> **Information measures uncertainty.** Furthermore (and this is a tricky point to grasp), in information theory, information does not measure the amount of "stuff" in a message. It does not measure the knowledge contained in a message—it measures uncertainty instead. As Littlejohn notes, "When a situation is completely predictable, no information is present."

The first point, *meaning is irrelevant to information,* is the easier of the two to digest. Information theory concerns signal transmission—it is a formal way of looking at the mathematical structure of a signal, rather than a semiotic way of looking at its content. Remember the example of changing the suits on a deck of cards in *Defining Rules?* As long as the mathematical structure of the cards remained the same, we could change the content of the suits and still play a card game with the deck. Information theory looks at communication signals in a similar way, highlighting the formal structure while ignoring its content. Because information theory looks at mathematical data

and not at meaning, it can be applied to any form of communication: "written letters or words, or musical notes, or spoken words, or symphonic music, or pictures."[4] In information theory the format of the data is irrelevant to the analysis.

What about the second point: *information measures uncertainty?* This concept is subtler to grasp. According to information theory, information is a measure of how certain you can be about the nature of a signal. A completely predictable signal has a very low amount of information, whereas one that could contain anything has high informational content. What does it mean that parts of a signal are predictable or unpredictable? Consider telegraph messages. For years, people sent telegraph messages leaving out non-essential words such as "a" and "the." These words had a high degree of certainty, and therefore conveyed very little information to the receiver. Similarly, predictable letters were sometimes left out as well, such as in the sentence, "Only infrmatn esentil to understandn mst b tranmitd."[5]

As a thought experiment, imagine a stranger named J.L. If you are trying to guess whether or not J.L. had eaten breakfast today, there are two possible answers to the question: "yes" or "no." You would have a fair degree of certainty as to what J.L. might answer, because there are only two possible units of information to choose from—and that means the amount of information contained in the answer would be low. If you are trying to guess J.L.'s favorite color, you are still just guessing at a single word, but there are more possibilities and therefore there is more uncertainty in your guess. The amount of information in the answer would be higher because you would be selecting J.L.'s favorite color from a larger set of possible answers. If you try and guess J.L.'s favorite word from among all of the words in the English language, the amount of information contained in the answer is even higher still, because there is so much uncertainty about what it might be. As Weaver puts it, information "relates not so much to what you *do* say, as to what you *could* say."[6]

If you were going to make a correct guess about J.L.'s breakfast, favorite color, or favorite word, think about the amount of uncertainty that is reduced with a correct answer. If you correctly guessed whether or not J.L. had eaten breakfast, you wouldn't be reducing much uncertainty, because there was very little to begin with. But if you correctly guessed J.L.'s favorite word, uncertainty would be greatly reduced. In this example, the signal that correctly guesses J.L.'s favorite word contains the most information, because it also reduces the highest degree of uncertainty.

On the other hand, if you already know everything about J.L., including his favorite word, his favorite color, and whether or not he ate breakfast today, then a response to the question would actually contain no information at all. The answer is already certain before the guess takes place, and therefore the guess is not really a guess. The degree of uncertainty about the truth would not decrease as the result of a right or wrong answer.

This is precisely what Weaver means when he says that, "information is a measure of one's freedom of choice when one selects a message."[8] No freedom of guessing (because we already know the answer) means no information: uncertainty has not decreased. With a simple yes or no answer, there is a little more freedom in what can be sent as a message, but not much. In moving toward picking a favorite color or picking a favorite word, the freedom of what might be offered as an answer increases, and the amount of information in the message increases as a result.

How does information theory's concept of "information" connect with games? Think about this: information is a measure of freedom in decision making. Games are contexts which provide players with the ability to make meaningful decisions. In a sense, the information in a communication system is analogous to the space of possibility in a game. The sender of an information-rich message is choosing from many potentially meaningful options. The player in a game with a large space of possibility is selecting an action from among many possible meaningful options as well.

Probability and Guesswork

Another important connection between games and information theory is that information is a measure of uncertainty. We know that meaningful play in games requires some degree of uncertainty on the macro-level. If the outcome of a game is known in advance, there really isn't a game at all. If one player is trying to win a simple game by correctly guessing whether a penny is heads-up or tails-down, there are two possible messages the penny can generate (*heads* and *tails*). However, if both players know that it is a two-headed coin, the amount of uncertainty drops to zero. Suddenly there is no game to be played, just as there is no information to be generated by the coin. We know this from the example of J.L.: if you already know his favorite color, your answer contains no information.

We can also make a connection on the micro-level of uncertainty. Uncertainty, information, and probability all share a set of formal relationships. Think about a die roll as an information theory signal. If one die is rolled, there is less information (and uncertainty of the outcome) than if two are rolled, where the set of possible outcomes is greater. Two die rolls—more possibilities and more uncertainty—equals more information. Because guessing games rely on uncertainty, they make good information theory case studies.

Take a game such as Mastermind. Each turn, one player attempts to guess the correct answer. By receiving coded feedback in the form of black and white pegs, her opponent tells her how correct or incorrect her guess was. The goal of the game is to arrive at the correct answer within a limited number of turns. Understood as an information theory system, Mastermind is a wonderful structure which puts information at play. With each guess, the guesser narrows down the possible answers (decreasing uncertainty), carving out a single guess from a range of all possible guesses. By narrowing the degree of uncertainty, the guesser navigates the space of all possible answers, hopefully arriving at the correct answer before it is too late. Because the answer remains fixed, as long as the guesser doesn't make any logical mistakes, each guess is progressively more certain. Imagine for a moment a variation on Mastermind, in which the guesser's opponent rearranges the solution pegs each time. In this game, a non-winning guess would not reduce the amount of uncertainty, because the system is "reset" every turn. Like a gambler betting on a single Roulette number over and over again, the amount of uncertainty would remain fixed and would not be reduced by successive guesses.

It is even possible to think of cultural information in information theory terms. Take the classic guessing game Twenty Questions, which Bertalanffly uses as an example in *General Systems Theory.*[8] In this simple game, one player has a piece of information, the answer, and the other player tries to guess that piece of information. Each turn, the guesser can ask a yes or no question, and the goal is to arrive at the correct answer within 20 questions. "Is it a vegetable?" *"No." "*Is it an animal?" *"Yes." "*Is it a mammal?" *"Yes." "*Is it a rodent?" *"No."* As with Mastermind, the answer remains fixed as the guesser tries to narrow down the possibilities through clever queries. In this case, however, the answer does not reside within an abstract mathematical system, but instead is an object that exists in the world, in language, in the shared culture of the two players. It is striking that the vast realm of possible solutions can be reduced so quickly and so efficiently through a series of yes/no guesses—usually, fewer than twenty!

If meaning is irrelevant to information theory's concept of "information," how is it possible to use information theory to look at a game such as Twenty Questions, a game that relies on culture for its content? Because information is an abstract formal quantity, it can be applied to any form of communication. In the case of Twenty Questions, it is not the linguistic, historical,

or cultural relationships that interest information theory, just the mathematical ones. If we really wanted to reduce the game to its formal essence, we could plot the mathematical interrelationships between any possible Twenty Questions query and every possible yes or no answer, using a nonsense language instead of speech. Although this would empty out the cultural content from the game, the informational structure would remain the same. The beauty of Twenty Questions is that such a reduction does occur on some level as the game is played. The game suspends language in a formal web of informational connections. Each guess is a deductive gesture that narrows the focus of the guesser's pursuit until the uncertainty of culture resolves itself into a single coherent answer that, finally, marks the end of the game.

Noise in the Channel

Up to this point, we have discussed information itself as a concept. But how are informational signals sent and received? How does information get from one context to another? One of information theory's most enduring concepts is the model of signal transmission developed by Warren Weaver and Claude Shannon. Signal transmission looks at the path of a signal as it departs from its origin and arrives at its target.

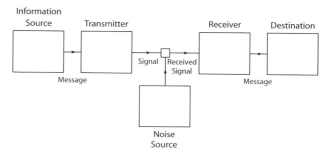

Each element of the model represents a different stage of the process by which a signal is transmitted and received. For example, if a signal is a spoken word, the source is the mind of the speaker, which activates the vocal cords, a signal which is carried by airwaves, received by the ears of the listener, and interpreted in the mind. If we look at the circumstance of a driver regarding a stoplight, the signal is a visual signal. The timing mechanism of the stoplight is the source, which activates a light bulb, a signal that travels as light to the driver's eye, where is it is interpreted by the mind.

As information theory systems, games are rife with instances of signal transmission and reception. Players communicate with each other through speech, written words, and gesture. They also communicate with the system of the game itself. During a turn in Monopoly, players roll the dice and receive the visual signal of the black dots on the die cubes, interpreting it as a numerical value. Signals manifest as speech between players, as written text on cards, and even as visual information: players look at the board in order to see their positions relative to properties, houses, hotels, and each other.

However, signal transmission is hardly ever clean and pure. The one element in Shannon and Weaver's model not yet mentioned, *noise,* addresses this important aspect of communication. Noise is interference in the signal that enters into a channel of transmission. In affecting the transmission process, noise affects the amount of information in a message.

> How does noise affect information? Information is, we must steadily remember, a measure of one's freedom of choice in selecting a message. The greater this freedom of choice, and hence the greater the information, the greater is the uncertainty that the message actually selected is some particular one. Thus greater freedom of choice, greater uncertainty, greater information go hand in hand. If noise is introduced, then the received message contains certain distortions, certain errors, certain extraneous material, that would certainly lead one to say that the received message exhibits, because of the effects of the noise, an increased uncertainty.[9]

Noise, as Weaver points out, increases the amount of information and uncertainty in a message. In the example of a vocal signal, strong wind or loud traffic could interfere with the transmission of the message from sender to receiver through the introduction of audio noise. With the driver and stoplight example, noise might take the form of darkness, fog, or dirt on the windshield of the driver's car. In all of these examples, noise increases the uncertainty of the signal, and therefore the amount of information it contains.

We can also understand the phenomenon of noise another way. Noise is directly related to the amount of freedom that the sender has in choosing a signal. Classical information theory, as an engineering discipline, was generally concerned with sending and receiving messages of the greatest possible clarity. Noise in the channel was something to be minimized, so that people could have clear telephone conversations and watch their televisions free of static and snow.

If games are framed as a system of information, however, noise is not necessarily a negative element. Sometimes entire games are premised on the notion of putting noise into a channel of communication. Take the informal play activity of Telephone, in which people whisper a message around a circle. The point of the activity and the pleasure for the participants comes from the noise in the system. The original message receives noise as it passes from person to person, transforming the message a little bit each time. By the time the message reaches the last person, the noise has impacted the identity of the original signal. In most cases, the signal that emerges from the long chain of whisperers undergoes a radical transformation—and that is exactly the fun of the game.

Similarly, Charades is based on the transmission of signals from one form to another. At the start of the game, players write the

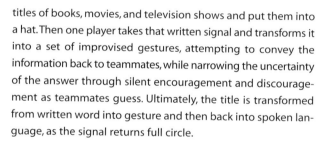

titles of books, movies, and television shows and put them into a hat. Then one player takes that written signal and transforms it into a set of improvised gestures, attempting to convey the information back to teammates, while narrowing the uncertainty of the answer through silent encouragement and discouragement as teammates guess. Ultimately, the title is transformed from written word into gesture and then back into spoken language, as the signal returns full circle.

In Telephone, pleasure emerges from the addition of noise. In Charades, the players fight against the noise inherent in the structure of the game, as they attempt to overcome communication hurdles and complete the circuit of transmission. The pantomime gestures of Charades introduce noise into the system through their inherent ambiguity. The many competing and contradictory guesses contribute noise as well. Sometimes the guessing team misinterprets a clue and gets off track, introducing yet more noise. With all of the opportunities for noise, it is a wonder that signals are transmitted at all! But it is this struggle against noise and uncertainty that makes Charades fun to play. The instant that the correct answer rings out—the signal

coming full circuit, the noise and uncertainty finally overcome—is a deeply satisfying moment of play.

The phenomenon of noise as a desirable component of a game system is a function of the lusory attitude, the state of mind that players take on in order to enter the magic circle and play a game, the shared attitude that accepts the paradoxically "inefficient" means for achieving the goals of a game. The fact that Charades' players enjoy the difficulty of indirect communication, rather than just speaking the correct answer out loud and saving themselves the trouble of guessing, is a great example of how the lusory attitude manifests in the experience of play.

Redundancy in the System

Whereas noise negatively impacts the successful transmission of a signal, information theory also identifies its opposite, the counterbalance to noise known as *redundancy*. Redundancy refers to the fact that in information systems, the message can be successfully transmitted even if some of the signal is lost, because redundant information patterns compensate for "holes" in the data of the signal.

In most communication systems, such as spoken language, much more information is transmitted in a single statement than is minimally required to convey the signal. As Weaver notes, "the redundancy of English is just about 50 per cent, so that about half of the letters or words we choose in writing or speaking are under our free choice, and about half (although we are not ordinarily aware of it) are really controlled by the statistical structure of the language."[10]

If someone shouts, "GET OUT OF THE ROOM RIGHT ___!" and you don't quite hear the final word, you will most likely be able to infer the missing "NOW" and exit the room. The sentence could lose even more words and still convey its intended signal. This kind of redundancy exists on many levels of language: it is also the case with letters. For example, you can s ill read th s sente ce even thou h som of th let ers are m ssing.

Noise and redundancy together contribute to the ability of a system to transmit signals. In the case of games, redundancy is just as important a concept as noise. In a system filled with modular, interlocking informational elements, redundancy becomes important, because a system with a lot of redundancy is more flexible than one with less. Crossword puzzles, for example, take advantage of redundancy. Instead of the Twenty Questions-style single-answer guess, in a crossword puzzle there are many clues, each with its own answer. Yet the answers overlap with each other, and there is redundancy in the system that can "fill in the holes" and compensate for a clue that is too difficult to decipher. The name of an obscure capital city is much easier to figure out when previous answers have already determined some of the letters. In *The Mathematical Theory of Communication,* Warren Weaver explicitly draws the connection between crossword puzzles and redundancy:

> It is interesting to note that a language must have at least 50 per cent of real freedom (or negative entropy) in the choice of letters if one is to be able to construct satisfactory crossword puzzles. If it has complete freedom, then every array of letters is a crossword puzzle. If it has only 20 per cent of freedom, then it would be impossible to construct crossword puzzles in such complexity and number as would make the game popular.[11]

By 50 percent redundancy, Weaver means that half of the letters in a word or statement could be removed without a loss of understanding. This is because not every letter combination appears in English. There are no words, for example, in which "G" follows "T." On the other hand, letters such as "H," "R," and "E," very commonly follow "T." When we start to write a word with the letter "T," we have already cut out many possible letters that might follow it—about 50 percent of them, according to Weaver.

As Weaver points out, if a language had 100 percent freedom, then every possible combination of letters would be a crossword puzzle. If this were the case, crossword puzzles would be far easier and less satisfying: when we figured out a clue and filled in the letters of a word, we would gain little or no benefit from all of the other blank words that it intersects. On the other hand, Warren points out that if the redundancy in English were too low, there simply would not be enough flexibility to properly design crossword puzzles. We could presumably construct some kind of word puzzles with 100 percent or 10 percent redundancy, but they simply would not be crossword puzzles as we know them. Crossword puzzles contain a delicate balance that keeps them just flexible enough to allow for numerous combinations, but still rigid enough so that one correctly answered clue leads to others, and yet others, until the crossword puzzle is solved.

Balancing Act

Information, signals, noise, redundancy: the relationships between games and information theory offer subtle but powerful ways of thinking about design. Successful signal processing requires balancing noise and redundancy. It requires tuning a communication system so that there is enough uncertainty to ensure a sufficient amount of information passing through the channel, but not too much information, so that the signal gets lost in vast oceans of uncertainty. This is the balance found in the interconnected informational grids of crossword puzzles.

Information theory studies is closely linked to systems theory and it should be no surprise that our observations in this schema bear some resemblance to *Games as Emergent Systems.* A complex, emergent system can only exist somewhere between the rigidity of fixed, periodic systems and the hyperflexibility of chaotic systems. Too much structure and a game is overdetermined: there is not enough uncertainty or freedom for the players. Too little structure and the game turns chaotic: there is too much uncertainty, too much freedom, and no sense of how the player's decisions should proceed from one moment to the next.

All of which leads us back to meaningful play. It is significant that Weaver links uncertainty and information to what he calls "freedom," the ability of a person to make choices in a system. In a system with too much rigidity, a player doesn't have enough freedom: there are choices, but not enough of them, and not enough uncertainty in the system to ever give a player doubt about the outcome. By contrast, in a system where chaos reigns, there can be no meaningful relationship between action and outcome. The system's outcome is perpetually uncertain, and nothing the player does will affect it. In both of these cases, meaningful play is impossible.

Meaningful play requires that players choose actions from among a palette rich enough to support a large space of possibility but limited enough to properly structure their decisions. Finding the sweet spot between too much and too little freedom, designing constraints that provide enough (but not too much) challenge for players, is an elemental problem of game design. Information theory is one useful way to make sense of these eternal design dilemmas.

Further Reading

Grammatical Man, by Jeremy Campbell *(see page 169)*

> *Recommended:*
>
> Part One: Establishing the Theory of Information
>
> Part Two: Nature as an Information Process

The Mathematical Theory of Communication, by Claude E. Shannon and Warren Weaver

The Mathematical Theory of Communication is the foundational text of information theory. While much of Shannon's contribution is highly mathematical, Warren's introduction to the book details the basic tenants of the field in non-technical language.

> *Recommended:*
>
> Some Recent Contributions to the Mathematical Theory of Communication

Theories of Human Communication, by Stephen W. Littlejohn

Littlejohn's volume is a textbook for communication studies, and as such provides a great deal of information at a somewhat shallow depth. That said, his explication of basic systems theory, information theory, and cybernetics provide the most lucid articulations of these complex fields that we have encountered.

> *Recommended:*
>
> Chapter 3: System Theory

Notes

1. Stephen W. Littlejohn, *Theories of Human Communication,* 3rd Edition (Belmont, CA: Wadsworth Publishing Company, 1989), p. 45.
2. Claude E. Shannon and Warren Weaver, *Mathematical Theory of Communication* (Champaign: University of Illinois Press, 1963), p. 8–9.
3. Littlejohn, *Theories of Human Communication,* p. 46.
4. <www.lucent.com/minds/infotheory/>.
5. Weaver and Shannon, *Mathematical Theory of Communication*, p. 25.
6. Ibid. p. 8–9.
7. Ibid. p. 8–9.
8. Ludwig von Bertalanffy, *General Systems Theory Foundations* (New York: George Braziller, 1968), p. 42.
9. Shannon and Weaver, *Mathematical Theory of Communication*, p. 19.
10. Ibid. p. 13.
11. Ibid. p. 14.

Games as Information Theory Systems

SUMMARY

- **Information theory** is a mathematical, structural way of looking at signals that disregards the knowledge-content or meaning of a message.

- In information theory, **information measures uncertainty.** Information is a measure of all of the possible messages an act of communication might contain. The answer to a yes/no question contains less information (and less uncertainty) than an answer to a question about a favorite color, because there are fewer possible answers to the yes/no question.

- Information Theory studies signal transmission from a source to a target. Part of this process is **noise,** in which distortion enters into the signal from an outside source. Noise increases the uncertainty and the therefore the amount of information in a message.

- Although noise in the engineering of signal transmission is usually undesirable, in games noise can be a productive design element. According to the lusory attitude, players seek out inefficient activities in a game. Thus noise, which makes communication more difficult and uncertain, makes games such as Charades possible, in which difficulty in communication is the premise of the game.

- **Redundancy** in a system acts to balance out noise by ensuring that not every component of a message is necessary. The English language as a form of communication contains about 50 percent redundancy.

- In an information theory system of communication, greater freedom of choice, greater uncertainty, and greater information all increase together. The concept of choice in this sense relates directly to the space of possibility and meaningful play. As a complex system, a game design must strike a balance between too little and too much uncertainty, flexibility, and information.

Unit 2: **Rules**

GAMES AS SYSTEMS OF INFORMATION

perfect information
imperfect information
information economy
objective information
perceived information

17

*All card games hinge on the fact that a card has two sides, one of which **reveals** its identity (Ace of spades, Queen of hearts, etc.), while the other **conceals** it, being indistinguishable from the reverse of any other card in the pack....*

This element of secrecy puts cards into the category of "games of imperfect information," by contrast with board games such as Chess, in which each player always knows exactly what his opponent's resources are....

*This suggests that "information" and its acquisition are what card games are all about.—**David Parlett,** The Oxford Dictionary of Card Games*

Introducing a Different Kind of Information

Our second "information" schema, ***Games as Systems of Information,*** builds on the connection between games and information begun in the previous chapter. However, within this schema we shift to a very different understanding of "information." This shift should be relatively painless, because we are moving away from the counter-intuitive concepts of information theory and toward a much more commonsense understanding of information.

Rather than thinking about "information" as a measure of uncertainty, we now do just the opposite. "Information," for the purposes of this schema, means *knowledge,* the informational content or data of a game. Within classical information theory, games are signal-processing systems, balancing noise and redundancy. But in this schema, we consider games as interactive systems that put knowledge or information at play. Depending on the game, information can be randomized, acquired, transformed, hidden, rearranged, remembered, or forgotten.

In the quote that opens this chapter, David Parlett describes playing cards as objects designed to conceal and reveal information. Earlier, in ***Defining Rules,*** we pointed out that we could still play the game of Poker even if we altered the "content" of the system by renaming the suits. Poker also came up in our schema on emergence, in which the activity of bluffing arose during play, even though it was not specified in the rules. If we had wanted to, we could have framed Poker as a system of uncertainty as well, perhaps charting the percentage chance of being dealt a particular hand. But by considering Poker within ***Games as Systems of Information,*** we can take a cue from game historian David Parlett and explore information as a commodity to be hidden or shared. How do players hide information in the cards they hold? How is information concealed, revealed, disguised, and deduced?

Although Poker is premised on the manipulation of information, we can consider any game along similar lines. As a system of information, Chess is an array of data spread out on the gameboard grid, in public view of both players. The system of information known as Chutes and Ladders is constructed from the steady stream of data flowing from successive die rolls, and the way that this information is recorded and transformed into player movement on the board. A console adventure game such as Jak and Daxter brokers information in many complex ways, from hidden sections of the world revealed as the player unlocks them to special powers and abilities that are unknown to the player when the game begins.

Perfect and Imperfect Information

*Such games have **perfect information**: Each player, when deciding his move, must have complete information about the current position of the board (I include in "position" qualities that may be physically undetectable, such as whether a player may castle), or equivalently, about the original position of the board and all moves made so far. Examples of perfect information games would include Chess and Backgammon; games like Stratego, Kriegspiel, or the recent Stealth Chess are not perfect information games.*—***J. Mark Thompson,** "Defining the Abstract"*

Parlett describes card games as games of "imperfect information," due to the fact that the two-sided nature of cards permits them to hide their informational value. In the quote above, mathematician and game aficionado J. Mark Thompson[1] points out the opposite kind of system: games of "perfect information." Perfect and imperfect information refer to the relationship a player has to the information contained in the formal system of the game.

Perfect information exists in a game when all players have complete knowledge about every element in the game at all times. Thompson includes Chess and Backgammon in this category. In games of *imperfect information,* some of the information may be hidden from players during the game. Thompson names Stratego, a game in which the value of each piece on the gameboard is kept hidden from each player's opponent, as a game of imperfect information. Card games are also good examples of games of imperfect information. Although it would be possible to design a card game in which all of the cards are visible for the entire game, almost every card game does feature imperfect information in some form.

Games of perfect and imperfect information can both provide meaningful play, but they do so in different ways. Games of perfect information tend to be more analytically competitive games, in which players are pitted directly against each other, each player's moves and strategies available for the other to see. Games of imperfect information add an element of mystery and uncertainty to a game. Imperfect information invites treachery, trickery, and deception, and can be used as a design element in games meant to inspire mistrust among players.

Although imperfect information can heighten a feeling of uncertainty in a game, actual randomness is not intrinsically tied to either perfect or imperfect information. A game can have chance mechanisms as part of the game and still possess either perfect or imperfect information. As Thompson points out, both Chess and Backgammon are games of perfect information, even though Backgammon makes use of die rolls every turn. An imperfect information game such as Stratego does not use any kind of chance mechanism, whereas Poker does, in the form of a shuffled deck.

Chance is not related to our definitions of perfect and imperfect information. But whether or not a game has a random element does affect the kind of information that exists in a game. In *The Interactive Book,* designer and scholar Celia Pearce presents a different typology for understanding the ways games manifest information. She proposes four scenarios:

- *Information known to all players:* In Chess, this would consist of the rules of the game, board layout, and piece movement parameters.

- *Information known to only one player:* In Gin, this would be the cards in your hand.

- *Information known to the game only:* In Gin, this would be unused cards in deck. In Space Invaders, this would be the paths and frequency of alien space ships.

- *Randomly generated information:* In Backgammon, this would be the roll of the dice.[2]

Pearce's categories offer another way of describing the informational component of a game. She differentiates between two kinds of hidden information, one in which each player possesses private information and another in which the game system itself hides information from all of the players. As she illustrates through her example of Gin, any card game with a shuffled deck and private hands for each player contains both kinds of hidden information. Pearce also designates randomly generated information within its own informational category.

One disagreement we have with Pearce's typology regards the inclusion of the rules of a game in her information model. Pearce states that the rules of Chess should be considered information known to all players. Although this is arguably the case, we don't feel that including rules as part of the perfect information of a game is particularly useful, since in all games, some or all of the game rules are known to all players. There may be hidden strategic relationships in a game that are gradually uncovered (like the strengths and weaknesses of particular unit combinations) but these are not rules. Rules are the formal foundation of a game that allows players to manipulate information. Rules generally do not constitute the information being manipulated during play.

There are other slightly ambiguous aspects of her model as well. For example, although a deck of cards in Gin might contain information "known to the game only," one could imagine a deck of cards that is reshuffled every turn, functioning in exactly the same way as a random die roll—Pearce's "randomly generated information." Perhaps the subtle difference between these two types of information is whether or not the exact makeup of the remaining deck is completely known to all players. If it is, then the deck would function like a random die roll, in which the precise chance to roll a particular number (or draw a particular card) is known to all players. On the other hand, when players draw cards in Gin, the face-down deck contains information known only to the game.

Despite our critique of Pearce's model, the four categories she proposes are in fact quite useful. For example, information is not always either public or private, and often moves between categories. As a deck of face-down cards are exposed to players, there is movement from once-private information to information that is public and shared. Similarly, in Battleship, both players try to uncover information that is hidden from them, but known to their opponent. As Battleship proceeds, the positions of the players' ships gradually become public knowledge.

Enchanted Information

Whether you prefer a model of perfect and imperfect information or Pearce's four categories, it is important to consider the ways that games manipulate information to generate meaningful play. Consider the game Enchanted Forest, a children's board game that uses information in a number of ways. The game is summarized below:

> In Enchanted Forest, players are seeking a number of treasures that are hidden on the board. When a game begins, a set of tree objects are shuffled and placed in set locations on the board. On the bottom of each tree is an image of one of the treasures in the game. There is also a deck of cards, each card containing the image of one of the treasures. At the start of the game, the deck is shuffled and the top card is turned over. This is the treasure that all of the players are initially seeking.

> By rolling two dice and moving on a network of paths, players maneuver their pieces to specific trees. When a player lands on a tree, she can privately look at the treasure under the tree. If a player

thinks that she knows the location of the treasure pictured on the face-up card, she can in subsequent turns travel to the castle on one end of the board and pick up the tree where she thinks the pictured treasure is hidden. If she is correct, she shows the tree to the other players, puts it back on the board, keeps the card, and turns over a new card, which becomes the next treasure for all of the players to seek. If she is not correct, she puts the tree back without revealing it to the other players and moves her piece to the village, which is located on the far end of the board from the castle. The first player to collect three cards and get to the castle wins.

> Other special rules in the game allow a player to bump another player back to the village by landing on his piece. Rolling doubles allows a player to optionally take a special action instead of moving. Special actions include shuffling the card deck and picking a new card, looking under any tree, and moving directly to the castle.

Enchanted Forest manipulates game information in a variety of ways. Let's use Pearce's four categories to analyze the use of information in the game. Enchanted Forest contains all four kinds of information:

- *Information known to all players:* There are many elements of Enchanted Forest not hidden from players. For example, the networks of paths on the boards, the locations of the players' pieces, the cards each player has collected, and the treasure that players are currently seeking represent information known to everyone.

- *Information known only to one player:* The one kind of information that is known only to one player is the locations of the treasures that players secretly uncover as they move about the forest. In most games that make use of private information, that information is kept in a hand of cards or an otherwise concealed collection of game components. In Enchanted Forest, however, the privately held information is something that each player keeps in memory, adding to the challenge of using the information.

Enchanted Forest

- **Information known to the game only:** Initially, the locations of the treasures under each tree are kept hidden from all of the players. However, as the game proceeds, the hidden information about the treasure locations shifts subtly from this category to the others. As they move about the board, each player begins to piece together a larger picture of the information hidden under the trees. Sometimes, when a player correctly guesses the location of a treasure, the information is temporarily made public.

- **Randomly generated information:** Enchanted Forest creates random information through a two-die roll. Players use each die separately when deciding where to move, so that rolling a 4 and a 5 can be used to move one space (moving five in one direction and then doubling back four spaces). These flexible rules of movement offer players many possibilities for navigating the network of paths on the game board. Moving onto a particular space can let a player look at a tree, enter the castle, or bump another player back to the village. Rolling doubles also allows special actions. Even the raw, randomly generated information of the die roll is used in a number of ways in the game.

As a game of Enchanted Forest proceeds, players gradually discover the hidden information stored under the trees, allowing them to build their own personal system of information and accompanying strategies. How will you navigate the board? Do you want to seek out trees that no other player has looked at, so that you have an informational advantage? Or perhaps you want to shadow other players and make sure that no one else has an advantage over you. Maybe you should just look at the trees near the castle, so that you can more quickly move there if a treasure you have seen turns up on a card.

If each player were allowed to take notes and store the data they gather, then a gradual accumulation of the game's hidden information would be inevitable. However, because players are storing all of this information in their memories, it is easy to forget exactly where a treasure is, even after they have seen it. The fact that players must memorize the locations of the treasure under each tree forces them to focus their attention on the game, making each guess in the castle a little bit risky. Furthermore, because strategic use of information dominates the game, there are many ways to acquire information, beyond looking under trees. If another player has just looked under a tree and is now heading for the castle, is it because she has just seen the treasure that is on the current face-up card? If you are closer to the castle, can you beat her there and make an edu-cated guess based on her behavior? Or is it all a bluff to get you to waste your time making a false guess so that you will be sent back to the village?

The same kind of dilemma confronts you when you roll dou-bles and can take a special action instead of moving. If another player is about to reach the castle and make a guess, you can shuffle the deck and draw a new card. But that might only reveal a card that the player already knows. If you think you know the tree where the treasure is, you can teleport next to the castle. Or perhaps you just want to ignore the other player's movement toward the castle and use your doubles to look under a tree on the far side of the forest.

Each turn, Enchanted Forest players must make tough decisions about what action to take. This is a good sign that meaningful play is taking place. Each choice a player makes in Enchanted Forest is bound up in the fluid flow of information, as direct knowledge and educated hunches are balanced with strategic navigation, challenging memorization, and risky guesswork.

Economies of Information

The other informational component of Enchanted Forest is the deck of cards that is uncovered as the game progresses. Because players know that each card in the deck corresponds to one of the treasures, the predictability of the identity of the next card being revealed changes as the game proceeds. At the beginning, there is a low chance that a particular card might turn up. But near the end of the game, when there are only two or three cards left in the deck, there is much less uncertainty about the possible outcome. That means that using a special action to reshuffle the information in the deck, as a way of mak-ing a particular card appear, is a more effective strategy later in the game.

This strategic phenomenon occurs because the information contained on each card does not exist in isolation from the others. Instead, the information is part of a larger system: an *economy of information* that grants each card its relative value. Meaning in a game, or in any system, for that matter, emerges out of relational identity. To use a non-game example, the meaning of the word "bird" depends on the larger sentence and performative context of use. Its relationship to other words and meanings will determine whether "bird" references a feathered animal, the jazz musician Charlie Parker, a rudely flipped-up middle finger, or a slang term for "woman."

In a game, the same holds true: the value of the information known to a player gains meaning within the larger system of the game. Furthermore, the systemic nature of information in a game and the way that it helps generate meaningful play has two facets: the actual make-up of the information structures in a system, and the apprehension of that information by players. We call a game's information structures *objective information* and the player's understanding of these structures *perceived information*. The interaction of these two aspects of game information determines the way that information operates within the system of a game.

In a trick-taking game such as Euchre, for example, if all of the trumps have already been played during a round, the once-private but now-public information regarding the location of the trumps becomes extremely important for making game decisions. The fact that any given card can be a trump or non-trump is a function of the *objective information* of the game. But the systemic fact that the trumps have all been played is only meaningful because of the player's ability to turn the objective information into *perceived information* and make decisions accordingly. Good Euchre players track not only the trump cards, but every card that is played in the game. This informa-tion determines the potential value of the cards you are holding in your own hand, as well as the cards you think other players will play next, directly informing your decision-making process. Euchre contains a tightly woven system of information, in which meaningful play emerges from the elegantly architected value of the card deck, as well as from players' shifting certainties, speculations, and ignorance about the cards left to be played.

The game of Scrabble also contains objective informational structures that are gradually revealed to players as perceived information over the course of play. For example, knowledge about the ratio of the letters in the overall mix is part of how you play the game. If you desperately need to pick a Z tile to make a 7-letter word and get a big bonus, you need to decide whether to play a single letter, make a small score this turn, and hold out for that Z, or else abandon the large-word strategy altogether. Your judgment will involve not only the probability of drawing a Z (dependent on the objective informational economy of the pool of letters), but also on perceived information: whether or not you know that the single Z has already been played on the board. The fact that the ratios of letters are printed on the Scrabble game board, next to the grid where letters are placed, points to the way that the structure of Scrabble's informational system is central to the play of the game.

When you create information in your game, its value for the players emerges from both its objective and perceived status: its structural position within a larger informational economy and the player's knowledge about that economy. Shaping these aspects of your game's design is a key component in creating meaningful play.

Hiding and Revealing Systems

We conclude our discussion of games as information systems by looking at some examples of digital games that successfully integrate information into the overall game design. These games take advantage of the ability of digital games to manipulate information in complex ways to engender meaningful play:

- **The Fog of War:** A wonderful method by which digital games manipulate information is the "fog of war" feature in real-time strategy games such as Starcraft. Although a real-time strategy game level might take place on a large map of terrain, the game only reveals information about the map near a player's own units. Initially, you only know about your own local area of the playfield. Sending out scouts and spies to learn more about the terrain and the location of your enemies becomes an important part of the game. The strategic unveiling of hidden information adds suspense and tension to the game experience.

- **Secret Locations and Hidden Moves:** Many digital games possess locations and features which are hidden to players at the beginning of a game and are slowly revealed through play. In Super Mario 64, not only does the player slowly gain enough coins to unlock new game worlds, but some of these worlds contain items that give Mario new powers and abilities. Although any level-based game could be considered a system of information revealed to players over the course of a game, Super Mario 64 masterfully integrates the uncovering of this information into the geography of the overall game space. Such an approach creates a rhythm of discovery that keeps players engaged throughout the game.

- **Item Economies:** Many digital games feature complex economies of items. In LEGO Drome Racing Challenge, a multiplayer online game in which players customize their cars by purchasing parts, the game limits a player's ability to purchase car parts based on their License Class: as a player progresses, they gain the ability to purchase more and more powerful parts. But the game doesn't limit the informational access to all of the parts: players can "browse" the more powerful parts, but not acquire them. Although this is the opposite design strategy that Super Mario 64 takes, it works well in the context of this particular design. By granting access to the entire set of part information, this structure gives players a better under-standing of the relative value of the items available for purchase, while also allowing them to make meaningful decisions about what to buy. Rather than purchasing a currently accessible item, a player can choose to "save up" for a more expensive item that can only be purchased once he or she has advanced to another License class.

· *Rules as Information:* The automated nature of game sys-tems, combined with their ability to manipulate informa-tion, forms a powerful design tool: the ability to reveal not just static information, but dynamic behaviors and rela-tionships as well. In the game FLUID, the player has little information at the beginning of the game experience. The interaction consists of poking, stroking, and prodding a touchscreen, interacting with the elements of the game. Each game element is part of a miniature ecosystem; as the player plays with FLUID, interaction and observation reveals the underlying principles of the system. In this case, the hidden information gradually revealed through play is the rules of the simulation itself. Part of the play of FLUID is the discovery of the game rules as information.

Many digital games rely on vast sets of information rewards for player interaction. Huge worlds to explore, complex economies of items, and hidden fighting moves are the "stuff" with which digital game designers fill their systems. One challenge for dig-ital game designers is not to rely so much on hidden content in order to generate player interest. Making use of information systems within your games requires that the information be made meaningful through player interaction. If there is too much information, or if the information is neither discernable nor integrated, the design has failed to support meaningful play. In contrast, non-digital games typically consist of more limited, replayable systems: imperfect information might be a core component of Poker, but you are not going to uncover a previously hidden card in the deck after 30 hours of play.

Drome Racing Challenge

The kind of information system you design, therefore, depends on the kind of game you want to create. A simple game system that players fully know from the start can create the obsessive play of Tetris or the opportunities for mastery of Go. On the other hand, a game that contains large amounts of information —strategically unveiling informational complexity, rewarding progress via new levels, powers, or narrative segments—can let players slowly come to know the game without feeling over-whelmed. Your challenge as a game designer is to identify the kind of experience you want to create and design a system that finds the proper balance of meaningful informational play.

Notes

1. <http://www.flash.net/~markthom/html/game_thoughts.html>.
2. Celia Pearce, *The Interactive Book* (New York: Macmillan Technical Pub-lishing,1997), p. 422–423.

Games as Systems of Information

SUMMARY

- In this schema, the concept of **information** refers to knowledge or content that is manipulated, acquired, hidden, and revealed during play.

- In a game of **perfect information** such as Chess or Backgammon, players publicly share all knowledge in the game. In a game of **imperfect information** such as Poker or Memory, some information is hidden from some or all players.

- Games of perfect information tend to be analytically competitive, whereas games of imperfect information tend to have more uncertainty and inspire distrust among players.

- Celia Pearce identifies four kinds of information in a game: **Information known to all players, information known to only one player, information known to the game only,** and **randomly generated information.**

- Information in a system does not have an intrinsic value but instead gains its value from its relationships to other units of information in the system's **information economy.**

- Information can contribute to meaningful play in two ways: **objective information,** the game system's internal informational structure; and **perceived information,** the information that a player observes and acquires through play.

- Digital games are particularly adept at manipulating complex sets of information. Because they are more automated than non-digital games, digital games can make the discovery of hidden game rules and mechanisms themselves part of the game experience.

Unit 2: **Rules**

GAMES AS CYBERNETIC SYSTEMS

cybernetic feedback loop
positive feedback
negative feedback
dynamic difficulty adjustment

18

Cybernetics enforces consistency. It permits change, but the change must be orderly and abide by the rules.—**Jeremy Campbell,** *Grammatical Man*

Introducing Cybernetic Systems

Cyberspace. Cyberpunk. *A Cyborg Manifesto.* The term *cybernetic* has been appropriated by science fiction and technoculture to mean anything associated with computer technology. In point of fact, the field of cybernetics precedes the advent of digital computers. Mathematician Norbert Weiner coined the term "cybernetics" in his 1948 book *Cybernetics or Control and Communication in the Animal and the Machine.* The word is derived from the Greek word for *steersman* or *navigator,* and appropriately enough, cybernetics studies the regulation and control of systems.

Cybernetics grew out of systems theory and information theory, and like these fields, cybernetics studies a range of subjects, from mechanical and electrical systems to social and biological systems. In looking at the basic principles of cybernetics, we are touching on a field filled with great debates and a rich history, a field that greatly influenced contemporary ideas about computer technology and society.

This chapter can only offer a brief introduction to cybernetics, focusing on the ways dynamic systems change over time and the formal structures that allow these changes to occur. What are the rule structures that monitor change within a game system? How does a game system adjust to change over time? What constitutes feedback within a game? How can positive and negative feedback loops be used in the design of meaningful play? Within this schema on **Games as Cybernetic Systems,** we bring cybernetics to bear on these important game design questions.

Elements of a Cybernetic System

Cybernetics deals with the ways a system gauges its effect and makes necessary adjustments. The simplest cybernetic device consists of a sensor, a comparator, and an activator. The sensor *provides* feedback *to the* comparator, *which determines whether the machine is deviating from its established norm. The comparator then provides guidance to the* activator, *which produces an output that affects the environment in some way. This fundamental process of output-feedback-adjustment is the basis of cybernetics.—**Stephen Littlejohn,** Theories of Human Communication*

As communications theorist Stephen Littlejohn makes clear, cybernetics studies particular kinds of systems. The cybernetic conception of a system is based on the interaction of inputs and outputs with the internal mechanism of a system. Inputs are how the system monitors the environment—they allow the environment to influence the system. Outputs are the ways that the system takes action—they are how the system influences the environment. Through the back-and-forth exchange between the environment and the system, the system changes over time.

A cybernetic system contains three elements: a *sensor,* a *comparator,* and an *activator.* The sensor senses something about the environment or the internal state of a system. The comparator decides whether or not a change to the system needs to be made as a result of the sensor's reading, and the activator activates that change. Together, these three elements regulate how a system operates and changes over time.

A common example of a cybernetic system is a thermostat. Imagine a hot summer day and a room with an air conditioner that is attached to a thermostat. The thermostat contains the system's *sensor,* a thermometer. The thermostat also contains a *comparator* it can use to compare the temperature of the room to a user-set temperature. If the thermostat measures the air temperature above the set amount, it activates the air conditioner, the *activator* of the system, which cools down the room.

As the air begins to cool, the system continues to monitor the room temperature. When the room is sufficiently cooled so that the thermostat's sensor doesn't register the temperature as being above the set limit, the thermostat no longer sends a signal to activate the air conditioner, and so shuts off the cold air. However, the hot summer sun will begin to heat up the room again. When the temperature rises above the thermostat's limit, the air conditioner will again be activated. This cyclic behavior of the system is the "process of output-feedback-adjustment" Littlejohn describes. The fact that the cybernetic system is running as a circuit, constantly monitoring itself to see whether or not conditions have been met, is the reason why cybernetic systems are sometimes called *feedback systems,* or *feedback loops.*

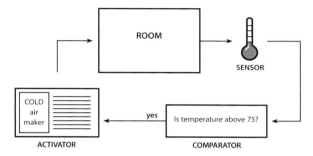

Negative feedback air conditioning system

In every feedback loop, information about the result of a transformation or an action is sent back to the input of the system in the form of input data. With the thermostat, the input data is information about air temperature. If this data causes the system to continue moving in the same direction (the temperature continues to rise), then it is *positive* feedback. This means that the effect is *cumulative.* If, on the other hand, the new data produces a result in opposition to the previous result (the temperature is rising, it will now be lowered), the feedback is *negative.* The effects of negative feedback *stabilize* the system.

Positive feedback loops create an exponential growth or decline; negative feedback loops maintain an equilibrium. As cyberneticist J. de Rosnay explains,

> Positive feedback leads to divergent behavior: indefinite expansion or explosion (a running away toward infinity) or total blocking of activities (a running away toward zero). Each plus involves another plus; there is a snowball effect. The examples are numerous: chain

reaction, population explosion, industrial expansion, capital invested at compound interest, inflation, proliferation of cancer cells. However, when minus leads to another minus, events come to a standstill. Typical examples are bankruptcy and economic depression.

> Negative feedback leads to adaptive, or goal-seeking behavior: sustaining the same level, temperature, concentration, speed, direction. In a negative loop every variation toward a plus triggers a correction toward the minus, and vice versa. There is tight control; the system oscillates around an ideal equilibrium that it never attains. A thermostat or a water tank equipped with a float are simple examples of regulation by negative feedback.[1]

The thermostat example represents a negative feedback system. The system is negative because it seeks to sustain the same temperature. Instead of letting the room get hotter and hotter from the sun, the system acts to return the room to its normative state.

A positive feedback system works in the opposite fashion. Instead of bringing the system to a steady state, a positive cybernetic circuit encourages the system to exhibit more and more extreme behavior. For example, if the thermostat were reversed so that it only activated the air conditioner when the room was *below* a certain temperature, we would have a positive feedback system. If the room temperature ever went below the comparator's threshold, it would continue to run, making the room colder and colder, so that the temperature would steadily get lower and lower. Brrr!

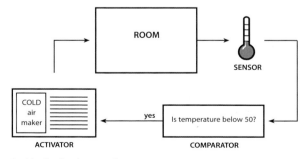

Positive feedback air conditioning system

We could also construct negative and positive feedback loops with a heater. In a negative feedback loop, the heater would turn on when the temperature was *below* a certain level, raising the temperature until it reached its original state, at which point the heater would shut off. In a positive feedback loop, the heater would turn on when the temperature rose *above* a certain level, continuing to heat the room indefinitely. Hot hot hot!

Now imagine what would happen if we combined two simple cybernetic systems using an air conditioner and a heater. This dual system would have a sensor to detect the temperature, a double-comparator to compare the room temperature to a pre-established setting, and heating and cooling activators. Using a dual system allows us to control the room temperature in more subtle ways. If both sub-systems were negative feedback systems, the room temperature would be very stable, as both would seek to sustain a middle room temperature. The cooler or heater would turn on when the room became too hot or too cold, and the temperature would always be brought back to its normative position. The system would never let the temperature vary too greatly. This is, in fact, how central heating and cooling works in many homes.

Alternately, both the heating and cooling circuits could be made into positive feedback sub-systems. Whenever the temperature became too hot or too cold, one of the activators would turn on and keep pushing the temperature in that direction. If the temperature setting for the heater were above the temperature setting for the air conditioner, once the room temperature strayed from the middle range, it would never reach the center again. On the other hand, imagine that the heater's activation temperature was below the air conditioner's activation temperature. If the room started out in a middle temperature range somewhere between the two activation temperatures, when the two systems were turned on, both activators would begin battling with each other in a tug-of-war to either raise or lower the temperature.

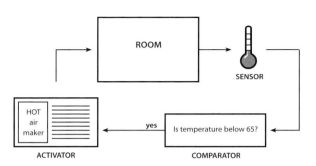

Negative feedback heating system

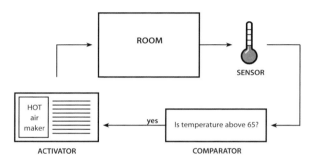

Positive feedback heating system

The important thing to notice in all of the heating and cooling examples is that cybernetic systems affect phenomena like temperature in very specific ways. When more than one cybernetic system is operating together, things get complex quite quickly.

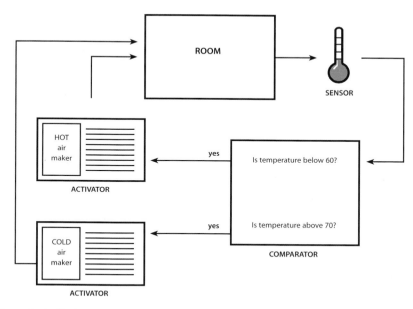

Hot and cold negative feedback system

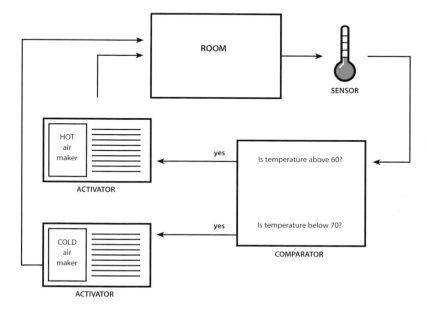

Hot and cold positive feedback system

Feedback Systems in Games

How do feedback systems operate in games? As a cybernetic system, the rules of a game define the sensors, comparators, and activators of the game's feedback loops. Within a game, there are many sub-systems that regulate the flow of play, dynamically changing and transforming game elements. Do you want your game to move toward a balanced, steady state? Or do you want it to spin wildly toward one extreme or another? Designing feedback loops within your game can help you shape these tendencies. Feedback loops can be tricky to grasp, but they offer a crucial way of understanding how formal game systems function.

Game designer Marc LeBlanc has done a great deal of thinking about the relationship between game design and feedback systems, and this schema is indebted to LeBlanc's important work on the subject. In 1999, LeBlanc gave a presentation at the Game Developer's Conference, titled "Feedback Systems and the Dramatic Structure of Competition."[2] In this lecture, LeBlanc proposed a way of thinking about games as feedback systems, summarized in the following chart:

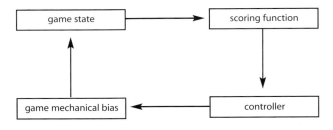

In this model, the *game state* represents the current condition of the game at any given moment. In a Chess game, for example, the game state is represented by the arrangement of the pieces on the board, the captured pieces, and which player is about to move next. In a console fighting game such as Virtua Fighter 4, the game state includes which two combatants were chosen, the health and other fixed and variable stats of the two

fighters, their relative spatial positions, and the arena in which they are fighting. The game state is a *formal* way of understanding the current status of the game, and does not take into account the skills, emotions, and experience of the players. Of course, these player-based factors will definitely affect the game state. If you are a masterful Virtua Fighter 4 player and your opponent is not, this will be evident in the play of the game. However, the game state itself refers only to the formal, internal condition of the game.

The other elements of LeBlanc's model correspond directly to the components of a cybernetic system as we have discussed them. The *scoring function* is the system's *sensor* that measures some aspect of the game state. The *controller* is the *comparator*, which looks at the sensor's reading and makes the decision whether or not to take action. The *game mechanical bias* is the *activator*, a game event or set of events that can be turned on or off depending on the decision of the comparator.

When looking at games as cybernetic systems, it is important to note that we are not necessarily considering the entire game as a single feedback system. Instead, our emphasis is on the ways that cybernetic systems are embedded in games. Embedded cybernetic systems affect a single aspect of a larger game, such as determining which player goes first next round or the relative speed of players in a race. We know from our study of systems that all parts of a game are interrelated in some way. A cybernetic system within a game that directly affects just one component of a game will indirectly affect the game as a whole.

Positive and Negative Basketball

To bring this abstract discussion closer to game design, let's look at several game examples. In his talk "Feedback Systems and the Dramatic Structure of Competition," LeBlanc invented two variations on the formal structure of Basketball: Positive Feedback Basketball and Negative Feedback Basketball. Each variation adds just a single rule on top of the existing formal structure of the game:

Negative Feedback Basketball: For every *N* points of difference in the two teams' scores, the losing team may have an extra player in play.

Positive Feedback Basketball: For every *N* points of difference in the two teams' scores, the winning team may have an extra player in play.

How do the addition of these rules change the game? Say, for example, that *N* is 5. In a game of Negative Feedback Basketball, when Team A fell behind by 5 points, it would gain a player on the court and begin to play with a team of 6. As soon as Team A scored points that put it behind by less than 5, it would drop its extra player. On the other hand, if Team A continued to do poorly, when its score was 10 points behind the other team, it would gain a second extra player. Why is this an example of negative feedback? Because the adjustments in the system (gaining and losing players) encourage the system to move toward a stable, steady state. A losing team gets extra players, which helps it catch up to the winning team; when it moves to within 5 points, the two teams are evenly matched. The steady state of this system is not that the total points tend towards zero, but that the *difference* between the two teams' scores stays near zero. The end result is that Negative Feedback Basketball games would tend to be very close games.

Positive Feedback Basketball creates the opposite situation. As soon as one team increased its lead, it would gain additional players. These new players would help the team do even better against the opposing team, which would increase the winning team's lead even more, which would result in yet more players for that team. Eventually, the court would be absurdly crowded with members of one team, who would completely overwhelm and defeat the team with only five players. Positive Feedback Basketball encourages a large difference between the two teams' scores, so that there is a runaway, devastating victory instead of a closely matched game.

As in the examples of heating and cooling, there are many ways to transform the game system. We could, for example, change the rules to remove players instead of adding them. In this case, in Negative Feedback Basketball, when one team pulls ahead by *N* points, it would lose a player, making it easier for the other team to catch up. In Positive Feedback Basketball, the team that was behind by *N* points would lose a player, encouraging them to fall further behind, which would result in the loss of even more players. Eventually, one team would fall so far behind that none of its players would be left on the court. In both games, even though players are removed rather than added, the end results remain the same: Negative Feedback Basketball tends toward stable, close matches and Positive Feedback Basketball tends toward unstable, unbalanced matches. Each variation on the game of Basketball would result in vastly different player and spectator experiences. Yet all we did was add one rule that affected the behavior of the system. Feedback systems offer game designers a powerful tool to affect a game's formal structure and the way that structure manifests in play.

Racing Loops

Positive Feedback Basketball and Negative Feedback Basketball were variations on the game of Basketball. But many existing games already make use of feedback systems in their designs. Here, we look at the use of cybernetic systems in two digital racing games.

Wipeout is a science-fiction racing game originally released for the Playstation, in which the player pilots a fast-moving hover vehicle around a track, trying to beat the computer-controlled vehicles and come in first place. It is common in racing games such as Wipeout for the program to employ feedback mechanisms. Obviously, a computer program can drive a vehicle as poorly or as skillfully as the game designer wants. It would be simple to program the computer-driven cars so that they drove in a mathematically optimal fashion and always beat the player. However, that would simply not be fun. Instead, in racing games the computer vehicles are programmed to drive in a

Wipeout

less than "perfect" manner, sometimes not steering or accelerating efficiently, in order to provide a challenge that a human player can overcome.

One way to create a scaled challenge for the player would be to program different skill levels for the computer-controlled vehicles. Some vehicles would be easy for a beginner to beat whereas others could only be bested by experienced players. Programming a static skill level for each opponent vehicle, however, is not yet a cybernetic feedback loop. Why would we want to add a feedback system to a racing game? In order to keep the flow of play exciting, of course. Part of the fun of a racing game such as Wipeout is jockeying for position among a dense cluster of hover vehicles, battling for first place with another racer who is hot on your tail or dead ahead in your sights.

Without a feedback loop, these moments are unlikely to occur. What if a player crashes early in a race—will she ever catch up to the computer-controlled vehicles? Or what if a player's skill far outmatches the pre-programmed computer opponents? Once she gains a lead early in the race, she might as well be racing alone, because the computer opponents will never catch up to her.

This is precisely why Wipeout (and many other digital racing games) make use of cybernetic feedback systems to control the speed of the computer opponents. There are two general rules we can abstract from the behavior of the computer-controlled vehicles in the game. Although these are not the only factors determining their speed, they do have a clear impact on the experience of the game:

·   If the human player is in first place, the vehicle in second place will accelerate and catch up to the human player's vehicle.

·   If the human player is in last place, the last few vehicles will slow down to let the player catch up to them.

The result of these two rules is a negative feedback system. Like Negative Feedback Basketball, together these two rules operate to reduce the distance between vehicles in the game, eliminating the "extremes" of the player being very far ahead or very far behind the computer opponents.

In this system, there are three states that the comparator needs to monitor: when the player is in first place, when the player is in last place, or when the player is in neither first nor last place. If the player is somewhere in the middle of the pack, then no special activator event comes into play. But if the player is in first or last place, vehicle behavior adjusts accordingly. The outcome of this feedback system is that racing in Wipeout tends to offer exciting and satisfying play. Significantly, Wipeout only affects the computer-opponent vehicles, not the hovercraft that the player is driving. In essence, the program carefully adjusts the competitive backdrop, rather than boosting or handicapping the player directly. However, there are games that apply a negative feedback system more directly to a player's abilities.

One example of such a game is Super Monkey Ball for the Nintendo GameCube. Super Monkey Ball contains several different game modes; one of them is a racing game in which up to four players simultaneously race monkey characters through

Super Monkey Ball

Powerstone

a series of tracks. When players drive through a power-up object on the track, they gain a special power that can be used one time. These powers range from forward-firing attacks (shoot a bomb at another player ahead of you) to rear-based attacks (drop a banana peel, hoping a player behind you will run over it and slip) to non-attack powers (a speed-up that temporarily boosts a player's velocity).

Whereas many racing games use this power-up convention (including Wipeout), Super Monkey Ball uses a feedback system to determine which power-up a player will receive, depending on whether the player is ahead or behind other players. If a player is in last place, the player is much more likely to receive the speed-up power, which will help that player catch up to the other competitors. On the other hand, a player in first place is more likely to get forward-firing attacks, rather than speed-ups or rear-based attacks. The lead player thus receives the least useful kind of power-up: a player in first place can't use a forward-firing attack to better his position, because no one is ahead of him. These rules add up to a negative feedback system. As with Wipeout, Super Monkey Ball's feedback loops encourage a close race, in which no player is too far ahead of or behind the others.

In Super Monkey Ball and Wipeout, negative feedback loops are used to engender meaningful play. As we know from **Games as Systems of Uncertainty,** the outcome of a game needs to be uncertain for meaningful play to occur. If, as a player, you fall so far behind or ahead of the other players that the outcome is a foregone conclusion, meaningful play is diminished, because decisions you make won't have an impact on the outcome of the game. This does not mean that feedback systems guarantee a close race every time: skill plays an important role in racing games, and it is possible for a player in Super Monkey Ball to fall so far behind that there is very little chance of victory. There is no universal strategy for crafting meaningful play. But in Wipeout and Super Monkey Ball, feedback systems support meaningful play by making the game responsive to the ongoing state of the game.

Positive Feedback in a Game

Not all games use negative feedback systems. Some make good use of positive feedback systems as well. Powerstone is a console fighting game for up to four players that features cartoony, fast-paced brawling action. In Powerstone, when a player is successfully hit by a powerful attack, the target of the attack will be stunned for a short time, during which the target player cannot move his or her character, and the attacker can continue to strike the stunned character. A stunned character cannot move out of the way, defend, or counterattack, and is much easier to hit. This is, in effect, a positive feedback system: because a player successfully launches a powerful attack, the player has a better chance of launching yet more attacks as the target remains stunned and easier to hit. The new attacks continue to stun the target, increasing the ability of the attacker to deliver more damage. Positive feedback creates dramatic results, in which a player can be devastated by a rapidly delivered series of attacks. This kind of slapstick action makes sense in a lighthearted and humorous game such as Powerstone.

However, if the positive feedback system were permitted to play itself out until the end of a match, then the game as a whole wouldn't work. Once your character was hit for the first time, you would remain stunned while an opponent continued to attack you. In effect, the first blow landed would determine your fate and the game would lose the back-and-forth struggle that is an important ingredient of fighting games. Powerstone gets out of this feedback trap by adding a different behavior to the game system. After receiving a certain number of attacks, a stunned character will be hurled across the playfield, making it impossible for the attacker to indefinitely continue rapid-fire strikes. The attacker can pursue the character that flew across the playfield, but the far-flung character is usually no longer stunned by the time the attacker gets there.

Because positive feedback systems are inherently unstable and push a game system toward an inevitable outcome, they are usually dampened by other game factors that limit the acceleration of the feedback loop. In real-time multiplayer strategy games such as Warcraft II, players gather resources, which allow them to build more units that can gather yet more resources, increasing the acceleration of resource-gathering. In this way, all of the players are building their own positive feedback loops, joined together in an arms race to see who will gather enough resources and be the first to front an army capable of winning the game.

In Warcraft II, potentially unstable positive feedback loops are balanced by the fact that each player is creating his or her own feedback loop in parallel. Furthermore, these feedback loops help bring the game to conclusion. Because of their complexity, real-time multiplayer strategy games can sometimes drag on interminably, with players evenly matched and unable to get an upper hand. Because of the way that positive feedback systems can quickly grow out of control, a player that can gain a slight advantage (such as capturing a resource-rich gold mine from another player) can use the advantage to overwhelm an opponent. Obviously, there are many strategic factors other than the resource-feedback loops that determine the outcome of Warcraft II. (For example, skillful battle tactics can help defeat a more resource-powerful opponent.) However, positive feedback systems are clearly a key element of the game design and contribute to the successful play of the game.

Dynamic Difficulty Adjustment

Increasingly, digital game designers are incorporating more sophisticated feedback techniques into their game designs. The game developer Naughty Dog Entertainment is known in the game industry for what it calls "Dynamic Difficulty Adjustment," a technique it has used in the Crash Bandicoot series of games, as well as the more recent Jak and Daxter.

Dynamic Difficult Adjustment, or DDA, uses feedback loops to adjust the difficulty of play. For example, in the original Crash Bandicoot game, the player is generally maneuvering the character Crash through a series of jumping and dodging obstacles, trying to overcome damaging hazards and reach objectives to finish the level. When a player dies, the game restarts at the beginning of the level or at the most recent "save point" reached in the level.

The danger in designing this kind of game is that players possess widely varying skill levels. An experienced gamer might breeze through a level, whereas a beginner might become frustrated after dying several times without making any progress.

The DDA operations in Crash Bandicoot evaluate the number of times that a player is dying at a particular location in a level, and make the game easier as a result. A player having trouble might suddenly find that there are more helpful objects nearby, or fewer enemies to avoid. This kind of attention to the balancing of player experience is evident in the play of Crash Bandicoot games, and it helps explain the fact that a wide audience of both hardcore and less experienced players enjoys them.

Using DDA and other feedback mechanisms in games raises some fascinating game design issues. If we consider the millennia-old tradition of pre-computer play, games are traditionally about a player or players competing within a formal system that does not adjust itself automatically to player performance. As you play a game such as Baseball or Othello, your fluency with the system and your ability to manipulate it grows. The game itself and the other players provide the challenge for you. As your play deepens, you find new forms of play, new ways of expressing yourself within the system of the game.

DDA points to a different kind of game, a game that constantly anticipates the abilities of the player, reads the player's behavior, and makes adjustments accordingly. Playing a game becomes less like learning an expressive language and more like being the sole audience member for a participatory, improvisational performance, where the performers adjust their actions according to how you interact with them. Are you then playing the game, or is it playing you? Is a game "cheating" if it constantly adjusts its own rules? Could such a scheme be designed into a multiplayer experience and still feel "fair" for everyone involved? These questions have no definitive answers, as there are always many solutions for any given game design problem. Dynamic Difficulty Adjustment could be considered a heavy-handed design tool that takes agency away from the player, or it could be considered an elegant way of invisibly shaping game play so that every player has an optimal experience. Regardless of your opinion on the matter, DDA is

an important tool, and as digital games rely more and more on their ability to automate complex processes, this kind of design strategy will become more common.

A Simple Die Roll

Because most of the examples used so far have come from complex digital games, we wanted to finish by looking at a cybernetic feedback system within a more minimal game context. Sometimes in games, there is no game AI or referee to sense and activate the changes in the game state. However, elegant feedback systems can still emerge directly from the game rules.

Let us take a look at one of our favorite examples, Chutes and Ladders. Chutes and Ladders is an extremely simple game of pure chance. But can you spot the feedback system in it? It is not the actual chutes and ladders. Yes, those seem like they regulate the positions of the players, but they do not act in a cybernetic way. They merely randomly shift the position of the players on the board. The chutes and ladders do not constitute a dynamic feedback loop.

The feedback loop in Chutes and Ladders occurs at the very end of the game, when players must land exactly on the final square in order to win (rather than being able to overshoot the final space and land there anyway). This rule creates a kind of negative feedback system. The exact landing rule serves as negative feedback on the distance between players. In a game of Chutes and Ladders, the player that is farthest ahead will eventually be within six spaces of the finish square and will usually end up spending a few more turns trying to make the exact roll, or possibly inch ahead by rolling small numbers. During this time, the other players often catch up. The overall effect is to level out the playing field by reducing the difference between the positions of the players. The result of stretching out the end of the game in this way is a closer and more dramatic finish.

Think about the game without this rule. If players can over-shoot the final space and still win, imagine that you are playing against someone who is just three spaces away from the last square. Even if that player has very bad luck (rolling three 1s in a row), that player is no more than three turns from winning the game. If you are more than 18 spaces away (the total of rolling three 6s in a row), there is no way you can win. On the other hand, if your opponent has to make an exact roll, then he has a 50 percent chance of rolling too high so that he has to stay put, as you keep getting closer. The game is prolonged, the outcome remains uncertain, and in general, the game is more satisfying to play. Those last few die rolls become dramatic, nail-biting game events.

We should point out that this is not a true example of a cyber-netic feedback system. An orthodox systems theorist would point out that there is no sensor, comparator, and activator in actual operation. As a counter-example, if there were a rule requiring that the player in first place subtract 1 from his die roll, we would have a true feedback loop, in which a procedural change is enacted when certain conditions are met. Here the player is the sensor, the rule itself the comparator, and the acti-vator is the action of subtracting one from the die roll.

Coming back to our exact landing rule, if we frame the rule in the following fashion, we might consider it to have a feedback loop: "If a player is fewer than 6 spaces from the final space, then rolling higher than N, where N is the number of spaces between the player and the final space, has no effect."

The rule now feels more like a feedback loop, where the player senses proximity to the finish and the rule acts to limit the effectiveness of the die roll. Ultimately, it does not really matter whether an orthodox systems theorist would approve of this example or not. As designers, the value of a schema is its ability to solve design problems. The rule that requires players to land by exact count on the final space does create more meaningful play. Understanding the rule as a cybernetic feedback loop, or even a pseudo-cybernetic feedback loop, can only enhance our appreciation for the game's design.

Putting Feedback to Use

As a game design schema, **Games as Cybernetic Systems** is one of the most practically applicable frameworks presented in this book. Cybernetic feedback systems can be wonderful ways of balancing your game to arrive at a particular result. What is wrong with your game: Is it ending too soon? Running on for too long? Is it too uncertain? Not uncertain enough? Is it too easy or too difficult for players to gain an advantage? You can address all these fundamental questions by looking for feed-back loops existing within the formal structure of your game's design, or by adding additional loops of your own.

In his lecture, Marc LeBlanc boiled down the relationship between game design and feedback systems to a set of design "rules." These rules offer a useful set of guidelines for integrat-ing feedback systems into your design. Here are a number of LeBlanc's "rules" and some of our comments on each of them:

- **Negative feedback stabilizes the game.**

- **Positive feedback destabilizes the game.**

These two observations form perhaps the most fundamental cybernetics insight for game design. As a designer, you should be aware of the ways that your game creates stabilities and instabilities. If your two-player card game lets the most power-ful player take cards from the weaker player, then you have cre-ated a positive feedback system where the most powerful player will quickly dominate. The game is unstable, and will rapidly fall out of balance. Perhaps the solution is to add more players to the game and allow them to team-up on the player that is ahead. This would be adding a negative feedback sys-tem to re-balance the game and make it less likely that a player who gains a small advantage will end up winning.

Although our examples have emphasized negative feedback as a useful game design tool, too much negative feedback can make a game too stable. Imagine a variation on Chutes and Ladders in which, whenever a player is ahead of another player, all of the players go back to the start. Although this rule would certainly add negative feedback to the game, ensuring that no player would get ahead of the others, it stabilizes the game to the point of stasis, so that the game doesn't move forward at all. Finding a balance of negative and positive factors for your game is crucial in designing meaningful play.

- **Negative feedback can prolong the game.**

- **Positive feedback can end it.**

LeBlanc's next two "rules" should follow intuitively from our many examples of feedback systems. Positive feedback can rush a game to conclusion, rewarding a player that is already ahead, as in Warcraft II. Negative feedback, as in the Chutes and Ladders exact landing rule, makes it easier for a losing player to catch up, prolonging the game by reducing the winning player's lead.

- **Positive feedback magnifies early successes.**

- **Negative feedback magnifies late ones.**

These two "rules" follow closely from the last pair. In Warcraft II, an early advantage in establishing positive feedback resource loops can put a player too far ahead of the other players. In Chutes and Ladders, on the other hand, negative feedback at the very end can allow a player that has been behind the whole game to catch up.

How can you apply these ideas to your own game design? It depends on the kind of game experience you want to create. There are no universal guidelines for the proper length of a game. Wargamers might play a game for weeks, whereas less hardcore gamers might think an hour is a long time to be play-ing a single game. Similarly, there are no fixed rules that tell you to make the opening moves or the ending moves the most important ones in the game.

Your guide to making these kinds of decisions should be the core principles of meaningful play. Regardless of the length of your particular game, you should strive to create meaningful play at *all* moments, where the game outcome is uncertain until the end and every action a player takes can help determine that outcome in an integrated way. In general, players that play well should be rewarded with victory. But perhaps there is always a chance for a dramatic turn of events at the end, where the first becomes the last and the last becomes the first.

- **Feedback systems can *emerge* from your game systems "by accident." Be sure to identify them.**

- **Feedback systems can take control away from players.**

LeBlanc's final few "rules" are crucial. Game systems are complex and unpredictable and you can never be sure what feedback systems might be hiding out in the space of possibility you are constructing. Feedback systems can be great ways of shaping player experience, but as LeBlanc warns, as you incorporate systems into your game that actively reshape the experience, you run the danger of removing player agency, leaving your players feeling powerless. Some feedback systems, such as the last space rule of Chutes and Ladders, are relatively innocuous. But many game players will feel "cheated" if they can detect a game adjusting itself to their play. If that second place car is *always* on your tail, does it really matter how well you perform? Perhaps there should be limits on the speed of the second place car, so that a truly masterful player can have the satisfaction of driving far ahead of the rest of the pack.

As this last example clearly demonstrates, the most important thing about players and control is not their actual control in a game, but their *feeling* of control in the experience of play. We explored this phenomenon in the schema on *Uncertainty,* and it is just as valid here. Meaningful play is, after all, measured by what a player experiences, not by the underlying rules of a game.

Afterword: Don't Forget the Participant

Before departing a discussion of cybernetic systems entirely, we would like to make a few critical comments on the field. Cybernetics is clearly a formal way of understanding systems, which is why the schema of *Games as Cybernetic Systems* belongs within our **RULES** primary schema. However, as with all formal schemas, there are many things that cybernetics fails to address.

As a field, cybernetics initially considered a system as a completely self-contained entity. Cybernetics played into the classical scientific idea that the observer of a system had no effect on the operation of the system. This initial model of a cybernetic system was rocked by the introduction of second-order cybernetics into the field. Second-order cybernetics took the observer into account as a part of the system itself, undermining the "objective" stance of classical cybernetics. The insight of second-order cybernetics is that to observe a system in operation is to be part of that system. Although many thinkers, such as Katherine Hayles in her book *How We Became Post-Human,* have since criticized second-order cybernetics for falling into many of the same objectivist traps as its predecessor, second-order cybernetics went far in attempting to understand systems within a larger context.

What does all of this mean for game design? For the purposes of this schema, we made use of the more "classical" first-order cybernetics. We looked at games as self-contained systems, ensconced entirely within the magic circle demarcated by the rules. Occasionally we peeked a bit at the way formal changes play out in the experience of a game, but by and large we kept to the formal mechanics of game systems. This formal emphasis, of course, is what the **RULES** schemas are all about. The conceit of looking at games as formal systems is to leave out all of the emotional, psychological, social, cultural, and contextual factors that influence the experience of the game for the players. In the **PLAY** and **CULTURE** sections of this book, we do in fact look at games as much more than self-contained systems. For the time being, however, we continue our rules-based investigations. Even considered as purely formal structures, there are still many layers to the complex phenomena of games for us to uncover.

Further Reading

How We Become Post-Human, by Katherine Hayles

Hayles' book is less an explication of cybernetic theory and more an ideological critique of the field. However, her detailed research on the development and evolution of cybernetics and second-order cybernetics provides a great deal of insight to how these movements intersect with cultural beliefs about technology. In this complex book, Hayles also relates these subjects to literary theory and contemporary ideas about computer technology, virtuality, and identity.

> *Recommended:*
>
> Chapter 3: Contesting for the Body of Information: The Macy Conferences on Cybernetics
>
> Chapter 4: Liberal Subjectivity Imperiled: Norbert Wiener and Cybernetic Anxiety
>
> Chapter 6: The Second Wave of Cybernetics: From Reflexivity to Self-Organization

Theories of Human Communication, by Stephen W. Littlejohn *(see page 200)*

> *Recommended:*
>
> Chapter 3: System Theory

Notes

1. <pespmc1.vub.ac.be>.
2. Marc LeBlanc, presentation at Game Developer's Conference, 1999.

Games as Cybernetic Systems
SUMMARY

- Cybernetics studies the behavior of self-regulating systems. A cybernetic systems consists of three elements:

  - A **sensor** that measures some aspect of the system or its environment

  - A **comparator** that compares this measure to a set value and decides whether or not to take action

  - An **activator** that creates a change in the state of the system

  For example, in an air conditioner, the sensor and comparator are in the thermostat, which activates the air conditioner activator to cool down a room when the temperature gets too high.

- **Cybernetic feedback systems** can be positive or negative:

  A **negative** feedback system is **stabilizing** and brings a system to a fixed, steady state. The air conditioner example, which keeps a room from getting too hot, but shuts off when the room cools down, is a negative feedback system. The temperature remains within a narrow range.

  A **positive** feedback system is **cumulative** and makes a system unstable. If the air conditioner turned on when the temperature was **below** a certain number, then the room would become colder and colder, moving away from a stable state.

- A game can contain many feedback systems that interact with each other within the larger system of the game.

- Many game feedback systems are negative, reducing the advantage or disadvantage of a player or a team. This phenomenon is common in digital racing games.

- Games also make use of positive feedback systems for dramatic effect or to bring a game to conclusion. Often, a positive feedback system is countered by a negative feedback system in a game. Powerstone's stunning and hurling features demonstrate positive and negative feedback systems working together.

- **Dynamic Difficulty Adjustment,** or **DDA,** is the modification of a game's challenge according to player performance. It is most often used in complex single-player digital games.

· Game Designer Marc LeBlanc outlines a number of design "rules" that apply cybernetics to game design. These "rules" include the following:

- Negative feedback stabilizes the game.
- Positive feedback destabilizes the game.

- Negative feedback can prolong the game.
- Positive feedback can end it.

- Positive feedback magnifies early successes.
- Negative feedback magnifies late ones.

- Feedback systems can emerge from your game systems "by accident." Be sure to identify them.

- Feedback systems can take control away from the players.

· In the field of cybernetics, the more classical **first-order cybernetics,** which considers a system as a self-contained entity, was challenged by **second-order cybernetics,** which includes the observer of a system as an element of the system. Within this formal schema, we have not made use of second-order cybernetic thinking.

Unit 2: **Rules**

GAMES AS GAME THEORY SYSTEMS

decision tree
strategies
utility
payoff matrix
zero-sum
saddle point
degenerate strategy
mixed strategy

19

These are the main problems: How does each player plan his course—i.e., how does one formulate an exact concept of a strategy? What information is available to each player at every stage of the game? What is the role of a player being informed about the other player's strategy? About the entire theory of the game?—**Oscar Morganstern and John Von Neumann,** *Theory of Games and Economic Behavior*

Introducing *Game Theory?*

Perhaps you thought that this entire book was about game theory. If that were the case, what does "Games as Game Theory Systems" mean? Actually, game theory is not what it may appear to be. It is not a general term that means theoretical approaches to games. Game theory means something quite specific: it is a branch of economics that can be traced back to the work of two mathematicians, Oscar Morganstern and John Von Neumann. The classic text in the field is *Theory of Games and Economic Behavior,* published in 1942.

Game theory is the mathematical study of decision making. It looks at how people behave in specific circumstances that resemble very simple kinds of games. The founders of game theory intended to create a new kind of mathematical approach to the study of economics. Morganstern and Von Neumann were writing during a time when Marxism was very much in vogue in the field of economics, and *Theory of Games and Economic Behavior* was, in many ways, an attempt to replace the ideological approach of Marxism with a more rational and scientific set of techniques. Although it caused quite a sensation when it was introduced, the promises of game theory were never quite fulfilled, and it has largely fallen out of favor as a methodology within economics. But game theory can still be quite useful for game designers.

> The theory of games is a theory of decision making. It concerns how one should make decisions and, to a lesser extent, how one does make them. You make a number of decisions every day. Some involve deep thought, while others are almost automatic. Your decisions are linked to your goals—if you know the consequences of each of your options, the solution is easy. Decide where you want to be and choose the path that takes you there. When you enter an elevator with a particular floor in mind (your goal), you push the button (one of your choices) that corresponds to your floor.[1]

As a formal game design schema, **Games as Game Theory Systems** looks at games as systems of rational choice. It is potentially useful to game designers for two chief reasons.

First, it analyzes situations that resemble simple games in a very detailed way. Even more importantly, as game theorist Morton D. Davis points out in the previous quotation, game theory specifically focuses on relationships between decisions and outcomes. We know from our earlier discussion of interactivity that actions and outcomes are the building blocks of meaningful play. Within this schema, we explore questions of how players plan their course of action within a game and how they formulate strategies and make decisions. From decision trees to degenerate strategies, we will look closely at the application of game theory concepts to the design of meaningful play.

Decision Trees

As a formal approach to understanding games, game theory looks at games as a series of strategic decisions made by the players of a game. What does it mean to reduce a game to its strategic decisions? One common game theory method is to create a *decision tree* for a game. A decision tree is a branching tree-style diagram that outlines all of the possible moves a player can make in a game. Decision trees are a common way of flow-charting interactive experiences. For example, if you are programming an interactive story that has a hypertext structure, you might draw a diagram that shows all of the links between the different parts of your story. This kind of diagram would be a decision tree.

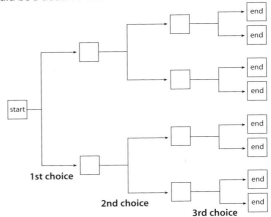

Creating a decision tree for a game is more complicated than creating a decision tree of a hypertext structure. The difference is that in a typical hypertext, the links and the actions that a player can perform at any location in the larger structure do not change as the participant moves through the structure. A reader's first choice in a hypertext structure does not change the way that the other hypertext links function. The only thing that changes is where the reader is positioned in the structure.

A game is more complex. In a game, what you can do at any given moment depends on what has already happened in the game. At the beginning of a game of Chess, for example, you can't move either of your rooks because they are both blocked by pawns. Later in the game, you might be able to move your rooks if your pawns have been maneuvered out of the way. The complexity of games leads to a system of many possible actions. Which actions can happen at a given moment is contingent on the current state of the game.

Because Chess is a complicated game to diagram as a decision tree, let's start with a simpler example: Tic-Tac-Toe. In *Prisoner's Dilemma,* a book about game theory and its historical context, writer William Poundstone leads us through the process of making a decision tree of the game of Tic-Tac-Toe.

> Ticktacktoe starts with the first player ("X") putting a mark in any of nine cells. There are consequently nine possible first moves. The nine choices open to Player X on the first move can be diagrammed as nine lines radiating up from a point. The point represents the move, the moment of decision, and the lines represent the possible choices.
>
> Next it's Player O's move. There are eight cells still open—which eight depending on where the X is. So draw eight secondary branches at the top of each of the nine primary branches. That leaves seven open cells for X on his second move. As the diagram of possible moves is continued upward, it branches like a very bushy tree.

As you continue the process, you will eventually diagram moves that put three markers in a row. That's a win for the player who moves. It's also the termination of that particular branch in the diagram, for the game ends when someone gets three in a row. Mark that point (call it a "leaf" of the diagram) as a win for X or O as the case may be.

Other branches of the diagram will terminate in a tie. Mark them as ties. Obviously, the game of ticktacktoe cannot go on forever. Nine moves is the maximum. So eventually, you will have a *complete* diagram of the game of ticktacktoe. Every possible ticktacktoe game—every game that ever has been played or ever will be played—must appear in the diagram as a branch starting at the "root" (X's first move) and continuing up to a "leaf" marked as a win for X, a win for O, or a tie. The longest complete branches/games are nine moves long. The shortest are five moves (this is the minimum for a win by the first player).[2]

Creating a decision tree can be a powerful way of understanding the formal structure of a game. It is in essence a way of mapping out a game's formal space of possibility. For a simple game such as Tic-Tac-Toe, the complete space of possibility can in fact be diagrammed. However, not all games can be mapped out in this way.

Being able to make a decision tree of a game or other interactive structure implies that the decisions participants make are discrete decisions that lead to knowable outcomes. For example, a game that involves physical skill, such as American Football, does not have self-contained moments of decision making that can be diagrammed like the alternate turn-taking of Tic-Tac-Toe. Instead, the game exists as a continuous flow of action. When the ball is hiked, a quarterback does not take a single discrete action. Instead, the game flows forward in a complex web of activity. Perception, movement, and the granularity of the real world creates a non-discrete game space.

Although the moment-to-moment play of Football is continuous, the game can be broken down into a system of separate plays. Does that mean it is possible to create a decision tree of Football by widening the frame of analysis, so that each decision point on the chart represents the choice of a play by one team's coach? The answer is no. The problem with this proposal is that to create a decision tree, the result of a decision needs to be a knowable outcome or set of outcomes. Think about a game of Tic-Tac-Toe. When a player makes a decision to place an X or an O in a particular square, there isn't any doubt that the player will finish the action and make the mark. On the other hand, just because a Football team picks a certain play does not mean that they will be able to successfully complete it, or complete it in a way that can be predicted with any accuracy. The outcome of picking a particular play in a Football game could result in a yardage loss or gain, a penalty, a fumble, a reversal, or a touchdown, making it impossible to diagram the outcome in the same way that we could Tic-Tac-Toe. (Note also that "X and O" play diagrams that show where players will run on certain plays can be used to schematize the play of Football. But these play diagrams do not qualify as decision trees.)

What kinds of games can we turn into decision trees? Decision trees work for any game that has the following qualities:

- Time in the game takes place in turns or other discrete units.

- Players make a finite number of clear decisions that have knowable outcomes.

- The game is finite (it can't go on forever).

Although this disqualifies many games (including Football), it does include a wide variety of games, such as turn-based strategy games like Tic-Tac-Toe, which clearly fulfills all three criteria listed above. What about Chess? Chess takes place in turns and decisions have clear outcomes, but is it finite? Chess might seem like an infinite game (imagine an endgame with two kings shuffling back and forth between the same squares for-

ever), but in fact there are rules that resolve the game in a stalemate when a certain number of moves have elapsed without a capture. How about a game such as Chutes and Ladders? It seems to fit the three criteria, but it does have a random die roll. Could we map it out with a decision tree? Surprisingly, yes we could. The first point or "root" of the decision tree would have six branches coming out, depending on what the first player rolled. Each of those six branches would have six more, depending on what number the next player rolled. And so on. Of course, there would have to be a different tree for a two-player game, a three-player game, and a four-player game.

Although the decision tree for games as simple as Tic-Tac-Toe might seem large, a decision tree for a game such as Chess or Chutes and Ladders would be extraordinarily vast and complex. Remember that the decision tree contains all of the possible games that have ever or will ever be played. The decision tree for Chutes and Ladders would have to contain every possible die roll at every possible moment in the game with every possible arrangement of players on the board, in every possible sequence that could logically occur. The decision tree for Chess would have to contain every possible move and every possible response to every possible response to every possible move. The decision trees for these games would be immense. According to Poundstone, if a decision tree for Chess were graphed out on paper at a legible size, the diagram would span the solar system.

If decision trees for games are so unwieldy in the real world, how are they possibly useful for game designers? Decision trees are more theoretical constructs than engineering tools. At the same time, the ability to understand what a decision tree is and how it works is crucial to game design. Why? *Because a decision tree is also a diagram of the formal space of possibility of a game.* Being able to conceptualize the space of possibility you are designing is an important game design skill.

Even though true decision trees are usually impossible to create, often you can create very useful decision trees for sections or aspects of a game. For example, say you are designing a mission-based strategy game that contains many level "missions" that the player has to complete. A player can succeed or fail at a mission, and the next mission depends on the outcome of the most recent mission. While it might be impossible to draw a decision tree of the battle that takes place within an individual mission, it would be extremely useful to chart out the relationships between missions.

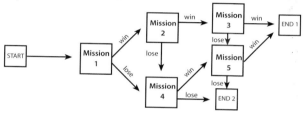

Making a decision tree of the game's missions will tell you, for example, how many missions a single player will play through in an average game. Or it will help you eliminate game designs that loop back on themselves. When you can make use of them, decision trees are a straightforward and useful way of understanding the structure of a game. Perhaps more importantly, however, decision trees are an important part of understanding game theory.

Strategies in Game Theory

Decision trees help us understand how players move through the space of possibility of a game. To see how this works, think back to the Tic-Tac-Toe decision tree. The tree contains every conceivable move, in every possible iteration of the game. This is actually more information than we need. Most players will not randomly pick their next square, but will actively try and score three in a row while keeping an opponent from doing the same. With this in mind, we can start to trim all of the "stupid move" branches from our tree. Poundstone describes what this process of "trimming" would be like:

Go through the diagram and carefully backtrack from every leaf. Each leaf is someone's last move, a move that creates a victory or a tie. For instance, at Point A, it is X's move, and there is only one empty cell. X has no choice but to fill it in and create a tie.

Now look at Point B, a move earlier in the game. It is O's turn, and he has two choices. Putting an O in one of the two open cells leads to the aforementioned Point A and a sure tie. Putting an O in the other cell, however, leads to a win for X. A rational O player prefers a tie to an X victory. Consequently, the right branch leading upward from Point B can never occur in rational play. Snip this branch from the diagram. Once the play gets to Point B, a tie is a forgone conclusion.

But look: X could have won earlier, at Point C. A rational X would have chosen an immediate win at Point C. So actually, we can snip off the entire left branch of the diagram.

Keep pruning the tree down to the root, and you will discover that ties are the only possible outcomes of rational play. (There is more than one rational way of playing, though.) The second player can and will veto any attempt at an X victory, and vice-versa.[3]

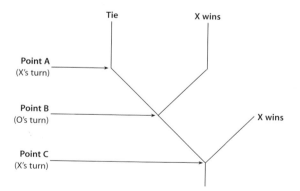

From this pruned-down version of Tic-Tac-Toe, it is possible to create what game theory calls a *strategy*. A strategy in game theory parlance offers a more precise meaning than what is commonly meant by "strategy." A common understanding of a strategy in Starcraft might be: "If you're playing the Zergs, create a lot of Zerglings at the beginning of the game and rush your opponent's central structures before they have time to build power." A strategy in this casual sense is a set of general heuristics or rules of thumb that will help guide you as you play. However, a strategy in game theory means a *complete* description of how you should act at every moment of the game. Once you select a strategy in the game theory sense of the word, you do not make any other choices, because the strategy already dictates how you should act for the rest of the game, regardless of what the other player does. This can make game theory strategies quite intricate. Poundstone lists a sample strategy for Tic-Tac-Toe for the first player X.

> Put X in the center square. O can respond two ways:
>
> 1. If O goes in a non-corner square, put X in a corner cell adjacent to O. This gives you two-in-a-row. If O fails to block on the next move, make three-in-a-row for a *win*. If O blocks, put X in the empty corner cell that is not adjacent to the first (non-corner) O. This gives you two-in-a-row two ways. No matter what O does on the next move, you can make three-in-a-row after that and *win*.
>
> 2. If instead O's first move is a corner cell, put X in one of the adjacent non-corner cells. This gives you two-in-a-row. If O fails to block on the next move, make three-in-a-row for a *win*. If O blocks, put X in the corner cell that is adjacent to the second O and on the same side of the grid as the first O. This gives you two-in-a-row. If O fails to block on the next move, make three-in-a-row for a *win*. If O blocks, put X in the empty cell adjacent to the third O. This gives you two-in-a-row. If O fails to block on the next move, make three-in-a-row for a *win*. If O blocks, fill in the remaining cell for a *tie*.[4]

As you can see, the strategy for even a simple game such as Tic-Tac-Toe is somewhat complex. A complete strategy is ultimately a methodology for navigating the branches of a decision tree. A strategy proscribes exact actions for the player utilizing the strategy, but it also has to take into account all of the possible branches that an opposing player could select. In Poundstone's example, the strategy dictates the way that the first player would move from the root of the tree to the first of nine possible points. From there the opposing player could move to any of the other eight points, a move that the strategy has to take into account.

A complete strategy for a game such as Chess would be mindbogglingly huge. However, game theory does not study games as strategically complicated as Chess. In fact, the games that game theory studies are remarkably simple. But as we already know, even very simple games can play out in quite complex ways.

Game Theory Games

Game theory demands a sacred character for rules of behavior which may not be observed in reality. The real world, with all its emotional, ethical, and social suasions, is a far more muddled skein than the Hobbesian universe of the game theorist.—**Richard Epstein,** The Theory of Gambling and Statistical Logic

Now that we have outlined decision trees and strategies, we are ready to take a look at what it is that game theory calls a game. As the mathematician Richard Epstein points out, game theory games are not about real-world situations or about all kinds of games. Game theorists look at very particular kinds of situations in a very narrow way. What kind of situations? We can summarize a game theory game in the following way: a game theory game consists of *rational players* who *simultaneously* reveal a *strategy* to arrive at an *outcome* that can be defined in a strict measure of *utility*. Usually, game theory limits itself to games with only *two players*.

Rational play, simultaneity, strategy, outcome, utility, and *two players.* Let us look at each of these elements separately. First, game theory focuses its attention on *rational players.* Rational players are perfectly logical players that know everything there is to know about a game situation. Furthermore, rational players play to win. As Poundstone puts it, "Perfectly rational players would never miss a jump in checkers or 'fall into a trap' in Chess. *All* legal sequences of moves are implicit in the rules of these games, and a perfectly logical player gives due consideration to *every* possibility."[5] As we know from our detailed investigation of Tic-Tac-Toe, if two rational players played the game, the outcome will always end in a draw, because both players would select strategies that would stalemate the other player. Rational players are a fiction, of course, as Epstein makes clear. Real-world players are not like game theory players, as rational as Mr. Spock, completely immune from "emotional, ethical, and social" liabilities. But rational players are still a useful theoretical construct, for they allow us to look at games in a very isolated and controlled way.

The fact that rational players follow a *strategy* is an important aspect of a game theory game as well. As we mentioned previously, a strategy is *comprehensive.* It is a complete plan for playing an entire game, from start to finish. A strategy includes explicit instructions for playing against any other strategy an opponent selects. In a game theory game, both rational players *simultaneously* choose and reveal their strategies to each other. In other words, instead of the "I take my turn, you take your turn" pattern of many games, in a game theory game, players only make one decision, at the same time, without knowing what the other player will do. In making a simultaneous decision, a player has to take into account not just the current state of the game, but also what the opponent is thinking at that very moment. A classic example of a simultaneous decision game is Rock-Paper-Scissors, in which both players have to decide what they are going to do based on the anticipated action of the other player.

So although game theory does not study psychology directly, there is a psychological element in game theory games, where players might consider "bluffing" or using other indirect strategies against each other. Though they might take these kinds of actions, rational players are still psychologically predictable. Players in a game theory scenario are never going to be vindictive, forgetful, self-destructive, or lazy, as this would change their status as rational players. In game theory games one can always assume that both rational players are acting in their own best interest and are developing strategies accordingly.

Why would game theory choose blind, simultaneous decision making as the game play process that it studies? Remember that game theory is not a form of game design: it is a school of economic theory. Within an economic situation, decisions have to be made without knowledge of how the other "players" are going to act. Should you sell your stock in Disney, or buy more shares? Should you purchase two gallons of milk this week, or buy one and wait to see if the price goes down? Should a nation increase or decrease import taxes? All of these micro- and macro-economic scenarios involve making decisions. But the outcome of the decision is based on factors outside the decision maker's direct control. Simultaneous, blind decisions offer a way of simulating this decision making context, a context that lies at the intersection of mathematics and psychology. As Morganstern and Von Neumann explain,

> It is possible to describe and discuss mathematically human actions in which the main emphasis lies on the psychological side. In the present case, the psychological element was brought in by the necessity of analyzing decisions, the information on the basis of which they are taken, and the interrelatedness of such sets of information (at the various moves) with each other.[6]

Another important component of a game theory game is *utility,* which is a mathematical measure of player satisfaction. In order to make a formal theory of decision making, it was necessary that Von Neumann and Morganstern numerically quantify the desire of a player to achieve a certain outcome. In a game theory game, for every kind of outcome that a decision might have, a utility is assigned to that decision.

> A utility function is simply a "quantification" of a person's preferences with respect to certain objects. Suppose I am concerned with three pieces of fruit: an orange, an apple, and a pear. The utility function first associates with each piece of fruit a number that reflects its attractiveness. If the pear was desired most and the apple least, the utility of the pear would be greatest and the apple's utility would be least.[7]

Utility can become more complex when multiple factors come into play. For example, if you were building a house for yourself on beachfront property, thinking in game theory terms, you could measure different locations of your house in terms of utility. You might be able to get the highest utility, say +10, if you built right on the beach. There might be a lower utility, such as +5 or +2, if you had to build it several meters away from the shoreline.

On the other hand, if you had to build the house so far away from the beach that the ocean was no longer in view, your utility might go into the negative numbers, indicating an outcome that you would find unpleasant. Of course, you might not have the money to afford the situation with the highest utility. For example, you might require a house of a certain size and if it were directly on the beach it couldn't have a basement and would have to be smaller. Or the cost of the house might be higher on the beach because of the extra architectural complexity required to build in the sand. Cost, size, and location would all be assigned different values. In making your decision, you would try and maximize the total utility given your available options.

These examples touch on the ways that game theory employs the concept of utility. It might seem silly to turn something like human satisfaction into a numerical value, given the innumerable complexities that go into our feelings of pleasure, but

Morganstern and Von Neumann felt very strongly that a scientific theory of economics necessitated such an approach. In their book, they use an analogy to physical properties such as heat. Before scientists developed a way of conceptualizing and measuring heat, it was an unknown, fuzzy property that seemed impossible to measure: a sensation that occurred as one approached a flame. But the precise measurement of heat is now an important part of contemporary physics. The aim of Von Neumann and Morganstern was to begin a similar revolution in economics, by quantifying pleasure as a measure of utility.

Utility may well be an oversimplification of human desire, but it does make a good fit with the formal qualities of games. As we know from our definition of games, all games have a *quantifiable outcome:* someone wins, or loses, everyone wins or loses, or player performance is measured in points, time, or some other numerical value. The concept of assigning a numerical utility to decision outcomes is really just another way of creating a quantifiable outcome. When looking at games through a formal frame, we do not have the luxury of being non-numerical. The formal systems of both digital and non-digital games require an exactness that does in fact come down to numbers. How many kills did you earn that round? What qualifying time do you need on the next heat in order to continue the race? Which team won the game? These very simple game results are all quantifiable outcomes, and are all examples of utility as well.

The last component of most game theory games is that they are usually played by only two players. This was not part of the original formulation of game theory as proposed in *Theory of Games and Economic Behavior.* The original idea was that the theory could cover n-player games, where n was a number of any size that indicated the number of players. But Von Neumann and Morganstern found that, as with the problem of three planetary bodies discussed in **Games as Emergent Systems,** their theory became vastly more complex when it took three or more players into account. As a result, most game theory work has focused on two player games. We follow suit in the material to follow.

Cake Division

It is finally time to take a look at a real game theory game. The following description is taken from *Prisoner's Dilemma* and is the classic "cake division" game theory problem:

> Most people have heard of the reputed best way to let two bratty children split a piece of cake. No matter how carefully a parent divides it, one child (or both!) feels he has been slighted with the smaller piece. The solution is to let one child divide the cake and let the other choose which piece he wants. Greed ensures fair division. The first child can't object that the cake was divided unevenly because he did it himself. The second child can't complain since he has his choice of pieces….
>
> The cake problem is a conflict of interests. Both children want the same thing—as much of the cake as possible. The ultimate decision of the cake depends both on how one child cuts the cake and which piece the other child chooses. It is important that each child anticipates what the other will do. This is what makes the situation a game in Von Neumann's sense.
>
> Game theory searches for *solutions*—rational outcomes—of games. Dividing the cake evenly is the best strategy for the first child, since he anticipates that the other child's strategy will be to take the biggest piece. Equal division of the cake is therefore the solution to this game. The solution does not depend on a child's generosity or sense of fair play. It is enforced by both children's self interest. Game theory seeks solutions precisely of this sort.[8]

The cake division problem contains all of the elements of a game theory "game" listed earlier. There are two *rational players* (the children motivated by self interest). These two players choose a *strategy* about how to behave (how to cut or select the pieces). These strategies result in some kind of *utility* for the two players, measured in how much cake they get. Note that even though the "play" of this very simple game consists of a two-part action (first slice the cake and then choose a slice),

the two players can still reveal and enact their strategies simultaneously. For example, the strategy of the player that chooses from the two pieces is always going to be "take the bigger piece." A rational piece-choosing player is going to choose this strategy regardless of the strategy that the cake-cutting player takes. (Note that although these "strategies" may seem like forgone conclusions rather than choices, this is because this game theory game has a *saddle point,* a concept explained in detail later on.)

A powerful analytical tool provided by game theory is to map this decision making process into a grid. One axis of the grid represents one player's decision. The other axis represents the other player's decision. The cells in the grid represent the outcomes reached depending on which decisions were made. A game theory table of this sort is called a *payoff matrix* (payoff being another term for utility). Figure 1 shows a payoff matrix for the cake division problem, taken from *Prisoner's Dilemma*. Note that William Poundstone makes the assumption that the cake slicing is going to happen in an imperfect world, so that even if the child that cuts the cake tries to slice it evenly, the two resulting slices will still differ a tiny bit, say by one crumb.

Along the left side of the matrix are strategies that the cutter can take: either cut the cake evenly or cut it unevenly. Although there are any number of ways to cut the cake, these are the two essential strategies from which the cutter can choose. Across the top of the matrix are strategies the chooser can take: choose the bigger piece or choose the smaller piece. The cells show the utility or payoff for only one of the players (the cutter), but it can be assumed that the inverse payoff would happen for the chooser. If the payoff matrix indicates that the cutter receives the "small piece," the chooser would therefore receive the "big piece." This is also true for half of the cake plus or minus a crumb.

Figure 1: Cake Division payoff grid

Chooser's Strategies

	Choose bigger piece	Choose smaller piece
Cut cake as evenly as possible	Half the cake minus a crumb	Half the cake plus a crumb
Make one piece bigger than the other	Small piece	Big piece

Cutter's Strategies

The cake division problem illustrates two important game theory concepts. The first is the concept of a *zero-sum game*. In a zero-sum game, the utilities of the two players for each game outcome are the inverse of each other. In other words, for every gain by one player, the other player suffers an equal loss. For example, playing a version of Poker in which everyone puts money into a pot is a zero-sum game. At the end of the game, every dollar won by one player is a dollar lost by another player. A group of gamblers playing Roulette is not a zero-sum game between the players, because they are not playing directly against each other. On the other hand, if we frame Roulette so that one player is playing against the casino, then it is a zero-sum situation: if a player wins a dollar, it is taken from the house, and vice-versa.

Many games are zero-sum games, even those that do not involve money. When one player wins a game of Checkers and the other player loses, the loss by one player equals a gain for the other player. In this case, game theory would assign a utility of −1 for the loss and +1 for the gain. The utilities add up to zero, which is exactly why it is called a "zero-sum" game. Some games, such as the cooperative board game Lord of the Rings, are not zero sum games. In the basic version of Lord of the Rings, players cooperate against the game system itself. Players

either all lose, or they all win. Because the players are not competing against each other, they either all get a −1 for losing or all get a +1 for winning. The losses and wins among the players do not add up to zero; it is therefore not a zero-sum game.

Not all game theory games are zero-sum games, but many are. Cake division is clearly a zero-sum game. Consider the problem intuitively: there is only so much cake, which is all going to be divided into two slices and eaten. The more cake that one player eats, the less the other player eats. We could assign the following utilities to the four cells of the diagram:

-1	+1
-10	+10

We know that the two player outcomes are inverses of each other. If one player receives half of the cake minus a crumb (-1) the other player will receive half of the cake plus a crumb (+1). The total is zero. Cake division is a zero-sum game.

Why is this important? Because, according to game theory, every finite, zero-sum, two-player game has a *solution* (a proper way to play the game), the strategy that any rational player would take. What is the solution to the cake division problem? The game will always end in the upper left corner. The cutter will get half of the cake minus a crumb and the chooser will get half of the cake plus a crumb. Why is this so? Look at the cutter's strategies. The cutter would love to end up with the lower right cell, where he gets the big piece. So perhaps he should choose the strategy of cutting the pieces unequally. But the cutter also knows that if the chooser is given the chance to choose, the chooser will always choose the bigger piece. As a result, the cutter has to minimize the bigger piece that the chooser will select by cutting the cake as evenly as possible. The game resolves to the upper left corner.

This situation clearly illustrates another key game theory concept: the *saddle point* property of payoff grids. In cake division, each player is trying to maximize his own gains while minimizing the gains of the other player. When the choices of both players lead to the same cell, the result is what Von Neumann and Morganstern call a saddle point. A saddle point refers to a saddle-shaped mountain pass, the intersection of a valley that goes between two adjacent mountains. The height of the pass is both the minimum elevation that a traveler going across the two mountains will reach, as well as the maximum elevation that a valley traveler crossing the mountain pass will achieve. The mathematical proof of saddle points in games is called the *minimax theorem,* which Von Neumann first published in 1928, many years before the 1944 publication of *Theory of Games and Economic Behavior.*

The concept of saddle points is extremely important in game design. In general, you want to avoid them like the plague. Remember, a saddle point is an optimal solution to a game. Once a player finds it, there is no other reason to do anything else. Think about the cake division saddle point: if either player deviates, that player will lose even more cake. If you think of the space of possibility that you are crafting as a large 3D structure carefully crafted to give a certain shape to the experience of your players, saddle points are short-circuits in the structure that allow players to make the same decision over and over. That kind of play experience does not usually provide very meaningful play. Why? Because if there is always a knowable saddle point solution to a game, a best action regardless of what other players do or what state the system is in, the game loses the uncertainty of possible action. Meaningful play then goes out the window.

Saddle points do not just occur in game theory games. Many fighting games are ruined, for example, because despite all of the special moves and combinations that are designed into the game, the best strategy to use against opponents is simply to use the same powerful attack again and again and again. Saddle point! Another common occurrence of saddle points involves the programming of computer opponents. In many real-time strategy games there are "holes" or weaknesses in the AI that allow for saddle points. If a player discovers that the computer opponent does not know how to defend well against a certain type of unit, he is likely to abandon all other game strategies and simply hammer on the AI's weakness over and over, regardless of how much care went into carefully designing missions that require different kinds of problem-solving. Saddle point!

This style of play, based on exploiting a strategic saddle point, is called an *exploit* or *degenerate strategy.* A degenerate strategy is a way of playing a game that ensures victory every time. The negative connotation of the terms "exploit" and "degenerate" imply that players are consciously eschewing the designed experience in favor of the shortest route to victory. There are some players that will refuse to make use of degenerate strategies, even after they find out about them, because they wish to play the game in a "proper" manner. On the other hand, many players will not hesitate to employ a degenerate strategy, especially if their winnings are displayed in a larger social space outside the game, such as an online high score list.

Degenerate strategies can be painful for game designers, as players shortcut all of the attention lavished on a game's rich set of possibilities. Try to find degenerate strategies and get rid of them! We learned in the previous schema that positive and negative feedback systems can emerge unexpectedly from within a game's structure and can ruin a game experience for players. The same is true of degenerate strategies. A close analysis of your game design can sometimes reveal them but the only real way to root them out is through rigorous playtesting. If you see players drawn to a particular set of strategies again and again, they may be exploiting a weakness in your design.

Playing for Pennies

Not all game theory games have a saddle point. Consider a simple game that requires a more complex playing strategy: Matching Pennies, another classic game theory problem. Here is how the game works: two players each have a penny. Hiding their penny from view, both players pick a side, heads up or heads down, and then simultaneously reveal their pennies. If they match, Player 1 gets both pennies. If they don't match, Player 2 gets them. We can graph this game on a payoff grid :

Player 1's choices

	Heads	Tails
Tails	−1 cent	1 cent
Heads	1 cent	−1 cent

(Player 2's choices)

This table shows the outcomes for Player 1, the player that wins if the pennies match. Because this is another zero-sum game, the utility for Player 2 is the inverse of Player 1's payoff. What is the proper way to play this game? What strategy should a rational player choose: heads or tails? There does not seem to be a single best answer to the question. If one player decided to pick heads or tails as a permanent strategy, the other player could take advantage of this strategy and win every time. But Matching Pennies is a finite, zero-sum, two-player game, and game theory should be able to solve this game and provide the proper strategy for two rational players. The solution turns out to be more complex than the cake division problem: players do not choose a single, fixed strategy, but select a mixed strategy. In a *mixed strategy,* players choose one of their options accord-

ing to a certain probability ratio. For Matching Pennies, the mixed strategy requires rational players to randomly pick heads or tails, with a 50/50 chance of selecting either one.

Remember that rational players will attempt to maximize their own gains in utility while minimizing the gains of their opponents. If rational players play many, many games of Matching Pennies, they will end up with an average utility of zero. This means that neither player will ever come out ahead, but that is the best that they can hope for in this "game."

The Prisoner's Dilemma

Of course, it is possible to construct payoff grids in many different ways, and they do not always have to be zero-sum. In fact, constructing game theory problems that are intentionally less symmetrical than Mixed Pennies and Cake Division can lead to some very perplexing "games." One famous game theory problem is called the Prisoner's Dilemma. It is from this problem that William Poundstone takes the title of his book. He describes the "story" behind this game as follows:

> Two members of a criminal gang are arrested and imprisoned. Each prisoner is in solitary confinement with no means of speaking to or exchanging messages with the other. The police admit they don't have enough evidence to convict the pair on the principal charge. They plan to sentence both to a year in prison on a lesser charge. Simultaneously, the police offer each prisoner a Faustian bargain. If he testifies against his partner, he will go free while the partner will get three years in prison on the main charge. Oh yes, there is a catch. . . . If *both* prisoners testify against each other, both will be sentenced to two years in jail.

> The prisoners are given a little time to think this over, but in no case may either learn what the other has decided until he has irrevocably made his decision. Each is informed that the other prisoner is being offered the very same deal. Each prisoner is only concerned with his own welfare—with minimizing his own prison sentence.[9]

	B refuses deal	B turns state's evidence
A refuses deal	1 year, 1 year	3 years, 0 years
A turns state's evidence	0 years, 3 years	2 years, 2 years

The payoff grid shows the utilities for both prisoners, listing Prisoner A first and Prisoner B second. For ease of use, the utilities are displayed as years of jail time rather than as positive and negative utility values.

Look closely at this situation. First of all, is it a game in the game theory sense? Yes, it is: there are two rational players who are only interested in their own welfare (and not in abstract concepts such as cooperation or loyalty), both players have to choose a strategy simultaneously, and each possible outcome of their decision is measured in discrete numbers—in this case, in terms of years of jail time. Because the two prisoners want to minimize their sentence, they desire the lowest possible number.

Next question: Is Prisoner's Dilemma a zero-sum game? The answer is no. Look at the upper left and lower right cells. With these outcomes, both "players" in our game do not have inverse outcomes. The gains of one player are not equal to the losses of another player in every case, so the game is not a zero-sum problem.

Now think about what each prisoner might decide to do in this situation. First of all, it seems like it is better to turn state's evidence, to "defect" rather than "cooperate" with the other prisoner. If the other player cooperates, then the defector receives the best possible outcome, which is to receive no jail time at all. But both players are rational and will be thinking the same thing, which means both prisoners will "defect" and turn state's evidence. This means that both of them will receive two years. But if they both cooperated, they could have received only one year each!

Game theorists do not agree on the proper solution to the Prisoner's Dilemma. There are two ways of thinking about this problem. Using a minimax approach, it is clear that it is always better to defect, no matter what the other prisoner does. If you defect and the other prisoner does not, you get the best possible outcome. But if the other prisoner decides to defect, then it is a good thing you did too, because you saved yourself from the worst possible outcome. According to this logic, both players will defect and the rational outcome is the lower right cell of the payoff grid. The other approach is to say that because both players are rational and because the payoff grid is symmetrical, both players will make the same choice. This means that the two players are choosing between the upper left and the lower right cells. Given this choice, two rational players will end up choosing the better of their two options, the upper left, where they receive only one year of jail time.

The Prisoner's Dilemma remains an unsolved game theory problem. It clearly demonstrates that even very simple sets of rules can provide incredibly complex decision-making contexts, which raise questions not just about mathematics and game design, but about society and ethics as well.

Game Theory and Game Design

Game theory is a curious thing. It promises to be a detailed theory of decision making in a game context. At the same time, its relationship to real-world games seems incidental: the "games" that game theory studies are far removed from the kinds of games that most game designers would like to create.

Does that mean that game theory is irrelevant to game design? Absolutely not. This schema on *Games as Game Theory Systems,* like most of our other RULES-based schema, borrows concepts and theories from disciplines that make a formal study of systems. Like systems theory, complexity theory, information theory, and cybernetics, game theory was not created in order to assist in the game design process. But that doesn't mean that it isn't relevant to designers.

Decision trees that mark out a game's formal space of possibility; utility that measures the desire of a player for a given game outcome; saddle points that erase meaningful play—game theory is rife with connections to some of our core design concepts. Game theory games are microcosms for game design problems, an opportunity to plot out a simple decision in great detail and appreciate the complexity that even elementary moments of choice can generate. Game theory, as a formal approach to understanding decisions, is an extremely useful game design tool.

The rules of games constitute systems of incredible subtlety and complexity. As a design discipline with a very young history, game design must turn to these more established ways of thinking in order to try and make sense of the phenomena of games. Perhaps as the field matures, the theoretical borrowings that take place in this book will be replaced by more game-centric schools of thought. At least, we certainly hope so.

Further Reading

Emergence: From Chaos to Order, by John Holland *(see page 169)*

> *Recommended:*
>
> Chapter 2: Games and Numbers
>
> Chapter 3: Maps, Game Theory, and Computer-Based Modeling

Prisoner's Dilemma, by William Poundstone

Prisoner's Dilemma combines a biography of John Von Neumann with an analysis of Cold War politics and a detailed explanation of game theory. It is the clearest non-technical book on game theory we have found, with a range of detailed examples. Taken as a whole, *Prisoner's Dilemma* helps put game theory in its proper historical and cultural context.

> *Recommended:*
>
> Chapter 3: Game Theory
>
> Chapter 6: Prisoner's Dilemma
>
> Chapter 12: Survival of the Fittest

Notes

1. Morton D. Davis, *Game Theory: A Nontechnical Introduction* (Mineola: Dover Publications, 1970), p. 3.
2. William Poundstone, *Prisoner's Dilemma* (New York: Doubleday, 1992), p. 45.
3. Ibid. p. 46.
4. Ibid. p. 48.
5. Richard Epstein, *The Theory of Gambling and Statistical Logic* (San Diego: Academic Press, 1995), p. 118.
6. John Von Neumann and Oscar Morganstern, *Theory of Games and Economic Behavior* (Princeton: Princeton University Press, 1944), p. 77.
7. Davis, *Game Theory: A Nontechnical Introduction,* p. 62.
8. Poundstone, *Prisoner's Dilemma,* p. 43.
9. Ibid. p. 118.

Games as Game Theory Systems

SUMMARY

- **Game theory** is a branch of economics that studies rational decision making. It often looks at game-like situations, but it is not a general theory of games or game design.

- A **decision tree** is a diagram that maps out all of the possible decisions and outcomes that a player can take in a game. A completed decision tree is equivalent to the formal space of possibility of a game. A game must have the following characteristics to be reducible to a decision tree:

    - Time in the game takes place in turns or other discrete units.

    - Players make a finite number of clear decisions that have knowable outcomes.

    - The game is finite (it can't go on forever).

    Even if a game meets these criteria, most games are too complex to be diagrammed as a decision tree. Decision trees are most useful for mapping aspects of games, or as conceptual tools for thinking about the formal structure of a game.

- A game theory game is limited to **rational players** who **simultaneously** reveal a **strategy** to arrive at an **outcome,** which can be defined in a strict measure of **utility.** Usually, game theory limits itself to games with only two players.

    - A **rational player** doesn't exist in the real world. A rational player is a completely logical player that plays only to maximize winnings, regardless of emotions, ethics, and social attachments.

    - A game theory **strategy** is a complete plan for playing a game. A strategy explicitly and comprehensively covers every possible situation that a player might encounter in the course of playing a game, including every possible strategy that an opponent might select.

    - In a game theory game, rational players make a **simultaneous decision** about what strategy to take. They know the complete rules of the game and the possible outcomes of their decisions, but they do not know the strategy that the other player will take.

    - The results of a game theory game are measured in **utility,** which is a numerical representation of the players' desire for a certain outcome. Attractive outcomes are assigned higher positive numbers, and less attractive outcomes are assigned lower numbers. Negative numbers represent an unpleasant utility.

· A **payoff matrix** is a grid of cells used to diagram the possible outcomes of a game theory problem.

· In a **zero-sum** game, the winnings of the victor are equal to the losses of the loser. Games such as Chess with a single winner and a single loser are zero-sum games.

· Every two-player, zero-sum game theory game has a **solution,** a proper way to play the game that will maximize winnings for the player every time. When there is a single best solution to a game for both players, the solution is known as a **saddle point.**

· Saddle points in any game can lead to **degenerate strategies,** also called **exploits.** A degenerate strategy is a way to play a game that leads to victory every time. Generally, degenerate strategies are to be avoided in games because they diminish uncertainty and meaningful play.

· Some game theory solutions consist of **mixed strategies,** where players select among different strategies with a weighted percentage.

Unit 2: **Rules**

GAMES AS SYSTEMS OF CONFLICT

competition and cooperation
systemic cooperation
player cooperation
game goals
victory and loss conditions
level playing field

20

Conflict arises naturally from the interaction in a game. The player is actively pursuing some goal. Obstacles prevent him from easily achieving this goal. Conflict is an intrinsic element of all games. It can be direct or indirect, violent or nonviolent, but it is always present in every game.—**Chris Crawford,** *The Art of Computer Game Design*

Introducing Conflict

What does it mean to consider games as *Systems of Conflict?* First of all, we agree with Chris Crawford. Conflict is an intrinsic element of every game. Conflict, a game as a contest of powers, is a core component of our very definition of the term "game." While conflict outside of games can sometimes be destructive, in games we find the wonderful paradox of a *staged* conflict, resulting in meaningful play.

Game conflict emerges from the unique circumstances of a game. The magic circle imbues games with special meanings. One of the most important meanings to emerge is the game's victory conditions. Winning the game might only have value within the magic circle, yet players pursue it. By virtue of their participation in the game, they have taken on as *meaningful* the game's presumptions and proscriptions, including everything associated with winning. The struggle among the players to achieve the goal of a game and become winners is the competitive activity that drives a game's system of conflict.

The fact that this activity is a *struggle* derives from the intrinsic challenge presented by the conflict of a game. As we know from our study of the lusory attitude, games are constructed so that their goals are difficult to achieve. The conflict of a game arises as the game players struggle toward achieving the goal, often in opposition to each other, sometimes struggling together or in parallel.

What are the shapes of conflict that occur in games? Struggle in a game can take many forms:

- *Single player vs. single player:* a Chess game or Boxing match

- *Group vs group:* Basketball, Soccer, and other team sports

- *One against many:* Tag or Mother May I?

- *Every player for themselves:* a footrace or the strategic board game Risk

- *Single player competing against a game system:* Solitaire or Tetris

- *Individual players competing side by side against the game:* casino Blackjack

- *A group of players cooperating against a game:* Lord of the Rings Board Game

Many games mix and match these forms, such as a wrestling meet, in which individuals compete against each other in pairs, but their scores are added up and applied to the team as a whole. Some games can accommodate more than one of these game modes, such as the arcade game Double Dragon, in which one player can compete against the program, or two players can cooperate against it. Still others have competitive structures that change over time, such as the television show *Survivor*, in which players are initially divided into two competitive teams, eventually becoming a single group from which a single winner emerges.

Conflict in a game can be direct or indirect. In an arm wrestling match, players are pitted directly against each other, trying to pin the other player's arm while avoiding being pinned themselves. The back and forth movements of the players' locked hands is a direct meter of the struggle, indicating how near or how far either one of them is from achieving the winning conditions of the conflict. In a figure skating contest, the conflict is indirect. Competitors each have their own turn to perform and be judged. They cannot directly interfere with each other's success, and winning the competition means receiving the highest score from the judges.

Still other games mix direct and indirect conflict. In a real-time strategy game such as multiplayer Starcraft, players compete against each other, though they are not always directly interacting. Players have to think offensively and defensively, building their resources and defenses, anticipating the actions of other players. As a game proceeds, the solo activities of each player evolve into direct conflict, as the units controlled by the players come into contact. Further, there is more than one way to configure the conflict in Starcraft: the game lets players set up team vs. team games, one player vs. many players, human players vs. computer opponents, and so on.

Conflict Case Studies

As these examples illustrate, more than one form of conflict can exist within the scope of a single game design. Next we take a detailed look at three different games, focusing on the ways each one configures competition and cooperation between players. All three games are arcade games from the 1980s: Centipede, Joust, and Gauntlet. Each game weaves its own surprisingly complex fabric of player conflict.

Centipede

Our first example is the arcade game Centipede, in which the player uses a trackball controller and fire button to move a character at the bottom of the screen and shoot at objects coming down from the top. Centipede might seem at first glance to have a simple and straightforward structure of conflict. But in fact, the formal system provides many ways for players to struggle and pursue goals.

- As a single-player experience, you compete against the program. The game compiles an ongoing "score" based on your performance, and the presumed goal of the game is to achieve the highest score.

- There are many ways that you might pursue goals related to the high score goal of the game. You might have a general idea of what constitutes a "good score," which you try to achieve. Or you might try to surpass your previous game's score, or attain a new personal best score.

- You might set other goals besides those involving your score. For example, you might try to play for a certain amount of time, get to a certain level in the game, or destroy every enemy of a particular type that appears. Several of these goals might co-exist with each other and with the score-oriented goals.

- Centipede can be played as a two-player game. Both players alternate play, switching places when the current player loses a life. If you compete against another player in this way, the quantifiable outcome of the game (your score) has new meaning. It is no longer only an indicator of your personal success but becomes a way to compare your performance to that of the other player. Two-player Centipede is a zero-sum competition, where one player wins and the other player loses. In this sense, the actual game scores are important only insofar as they are used to determine the winner. The numeric scores of the players are translated into binary win/lose values.

- Aspects of the single-player competition can be combined with aspects of the two-player competition. You might have lost to your opponent, but you might also have gotten your best score ever, in which case you won in your own self-competition, even while losing to the other player in the zero-sum conflict of the two-player game.

- The fact that players can enter their initials into a high score list creates a different kind of competition: you compete against previous players, whom you probably have never met. This competition is more indirect: you compare your score with their scores, and if you are one of the top eight players, you get to enter your initials into the game for other players to see, bumping off the player at the bottom of the list. However, you might later be bumped off as well. Here, your numeric score is translated into a scaled rank: either your score wasn't high enough to put you on the list, or you entered the list at a specific rank.

- There are other competition scenarios as well. For example, you might play as a single player and set the goal of making it onto the high score list. In this case, you turn the game into a system of competition with a binary win/loss condition: either you make it onto the high score list or you don't.

• You might have an ongoing rivalry with a friend about who can achieve the higher score on Centipede. The two of you are not good enough to get on the high score list, but you can still keep track of your relative scores. Your score in this scenario is translated into a rank between you and your friend, a rank that changes as one of you bests the other's higher score.

Joust

Who knew so many different forms of conflict were lurking under the surface of a simple arcade game? Our next example adds even more. In Joust, two players maneuver bird-mounted knights, attacking enemies controlled by the program. Both players can play the game simultaneously, instead of alternating turns. This structure opens up whole new forms of competition.

• Joust can be a single-player game. Individual players receive a score and there is a list of player high scores, including separate rankings for daily high scores and "all time" high scores. Most of the forms of competition in Centipede also occur in Joust.

• Two players could compete to see who gains the higher score over the course of a game. Because players do not alternate turns but compete simultaneously, the scores of both players are visible at all times, heightening the drama of this form of competition.

• The simultaneous two-player structure opens other possibilities for conflict. Two Joust players can attack each other if they wish. One way to play the game is as a fighting game, where players directly attack each other, killing their opponent with a successful attack. The goal of the competition in this case is to kill your opponent more times than you are killed. Playing the game in this way turns Joust into a zero-sum game. Numerical scores do not matter, only who is left alive at the end.

Joust

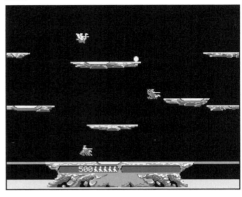

• It is also possible for two players to refrain from attacking each other and instead work together to defeat the computer-generated enemies, strategically coordinating their actions. In this case, the two players compete together against the computer. They might set a goal of reaching the highest level or for playing as long as possible.

• Even if players cooperate, they might still compete in other ways. For example, two players coordinating their actions against the computer might compete to get the higher score.

• Often, these different kinds of competition overlap. The game design of Joust makes it easy for a player to kill another player: if they collide, the one that is in a higher position destroys the other one. Even cooperating players sometimes accidentally kill each other, an event that usually affects the competitive flow of the game. After an accidental killing, one player might become resentful and aggressive and the game might transition into the "fighting game" version of Joust. Or the accidental killer might let his opponent kill him one time, just to balance things out. The game might also just continue as usual.

- Competitive tensions persist throughout the game. Because both players are operating on the screen at the same time, there may be competition about where and how they should play, even if they are not actively trying to kill each other. For example, two players might both wish to occupy a certain section of the screen or attack a specific group of enemy characters. An accidental player-killing (or the threat of one) can enter the game as a result, opening up additional competitive complexities.

Gauntlet

In Joust, the two-player simultaneous structure adds new layers to the possibilities of game conflict. In Gauntlet, our third arcade game example, up to four players can play at once. The players take fixed roles (Warrior, Valkerie, Thief, or Wizard) as members of a team. Together the team explores the game spaces, fights computer-generated enemies, and gathers resources that boost their abilities to let them explore further.

- Like Joust and Centipede, Gauntlet can be played by a single player. Gauntlet players also receive a score; if the score is high enough, players record high scores and player initials. All of the single-player and high score list forms of competition apply to Gauntlet as well.

- Unlike Joust, Gauntlet players can only attack computer-generated opponents—their attacks do not affect the other players. As a result, Gauntlet lacks the "fighting game" as a possible form of conflict. Instead, the players consistently work together, usually with the goal of seeing how many levels of the game they can explore.

- Because Gauntlet players receive a score, players might also compete to see who has the highest score at the end of the game. As with Joust, the scores are displayed throughout the game, allowing players to constantly check their relative scores.

- Whenever players clear a level of the game, the game pauses to display the relative points of each player and

Gauntlet

their overall performance in the game, showing, for example, which player received the most treasure in the last level. These moments highlight score-based and stat-based competition between players, encouraging them to compare their performances against each other and invent competition around the many kinds of statistics in the game.

- During the actual play of a game, another form of competition takes place over in-game resources. As players progress in the game, a number representing their health is slowly reduced. When a character touches an enemy, health is lowered even more. However, there are many "food" items scattered throughout the game that raise a character's health. Players sometimes compete directly for food, trying to be first to reach the item. Players might also discuss who among them needs the food most and let that player acquire the item. The same is true for other special objects in the game, such as keys and magic potions. These forms of resource-based competition are heightened by the statistic comparisons between levels: at these moments, players take stock of how resources have been distributed among the group and can accuse each other of being "unfair" or "greedy."

- A final form of competition unique to Gauntlet involves players spending money on a game. In many arcade games, prestige comes from being able to play for a long time on a single quarter. But unlike Joust and Centipede, Gauntlet lets players extend their current game via cash additions. Players can put quarters into the game during play to add to their characters' health or to resurrect their characters after they have died. This means that as long as players want to continue spending money, they can keep on playing, exploring more game levels. The escalating difficulty of the game ensures that players will need to spend more and more money as they play. This can turn Gauntlet into a completely different kind of conflict, one in which players compete to demonstrate their tolerance for putting money into the game, a form of conspicuous consumption much like high-stakes gambling. Conversely, players might compete to see who can play the longest before having to spend more money to continue, because skillful players will avoid being killed. In this case, spending less money for the same amount of time would be the goal.

There are obviously many, many more models of competition in games. However, even within these three similar examples there is a wealth of ways that conflict can manifest. The point of these examples is to demonstrate how the design of a game leads to forms of conflict. In each case, formal decisions about the game's structure directly shape the nature of conflict emerging from the game. For each game, the following kinds of questions determine the essential formal structures:

- How many players can play?

- Do they play simultaneously or do they alternate playing the game?

- Is there a high score list?

- Are players given constant feedback about their relative scores?

- Does the game pause to allow players to directly compare their scores and other game statistics?

- Are there computer-generated opponents and obstacles that players face together or do the players serve as opponents for each other?

- Does the structure of the game allow players to have direct conflict with each other?

- Are there resources for which players can compete?

- Can players spend money to continue the game or enhance their play?

The forms of conflict we observed follow directly from the way that each game answers these design questions. Take Gauntlet: if players were allowed to damage each other through attacks, the game would lose its enforced cooperative spirit, and inter-player fighting might become common. If players could not continue their game by paying another quarter, competition for in-game resources would be much fiercer, as players would vie against each other to stay alive until the game ended. What is surprising in all three examples is just how rich and multi-layered conflict can be in a game. This richness comes from the fact that players can derive and construct their own forms of conflict in a game. Some of the goals we outlined are explicitly defined by the game rules. Others are emergent forms of competition that arise from the player's active engagement with and manipulation of the game structure.

Back in *Defining Games,* in discussing whether or not Sim City was a game, we concluded that it was a borderline case. Although Sim City does not formally define goals with quantitative outcomes, it does provide a space within which players form their own goals and arrive at their own outcomes. As the investigation of Centipede, Joust, and Gauntlet demonstrates, in many ways all games can function like Sim City, with players inventing their own goals and layering these goals on top of those defined directly by the rules of a game.

A game's space of possibility is a space of possible conflict. Part of playing a game involves selecting game goals as a means of navigating and exploring forms and degrees of conflict. What is the best form of conflict to provide your players? As with other aspects of games, there is no single formula that will work best for all players in all contexts. However, providing a rich space of possibility that supports a range of conflict increases the potential variety of players and the ways that they might find your game meaningful.

Competition and Cooperation

So far, we have spoken somewhat loosely about competition and cooperation as they relate to the conflict in a game. But what do these terms really mean? Competition occurs when players struggle against each other within the artificial conflict of a game. Perhaps our clearest model of competition comes from game theory: the zero-sum game. In a zero-sum game, one player's winnings equal another player's losses. If one player is the victor in a two-player zero-sum game, the other player will necessarily lose. Winning is always equally balanced by losing, making the end sum zero.

A common criticism leveled against games is that they are all competitive, and that competition is somehow undesirable. Framed in this way, competition is something to avoid in order to ensure a positive play experience. Bernard DeKoven, game designer and author of *The Well-Played Game,* states this position eloquently:

> It is clear to me now, that the result of such a union [playing to win] is separation, always separation. It divides us into winners and losers, those who have achieved and those who have failed. The division then leads us into further division. It becomes difficult, now that some of us have won and some of us have lost, to find a game that we are all willing to play well together. It was never our focus at all. Though what we have always cherished most is the game in which we are playing well together, winning takes precedence.[1]

DeKoven's point is that when the winning and losing of competition enters into the conflict of a game, it becomes the paramount concern of the game's participants, eclipsing everything else the game has to offer. With all due respect, we disagree. It seems quite clear to us that competitive games can offer genuinely meaningful experiences. Sometimes that meaning can stem from the joy of play itself (DeKoven's "playing well together"), but certainly much meaning derives from the competitive struggle of a game, from trying to become a winner while avoiding a loss.

The competitive striving toward a goal is fundamental in giving shape to the structure of a game and the way that the game creates meaning. The idea, for example, that in meaningful play a player's actions are *integrated* into the larger context of a game is dependent on the competitive nature of games. Without a goal toward which players strive, it is very difficult for a player to measure his or her progress through the system of a game. Without a measure of progress to give a player feedback on the meaning of his or her decisions, meaningful play is not possible. Remember the "horrible" game The Grid in *Games as Emergent Systems*? That game had no goal, and no way for players to compete with each other. There was nothing to motivate players to move their pieces *this* way instead of *that* way. Meaningful play was impossible.

Our opinion is that all games are competitive. All games involve a conflict, whether that conflict occurs directly between players or whether players work together against the challenging activity presented by the game system. Without a clearly defined goal, games generally become less formalized play activities. However, just because all games are competitive does not mean that they are not cooperative as well. Although we can assert with confidence that *all games are competitive,* it is equally true that *all games are cooperative.* Are these two statements contradictory? Can all games be both competitive and cooperative? The idea that games are both competitive and cooperative is only contradictory if the two terms are mutually exclusive, which they are not. The root of the word "compete" is the Latin *con petire,* which means "to seek together."[2]

In what ways are all games cooperative? Recall the magic circle and the lusory attitude, and the way that these aspects of a game create meaning. To play a game is to submit your behavior to the rules of the game, to enter into the time and space that the game demarcates, to traffic in the special meanings that the game offers up. To play a game is to participate in the discourse of the game with the other players. Players can play Basketball together because they both speak the "language" of Basketball. When two players hit the courts for a game of one-on-one, that is exactly what they are doing.

Therefore, to play a game is to cooperatively take on the artificial meanings of the game, to communicate to the other players through the artificial discourse that the game makes possible.

Terminological Aside: Two Forms of Cooperation

We use the term "cooperation" here in a slightly different way than at the beginning of this chapter. Saying that all games are cooperative refers to the mechanisms that underlie all games, and the way these structures ensure a shared discourse and cooperative spirit among players. We call this form of cooperation *systemic cooperation* because it occurs in all games at a fundamental level.

However, when we said that the Lord of the Rings Board Game, in which players work together to defeat the game system, was cooperative, we used the word in its more common sense. Unlike a directly competitive, zero-sum game such as Chess, players in Lord of the Rings win or lose as a group. We call this form of cooperation *player cooperation* because it describes specific player relationships that do not occur in all games.

The two uses of the word are not ultimately dissimilar. Player cooperation is really just a literalized manifestation of systemic cooperation. Systemic cooperation, as a phenomenon intrinsic to all games, occurs "under the hood" of the experienced game structure, whereas player cooperation happens at a higher level, incorporated more consciously into a player's understanding of a game.

In this sense, the very act of playing a game is an act of cooperation. It is only through the shared efforts of the players that a game's fragile magic circle takes shape and is sustained over the course of play. There is a wonderful paradox here. Within the magic circle set aside for the game, within the arena spelled out by the rules, a conflict takes place. The players cooperatively form the space of the game, in order to create a competition for their own amusement. Game conflict is like a duel between actors in a play: it is an elaborately staged competitive artifice, enjoyed in part because of its artificiality. There is genuine conflict in a game, but only within a larger cooperative frame sustained by the participation of the players.

New Games

In the earlier critique of Bernard DeKoven's ideas about the negative aspects of competition, we were not quite playing fair. It is true that DeKoven questions traditional forms of competitive play. It is also true that we do not agree with all of his ideas on the subject. But DeKoven's concepts have to be understood within the larger context of his important work on games. In his book *The Well-Played Game,* DeKoven argues for a new understanding of play, governed by a shift in emphasis away from competition. Instead, DeKoven is an advocate for more improvisational games in which players take on the role of game designers.

DeKoven was not alone in his ideas. He was one of the early members of the *New Games Movement,* a group of game designers and play advocates that had a tremendous impact on the culture of games. Founded by Stewart Brand (the same man who started *The Whole Earth Catalog*) in the late 1960s, the New Games Movement was an organization dedicated to the promotion of play and its positive impact on society. During the late 1960s and 1970s, the New Games Movement organized a number of large-scale public game "tournaments" in the San Francisco Bay Area and other parts of the world. Part art happening, part community action, and part playground carnival,

New Games Movement Tournaments embodied a uniquely game-centric, community-based politics of a scale that has not been seen since.

The New Games Movement had a large impact on physical education and the integration of games and play into schools. If you grew up playing with a parachute or huge rubber "Earth Ball" in your elementary school gym class, it is probably due to the direct or indirect influence of the New Games Movement. The New Games Movement published two books (*The New Games Book* and *More New Games*) that cataloged their playful game designs. How does the New Games Movement fit into an understanding of games as systems of conflict? The New Games Movement confronted the idea of competition and cooperation head on, creating games and ways of thinking about game design that challenged conventional notions of games as conflict.

> Many people think of New Games as non-competitive. Of course this isn't the case. Most of the games in this book involve competition—it's what gives New Games its vitality.... The effort each player makes to overcome the resistance and achieve the goal is the heart of the game and what makes it enjoyable and gratifying. In most games, the resistance is supplied by your opponent trying to achieve her goal. Your opponent is therefore your partner in the game. The best games are those in which you can play your hardest and still count on our opponent to meet your effort—to compete with you.[3]

Although DeKoven may rail against competition in some of his writings, he also helped instill in New Games the more balanced notions of competition embodied in the quote above, taken from an essay he wrote for the *New Games Book*. DeKoven's main point is that in the context of a game, the struggle of players *against* each other is also a struggle *with* each other, as players meet the challenges that they provide for one another. In this way, New Games affirms the interdependent relationship between competition and cooperation, the systemic cooperation that is part of all games.

But the central focus of New Games wasn't game philosophy: it was the design and play of games themselves. The movement produced some extraordinary game designs. Take, for example, a game called Catch the Dragon's Tail:

> You'll need a good-sized area for this event, clear of sudden pits and immovable oaks. About eight to ten people line up, one behind the other. Now, everyone puts their arms around the waist of the person in front of them. (You can't be ticklish around dragons.) The last person in line tucks a handkerchief in the back of his belt. To work up steam, the dragon might let out a few roars—fearsome enough, we wager, to put Hydra to shame.
>
> At the signal, the dragon begins chasing its own tail, the object being for the person at the head of the line to snatch the handkerchief. The tricky part of this epic struggle is that the people at the front and the people at the back are clearly competing—but the folks in the middle aren't sure which way to go. When the head finally captures the tail, who's the defeated and who's the victor? Everyone! The head dons the handkerchief and becomes the new tail, while second from the front becomes the new head.[4]

Catch the Dragon's Tail purposefully blurs the lines between competition and cooperation. On the one hand, all of the players are cooperating to hold on to each other to become a single dragon. But at the same time, the front part of the dragon is chasing the rear part, with the people in the middle not given a clear role to play in the conflict. Catch the Dragon's Tail makes playfully explicit the ways that players must work together even as they compete within the limited space of a game. Catch the Dragon's Tail also embodies an important lesson for game design: all of our preconceptions about games can be questioned. Normally we might think that all players of a game must have a clearly defined goal, or that lines of competition must be sharply defined, or that a game with player cooperation cannot also have vigorous competition—but Catch the Dragon's Tail debunks all of these assumptions. If nothing else, game design is about playing with ideas, and even seemingly fundamental ideas about competition in games are subject to playful intervention.

The Goal of a Game

In addition to competition and cooperation, another essential component of a game as a system of conflict is a *goal*. Goals are fundamental to games. In the explication of Centipede, Joust, and Gauntlet, goals figured into each form of conflict. At the outcome of a game, the goals are either reached or not reached, and this quantifiable outcome is part of our definition of games. Very often, it is a clear and quantifiable goal and outcome that distinguishes games from other play activities. Add a goal to informal play and usually you will have a game. Casual skiing for fun is a leisure play activity. But race your friend to the bottom of the mountain and suddenly you're taking part in a game.

A game's goal is defined by its rules and is tightly interwoven into the formal structure of the game as a whole. A game's goal is a central feature of its formal structure. When players come together to play a game, the goal is at the center of the magic circle, the pole that holds aloft the circular tent of the game while the players are inside the structure, at play with one other. The goal sustains their interest, their engagement, and their desire. Without a clear goal, meaningful game play is not possible; if players cannot judge how their actions are bringing them closer to or farther away from winning the game, they cannot properly understand the significance of their actions, and the game collapses into a jumbled heap of ambiguity.

A game's goal defines its endpoint; once it is reached, the game is over. In this sense, a game's goal is the death of play, the mark of the end, foretelling the moment the magic circle will disappear. There is a curious poetic quality to the struggle of game players as they make their way through the system of a game, playing to no end but the one provided by the game itself, even as their joyful pursuit of that end means the death of their pleasure. Until, of course, the next game begins.

Most games have an end in which one or more players achieve victory. However, in games such as Space Invaders, in which the game structure repeats itself with increasing challenge to the player, there is no single victorious endpoint. In this form of game, the goal is to play as long as possible or achieve the highest score. This formal structure heightens the sense of inevitable death. The player is living on borrowed time, staving off the inevitable end of a game that occurs when conditions of failure are met.

The space of possibility of a game is a plane stretched between two anchorage points: the beginning and the end of the game. The players journey from one end to another, making their way from the start to the finish. In a well-designed game that supports meaningful play, this journey between points should be taut and efficient, with every element contributing directly or indirectly to the larger experience.

In case this all sounds too goal-oriented, we must acknowledge that goals are not the only reason people play games. Play can be an end in itself, or a way to achieve social interaction, or affect cultural change. We address each of these motivations for play in later chapters. But seen as a formal system, the goal of a game needs to be recognized as a primary structure that shapes the game as a whole.

Case Study

Beating Loop

It is easy enough to state that the goal of a game is an important part of the overall design. But it is often very difficult to figure out the exact victory and loss conditions for a particular game. One play pattern can lend itself to different winning conditions, each one shaping the game experience differently.

LOOP is an online single-player game about catching butterflies. In the development of LOOP, the core game play was invented before a decision had been made concerning victory and loss conditions. The game development began with the idea of drawing lines to loop butterflies, scoring points by looping special groups of them (such as butterflies of the same color). The first prototype demonstrated the game interactivity but the start and finish conditions of the game had not been defined. Many options for the victory conditions were discussed and were narrowed down to three scenarios:

1. The player has to catch a certain number of butterflies to finish a level.

2. The player has to clear the screen of all of the butterflies to finish a level.

3. There are no levels: the player has to keep on catching butterflies forever.

Each of these endpoints entailed different kinds of player experiences. For example, scenarios 1 and 2 presumed that the game proceeded as a series of discrete levels, whereas scenario 3 provided a single, continuous game, as in Tetris. There were other unsolved questions too: for example, in scenario 2, what would happen if a player were left with only one butterfly? And what was the loss condition? If the game did have levels, there needed to be victory and loss conditions for finishing a level; if it did not have discrete levels, there only needed to be a loss condition for the game as a whole. In considering the loss conditions, two primary schemes were proposed:

1. A player has a certain amount of time to attain the victory conditions.

2. Butterflies appear as the player proceeds. If too many appear, the game is over.

Many of these variations were playtested in different combinations. For the loss conditions, a time limit was selected, rather than the option of having the screen overrun with butterflies, because it gave the game a clearer sense of progression. In Tetris, it is clear that when the bricks pile up near the top of the screen, you are about to lose. In the prototype of LOOP, it was never quite clear when there were too many butterflies on the screen. A

The Level Playing Field of Conflict

Competition and cooperation, goals and struggle, victory and loss: how does it all add up? What are the general conditions of a game conflict? One core principle of conflict in games is that it is *fair*. Game conflict is impartial conflict: it is premised on the idea that all players have an equal chance at winning, that the game system is intrinsically equitable, that the game's contest takes place on a *level playing field,* which does not favor one side over the other. Anthropologist Roger Caillois points this out in speaking about competitive forms of play: "A whole group of games would seem to be competitive, that is to say, like a combat in which equality of chances is artificially created, in order that the adversaries should confront each other under ideal conditions, susceptible of giving precise and incontestable value to the winner's triumph."[5]

Why would a game strive so forcefully to create equality in this way? As our definition states, a game is an *artificial* conflict. The game structure creates an artificial arena, in which everything is removed except for the factors involved in the conflict. Chess is a context for intellectual strategic competition. In a gymnastics competition, only gymnastics skills matter.

In real life, the conflicts and struggles faced are never so clearly articulated and understood as in a game. The idea that players are entering into a fair conflict, where they won't be fooled or tricked by the game itself, is a key component of the lusory attitude. Even though games may have elements of uncertainty, the structure within which that uncertainty plays out is known in advance. The qualities of rules themselves make this so. As we know from **Defining Rules,** rules of a game limit player action, are explicit, unambiguous, binding, and shared by all players. Within the magic circle, players experience a kind of equality and fairness that is not present outside games.

Is it really true that games strive to create spaces of equality, where only the play of the game can determine the winner of a game? Are games so pure and separate from the real world that no other factors possibly enter into the play? Generally speaking, no. But in this chapter we are analyzing games on a

LOOP

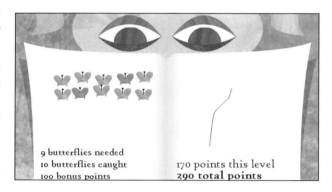

LOOP

"meter" that kept track of the number of butterflies and displayed how close the game was to being overcrowded could have been added, but that seemed to unnecessarily complicate the game interface.

Having made a decision about the loss conditions (a timer), it was determined that the game would be given discrete levels, with the goal of each level to catch a certain number of butterflies. It was decided that the number of butterflies did not decline over the course of a level: every time you caught a group, the same number of butterflies immediately flew in from the side of the screen. There were several reasons for these decisions. First, there was a desire to create a game that seemed full of possibilities. If the goal of the game was to clear the screen, then the game would have gradually emptied out as the player proceeded through a level. The game would have felt less dynamic and alive: given any set of butterflies, there would have been a single best solution for clearing the screen—and as a level proceeded, the possibilities for different actions decreased. The solution to keep the number of butterflies constant kept the game exciting and full of alternate strategies.

Even though a level ended when a quota of butterflies had been captured, it was possible to exceed the level's victory conditions by going over the quota. You could, for example, strategically capture enough butterflies so that you only had to capture one more to reach your quota—and then snatch a large group of them for your final loop, putting you well above the quota. Butterflies captured beyond your quota earned you large bonus points. The best players managed their butterflies carefully, creeping up on the quota and then scoring a large group at the end that took them well over the quota amount. This kind of careful play was only made possible by the particular structures that had been designed into the game.

Digital games tend to proceed as a series of levels and have loss conditions that end the game, LOOP being one such example. Deciding what constitutes success in a level and what ends the game are absolutely crucial game design decisions. Too often, game designers take these decisions for granted, following design conventions instead of inventing new ones. What about a game in which there are multiple loss or win conditions? What if the goal of the game is to lose as quickly as possible, or run out of points? Just as Catch the Dragon's Tail played with traditional ideas of competition and cooperation, your games can play with traditional ideas of winning and losing as well.

formal level, removed from consideration of their relation to the outside world. And in a formal sense, yes, games are spaces of pure conflict, separate from the outside world.

Given the artificial nature of games, is fairness possible? Does the magic circle offer a truly level playing field? Caillois thinks not:

> As carefully as one tries to bring it about, absolute equality does not seem to be realizable. Sometimes, as in checkers or chess, the fact of moving first is an advantage, for this priority permits the favored player to occupy key positions or to impose a special strategy. Conversely, in bidding games, such as bridge, the last bidder profits from the clues afforded by the bids of his opponents. Again, at croquet, to be last multiplies the player's resources. In sports contests, the exposure, the fact of having the sun in front or in back; the wind which aids or hinders one or the other side; the fact, in disputing for positions on a circular track, of finding oneself in the inside or outside lane constitutes a crucial test, a trump or disadvantage whose influence may be negated or modified by drawing lots at the beginning, then by strict alternation of favored positions.[6]

There is indeed a contradiction at work in the idea of equality within games. As Caillois points out, equality is something that is sought after in games, but somehow never quite achieved—at least, in the non-digital game examples he cites. What about digital games? In some ways, they have an advantage when it comes to creating a level playing field. The constrained context of a computer system allows for greater control over the exact conditions of play. On the other hand, the complex automated nature of digital games can place players at some distance from the rules. Players can easily grow suspicious of an unfair network lag, a "cheating" AI, or a low processing speed "stutter." This kind of player distrust, whether or not it is based in reality, can ruin a game.

The magic circle is fragile, easily dispelled when players fail to invest faith in the game. If your players feel that your game is unfair, that it lacks a level playing field, it is unlikely that they will want to play. Within the magic circle, a game is suspended between the ideal notion of a level playing field and the reality of inevitable unfairness, a reality that creeps into every game, even while the magic circle's border holds it at bay. Perhaps games do not take place on an absolutely level playing field. But they are premised on the very real idea of fairness and equality. This struggle is part of what gives games their vitality.

All games participate in this conflict between fairness and unfairness, a struggle that reaches its climax in rule-breaking, a phenomena explored fully in the next schema. But even within a more limited game design context, establishing a sense of fairness is crucial to successful game play. The following case study looks at one example of this problem in detail.

Pig Redux

We first examined the game Pig in *Games as Systems of Uncertainty.* In Pig, the goal of the game is to score points by rolling a die and adding to your score until you reach 100 points. If you roll a 1, then you lose the points you earned that turn and pass the die. Otherwise, you keep rolling to try to increase your score. You can always decide to stop rolling, at which point you add your current total to your overall score and pass the die to the next player.

The game is very simple. But is it truly fair? Does the first player have an advantage? Because Pig is about accumulating a score, turn after turn, it does favor the first player: that person has an added chance of reaching 100 first. If there are five players and on the tenth turn the player that went first scores 100 points or more, that player wins. But some of the other players, who only got to play nine rounds, might have reached 100 if they had been allowed a tenth turn as well.

Pig embodies the classic game design problem of creating a level playing field. Ideally, every player should have an equal chance of winning. So what is the solution? There are a few possible game design adjustments. One solution is that the winner of the previous game gets to go first, as an added reward. But this does not solve the problem of deciding who goes first in the very first game. Should the winner be rewarded in this way? Doing so creates a positive feedback loop, which might unbalance the game. Should the player with the lowest score go first? Neither of these solutions create fairness for all players.

Another solution is using a random die roll to determine player order. The player that rolled the highest number goes first. Even though a great many games use this method, it is not necessarily the best solution to the problem. Will it feel fair to all of the players? For example, because play proceeds around the circle of players, the player that rolled the lowest number may end up as the second player, if that player is sitting next to the person that rolled the highest number. In any case, even if the order of players is randomly determined, the player moving first still has an advantage over the other players, and the inequality remains.

Yet another solution would be to play the game a number of times equal to the number of players at the table, rotating which player goes first. If there were ten players, they would play the game ten times. Each time, a different player would go first. Players would either add up their scores for a grand total or the player who won the most times would be named the overall winner. This solution works mathematically to equalize the game, but it suddenly transforms the casual experience of Pig into a structured tournament. What if you only want to play a game or two and not an entire series of games?

We borrowed the game of Pig from Reiner Knizia's book *Dice Games Properly Explained.*[7] Knizia notes this very inequality and suggests the following as a variation: when a player reaches 100, all of the rest of the players get to roll once more and finish the round. If more than one player ends up exceeding 100, the player with the highest score wins. This is better than any of the previously proposed adjustments, but even this well-designed solution is flawed. In Knizia's solution, it is best *not* to be the first player to reach 100, because all of the other players know exactly the score that they need to win, and they will push their luck in order to beat the player that is about to win. It is actually best if you roll last during the final round. Because the player that went first at the beginning of the game is mathematically more likely to be the first to reach 100, it ends up being a slight disadvantage to be the first player.

Even in a very simple game such as Pig, there is no perfect solution that offers absolute equality for all players. But luckily, players are not perfectly rational beings. They are human, and the best solution is not necessarily the best mathematical answer to the question of equality, but the one that *feels* right within the context of a game. Absolute equality, like pure randomness in a computer algorithm, may be a myth. But as long as the *feeling* of equality persists within the game, players will keep the faith and enter into the magic circles you design for them.

As a final thought, is fairness itself something that can be put at play in a game? We have suggested that other components of game conflict, such as competition and cooperation, or achieving game goals, could be challenged through innovative game designs such as Catch the Dragon's Tail. Does this extend to the level playing field of a game as well? Perhaps. But it is a very complicated question. In the next schema, ***Breaking the Rules,*** we do our best to answer it.

Further Reading

Homo Ludens, by Johann Huizinga *(see page 99)*

> *Recommended:*
>
> Chapter 1: Nature and Significance of Play as a Cultural
> Phenomenon

The New Games Book, by Andrew Fluegelman and Shoshana
Tembeck *(see page 21)*

> *Recommended:*
>
> "Creating the Play Community," Bernard DeKoven
> "Theory of Game Change," Stewart Brand

Notes

1. Bernard DeKoven, *The Well-Played Game* (New York: Doubleday, 1978), p. 11.
2. Mihaly Csikszentmihalyi, *Flow: The Psychology of Optimal Experience* (New York: HarperCollins Publishers, 1991), p. 72–3.
3. Andrew Fluegelman and Shoshana Tembeck, *The New Games Book* (New York: Doubleday, 1976), p. 87–88.
4. Ibid. p. 47.
5. Roger Caillois, Man, *Play, and Games* (London: Thames and Hudson, 1962), p. 14.
6. Ibid. p. 14–15.
7. Reiner Knizia, *Dice Games Properly Explained* (Tadworth, Surrey: Right Way Books, 1992), p. 128–30.

Games as Systems of Conflict SUMMARY

- **Conflict** is an intrinsic element of every game. The conflict in a game emerges from within the magic circle as players struggle to achieve the goals of a game.

- Game conflict comes in many forms. Conflict can be individual or team-based, cooperative or non-cooperative, direct or indirect. Many games mix and match forms of conflict within a single game structure.

- The forms of conflict occurring within a game are a direct outgrowth of its rules. One way of framing a game's space of possibility is that it is a space of possible forms of conflict. Players take part not just in the forms of conflict that the game design proscribes, but will also find their own forms as well.

- All games are **competitive** in that players struggle against each other or against a game system as they play. Without this sense of competition, meaningful play would be difficult because players would not be able to judge their progress through the space of possibility of a game.

- All games are **cooperative,** in that playing a game means engaging with the shared meanings of the game, "speaking the language" of the game with other players in order to play.

- **Systemic cooperation** refers to the fundamental, discursive cooperation that is intrinsic to all games. **Player cooperation** refers to games in which players all work together to achieve the goal. Not all games exhibit player cooperation.

- The goal of a game is a fundamental element that shapes the game's formal structure. The goal is at once that toward which players strive, while also that which represents the end or symbolic death of a game.

- Shaping **victory and loss conditions** is an important component of game design. Victory and loss conditions directly shape the possible outcomes of a game.

- Game conflict is premised on a **level playing field** where all players have an equal chance of winning. A truly equitable game is virtually never possible in the real world, creating an intrinsic tension in regards to the fairness of any game. Players will generally refuse to play a game they perceive to be unfair.

BREAKING THE RULES

standard players
dedicated players
unsportsmanlike players
cheaters
spoil-sports
degenerate strategies
exploits

21

*[The rules that players verbalize] are an idealized set of rules—they are the rules by which people **should** play rather than the ones by which they **do** play....we may have to know **two** sets of rules: the ideal ones **and** those by which the ideal rules are applied, misapplied, or subverted.—**Kenneth Goldstein,** "Strategies in Counting Out"*

*When you **have** to win, you're willing to break whatever rules you can if that would help you get closer to the goal. When you have to win, you're not concerned with fairness, feeling, the community, or even play. When you have to win you can't leave the game until you have finally, ultimately won.*

*What's amazing to me about all this is that the game itself doesn't change. The rules and the conventions are the same. But the manner of playing the game is completely different.—**Bernard DeKoven,** The Well-Played Game*

Introducing Rule-Breaking

This schema opens with a pair of quotes from two thinkers we have heard from before. Folklorist Kenneth Goldstein first appeared in the schema on **Uncertainty,** where he looked at the ways that children subvert the ritual of counting-out through a number of subtle and devious strategies, such as adding an extra "eenie-meenie-minee-moe" in order to avoid becoming "it." We introduced Bernard DeKoven in the previous schema on **Conflict** as a leading figure in the New Games Movement.

Goldstein points out that although games have rules, they should be considered to have two sets of rules: the ideal rules of play and the actual rules of play, which sometimes misapply and subvert the ideal rules. DeKoven comes at the same set of issues from a different point of view. He points out that some players are so motivated to win that they disregard usual notions of fairness. What seems to intrigue DeKoven the most is that such opposing styles of play can occur alongside normal play within the same game structure.

Whether we are talking about ideal rules versus actual rules or honest players versus cheating players, both writers point to an important game phenomenon. So far in this book, we have described game players in an almost naïve way: we have assumed that every player is an earnest player, carefully and honestly playing by the rules. Although this does describe many game players, it is certainly not true of every single one. Take the children that Goldstein studied in his analysis of counting-out games. In manipulating rhymes in order to achieve certain desired results (*he* is going to be "It," not me!), what were these players actually doing? Were they stretching and altering the rules of counting-out in order to win? Were they cheating at the game? Or were they simply playing the game very well? This final formal schema, **Breaking the Rules,** takes a direct look at how players bend, cheat, and break those carefully crafted systems of rules that we have so thoroughly investigated in the last several chapters.

In so many different ways, breaking the rules seems to be part of playing games. Whether it is trying to sneak in a foul while the referee isn't looking, altering a board game to play with a special set of "home rules," or making use of an ace of spades hidden up your sleeve, reconfiguring, breaking, and ignoring the rules seems to be an intrinsic part of games themselves. But what guides a player to break the rules? What is the effect of rule-breaking on game play? How does a game's design either encourage or discourage players from breaking the rules? Lastly, can rule-breaking be used as a creative strategy for game design? We investigate these questions in the following pages.

Kinds of Rule-Breaking

Rule-bending and rule-breaking manipulate the structure of a game. To cheat or transgress in a game means to break the rules, to have a relationship to the formal system that is different than the relationship that the formal system itself presupposes and endorses. In considering the ways that game rules are broken, we can divide players into different player "types." Each type of player is defined by his or her relation to the formal systems of a game, along three related axes of behavior and attitude:

- The rule-breaking player's adherence to the rules

- The rule-breaking player's interest in winning

- The rule-breaking player's degree of lusory attitude

Player Types

The Standard Player: This player type is a "standard" and honest game player that plays the game as it was designed to be played, following the rules and respecting their authority.

The Dedicated Player: This close cousin of the standard player studies the formal systems of a game in order to master and perfect his or her play of the game, often finding and exploiting unusual strategies in order to win. *Examples: professional athletes, hardcore gamers.*

The Unsportsmanlike Player: This third type of player follows the rules of a game, but does so in a way that violates the spirit of the lusory attitude. *Examples: The older sibling that never lets the younger sibling win, or the baseball catcher that tries to distract the batter's concentration at the plate.*

The Cheat: The cheater, unlike the other kinds of game-players, actually violates the formal rules of the game, but does so in order to win the game. *Example: The hide-and-seek player that peeks while the other players are hiding.*

The Spoil-Sport: This kind of game player is hardly a player at all. Unlike the cheat, the spoil-sport refuses to acknowledge the magic circle of the game and does not care about winning or about following the rules. *Example: The frustrated Twister player that ruins a game by pushing over the other players.*

In the sections that follow, we describe each kind of player in more detail. But before moving on, it is important to recognize that these categories are neither fixed nor mutually exclusive. The boundaries between them are quite fuzzy, and often contextual. A player that is a dedicated hardcore gamer among gamer friends might be seen as an unsportsmanlike, overly competitive "power gamer" when playing a game with more casual players. Likewise, a player might shift between categories over time, or even within the course of a single game. Despite the fluid boundaries between them, however, these categories provide a useful typology for understanding the ways players stretch, bend, and break game rules.

Standard Players

The *standard player* is the test case against which all other types of players are contrasted. The standard game player attempts to follow the rules as best he or she can, respecting their authority and honoring the limits they set. In terms of rules, goals, and possession of the lusory attitude, the standard player is a most law-abiding citizen.

Do most players fit this description? Actually, they do. The magic circle is fluid, but when most players play a game, especially a game with other players that can be seen face-to-face, they respect the rules and play the game from beginning to end. Why is face-to-face interaction important? A game is a kind of social contract. The presence of other players is important to maintaining the authority of the magic circle, because if a group of players are all obeying the rules, they implicitly police and enforce proper play. Why? Because if they have decided to invest the game with meaning in order to play, they all have a vested interest in maintaining the level playing field of conflict created by the rules. This does not mean that most players are mindless slaves to the rules of a game, but generally speaking, looking across all phenomena of games, players do follow the rules. If this were not the case, then cheating at games would be the rule and not the exception.

You may well disagree with our contention that most players do not break the rules. One could also take the position, for example, that cheating exists in all players, that the force of game-playing desire that drives a player to win contains the seeds of cheating. Cheating, in this view, would be an intrinsic aspect of game-playing, even if it did not always rise to the surface in the form of genuine rule-breaking. But whether the "standard player" is really the majority case or a fiction that doesn't exist in the real world, the notion of the "standard player" is still important. The *idea* that there is a standard player, a game player that earnestly follows the rules without trying to bend and break them, provides the backdrop against which less rule-governed styles of play can be understood.

Dedicated Players

The next type of game player is the *dedicated player*. The dedicated player is really more of a special case of the standard player than a completely different player type. The dedicated player desires to become an expert at a game, and diligently studies the rules of play in an attempt to maximize the chances of winning. Whereas standard game players exhibit a desire to win and an interest in the rules of a game, dedicated players apply themselves to this task with a certain kind of zeal, to a degree that more casual players might not find enjoyable. If the game permits, dedicated players tend to practice their play, testing out strategies and perfecting their knowledge of the game.

A typical Las Vegas tourist who wants to enjoy Blackjack might play a few games here and there, browsing different casinos and tables, relying on intuition to guide him as he plays. A dedicated Blackjack player, on the other hand, won't merely play a few casual rounds of the game, but is likely to study a Blackjack "system" or two and implement it diligently in play, finding tables with advantageous rule variants, counting cards during play, and spending long hours at the Blackjack table in order to balance out his odds of winning. The difference between dedicated and standard players is a matter of degree, not kind.

Recall that the differences between types of players is drawn along three axes: their relationship to the lusory attitude, their respect for the authority of the rules, and their interest in attaining the goal of the game. Within each of these categories, dedicated players resemble standard players. But dedicated players have a deeper engagement with the game, a greater zeal for play. It is more important for dedicated players to win, and in order to do so, they will generally learn and master the rules of a game. At the same time, dedicated players tend to invest the magic circle with more authority, because of the value of their investment in the game as a whole. They possess extra amounts of the lusory attitude, relishing the inefficiencies of games as important challenges to overcome as proficiently as possible.

Who are dedicated players? Professional athletes and professional gamblers—those that make their living as game players. So are so-called "hardcore gamers," from grognard historical wargamers to deathmatch clan leaders with tricked-out custom PCs. In general, dedicated players require more depth and complexity, a richer space of possibility in their games. This is why non-gamers often find the gaming fare of hardcore gamers bafflingly complex and unapproachable.

Dedicated players tend to play with a zeal that often puts off less dedicated players, who sometimes wonder if dedicated players are taking the game just a bit too seriously. The dedicated Blackjack player we described, who might spend most of a Las Vegas vacation at the Blackjack tables, might seem incomprehensible to the casual, standard player, who looks at games as a form of relaxation and leisure. A casual player does not wish to spend so many waking hours inside the magic circle of a game.

There is a very fuzzy line between dedicated game players and standard game players, and the difference is often contextual. Among your dedicated bowling buddies, you might fit in just fine as a standard player, scoffing at the league players that wear matching shirts and play the game "too seriously" to have fun. But when you end up in a game with a group of beginners who want to abandon a match in the middle to go see a movie, you might find yourself being accused of playing "too seriously" when you demand that they stay to the tenth frame and finish what they started.

As game designers, it is important to understand the range of player types that encounter your game, and the kinds of relationships they have to the rules, goals, and magic circle that your game delineates. Some games clearly appeal to both standard and dedicated players, such as Scrabble. Scrabble is often played as casual family fare, but it also supports an international tournament culture of hardcore players. Other kinds of games tend to attract one kind of player over another. The players that enjoy the low-pressure, exploratory pacing of Myst are generally not the same kind of dedicated player audience that would spend the many hours required to understand and master Myth: The Fallen Lords. There is a similar divide off the computer between players of party games such as Pictionary and fans of complex wargames and role-playing games.

The first two categories of game-players—standard and dedicated players—are not ultimately rule-breakers. They are "classical" game players, the kinds of players for whom designers usually design games, loyal functionaries of the rules. Like standard players, dedicated players are indeed rule-abiding. But as we'll see soon enough, even though they seem more invested in the magic circle of a game, their dedication takes them one step closer to actual rule-breaking.

Unsportsmanlike Players

The third type is the *unsportsmanlike player*. Unsportsmanlike players do anything they can to win. They try to find shortcuts to victory, exploiting the rigidity of the rules to locate holes that they can slip through to end up ahead. An unsportsmanlike boxer, for example, might constantly grab at the ropes or go into a clinch whenever the opponent advances aggressively. Note that the boxer stops short of actually violating the rules of the game. In fact, some might consider this approach a valid strategy for Boxing. But somehow, the unsportsmanlike boxer violates the spirit of the contest of Boxing, marring the purity of the battle between the athletic skills of the two players.

Unlike standard and dedicated players who generally engage openly with the "fun" quality of play, there is something negative about unsportsmanlike behavior. The unsportsmanlike player turns the special zeal of dedicated players into something that seems to run counter to the joyful nature of play and games. An unsportsmanlike player is not a cheat. The unsportsmanlike player does follow the rules of a game, but in a way that violates the spirit of the game. By attempting to shortcut the challenges of a game, the unsportsmanlike player refuses to surrender completely to the lusory attitude, in which the inefficiencies of play are readily accepted.

Unsportsmanlike behavior is a violation of the "unwritten" rules of a game, the *implicit rules* that are not actually written out, but are observed by all players. This is how the unsportsmanlike player "technically" avoids designation as a cheater, while still failing to completely respect the lusory attitude. One of the implicit rules of Tic-Tac-Toe we discussed in **Rules on Three Levels** is the implied time limit between turns. Even though the operational rules do not mention a time limit, the idea that a player must take a turn in a "reasonable" amount of time is an implicit rule of the game. Imagine an unsportsmanlike player that is about to lose a game of Tic-Tac-Toe, but refuses to take a turn. The player might state that he is "thinking" about his next move, and claim that because the rules do not state a time limit, he can take as long as he wants, even years, before he has to move. This kind of behavior, although not violating the operational rules, clearly violates the spirit of the game.

Degenerate Strategies

Dedicated and unsportsmanlike players have particular ways of engaging with the system of a game. One common behavior these player types exhibit is to make use of *degenerate strategies* or *exploits*. We first encountered degenerate strategies in **Games as Game Theory Systems**. A degenerate strategy is a way of playing a game that takes advantage of a weakness in the game design, so that the play strategy guarantees success.

Degenerate strategies often appear in complex games, where the numerous permutations of play sometimes afford shortcuts in the space of possibility. For example, you are playing a real-time strategy game against the computer and you realize that the program's AI does not handle pathfinding well. (Pathfinding refers to the aspects of the program that plot navigational paths for the computer-controlled characters through obstacle-filled terrain.) Whenever the computer-controlled troops move around obstacles, they begin the march in formation but end up disorganized, with individual units trapped in irregularly shaped pockets of the terrain. It is not difficult for you, however, to make the small corrections necessary to keep your units together. If you decided to take advantage of this weakness by strategically leading the computer-controlled opponents into obstacle-filled parts of the map, you would be using a degenerate strategy.

Taking advantage of the game's weakness in this way would not exactly constitute cheating, but it does exploit the game's structure as a means of winning. Although games are not designed to be exploited by players, what makes a degenerate strategy degenerate is not just that it goes against the intentions of the designers. Using an exploit is a way of playing that violates the spirit of the game, similar to taking advantage of the implicit rule governing time between Tic-Tac-Toe turns.

Degenerate strategies appear in non-digital games as well. In early editions of Magic: The Gathering, certain card combinations were simply too powerful and could destroy a player on the first turn, before a match had a chance to develop. Wizards of the Coast, the publishers of the game, declared certain cards "officially" illegal, most notoriously the Black Lotus card, in order to keep this kind of play experience in check. In regulated tournament play, the outlawed cards were not used. But in more casual games, players continued to include them in their decks for years.

Why isn't using a degenerate strategy considered cheating? Degenerate strategies take advantage of weaknesses in the rules of a game, but do not actually violate the rules. What kind of player would play in this way? The answer is both a dedicated player, who is overzealously seeking the perfect strategy, and an unsportsmanlike player, who has found a hole in the rules to exploit, even though he understands that he is not playing the game the way it was intended. These two kinds of players can both make use of degenerate strategies, depending on the context.

The difference between a dedicated player and an unsportsmanlike player is the degree to which the player subscribes to the lusory attitude. Dedicated players follow rules on all levels. Unsportsmanlike players follow the operational rules, but they do not follow all of the implicit ones. Dedicated players loyally uphold the magic circle of a game, but unsportsmanlike players fail to do so, occasionally stepping just outside its borders in order to bend the rules.

Often, whether or not a degenerate strategy is a "proper" way to play depends on how the game experience is framed. When it was discovered that Pac-Man could be played by memorizing patterns of movement instead of through improvisational moment-to-moment tactics, player reaction fell into two camps. Some frowned on using memorized play patterns as a violation of the spirit of the game. Other players, however, capitalized on patterns in order to get higher scores. These pattern players did not consider themselves to be unsportsmanlike at all: they saw themselves as dedicated players who had simply found a better (and more demanding) way to play the game.

One more example: remember the hypothetical fighting game from our earlier investigation of degenerate strategies? The game could be beaten by using one technique over and over, rather than exploring the carefully orchestrated system of fighting moves created by the game's designers. It could be said that the player making use of this degenerate strategy is behaving in an unsportsmanlike manner, improperly playing the game, sacrificing "fun" in exchange for a shortcut to victory. It could also be said, however, that the exploit was being used by a dedicated player who had "solved" the fighting game like a puzzle. As with the Pac-Man pattern players, instead of playing the game the way it was designed to be played, the dedicated player simply invented a new method of interaction. This is arguably an example of transformative play, an important game phenomena we will investigate in chapters to come.

Whether or not a particular degenerate strategy is considered proper is often contextual. For example, the use of the single-technique exploit to beat all of the computer opponents in our hypothetical fighting game might be admired by a group of players for its elegance. On the other hand, if the degenerate strategy were used against other human players, fighting bouts would devolve into uninteresting games, with both players relying on the one exploitable technique again and again. In this social context, the exploit would be frowned upon as unsportsmanlike behavior, a violation of the implicit rules and the enjoyable spirit of the game. The *meaning* of a game action, even if the action is the selection of a general strategy, is always influenced by the context in which it occurs. In a social context, the exploit unbalances the level playing field of conflict and shrinks the space of possibility to a very narrow range, threatening the meaningful play of the game.

Degenerate Strategy Ecosystems

As a rule of thumb, you want to be on the lookout for degenerate strategies and keep them out of your game. The ability to win a game by playing in a singular way demonstrates a poor game design, a space of possibility with an unintended, limiting short-circuit. There is, however, an extremely fuzzy line between degenerate strategies and imaginative ways to play a game. There is something exciting about having players explore the space of possibility of your game, rooting around for new strategies and new ways to play. If the game is complex enough and the community of players is large enough, degenerate strategies that do emerge can be countered by new strategies created specifically to oppose the exploits. An ecosystem emerges from the community, in which different styles of play compete for dominance.

In real-time strategy (RTS) game player communities, for example, players constantly look for ways to get ahead on the rankings boards. Command and Conquer, like most RTS games, was intended to emphasize steady planning and gradual development. But over time a degenerate strategy evolved called the "tank rush." Instead of slowly building up forces, a player using the "tank rush" strategy could quickly create a group of tanks and wipe out his opponent's base camp in the early game, before his opponent had a chance to prepare his defenses. Although the tank rush degenerate strategy ruined the games of many players that desired a more typical long-term conflict, it also spawned new kinds of defensive strategies. The introduction of a degenerate strategy enlarged the overall space of possibility of the game.

Although some player communities are resourceful enough to create their own antidotes to degenerate strategies, it is often necessary for the designers to step in and correct the breach themselves, as in the case of Magic's Black Lotus card. With popular games, play strategies sometimes evolve in a way that necessitates a refinement of the formal structure, like a gardener pruning branches of a tree to improve the overall health of the plant. The process of degenerate strategy correction is ultimately part of the iterative process of game design. One game that has undergone constant refinement is professional Basketball in the U.S.

Over the last several decades, Basketball has undergone a number of rule changes. For example, in the 1960s and 1970s, most of the action took place right under the basket, where the chance of scoring was greatest. Play was dominated by tall players that could control this space with the greater offensive and defensive capabilities their height provided. Two rules were introduced that shook up the play of the game and defused degenerate strategies that were beginning to crop up. The three-point line incentivized players to play away from the basket, daring them to risk a longer shot in order to gain an extra point. At the same time, the three-second rule, which kept offensive players from spending more than three seconds parked in the paint under the basket, helped unclog the scoring zone traffic jam. The end result of these two rules is that quick players who could weave into the zone and out from under the basket, perhaps darting back to the three-point line to take a shot, became more important than static, towering giants. The space of possibility of the game expanded to include not just more diverse strategies of play but more diverse physical types of players to implement them.

Basketball has plenty of other rules that have been modified over time as well, from the introduction of dribbling near the beginning of the century to the more recent innovation of the shot clock and the back-and-forth controversies over zone defense. In his essay "The Heresy of Zone Defense," cultural critic Dave Hickey eloquently addresses this process of rule iteration:

> The "illegal-defense rule" which banned zone defenses, however, did more than save the game. It moved professional basketball into fluid complexity…leaving the college game with its zoned parcels of real estate behind. Initially, it was feared that this legislated man-to-man defense would resolve competition in terms of "natural comparative advantage" (as an economist might call it), since if each player is matched up with a player on the other team, the player with the most height, bulk, speed, or quickness would seem to have a permanent advantage. But you don't have to guard the same man all the time; you can switch, and this permission has created the beautiful "match-up game" in which both teams run patterns, picks, and switches in order to create advantageous situations for the offense or the defense—to generate shifting interplay.[1]

Degenerate strategies can lead to iterative design. It is beautiful to think of a game design as a design in process, which can grow and evolve over time, remaining fresh in response to changing needs and invented strategies. As the athletic abilities of players and the strategic acumen of coaches tested the limits of the system, the rules of Basketball were refined. Changes in rules maintained the tautness of the space of possibility while allowing players to move freely within it. Even today, regular changes in the rules continue to keep the game fresh. The act of rule-modification itself—by game designers, players, or administrative bodies—is an important kind of game design which will be addressed further in the pages to come.

Cheats and Spoil-Sports

*The player who trespasses against the rules or ignores them is a "spoil-sport." The spoil-sport is not the same as the false player, the cheat; for the latter pretends to be playing the game and, on the face of it, still acknowledges the magic circle…the spoil-sport shatters the play-world itself. By withdrawing from the game he reveals the relativity and fragility of the play-world in which he had temporarily shut himself with others.—***Johann Huizinga,** Homo Ludens*

The final two categories of players are the cheater and the spoil-sport. Up to this point, we have had to look very carefully at the players' behavior to decide whether or not they are violating the formal system of the game and are actually breaking the rules. With these final two categories of players, things become more explicit.

What defines the *cheating player?* The cheater breaks rules. Unlike the unsportsmanlike player, who merely violates the implicit, unspoken rules of a game, the cheater transgresses the operational rules, the actual rules of play. The cheater is the player that secretly moves a piece when her opponent looks away from the board, the player that steals Monopoly money from the bank and hides it for future use, the player that uses a non-regulation golf ball in a tournament in order to gain a little more distance. The cheater surreptitiously takes actions that are not proscribed by the rules, in order to gain an advantage.

Does cheating destroy a game? The unexpected paradox of cheating is that, as Huizinga points out, the cheater is still in some way playing the game. The cheater breaks rules, but only to further the act of winning. So while the cheater sheds enough of the lusory attitude to disrespect the authority of the rules, the cheater still has faith in the sanctioned conflict of the game: being the victor still has meaning to the cheater. This may seem like bizarre behavior. What is the point of hanging onto the authority of the quantifiable outcome when the proscribed steps for getting there are thrown out the window?

It turns out that the cheater is only one step removed from the dedicated player. It is possible to sympathize with a cheat, for he or she too has a passion for winning. A cheater craves winning, but too much, committing crimes in order to attain the object of desire. Of course, the motivations for cheating are many. Cheating might grow from a desire to beat the game system itself, to show up other players, or to reap rewards of glory external to the game. But no matter what the psychological motivation for cheating, all cheating behavior shares a particular set of formal relationships to rules, goals, and the magic circle.

The *spoil-sport* is the category of player furthest from the standard player. As game designer Mark Prensky explains, "What spoils a game is not so much the cheater who accepts the rules but doesn't play by them (we can deal with him or her), but the nihilist who denies them altogether."[2] The cheater breaks the rules but remains within the space of play. The spoil-sport is more destructive, refusing to acknowledge the game altogether. The spoil-sport is the frustrated player that knocks all of the pieces off the Chess board, the player that reveals the hidden information of Charades, the player that answers when it isn't his turn, the player that hacks into the game database to erase all of the player records. The cheater is a conniving actor, a spy within the magic circle, carefully pretending to obey all of its regulations even as he breaks them. But the spoil-sport has no such compunction. His destruction of the game does not

require concealment, because the rule structure that would condemn his action as illegal is exactly the authority the spoil-sport wishes to undermine.

When a set of Chess pieces are placed in their proper positions on the board and a game begins, the pieces gain meaning. But if, during a game, the action of a spoil-sport wipes the Chess pieces from the board, meaning is violently erased. Removed from their grid positions, the Chess pieces merely represent a collection of scattered figurines. The spoil-sport returns the game to its pre-game state as a collection of parts, no longer the embodiment of the space of possibility set out by the rules of the game.

The spoil-sport, more than any other kind of player, demonstrates the fragility of the magic circle. Not bound by a faith in the game, an interest in the lusory attitude, a respect for the rules, or even a concern for the outcome, the spoil-sport is the representative of the world outside the game. Armed with a powerful lack of belief, the spoil-sport has no qualms about ruining the play of others. The cheat may hack into a multiplayer deathmatch to up his ping time and secretly improve his play performance. But the spoil-sport will unleash a virus that brings the game servers to a halt, making play impossible for all players.

Five Player Types Compared

On the following page is table that summarizes the five kinds of players discussed in this schema. Several fascinating patterns arise when we compare player types in this way. The slippery slope between the dedicated player and the cheat becomes particularly clear. An enthusiasm for playing a game can quickly become a zealous winning-for-its-own-sake, which can lead to unsportsmanlike behavior and outright cheating. In their shared investment in the outcome of the game, players and cheaters have a great deal in common.

	Degree of lusory attitude	Relationship to rules	Interest in winning
Standard Player	Possesses lusory attitude	Acknowledges authority of rules	Typical interest in winning
Dedicated Player	Extra-zealous lusory attitude	Special interest in mastering rules	Intense interest in winning
Unsportsmanlike Player	Sometimes resembles the Dedicated player, sometimes resembles the Cheat	Adherence to operational rules, but violates implicit rules	Intense interest in winning
Cheat	Pretends to possess lusory attitude	Violates operational rules in secret	Intense interest in winning
Spoil-Sport	No pretense about lack of lusory attitude	No interest in adhering to rules	No interest in winning

It is sometimes difficult to identify exactly when an instance of cheating is a true transgression of the magic circle or merely part of the play of a game. Is hacking into an online server to inflate a high score on a public ranking board cheating? The transgression is not taking place within the magic circle of a particular game, but it certainly demonstrates an overly serious interest in the act of winning. How about fouls in sports? And what about games that encourage rule-breaking as part of their play? Where do they fit into our understanding of formal transgressions? We end this chapter by looking at a series of games that incorporate rule-breaking into the game design itself.

Sanctioned Violations: Professional Sports

In most games, rule violations threaten to destroy the magic circle. However, there is one category of game in which rule-breaking by players and punishments for violations of the rules are an important part of the overall game structure: professional sports. Double-dribbling in Basketball, icing in Hockey, using hands in Soccer—these are all rule-violations, but they are violations that are punished within the game itself, in ways that let the play continue. It is expected, and even anticipated

that these kinds of events will occur in a sports game. It would be extremely unusual for an entire Basketball game to occur without a single foul being committed.

What is interesting about the way that sports handle rule-breaking is that there is always a sliding scale of severity for different rule violations, and often extra punishment for repeated offenses, as when a basketball player "fouls out" and cannot play in a game after committing six personal fouls. A single foul might be the result of an "honest mistake" and is therefore treated somewhat lightly. Six fouls, on the other hand, creates a pattern of rule-breaking behavior, and the player is ejected from the magic circle entirely. Sports referees, as extensions of the formal system of a game, have authority to decide when violations occur and how to interpret the rules to mete out punishment. For example, referees generally have the authority to throw players and coaches out of games if their behavior becomes too extreme.

When rule-breaking becomes sanctioned, as it is in sports, a whole new layer of implicit rules enters into the space of play. Whereas it is considered aggressive play (and a foul) to elbow an opponent on a Basketball court, it is truly bad sportsmanship to punch that same opponent in the face. As rule-breaking is integrated into a game, it is incorporated into the space of possibility. Depending on the particular game, players may strategically transgress rules, accepting a short-term punishment for a long-term strategic or psychological advantage.

This intentional brokering of rule-breaking can be quite complex. In Basketball, the players can attempt to "draw fouls" from opponents. This risky practice can result in the player who is attempting to draw a foul committing a foul himself. Players who charge the basket on offense hoping to be fouled on their way to the hoop are often called for "charging," an offensive foul that results in the loss of the ball for the offensive team.

In professional sports, the complex system of violations and punishments within a game is also reflected in the professional legislative bodies which can sanction penalties for larger violations. Outside the scope of an individual game, these organizations govern more serious offenses. If a professional athlete is found to be fixing games or is convicted of a criminal act, he can be banned from the sport for life by the game's professional body.

Why is there so much attention to breaking the rules in sports, particularly professional sports? One answer is the nature of athletic game play. On a Chess grid, there is little or no ambiguity about which square a piece occupies; a Chess player will not gain an advantage by having a little corner of his Rook peek into an adjacent square. But in the infinitely granular space of the real world, milliseconds and millimeters can mean the difference between winning and losing. The runner does not want to start running before the starting gun fires, but springing forward as close to that moment as humanly possible will certainly offer an advantage. As a result, many false starts occur in races. Most sports fouls are motivated by an attempt to maximize an offensive or defensive advantage.

In looking for a motivation behind the prominence of rule-breaking in sports, we must also acknowledge the economic component of the games. A great deal of capital is connected to professional sports, from player salaries to ticket sales to network advertising. When the external stakes of a game are high, it is especially important to maintain and enforce the level playing field of conflict. The premise of a professional sport, even more than with most games, is that it is being played fairly. This emphasis on fairness extends naturally to its opposite: an emphasis on breaking the rules.

Sanctioned Cheating: Illuminati

For a different approach to the integration of rule-breaking into a game, we turn to Illuminati, a humorous strategic tabletop game based on the *Illuminatus* books by Robert Anton Wilson. In the game, players take on the role of all-powerful Illuminati, the shadowy power brokers pulling the strings behind world governments. The original edition of Illuminati contained an optional set of rules for cheating:

Cheating:
Some fiendish people think Illuminati is even more fun when nothing, not even the bank, is sacred. In this variant of the game, most forms of cheating are permitted.

Exceptions:
- You may not tip over the table or disarrange opposing power structures.

- You may not bring in counterfeit money or money from other sets.

- You may not cheat on the amount of money drawn from the bank during setup or the income phase (this would slow things down too much).

- Anything else goes. Anyone caught in the act must undo that cheat. There is no other penalty.

  Suggested methods for cheating include:
- Accidentally misread the dice.

- Steal from the bank (other than during the income phase).

- Lie about the amount of power or resistance your groups have.

- Stack the deck or peek ahead.

- If anyone leaves the table, anything goes!

- We recommend you play the cheating game only with very good friends or with people you will never see again.[3]

These "rules" for cheating in Illuminati provide a fascinating example of the relationship between rule-following and rule-breaking. Normally, cheating is considered something that runs counter to the spirit of the game rules. But in Illuminati, the sanctioned formal system of the game actually contains rules for cheating.

Illuminati's rules for cheating are different than rule-breaking in professional sports. In sports rule violations, most fouls are committed by players performing as close as possible to the limits of what the rules allow. In the real-world context of athletic performance, sometimes players miscalculate and end up breaking a rule. But in Illuminati, the suggested modes of cheating focus explicitly on player deception. The rules above directly suggest out-and-out, down-and-dirty cheating. The rules are not descriptions of penalties for fouls: they are proscriptions for different ways to cheat! In fact, there is no explicit penalty for being caught cheating, other than undoing the effect of the cheat.

Sanctioned cheating can easily destroy a game. Are Illuminati's "cheating rules" a recipe for anarchy, or are they a well-designed extension of the rest of the rulebook? It seems like a contradiction that the rules themselves contain suggestions for transgressive play. But a close look at the rules reveals the care taken in crafting this section of Illuminati's formal structure.

Illuminati places numerous formal restrictions on the scope of possible cheating. Forbidding players from tipping over the table (a classic spoil-sport action) lets players know that they cannot completely disrupt the game for the other players. Keeping players from inflating their income ensures that the game will not get too bogged down in mathematical squabbling. Permitted cheating focuses on keeping the rule-breaking play constrained, so that things do not swing too wildly outside the magic circle. For example, the rule that keeps players from smuggling money in from other sets of the game performs a number of regulatory functions. It keeps the designed economy of the game intact, while not letting players with "outside" resources (such as their own copy of the game) from gaining an unfair advantage. The result is that even with cheating, the game is contained within the magic circle, so that all of the players have an equal chance of being skillful cheats. The magic circle is such a strong focus of the cheating rules that when a player actually leaves the physical space of the game by getting up from the table, the rules state that "anything goes." Players are clearly discouraged from exiting a game in progress.

In addition to formal restrictions, the cheating rules go so far as to shape the lusory attitude of the players that might want to use them. The statements that begin and end the cheating rules place it within a particular context. The opening statement, which implies that only "fiendish" players would play this game variation, and the suggestions at the end, which imply that only good friends or near-strangers play this version of the game, are revealing. By removing the artificial nature of the game conflict, cheating can destroy the implicit camaraderie of the magic circle, letting its conflict leak out to infect the real-world relationships of players. Only friendships strong enough to weather such an experience or more disposable relationships in which further contact is not desired are appropriate.

The very notion that the rules could sanction cheating is a bit outrageous, but it ultimately fits the spirit of the game and its narrative world quite well. Illuminati is a parodic game about hidden organizations that rule the world, where the players are secret power brokers manipulating governments, media, and culture to their own devious ends. Seen in this light, the idea that the rules themselves are also subject to manipulation fits within the overall narrative trajectory of the game. Rule-breaking is a way of expressing the humorous critique of power that Illuminati the game embodies.

In the right context, sanctioned cheating can be an innovative way to enrich a game design. But it must be done with great care. Beneath the light-hearted tone of Illuminati's rules is a careful design allowing only those forms of cheating that leave the game intact, playable, and meaningful. Cheating in Illuminati does not remove all rules and boundaries from the game: it serves to re-draw them. Although the new boundaries might be drawn in lines that are considerably more fuzzy, a clear formal system remains. Even cheating is something that can be intentionally designed to facilitate meaningful play.

Hacks, Cheats, and Mods: Digital Rule-Breaking

When it comes to forms of rule-breaking incorporated into the design and experience of games, computer and video games offer a cornucopia of examples. Following are some sample instances of digital game rule-breaking, ranging from the timidly transgressive to the truly unlawful.

Easter Eggs

Easter eggs are secrets hidden in a game that players can discover. The first Easter egg was created by game designer and programmer Warren Robinett for the Atari 2600 game Adventure. In defiance of Atari's refusal to give credit to the creators of their games, Robinett programmed a secret room that could only be found with great difficulty. When players reached it, his initials were displayed. Hidden messages, images, and spaces are now a standard feature of digital gaming. In a mild kind of way, Easter eggs break a game's rules because they violate the otherwise internally consistent world of a game. Part of the pleasure of finding an Easter egg is a sense of transgressive discovery: by bending the rules of the game in just the right way, the player gets to see or experience something that more lawful players would not.

Cheat Codes

Although Easter eggs usually do not impact the strategic play of a game, cheat codes do. Like Easter eggs, developers design cheat codes into a game. Some of the best-known instances of cheat codes come from the first-person shooter DOOM, where a player can type special key combinations to gain weapons, health, and invulnerability. Sometimes a cheat code is a leftover tool from the game's development process, but often they are added just for the benefit of players. Although the name "cheat code" implies that these shortcuts to power are rule infringements, cheat codes frequently appear in game magazines and on official game websites, making them a form of officially sanctioned "cheating." The result is a rich culture of insider game knowledge, with fans scouring magazines and websites for the latest, coolest cheats.

Game Guides and Walkthroughs

Related to cheat codes are the sources of information that players turn to for help with a difficult or lengthy game. These resources appear on the web and in print, and range from elaborate color maps and strategy guides to fan-generated text files that cover every conceivable aspect of a game. Game walkthroughs are step-by-step instructions for finishing a game, particularly useful to players of adventure games and role-playing games that have a more linear structure. Some players view these resources as unfair techniques that breach the spirit of a game. At the same time, walkthroughs have raised the bar of difficulty and complexity in certain game genres. Many digital games are so challenging that they seem designed to require a guide.

Workarounds

The complexity of digital games often makes it impossible for designers to test or anticipate every possible permutation of play before releasing a title to the public. Furthermore, players are infinitely creative in finding ways of "legally" working around game structures. In "The Future of Game Design," Harvey Smith writes about how players discovered new ways to play Deus Ex. For example, the proximity mine object is an explosive device that can be "stuck" onto walls in the game space. After the game's release, players realized something that the game's developers did not anticipate. Exploiting the game's physics and interactivity, players learned to climb up on proximity mines, and using (or misusing) a series of these objects like a ladder, they could ascend the game's vertical surfaces, ruining many of the carefully designed levels. Workarounds are on the borderline between dedicated play and unsportsmanlike play, and include degenerate strategies. Is it cheating to purchase game power by buying an EverQuest character on eBay, or is it simply a workaround that converts labor to capital?

True Cheating

In addition to fuzzier types of "cheating" behavior, there is plenty of bona fide cheating in digital games. More than clever workarounds or sanctioned cheat codes, true cheating breaks the rules of the game. In a multiplayer environment, guidelines for what constitutes cheating are generally made known to all players; cheaters are usually removed immediately and permanently from a game. In SiSSYFiGHT 2000, the most common form of cheating is multi-sessioning, in which a single player opens up two game windows on two different computers, playing two characters at once and gaining very strong play advantages. Although it is difficult to spot, multi-sessioning is outlawed in the game, and there are vigilante fan websites devoted to maintaining lists of known game cheaters.

Hacks

Hacking into a digital game goes beyond simply breaking the rules—it does so through intervention at the level of code. A player might hack a high score list, for example, to place her name at the top. Or she might modify the code of a first-person shooter to gain an unfair advantage in a deathmatch. If too many players hack a game, all sense of fairness can be destroyed. Therefore, the administrators of commercial multiplayer games put great effort into eliminating cheating and hacks from their games. According to massively multiplayer online game designer Ralph Koster, tracking down cheaters and hackers can occupy approximately half of all of the resources spent on maintaining and improving an online game.

Spoil-Sport Hacking

Most hacking is done in the spirit of the cheat: players want to do well in a game and do not mind breaking the rules in order to get ahead. Occasionally, game hackers can take the role of a spoil-sport as well, bringing down an entire game or game network. In this case, the aim is to dispel the magic circle for all players involved, not to better one's own performance.

Why are digital games so fertile a ground for these varieties of rule-breaking? First and foremost, code is a plastic and pliable medium. The complex processes that give digital games their uniquely automated quality leave gaps for hacking into the system, whether it is through officially distributed cheat codes, clever workarounds, or genuine code-breaking. The anonymous nature of digital game play, where computers and networks mediate players, encourages rule-breaking as well. The reduced physical presence of other players permits a greater sense of social autonomy, which can facilitate the surreptitious activities of rule-breaking. Lastly, digital games are pop culture with a rich fan base: game fans deconstruct and reconstruct the codes and structures of the works that interest them. Cheating and hacking in this sense is similar to the ways that Star Trek fans re-mix the narrative universe of the television show to invent new stories and characters.

The blessing and curse of digital gaming media is that they provide a pliable space in which to play. With so many ways to gently bend and forcefully break the rules of a game, in playing a computer or video game players must decide what constitutes proper game behavior, navigating the space of possible rule violations. Is it acceptable to download a walkthrough guide? Do you use cheat codes to short-circuit your way through tough game levels? If you were offered a cracked version of the game that let you cheat, would you use it? As a digital game designer, you need to decide what kinds of rule-breaking you want to engender and what kinds you want to outlaw. Can you foster fan communities by offering sanctioned ways to violate the game without letting things get out of hand altogether? Ethics and game design collide in this rich space of rule-breaking possibility.

Rule-Breaking as a Game Design Practice

Our discussion of rule-breaking is not just an explication of the ways in which players break the rules of a game. It is a game design schema, a way of looking at *all* games that offers a framework for solving particular game design problems. However, it is a different kind of chapter than the other formal schema we encountered in our investigation of **RULES**. Framing games as systems of rule-breaking questions many of the unspoken assumptions of earlier schemas. We did not, in considering games as emergent systems, information, or cybernetic feedback loops, ever consider that players might disrespect or transgress the authority of the rules and the magic circle.

Player behavior is not universally law-abiding. Given any particular game, there are many ways to play it and many ways to bend and break its rules. For game designers, this means that you should never take players' behavior for granted. You need to assume that your game will be played not just by earnest rule-followers, but by zealously dedicated players, inappropriately unsportsmanlike players, brilliantly secretive cheaters,

and uncaringly nihilistic spoil-sports. Some of these player types can help expand your game's space of possibility, whereas others can wreck the game for everyone involved. How do you take these possibilities into account in your game design? As always, there is no single solution. But framing your game as a system of rule-breaking lets you formulate your own answers.

There is yet another way to frame rule-breaking: as an attitude toward playing and designing games. We have seen a number of examples of how rule-breaking can enhance meaningful play. In professional sports, digital games, and in the cheating variant of Illuminati, breaking rules is part of the game itself. In all of these cases, through rule-breaking the space of possibility fills with alternative modes of play. What is the lesson here? Perhaps it suggests a shift in the way that we think about game design. In *The Well-Played Game,* Bernard DeKoven advocates a fundamental adjustment in players' attitudes towards the rules of a game:

> You're not changing the game for the sake of changing it. You're changing it for the sake of finding a game that works.
>
> Once this freedom is established, once we have established why we want to change a game and how we go about it, a remarkable thing happens to us: We become the authorities.
>
> No matter what game we create, no matter how well we are able to play it, it is our game, and we can change it when we need to. We don't need permission or approval from anyone outside our community. We play our games as we see fit. Which means that now we have at our disposal the means whereby we can always fit the game to the way we want to play.
>
> This is an incredible freedom, a freedom that does more than any game can, a freedom with which we nurture the play community. The search for the well-played game is what holds the community together. But the freedom to change the game is what gives the community its power.[4]

Rather than obeying game rules as an ultimate authority, DeKoven would like players to assume authority over the rules. Once they feel confident and in control of the rules, players can break them and modify them in the course of playing a game. They do so not out of a mischievous desire to disrupt the authority of the rules, but out of a directed attempt to create a deeper experience of play. This beautiful vision for games does not describe the way that most people normally play. However, there is one type of game player that already has this attitude: game designers. Game designers, particularly those that design through an iterative process, already posses a methodology in which playing a game means breaking, tweaking, and modifying rules. In a sense, DeKoven is advocating that game players become more like game designers.

How are game designers rule-breakers? Being a game designer means that you are constantly testing the limits of a game you are creating. Which aspects of the rules are working and which are not? Do you need to add a feedback loop, or modify the amount of randomness in the game? Are players being faced with meaningful decisions at every moment? The best way to answer these game design questions is by changing the rules of your game, trying out new variations, and seeing what happens.

Of course, DeKoven's vision for dethroning the authority of a game extends beyond just professional game designers. He would like to see all game players adopt this attitude toward play. What would it mean if all players felt free to break the rules of a game, to play not just inside the space of a game, but to modify and change the shape of that space itself? One answer to this important question is that it would require a fundamental alteration in the attitudes of game players and game designers. If players regularly break the rules, are they really rules at all? If players no longer stay inside the magic circle, are they really playing a game? Making this shift might be liberating, but it would certainly change the way we conceive games, game play, and game design.

Yet another answer to DeKoven's challenge is that perhaps the phenomenon he describes already exists. Perhaps all players already play, not just inside the frame of a game, but with the frame of a game itself. If this is indeed the case, then all the varieties of rule-breaking players, from dedicated and unsportsmanlike players to cheaters and spoil-sports, are natural extensions of the flexibility of game structures. Rule-breaking is simply one of the ways that we play.

Lastly, rule-breaking can be considered not just a way to play or design games, but a more general attitude about game design itself. If the conventions and genres of game design are the rules by which most designers "play," then the innovators are those designers that manage to break the rules. Games hold great promise, but only if we are bold enough to truly break the rules of our field. This is harder than it seems. We know that to skillfully break rules requires an intimate knowledge of the rules themselves. And our hope is that this book provides some of those "rules of play"—rules that you will mercilessly and playfully violate in order to expand the space of game design's possibilities.

With this chapter, we finish our first Primary Schema. In **RULES**, we consciously limited our gaze to the strictly formal boundaries of the magic circle, generally ignoring the player experience and the larger contexts in which a game takes place. But as we move forward, we will slowly widen the scope of our investigation, as we include those aspects of games that have been left out. How stable is the authority of a game's rules? How permeable is the boundary of the magic circle? How is it possible to not just play a game but play with the very structures of gaming? We directly address these questions and many more in the **PLAY** and **CULTURE** schemas to come.

Further Reading

Grasshopper: Games, Life, by Bernard Suits *(see page 98)*

    Recommended:

    Chapter 4: Triflers, Cheats, and Spoilsports

The Well-Played Game: A Player's Philosophy, by Bernard DeKoven *(see page 21)*

    Recommended:

    Chapter 2: Guidelines

    Chapter 3: The Play Community

    Chapter 5: Changing the Game

Notes

1. Dave Hickey, *Air Guitar: Essays on Art and Democracy* (Los Angeles: Foundation for Advanced Critical Studies, 1997), p. 160–1.

2. Marc Prensky, *Digital Game-Based Learning* (New York: McGraw-Hill, 2001), p. 119.

3. *Illuminati: The Game of Conspiracy,* Fourth Edition (Austin: Steve Jackson Games, 1991), p. 9–10.

4. Bernard DeKoven, *The Well-Played Game* (New York: Doubleday, 1978), p. 68.

Breaking the Rules
SUMMARY

- Breaking the rules is a phenomenon that occurs in almost every kind of game.

- Relative to rule-breaking, there are **five player types.** Each type of player has a particular relationship to the following aspects of a game:

    - adherence to the rules

    - interest in winning

    - degree of lusory attitude

- The **standard player** is the typical rule-following player that obeys the restrictions of the game and possesses the lusory attitude. Even if the standard player is a theoretical fiction, it is important to acknowledge this player position, which stands in contrast to the other four types.

- A **dedicated player** is similar to the standard player but has an extra zealousness toward succeeding at a game. The dedicated player follows the rules, is interested in winning, and possesses the lusory attitude.

- **Unsportsmanlike players** violate the implicit rules of a game without actually breaking operational rules. Their strong interest in winning gives them license to violate rules of etiquette and proper game behavior.

- **Cheaters** break operational rules of a game in order to win. Cheating players thus possess a strong interest in winning, but will forgo the normal means of achieving victory. Acknowledging that other players can invoke the authority of the rules, cheaters break rules secretly.

- A **spoil-sport** is a player that refuses to acknowledge the authority of a game in any way. These nihilistic players do not hesitate to destroy the magic circle of a game.

- The five player types are not always distinct. During a single game, a player can move from one category to another. The same behavior in different contexts can fall into different player categories.

- A **degenerate strategy** or **exploit** is a way of playing a game that ensures victory every time. Dedicated players and unsportsmanlike players make use of degenerate strategies. In general, degenerate strategies are detrimental to a game. However, within a community of players, degenerate strategies can sometimes act to expand the space of possibility.

- There are many examples of the integration of rule-breaking into game design and player experience, including professional sports, digital games, and games that sanction cheating such as Illuminati.

- Game designers need to recognize that rule-breaking is a common phenomenon in gaming and incorporate it into their game design thinking. One solution, which comes from the New Games Movement, is to empower players to be more like game designers by creating games with rules that are meant to broken and modified.

Ironclad
A game for 2 players

Overview

Ironclad is a game of arena combat between opposing teams of massive, armored robots. It is also a game about two logicians attempting to resolve a philosophical disagreement. The two "sub-games" occupy different dimensions of the same space. The gameboard is a grid: the robot combat occurs in the squares of the grid, whereas the philosophical debate occurs on the intersections of the grid. The two sub-games occur in separate and unrelated domains, but each exerts a subtle and crucial influence on the other.

Rules

The Board

The gameboard is a 6 x 8 (48-square) checkerboard, positioned between the players with the two narrow ends facing either player. You can create an Ironclad gameboard simply by marking off two outside rows of a checkerboard with masking tape.

The Pieces

· 24 checkers (or any other stackable piece): 2 colors, 12 of each color
· 64 stones (or any other small marker): 2 colors, 32 of each color
· a 6-sided die

Setup

Each player chooses a color of checker and a color of stone. Organize the checkers into six stacks as follows: two stacks of three checkers, two stacks of two checkers, and two stacks of one checker. Place the stacks according to the diagram below. Collect the stones in two bowls and set them beside the board.

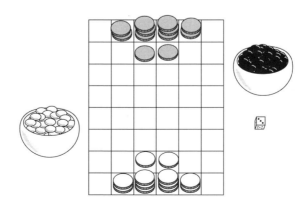

Structure of Play

·   Players alternate turns.

·   During a player's turn, he or she chooses one of the two sub-games and makes a move in this sub-game.

·   The player's opponent then makes any legal move for the player in the other sub-game.

·   As soon as a player achieves a winning condition in either sub-game, that player immediately wins the overall game.

Playing Ironclad: The Spectacle of Mechanical Destruction

Beneath its hermetically sealed dome, the Grid is a clockwork battlefield littered with the steel corpses of recombinant automata. They re-assemble nightly to battle for the horror and amusement of an audience that has long since crumbled into dust.

Explosions shake the foundation of the Grid. With thundering tread, massive automated Warsuits stride through columns of smoke and the incandescent latticework of laser fire. Flocks of nervous cameras drift and scatter around their shoulders. Colorful insignia decorate scorched breastplates. Periodically these giant predator machines freeze, helms bowed, listening for the silent word of sponsorship.

Objective

To move one of your robots onto any of the six squares on the opposite side of the grid (your opponent's first row).

How to Play

You control a combat squad of giant robots, each robot represented by a stack of chips. During your turn you move one of your robots or fire on one enemy robot.

Moving

Robots can move one square in any direction horizontally, vertically, or diagonally. They may not move into a square already occupied by another robot.

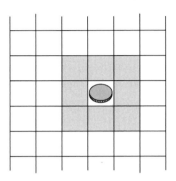

Robot movement

Firing

A robot can fire on any enemy robot that is within two squares in a straight line horizontally, vertically, or diagonally. If there is at least one enemy robot within range of one of your robots, you may choose to fire during your turn instead of moving. To fire, choose a target. Only enemy robots within range of one of your robots can be selected as a target. The target takes one point of damage from each of your robots that are within range. Robots may fire "through" friendly or enemy robots with no effect.

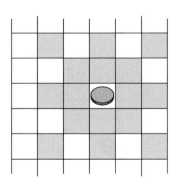

Robot range

Damage

For each point of damage a robot takes, remove one checker from the stack representing that robot. If, during one turn, a robot takes more damage than the number of checkers in its stack, remove all of the checkers from that stack.

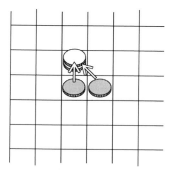

Robot combat
The two black robots attack a white target, destroying it.

Terrain

The grid contains terrain represented by stones located on some of the grid intersections. A robot located on a square whose corner points contain one or more stones receives a defensive bonus from this terrain. Each stone gives one terrain bonus. If this robot is the target of enemy fire, the firing player must roll the die one time for each robot that is firing on the target. The number showing on the die must be greater than the target's terrain bonus, in order for that robot to damage the target.

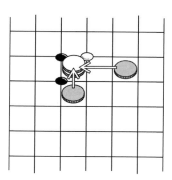

Defensive terrain
Again, the white target is under attack. This time, the target has a terrain bonus of 3. The black player must roll twice, once for each attacking robot. The target only takes damage on a roll of 4, 5, or 6.

Playing Ironclad: The Technique of Scholarly Discourse

The Grid is a formal system for philosophical disputation. It has been handed down through countless generations by the ones who live and die in pursuit of enlightenment. Its borders, once engraved with axiomatic symbols, are now worn smooth by the motion of a thousand cuffs. The Laws of Inference determine the position and motion of the stones. Shifting constellations trace the arguments of Scholars as they fight to establish the irrefutable truth of propositions whose meanings have long since been forgotten.

Object

To form an unbroken string of stones, running from any one side of the grid to the opposite side.

How to Play

You are attempting to manipulate stones (representing logical statements) on a grid (representing a formal philosophical system). Each turn you must place a stone of your color onto the grid. If you cannot place a stone you must move one stone of either color.

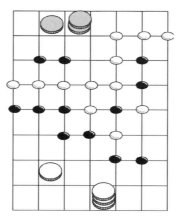

Winning position
White has an unbroken string running from one side of the board to the opposite side.

Placing

Stones can be placed onto any unoccupied intersection of the grid, including those around the edges of the grid. The only limitation on stone placement is the *Rule of Negation*.

The Rule of Negation

You may not place a stone on the corner point of any square that contains one or more checkers.

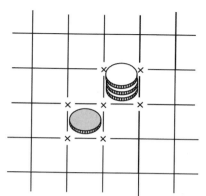

Rule of Negation
No stones can be placed on intersections shown marked with an X.

Movement

If during your turn you cannot place a stone, you must move one stone of either color from one intersection of the grid to another. In order to move, a stone must be situated next to an open intersection. You may move a stone in the direction of any open intersection as far as you want, until it is blocked by another stone. The Rule of Negation has no effect on stone movement.

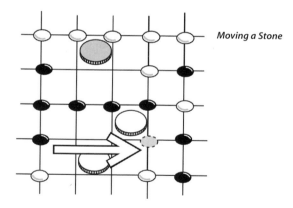

Moving a Stone

The Rule of Circularity

You may not move a stone if that stone was the last stone moved.

Forfeit

If during your turn you cannot place or move a stone, your opponent wins.

Ironclad

It seemed like a good idea at the time. The original concept for Ironclad was a game that had a single rule-structure but two completely different "themes." Both players would manipulate identical, abstract pieces and cards according to identical rules, but the pieces and rules would represent something different for each player.

Here was my original idea:

The game is a card game for two people. The game has two separate sets of rules, one for each player, and in a sense the two players are playing different games. Although structurally similar, the motif and narrative surface of the two games are entirely different. One player is playing a game about an argument between two philosophers; the other is playing a game about giant robots battling in arena combat.

The cards use abstract symbols and numbers. A card that represents a "Premise" in the philosophy game might represent a "Base" in the battling robots game, "Irony" vs. "Camouflage Armor," and so on. All game actions would share the same mechanic but have different names.

The players compete to determine which game is being played.

The game mechanic involves building a network of cards across the table towards a player's opponent. The game mechanic will probably include hidden information (such as cards hidden underneath other cards) because I want there to be a bluffing element. Also it may include shared resources, such as asking each player to design a deck, with both players drawing from either deck.

I will attempt to make the game as simple as possible. I'm thinking of using fewer than 10 different card types with some variations, such as strength or direction.

I have for many years been haunted by the image of massive, futuristic philosopher-robots engaging in combat that represents an abstract clash of ideas and beliefs. (The Nietzsche mech: enormous and overpowering, but piloted by a shriveled homunculus who is crawling over the monster's surface wrenching off parts of the machinery and using them to jam his own gears. The Derridean mech: a swarm of robots who scatter to the edges of the arena and begin to disassemble its walls and floor, etc.) It's one of those idée fixe that I knew would come out somewhere but never knew when it would appear.

I love the high-culture/low-culture friction of the game, and I also think that the concept gets at something about games and representation that is hard to put into words but is an important and unique aspect of games.

I considered a number of different names for this game, including 2-Player, or 2-P, but eventually decided on the name Ironclad.

I wanted the design to adhere to specific constraints relating to the context of the game. Because players would only be given a ruleset (and possibly some printed elements), I wanted to keep the game materials minimal. My intention was to make a game that was ambitious and unusual, but I wanted people to actually play it, not just read it, and so I made the materials as simple as possible.

Ironclad began life as a two-player card game, with a high concept and a game play mechanic that was vague to the point of non-existence. And here was the problem—I wasn't really interested in the mechanic, I was completely focused on the "big idea." I could picture the way the rules would be laid out: two sets of rules, one for each player. Each player would have the same instructions about the goal of the game and the types of actions allowed in terms of manipulating pieces, but their mental image of what those actions *represented* would be completely different.

Because of this interest, I set out to find a straightforward structure that would be flexible enough to bend both ways. The first hurdle was the problem of *space*. Robots occupy space and move through it, philosophical debates don't. Any structure that had pieces moving around would evoke the robot game to the detriment of the philosophers' game, so I needed something more abstract. A card-based structure seemed to be the perfect solution. I was thinking of how the card game Milles Bournes creates the image of a car race without any spatial maneuvering.

My initial plan was for a set of 30 cards: 15 base or premise cards, and 15 attack or argument cards. Each card would have a numerical value; players would lay the cards out on the table in various arrangements in an attempt to destroy their opponent's bases (or invalidate their arguments) in the most efficient way. The cards would have abstract symbols in the center and a different caption and "flavor text" facing each opponent. One direction would say "EMP Blast" the other would say "Occam's Razor." Imagine Richard Garfield's NetRunner, only not as much fun.

At this point I had a game that was almost working but wasn't at all enjoyable. More importantly, the game was supposed to be about one structure and two representations, but the structure really didn't fit *either* representation. After a few weeks of ruminating on this problem I wasn't able to come up with a different structure that would work. More importantly, the whole project felt wrong to me. Normally it's a lot of fun to think about how the structure of a game system relates to its theme, but trying to come up with a structure that would serve as the fulcrum for two opposing themes was not fun. There was something unpleasant about it, something particularly forced, overly deliberate, and awkward.

I began to think a lot about how structure and representation work in games. There was a notion buried in my original idea, the idea of a fundamental separation between a game's structure and whatever subject matter or activity or setting the game represents. The implication was that you could take any number of different structures and match them up with various themes for different effects, but there wasn't any *deep, essential* relationship between any particular theme and any particular game mechanic. Upon subsequent examination of this notion, I recognized that there was a kind of hidden agenda driving it, a pro-structure/anti-theme agenda. The agenda goes like this: the really interesting thing about a game is the structure, the system, the math, the topological convolutions of phase-space, whereas theme is just so much make-believe, fantasy, and pretend. Look player, you don't really want to swing a giant sword and kill monsters, you want to manage limited resources and calculate recursive probabilities! This notion wants to pry structure and theme apart so that structure can evolve on its own, released from subservience to the surface concerns of theme, or at least freed up to enter into new and more dynamic arrangements with these concerns. Picture the changing relationship of form to subject matter in twentieth century painting, only with orcs instead of nude women.

After a couple months of banging my head against it, this notion seemed less certain, or at least less interesting. I mean, sure you could do what I set out to do, but it was starting to seem like an empty and somewhat grotesque trick, like running electricity through a dead frog's legs and calling it ballet.

There are, of course, many relationships between theme and structure in a game. Whether or not any of those relationships are *essential,* they are complex and vital enough to resist my attempt to lightly shuffle them around. For example, there is the symbiotic relationship by which theme and structure assist each other. Theme can provide the entry point into a complex structure whose rewards are deeply buried: first it's all about the sword—the calculations are only there to conjure up the sword. Eventually the game becomes about the calculations and the sword fades away. Then there is the fact that representation can be used as a shortcut to embody a complicated structure that might otherwise be too much for the player to assimilate. If the red squares are "lava," then the player won't forget they are out of bounds. Why do the pieces in Tetris move from the top of the screen to the bottom? They're bricks! Theme can add arbitrary limitations to the structure, and arbitrary limitations are often a good thing.

Sometimes games actually *are* the things they represent. A painting of a bowl of fruit, no matter how realistically it's painted, is never going to turn into actual fruit. But the line between a game's simulation of, for example, bravery, betrayal, or greed, and those actual things is not so clear. Kory Heath's game Zendo seems at first to be a somewhat whimsical representation of the spiritual discipline of Zen Buddhism; but in play it can become a form of actual meditation.

In any event, I was operating under the influence of this half-recognized agenda, this kind of half-hearted critique of the conventional one-to-one correspondence of structure to theme. And ironically, despite the pro-structure implications of this agenda, I had two themes I really liked and no structure I cared about. I was grasping around trying to find any old structure I could plug in that would dutifully carry my two precious themes!

So, I abandoned Ironclad and I retreated, with some relief, to a totally different idea that I had been idly thinking about for a while. Often, when I looked at a grid, I would imagine a board game that was two different games at once. One set of pieces would move, like Chess, from square to square, while another set of pieces would move along the lines from intersection to intersection. I thought that there should be little or no contact between the two sets of pieces, and I pictured them simultaneously occupying two dimensions of the same space, affecting each other in some subtle and oblique fashion. I imagined the square pieces feeling the presence of the line pieces like the chill you feel when a ghost is in the room.

Now I had a structure I was excited about and a theme that emerged from the structure, rather than one that felt "applied." The two sets of pieces were "bodies" occupying the material realm of the squares of the grid, and "spirits" occupying the non-space of the intersections between the squares. Early versions of this idea involved bodies attacking and killing each other, resulting in the release of spirits that would flutter around subtly influencing subsequent combat. The goal was to get a body across the board to your opponent's side. Each turn a player would decide which type of piece to move. I tried a few variations of this and it played pretty well, leading to a game of strategic sacrifices.

I then began to toy with refinements to this theme: pawns and stones, bodies and souls, the material and the metaphysical, objects and ideas. Wait, objects and ideas? Without intending to, I had bounced back, hard, to Ironclad. It was obvious to me that the two sets of pieces were robots and concepts. From this insight the final form of the game began to take rough shape. I needed to pull the two "realms" apart a bit more. I gave the stones their own goal—to link two opposite sides of the board together as in Hex. This seemed to fit well with the idea of a "chain" of reasoning and was nicely reminiscent of the metaphysical contests of Herman Hesse's fictional Glass Bead Game. If the pawns were going to become giant, lumbering battle-mechs they needed to act the part more—they needed to shoot, and they needed to take damage, not just disappear. A stack of pieces seemed like an easy way to show energy or health, so the pawns became stacks of checkers. For the robots the stones operated as terrain, giving a defensive bonus that made them harder to hit. For the philosophers the robots operated as interruptions, gaps in the grid on which no stone could be played. Now instead of having one game with two different "surfaces" (but not really), I had two games occupying the same space (but not really). Ironclad had become a game about superimposition, an experiment in game play collage.

Early playtesting indicated that whichever sub-game "heated up" first would dominate, leaving the other one abandoned in a more stable position, in which any individual move was less likely to disturb the equilibrium and was therefore less valuable. I needed to make sure both sub-games moved forward at roughly the same rate. Rather than force each player to move in each sub-game every turn, I decided that on her turn a player would pick a sub-game in which to move and her opponent would move for her in the other sub-game. This made the choice of which sub-game to move in more interesting: because your opponent was trying to make the worst possible move for you in the other sub-game you were sure to eventually respond. This structure led to a nice back-and-forth between the two sub-games as the players' attention oscillated between them. I also like the way that moving for your opponent blurs the lines between the two players in a game that is already about double-vision on many levels.

Final playtesting enabled me to work out the remaining details. The "choose a target" method of firing was developed to allow for combined fire without adding extra steps to a turn in the robot sub-game (multiple robots can fire with a single move.) In the last stages of the design I fixed the size of the grid and the number of starting pieces, and ironed out any ambiguities in the rules.

In its stereoscopic use of the grid, Ironclad resembles a collision between Chess and Go. But there is a deeper connection. Two ideas from Chess and Go were a major influence on the game. The first is Bughouse, the Chess variant in which two games are played simultaneously and captured pieces in one game show up as new pieces in the other. The second is the Go concept of *tenuki*. Because of its deep complexities, Go can almost be thought of as a collection of multiple, simultaneous games. Tenuki is a term that describes a player leaving a "local" situation to move somewhere else on the board.

A final note: although the philosophers have long ago forgotten what they are arguing about, I happen to know that it's the mind/body problem. The robots are fighting because that's what robots do.

Frank Lantz

Frank Lantz is a freelance game designer based in New York City. For the past 3 years Frank has been lead designer on a variety of projects for two independent game developers—gameLab and Pop. Prior to that, he was Creative Director of New York design firm R/GA Interactive, where he worked on several games including the PC titles Gearheads and The Robot Club. Frank is a member of the faculty of NYU's Interactive Tele-communications Program, where he teaches classes in game design and interactive narrative.

Unit 3: PLAY

*[Play] is a **structuring** activity, the activity out of which understanding comes. Play is at one and the same time the location where we question our structures of understanding and the location where we develop them.—**James S. Hans,** The Play of the World*

How do the rules play out?

Ultimately, game design is play design. The rules of a game are relevant because they facilitate the experience of players. Within this primary schema, we expand our understanding of games considerably, delving into topics like pleasure, narrative, and social interaction. In the movement from the primary schema of **RULES** to **PLAY,** we loosen our tight focus on rules as a formal system to examine the ways that rules become a meaningful experience for the players of a game.

Unit 3: **Play**

DEFINING PLAY

game play
ludic activities
being playful
free play
transformative play

22

Any earnest definition of play has to be haunted by the possibility that playful enjoinders will render it invalid.—**Brian Sutton-Smith,** *The Ambiguity of Play*

Introducing Play

The design of meaningful play, in whatever form the play might take, demands an understanding of how rules ramify into play. The play of a game only occurs as players experience the rules of the game in motion. Before a game begins, the many formal components of the game-system lie in wait: an empty football stadium; Chess pieces resting in their starting positions; a game program installed on a hard drive. Only when the players enter into the game does the system come fully to life. Athletes and fans spill into the stadium; Chess pieces sally forth one by one from their starting positions; a saved game file is loaded and the game fills the screen. Dormant relationships spring up between game elements as players inhabit, explore, and manipulate the game's space of possible play.

From a formal point of view, the rules of a game indeed constitute the inner "essence" of a game. But there is a danger in limiting the consideration of a game solely to its formal system. The complexity of rules has an intrinsic fascination, the hypnotic allure of elegant mathematics and embedded logic. However, it is crucial for game designers to recognize that the creation of rules, even those that are elegant and innovative, is never an end in itself. Rules are merely the means for creating play. If, during the process of game design, you find yourself attempting to perfect an elegant set of rules in a way that fails to impact the experience of the player, your focus has become misdirected. The experience of play represents the heart and soul of the game designer's craft, and is the focus of all of the chapters collected under the Primary Schema of **PLAY.**

Following this introductory chapter are a number of schemas, each one framing games from a different perspective. Within **PLAY,** we explore games as systems of experience and pleasure; as systems of meaning and narrative play; and as systems of simulation and social play. We are aware of the near-infinite variety of ways to frame games as experience and we make no pretense that our set of **PLAY** schemas offer a complete list. There are experiential schemas that offer valid ways of under-

standing games which we did not include. We don't, for example, look at play as an experience of learning, or at play as a kinesthetic system of movement. The schemas included offer a starting point for an ongoing discussion of game design and play, a discussion that is only just beginning.

What Is Play?

As psychologist J. Barnard Gilmore notes in *Child's Play,* "Certainly everyone knows what play is not even if everyone can't agree on just what play is."[1] The psychological and anthropological study of play has resulted in a range of definitions, from a formulation of play as "activities not consciously performed for the sake of any result beyond themselves" to a conceptualization that "play refers to those activities which are accompanied by a state of comparative pleasure, exhilaration, power, and the feeling of self-initiative."[2] Although these definitions may tell us something about play, we want to build a more design-centric definition of the concept, one that will help us create an experience of meaningful play in our games.

Let us start by looking at how play is used in everyday speech. As with "game," the word "play" is used in many and varied ways:

- the act of creating music, such as *playing* the radio or *playing* a musical instrument

- pretending: *playing* at being angry, *playing* the fool

- activating a process: putting something into *play*

- taking a risky action: *playing* fast and loose

- the course of events or fate: letting things *play* out, *playing* into the hand of fate

- stalling: *playing* for time

- being joking or not serious: just *playing* around, *playing* tricks

- gambling: *playing* the horses

- a subtle effect: a smile *playing* on the lips, the *play* of light on the wall

- the loose space between gears or cogs: the *play* of a car's steering wheel

- fooling or deceiving someone: *playing* someone for all they're worth, *playing* on someone's feelings, *playing* up to someone

- being artful, clever, or youthfully jubilant: dressing in a *playful* style, engaging in *wordplay* and, of course,

- *playing* with toys or *playing* a game

Whereas we "play" games such as Metal Gear Solid, Racquetball, and UNO, there seem to be many other activities that fall under the category of play and playing as well. What is the connection between the terms "play" and "game"? When we defined the word *game* in chapter 7, we posited two possible relationships between games and play:

> **Games are a subset of play:** Games constitute a formalized part of everything we might consider to be play. Playing catch or playing doctor are play activities that fall outside our definition of games (a contest of powers with a quantifiable outcome, etc.). However, although not all play fits the category of games, those things we define as games fit within a larger category of play activities.

> **Play is an element of games:** In addition to rules and culture, play is an essential component of games, a facet of the larger phenomenon of games, and a primary schema for understanding them.

Neither one of these two relationships is more correct than the other. The first is a *descriptive* distinction that places the phenomenon of games within a larger set of real-world play activities. The second is a *conceptual* distinction that frames play as an important facet of games. However, the common uses of "play" in English point to other understandings of the concept, which fall completely outside these two framings of "game" and "play." Making a *playful* gesture, for example, or the *play* of the waves on the beach—these examples don't seem to have anything at all to do with games. Or do they? Looking over all of the ways that play manifests, we can group them into three categories of "play:"

Game Play

This form of play is a narrow category of activity that only applies to what we defined already as "games." Game play is the formalized interaction that occurs when players follow the rules of a game and experience its system through play.

Ludic Activities

The word ludic means *of or relating to play* and like the title of Huizinga's book *Homo Ludens,* it is derived from *ludus,* the Latin word for play. Ludic activities are play activities that include not only games, but all of the non-game behaviors we also think of as "playing:" a kitten batting a ball of yarn, two college students tossing a Frisbee back and forth, children playing on a jungle gym.

Being Playful

The third category of play is the broadest and most inclusive. It refers not only to typical play activities, but also to the idea of being in a playful state of mind, where a spirit of play is injected into some other action. For instance, we are being playful with words when we create nicknames for friends or invent rhymes to tease them. We might dress in a playful way or deliver a critique of a sibling in a playful tone. In each case, the spirit of play infuses otherwise ordinary actions.

Each of the three categories of play is successively more open and inclusive. As a category, ludic activities includes game play, and the category being playful includes both of the previous two. Game play is really just a special kind of formalized ludic activity. Similarly, ludic activities are formalized, literal ways of being playful.

A General Definition of Play

Although these three categories bring the many expressions of play into focus, we still lack a general definition to assist us in designing experiences of meaningful play. There is, in fact, a way of defining play that does justice to all three categories:

Play is free movement within a more rigid structure.

At first glance, this definition might seem a little spare and abstract for such a rich and complex topic such as play. But it is an extremely useful way to think about the design of play. Where does the definition come from? Think about the use of the word "play" in the sense of the "free play" of a gear or a car's steering wheel. The "play" is the amount of movement that the steering wheel can move on its own within the system, the amount the steering wheel can turn before it begins to turn the tires of the car. The play itself exists only because of the more utilitarian structures of the driving-system: the drive shaft, axles, wheels, and so on. The "rules" created by these elements make the free movement of play possible. Play emerges from the relationships guiding the functioning of the system, occurring in the interstitial spaces between and among its

components. Play is an expression of the system, one that takes advantage of the space of possibility created from the system's structure.

As a formal way of conceptualizing play, this definition applies to all three categories of play:

> *Game Play:* Playing a game such as Chutes and Ladders occurs only when players set the rigid rules of the game into motion. But the game play itself is a kind of dance that occurs somewhere between the dice, pieces, board, and the rules themselves, in and among the more rigid formal structures of the game.

> *Ludic Activity:* Think of bouncing a ball against a wall. This play activity has a less formal structure than a game, but the definition of play still applies. In experiencing the play of the ball, the player is playing with structures such as gravity, the material identity of the ball, the architectural space, and his or her own physical skill in throwing and catching. To *play* with the ball is to play with all of these structures, testing their limits and boundaries, finding ways of moving around and inside them.

> *Being Playful:* Even in this broad category of play the definition is relevant. Using playful slang, for example, is to find free movement of words and phrases within the more rigid rule structures of grammar. Being playful while walking down the street means playing with the more rigid social, anatomical, and urban structures that determine proper walking behavior.

In every case, play exists *because* of more rigid structures, but also exists somehow in *opposition* to them. Slang is only slang because it departs from the grammatical norm. It is oppositional to the more staid and conservative "official" uses of language, and gains its identity through its difference from them. Similarly, bouncing a ball against a wall is at odds with more utilitarian uses of the architecture. At the same time, the action conforms to certain rules afforded by the formal structure of the building, leading to a particular type of interaction. The play of a game, as we have explored in detail, is only possible because of rules. Yet paradoxically game play is in many ways the opposite of rules. In all of its many guises, play opposes and play resists. But it does so *playfully,* making use of existing structures to invent new forms of expression.

Transformative Play

When play occurs, it can overflow and overwhelm the more rigid structure in which it is taking place, generating emergent, unpredictable results. Sometimes, in fact, the force of play is so powerful that it can change the structure itself. As philosopher James S. Hans notes, "The role of play is not to work comfortably within its own structures but rather constantly to develop its structures through play."[3] A playful slang term can become an idiom, for example, and may eventually be adopted into the dictionary, becoming part of the larger cultural structures it originally resisted. We call this important form of play *transformative play.*

Transformative play is a special case of play that occurs when the free movement of play alters the more rigid structure in which it takes shape. The play doesn't just occupy and oppose the interstices of the system, but actually transforms the space as a whole. A cyberfeminist game patch that creates transsexual versions of Lara Croft is an example of transformative play, as is the use of the Quake game engine as a movie-making tool.

Although every instance of play involves free movement within a more rigid structure, not all play is transformative. Often, whether or not we can consider play as transformative play depends on the way we frame the play experience. Take the familiar example of Chess. Some aspects of play in Chess are, by and large, not transformative at all. As with most games, the formal rules of Chess do not change as a result of playing a game of Chess. If the play of Chess is considered purely as an exercise in the strategic logic of Chess, then the system (the rules) remains the same each time the game is played. However, once human players come into the equation, transformative play can occur across many levels. A player's thinking skills might be transformed as a result of playing Chess over a long period of time. Social relationships with other players (or non-players) might undergo a transformation. The play of Chess might even transform the way a player perceives objects in space. (Just ask any Tetris addict!)

Transformative play can occur in all three categories of play:

Game Play: In professional Basketball, as players find new ways of playing the game, the rules are adjusted to keep the game challenging and entertaining. There are many examples of games, from Flux to 1000 Blank White Cards, where inventing and transforming the rules are part of the game's design.

Ludic Activity: In informal, imaginative children's games, such as House or Cops and Robbers, the rules and possible behaviors are often improvised, transforming the play of the game from session to session.

Being Playful: In fields and activities outside what we normally think of as play and games, being playful can have a transformative effect. In fashion design, there is a reflexive relationship between marginal forms of dress and the fashion establishment. A subcultural style of dress can challenge notions of taste and etiquette (think Punk), while helping to define new forms of expression within the very context it opposes.

In the remaining sections of this chapter, we explore the three types of play in more detail, with an eye to discover how each category intersects with our general definition of play, transformative play, and game design.

Being Playful

If we examine how the word "play" is used and concentrate on its so-called transferred meanings we find talk of the play of light, the play of the waves, the play of the components in a bearing case, the inner play of limbs, the play of forces, the play of gnats, even a play on words…. This accords with the original meaning of the word "spiel" as "dance," which is still found in many word forms. —Brian Sutton-Smith, **The Ambiguity of Play**

We start with the largest of the three categories: simply being playful. The preceding quote from Sutton-Smith points to some of the many contexts outside of games, toys, and ludic behavior to which we can apply our general definition of "play." Like the "free play" of a gear, the instances of play identified by Sutton-Smith are all moments when a system is in motion, in a kind of dance. ("Spiel," the German word for play, originally meant *dance,* as Sutton-Smith points out.)

Take Sutton-Smith's example of a "play on words." There are many kinds of wordplay, from the nonsense rhymes of Dr. Seuss, to the rhythmic intricacies of freestyle rap, to the semantic doubling of a children's riddle. In every case, the wordplay embodies free movement within a more rigid structure. If you will pardon the cheesy humor, consider the following joke:

Q: Why is six afraid of seven?

A: Because seven ate nine.

The "play" of this particular joke rests in the fact that "ate" and "eight" are homonyms. Saying "seven eight nine" is merely counting, whereas "seven ate nine" becomes a genuine cause of alarm for our personified numerals. What is happening in this instance of play? Within the more rigid and fixed sets of linguistic meanings, the joke has managed to carve out a space of play, a movement in which unexpected characters come to life and express double meanings usually repressed within more utilitarian communication. The joke "plays" on our expectations of language. But without the larger context of conventional language use in which the joke takes shape, the joke would lose its humor and sense of play. The play exists both *because of* and *in opposition to* the structures that give it life.

Even if we use some of Sutton-Smith's more abstract examples, such as the play of light, our definition of play still applies. Imagine light reflecting from your wristwatch to make a bright spot on the wall: we say that the light is *playing* on the wall. From within the structures of the physics of light, perception, and architecture emerges the unusual circumstance of a floating speck of light on the wall. The light playfully calls attention to itself, changing the relationship between your wristwatch and the architectural space. Your instinct is to play with the light, even for just a moment, to experience this new set of relationships between the movements of your body and the surface of the wall. The play of the light, and your play with the play of the light, is only made possible by the ordinary sets of experiential relationships that this instance of play transforms.

Are these examples of "being playful" transformative as well? Possibly. Maybe the play of the light transforms your behavior: perhaps you make a habit of sitting in the same room at the same time the next day to enjoy the possibilities of the play. Or maybe telling the "seven ate nine" joke at dinner leads to an entire evening of math jokes that wouldn't otherwise have occurred. Every instance of play carries with it the seeds of transformative play.

How is this general understanding of being playful relevant to game design? When you are designing a game, you should maximize meaningful play for your participants at every possible moment. Often, this means thinking about how you can inject the proper spirit of playfulness into an otherwise ordinary behavior. You Don't Know Jack, for example, took the normally chore-like routine of entering in player names, loading game data, and outlining game rules and turned it into an entertainingly playful series of events that even experienced players of the game continue to enjoy. Could you make an entire game out of an experience that is typically ordinary or tedious? How about a game designed to be played while waiting in line? Or watching the news? Or driving a car? Once you understand that play is latent in any human activity, you can find inspiration for play behaviors and contexts anywhere.

Ludic Activities

The second category of play, *ludic activities,* brings us closer to the play of games. Games represent one type of ludic activity, a particularly formalized variety of play. But there are many less formal versions of play as well, from two dogs chasing each other in a park to an infant playing peek-a-boo with his father. What most often distinguishes games from these other forms of play is the fact that games have a goal and a quantifiable outcome. Generally speaking, non-game forms of ludic activities do not.

Even though ludic activities constitute a type of play phenomena more narrow than simply being playful, there is still a relatively wide range of activities contained within this category. How might these activities be organized and understood within the larger rubric of play? Anthropologist Roger Caillois suggests a useful model for organizing various forms of play. In his book *Man, Play, and Games,* he provides a powerful framework for classifying play activities. Caillois' model is one of the most theoretically ambitious attempts to organize the many forms of play.

Caillois' model begins with four "fundamental categories" of play:[4]

- *Agôn:* Competitive play, as in Chess, sports, and other contests

- *Alea:* Chance-based play, based in games of probability

- *Mimicry:* Role-playing and make-believe play, including theater and other exercises of the imagination

- *Ilinx:* Playing with the physical sensation of vertigo, as when a child spins and spins until he falls down

Here are some of Caillois' thoughts about each fundamental category:

Agôn. A whole group of games would seem to be competitive, that is to say, like a combat in which equality of chances is artificially created, in order that adversaries should confront each other under ideal conditions, susceptible of giving precise and incontestable value to the winner's triumph.[5]

Alea. This is the Latin name for the game of dice. I have borrowed it to designate, in contrast to *agôn,* all games that are based on a decision independent of the player, an outcome over which he has no control, and in which winning is the result of fate rather than triumphing over an adversary. More properly, destiny is the sole artisan of victory, and where there is rivalry, what is meant is that the winner has been more favored by fortune than the loser.[6]

Mimicry. Play can consist not only of deploying actions or submitting to one's fate in an imaginary milieu, but of becoming an illusory character oneself, and of so behaving. One is thus confronted with a diverse series of manifestations, the common element of which is that the subject makes believe or makes others believe that he is someone other than himself. He forgets, disguises, or temporarily sheds his personality in order to feign another.[7]

Ilinx. The last kind of game includes those which are based on the pursuit of vertigo and which consist of an attempt to momentarily destroy the stability of perception and inflict a kind of voluptuous panic upon an otherwise lucid mind…. Every child very well knows that by whirling rapidly he reaches a centrifugal state of flight from which he regains bodily stability and clarity of perception only with difficulty.[8]

Caillois' categories cover a wide range of play activities. Some of them, such as the game contests of agôn and the chance-based games of alea, resemble many of the games we have already discussed. Other activities he mentions, such as the make-believe play of mimicry and ilinx activities like leapfrog and waltzing, clearly fall outside the boundaries of games. Although many games include elements of mimicry and ilinx, these categories go beyond a description of games—but they do outline a model for understanding many kinds of ludic activities.

Caillois doesn't limit his classification system to these four categories. He enriches his taxonomy by adding the pair of concepts *paida* and *ludus*. Paida represents wild, free-form, improvisational play, whereas ludus represents rule-bound, regulated, formalized play. Caillois writes: "Such a primary power of improvisation and joy, which I call *paida,* is allied to the taste for gratuitous difficulty that I propose to call *ludus,* in order to encompass the various games to which, without exaggeration, a civilizing quality can be attributed."9 Caillois crosses his four fundamental categories of play with the concepts of *paida* and *ludus,* resulting in a grid on which he charts a wide variety of ludic activities. A rule-bound game of chance such as Roulette falls into the alea/ludus section of his model. Unstructured make-believe play like wearing a mask would fall under mimicry/paida.

	Paida	Ludus
Agôn (Competition)	Unregulated athletics (foot racing, wrestling)	Boxing, Billiards, Fencing, Checkers, Football, Chess
Alea (Chance)	Counting-out rhymes	Betting, Roulette, Lotteries
Mimicry (Simulation)	Children's initiations, masks, disguises	Theater, spectacles in general
Ilinx (Vertigo)	Children "whirling," Horseback riding, Waltzing	Skiing, Mountain climbing, Tightrope walking

Examples taken from Man, Play, and Games

How does Caillois' model fit into our definition of play? A look at the four fundamental categories of play shows that each embodies free movement within a more rigid structure:

- *Agôn* and *alea* are categories that generally contain games. As a result, play emerges from the players' movement through the rigid rule-structures of the game. In a competitive game, players do their best to win by playing within the behavioral boundaries set by the system of rules. In a game of chance, players set the game in motion through their participation, hoping the system plays out in a fortuitous manner.

- The free of play of *mimicry* is the play of representation. If you wiggle your index finger and say "hello," pretending that your finger is a little person that can talk, you are playing with the fixed representational categories of finger and person, finding free movement within these more typically rigid sign systems through imaginative play.

- Play in *ilinx* emerges as the play within physical and sensual structures. The spinning player abandons more typically tame behavior to find new sensation in the interplay between bodily movement and perceptual input.

Terminological Aside: "Play" and "Games" in French

Man, Play, and Games was written in French, Caillois' native tongue. Many languages do not have separate words for "game" and "play." In French, for example, game is "jeu," and play is "jouer," the verb form of the same word. The original title of his book is *Les Jeux et les Hommes* (Games/Play and Man); the English translation of the title as *Man, Play, and Games* does an admirable job of expressing the broad array of play forms Caillois investigates.

It is important to note the difference between the French and English titles of Caillois' book because although the English translation generally uses "game" to describe what Caillois is studying, for our purposes he is, in fact, studying play. Some of the phenomena listed by Caillois are bona fide games and sports. Others, like theater and public festivals, do not fit our narrow definition of game. They are all, however, ludic activities.

Furthermore, the categories of *ludus* and *paida* directly address a structural understanding of games, a continuum of relationships between structure and play. As play edges closer to the ludus end of the spectrum, for example, the rules become tighter and more influential. Located on the other end of the spectrum, paida-based play eschews rigid formal structures in exchange for more freewheeling play. In both cases, Caillois defines play by virtue of its structural identity.

There is a good deal of correspondence between Caillois' model and our own. However, the two models do not offer identical ways of conceptualizing play. For example, our distinction among game play, ludic activities, and being playful is not relevant to Caillois' organization of play activities. Although we can frame his categories under the rubric of our "free movement" definition, he never explicitly constructs play in this way.

Caillois is a tremendously important game scholar. His system for classifying forms of play is one of the most inclusive and robust we have encountered. Furthermore, Caillois' model can be very useful for understanding the kinds of play experiences your game is and is not providing. Although Caillois tends to place an entire game or play activity into a single section of his grid, most games have elements from several of his categories. Maybe your hardcore agôn strategy game could be leavened with a bit more alea. Or perhaps you could enrich your mimicry-based role-playing game by considering the kinds of ilinx sensations your players might experience at key dramatic moments. Any model that helps you to frame your design problems in a new way can be a valuable game design tool.

Game Play

The third and final category of play is game play. Just as ludic activities constitute a special subset of the larger category of being playful, game play is a special subset of the category of ludic activities. Game play only occurs within games. It is the

Delimitation of our project

Although the number of writings on game design is somewhat limited, in the past few decades, there has been a tremendous amount of study on the nature and function of play. Scholarship comes from a wide variety of fields: animal behaviorists studying the adaptive advantages of play, developmental psychologists studying the cognitive and social skills that children learn through play, sociologists studying the way play fits into larger social needs.

By and large, these studies of play focus on identifying the function or purpose of play. The implicit assumption is that play serves a larger purpose for the individual psyche, the social unit, the classroom, the species, and so on. In *Child's Play,* Frank A. Beach indexes some of the functions that are typically associated with play across many fields:

- a release of surplus energy

- an expression of general exuberance, or joie-de-vivre

- expression of sex drive, aggression, or anxiety

- youthful "practice" for adult life skills

- necessary context for exploration and experimentation

- a means of socialization

- tool for self-expression and diversion[12]

Studying the function and purpose of play is important and fascinating work, but we will not address it in this book. The schemas we present for understanding play and other aspects of games focus on the challenges of creating meaningful play, rather than on investigating the social or psychological *purpose* of games. There is a tremendous amount of literature available on the function of play and we have included many of these references in our bibliography, as it should be a part of the way that game designers understand games.

experience of a game set into motion through the participation of players. The other two categories of play, being playful and ludic activities, contain a vast and diverse array of play forms. Yet even though game play is the smallest category of the three, the play of games takes on a multitude of forms as well: the strategic competitive play of Settlers of Catan; the performative social play of Charades; the physical sporting play of Cricket; the lush narrative play of Final Fantasy X—all are examples of game play.

Game play clearly embodies the idea of play as free movement within a more rigid structure. The particular flavor of a game's play is a direct result of the game's rules. The rules of Charades, written out as text on paper, could not be more different from the exuberant, free-wheeling activity of the game itself. Yet these rules provide the rigid structure within which the play resides, the rules that guide and shape the game play experience. As Caillois himself states, within a game a player is "free within the limits set by the rules."[10]

Because play involves human participation, it is an endlessly rich and complex locus for study. Even within a single game, there are innumerable ways to delineate its play. In the following excerpt, taken from *The Study of Games,* Norman Reider begins an in-depth study of Chess by touching on many of its characteristics:

> The fascination and the extent of the addiction to the game; the psychological factors involved in its historical development; its social and therapeutic value; its legal involvements; its relation to love and aggression; the problem of genius in chess; the characterological problem of its players and their style of play; and ego functions as manifested in play, especially the distinctions between the psychological meanings of the game, its pieces and rules, and the psychology of the players.[11]

Most or all of the "facets" Reider lists are ways of understanding the operation of play in a game. The psychology of play, the expression of love and aggression, the way that the game facilitates individual styles of play, are part of the play experience of Chess. Understanding the experiential qualities of play, engendered by rules and given life through game play, is the precise focus of the rest of this Primary Schema. Are you ready to play?

Notes

1. J. Barnard Gilmore, "Play: A Special Behavior." In *Child's Play,* edited by R.E. Herron and Brian Sutton-Smith (New York: John Wiley & Sons, 1971), p. 311.

2. Ibid.

3. James S. Hans, *The Play of the World* (Boston: University of Massachusetts Press, 1981), p. 5.

4. Roger Caillois, *Man, Play, and Games* (London: Thames and Hudson, 1962), p. 12.

5. Ibid. p. 14.

6. Ibid. p. 17.

7. Ibid. p. 19.

8. Ibid. p. 23.

9. Ibid. p. 27.

10. Ibid. p. 8.

11. Norman Reider, "Chess, Oedipus, and the Mater Dolorosa." In *The Study of Games,* edited by Elliott Avedon and Brian Sutton-Smith (New York: John Wiley & Sons, 1971), p. 440.

12. Frank A. Beach, "Current Concepts of Play in Animals." In *Child's Play,* edited by R.E. Herron and Brian Sutton-Smith (New York: John Wiley & Sons, 1971), p. 311. p. 204–208.

Defining Play SUMMARY

- The play of a game is the **experiential** aspect of a game. Play in a game occurs as the game rules are set into motion and experienced by the players.

- The relationship between games and play can be structured in two ways:

  - **Games are a subset of play:** Games constitute a formalized part of all activities considered to be play.

  - **Play is an element of games:** Play is one way to frame the complex phenomenon of games.

- All of the different phenomena of play behavior can be organized into three categories:

  Game Play: the formalized, focused interaction that occurs when players follow the rules of a game in order to play it.

  Ludic Activities: non-game behaviors in which participants are "playing," such as two tussling animals or a group of children tossing a ball in a circle. Game play is a subset of ludic activities.

  Being Playful: the state of being in a playful state of mind, such as when a spirit of play is injected into some other action. This category includes both game play and ludic activities.

- A general definition of play: **play is free movement within a more rigid structure.** Play emerges both *because of* and *in opposition to* more rigid structures.

- **Transformative play** is a special kind of play that occurs when the free movement of play alters the more rigid structure in which it takes shape. The play actually transforms the rigid structure in some way. Not all play is transformative, but all forms of play contain the potential for transformation.

- Anthropologist Roger Caillois classifies play according to four "fundamental categories:"

  - **agôn:** competitive play

  - **alea:** chance-based play

  - **mimicry:** simulation or make-believe play

  - **ilinx:** vertigo or physically-based play

  Each of these categories can be plotted along an axis that runs from **ludus,** or rule-bound play to **paida,** or free-form play. Many games possess several of these characteristics of play at once.

Unit 3: **Play**

GAMES AS
THE PLAY OF EXPERIENCE

interactivity
input/output/internal processes
core mechanic
repetition
second-order design
core mechanic variations

23

I rise with the first shot, no problem, pushing my head up toward the peak of its ascent, and the ball hits the brick. No it doesn't. I wish it struck the barricade, wish it surged forward and surged back, so as I surge along pushing and recoiling there wouldn't be those blank spaces while I wait for the ball to catch up or fall behind. It has a rhythm filled with empty time, while mine is compacted, full and dense....

I'm rising with the shot then, the volume turned up high now, filling the room with bleeps, and I'm putting the shoulders and head into the action, singing a song with this ten-second sequence.... Hum the sixteen-note melody created by the bleeps when the ball hits paddle, bricks, and side wall. **Bleep,** *the serve...***bloop,** *the return...***blapbleep***...a quick brick bounce off the side wall down to...***bloop,** *the next return after the beat, and then up, down, off the side down up. Throw yourself into the unfolding melody, carry the hand smoothly from one point to the next, ride with the ball through the whole five places.—**David Sudnow,** Pilgrim in the Microworld*

Introducing Experience

To play a game is to *experience* the game: to see, touch, hear, smell, and taste the game; to move the body during play, to feel emotions about the unfolding outcome, to communicate with other players, to alter normal patterns of thinking. Unlike the clean mathematical forms of rules, the experiential play of a game is fuzzy, murky, and messy. Yet it is in this realm that players actually take part in a game, engaging in meaningful play. In *Games as the Play of Experience,* we build on the somewhat abstract definition of *play as free movement within a more rigid structure* to look concretely at the ways that games build experiences for players. In order to do so, our focus narrows. In the previous chapter, we defined play not just in games, but in the broadest sense of the word. As we move forward, we will limit the scope of our investigation to the play occurring in games.

What does it mean to experience game play? The passage that opens this chapter is from *Pilgrim in the Microworld,* a book that describes, in loving detail, a player's waxing and waning addiction to the video game Breakout. Breakout was one of the earliest video games, first released as an arcade game in 1976 by Atari, and then published for the Atari 2600 home video game system a few years later. In this Pong-like game, a player moves a paddle back and forth across the bottom of the screen, bouncing a ball into rows of bricks positioned along the top of the screen. Each time the ball hits a brick it disappears; the goal of the game is to move through as many screens as possible, clearing every brick on the screen.

Throughout his extraordinary book, author David Sudnow vividly evokes the experience of playing Breakout. His highly personal account describes the complex experience of play with a nuance and insight rarely found in writing about games. In his observations, Sudnow uncovers a flurry of experiential elements: the kinesthetic movement of his body as he plays; his multi-layered emotions of hope and anxiety, his altered sense of time; the visual and audio rhythms of the game; the minute controlling motions of his hand on the paddle; and even a kind of perceptual identification with the ball itself.

In the sensory blur of game play, the formal system of the game only reveals itself through its experiential effects. The programmed code, paddle controller, console hardware, television screen, and audio speakers become elements of a larger system that includes the player himself. The space of possibility for Sudnow is a visceral space of experiential potential, a space he explores through play, his state of being in some way extended though the input, output, and logic of the game.

The experience of play is just that: an experience. The word "experience" commonly refers to:

1. The apprehension of an object, thought, or emotion through the senses or mind;

2. Active participation in events or activities, leading to knowledge or a skill;

3. An event or a series of events participated in or lived through.[1]

In other words, experience is *participation*. Every game creates its own kind of experience, from the theatrical interventions of live-action role playing, to the international spectacle of the Olympics, to the vast virtual communities of Phantasy Star Online. There is no single, proper kind of experience that all games should try and provide. Yet there are principles of meaningful play that we can apply to games in a variety of design contexts. In this chapter, and in the **PLAY** schema that follow, we investigate the design of experience as a fundamental principle of game design.

Qualities of Experience

The experience of play comes in so many diverse forms that creating a single catalog that takes all of them into account would be an impossible task. However, this does not mean that systems for categorizing play cannot be a useful tool for solving design problems. The classification model developed by Roger Caillois, outlined in the previous chapter, provides one typology for the variety of experiences found in games. In *Toys* as Culture,[2] Brian Sutton-Smith presents another model, one that lists the psychological processes by which games are experienced. Although Sutton-Smith is looking specifically at video games, his model is relevant to other kinds of games as well. His five elements of game experience are:

· *Visual scanning:* visual perception, especially scanning the entire screen at once.

· *Auditory discriminations:* listening for game events and signals.

· *Motor responses:* physical actions a player takes with the game controls.

· *Concentration:* intense focus on play.

· *Perceptual patterns of learning:* coming to know the structure of the game itself.

Sutton-Smith offers a relatively succinct list of the elements that constitute the experience of play within a digital game. Visual scanning and auditory discrimination represent the sensorial activities of the player, motor responses represent the player's physical actions, and the other two elements (concentration and perceptual patterns of learning) represent cognitive mechanisms internal to the player that link these inputs and outputs. How do these categories apply to the experience of a particular game? If we look back at Sudnow's observations of Breakout one more time, we can find examples from all of Sutton-Smith's five categories of experience:

> **Concentration and auditory discriminations:** *"I'm rising with the shot then, the volume turned up high now, filling the room with bleeps, and I'm putting the shoulders and head into the action, singing a song with this ten-second sequence."* Sudnow is deeply engaged in play, to the point where he feels like he is part of the game system. He moves his body in synch with the action on screen, humming along to its blips and bleeps, focusing all movement and energy on control of the ball.

> **Visual scanning and motor responses:** *"Throw yourself into the unfolding melody, carry the hand smoothly from one point to the next, ride with the ball through the whole five places."* Sudnow perceives the screen as a single field of space within which he guides the ball. As his eyes scan the screen he takes action through the game controller, moving the paddle into strategic position. Sudnow psychologically integrates the horizontal movement of the virtual paddle onscreen with the physical motion of twisting the game control knob.

> **Perceptual patterns of learning:** *"At first it felt like my eyes told my fingers where to go. But in time I knew the smooth rotating hand motions were assisting the look in turn, eyes and fingers, in a two-way partnership."* The coordination Sudnow achieves between perception and action is a quality of deeply engaging play. His eyes work in concert with his hands to control the action onscreen. The resulting experience of play offers a seamless transition between input and output, between the action and outcome of player choice.

Although Sutton-Smith's five categories do a good job of describing the experience of early, single player console games, they are certainly not inclusive of all games. A game might be invented, for example, that involves smell-based sensory input. There are also plenty of games that involve social communication between players, which Sutton-Smith's model does not take into account.

However, we can abstract elements from Sutton-Smith's thinking that are more widely applicable. His model in essence posits relationships between inputs, outputs, and internal player mechanisms. This three-part model is a useful general structure for understanding how players experience a game. The way that a player perceives a game and takes action in it is always going to be specific to a particular design. But these details are contained within a larger system of experience that always includes some kind of sensory input, player output, and internal player cognition.

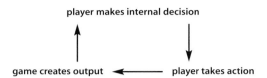

All three components of this model can be considered in isolation, but they only generate meaningful play as part of a larger designed system. What kind of play experience do you want to create? A rhythm-based dance game such as Bust-a-Groove locates player experience within a finely tuned set of visual, auditory, and physical cues designed to involve players within the full-body rhythms of structured beats. A word game such as Scrabble forces players to think strategically and linguistically, scanning the board for openings, rearranging letters in their head and in their hand, making language tactile by manipulating smooth wooden tiles. An arcade shooter such as House of the Dead emphasizes the ability to quickly scan and isolate elements on screen, responding to game events with rapid and repetitive motor responses. Identifying the qualities of play you want your players to experience is a useful way of framing any game design problem.

Designing Interactive Experiences

The challenge, of course, is that the experience of play is not something that a game designer directly creates. Instead, play is an emergent property that arises from the game as a player engages with the system. The game designer creates a set of rules, which players inhabit, explore, and manipulate. It is through inhabiting, exploring, and manipulating the game's formal structure that players experience play. We made this point in earlier chapters, but it is important enough to repeat here within the context of experience. The game designer only *indirectly* designs the player's experience, by *directly* designing the rules.

So how do game designers shape player experience? We have already covered the basics. In the chapter on *Interactivity,* we discussed in detail how sequences of action > outcome units in a game add up to a larger system of meaningful play, especially when the outcome is both discernable and integrated into the game as a whole. If we highlight the experiential dimensions of these choice-based mechanisms, we can frame games as systems whose meaning emerges from the experience of players as they make choices in a game. Every component of a choice, from the representational elements displaying actions and related outcomes, to the systemic elements determining the internal logic of a choice's result, are experientially relevant.

Creating great game experiences for players—creating *meaningful* experiences for players—requires understanding how a game's formal system transforms into an experiential one. Doing so means considering both micro- and macro- dimensions, from the small moment-to-moment interactions confronting a player to the way these core interactions combine to form a larger trajectory of experience. Throughout **PLAY,** we cover the many dimensions of the micro- and macro- components of designed game play. The rest of this chapter will take a very close look at the fundamental micro-interactions of a game, known as the core mechanic.

The Core Mechanic

Every game has a *core mechanic.* A core mechanic is the essential play activity players perform again and again in a game. Sometimes, the core mechanic of a game is a single action. In a footrace, for example, the core mechanic is running. In a trivia game, the core mechanic is answering questions. In Donkey Kong, the core mechanic is using a joystick and jump button to maneuver a character on the screen. However, in many games, the core mechanic is a compound activity composed of a suite of actions. In a first-person-shooter game such as Quake, the core mechanic is the set of interrelated actions of moving, aiming, firing, and managing resources such as health, ammo, and armor. Baseball's core mechanic is composed of a collection of batting, running, catching, and throwing skills. In a real-time strategy game such as Starcraft, the core mechanic combines resource management with wargame strategy and rapid mouse and keyboard command skills.

A game's core mechanic contains the experiential building blocks of player interactivity. It represents the essential moment-to-moment activity of players, something that is repeated over and over throughout a game. During a game, core mechanics create patterns of behavior, which manifest as experience for players. The core mechanic is the essential nugget of game activity, the mechanism through which players make meaningful choices and arrive at a meaningful play experience. It is therefore very important to be able to identify the core mechanic at the beginning of the design process, even if it changes as the game develops. Pinpointing the core mechanic of the game allows designers to generate a summary profile of the game's interactivity. Very often, when a game simply isn't fun to play, it is the core mechanic that is to blame.

The notion of a core mechanic is a crucial game design concept, and one frequently taken for granted in the design process. Concepts for games, particularly digital games, often begin with an idea for a story or character, to take place within an established commercial genre. This is a valid way to start a design process. However, in focusing on the "high level," narrative elements of a game, game designers can miss equally fundamental questions that concern the core mechanic and play experience. Game designers don't just create content for players, they create *activities* for players, patterns of actions enacted by players in the course of game play.

Core Mechanics in Context

Designing the activity of play means creating the system that includes the game's sensory output to the player and the player's ability to make input, as well as guiding the internal cognitive and psychological processes by which a player makes decisions. The core mechanic is not limited to just one component of this experiential process, but exists as an activity that permeates all three. Following are several game examples, each one utilizing an extremely different core mechanic.

Tag

In Tag, one player is "It." This player chases all of the other players within a limited boundary; when another player is tagged by "It," he or she becomes "It." The core mechanic of Tag is incredibly simple: chase and be chased. Because Tag is a physical game, the experiential component is very rich. As input, the player senses the entire field of play, the position of other players (especially the player that is "It"), as well as his or her own state of exhaustion. The output involves a player's entire body, and usually involves running, dodging, and other evasive maneuvers.

The simple rules leave no room for ambiguity. If you are not "It," you avoid being tagged at all costs. If you are "It," your goal is to shed this role by giving it to another. Chasing and running. Running and chasing. And then, the occasional tag. The repetition of the core mechanic enacted over the course of a game builds into larger patterns of experience as players run about the field, avoiding the player that is "It," exchanging roles of the hunter and the hunted when a tag takes place. As an experienced game system, Tag's mythic simplicity is part of its appeal.

Verbal Tennis

Verbal Tennis is an unusual game in which two players carry on a conversation, taking turns making statements. The only rules are that each statement must be in the form of a question and cannot repeat another statement that has already been made. If a player gets stuck and cannot make a coherent response to the previous statement, he or she loses. A game might begin as follows:

PLAYER 1: Are you feeling well today?

PLAYER 2: Don't I look well?

PLAYER 1: If I knew that, why would I have asked you?

PLAYER 2: Why do you care how I'm feeling?

PLAYER 1: Is it impolite to ask?

PLAYER 2: Can't you figure that out for yourself?

PLAYER 1: What?

PLAYER 2: Didn't you hear what I said?

etc.

The entertaining challenge of verbal tennis is to continue the conversation as a logical chain of statements. Taking part in the conversation, or taking an action in the game, involves a uniquely engaging core mechanic. The player's experiential input and output are simple conversational statements. But the internal process of the player involves complex thinking, in which he or she quickly assimilates the previous statement and composes a new one that extends the conversation, shaping his or her response into a question.

In Verbal Tennis, the actual *activity* of the player is merely to listen and to speak, something that players do in their ordinary lives many times a day. The elegance of the game is that a simple set of rules transform this action into the puzzle-like experience of Verbal Tennis, resulting in an intellectually challenging and theatrically engaging game experience.

LOOP

The game of LOOP is a single-player computer game where the player uses the mouse to draw lines around fluttering butterflies and capture them. Butterflies come in different colors, and a player can only capture groups of butterflies of the same color. There are additional ways to score, special bonuses, hazards, and bonus levels, but the core mechanic—looping—remains the same throughout the game.

The core mechanic of a computer or video game involves a hardware input device in some way, and LOOP is no exception. The essential activity of the game is to use the mouse to roll the cursor about the screen, drawing lines to make loops around the moving butterflies. The player perceives visual information on the screen and responds through motor movement, generating additional audio and visual feedback. Instead of a drag-and-click, cursor-style interaction, LOOP engenders a fluid series of wrist and arm gestures. The design of LOOP emphasizes this core activity throughout: if the player clicks during a game, the game pauses; on the game's main menu, the player does not click on a button but instead loops around it to make a selection.

One challenge of designing computer game interactivity lies in inventing new forms of player interaction, new core mechanics that lead to alternative game experiences. Just as Verbal Tennis turns an ordinary conversation into dueling wordplay, LOOP appropriates conventional mouse interaction and twists it to playful effect.

Just because a game's input is limited to mouse and keyboard or console controller input does not mean that it has to rely on the conventions of other games. What if mouse movement was the inverse of cursor movement? What if the keyboard was used as a physical input grid? What if the player had to hold the console controller upside-down? Designing inventive core mechanics, on or off the computer, often comes from questioning existing conventions.

Breaking Out of Breakout

Line up your extended finger with the lower left corner of the TV screen a comfortable six feet away. Now track back and forth several times in line with the bottom border and project a movement of that breadth onto an imagined inch and a half diameter spool in your hands. That's how knob and paddle are geared, a natural correspondence of scale between the body's motions, the equipment, and the environs preserved in the interface. There's that world space over there, this one over there, and we traverse the wired gap with motions that make us nonetheless feel in a balanced extending touch with things.—**David Sudnow,** *Pilgrim in the Microworld*

Breakout

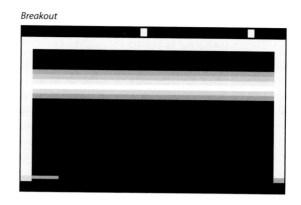

This chapter concludes with a detailed look at two digital games, and an examination of how the core mechanic helps create an experience of meaningful play. The first game is Breakout for the Atari 2600, the game David Sudnow details in his book. Breakout's core mechanic is both simple and elegant; it is one of the keys to what makes the play of the game so meaningful. The player uses a paddle controller to move a bar on the bottom of the screen left and right, trying to intercept a "ball" that is bouncing around the game space.

It would be difficult to find a core mechanic more stripped down than in Breakout. In the game, players are not moving an animated character through a richly textured 3D space; they are not even moving in 2D. Players are moving a blocky, rectangular shape in one dimension along a line. Players don't have a range of actions and powers. They don't have a complex set of tasks to complete or resources to manage. All players do is turn the knob, move the line, and avoid missing the ball. Despite this spare interactive scheme, Breakout manages to generate meaningful play.

The simplicity and immediacy of the design creates an interactive circuit between the player and the game. The response of the paddle on the screen to the movements of the knob in the player's hand is intuitive and instantaneous. The screen, the

controller, and the player enter into a larger set of experiential relationships, forming a system that bridges the "wired gap," as Sudnow puts it, between the player's world and the televised world of the game. But if that were everything there was to Breakout, a line moving on a screen, it wouldn't be a game. It wouldn't have meaningful play. And it certainly wouldn't generate the obsessive attachment Sudnow documents. On top of this core mechanic, the simple action of knob-turning and ball-blocking, Breakout builds a more complex game experience.

> Of course the lights didn't obey the laws of physics governing solid objects, like billiard balls, say. But Atari had rather decently simulated a sense of solidity. The light [ball] came from a certain angle toward the side wall, and then followed out the triangulation by going in the direction you'd predict for a real ball. What about the paddle? Hit on an off-centered portion of a tennis racket or hand, a ball will deflect on a different path and you can thereby place shots. Sure enough they'd programmed the trajectories and different parts of the paddle surface to match, so the light-ball behaved rather like a tangible object, refracting and deflecting so it seemed you could at least somewhat control the ball's direction.[3]

At first, playing Breakout is simply a matter of hitting the ball, trying not to let it pass by the paddle. If a player misses the ball five times, the game is over. But as play continues, the game play grows deeper. The paddle is divided into five sections, each of which ricochets the ball at a different angle. Using the simulated physics of the game, players can learn to direct shots. When the ball hits a brick, it disappears and the player gains points. The goal of the game is to direct the ball to remove as many bricks as possible, gaining points along the way. Because the brick patterns at the top of the screen change each time the player hits and removes a brick, the playfield gradually shifts from full to empty as a level progresses, each new arrangement offering different possible trajectories for the ball to follow.

Many patterns and rhythms of play emerge. A skilled player will concentrate on one side of the screen, creating a hole in the wall of bricks that allows the ball to "break out" and bounce back and forth along the top of the screen. Other kinds of strategies are required for the endgame, in which only a few bricks remain: the center of the paddle is used to hit the ball in a nearly vertical trajectory, cutting a slow path across the screen toward the remaining bricks. More than just a simple system of interaction, the game rules create multiple levels of play experience, layering strategic thinking and gradual skill acquisition on top of the physical and perceptual components of the core mechanic.

All of this experiential complexity in such a simple game! Yet the player's action, the essential activity, the core mechanic, remains strikingly spartan: rotate the knob with the wrist. Out of this basic interactivity blossoms an entire structure of play. This is precisely how meaningful play emerges on the level of experience: through player action, input, and output. In the end, the system of play becomes more than the sum of its parts.

Variations on a Core Mechanic

Working with an existing core mechanic is a common game design problem. Perhaps there is a core mechanic that you want to borrow. Or maybe a publisher is funding a digital game project that needs to resemble an existing game genre. Or it could be that you have already designed an original core mechanic, but you don't know how to extend it into a full game experience. In this section, we look at examples of how to modify and re-mix a core mechanic to create new game experiences, using Breakout as a touchstone. The version of the game Sudnow describes is Breakout for the Atari 2600. Although he only plays the "basic" version of the game, the original Atari cartridge includes many play variations.

The inclusion of game variations was a common design strategy in early console games for platforms such as the Atari 2600. Typically, designers extended the basic game interaction, creating numerous variations for play. For this reason, Atari games are excellent examples of game designs that take a core mechanic and spin out many variants. The alternate versions can be clever and engaging or gratuitous and unplayable. But there is much to learn from both successful and unsuccessful attempts at creating core mechanic variations. On the original Atari 2600 Breakout cartridge, there are twelve different game variations. We list the mechanics for each below:

Timed Play

Breakout on the Atari 2600 is a finite game. The goal is to clear the bricks from one screen, which leads to a second screen of bricks. If that screen is cleared, the game ends. Because players score points for each brick eliminated, the score at the end of a finished game is always the same (864 points). One problem with this game design is that an expert player will be able to clear both screens and will eventually lose interest in the game. Even though the core mechanic might be engaging enough to encourage repeat play, it is more likely that the player will feel as if the game has been "solved." The game's space of possibility will become too familiar, and is unlikely to offer any more surprising challenges.

To address this potential problem, the cartridge includes a "timed" version of the game. In addition to a point score, the game keeps track of how long a player has been playing. The goal of a timed game becomes not only reaching the maximum number of points, but doing so as quickly as possible, adding a quantifiable tool for judging performance to the same essential game play. The result is that timed Breakout becomes a more engaging game for advanced players, who may have reached a scoring ceiling in terms of points. The game variation allows players to continue exploring strategies for reducing their overall time.

It is significant to note that the timer could have been included in the basic game as well. The timer doesn't structurally change the actual interaction—it merely displays a new kind of data. But the timer does change the experience of the game, psychologically placing players under more pressure as the seconds tick by. Breakout can be a very difficult game for beginners, and it was a smart design decision to keep the timer element out of the basic game. That way, beginners feel a bit more comfortable as they learn the game's basic interaction. Conversely, advanced players feel as if they have "graduated" to a new level when they take up the timed version of the game.

Breakthru

Another variant on the Breakout core mechanic is the "Breakthru" version. In this game, the player's core interaction with the paddle remains the same, but the behavior of the elements in the game change. When the ball hits a brick, it eliminates the brick—but instead of bouncing back, the ball keeps on going until it hits a wall. That means that a ball will travel right through the wall of colored bricks, leaving a trail of empty brick spots as it plows through them.

What is the reason for this design variation? In the normal version of Breakout, it feels satisfying to eliminate bricks, a satisfaction that extends over the course of the game. One by one, brick by brick, you chip away at the wall. Breakthru accelerates this satisfaction, allowing you not just to nip at the wall, but to gouge out whole sections in

a single gesture. Although it makes the game much easier, this variation adds a new degree of experiential pleasure to the game. It is significant that the designers chose the more delayed gratification of the basic version to be the default structure for play.

Steering, Catching, and Invisible Bricks

Atari 2600 Breakout includes other variations as well. In some, the player can use the paddle to affect the ball while it is in the air, nudging its path to the left or right. In others, the player uses a button on the paddle to "catch" the ball, making it stick to the paddle until it is released. In a third variation, the bricks are invisible until they are hit, at which point all of the remaining bricks light up.

Each of these versions of Breakout has a strong impact on the play of the game. Steering and catching give the player an additional way to control the ball, increasing the complexity of the interaction slightly, while also decreasing the game's overall level of difficulty. The invisible brick variations make the game much harder, especially when there are only a few bricks left and players must use their memory to aim at them.

All of these variations (timer, breakthru, steering, catching, and invisible bricks) offer not only individual variants, but are mixed and matched to provide many versions of Breakout. Each of the dozen games on the cartridge is either basic Breakout, timed Breakout, or Breakthru; each of these three general types manifests four times: with no additional modifications, steerable balls, catchable balls, or invisible bricks. This system offers a total of twelve different Breakout games, eleven variants on the basic version, each one modifying the game's core game mechanic. Obviously, one effect of including variations is to greatly expand the overall space of play; each version of the game provides new strategic and experiential possibilities. Playing Breakout takes place on two levels: not only do players explore the structure of an individual variant, but they also explore the larger set of variants as a whole.

For example, perhaps you like the satisfaction of the Breakthru version of the game, but you find it too easy. You might balance the difficulty by playing Breakthru with invisible bricks. If you are a strategic player that enjoys the pressure of the clock, timed versions of the game with steerable or catchable balls might work well for you. Providing variations for players lets them design their own experiences in a limited way. Although it is not the right solution for every game, it is certainly part of the appeal of many Atari 2600 cartridges. In the case of Breakout, the variations offer a great lesson in altering a core mechanic in order to enlarge the space of possibility.

Beyond the original Breakout arcade game and the Atari 2600 version of Breakout, there are many other versions of the game that borrow the same core mechanic. For example, the sequel release, Super Breakout for the Atari 2600, refines the play in many ways. In Super Breakout, games are no longer limited to two walls of bricks, but can continue on indefinitely. Super Breakout also adds new game variants, such as more than one ball in play at once, more than one paddle on the screen at the same time, bricks that slowly move downward toward the player, and a special "children's version," in which the ball moves more slowly. The number of variations that could be designed for the core mechanic of Breakout is nearly infinite.

For a last look at Breakout, we turn to Alleyway, a game published in 1989 for the Nintendo Game Boy. The essentials of the game are the same as in the Atari 2600 version: the player uses the directional pad on the Game Boy to move a paddle back and forth at the bottom of the screen, bouncing the ball into a wall of bricks to make them disappear. Alleyway offers its own variation on the game, while still remaining true to the Breakout core mechanic.

Breaking Out

The moment in Breakout when the ball actually "breaks out," when a player carves a narrow path that allows the ball to bounce along the top of the screen, is one of the experiential climaxes of the game. When breakout happens, the ball goes into a brick-clearing frenzy, as the player sits back and watches the system do the work. In the Atari 2600 game, breakout is difficult to achieve, meaning that only advanced players get to experience its thrill. Sometimes, by the time a player hits the top of the screen, there are only scattered bricks remaining, so that the satisfying rapid-fire breakout bouncing never occurs.

Alleyway addresses this design challenge by providing levels that encourage breakouts to occur. For example, the very first level of the game features the classic wall of bricks, but with columns of bricks removed from the left and right sides of the brick wall. Instead of a closed wall that stretches the length of the screen, the wall of bricks has open sides. A well-placed ball can angle into this gap, travel to the top of the screen, and achieve breakout. This brick arrangement makes it much more likely for breakout to occur early in the game.

Furthermore, when breakout happens, the audio design of the game highlights the event for the player. As in the original Breakout, when the ball hits a wall or brick, there is a collision sound effect. In Alleyway, the top border of the screen makes a very different, high-pitched bell-like sound when the ball hits it. This means that when the ball breaks out, the speedy back-and-forth bouncing produces an appropriately celebratory "ding! ding! ding!"

The first variation on the design—removing the sides of the brick pattern from the initial game level—changes the game's structural logic in order to make the satisfying breakout experience more likely. The audio feedback helps emphasize this event when it does occur.

Repetitive Play

One common criticism of early digital games like Breakout is that they are too repetitive. Although the core mechanic of the game is quite satisfying on its own, each level is essentially identical. There might be many variations of the core game in Breakout and Super Breakout, but once a player has selected a version of the game to play, each set of bricks will be the same from screen to screen.

Alleyway's solution to this design problem was to design many different level variations, so that each time a player clears a level and gets a new wall of bricks, the arrangement (and sometimes behavior) of the bricks is different. Alleyway is certainly not the first title to create unique levels for a Breakout-style game, but the progression of levels is particularly well-designed.

Some levels in Alleyway feature bricks that fly steadily across the screen from right to left. Others have bricks that slowly move down the screen toward the player's paddle. In the timed bonus levels, the walls are replaced by portraits of Nintendo characters made out of bricks that the player must eliminate, breakthru style: the ball passes straight through the bricks and only bounces back when it hits a wall.

The levels in Alleyway follow a repeating pattern. For each structural arrangement of bricks (such as the open-sided wall of the first level), the player plays a "standard" version of the game, then a version with horizontally moving bricks, then vertically moving bricks, before reaching a bonus level. The next level introduces a new structural arrangement, and the player cycles through the set of variations again, followed by another bonus level. This pattern of levels creates a wonderfully heterogeneous playing experience, providing both familiarity (the variations cycle in a consistent way) and newness (every four levels, a new structure appears). The engaging, repeatable core mechanic of Breakout is enhanced through a system of levels that adds an element of discovery to the overall experience.

Alleyway

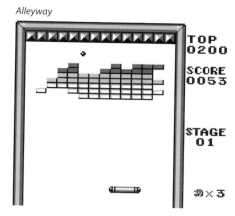

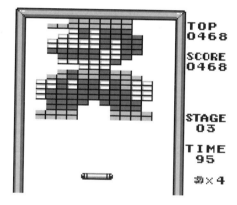

Adjustments to a core mechanic, whether in a digital or non-digital game, can be subtle or overt. They can create meaningful variations on an existing game, or a new game altogether. The key to taking a core mechanic and modifying it within a game relies on an iterative process. As you experiment with variations, ask yourself what is successful or unsuccessful about the existing core mechanic. Then try out your best guesses to see whether or not adjustments to the core mechanic result in more meaningful play.

Putting It All Together

This chapter has introduced some general frameworks for thinking about the experience of play: how rules become play, the core mechanic, and game inputs, outputs, and internal player mechanisms. In the **PLAY** schemas that follow, we take more specific approaches to understanding how a player occupies the space of a game during play. But before moving on, we would like to bring our ideas about the play of experience together in a final, detailed look at a particular digital game: Centipede.

In the early arcade game Centipede, the player's input occurs though a trackball device and a single button for firing. The player uses the trackball to move a bug-like character on the screen, firing shots upward at a variety of objects. Player input in Centipede is very simple: move and fire. Output, in the form of a video screen and audio speakers, is typical for an arcade game. The resulting core mechanic is somewhat generic: shoot enemies to score points and avoid enemies to stay alive. Despite the seemingly simple elements that make up the core mechanic, the game design of Centipede engages the player on a number of levels. The following analysis of Centipede relies heavily on observations made by game designer Richard Rouse III in his book *Game Design: Theory and Practice*.[4] He devotes an entire chapter to Centipede, providing a rigorously detailed reading of the game's design.

How does a player take action in Centipede? There are some wonderful restrictions designed into the game. The trackball itself was a novelty when Centipede was first released, and even today, the large ball promises tactile, fluid motion. Ironically, however, the player cannot move the character anywhere: movement is restricted to the bottom 20 percent of the screen. By limiting the character in this way, the game retains a tight structural focus. As in games such as Space Invaders and Breakout (other games where the player moves along the bottom of the screen), game objects occupy the rest of the space above the player. In Centipede, this space contains both inert obstacles like Breakout bricks, as well as descending enemies like the aliens of Space Invaders. Even though movement is limited, the fact that the player can maneuver a little bit in the vertical dimension increases strategic opportunities and gives the player a much greater sense of freedom than in games that limit movement to a single spatial dimension. Yet the freedom of movement is just enough: if the player was given access to the entire screen, the game enemies and obstacles (which are focused downward towards the player's narrow strip of free action), would not function as successfully.

Centipede's shooting mechanism also places important restrictions on player action. The player can hold down the fire button for a continuous stream of shooting, but only one shot can appear on the screen at a time. Because objects can be very close to the player or very far away, timing shots becomes a focus of game play. Sometimes, a stream of rapid, short-range shots are necessary. However, a shot that goes all the way up to the top of the screen can waste a maddening amount of time, as a player impatiently waits to gain the ability to fire again. The result of this simple design decision (only one shot on the screen at once) forces players to manage their shots like a resource, greatly enriching the decision-making process of the player.

What distinguishes Centipede's well-designed play from a more generic 2D shooter is what Rouse calls the "interconnectedness" of the elements that appear in the game. There are five basic game elements, apart from the player's unit:

- *Mushrooms* are immobile objects that clutter up the screen. It takes four shots from the player to destroy a mushroom, each shot taking away a quarter of the mushroom.

- *Centipedes* are multi-segmented creatures that descend from the top of the screen and move back and forth, descending toward the player. When a centipede hits a mushroom, it drops a row downward, toward the player, meaning that the more mushrooms there are onscreen, the more quickly the centipede will descend. If a centipede segment is shot, it turns into a mushroom, creating a game play loop in which the player is constantly trying to clear mushrooms from the screen in order to slow the centipede's descent, but is also creating more mushrooms by shooting the centipede. When a player shoots a segment of a centipede that is not the head or tail, the centipede splits into two creatures, becoming a multiple threat.

- *Fleas* descend in a straight line from the top of the screen, leaving behind a dense column of mushrooms in their wake. Fleas only appear when the number of mushrooms in the lower half of the screen is below a certain amount, ensuring that there will always be enough mushrooms to create a challenging playfield.

- *Spiders* move in a zig-zag style near the bottom of the screen, directly threatening the player's unit. But spiders eat mushrooms, so the player always has to decide whether it is better to kill a spider right away or to let it eat mushrooms while risking a collision with it.

- *Scorpions* cross the screen horizontally above the player, so they do not pose a direct threat. However, they poison any mushrooms they encounter. If a centipede hits a poisoned mushroom, it will immediately move directly downward toward the player. As a result it is best to remove poisoned mushrooms from the screen.

Each of the five elements plays a role in the game's tightly designed system. The experience of play, a composite of all of the decisions made by the player, emerges from the possibilities mapped out by this system. For example, it is best to keep the overall number of mushrooms low, because the more mushrooms that are on the screen, the more rapidly a centipede will descend and the more mushrooms a scorpion is likely to poison. The mushrooms at the top of the screen are particularly difficult to reach, because they are blocked by lower mushrooms, and the limitation on the player's rate of fire makes it difficult to rid the screen quickly of mushrooms that

are far away. It is easier to clear mushrooms from the bottom of the screen, but if the player clears too many, a flea will descend, dropping mushrooms across the entire height of the screen, including the top, where they are difficult to clear. The player must carefully prune mushrooms from the field of play, while retaining just enough to keep the flea from appearing.

As Rouse writes, "…each of the creatures in the game has a special, unique relationship to the mushrooms. It is the interplay of these relationships that creates the challenge for the player."[5] He cites many examples of this interplay:

> If the player kills the centipede too close to the top of the screen, it will leave a clump of mushrooms which are difficult to destroy at such a distance and which will cause future centipedes to reach the bottom of the screen at a greater speed. However, if the player waits until the centipede is at the bottom of the screen, the centipede is more likely to kill the player. With the mushrooms almost functioning as puzzle pieces, Centipede becomes something of a hybrid between an arcade shooter and a real-time puzzle game.[6]

In looking at the system of Centipede, it is striking to see how a simple set of rules generates complex play. More than just a complex formal system, such rules ramify into a particular *experience,* a set of relationships that give the player's actions meaning. Shoot this mushroom or that one? Kill the centipede at the top of the screen or the bottom? Let the spider eat mushrooms or not? Furthermore, Centipede is an *action* game: all of this rich decision making happens in an extremely compressed space of time, resulting in the blend of action-shooter and strategy-puzzle experience Rouse describes.

But there's more. In his explication of the game, Rouse goes on to describe not just the basic relationships between game elements, but also how they create what he calls "escalating tension" over time. Centipede's design carefully orchestrates the experience of play, creating tension across many levels of the game at once. For example, there is an immediate sense of tension created through the way that the flea and the centipede respond to being hit:

- The first time the flea is shot, it will accelerate its descent, only being destroyed by a second shot.

- Hitting a central segment of the centipede creates two centipedes.

In both of these cases, the result of a shot helps the player by bringing an enemy closer to destruction, but also adds additional danger to the game. As the centipede descends toward the bottom of the screen, anxiety slowly builds up. If the centipede reaches the bottom, extra centipede heads appear, making things dangerously crowded. However, once a level is complete, the player gains a brief respite before the next level begins, a relief that only accentuates the escalating tension that will immediately follow.

Tension also escalates across an entire game. As the game proceeds, more and more mushrooms crowd the game space, until the top of the screen is quite dense with them. Of course, this makes the game more difficult in several ways. Additionally, the creatures become more challenging as the game wears on: the centipede moves faster and eventually begins a level already split into several independent pieces; the spider travels more quickly and in a tighter pattern, making it more difficult to kill. Centipede creates overlapping rhythms of pressure and relief, frustration and achievement, whether in a single game moment, on an individual game level, or across the game as a whole. *This is play: the experience of rules set in motion.* Players *experience* this system: as blinking pixels on a screen, as sharp electronic sounds from a speaker, as sweaty fingers on a trackball and button, as lightning-fast strategic planning. Play culminates in a whirl of perceptions and emotions, thoughts and reflexes, inside the mind and through the body of the player.

Too often, game designers forget that they are creating, above all, an experience of play. It is not enough to tell a story. It is not enough to create pretty pictures or use dazzling technology. A game designer creates an interactive system, a set of choices, an

activity. When you are making a game, ask yourself fundamental questions: What is the player *actually* doing from moment to moment in the game? How are these moments connected in a larger trajectory of experience? How does the experience of play become meaningful? What, above all, is the play of the game? Although there are no easy answers to these questions, focusing on the play of a game's core mechanic is a good starting point for designing powerful player experiences.

Further Reading

"Formal Abstract Design Tools," by Doug Church *(see page 68)*

Man, Play, and Games, by Roger Caillois *(see page 82)*

    Recommended:

    I. The Definition of Play

    II. The Classification of Games

Pilgrim in the Microworld, by David Sudnow *(see page 68)*

    Recommended:

    Memory

    Interface

    Cathexis

    Eyeball

    Coin

Notes

1. *American Heritage Dictionary* (Boston: Houghton Mifflin, 2000).
2. Brian Sutton-Smith, *Toys as Culture* (New York: Gardner Press, 1986), p. 69–72.
3. David Sudnow, *Pilgrim in the Microworld* (New York: Warner Books, 1983), p. 37.
4. Richard Rouse III, *Game Design: Theory and Practice* (Plano, TX: Wordware Publishing, 2001), p. 68.
5. Ibid. p. 68.
6. Ibid. p. 68.

Games as the Play of Experience

SUMMARY

- Play is experienced through **participation.** When a player interacts with a game, the formal system is manifest through experiential effects.

- Sutton-Smith's model for the psychological processes by which video games are experienced:

  - **Concentration**

  - **Visual scanning**

  - **Auditory discriminations**

  - **Motor responses**

  - **Perceptual patterns of learning**

- This model can be abstracted into three components that constitute the system of experience of any game:

  - **input** by which a player takes action

  - **output** of the system to the player

  - **internal processes** by which a player makes decisions

- Game design is a **second-order** design problem. A game designer only *indirectly* designs the player's experience, by *directly* designing the rules. Creating meaningful experiences means understanding the ways a game's formal system transforms into an experiential one.

- The **core mechanic** of a game is the essential moment-to-moment activity players enact. A core mechanic is repeated over and over in the course of a game to create larger patterns of experience.

- A core mechanic can be a single activity, such as running in a footrace. A core mechanic can also be a compound activity, such as the military tactics, resource management, and mouse and keyboard skills of a real-time strategy game.

- Too often, game designers do not consider a game design on the level of the core mechanic, instead relying on conventional interactivity to determine the key player activity.

- A core mechanic can be extended and enlarged through the design of variations. Breakout provides a good example of a simple core mechanic that is intrinsically successful, but which has been successfully modified into many variations.

Unit 3: **Play**

GAMES AS THE PLAY OF PLEASURE

autotelic
extrinsic vs. intrinsic
double seduction
typologies of pleasure
flow
same-but-different
entrainment
short- and long-term goals
conditioning
reinforcement schedules

24

It's not that you have to "care" in order to get good, but rather that you have to be kept caring. You've got to be kept in the right state so you'll get to some places a little bit better all the time, so that a goal remains alive by always moving just ahead out of reach and you keep wanting to attain it without having to spend a fortune.—
David Sudnow, *Pilgrim in the Microworld*

Introducing the Play of Pleasure

Video game arcades are sites of lucratively programmed caring, worlds of fun nourished by a seemingly endless stream of quarters, tokens, and plastic swipe cards. Players enter, they play, and if the game designers have done their job well, they stay to play some more. The carefully crafted arc of rewards and punishments that draws players into games and keep them playing connects pleasure to profitability.

Such intricate games of pleasure and play are not unique to the arcade. Pleasure is, perhaps, the experience most intrinsic to games. From the visceral excitement of an online deathmatch to the satisfying clink of a Go stone on wood, games provide an abundant variety of pleasures. We often take it for granted that games are fun to play, that they provide pleasure, that they embody enjoyable experience. Players derive many kinds of satisfaction from play, from the imaginative adventures of a narrative role-playing game to the social camaraderie of a team sports match. But what is the pleasure that underlies the appeal of games, the pleasure at the core of game play, the pleasure that provides the enticement to begin play and to continue playing? What connects pleasure to the design of meaningful play?

The word "pleasure" evokes associations with activities of leisure or self-indulgence. Sex, drugs, and rich foods come to mind, as do stolen naps, deep friendships, or dancing to a favorite song. Pleasure is commonly understood as a fundamental feeling that is hard to define but that people desire to experience.[1] Words such as delight, amusement, gratification, satisfaction, or happiness describe the kinds of feelings pleasure evokes. When we speak of pleasure in games, we are referring to the fundamental feelings derived from the intense concentration of a game of Memory, the exhilaration of a winning touchdown, the charged socio-sexual maneuvers of Twister, the hypnotically satisfying patterns of Tetris. Pleasure can include any physical, emotional, psychological, or ideological sensation. Of course, pleasure's opposites (pain, frustration, despair) are equally important in understanding the play of pleasure in a game.

Within *Games as the Play of Pleasure,* a game's space of possibility is defined as more than a mathematical entity. It is a space in which a player's emotions and sense of desire undergoes manipulation and coercion, teasing and seduction, frustration and reward. As the sculptor of the space of possible pleasure, the game designer faces a truly challenging set of problems. Managing the pleasure of a game's players means translating the formal intricacies of the rules into an engaging experience of play. Although the emergent math of formal rulesets may be complex, the tangled puzzles of pleasure and desire are surely enigmatic dilemmas of an even higher order.

Rule-Bound

Picture a child poised excitedly at the starting line of a footrace, ready to run down the track, breathlessly awaiting the starting signal. Rather than giving in to her intense desire to leap from the starting line, she waits for the signal that the race has begun. What's going on here? Why does our player anxiously hold back when she really desires to run?

Developmental psychologist L. S. Vygotsky notes that "Play continually creates demands on the child to act against immediate impulse, i.e., to act on the line of greatest resistance."[2] Certainly the child in our example wants to begin running, but the rules of the game order her to wait. At the same time, the runner knows that the rules are artificial, describing systems that are in some way outside ordinary life. So why follow the rules? Vygotsky argues that players accept the rules of the game not in order to restrict pleasure, but instead to maximize

---

Footnote to a Footnote

In *Defining Play,* we noted that we would not be investigating the purpose or function of play in this book. Rather, we focus on the way that play creates meaningful experiences for players, when considered from a game design perspective. Likewise, in the study of the play of pleasure, we will not suggest a root cause or mechanism, nor argue a unified theory of pleasure. There is a tremendous amount of existing research on the philosophical, psychoanalytic, cognitive, and cultural qualities of pleasure, some of which we reference in this chapter.

it. "To observe the rules of the play structure promises much greater pleasure from the game than the gratification of an immediate impulse."[3] Through mechanisms of restraint and the withholding of immediate impulses, games transform the player's experience of constraint into one of abundant pleasure.

The notion that pleasure is an effect of submitting to the rules of a game, that pleasure delayed and constrained is pleasure enhanced, offers a powerful model for understanding all kinds of pleasure. Think of examples from your own experience: waiting to eat a particularly enticing dessert until completing the main course, or not skipping ahead to the end of a suspenseful murder mystery. The delayed gratification of orgasm is heightened when it is initially resisted, as is the urge of opening a fine wine before it has properly aged.

Submission to constraint is certainly not the only way to understand pleasure, but it is an appropriate starting point for a discussion of the play of pleasure in games. Consider, for example, how the notion of constraint intersects with several core game design concepts:

- *Rules and Play.* The idea that players subordinate their behaviors to the restrictions of rules in order to experience play—and its pleasures—is a fundamental aspect of games. The restrictions of rules facilitate play, and in doing so, generate pleasure for players.

- *Free Play.* A player's sense of pleasure is explicitly derived from being a part of the system of a game, from being "at play" within the more rigid structures of a game. In *Man, Play, and Games,* Caillois makes an explicit link between a player's free action within the limits set by the rules and player gratification: "This latitude of the player, this margin accorded to his action is essential to the game and partly explains the pleasure which it excites."[4] Free play is dependant on, yet also resists, the rigid structures that give rise to it.

- *The Lusory Attitude.* Playing a game means abiding by artificial restrictions, which make game actions seemingly inefficient. Runners not only wait for the starting gun, but, as Bernard Suits points out in *Grasshopper,* they also run around a circular track, instead of cutting through the middle of the field to reach the finish line first. Games are constituted by these kinds of constraints, which simultaneously restrain and enable pleasure. The willingness of players to step into these artificial systems in order to experience the resulting pleasure is at the heart of the lusory attitude.

- *Stylized Behavior.* Although play is a free and improvisational activity, the rules of a game stylize the actions and behaviors of players in very particular ways. Think about the patterned movement of players engaged in a game of Ping Pong, or the tightly constrained movements of Simon Says. There is something very pleasurable in the way that games stylize play through a ritualistic, collective orchestration of movement and action. Children derive pleasure not just from the dramatic tension at the start of a race, but also from the collective experience of running together in formation, pumping their arms and kicking their heels toward the finish line.

Rules give rise to the dramatic structure of pleasure, the link between constraint and pleasure binding tightly the formal and experiential qualities of a game. But players don't simply stumble into a game. Unlike other forms of ludic activities (such as playing with a toy), a game demands that players know the rules before play begins. What provides the enticement to begin play? What makes players stay in a game once it starts?

Autotelic Play

The magic circle of a game is, by definition, removed in some way from what Huizinga calls "ordinary life." The victories and losses, the triumphs and failures that a player experiences in a game are in a very real sense contained within the magic circle. As DeKoven puts it, a game provides "a common goal, the achievement of which has no bearing on anything that is out-side the game."5 We know, of course, that there are many ways winning or losing games can impact players: affecting their lifestyles, their sense of self, their relationships to friends, even the amount of money they have in their pockets when the game is over. There are certainly *extrinsic* ways that winning a game matters. At the same time, every game implicitly asserts the premise that the value of the game is *intrinsic,* that the game is self-contained, that the fiction of the magic circle will be upheld, that winning or losing the game is separate from everyday lived experience.

If one considers the self-contained nature of the magic circle, the way that games create their own meanings and provide their own goals, it is clear that games are strongly *autotelic.* We borrow the term from psychologist Mihaly Csikszentmihalyi, who in his book *Flow* explains that "The term 'autotelic' derives from two Greek words, *auto* meaning self and *telos* meaning goal. It refers to a self-contained activity, one that is done not with the expectation of some future benefit, but simply because the doing itself is the reward."6 When an experience is autotelic, it is participation in the activity alone that counts. Games are, to a greater or lesser extent, pursued for their own sake, for their own intrinsic stimulation. Although there are always some extrinsic reasons for play, there are always intrinsic motivations as well. In playing a game, part of the incentive is simply to play—and often, it is the prime motivator.

Because they have such a strong autotelic component, games are largely non-utilitarian. Most forms of design serve an exter-nal function, or utility. Architecture houses and shelters our families, government, and industries. Typography enables visual communication. Automotive design supports mobility through the design of cars. Game design, on the other hand, simply enables its own play. Please note, in saying that game design exists in contrast to other forms of design, we are *not* proposing that games do not serve external functions, or that other forms of design don't also serve non-utilitarian ends. Our point is that

games posit their own intrinsic needs or goals, such as abstract winning conditions, which gives them a distinctly artificial and non-utilitarian status.

Contrast an online medical database program with an online multiplayer game. A hospital worker looking for a particular patient's record comes to the software experience with a clear extrinsic goal in mind, such as finding out what meds the patient needs to take that day. The database does not contain its own set of goals; it supports the goals of the user. The data-base program is used as a tool, as a means to an end, rather than as an end in itself. When the worker finds the record he is looking for and extracts the prescription information, the data-base has successfully fulfilled a goal that was brought to the system from an external context. In an online multiplayer game, on the other hand, there is no clear utilitarian purpose that the game serves. Why is the player exploring the game world, customizing her character, killing monsters, and accu-mulating treasure? Because she is playing the game. The game is not a tool being used to fill an external, utilitarian need. The player is not playing the game in order to feed her cats, or tune her car's engine. The explicit interaction of the game is not a means to an end, as in the case of the medical database pro-gram; rather, the play of the game represents an end in itself. We play, in some measure, for play's own sake.

Consider the way that the experience of play as an end, rather than a means, has affected the development of digital game technology. One of the reasons why games have been so inno-vative—pushing the envelope of computer processing power, creating experimental hardware interfaces, pioneering graphics rendering and spatial audio—is because games must provide their own motivations and pleasures. The medical worker will suffer through an awkward interface and ugly visual design in order to find the record he needs. A game player, on the other hand, is a much more fickle user: why play a game that isn't fun? The computer and video game industry is continually spurred on by an audience hungry for ever-more spectacular games and ever-more meaningful interaction. People play games because they want to; game designers must create experiences that both feed and satisfy this sense of desire.

Enter. Play. Stay.

Why go to such lengths about the non-utilitarian nature of games? In order to make a larger point about the challenge of bringing players into a game and keeping them at play. Because games are premised on needs *intrinsic* to the game, it is necessary for game designers to both entice the player into crossing the boundary of the magic circle and also keep them there until the goals of the game have been met.

Beginning a game means entering into the magic circle. Players cross over this boundary to adopt the artificial behaviors and rituals of a game. During the game, the magic circle persists until the game concludes. Then the magic circle dissolves and players return to the ordinary world. These two actions, crossing into the magic circle as well as maintaining its existence, represent two of the chief challenges of designing meaningful play. The two actions require a carefully orchestrated double seduction. First, players are seduced into entering the magic circle of a game. Second, players are seduced into continuing to play.

Both events are challenging to design. The first seduction, bringing players into the magic circle, requires players to cross a threshold that will take them out of their ordinary lives and into the world of the game. The difficulty in making this happen comes from the formal quality of game play. It is much easier to slip into and out of ludic activities that aren't games. Are you eating peanuts and feeling playful? Just toss one up and see if you can catch it in your mouth. How about those building blocks on your desk? Stack them up, knock them down, or just let them be. In **The Magic Circle,** we looked at the way a child might play with a doll, at how smoothly a player can slip in and out of play, at how permeable the borders are between playing and not playing. In games, however, the transition between not playing the game and starting to play the game is more clearly

defined. Games usually require formal preparation: finding players, reading the rules, opening a saved game file, shuffling cards, setting up the board, and so on. Players must learn the system and "officially" enter into the game and begin play. This is a genuine hurdle for players of your game: they must attend to the initial set of chores that lie on the border of the magic circle; they must properly perform the rituals of entry.

What does this mean for game designers? Designers create not just the game itself, but also the ways that players enter into the game system. This event involves consideration of not just the formal elements of the game, but also the way that the game interfaces with external contexts. How and when does a player enter into a game? Where does the initial seduction begin? Does it begin the first time a player sees a commercial or reads a review of a game that encourages or discourages the player to make a purchase? Does the seduction emerge from peer pressure and social values (*Barbie Fashion Designer is for girls! Quake is cool! Everybody is playing P.O.X.!*). Does it begin with the installation of a downloaded game, the first reading of a game's rules, or the menu screen of a console title? Does it start the moment a newbie shoots his first monster?

Clearly, there is no single factor to which the act of seduction can be attributed and no single, isolated moment when the player decides to begin play. Designing the seduction of a game means understanding all of the formal, social, and cultural factors that contribute to the player's experience. It is important, for example, to understand how marketing, promotion, and distribution work in the game industry. It is important to scout out what other game developers are creating and how it may impact the game you are designing. It is important to understand how the culture at large perceives and regards games and how new audiences might be brought to your games. There are no simple answers to the question of whether or not a player will decide to begin playing your game. This is one more challenge game designers face.

On the other hand, once players start playing your game, they have stepped out of the world at large and entered into the magic circle of the game's design. As we will see, keeping players in a game, understanding and sculpting their experience of pleasure, offers at least as great a challenge as getting them to play in the first place.

Typologies of Pleasure

It is difficult to generally speak about pleasure. It is especially hard to find the words that describe the pleasures we experience in games.

> Games evoke emotions of struggle, of competition. The kinds of things you feel aren't often given common names in our usual everyday parlance but they are important emotions that we feel and go through and enjoy and find in some mysterious ways enlarge our spirit. How about the anxiety that you feel when your chest suddenly swells as you realize you are going to be a master? How about the sense of self that develops as you concentrate all your being and the various parts of your body upon the task of overcoming obstacles? How about the dejection you feel, the despair when you fail utterly? And how about the exultation and the sense of triumph you feel when you actually succeed? And sometimes a little bit of awe as you maybe find that path out there. And there's another name for these emotions and game developers call them fun.[7]

Game designer Hal Barwood organizes all the varied emotions a game can produce under the heading of *"fun."* This term does make some sense. Good games are fun. Fun games are what players want. A fun game makes for a pleasurable experience, which is why people play. But not everyone sees the value of this word. Game designer Marc LeBlanc simply hates the term "fun." In several of his talks at the Game Developers Conference, he has called for a moratorium on the word. "Fun," according to LeBlanc, is merely a stand-in term for a more complex phenomenon that no one really understands.

Perhaps LeBlanc is right. Perhaps we are falling into a similar trap by our use of the word "pleasure." Is it possible to unpack the more general notion of fun and create a structure for categorizing pleasure? LeBlanc has done some thinking along these lines and has created his own typology, proposed as an antidote to the singular concept of "fun." In his typology LeBlanc lists eight categories that describe the kinds of experiential pleasure players derive from playing games.

1. Sensation: *Game as sense-pleasure*

2. Fantasy: *Game as make-believe*

3. Narrative: *Game as drama*

4. Challenge: *Game as obstacle course*

5. Fellowship: *Game as social framework*

6. Discovery: *Game as uncharted territory*

7. Expression: *Game as self-discovery*

8. Submission: *Game as masochism*[8]

Most of these categories are self-explanatory. Note, however, that "masochism" doesn't refer to sexual pleasure, but instead to the more general pleasure of submission to a system. Part of the hypnotic pleasure of Bejeweled or Solitaire, for example, comes from the ritualized act of behaving in a rule-based, stylized manner. That is what LeBlanc means by his category of Submission.

LeBlanc's model is intended not only to assist game designers in understanding the range of forms that "fun" can take, but also to provide a common language for marketing digital games. He has proposed, for example, that by rating each of these categories on a zero-to-ten scale and putting that information on the back of a product package, a consumer could quickly get a sense of the kinds of pleasures the game provides. A first-person shooter, for example, might have a high rating in Sensation, Fantasy, and Challenge, but a low rating in Expression, Narrative, and Fellowship. The challenge, of course, is that many of the categories seem to overlap. There is a very fuzzy line, for example, between Fantasy and Narrative. Other ambiguities persist as well. Categories such as Discovery and Expression might easily be applied to other categories: can't a social framework be uncharted territory? Doesn't self-discovery occur in a challenge? Moreover, even if these theoretical problems could be resolved, "officially" rating a game's pleasure in this way would be a highly subjective endeavor. Despite all of these criticisms, however, LeBlanc's eight categories do identify many of the components of game-induced pleasure and are useful as a way of understanding the range of pleasures games provide.

A different approach comes from psychologist Michael J. Apter, in his essay "A Structural-Phenomenology of Play." In focusing on the cognitive arousal play provides, Apter compiles the following list, amended with our brief paraphrasing in italics:

1. Exposure to Arousing Stimulation: *intense and overwhelming sensation*

2. Fiction and Narrative: *emotional arousal from character identification*

3. Challenge: *difficulties and frustrations arising from competition*

4. Exploration: *moving off the beaten track into new territory*

5. Negativism: *deliberate and provocative rule-breaking*

6. Cognitive Synergy: *imaginative play*

7. Facing Danger: *risk within the "protective frame" of play* [9]

Apter admits in his essay that these categories offer only a partial list of cognitive arousals, and that there is considerable overlap between categories. Despite these delimitations, Apter's model gives us another framework within which to consider pleasure in games, one that emphasizes cognition. Some of his categories, such as Challenge and Exploration, appear similar to LeBlanc's. Others, such as Negativism and Facing Danger, clearly identify alternate approaches.

A third typology of pleasure comes from the classification of games by anthropologist Roger Caillois. In **Defining Play,** we introduced his four "fundamental categories," which purport to describe the phenomena of play:

1. *Agôn:* competition and competitive struggle

2. *Alea:* submission to the fortunes of chance

3. *Mimicry:* role-playing and make-believe play

4. *Ilinx:* vertigo and physical sensation

In some ways, Caillois' compact categories offer a succinct distillation of the models LeBlanc and Apter propose. In agôn, alea, mimicry, and ilinx, there is a fusion of experiential and cognitive components that creates a useful critical framework.

There are many other typologies we could consider as well. Last chapter, we looked at Brian Sutton-Smith's five categories describing the psychological processes of video game players: concentration, visual scanning, auditory discriminations, motor responses, and perceptual patterns of learning. These too might be considered a list of the means by which games generate and support pleasure. There is no need to choose a single typology to represent pleasure in games. You should feel free to mix and match different models of experience and pleasure, depending on the needs of your design. These typologies are less useful for theorizing about pleasure or for classifying games, but they can be very handy as a way of organizing observations about the kinds of pleasures that a particular game provides. One model is not necessarily better than the others; each offers a different way of thinking about pleasure and its many motivations.

For example, let us employ one of these typologies—Caillois' four categories—in looking at an Unreal deathmatch. Do they apply to the pleasures of playing Unreal? Certainly the game contains a great deal of competitive, agônistic struggle. Mimicry plays a strong role as well, in the fact that each player is represented to the others through a customizable avatar in a fictional, virtual space. Unreal and games of its ilk are well known for representing physical movement through three-dimensional space in real-time, often creating vertigo in the form of motion sickness. There are arguably even elements of chance in Unreal as well, such as the particular players that happen to join an online deathmatch, or the layout and distribution of items on a level.

We can similarly apply the categories of LeBlanc and Apter. A game of Unreal provides all of the pleasures they list too, from the Fellowship that emerges out of hard-fought competition, to the creative Negativism of cheats, hacks, and mods. Pleasure is always already exceedingly complex: where we find one form of pleasure in a game, we will almost always find others. In general, most games provide many or all of the pleasures listed in any typology of game play experience. But at the same time, there is always a balance of factors, a particular ratio of ingredients that adds up to the unique flavor of an individual game experience. What meaningful pleasures is your game providing, or failing to provide? This is the utility of a typology of "fun:" offering a vocabulary for charting out the complex play of pleasure.

Game Flow

Listing categories is one approach to describing pleasure in a game. Are there other approaches? Is it possible to look at game pleasure in a more abstract way to synthesize the diverse pleasures of gaming into a single concept? Think again about the experience of playing a game. One aspect of game pleasure lies in the intensity with which it is experienced, the almost overwhelming sensation of play. Whether the pleasure rests in a cognitive response, an emotional effect, or a physical reaction, the experience of play, and especially play in games, can be strikingly deep. As writer J. C. Herz writes of classic arcade gaming, "Just the emotion, the survival nature of the videogame—you're tapping into the most powerful human instinct. Survival. Fight or flight. That is so hugely intense that in some ways it becomes too intense. People really lived the games. They dreamed the games."

All game players have experienced this feeling at one time or another, even if for only a short time. This level of engagement with a game suggests that the player has transcended an ordinary psychological state to arrive at a more profound relationship with the game. The psychologist and theorist Mihaly Csikszentmihalyi is best known for his research on what he calls *the flow state*—a particular state of mind in which a participant achieves a high degree of focus and enjoyment. His book *Flow: The Psychology of Optimal Experience* offers a great general introduction to his ideas. *Flow* is filled with anecdotal accounts of individuals achieving a flow state, documented over the years of Csikszentmihalyi's research.

The phenomenon of flow comes in many forms. Some people reported to Csikszentmihalyi that they reached flow through the rigors of perfecting an assembly line work task, or through the immersive problem-solving of law library research. Others say they achieved flow during the solitary exertion of rock climbing or through the exacting vocation of surgery. What exactly is *flow*? Csikszentmihalyi suggests that flow is something we have all experienced. It is a feeling of being in control of our actions, masters of our own fate. Although rare, when we achieve a state of flow we are deeply exhilarated. Csikszentmihalyi refers to this phenomenon as an *optimal experience*.

> It is what the sailor holding a tight course feels when the wind whips through her hair, when the boat lunges through the waves like a colt—sails, hull, wind, and sea humming a harmony that vibrates in the sailor's veins. It is what a painter feels when the colors on the canvas begin to set up a magnetic tension with each other, and a new thing, a living form, takes shape in front of the astonished creator.[11]

Flow is, more than anything else, an emotional and psychological state of focused and engaged happiness, when a person feels a sense of achievement and accomplishment, and a greater sense of self. What might be the relevance of flow for game design? In many ways, the heightened enjoyment and engagement of the flow state is exactly what game designers seek to establish for their players. In fact, many of Csikszent-mihalyi's examples come from games, such as professional Chess players, which were an early focus of his research. The connection between game design and the flow experience clearly appears in Csikszentmihalyi's description of the components of flow, the conditions that make flow possible. He lists eight components:

> First, the experience usually occurs when we confront tasks we have a chance of completing. Second, we must be able to concentrate on what we are doing. Third and fourth, the concentration is usually possible because the task undertaken has clear goals and provides immediate feedback. Fifth, one acts with a deep but effortless involvement that removes from awareness the worries and frustrations of everyday life. Sixth, enjoyable experiences allow people to exercise a sense of control over their actions. Seventh, concern for the self disappears, yet paradoxically the sense of self emerges stronger after the flow experience is over. Finally, the sense of the duration of time is altered; hours pass by like minutes, and minutes can stretch out to seem like hours.[12]

It should be immediately striking how every one of these eight components corresponds to an aspect of games. We can look at each in more detail, making use of Csikszentmihalyi's own language.[13]

A Challenging Activity that Requires Skills: Csikszentmihalyi emphasizes the fact that the flow activity is not passively experienced; it requires active and directed engagement. "The overwhelming proportion of optimal experiences are reported to occur within sequences of activities that are goal-directed and bounded by rules." This sounds remarkably like a description of a game.

The Merging of Action and Awareness: One distinctive feature of the flow state is that a person is so absorbed in the activity that it becomes "spontaneous, almost automatic;

they stop being aware of themselves as separate from the actions they are performing." This component of the flow experience is something that can occur in games as well. David Sudnow's account of his engagement with Breakout clearly describes this state of mind.

Clear Goals and Feedback: These two components evoke the goal-oriented nature of games and the discernable action-outcome sequence necessary for making meaningful choices. Meaningful play seems to be intimately related to flow.

Concentration on the Task at Hand: A common effect of flow is "a complete focusing of attention on the task at hand, thus leaving no room in the mind for irrelevant information." Like a game that removes itself from "ordinary life," flow activities carve out their own experiential spaces for participants.

The Paradox of Control: In an optimal experience, the participant is able to exercise control without completely being in control of the situation. If there is no chance of failure, the activity is not difficult enough. "Only when a doubtful outcome is at stake, and one is able to influence that outcome, can a person really know whether she is in control." As game players struggle against the system of artificial conflict, they attempt to assert control by taking actions. Yet the outcome of a game is always uncertain.

The Loss of Self-Consciousness: In flow, the participant's sense of self becomes subservient to the greater whole of the experience. "When a person invests all her psychic energy into an interaction... she in effect becomes part of a system of action greater than what the individual self had been before. This system takes its form from the rules of the activity; its energy comes from the person's attention." The fact that Csikszentmihalyi emphasizes the systemic quality of a participant's connection with the flow activity is reminiscent of the system-based nature of games.

When we consider a game as an experiential system, the player is a component of that system—a formulation echoed by Csikszentmihalyi.

The Transformation of Time: The participant's sense of time can stretch or shrink. Sometimes this feeling comes directly from the activity itself: "Most flow activities do not depend on clock time; like baseball, they have their own pace, their own sequences of events marking transitions from one state to another without regard to equal intervals of duration." Games not only change our perception of time but also offer freedom from its tyranny; losing track of time adds to the exhilaration we feel during a state of complete involvement.

In each of the eight components of the flow activity Csikszentmihalyi mentions, there are clear parallels with games. This doesn't mean that flow applies only to games, or that every game produces a flow state for its players. What it does mean is that games are one of the best kinds of activities to produce flow. The rules, goals, feedback, uncertain outcome, and other qualities of games make them fertile terrain for the flowering of a flow experience. We believe there is an intrinsic connection between game play and flow. Although the maximum flow "optimal experience" that Csikszentmihalyi describes is rarely achieved, all forms of play in some way partake of the flow experience. The conditions for flow are established as players find the interstices of a rigid structure, engaging with rules in order to play with them and transform them. Flow is one way of understanding that pleasure which draws players to a game and keeps them there.

Although he does not organize them this way, Csikszentmihalyi's eight categories can be divided into two groups. Four of the eight components of flow describe the *effects* of the flow state:

·   the merging of action and awareness

·   concentration

·   the loss of self-consciousness

·   the transformation of time

All of these effects occur in the player's experience once flow commences. These four facets of flow can diagnose whether a player has reached the flow state. If you are not sure if your game is truly producing flow, go down the list. If some or all of the four experiences listed are missing, you may need to adjust your design. But what kinds of adjustments are necessary? That's where the other four components come into play. Rather than being effects of flow, they represent flow's *prerequisites:*

·   a challenging activity

·   clear goals

·   clear feedback

·   the paradox of having control in an uncertain situation

These four prerequisite elements of flow are characteristics of the flow activity itself. Within them is the key to designing flow in games. Does your game contain the prerequisites of flow? Is there enough challenge to create real uncertainty? Do the players clearly understand the goals? As they move through the system, do their actions provide clear feedback and a sense of control? If your game supplies all of these mechanisms, you are well on your way to creating the necessary conditions for flow.

If your aim is to create a flow state for your players, we can summarize our advice quite simply: *design meaningful play.* The four prerequisites of flow bear a striking resemblance to the key components of meaningful play. "Clear feedback" is another way of stating the need for *discernable* choices and outcomes in an interactive experience. The goals, challenge, and uncertainty of a game provide the larger context within which choices are *integrated* and become meaningful. This is not to say that meaningful play is the same thing as flow. Flow is a state of mind and meaningful play is an approach to game design. But when it comes to games, the two are closely intertwined. If you want to create flow in a game, meaningful play must be present. If you want to design meaningful play, flow can be a useful diagnostic tool in the process of making your game.

Why would game designers want to create a flow state for their players? Being in flow represents a rich and meaningful engagement with the activity at hand. Generally, as a game designer, you are creating game systems meant for deep exploration. We should all be so lucky that players of our games invest enough effort and attention to achieve a state of flow. Remember that flow doesn't refer to just one kind of experience. The flow that surgeons feel is by all accounts radically different in sensation and emotion than the flow of a LARP combat. What unites all forms of flow, however, is the optimal happiness that participants experience. As an experiential goal for creating games, spreading happiness, focus, and a sense of well-being is certainly a worthy pursuit.

Sculpting Desire

If one problem with the concept of flow is that it is not as game-specific as we would like, what would it mean to take a more game-centric look at pleasure? Thinking of games as systems of pleasure implies that the game designer is an artisan of desire, shaping the pleasure of the players of a game. The designed system of the game, set in motion by the participation of players, becomes not just an experience of play, but also an experience of sensual, emotional, and psychological pleasure.

Achieving such an experience requires that a game designer not only pay attention to the immediate feelings of pleasure a game may produce, but also the way that a player's pleasure evolves and changes over the course of a single game, or across many games.

> Anyone can sit down at Quake and start shooting things. As he gains more experience, he realizes that if he stands in one place, he'll get killed, so he learns to start moving while shooting. Then he learns to circle-strafe. Then, to shoot while running backwards. Then, to figure out which weapons are better up close or far away.

Disclaimer: The Limits of Flow

As useful as it is, the concept of flow is not a skeleton key to unlock every mystery surrounding play and pleasure in games. Consider a few of the challenges in applying flow to game design:

> *Flow is not unique to games.* As Csikszentmihalyi's many examples from art, work, and non-game leisure demonstrate, flow can occur in many kinds of activities. Why is this a problem? If one of our goals as game designers is to understand and isolate the unique kinds of pleasures that only games can provide, then the flow state is not of much help.

> *Flow is more about the player than the game.* According to Csikszentmihalyi, flow depends at least as much on the attitude of the individual participant as the activity itself. Chess masters may achieve flow, but most Chess players do not. There is no guarantee that the game you design will be put to use by players that are ready or able to experience flow. A player's individual psyche is out of a game designer's control.

> *Flow is not a universal phenomenon.* It is easy to get carried away and assume that the flow state is the ultimate experience that every game design should try and induce. That is simply not the case. As Sutton-Smith points out in a critique of Csikszentmihalyi's work, "To say flow is universal might be like saying that all peak sex is everywhere the same, and that 'flow' is to play what orgasm is to sex. But who would be innocent enough of all the different contexts and acts that make sex meaningful to say something like that?"

Although flow is a useful conceptual tool for creating pleasure in games, it is but one of many possible tools. Flow offers a rigorous investigation into one kind of meaningful engagement, even if it doesn't represent a universal state of mind and even if it isn't completely unique to games.

Then he learns to rocket jump. As he progresses, he learns the characteristics of each weapon. He learns to "lead" his opponent. Anyone can pick up Quake and start having a good time within minutes, yet the longer he spends mastering the game, the more enjoyable it becomes.[15]

Quake is easy to learn but difficult to master. As game designer Bob Bates points out, it offers players a gaming experience that is pleasurable in both the short and long term. Because the core mechanic is relatively simple—move and shoot—players gain immediate access to the pleasures the game affords. Because playing the game well requires subtle skills that can only develop through repetitive play, long-term engagement with the game brings its own kind of pleasurable reward.

How does pleasure emerge and evolve over time in a game? All of the possible states and experiences of a game are contained within the theoretical construct called the space of possibility. A game player begins his or her journey through the space of possibility at the same place every time: the start of the game. But the experiential path that a player takes through the space will vary each time the game is played. Every play of the game will be unique, even though the rules of the game, its formal structure, remain fixed. This quality of games, that a game provides the *same* consistent structure each time but a *different* experience and outcome every time it is played, is a powerful engine that sustains and encourages play. We refer to this concept by the shorthand term *same-but-different*.

The same-but-different experience of play occurs both within an individual game, as well as across more than one game. Inside a game of Breakout, the player engages with the core mechanic over and over, exploring its permutations many times within the changing context of the game. Hit the ball again and again. Can you get that bank shot a second time from the side? Or slow things down by hitting the square in the

middle of the paddle? Can you control the flow of the volley? Within a game, given the same repetitive action of play, part of the pleasure that sustains the game is the player's ability to engage repeatedly with the same kind of interactivity—but with different results.

The core mechanic of a game provides its own inherent pleasure, whether it takes the form of the sensual click of a Tiddley-Winks flip or the simple, randomized drama of each round of the card game War. If a game's core mechanic is well-designed, players may not even care about winning. Players can enjoy Tennis just for the sake of a good volley, or Charades for the challenge of skillful pantomime and clever guessing. But to sustain pleasure over time, the repeated action of the core mechanic needs to embody the concept of same-but-different. It needs to continue to offer up new variations and experiences, even if they are as subtle as the gradual build-up of Tiddley-Winks skill or the deterministic playing-out of fate in War.

On a larger level, the same phenomenon occurs as a player plays a game more than one time. In this case, it is not the core mechanic that is repeated, but the entire formal structure of the game. The rules remain the same, but the play is different. It doesn't always happen, but if the play is meaningful enough, if the pleasure is rich and flowing, then a player will want to play a game again. With repeated play, the structure is increasingly familiar, and the player continues to play out the possible experiential permutations of the game. Within and between games, players discover the comforting familiarity of a fixed structure and the challenge and danger of an uncertain outcome. This same-but-different mechanism makes for an extremely powerful engine of desire. It is the itch of the same-but-different that brings you back, time and time again, for just one more round of play.

Furthermore, transformative play assists this process. In **Defining Play,** we established transformative play as the special case of play, when the free movement of play alters the more rigid structure in which it takes shape. When the structure of the game is altered, the possibilities for replayability increase. Even in a simple betting game, transformative play can ensure that new experiences continue to arise, as a player finds new patterns of betting, new places in which to bet, new patterns of life into which the betting activity fits, new circles of friends to support the activity. Still, the game remains familiar, even as it changes. Philosopher James S. Hans expresses this notion of the same-but-different experience of play quite well:

> In this regard, all play shares one thing with games: a familiar structure that allows one to play with the unfamiliar. This familiar structure is not universal; it is contingent upon the particular context of play. Nor is this familiar structure always the same. Indeed, it changes every time it is played with, for the occasion for new play introduces different elements into the activity that become part of the structure of any future play.... The structure of the familiar then permits the introduction of the different; play in one sense is no more than the infection of the familiar by difference.[16]

Although Hans is talking about all kinds of play, every game by our definition shares this quality. He makes explicit the idea that play is transformative, that through repetition, play itself changes. Hans calls this play of desire "the infection of the familiar by difference"—perhaps the heart of what makes games pleasurable. Within the magic circle, rules endow actions with meanings. But the free movement that is play transforms these meanings, even as they are experienced, putting pleasure "at play" at each moment of a game.

Patterns of Pleasure

The patterns of pleasure that emerge within and between games offer special kinds of enjoyments. Game designer Brian Moriarty uses the word *entrainment* to refer to this kind of rhythmic pleasure. Entrainment comes from the French word "entrainer" and has two meanings: *to carry along,* and *to trap.* The word has commonly been applied to a range of physical and natural phenomena, from circadian sleep rhythms to the sonic play of a thunderstorm. According to holistic thinker Dr. Stephan Rechtschaffen, "Rhythmic entrainment is one of the great organizing principles of the world, as inescapable as gravity. It explains how one rhythm works with another, and how separate entities, from molecules to stars, will fall into rhythm as automatically as a pulse beats or a butterfly flaps its wings."[17]

As used by Moriarty, entrainment is the process of falling into a patterned activity, such as when baseball fans spontaneously create a stadium-wide "wave" in a co-authored, massively multiplayer spectacle. One can also apply the concept to the play rhythms evoked when playing a game. In 1998, Moriarty gave a talk at the Game Developers conference about entrainment and game design:

> Rhythms and patterns exist in all games, if you watch. Watch someone playing a game sometime. Not the game itself, lest you be sucked in, but the player, and the space around him or her. Watch the rhythms emerge, and how the player and the game interact. It will become clear that a game is really an entrainment engine. The job of the gamewright, therefore, is to reinforce patterns, and dampen dissonance."[18]

The notion of entrainment combines pattern, interactivity, and the same-but-different quality of games into a rich and powerful design concept. If entrainment is a form of pleasure, it is a pleasure at once structural and experiential, both mathematically regular and playfully flexible. Entrainment is not a phenomenon completely unique to games, but it does come very close to identifying the curious structural pleasure that all game experiences seem to contain: the meditative patterns of Tetris; the turn-taking, clacking cadence of Billiards; the rhythmic shooting pattern of Space Invaders; the pulsing flow of cards, hits, and chips of Blackjack. Each of these game experiences—every game experience—can be framed as an instance of entrainment.

Entrainment is the experience of the same-but-different. As players explore the space of possible game pleasures, progress through the space occurs through patterned repetition, the drumbeat driving the heart of a game experience. Entrainment sometimes literally takes on form: the recurrent bleep of a laser blast, or the relentless throb of a marathon runner's steps. But ultimately, entrainment manifests in a more pervasive fashion, occupying not just perceptual sensations, but modes of thinking and feeling as well. The double-sided definition of the word entrainment, *to carry along* and *to trap,* is entirely accurate. The patterns of a game initially draw us in, moving us forward, encouraging us to play. But somehow, at some point, something changes. We find ourselves not just playing a game, but being played by the game as well. Pleasure is a mighty force, and it can carry along those trapped in its wake.

The Role of the Goal

How does this transition come about? How is it that a game can draw us in and take us hostage? Some of the most powerful mechanisms of pleasure that a game contains are derived from their constituent parts. The difference between games and other forms of play is most often the fact that a game has a goal and a quantifiable outcome. When it comes to understanding the pleasure of a game, the *goal* plays an absolutely crucial role.

A game's goal is often the largest single element that drives the pleasure of a player. The goal is the ostensible reason for playing, but the goal is never easily attained; rather, it is the obscure object of desire, the carrot held just out of reach, pulling players forward through the varied pleasures of game play. The goal helps move players through the space of possibility, a space stretched between the starting state of the game and its outcome like a billowing cloth staked to the ground. The goal acts to guide the players along the axis defined by the beginning and the end, letting them know if they are advancing or falling behind. In Chutes and Ladders, the player's position on the board clearly communicates proximity to achieving victory. In Chinese Checkers, the accumulation of pieces within a player's goal serves as a competitive marker toward winning. In an online deathmatch, ranking players by frag count shows which players are closest to victory.

A core component of pleasure in games lies in the creation and maintenance of a player's relationship to the goal. The game designer, by creating the game rules, indirectly engineers this relationship. Do you want to create a close game with a dramatic finish? Then engineer a negative feedback loop that punishes the lead player and closes the gap with players at the rear. Or perhaps you want to make use of hidden information, so that the outcome is in doubt until the very end. In the puzzle game Mastermind, each turn brings the player closer to the end of the track, where failure awaits after a set number of turns. Each turn also offers the player feedback and a glimpse of hope, signified by the black and white pegs, as he tries to puzzle out the correct solution. Between the inevitable, uncontrollable turn-by-turn movement, and the sometimes-backpedaling advancement toward the solution, the game unfolds as a journey of the player's desire. The result is the genuinely compelling play of Mastermind, in which the physical structure charts the player's progress through the game.

The classic arcade game Missile Command offers yet another example of the way games engineer dramatic experiences for players. As J. C. Herz writes in *Joystick Nation: How Videogames Won Our Hearts and Ate Our Quarters:*

> The most intense thing about Missile Command, though, was this weird crazy moment near the end, when the ICBMs were raining down and you knew you were just about to lose it, that was totally euphoric. Because you knew that you were going to die, that you were within seconds of everything going black. You're gonna die in three seconds. You're gonna die at this instant. You're dying. You're dead. And then you get to watch all the pretty explosions. And after

the fireworks display, you get to press the restart button, and you're alive again, until the next collision with your own mortality.[19]

Within the game the goal takes on enormous importance, but the goal itself as a formal construct is not the point: the goal is important only insofar as it serves to shape a player's experience. The goal is an artificial, invented condition that the players accept as their ultimate objective. In establishing the nature of that goal and the way that players overcome adversity to work toward it, the game designer has tremendous influence on crafting the character of the play experience.

Goals Within Goals

The goal is not the only source of pleasure in a game. In addition to the thrill that the pursuit of victory (or the agony of defeat!) can provide, games offer many pleasures that are parallel, or even tangential, to winning. Just as important as the final win condition, the macro-level goal, are the tiny moments of directed play, the micro-interactions that move a player though a game. These smaller moments of play emerge as the player engages repeatedly with the core mechanic, the same-but-different experience sustaining the interest and desire of the player.

If the macro-level of a game's pleasure is the player's pursuit of the goal, and the micro-level is the player's engagement with the core mechanic, then what is it that links these two levels of play? The answer is *short-term goals*. A game never simply provides a single long-term goal. Along the way, a player struggles toward short-term goals, each one providing a kind of pleasure that is less immediate than the instant gratification of the core mechanic, but more rapidly obtained than the long-delayed ultimate outcome of the game. Even in a simple game like Tic-Tac-Toe, there are short-term goals that help players gauge their progress through the system. Placing an "O" in the same row as another "O" to form two-in-a-row is a short-term goal that must be reached before one can achieve three-in-a-row (and victory). This short-term goal may sound uninterestingly

simple, and for adult players it usually is. But for young children struggling to comprehend the strategic complexities of the game, understanding short-term goals and the way these goals link the core mechanic of mark-making with the long-term goal of three-in-a-row is crucial to their enjoyment of the game.

The kinds of short-term goals that a player can achieve depend on the nature of the game and the way the goals are suspended between the core mechanic and winning. In a wargame such as Tanktics, the short-term goal might be outflanking the enemy's ranks in order to weaken their defensive position on the battlefield. In SiSSYFiGHT 2000, it might be making a social alliance with another girl to shift the wrath of the player mob onto a particular player. In the digital trading game Dope Wars, a short-term goal might be saving up enough cash to move up from selling pot to selling heroin.

A game can explicitly provide short-term goals, such as the medals a Pokémon player periodically earns by beating the best trainers in particular gyms. However, it is also very common for players to generate short-term goals themselves, in response to their current situation. A Pokémon player might be concerned with earning every medal in the game, but perhaps he invents a different short-term goal, such as capturing every species of Pokémon, or moving his Pidgeotto up to level 50.

Encouraging players to conceive and achieve goals gives them a sense of control in the game, as Doug Church points out in his essay "Formal Abstract Design Tools:"

> There are many ways in which players are encouraged to form their own goals and act on them. The key is that players know what to expect from the world and thus are made to feel in control of the situation. Goals and control can be provided and created at multiple scales, from quick, low-level goals such as "get over the bridge in front of you" to long-term, higher-level goals such as "get all the red coins in the world." Often players work on several goals, at different levels, and on different time scales. This process of

accumulating goals, understanding the world, making a plan and then acting in it, is a powerful means to get the player invested and involved.[20]

The way that players engage with goals as they play is a complex process. As Church mentions, at any moment during a game a player might be working on several nested, interrelated goals. As players construct and work toward short-term and long-term goals, they are actively charting a course through the space of possibility of a game.

In the landscape of a game defined by the space of possibility, short-term goals are navigational beacons that help orient players through two related experiential functions. First, players use short-term goals to make plans. Short-term goals allow players to plan ahead, scouting out future actions, generating hypotheses about how they should play the game. *(I'm playing Risk. What happens if I focus on conquering South America next turn?)* Second, short-term goals are sources of satisfaction for players. It is one thing to take on a short-term goal, but it is another thing to actually attain it. *(I did it! Now I'll get bonus reinforcements for controlling a whole continent.)* Short-term goals generate pleasure through both of these functions: making plans as well as achieving them.

Short-term goals are necessary because without them, a player can get lost in the landscape of a game. Are your players confused about what to do next? Perhaps you need to adjust the design to encourage the creation of short-term goals. An open-ended, massively multiplayer online role-playing game such as Ultima Online has an intimidatingly vast space of possibility, but it also provides innumerable opportunities for short-term goals. Are players trying to work their way into a guild? Trade up for an impressive suit of armor? Or just explore a particular section of the world? The game structure encourages each of these short-term goals, and the fact that players can author their own experiences in this way is part of the reason why UO provides such intense pleasure to its dedicated players.

The pleasure a player experiences in a game arises from many simultaneous factors: from the moment-to-moment core mechanic to the short-term accomplishments of play to the final outcome of the game. Each of these interrelated factors generates pleasure in its own way. The core mechanic might provide sensual entrainment, the short-term goals the satisfaction of gradual skill mastery, and the pleasure of winning the spoils of bragging rights. But what links these levels of pleasure is meaningful play. Without meaningful play, a player will never be able to take actions that have predictable outcomes, to choose *this* over *that* with a sense of how the choice plays out. Without the ability of players to progress, to have a sense of achievement and accomplishment, to know when they are moving toward or away from victory, your game's play experience will be dead in the water. The play of pleasure may seem free and spontaneous, the farthest thing from a careful, conscious design process, but creating a game that can nourish deep pleasure—that can truly entrain and enrapture players, that can lead to new forms of pleasure and meaning—is always a matter of sensitive and detailed game design.

Conditioned Pleasure

Meaningful play is key to designing pleasure in games, but it is only by making choices that meaningful play emerges. If you recall from **Interactivity,** a choice is made up of two primary components: the *action* that the player takes and the *outcome* of that action. Our exploration of the core mechanic focused on the action half of the equation: the actual activity that the player performs. So what about the other half—the outcome? One way of framing this facet of the moment of choice is that whenever a player takes an action, she ends up being rewarded or punished by the game as a result.

Psychologists have studied the connection between choice, action, reward, and punishment in a variety of contexts. One useful approach, known as *behavior theory,* emphasizes observable behavior, specifically the way that interaction with an environment shapes behavior. Ivan Pavlov and John B. Watson were early proponents of behavior theory and developed a series of experiments designed to study learned behavior. In one famous experiment, a bell would ring as dogs were fed a meal. Eventually, the dogs came to associate the bell-ringing with food, and would salivate at the sound of the bell. The dogs had been "conditioned" to provide their natural response to food (which was to salivate) even when the food was not present. Pavlov and Watson believed that the same principles could be applied to human behavior. This kind of conditioning, in which innate reflex responses are tied to a new stimulus, became known as *classical conditioning.*[21]

Psychologist B. F. Skinner refined the ideas of Watson and Pavlov by rejecting their exclusive emphasis on reflexes and natural conditioning. Instead, Skinner attributed a more active role to the learning subject. According to Skinner's theory of *operant behavior,* people learn to behave the way that they do because a certain kind of behavior has been rewarded in the past. If a lab rat learns that pressing a lever results in a food pellet appearing, it is going to develop a strong tendency to press that lever over time.

Behavior theory distinguishes between *positive reinforcements* (a positive reward, such as a rat getting a food pellet), *negative reinforcements* (the removal of something unpleasant, like silencing a loud, high-pitched noise), and *punishments* (the addition of something unpleasant, such as a sudden electric shock). Each kind of reinforcement can be effective in a particular context, usually when the reinforcement or punishment event immediately follows the behavior it is meant to condition. Reinforcements often function because their effects of pain and pleasure are linked to innate biological responses. However, punishments and reinforcements that operate on social and cultural levels can also have strong effects for people. For example, a nod and smile from a teacher can serve as powerful positive reinforcement. In games, these kind of non-biological reinforcements as the outcome of a game choice are common. For example, positive reinforcement in a game might involve giving a player bonus points or an extra life; a negative reinforcement might be eliminating a debilitating disease from a game character; a punishment might be a damaging attack on a player's character.

Games are systems of meaning. It is within their artificial boundaries that rewards and punishments are interpreted as positive or negative and gain force to shape player behavior. Operant conditioning reminds game designers to pay attention to the way a game encourages or discourages certain behaviors. In creating rewards and punishments, game designers shape the actions players are likely to take in the future. This is an important game design concept, especially in digital games, where the program automates so much of the play activity.

Rewards and Schedules

Operant conditioning not only affects the kinds of choices players make during the course of a game, but also their general motivation to continue playing. More than just shaping good and bad behaviors, rewards and punishments shape a player's sense of pleasure and overall play experience. Game designers Neal and Jana Hallford point out this design challenge:

> It's surprising how many developers forget that it's the victories and the treasures—not the obstacles—that make people interested in playing in the first place. If you stop giving out the carrots that will keep players excited, or even worse, if you start punishing them for their curiosity, you're only going to drive away the very people who want to enjoy your game.[22]

Keeping players engrossed in your game as they play is the second of the two seductions of game design. Hallford and Hallford are absolutely correct that players need to be rewarded, that they need to accomplish tasks and feel satisfaction as they play. Although punishments are important, on balance a play experience needs to be pleasurable. Otherwise, nobody is having any fun.

What kinds of rewards can games offer players? There are as many kinds of rewards as there are forms of play. Hallford and Hallford list four general types. Although these categories were written about computer role-playing games, they suggest the kinds of rewards other kinds of games might contain.

- *Rewards of Glory.* Glory rewards are all the things you're going to give to the player that have absolutely no impact on the game play itself but will be things they end up taking away from the experience. This includes winning the game by getting all the way to the end, completing a particularly difficult side quest, or defeating the plots of evil monsters.

- *Rewards of Sustenance.* Rewards of this nature are given so the player can maintain their avatar's status quo and keep all the things they've gained in the game so far. This might include health packs that heal injuries, mana potions that increase a player's magical abilities, high-tech armor that shields a player from e-mag radiation, robots that remove curses or diseases, or even storage boxes or beasts of burden that allow a player's avatar to carry more resources along with them.

- *Rewards of Access.* Rewards of access have three critical features: they allow a player access to new locations or resources that were previously inaccessible, they are generally used only once, and they have no other value to the player once they've been used. Keys, picklocks, and passwords are typical examples of this kind of reward.

- *Rewards of Facility.* Rewards of facility enable a player's avatar to do things they couldn't do before or enhance abilities they already possess. When well handled, they should increase the number of strategies and options that player will have for playing the game. A good example of a facility reward might be a magic orb that lets an avatar walk through a stone wall or a cybernetic software up-grade that lets them shut down enemy gun turrets from a distance.[23]

Punishments, negative reinforcement, and positive reinforcement are important game design tools. They not only teach players what actions to take and not to take in a game, but also craft larger structures of pleasure. These structures assure that players are properly rewarded for spending the time to take part in the experience designed for them. But using reinforcement successfully in a game means more than just knowing what kinds of pleasures to provide. It is equally important to know how to integrate rewards and punishments into the experiential structures of a game. How often does reinforcement occur? How powerful is the reward or punishment? Do reinforcement factors change over time or remain the same?

Behavior theory has devoted much study to *reinforcement schedules.* A reinforcement schedule refers to the rate a subject is given reinforcement over time. These reinforcement patterns, along with a network of integrated rewards and punishments, help shape the fabric of any game experience. There are two basic kinds of reinforcement: *fixed* and *variable.*

Fixed reinforcement means that rewards or punishments are occurring at a steady, continuous rate. A *fixed ratio* means that the outcome occurs a set number of times that the behavior is performed, such as a player getting a chevron for every five waves of aliens defeated. A *fixed interval* refers to a regular amount of time between reinforcements, as when a power-up appears in a game every 30 seconds as long as a player can stay alive.

With *variable reinforcement,* the rewards and punishments are coming at irregular intervals. *Variable ratio* means that the outcome happens after an irregular number of intervals, like slot machine payoffs that occur at a random rate. With a *variable interval,* the reward or punishment occurs at random time intervals, as in mechanical children's games like Don't Wake Daddy, in which daddy will wake up (with negative consequences) after a random amount of time.

A Hypothetical Case Study

A Game Called Unlocker

Let's invent a fictional game called Unlocker to illustrate several points about classical conditioning. Unlocker is a straightforward 2D computer game where the player controls an avatar seen from a top-down point of view. Moving through a series of rooms, the player must avoid traps, collect weapons, fight pursuing enemies, and collect keys that unlock doors to additional rooms and levels. Although combat can occur, it is not the intended focus of the game. The goal of Unlocker is to unlock as many doors as possible and earn the most points before dying.

Even this relatively simple game contains many kinds of objects and events: open and locked doors, hidden keys, mobile enemies, movement, combat, manipulation of an inventory, and so on. Because many players will not read the instructions (and just as many will forget them soon after reading), how do you teach players what they are supposed to do in the game? Rewards and punishments are one means of shaping their behavior.

The overall trajectory of the game is to open doors and move on to new rooms and new game levels. So you want your players to open those doors. Imagine the first time a player finds a key and uses it on a locked door. A sprite animation plays and the player sees the door swing open in the game space. The problem is that there is nothing in the game to let a player know that unlocking the door is a valuable action that brings the player closer to a positive outcome. The solution? Reward the player! Give the player bonus points for unlocking a door and make sure to add a *Ka-ching!* sound to emphasize the event. Make a gold star appear in the interface when a player unlocks a door—maybe five gold stars earn an extra life. Or flash a message on the screen that congratulates the player and shows a map to the next locked door. Each of these possible solutions represents a different way to reward the player for the action of unlocking. All of them combine internal, system-based rewards (points, extra lives, information about the next door location) with external, audiovisual rewards (sound effects, gold stars, congratulatory text). If you can craft the proper reward for your player, you will create a desire to achieve that satisfying reward event again, and the player's actions will follow suit.

The same is true of negative reinforcements and punishments. By providing unpleasant feedback, you can teach your player what *not* to do in your game. Let's say your intention

Fixed schedules are best at shaping behavior if the subject is being punished: sending a child to his room every time he performs an undesired behavior is much more effective than sending him to his room only some of the time. On the other hand, for many kinds of reinforcements, especially positive ones, variable schedules are more effective. In gambling, players are usually rewarded at variable ratios. The repeat play of gamblers is strong evidence of the power of variable reinforcement.

One game designer known for integrating ideas of operant conditioning and reinforcement schedules into his work is Gabe Newell, lead designer on the computer game Half-Life. During a panel discussion at an MIT conference on gaming, Newell discussed the way that Half-Life's design integrates these concepts:

> The rewards in Half-Life are getting to see new monsters, the plot is moving forward, getting to have a new fun weapon, getting to see something really cool…. You want to make sure that throughout the course of the game that they're getting rewards…. You want to look at it from the point of view of a reinforcement schedule and say OK, that makes sense. I mean there were points in the game before we shipped where there were long lulls where basically all you were doing was stuff that you'd already done before, which in our view didn't represent a reward. So we said we've got to put more fun stuff in here or eliminate that section from the game.[24]

Newell makes a number of important points. He begins by listing some of the chief rewards that Half-Life provides for players, which include what Hallford and Hallford call rewards of *facility* (new fun weapons), *access* (meet new monsters and experience plot twists), and *glory* ("getting to see something really cool"). He also emphasizes the fact that it is rewards that sustain players through the course of a game. When his design team felt like players were not consistently receiving substantive rewards, they either increased rewards in that section or removed it entirely from the game.

Half-Life utilizes principles of operant conditioning in other ways as well. Much of the success of Half-Life has been attributed to the way that it shapes player experience, creating a thriller-like tension while drawing the player slowly into its dangerous and mysterious spaces. For example, the intensely combative moments in the game are interspersed with uneventful stretches. As opposed to a typical "enemy lurking behind every door" structure, Half-Life creates uncertainty about when and where the terrifying mutant monsters of the game will appear. In some game levels, most doors *do not* open up to an opponent but instead to empty space. In these levels, Half-Life uses variable ratio punishments. Sometimes the player will be attacked when he opens a door or rounds a corner, but usually he is not. The experiential result of this design strategy is that in Half-Life, deadly threats seem to lurk in every dark shadow and beyond every closed doorway. Deploying enemies with restraint, creating a sparse pattern of unexpected, horrifying encounters, results in a more powerful experience through the use of fewer game elements.

The question arises: if rewards and pleasure are the keys to keeping players involved in a game, why don't tension-inducing punishments such as variable monster attacks drive players away? How can seemingly negative emotions create seductively positive play? We could answer by referring to similar pleasures in other media: the frightening ghost story or the gripping sci-fi cinema thriller. But there is a deeper principle at work. To play a game is to experience its pleasure. At the same time, we know from the lusory attitude that part of playing a game is to take on artificial challenges, inefficiencies adopted for no logical reason except that they make play possible. It is surely challenging to get a golf ball into a tiny little hole so many yards away on the green, but that hardly stops golfers from playing, just as the anxiety of Half-Life doesn't cause players to exit the program. On the contrary: challenge and frustration are essential to game pleasure. Without them, there would be no game conflict to struggle against and no pleasure would emerge from the process of overcoming adversity.

Unlocker

is that the game play of Unlocker is more about finding keys and unlocking doors than about combating enemies. In this case, you may need to find ways to punish players that go against the grain of the game. If combat is too rewarding, either in terms of structure (such as earning points) or experience (such as cool combat effects), your players will keep on fighting because the game intrinsically encourages them to do so.

What are some solutions to this dilemma? You could make the enemies tougher, but that might simply encourage players to rise to the challenge. There are better "punishments" that can steer your players away from fighting. For example, maybe players earn no points from killing enemies, only from finding objects and unlocking doors. Or perhaps when they die as a result of combat, they are sent back to an earlier level. Or when they die, they lose points and game resources. Obviously, you do not want to punish the player too harshly for fighting or dying, but you do want to nudge them in the direction that you designed for them. Of course, if you continue to observe your Unlocker playtesters engaging in too much combat and not enough door unlocking, it might be telling you something else. Maybe something about the game's core mechanic makes combat more compelling than the hunt-and-unlock activities you intended as the game's focus. Perhaps you should turn Unlocker into a combat game. On the other hand, you could always remove the combat component entirely. It's your design. You decide.

Reward and punishment are two sides of a coin, both of them necessary to craft the structure of meaningful experience for players. Finding that elusive balance between positive and negative experience—between anxiety and pleasure—is one of the deepest challenges of game design. In the following section, we engage directly with these important questions.

Boredom and Anxiety: Flow Redux

The concepts that come from behavioral psychology—operant conditioning, reinforcement schedules, positive and negative reinforcement—describe how individual rewards and punishments can affect a player's present and future behavior. The challenge of putting these concepts to use is that the actual context of a game is always more complex than any individual instance of behavioral conditioning.

At any moment in a game, a player is pushed and pulled in many directions at once, experiencing a complex mix of pleasures. Think about the layered pleasures of Half-Life: the terror of the lurking unknown, the vertiginous pleasure of moving in a 3D space, the satisfaction of gradual skill mastery, the strategic exploration of combat possibilities, the glory of finishing the game victorious. Some of these pleasures frustrate the player; others provide banquets of sensual delight. Yet others find their main significance in contexts outside the game. In order to bring the diversity of pleasure into a single understanding of the play experience, we turn once more to the work of psychologist Mihaly Csikszentmihalyi. In his book *Flow,* Csikszentmihalyi provides a general heuristic for understanding how a participant is pulled into and out of the flow state. Although we know that flow is not identical to meaningful play (or even play in general), the model is extremely useful for conceptualizing the play of pleasure in games.

Csikszentmihalyi looks specifically at the degree of *challenge* that a potential flow activity provides. Does the activity provide tasks that meet the abilities of the participant? What happens when an activity is too difficult, or not difficult enough? What

Terminological Aside: Behavior Theory and Cybernetics

If all of this talk about positive and negative reinforcement sounds familiar, it should. Cybernetics uses similar language when talking about feedback loops, which we first encountered in *Games as Cybernetic Systems.* Although there is a connection between behavior theory and cybernetics, there is also the possibility for linguistic confusion.

Behavior theory and cybernetics both address the way that repeated actions and outcomes affect the state of a system. If a thermostat keeps telling a heater to blow hot air into a room, that cybernetic system of positive feedback will continue to progress toward higher and higher temperatures. If a dog is continually rewarded with food for performing tricks, it will keep trying to perform tricks in order to get more food.

However, there are also differences in the kind of phenomena studied by each. Cybernetics is concerned with deviation from a stable state: negative feedback returns a system to stability and positive feedback moves the system away from stability. Behavior theory is concerned with intelligent learning behavior, which makes associations between specific actions and outcomes. Although they share some structural affinity, these two ways of thinking are not at all identical.

There are also differences in the way that each uses the terms "positive" and "negative." The term "positive" has happy connotations in behavior theory, as when a teacher rewards students with praise. Similarly, "negative" has unpleasant connotations, even implying punishment. But in cybernetics, the terms positive and negative are mathematical, and either one might result in an emotionally positive or negative experience for a player. If, in a car racing console game, the car in last place is given an automatic boost, that is an example of a negative feedback system (tendency toward a stable state where all cars are in equal place). The boost will most likely have a positive emotional impact on the losing player. "Positive reinforcement" and "negative reinforcement" are not universal terms, and mean very different things depending on whether you're referring to cybernetics or psychology. Be careful how you use them!

are the conditions under which someone can engage with the activity and enter a flow state? In answering these questions, Csikszentmihalyi charts a person's experience along two axes. One axis represents the degree of challenge an activity offers. The other axis represents the skills a participant possesses.

Both factors can range from a low to a high value, and as a player moves to different positions on the chart, he or she is navigating through different experiences of the activity. The narrow diagonal strip represents a potential flow state, those moments when a player's skills equally meet the challenges of the activity. On one side of this strip is the state of anxiety, where the activity's tests exceed the participant's skills. On the other side is boredom, the state in which the player's abilities outstrip what challenge the activity can provide.

Csikszentmihalyi uses the example of someone learning to play Tennis. When a Tennis player begins her study, she is at position 1 on the chart, possessing low skills, but also facing challenges appropriate to her abilities, meaning that she may have some initial experiences of flow. As she proceeds, however, she is likely to fall out of flow. If her Tennis skills exceed the challenge of her lessons, the result is an experience that does not fully engage her, and she finds herself in position 2 (boredom). On the other hand, if the sense of challenge she feels from Tennis is overwhelming, the result is a negative and intimidating experience, position 3 (anxiety). Only by finding a new balance between skill and challenge can the Tennis player arrive at position 4 and regain the flow state.

Csikszentmihalyi's model has a great deal of relevance to game design. How many times have you played a game and had a negative experience, either because it was too difficult to learn or play, or because it was not challenging enough for your skill level? Remember that for games, the concepts of skill and challenge should be interpreted broadly. Skill does not only mean hand-eye coordination or athletic ability. Increasing skill might take the form of greater knowledge of a game system's rules,

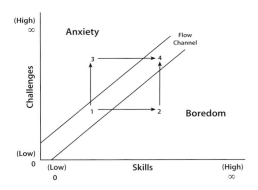

more detailed mapping of the game's narrative world, or increasing confidence to bet larger and larger sums of money at a gambling table.

One of the useful insights gleaned from Csikszentmihalyi's approach is that his model doesn't simply address an isolated moment in a game, but tracks a player's experience over time, over the course of many games. The best games manage to scale their challenge to the player. Ideally, games are simple to learn but difficult to master, providing an appropriate degree of challenge for beginners and advanced players alike. The two "traps" into which poorly designed games can fall—boredom and anxiety—are *extremely* useful ways of thinking about your players' game experience. Can you provide proper challenge at every stage of the game, for all levels of players? During playtesting, keep a sharp eye out for players encountering boredom and anxiety and note when these moments occur. What was the context? What kinds of decisions and outcomes were happening during these moments? What kinds of player strategies led to boredom or anxiety?

We can also frame boredom and anxiety in terms of meaningful play. Both states represent poorly designed moments of choice. If a player is feeling boredom, for example, she is not meaningfully exploring the space of possibility of a game.

Perhaps the outcome of a decision is not tied closely enough to the action, and so events in the game feel arbitrary. Boredom is "dead space" in a game, moments when the taut space of possibility falls limp, when the player is not being confronted with a rich set of choices in an entraining pattern of experience. Playing a game is a dance between a player and the system of the game. When a game is boring, the player's dance partner feels like a lifeless mass that has to be dragged about the dance floor. That doesn't sound like much fun.

Boredom can come from many different sources in a game. In the passage from Gabe Newell, he recalled the disappointing discovery of "long lulls where basically all you were doing was doing stuff that you'd already done before." Even though the player was actually quite busy, the lack of new kinds of rewards wasn't creating sufficient motivation for the player. But too many rewards can create boredom as well. Players often crave power, what Hallford and Hallford would call rewards of facility and sustenance. But too much power leaves players feeling tediously omnipotent and enormously bored, despite their fantastic abilities.

Anxiety operates in a parallel manner. Dramatic tension, as noted in Half-Life, can be a wonderful experiential tool for design. But there is a very thin line between meaningful challenge and truly unpleasant anxiety. Imagine if the tension in Half-Life never let up, if the player never received rewards to balance variable punishments, if the player was never able to feel an actual sense of accomplishment. The game experience would feel like a series of gratuitous attacks, with no justification or end in sight.

When the play of a game becomes synonymous with anxiety, the experience is surprisingly similar to boredom. No matter what choice a player makes, it feels like negative outcomes will always result, and choices in the game therefore feel arbitrary. The space of possibility becomes stifling and inert. To use the dancing metaphor once again, when game experience becomes synonymous with anxiety, the system of the game takes over the dance completely, like an overpowering robot, and the player is trapped in a series of actions over which she has no control. Once again, meaningful play fails to occur.

Anxiety sometimes results because in seeking to design a challenging game, game designers create games that are too challenging, especially for novice players. Remember the level playing field of conflict from **Games as Systems of Conflict?** It is important that players feel a sense of fairness as they play, that they win or lose because of the application of their own abilities within an equitable game system. This is why many games have handicapping rules or player classes, so that players of equal skill can be matched up against each other. With single-player digital games, it can be more challenging to anticipate and balance challenge and anxiety. In **Games as Cybernetic Systems,** we looked at an important approach to challenge management called Dynamic Difficulty Adjustment, used in games like Crash Bandicoot and Jak and Daxter.

Csikszentmihalyi's model of boredom and anxiety applies to games in many ways. It can help us understand how a player navigates the terrain of skill and challenge within a single game, for example, or to understand the way game skills are slowly built up over time. Csikszentmihalyi's model can also serve as a tool within the game design process. An iterative design process allows game designers to locate moments of boredom and anxiety in their game and re-shape the game experience to minimize moments of less meaningful play.

Anxiety and Boredom on the High Seas

In a wonderful essay published on Gamasutra.com, Jesse Schell and Joe Shochet of Disney Imagineering write about the process of designing Pirates of the Caribbean—Battle for the Buccaneer Gold, a game "ride" where a group of players stands on a motion-platform pirate ship surrounded by video projections. During the game, one player steers the ship while the other players operate a number of cannons, firing at monsters, forts, and enemy vessels. Pirates of the Caribbean is designed as a condensed five-minute experience, and it was essential that players feel properly challenged at every moment of the game.

In their design analysis, Schell and Shochet detail a number of design problems that had to be overcome in order to maximize player enjoyment. For example, during playtesting they identified as a problem the fact that the player steering the ship could take the ship to what they call "dull places," leading to a less engaging experience for all of the players. In the selected quotes below, Schell and Shochet outline some solutions to this problem:

Architectural Weenies: "Weenie" is a phrase coined by Walt Disney himself. It refers to the technique used on movie sets of guiding stage dogs by holding up part of a sausage… In the case of Pirates, [there are] three main "weenies," one for each island: a volcano, an enormous fort, and a plume of smoke coming from a burning town. No matter which way the boat is facing, at least one of these "weenies" is in view. Since the coolest action takes place at the islands, [we wanted] to guide the captains to go there.

Guide Ships: Since the short-term goal of the game is to fire on other pirate ships, captains strive to get near these ships so that their gunners can get a clear shot. Many of the ships in the Pirates world are "on their way" to the islands mentioned above. Many captains, in just trying to stay near these ships find that just as they have destroyed the ship, they have arrived at one of the islands, without even trying to get there.

Sneak attacks: What if the captain ignores the guide ships? Even if he heads toward one of the "weenies" it might mean as long as a minute during which the gunners have little to shoot at. For this reason, [we] created special "sneak attack" ships that "magically" appear behind the players' ship, and quickly pull up alongside, when no other boats are in range.

The Waterspout: This was [a] nickname for [a] "last ditch" forcefield that surrounds the game play area. If a captain tries to sail out of the main game play area and out to open sea, they hit the forcefield, and the ship is "magically" pointed back to where the action is. The few guests who see this don't even realize that anything unusual has happened. They are just pleased to have their boat going somewhere cool.[25]

Schell and Shochet are thinking in very experiential terms, using clever techniques to subtly guide player action in meaningful directions. At the time of its release, Pirates was a very high-tech production, featuring real-time 3D graphics, physically engaging cannon-firing interfaces, and a large motion platform to simulate a pirate ship rocking on the waves. Often in these instances, a desire to "properly" simulate a coherent 3D space or "correctly" output logical behavior for computer-controlled characters overshadows the design of the actual play experience. But Schell and Shochet had no hesitation in making pirate ships "magically" appear to guide the player, or abandoning "realistic" physics to have the player's ship turn on a dime to facilitate navigation. As they put it, "By choosing to be less concerned with reality and more concerned with what was fun, we created an experience that…is easier to adapt to, quicker to learn, and is a better show." In game design, player experience should always trump so-called "realism."

Boredom and anxiety, as game design watchwords, are wonderful because they speak directly to player experience. As you shape and sculpt your players' pleasure, you are guiding them between the Scylla and Charybdis of anxiety and boredom. This task is made all the more difficult because, as we know, the experience of play can only be indirectly designed. How do you create a set of rules that maximizes the play of pleasure for your audience?

Meaningful Pleasure

We can identify elements of the play of pleasure through concepts such as repetition and entrainment, short-term and long-term goals, rewards and punishments, and anxiety and boredom. Ultimately, however, a player experiences a more pervasive sense of pleasure and enjoyment; a total feeling of engagement that arises directly from play, the experiential whole that is more than the sum of the parts. Pleasure is emergent. Constructing the rules of a game, the formal system that produces this pleasure, is the challenge of game design. As usual, the key to understanding is meaningful play.

The core of meaningful play lies in the relationship between action and outcome. As a player uses core mechanics to take action, outcomes accumulate. These outcomes take many forms: sensory feedback, strategic achievement, emotional gratification, social relationships, and so on. As a player advances through a game, it is crucial that the game provide meaningful play at every moment. For example, as a player achieves a short-term goal, the movement toward, through, and beyond that goal should be clear. The game must communicate where the goal is, how it might be achieved, whether the player is making progress toward it, exactly when it was reached and completed, and its impact on future play. There is room in this experience for uncertainty and ambiguity, but a certain kind of clarity must underlie every action in a game. Even in the inexact, messy realms of pleasure and desire, every game choice must be discernable and integrated.

When game actions are discernable, the events of a game and the outcomes of choices are always evident. Discernable outcomes drive the experience of meaningful play and facilitate pleasure. In DOOM, for example, the monster opponents that players battle hardly exist on their own. Until the player enters a room full of monsters, they will "idle," walking in place, waiting for the player to enter so that they can spring to life and attack. Although some players regard this aspect of DOOM as comically impoverished, in fact it is key to the successful play of the game. Because monsters have little or no life "off camera," all of their important activity happens "in the face" of the player as he encounters them in battle. The game events that result in rewards and punishments for the player are always clearly communicated because they almost always occur in the presence of a player.

The need for events to be integrated into the larger fabric of the game experience is perhaps even more important than discernability in sustaining player pleasure. As long as a player understands the implications of the game's system of rewards and punishments, he or she can use that knowledge to set new short-term goals. This allows the player to maintain an overall sense of progress toward a long-term goal, such as winning. In the popular online game NeoPets, a player is continually rewarded for taking game actions, exploring the game world, caring for her pets, playing simple games, and interacting with other players. Each of these simple activities rewards the player with a small amount of points. These points are then used to facilitate new purchases, which in turn make new activities possible. The steady stream of incremental rewards forms a tight loop of desire, a compelling system of pleasure where short-term and long-term goals are constantly forming on the horizon of player action.

When game events are not discernable or integrated, boredom and anxiety, the enemies of pleasurable flow, can result. Does the game program know that a player just took an action? Why did all of those important events happen off-screen? Does it matter which piece a player just moved? Why is the game so hard? Designing for meaningful play comes down to treating players with great care and concern at every moment of the game. Too often, for example, a digital game just doesn't feel right. The interface is clunky, the player is not sure what to do when the game begins, or the first level is too hard. Retail digital games are usually designed for 30 to 40 hours of play. That kind of commitment demands a tremendous amount of trust. If the first five minutes are unpleasant, why would a player want to continue?

There is a reason why Myst was superior to all of the CD-ROM multimedia game clones that followed it, or why Super Mario 64 is still better than the scores of 3D over-the-shoulder, character-based console games that are released every year. Myst

NeoPets

and Super Mario 64, although very different in the experiences they provide, have one thing in common: they both treat the player with a tremendous amount of care. From the moment the game begins, the player has clear direction and purpose. As players explore their expansive worlds, both games provide a satisfying increase in challenge, while never leaving the player feeling lost or confused. There is clarity to the way that these games construct player pleasure.

Crafting this degree of pleasure is extremely challenging. Pleasure is difficult to design because it is an open-ended, multifaceted, and exceedingly complex concept. But that is also why it is such a fertile avenue for exploration by game designers. There are multitudes of game pleasures for you to create: pleasures that go deep into the hearts of your players; pleasures that transform your players and the ways that they understand the world; pleasures that expand the very medium of games. The process of discovering and inventing these pleasures is itself a unique form of bliss: the boundless joy of game design.

Against "Addiction"

The great damnation of the game [of Chess] has come from those who have been plagued by it. None has expressed so convincingly his sad and resigned self-denial as a minister who in 1680 wrote a letter, giving ten reasons why he refused to play the game. Among them is one of the most beautiful lines in English literature: "It hath not done with me when I have done with it." Truly this one sentence could be the motto for all addictions.—**Norman Reider,** *"Chess Oedipus, and the Mater Dolorosa"*

The play of pleasure in games is immensely complex, but we have done our best to trace some of its contours. Before ending this chapter, there is an additional issue we must address: addiction. Addiction and addictive play can mean many things. But by and large, among game designers, addiction is considered a positive trait, the mark of compelling play. In business terms, lots of addicted players mean that a game has a greater chance of being a commercial success.

Meaningful play can become addictive. If a player enjoyed the play of a game, he or she will probably want to play it again. If you create a space of possibility that rewards players for exploration, then you are likely to have players that want to see more permutations of how the rules play out. The same-but-different quality intrinsic to all games is at the core of a game's ability to engross players and bring them back into the magic circle again and again. "Addiction" in this sense is merely shorthand for a game experience that can support this depth of meaningful play.

As a game designer, it is flattering to find that players are addicted to your game. It might be that they use your game regularly to relax or unwind. Maybe they find your game a great way to interact with friends. Or perhaps they write fiction around your game's storyline and participate in the fan culture your game has spawned. All of these forms of so-called "addiction" are the mark of dedicated players, of meaningfully engaged people experiencing the play of pleasure provided by a game.

At the same time, there are negative connotations to the word "addiction" as well. Medically speaking, addiction is a genuine disorder, whether the addiction is to substances like alcohol or drugs, to negative behaviors like bullying or shoplifting, or to behaviors that are generally considered positive, like exercise or reading. Suffice it to say that the use of term "addiction," when used by professionals in the game industry, does not describe medically pathological behavior. Instead, it refers to engaged and repeated play, to players that enjoy a game and therefore play it more than one time.

Because of the negative connotations of the term, the repeatable play of games is sometimes naïvely compared to a genuine medical disorder. But the word "addiction" is a misnomer, as play scholar Brian Sutton-Smith points out:

> The persistent concentration we are talking about is sometimes mistaken for addiction. But its compulsive quality is the same experience by those who have fallen in love, or are taken by some hobby or sport.... It is not an addiction where what occurs is a surrender to outside forces over which one has no control. We must distinguish such compulsive avocations from addiction. Video games are of this first kind. Our proposal, then, is that video games, like all other forms of exciting play, lead to a compulsive and persistent attendance on the games themselves. In this, they are like all games and all play which has long been noted for holding children's attention when they should be coming inside for their supper, or leaving the playground to go into school.[26]

Play is intrinsically engaging. But that doesn't mean that it is negatively addictive. It is true that some forms of play can become pathological. People can become compulsive gamblers, or they can spend so many hours in an online MUD that they neglect aspects of their life outside the game. These rare cases, often highly publicized, are the exceptions that prove the rule. The overwhelming majority of play phenomena are not destructively addictive. This is true even for forms of play most commonly associated with pathological addiction, such as gambling. In *The Ambiguity of Play*, Sutton-Smith presents extensive research on gambling with the conclusion that "the majority of players gamble moderately and with positive results for family life and pleasure."[27] The existence of addictive play disorders doesn't mean that all play is bad for you. Eating disorders and addictions abound. But that doesn't mean that you should avoid the pleasure of dining.

To play is to find free movement within a more rigid structure. When a game activity becomes pathologically addictive, this movement is censured: free movement is shut down, the sense of free choice evaporates, and meaningful play abates. In this experiential sense, when a player becomes medically addicted to some form of play, play as we have defined it no longer exists. In other words, addictive play, in the negative sense used by the medical community, is not really play at all.

Case Study: The L Game

An Exception to Every Rule

One game that flies in the face of some of our ideas about meaningful play and pleasure is the L Game, designed by Edward de Bono, a writer and researcher who focuses on lateral thinking and creative problem-solving. The rules are summarized below.[28]

How to play the L Game

- *Pieces.* The Board is made up of 16 squares. Each player (only 2 can play) has an L piece that he must move when it is his turn. There are also two neutral pieces that either player can move.

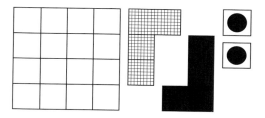

- *Object.* The object of the game is to maneuver the other player into a position on the board where he cannot move his L piece.

- *Starting Position.* Proceeding from the starting position, the first player (and each player on each move thereafter) must move the L piece first. When moving, a player may slide, turn or pick up and flip the L piece into any open position other than the one it occupied prior to the move. When the L piece has been moved, a player may move either one (but only one) of the neutral square pieces to any open square on the board. It is not required that the neutral piece be moved, this is up to the player! A player wins the game when his opponent cannot move his L piece.

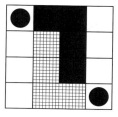

Further Reading

"Designing Interactive Theme Park Rides: Lessons From Disney's Battle for the Buccaneer Gold," by Jesse Schell and Joe Shochet *(see page 68)*

Flow: The Psychology of Optimal Experience,
by Mihaly Csikszentmihalyi

One of the great pleasures of games is the feeling of being in flow—a state of deep and all-encompassing absorption with the activity at hand. Csikszentmihalyi studies the qualities and conditions that allow for flow, which have many connections to the qualities and conditions of game play.

Recommended:

Chapter 3: Enjoyment and the Quality of Life
Chapter 4: The Conditions of Flow
Chapter 7: Work as Flow

Notes

1. Wordnet, Princeton University.
2. L. S. Vygotsky, "Play and its Role in the Mental Development of the Child." In *Play—Its role in Development and Evolution,* edited by J.S. Bruner, A. Jolly, and K. Sylva (New York: Penguin, 1976), p. 548.
3. Ibid. p. 548
4. Roger Caillois, *Man, Play, and Games* (London: Thames and Hudson, 1962), p. 8.
5. Bernard DeKoven, *The Well-Played Game* (New York: Doubleday, 1978), p. 3.
6. Mihaly Csikszentmihalyi, *Flow: The Psychology of Optimal Experience* (New York: HarperCollins Publishers, 1991), p. 67.
7. Hal Barwood, "Computer and Video Games Come of Age. A National Conference to Explore the Current State of an Entertainment Medium." February 10–11, 2000. Comparative Media Studies Department, MIT. Transcripts. Henry Jenkins.
8. Marc LeBlanc, Game Developers Conference, 2000.
9. Michael J. Apter, "A Structural-Phenomenology of Play." In *Adult Play: A Reversal Theory Approach,* edited by J. H. Kerr and Michael J. Apter (Amsterdam: Swets & Zeitlinger, 1991), p. 18–20.
10. J. C. Herz, *Joystick Nation: How Videogames Ate Our Quarters, Won Our Hearts, and Rewired Our Minds* (New York: Little, Brown & Company, 1997), p. 79.
11. Csikszentmihalyi, *Flow,* p. 3.
12. Ibid. p. 49.
13. Ibid. p. 49–67.
14. Brian Sutton-Smith, *The Ambiguity of Play* (Boston: Harvard University Press, 2001), p. 185.
15. Bob Bates, *Game Design: The Art and Business of Creating Games* (Roseville, CA: Prima Publishing, 2001), p. 37.
16. James S. Hans, *The Play of the World* (Boston: University of Massachusetts Press, 1981), p. 28.
17. Dr. Stephan Rechtschaffen, The Omega Institute. <www.omega-institute.com>.
18. <http://www.xyzzynews.com/xyzzy.16f.shtml>.
19. Herz, *Joystick Nation,* p. 64.
20. Doug Church, "Formal Abstract Design Tools." <www.gamasutra.com>, July 16, 1999.
21. Henry Gleitman, *Psychology,* 2nd ed. (New York: W.W. Norton & Company, 1986).
22. Neal Hallford with Jana Hallford, *Swords and Circuitry: A Designer's Guide to Computer Role Playing Games* (Roseville, CA: Prima Publishing, 2001), p. 158.
23. Ibid. p. 157–160
24. Gabe Newell, "Computer and Video Games Come of Age. A National Conference to Explore the Current State of an Entertainment Medium." February 10–11, 2000. Comparative Media Studies Department, MIT. Transcripts. Henry Jenkins.
25. Jesse Schell and Joe Shochet, "Designing Interactive Theme Park Rides: Lessons From Disney's Battle for the Buccaneer Gold." <www.gamasutra.com/features/20010706/schell_01.htm>.
26. Brian Sutton-Smith, *Toys as Culture* (New York: Gardner Press, 1986), p. 69–70.
27. Sutton-Smith, *The Ambiguity of Play,* p. 67.
28. < http://www.edwdebono.com/debono/lgame.htm>.

The L Game

It is difficult to get a sense of the L game without actually playing it, but the game essentially consists of players trying to place their pieces in such a way so as to keep their opponents from making a legal move. The two players end up shuffling pieces on the small but crowded board, taking turn after turn, until one of them hits upon a winning move.

The challenge of the L Game is that it does not provide clear feedback for players as they progress towards the goal. In Checkers, even a beginner can get a sense of the game's progress: if white has lost most of its pieces and black's pieces are all still on the board, then black is clearly progressing toward victory. But in the L Game, because the pieces are never removed and do not progress step by step toward a victory condition, it is very difficult to tell which player is gaining or losing ground. Playing the L Game can feel more like taking on an arbitrary, frustrating puzzle than playing a game.

Jeff Fedderson, a student in a class taught by Eric Zimmerman and Frank Lantz, analyzed the game. He found the game strategy so opaque that he wrote a program to play the L Game against itself. He experimented with strategies for his computer players and identified several patterns: for example, programs that attempted to occupy the center four squares of the board and avoided putting the long edge of an L shape on the edge of the board were much better at playing the game.

But even armed with these very short-term strategic goals, the L Game remains stubbornly resistant to providing meaningful feedback about progress toward the end goal. However, this strange feature of the L Game is actually what makes it so distinctive and compelling as a play experience. Despite the fact that the L Game seems to violate some of our most basic ideas about meaningful play, it still provides pleasure. Sometimes, when design rules are broken in a very original way, whole new modes of play can be invented.

Games as the Play of Pleasure **SUMMARY**

· **Pleasure** is intrinsic to games in many ways. The act of playing a game, submitting to a set of rules, is itself a form of pleasure. The restraint that limiting game behavior affords heightens the player's sense of pleasure.

· Games provide **autotelic** pleasures, experiences that are pursued for their own sake. Although it is true that games provide **extrinsic** pleasures that affect a player's life outside the game, all games also provide **intrinsic,** autotelic pleasures that are significant only within the artificial meanings that the game creates.

· Games must provide a **double seduction** for players. First, players must be seduced into entering the magic circle. Second, players must be continually seduced into remaining inside the circle of play.

· There are many established typologies that address the forms of pleasure provided by games. Typologies of game pleasure are generally less useful for theorizing pleasure and more useful for organizing observations about game experience.

· Psychologist Mihaly Csikszentmihalyi describes optimal experience as **flow.** Flow is the exhilarating pleasure that occurs when someone is engaged with an activity and feels in control of his or her actions. Although flow is not unique to games, it is a useful way of thinking about the creation of game pleasure.

· Csikszentmihalyi names eight characteristics of flow, each of which has a strong connection to games. Four of the eight characteristics describe the **effects** of flow:

    · the merging of action and awareness

    · concentration

    · the loss of self-consciousness

    · the transformation of time

· The other four characteristics describe the **prerequisites** of the kind of activity that will result in flow:

    · a challenging activity

    · clear goals

    · clear feedback

    · the paradox of having control in an uncertain situation

· Games possess a quality we call **same-but-different.** Every time one plays a game, the formal structure remains the same, but the way the rules play out are different. This quality of games makes it pleasurable for players to explore the space of possibility. Because play is often transformative, the continued exploration of a game can change the game structure itself, leading to a potentially endless sequence of same-but-different pleasures.

· **Entrainment** means both to *carry along* and *to trap.* Entrainment is the process of falling into the rhythmic patterns of pleasure that games can provide.

· The **goal** of a game is a key component in shaping the experience of pleasure. The goal is the object of desire held out to entice players to continue playing.

· Suspended between moment-to-moment core mechanics and the ultimate end goal are **short-term goals.** Short-term goals help players make plans in a game as well as provide moments of satisfaction when they reach them.

· **Behavior theory** is a branch of psychology that studies observable behavior. **Conditioning** is the acquisition of learned behaviors through rewards and punishments. Rewards and punishments can be used to teach players how to behave in a game from moment-to-moment, as well as create an experience that rewards players for their participation over time.

· **Reinforcement schedules** refer to the rate at which players receive rewards and punishments. Schedules can be either **fixed** or **variable** in regard to an **interval** of time or the **ratio** of action to outcome. Generally, variable reinforcement shapes behavior more powerfully than fixed reinforcement.

· **Challenge** is an important way to shape player pleasure. If the challenge of a game is too high for a player's skills, **anxiety** results. If there is not enough challenge, **boredom** results. Ideally, games provide a balanced challenge at all moments.

· A game designer can only indirectly design the pleasurable experience of a game through the creation of a game's rules. To provide meaningful play and pleasure, the actions a player takes must be **discernable** and **integrated.**

· The word **addiction** has different meanings in the medical community and the game community. For game designers, addiction is a positive quality that signifies players' meaningful interaction with a game. When pathologically addictive behavior emerges from a game, play is no longer possible.

GAMES AS THE PLAY OF MEANING

representation
systems of meaning
representational spaces
emergent meaning
cognitive frame
metacommunication

25

It's vital that we determine how games make meaning.—**Warren Spector,** *RE:PLAY*

Introducing the Play of Meaning

Game play takes place within a *representational* universe, filled with depictions of objects, interactions, and ideas out of which a player makes meaning. In Rock-Paper-Scissors a fist means "rock," an outstretched hand means "paper," and two fingers spread in a V-shape means "scissors." In the game of Mafia, an assassin's hand gesture that points to another player represents "kill!" and the act of keeping one's eyes closed "at night" marks a player as "villager." In a first-person shooter, the gun barrel emerging out of the bottom of the screen represents not only "a big-ass gun," but also denotes "you," the player.

To play a game is to rely on and interact with representations the game generates. This intersection between representation, meaning, and play raises a series of important game design questions. How does a player experience the representation of a game? What is the relationship between a game representation and the "real world?" What modes of representation can games provide? These questions are the focus of this schema: *Games as the Play of Meaning.*

We first touched on the way that games act as representational systems in *Design,* where we introduced a number of basic semiotic concepts. In this chapter, we elaborate on these ideas in order to gain a more detailed understanding of the way that games *represent*. The concepts we present here may seem slightly abstract, and this schema is certainly one of the more theoretical in this book. But the ideas initiated here find fruition in the more pragmatic schemas to follow, *Games as Narrative Play* and *Games as the Play of Simulation.*

Two Kinds of Representation

What exactly is the relationship between games and representation? There are two ways to think about it:

First, *games can represent.*

Second, *games are representations.*

Games can represent by creating depictions: of characters, stories, settings, ideas, and behaviors. Game representations gain meaning within the game universe, as they are experienced through play. Games represent by creating complex internal systems of meaning, so that in a GURPS fantasy role-playing game, for example, a sword is represented differently than a dagger. The difference in representation is not only achieved visually. A sword will certainly look different than a dagger (it is longer, for example), but its overall role in the game (how it is used, who uses it, what actions it allows) also contributes to its representation.

On the other hand, *games themselves are representations*. Mortal Kombat is a representation of hand-to-hand combat, Go is a representation of territorial conflict, and Pong is a representation of Table Tennis. *Games are representations* when we consider them as representational wholes.

These two ways of connecting games and representation are closely related. The forms of representation internal to a game work together to create a composite representation that emanates more generally from the game system. Sim City contains thousands of individual representations with which a player interacts over the course of game play (traffic jams, the city electrical grid, budget spreadsheets, and so on). These representations have meaning within the game, but also contribute to the meaning of the game as a representational object in its own right. The many internal representations of Sim City add up to create a single representation: the game depicts the process of urban planning.

Systems of Meaning

It should be self-evident that games contain representations. Think about the thousands of objects represented in a game such as Animal Crossing or Grand Theft Auto III. But games are not the only cultural forms that contain many internal representations. The text of a storybook is also composed of thousands and thousands of representations: the text doesn't just represent a single object, but is made up of a dense chain of signifiers (or signs), denoting complex networks of characters, objects, descriptions, and events. The words that make up the text of *The Little Prince* act as a representational system to depict the many characters and events of the story. Similarly, games are systems that give rise to representations of characters and events—representations at least as complex as those created through writing in a book.

Games can represent: this is a simple idea. However, because games are complex dynamic systems, the exact way representations operate within a game to generate meaning is quite complex. Even the most basic set of game signs are always bound up in larger systems of meaning. For example, consider one of the simplest elements of Virtua Fighter 4 for the Playstation2: the health bar. In the two-player "versus" mode of VF4, two players select a character and engage in hand-to-hand combat. Both characters begin the game with 100 percent health, represented by a full green bar. As a character is struck by attacks, her health is reduced; when a character's health reaches zero, she has lost the match. Both health bars are visible to both players; each one communicates to a player the status of his or her own health, as well as the health of his or her opponent. This information can suggest actions for the player to take, such as switching from an offensive to a defensive strategy if the player's own health is very low. Thus the "health bar" is a complex sign, which represents several things at once:

· The current level of health of a player's own character

· A meter measuring who is winning the match (who has more health)

· A display of how near the game is to finishing

· A display of how soon one or both characters will die

· The relative skill of both players

· The effectiveness of a player's current playing strategy

This example illustrates that even a simple game stat can have multiple, interrelated meanings. The health bar is part of a complex network of signs, which is why appreciating the meaning of the health bar requires an understanding of the larger system. For example, your character's health is at 30 percent. Are you about to die? Possibly, if your opponent is at full health. But perhaps your opponent's health is down to 5 percent. In these two scenarios, you would assume very different play strategies, perhaps falling back to a defensive posture or conversely, pressing the attack for a quick kill. The meaning of any one sign can only be understood in relation to a larger set of signs, which together form the densely woven fabric of meaning in a game.

We should point out that in Virtua Fighter 4 there are other ways to win the game besides reducing your opponent's health to zero. For example, in some of the arenas, you can win by knocking your opponent out of the ring. Every fight also has a pre-set time limit—when the limit is reached, the player with the most health wins, even if the health of one player's character hasn't been taken down to zero. These alternate victory conditions add even *more* meaning to the sign of the health bar. If your own health is very low, perhaps you should change your fighting style to try and push your opponent out of the ring. Or if you are ahead in health and the timer is almost up, you might want to stay away from your opponent, avoiding contact until the timed end of the match.

The meaning of the health bar affects the actions players take, actions which themselves can affect the meaning of the health bar, again leading to new actions and outcomes. In this way, meaning in the game sets up complex representational loops, generating representations that affect and are affected by player interaction. For this example, we used the single stat of a health bar, but we could have looked at any aspect of the game. When all of the elements represented in VF4 are considered at once, from the stances and maneuvers of the characters to the distances and spaces between them, the total system of meaning becomes staggeringly complex.

System and Context

The health bar in Virtua Fighter 4 is an individual sign. Individual signs are a key part of the way that meaning emerges from a game—but meaning requires more than just signs. Meaning requires a *formal system* to generate relationships between signs, as well as a *context* for interpretation. The formal system of a game is, of course, its rules. The rules describe actions and events whose meaning remains the same from game to game. Checkmate, for example, always means the end of a game of Chess. This is a meaning conferred by the unchanging formal system of the game. However, for the formal system of a game to be meaningful, the game has to be played—ultimately, the meaning of the formal system emerges from within a play context. The context affects interpretation, and can enhance, distort, or even radically alter the meaning conferred by the system. *Checkmate* might not just mean the end of the game. It might also mean that money passes hands if there was a wager on the game, or that reputations are gained and lost. It might not even mean final victory, if players are playing in a tournament for the best two out of three games.

Remember that the focus of this schema is how games can represent, how they create meaning for players through representation, and how these meanings can, in turn, be manipulated. To play a game is to move into the magic circle, to move from the domain of everyday life into a special place of meaning. Within this special space the player's experience is guided by a system of representation that has its own rules for "what things mean." The context of play affects how players understand and act upon the representations the game creates. The system and the context thus work hand-in-hand to support player interpretation. (Note that we are using the term *system* to designate the *structure* that organizes relationships between elements, an idea introduced in **Design**.)

The "X" in Tic-Tac-Toe, for example, means something quite different than an "X" in the game of Scrabble. The difference in meaning is conferred primarily by the system, which has rules for what an "X" means. In Tic-Tac-Toe, an X represents ownership of a square, a strategic movement towards victory. Yet as with Chess and Checkmate, the context of the "X" is also crucial in determining its meaning. Imagine a playful love letter that uses a Tic-Tac-Toe board to spell out "XXX." Rather than interpreting the three X's as merely a winning move in a game, the signs would also be read as symbols for kisses. The context of the "X" has shifted its meaning from a game move to a declaration of "winning" affection. The author of the love letter has played with the meaning of the sign "X" by shifting the context within which the sign is interpreted.

Emergent Representations

In the "X" of Tic-Tac-Toe and in the action of Checkmate, we see that games create meaning through the interplay of system and context—but this operation is not unique to games. System and context represent a general semiological approach to understanding how representation works. For example, consider spoken or written language. Language is structured by grammar, the formal system that gives its individual elements meaning. Yet the meaning of any utterance of language is also contextual. The phrase "Don't have a cow" means two different things when spoken by a dairy farmer or by Bart Simpson. The interpretation of the phrase relies both on grammatical structures and the context of the speaker.

Meaning is emergent. When we use language, as when we play a game, we are playing within the limits that the rules allow. To speak a sentence is to play with words—but only in ways that the rules of language permit. A paradox of meaning is that although simple rules shape every utterance, the total number of potential statements is nearly infinite. Both language and games represent complex emergent systems, in which possible outcomes far exceed the formal complexity of the rule-system, an idea we explored in **Games as Emergent Systems.** As Jeremy Campbell notes in *Grammatical Man: Information, Entropy, Language, and Life,* "A modest number of rules applied again and again to a limited collection of objects leads to variety, novelty, and surprise. One can describe all the rules, but not necessarily all the products of the rules—not the set of all whole numbers, not every sentence in a language."[1]

Representation in games emerges from the relationship between a rigid, underlying rule structure and the free play of meaning that occurs as players inhabit the system. Game designers must pay close attention to the play of meaning within a game, crafting individual instances of player interaction within a larger field of representation. As a game designer creates a system of rules, he or she is also creating a vast space of representational possibility, a space that becomes meaningful through player interaction.

The Context of Meaning

To see these abstract ideas in action, we'll turn to a thought experiment from *Swords and Circuitry: A Designer's Guide to Computer Role-Playing Games* by Neal and Jana Hallford. To illustrate how players learn what something "means" through interaction, Hallford and Hallford describe a player exploring a world in an adventure game. The player comes across a button set into an otherwise featureless wall. The curious player pushes the button to see what happens—and a secret door opens up in the wall. Pushing the button gives the player access to a new part of the game world.

Hallford and Hallford note that by providing the player with this scenario—push button, open door—the game designer has given the player a "rule" about how the game world works. The action *push button* results in the outcome *open secret door*. Armed with this rule, the player should be able to use this knowledge throughout the game to make informed decisions about how and when to push buttons. The meaning of the button press is both *integrated* and *discernable*, two requirements of meaningful play. The interaction is discernable, because the player clearly sees the secret door open as a result of the action of pressing the button. The interaction also appears to be integrated, because the player has discovered a universal rule about how buttons operate in the game.

Hallford and Hallford then ask us to imagine the player in another location somewhere later in the game. The player spies yet another partially hidden button along the edge of a wall. If the action > outcome meaning of the button were integrated, the player should expect that pushing the button will open a secret door. But when the player pushes the button, to his surprise a damaging fireball of doom comes out of the wall instead. What just happened? Why did the button unleash a lethal fireball, rather than open a secret door? Here is where Hallford and Hallford's analysis ties directly to the concept of play and representation. They write,

> If the designer hasn't provided some kind of clue about what sets this button apart from the door-opening variety, they've just violated a rule that's already been established by the game. The value of choice has been taken away from the player because they have no way of knowing whether pushing the button opens a door or whether it will do some catastrophic amount of damage. While this would certainly add a heightened degree of tension to the pushing of any buttons in the game, it really is nothing more than a way of arbitrarily punishing the player for being curious. Even worse, the value of the things that the player has learned are now worthless, making the winning of the game more a matter of chance than of acquired skill.[3]

When the meaning of an action is unclear or ambiguous, meaningful play in a game breaks down. How might meaningful play in this situation be reestablished? Hallford and Hallford suggest one way to remedy the situation by adding a small visual detail that gives the player some idea of the consequences for pushing a particular type of button. Blue buttons open secret doors. Red buttons unleash fireballs of doom.

This example demonstrates how game meanings can be engineered to create meaningful play. Color-coding buttons to denote consequence establishes a system of meaning. Players are, over time, able to determine which buttons are "good" and "bad," and can make informed choices about their actions in the world. This system implicates the player directly, for the *meaning* of a button is only ever established through player interaction. As Hallford and Hallford note, this design strategy "will also have the added bonus that players will pay a little closer attention to their environment to see if there's anything new around them that may lead to new kinds of experiences."[4] In short, the rules and context of interaction help to establish "what things mean." They do so by creating a very specific set of conditions within which a particular object or action becomes meaningful in the course of play.

Making sense of signs relies, in part, on the movement between known and unknown information. Players in Hallford and Hallford's hypothetical adventure game, for example, might come across a sign for which they don't have meaning (red button) within the context of signs for which they do (blue button). Familiar meanings generate new meanings due to the formal relations between known and unknown signs. What is important to note here is that players gain information about the game world by *interacting* with it, by *interpreting* it, by *playing* with signs to see what they might do or what they might mean. You find a button that is red *and* blue. What can you guess will happen if you press it? Will you take the risk to find out? Creating context as a mechanism for sense-making is a critical concept for game designers. It is why our definition of game design refers to the design of a context, rather than an artifact. The design of play is the design of an interactive context from which meaning can emerge.

Down the Rabbit Hole

In this schema, we frame games as the play of meaning, which is also a way of framing play as the process of making sense of the representational space of a game. What does it mean for a game to be a space of representation? Players interact with a game in order to make sense of it. Rules guide this interaction, establishing relationships between signs that tell a player what things mean. Meaning emerges as a player actively interprets the system established by the rules.

To illustrate this complex process of meaning-making, we take a detour through Wonderland. In Lewis Carroll's story *Alice in Wonderland,* there is a rich play of meaning, of sense and non-sense, that can shed light on the way games generate representations. In the story, Alice is lost in a fantastic realm of curious creatures, tripping and tumbling from page to page, through one non-sensical game to the next. Whether trapped in the elliptical language games of the Cheshire Cat or misplaying her way through a game of Croquet at the Queen's Court, Alice continually finds herself struggling to understand the rules of the game. Take the following excerpt in which Alice is challenged to a race:

> First it marked out a race-course, in a sort of circle, ("the exact shape doesn't matter," it said), and then all the party were placed along the course, here and there. There was no "One, two, three, and away," but they began running when they liked, and left off when they liked, so that it was not easy to know when the race was over. However, when they had been running a half an hour or so, and were quite dry again, the Dodo suddenly called out "The race is over!" and they all crowded round it, panting, and asking, "But who has won?"[5]

Wonderland has its own set of rules for determining not only what things mean but also for determining how they are made *meaningful.* Alice's descent down the rabbit hole can be metaphorically seen as an entry into the magic circle that is Wonderland, a realm of artificial meanings, marked off in time and space from the real world. The rules of the real world do not precisely obtain in Wonderland, even though Wonderland itself is in some ways a parody of the real world, a curious mirror of reality that playfully distorts our ideas about the logic of representation.

Each individual game that Alice encounters in Wonderland is a microcosm of this general scheme. The absurdly humorous contest Carroll describes is still recognizable as a race. It has a track, runners, a starting count, and a clear moment when the race ends. At the same time, it is like no race in the real world. The shape of the track doesn't matter, the runners can abandon the game at any moment, and even when the race is finished, no one is sure who won. As nonsensical as the race may seem, it is its own representational space, a space within which players struggle to make meaning. "But who has won?" they ask, seeking like all players to know the outcome of the game.

We have established that signs gain value from the system of which they are part. The structure and context of the system organize not only what those signs mean but also how they are used. The space of play defined by the borders of the magic circle operates as a space of representational possibility. This space of play gives life to a separate reality, a world of its own where its inhabitants can perform actions that are permitted to occur in that world, but that would not make sense anywhere else. It is only within the very strange context of Wonderland that such a contest could be called a race, and a winner could be so unknown and eagerly anticipated.

The complexity of using this example, of course, is that the game is not an actual game, but rather a fictional depiction of a game inside Carroll's story. But that is exactly why we have included it. The Wonderland race illustrates the process of meaning-making on two levels. First, it has its own curious internal mechanisms, its own "rules" for what constitutes the race to its participants. Second, the race also creates meaning for readers of the story by virtue of its relationship to the larger context of the real world. We know that Carroll is describing a race because we have a sense of what an ordinary race is like. It is our commonsense understanding of the real world that allows us to appreciate Carroll's playful nonsense. In this way, the meaning of the Wonderland race illustrates the paired interaction of system and context, the play between internal and external meanings that makes representation possible.

In the Queen's Court

Wonderland makes ideas about the artificiality of the play of meaning explicit. Alice's trip down the rabbit hole landed her in another context entirely, one where the rules of nonsense (rather than common sense) organized her play. Her life *outside* of Wonderland had its own set of rules and meanings. Adapting to life *inside* Wonderland meant transitioning into a radically different context with its own rules and procedures for representation. It is very much like entering into the magic circle of a game. When we play a game, we are doing more than just shuffling signs drawn from the domain of the real world; instead, we are shifting to another domain of meaning entirely. In the play of meaning, movement occurs both between signs and contexts. The magic circle is therefore a kind of Wonderland. Let's look at another game Alice plays during her visit:

> Alice thought she had never seen such a curious croquet-ground in all her life; it was all ridges and furrows; the balls were live hedgehogs, the mallets live flamingoes, and the soldiers had to double themselves up to stand on their hands and feet, to make arches. The chief difficulty Alice found at first was in managing her flamingo: she succeeded in getting its body tucked away, comfortably enough, under her arm, with its legs hanging down, but generally, just as she got its neck nicely straightened out, and was going to give the hedgehog a blow with its head, it WOULD twist itself around and look up in her face, with such a puzzled expression that she could not help bursting out laughing: and when she had got its head down, and was going to begin again, it was very provoking to find that the hedgehog had unrolled itself, and was in the act of crawling away: besides all this, there was generally a ridge or furrow in the way wherever she wanted to send the hedgehog to, and, as the doubled-up soldiers were always getting up and walking off to other parts of the ground, Alice soon came to the conclusion that this was a very difficult game indeed.[6]

Alice calls the game "very difficult indeed." But what is remarkable are *which* things Alice finds challenging. Consider that her chief difficulty was not imagining that a live flamingo could be used as a Croquet mallet, nor hedgehogs as balls. These she accepted easily as fitting into the representational logic of Wonderland. Her difficulty was simply in trying to play the game—in hitting a hedgehog with the head of a flamingo. It was not in recognizing this strange system of signs as "Croquet."

By this point in the story, Alice has largely accepted the non-sensical rules of Wonderland as her own. She has stepped into the magic circle of Wonderland and adapted her actions accordingly. Although the constant wanderings of the live game pieces across the Croquet-grounds made the game extremely challenging to play, their behavior in no way com-promised Alice's status as a player whose actions had meaning within the space of the game. In accepting the rules engen-dered by the magic circle, Alice acts within a field of represen-tation. As with the example of the race, the meaning of the Croquet game occurs on two levels. First, despite the ergonomic difficulties, the game of Croquet was an internally consistent game. It was never the case, for example, that a hedgehog was used as a mallet to hit a rolling flamingo. The game had its own rules, rules that Alice desperately tried to follow as she played. Second, the overall meaning of the game *to the reader* relies on a reader's knowledge of the normal play of Croquet. This larger context allows the reader to make sense of an otherwise non-sensical depiction of the game.

Poor Alice. Although the game of croquet might fail to provide her with meaningful play, it provides us with much insight into the machinations of play and meaning. Alice's inability to play the game in any logical way was, in fact, one of the points of Carroll's "design." Carroll was a master in the play of meaning. His use of game structures, whether that of playing cards, Chess, or Croquet, demonstrates the mechanisms of sense-making, revealing how the fields of representation denoted by games are ripe for playful interpretation.

Framing Play

It is time to climb out of the rabbit hole. Next stop: a concept that is critical to an understanding of play and meaning, the *cognitive frame,* which comes to us from the field of psychology. Taken most generally, a cognitive frame is a way of organizing how we look at the world. Cognitive frames create contexts for interpretation and affect how we make sense of things. In the story of Alice, for example, there are several frames at work. The cognitive frame "fairy tale" encourages us to see Alice's adven-tures as both fantastical and instructive. Carroll employs the cognitive frames of "game" and "play" throughout the story, to communicate that Wonderland is a space separate from reality, one where special rules abound. If you first had to read *Alice in Wonderland* for an English class, perhaps the cognitive frame of "exam" or "essay" shaped your interpretation and experience of the book.

The idea of a cognitive frame closely mirrors the concept of the magic circle. As a player steps in and out of a game, he or she is crossing that boundary, or frame, which defines the game in time and space. The cognitive frame is a concept connected to the question of the "reality" of a game, of the relationship between the artificial world of the game and the "real life" con-texts that it intersects. Additionally, a game's frame is responsible not only for the unusual relationship between the game and the outside world, but also for many of the internal mechanisms and experiences of game play.

How does the concept of the cognitive frame fit into a discus-sion of play and meaning? Anthropologist Gregory Bateson notes that, "play occurs within a delimited psychological frame, a spatial and temporal bounding of a set of interactive messages."[7] The frame of a game communicates that those contained within it are "playing" and that the space of play is separate in some way from that of the real world. A shove *inside* a game of Capture the Flag, for example, does not mean what it would normally mean *outside* the context of the game. Players engaged in play suspend the rules of everyday life when play begins. They then regulate their behavior according to a set of rules that operates only as long as the play frame is in force. We can understand play as a system of behaviors (with associated meanings) that get framed in particular ways, marked off and bound by rules regarding space, time, meaning, and consequentiality. Players acting within the frame of the game do so according to rules and the contexts that determine the meaning of those actions. But play has an additional function that helps shape how we communicate and make meaning, embodied in the act of *metacommunication*.

Metacommunication and Play

In his important essay "A Theory of Play and Fantasy," Gregory Bateson defines the concept of metacommunication. For Bateson, play not only grants distinctive meanings to actions but also communicates an attitude toward those actions. This attitude is a type of communication about how the actions associated with play should be interpreted and understood. Bateson's formulation was inspired by a visit to the zoo:

> What I encountered at the zoo was a phenomenon well known to everybody: I saw two young monkeys playing, i.e., engaged in an interactive sequence of which the unit actions of signals were similar to but not the same as combat. It was evident, even to the human observer, that the sequence as a whole was not combat, and evident to the human observer that to the participant monkeys this was "not combat."
>
> Now, this phenomenon, play, could only occur if the participant organisms were capable of some degree of metacommunication, i.e., of exchanging signals which would carry the message "this is play."[8]

Bateson saw play as an important step in the evolution of communication because it was "the point at which the organism is able to recognize the sign as a signal, that is, to recognize that the other individual's and its own signals are only signals."[9] To play, in other words, is not just to follow the rules and rituals of play, but also to continually communicate the idea that the play-actions are just play and not something else. Two dogs are

playing: one dog chases the other, catches up to it, and nips it on the neck. As an act of play and meaning, what is going on here? The playful nip connotes a bite: it means, *Aha! I pursued you, caught up to you, and bit you!* At the same time, the nip connotes the opposite: the nip also means, *I didn't really bite you. I'm just playing.* This double meaning, that the nip represents the bite but also exactly what the bite is not, is what Bateson means by metacommunication.

Metacommunication not only occurs with animals, but in games that people play as well. In Spin the Bottle, the ability of players to recognize that a kiss within the frame of the game at once *represents* but also *does not mean* the same thing as a kiss in the real world is an instance of metacommunication. We might say that players in a game of Spin the Bottle exchange signals that carry the message "This is a kiss," but at the same time convey the message "This isn't a *real* kiss—it's just a game."

This double consciousness is a product of the fact that the artificial game structure gives players license to kiss each other. Without the game, the kiss would probably not take place. The in-game kiss is a strange semiotic hybrid that could only emerge from the unique context of play. The kiss of Spin the Bottle has and does not have the meaning of a kiss in the real world. Like the nip and the bite, a Spin the Bottle kiss denotes a regular kiss *(I kissed that cute boy!)*, even as it simultaneously denotes what the kiss is not *(But it was only in a game.)*.

The concept of metacommunication is an absolutely critical idea that will greatly inform the following schemas, **Games as Narrative Play** and **Games as the Play of Simulation**. Play, as a form of metacommunication, reframes the events of the situation at hand, so that actions of "play" are related to, but are not the same as, other actions of "not play." Whenever we play, part of our play-activity involves the communication of the idea, "I am playing." This continual stream of communication between players, and between those playing and those not playing, helps sustain the magic circle. One of the functions of the magic circle is to actively demonstrate its own distinction from ordinary life. As Sutton-Smith notes, "Playfighting as an analogy to real fighting seems more like *displaying the meaning of fighting* than rehearsing for real combat. It is more about meaning than mauling."[10]

The exchange and recognition involved in arriving at the seemingly simple message "This is play" involves a range of interpretive acts. As in Wonderland, these interpretive acts connect "play" (events and actions within the magic circle) to "not play" (events and actions outside the magic circle). We need to take metacommunication into account when discussing the representational capacity of games, especially in the context of narrative, simulation, and immersion. The interpretative frame conditions how we "take" an event, or sign, as a communication. The point, in the end, is not what a play event means, but how we take its meanings.

Captured by the Game

Imagine a neighborhood game of Cops and Robbers. Everyone playing the game takes on a role of either a "cop" or a "robber." The cops designate a tree to represent the "jail" in the game. The rules of the game describe what players can do and when: how robbers can be captured by cops, placed into jail, and set free by other robbers. The game contains many representations: cops, robbers, and a jail, as well as actions such as capturing and making a jailbreak. The rules initially establish these representations, but they find their meaning through play.

The act of play is the act of interpretation. As players make their way through the game, representations shift and change: *I'm a mean Robber. I'm a helpless prisoner. I'm an escaped convict.* To play with representation in this way is to play the game. The meanings that emerge do so through the unique mechanisms of play. These representations refer to crime and punishment in the real world, but they are also artificial, uniquely enacted and interpreted within the magic circle of the game.

The players of Cops and Robbers know that they are playing. A captured robber player, clinging to the trunk of the jail tree and shouting "Set me free!" isn't just making a strategic move in the game. He is also signifying the fact that he is playing. If he really wanted to leave, he could just let go of the trunk and walk away. But he is bound within the chains of meaning that the game makes possible, taking part in the artificial conflict of the game. Being captured in the game signifies being placed inside a real jail, but it also signifies just the opposite: the player is not truly captured, because he is, after all, "just playing." If this all sounds complicated in theory, just remember how easy it is in practice. None of the players in the Cops and Robbers game have to understand the complex mechanisms games use to create meaning. All they know is that they are playing a game and enjoying themselves. The meanings they experience are wonderfully complex, but there is a simplicity with which they enter into the game and experience the effortless pleasure of play.

Game players inhabit that wonderland space where the frame of the game intersects the frame of the real world. Game designers have the supreme pleasure of creating their own rabbit holes, hoping players find their way down inside, in order to create their own meanings. Game designers are the architects, the meaning-makers, the storytellers that make the play of wonderland possible.

Further Reading

Nonsense: Aspects of Intertextuality in Folklore and Literature, by Susan Stewart

Stewart explores the labyrinthine relationships between common sense and nonsense, pointing to the ways interpretation and meaning are ordered and disordered through changes in formal and social context. Of particular interest is Stewart's discussion of the manipulation of context and meaning, and the role of the cognitive frame in shaping interpretation. Stewart examines a range of game-like structures, including palindromes, children's rhymes, puns, anagrams, code languages, and comic strips.

> *Recommended:*
>
> Part I. Common Sense and Fictive Universes, especially:
>
> "Framing in 'Life' and 'Art'"
>
> "Play and the Manipulation of Context"

"A Theory of Play and Fantasy," by Gregory Bateson, in *Steps to an Ecology of Mind*

Bateson's theory of play and fantasy suggests that play involves metacommunication—the use of signs that communicate about signs. He argues that what makes us human is our unique ability to use symbolic or abstract systems for representing experience. His important concepts of the cognitive frame and metacommunication, and their relationship to play, are wonderfully explored in this essay. The essay also offers a good introduction to the idea that play is a system of representation, in which interpretations are affected through their framing as "play".

Notes

1. Jeremy Campbell, *Grammatical Man: Information, Entropy, Language, and Life* (New York: Simon & Schuster, 1983), p. 127.

2. Bernard De Koven, *The Well-Played Game* (New York: Doubleday, 1978), p. 45.

3. Neal Hallford with Jana Hallford, *Swords and Circuitry: A Designer's Guide to Computer Role-Playing Games* (Roseville, CA: Prima Publishing, 2001), p. 152–4.

4. Ibid. p. 154.

5. Lewis Carroll, *Alice's Adventures in Wonderland* and *Through the Looking Glass* (New York: Signet Classic, 2000), p. 97–98, p. 173–74.

6. Ibid. p. 176.

7. Gregory Bateson, "A Theory of Play and Fantasy." In *Steps to an Ecology of Mind* (Chicago: The University of Chicago Press, 1972) , p. 191.

8. Ibid. p. 179.

9. Ibid. p. 178.

10. Brian Sutton-Smith, *The Ambiguity of Play* (London: Harvard University Press, 1997), p. 23. Our emphasis.

Games as the Play of Meaning
SUMMARY

- There are two ways of understanding the relationship between games and representation:

  - Games **can represent** (they contain internal depictions)

  - Games **are representations** (a game as a whole is a sign)

- **Meaning** in a game emerges from the interaction between system and context:

  - The **system** of a game's meaning is the set of formal relationships defined by the rules. It is the pre-existing structure of signs that does not change from game to game.

  - The **context** of a game's meaning is the space of experience where interpretation takes place. Interpretation in games is the act of play.

- This process of generating meaning is not unique to games. For example, meaning in language also emerges from the relationship between formal systems (grammar) and the context of interpretation.

- Because games are emergent systems, even a simple system can generate infinite meanings. The resulting set of possible meanings is the **space of representational possibility of a game.**

- Players in a game navigate this space of representational possibility through interaction. Game designers, by creating chains of actions and outcomes, build this space of possible meaning.

- The **magic circle** of a game is the space where special meanings obtain. It is the space where the rules of a game take hold, as well as the context for the interpretation of meaning.

- The meanings within the magic circle of a game are derived both from the internal formal system of the game as well as the ways that the game refers to the real world.

- A **cognitive frame** is a way of organizing how we look at the world. Game players take on a cognitive frame that affects how they interpret actions and events.

- **Metacommunication** is communication that takes place in the context of play. In addition to communicating game actions, players are also always communicating the fact that they are "just playing."

- Metacommunication helps generate the complex play of meaning in a game. Every game behavior signifies an action ("I just captured you!") but it also signifies what the action is not ("I didn't *really* capture you, since we were just playing.").

Unit 3: **Play**

GAMES AS NARRATIVE PLAY

situation
character
form
embedded narrative
emergent narrative
narrative descriptor
fictive worlds
story events
retelling play

26

Imagine you're in a one-man space shuttle traveling though the heavens at the speed of light. You and your tiny ship are totally engulfed in darkness, except for the luminance of an occasional passing star.

Suddenly, without warning, there's a brilliant flash straight ahead. You check the radar screen. Nothing. Pretty soon there's another flash, and another. Next thing you know the flashes have turned into one gigantic force field of some kind and it's dead ahead. You check the radar screen, still nothing.

The colors in this mysterious force field are so bright, they're almost blinding. And they seem to be in layers. But the strangest thing is that nothing shows up on the radar screen. What could that mean? Is it possible to travel through this mysterious force field or will you crash and be destroyed? And what about the layers? If you make it through one, can you make it through the next, and the next? It's decision time and there are only a few seconds to think about it. Turn back or blast ahead and try to make it through the layers of this brightly colored force field. It's up to you.—Atari Super Breakout Game Program Instructions

Introducing Narrative Play

Consider the card game War as an epic battle between the forces of good and evil, waged with a deck of cards and the laws of probability. Imagine Wipeout XL as a future sport circa 2097, in which corporate-sponsored, gravity-defying hoverships speed through impossible race tracks and hurl reality-warping weapons at each other for the pleasure of bloodthirsty fans. Experience Super Breakout as a conflict between a brave one-man space shuttle and a mysterious force field of blinding intensity, a gigantic array of color and light. Light up the engine. Energize the laser blaster. Check the radar screen. Blackness, a flash of light, and then…you are playing the game. The story, your story, begins.

Playing a game means interacting with and within a representational universe, a space of possibility with narrative dimensions. In Oddworld: Abe's Exoddus, players fight the Glukkons of the rapacious Magog Cartel to save their fellow Mudokens from a life of slavery in the mines of Necrum. In Driver: You Are the Wheelman, players take the role of Turner, a cop who goes undercover to infiltrate the Castaldi family, the underworld's most dangerous organization. In Monopoly, players are ruthless land barons vying for total economic domination of Atlantic City.

Formed by rules and experienced through play, a game is a space of possible action that players activate, manipulate, explore, and transform. When we frame this space of possibility as a narrative space, a special set of questions arise: Where do narratives in a game reside? How can one design games as narrative experiences? What kinds of narrative experiences do games make possible? What is the role of narrative in the design of meaningful play? We address these questions within this schema, *Games as Narrative Play.*

Each of these questions emphasizes a design-centric relationship between narratives and games. Because this chapter's potential terrain is so vast, we keep our investigation tightly focused. We do not ask, for example, "Are games stories?" or "How do we create better narratives?" These kinds of questions focus more generally on the nature of narrative itself, rather than on the role of narrative as experienced through game play. In this chapter, it is not a question of *whether* games are narrative, but *how* they are narrative.

Part of the challenge of talking about the experience of narrative in games are the many shapes it can take. Particularly in digital games, there is a proliferation of forms, often within a single game. For instance, how do players experience the "narrative" of DOOM? Is it by way of the "backstory" that we read on the back of the game box, concerning a lone soldier staving off an invasion of Earth by extra-dimensional demonic creatures? Do the opening title screen and between-level story updates play a role in the narrative experience? Is it through the play itself, a narrative structure that demands split-second timing, management of resources, navigation of space via POV and top-down maps, and a horrible death followed by rebirth at the last save point? What about the qualities and attributes of the game's characters, setting, and plot? As we discover, each of these elements contribute to the narrative play of a game in their own unique ways.

This schema is tied tightly to the chapters that precede and follow. *Games as the Play of Meaning, Games as Narrative Play,* and *Games as the Play of Simulation* together explore the ways that games operate as systems of representation. In *Games as the Play of Meaning,* we further developed our ongoing discussion of how games generate meaningful play through the process of signification. In this chapter, we pull back to look at larger questions of games and the experience of narrative representation. In the next chapter on simulation, we zoom back in to investigate the more atomic structures of games as representational systems, linking together signification, simulation, and storytelling.

Narrative Tensions

*Using other media as starting points, we may learn many things about the construction of fictive worlds, characters...but relying too heavily on existing theories will make us forget what makes games **games**: Such as rules, goals, player activity, the projection of the player's actions into the game world, the way the game defines the possible actions of the player. It is the unique parts that we need to study now.—**Jesper Juul,** "Games Telling Stories?"*

The intersection of the terms "narrative" and "game" has been surprisingly contentious in the study and design of games. In recent years, scholars and students of literature, film, and electronic narrative forms such as hypertext have gravitated toward the study of computer games. As disciplines outside of game design have studied games from the perspective of their own fields, debates have arisen over who has the right to make statements about games and narrativity, and exactly how to make such statements. These turf wars are symptomatic of the difficulty inherent in studying external media in the context of one's own discipline. Jesper Juul is correct in reminding us of the danger of relying too heavily on existing theories, particularly theories borrowed from other fields. For example, using literary theory to argue that all games are (or aren't) narratives ultimately doesn't offer much utility for game design.

Discussions of games as "interactive narratives" predictably fall into polarizing debates about linear vs. non-linear storytelling, of *games as stories* or *stories as games.* Some say that games and narrative are mutually exclusive concepts; others that some games are narrative whereas others are not. Consider the following excerpts from an online discussion of games and narrative by game designers/theorists Greg Costikyan and Brenda Laurel:

> *Greg Costikyan:* A story is best envisioned as "beads on a string," a linear narrative; a game is best envisioned as a triangle of possibility, with the initial position at one apex, and possible conclusions along the opposite side, with myriad, ideally, infinite paths between initial state and outcome. To the degree that you try to make a game more like a story by imposing arbitrary decision points, you make it less like a game.

> *Brenda Laurel:* I don't think the interactive game changes the popular understanding of what a story is. In popular culture, people talk about characters and worlds in relatively media-independent ways. In common speech, the name "story" actually refers to the central bundle of potential created by characters, worlds, situations, histories, and so forth, rather than to a specific instantiation (for example, *Star Trek, Care Bears, Myst*).[1]

While both Costikyan and Laurel make compelling points, the question underlying each of their statements is whether or not *games are narratives.* Our position in this schema is that the concept of narrative offers just one way of looking at games. Again, the question is not *if* games are narrative but *how* they are narrative. It is certainly possible to categorize all games as narrative objects—or as non-narrative objects—but as game designers we must ask how can we use such an understanding to generate meaningful play.

Over the last few years, several models regarding games and narrative have emerged. In "Games Telling Stories? A Brief Note on Games and Narratives," Jesper Juul summarizes these trends by identifying three arguments writers and scholars commonly make supporting an intrinsic connection between games and narrative:

1. We use narratives for everything.

2. Most games feature narrative introductions and backstories.

3. Games share some traits with narratives.[2]

The first argument offers a holistic view: we use narratives to make sense of our lives, to process information, and tell stories about a game we have played. Therefore, no genre or cultural form (including games) falls outside the idea of narrative.

The second argument centers on the story context provided by a game's opening cinematic or textual introduction. *(You are in a galaxy far, far, away…)* Backstories position a player in the context of a larger story; a player's action in a game is the means by which the larger story is realized. In Super Breakout, for example, the backstory written in the program instructions places players within a one-man spaceship, hurtling through the deep blackness of space, faster than the speed of light. The player encounters a mysterious force field, which blocks his way. Can he pass through it or will it destroy him? This text provides a narrative context within which the player acts, blasting away at the force field in order to resume his journey. Without this context, a player's actions in the highly abstract game of Super Breakout might lack narrative motivation. Although his actions certainly have interactive meaning—one pixel interacts with another, one action has a discernable and integrated outcome —they lack a designed experiential context within which these more formal meanings are framed as a story.

The third argument, that games share some traits with narratives, is exceedingly broad. This argument holds that games, like narratives, have quest structures, are experienced linearly, offer reversals of fortune, and contain other elements common to some, but not all narratives.

According to Juul, all three of these approaches have been used to justify a narrative approach to understanding games. Directly or indirectly, they all form a part of our own investigation of games as narrative play. However, unlike the approaches Juul summarizes, we are coming to the questions of games and narrative from a game design orientation. In previous chapters, we have framed and re-framed games from many points of view. Seeing games as information, conflict, pleasure, or meaning can help game designers to design meaningful play. The same is true when we look at games as narrative play.

A Framework for "Narrative"

Before we go any further, let's define the key term of this schema, *narrative*. Rather than coming up with our own definition, we borrow one from literary theorist J. Hillis Miller. In his essay "Narrative," he outlines a handful of components that constitute a narrative:

> There must be, first of all, an initial situation, a sequence leading to a change or reversal of that situation, and a revelation made possible by the reversal of the situation. Second, there must be some use of personification whereby character is created out of signs— for example, the words on the page in a written narrative, the modulated sounds in the air in an oral narrative. However important plot may be, without personification there can be no storytelling….Third, there must be some patterning or repetition of key elements.[3]

Miller's model for understanding narrative contains the following elements:

- *Situation:* A narrative has an initial state, a change in that state, and insight brought about by that change. This process constitutes the *events* of a narrative.

- *Character:* A narrative is not merely a series of events, but a *personification* of events though a medium such as language. Miller doesn't mean character in the usual sense of fictional persona, but rather the process by which "character is created out of signs." This component references narratives as not just events that take place in the world, but as represented events, events that occur via *systems of representation*.

- *Form:* Representation is constituted by *patterning and repetition*. This is true on every level of a narrative, whether it is the material form of the story or its conceptual themes.

Miller goes on to note that "even narratives that do not fit this paradigm draw their meaning from the way they play ironically against our deeply engrained expectations that all narratives are going to be like that."[4]

How do games relate to Miller's definition of narrative? From a formal perspective, they fit the definition very well. Take Chess, for example. Chess has a beginning state (when it is set up for a game), changes to that state (the game play), and a resulting insight (the outcome). It is a personified representation, a stylized depiction of war, complete with a cast of differentiated characters. The game also takes place in highly patterned structures of time (turns) and space (the checkerboard grid).

Miller's definition of narrative is succinct, but it is also very abstract. All games are narrative by this definition, as is literature, theater, and film. Many other kinds of experiences also fall into the wide net Miller casts, some of them activities or objects we might not normally think of as narrative, such as a marriage ceremony, a meal, or an argument. All contain situation, character, and form of the sort that Miller outlines. (A meal, for example, has a beginning, middle, and end, it comes to pass through systems of culinary representation, and it involves formal patterning on many levels.) The cleverness of Miller's definition lies in the fact that it is so inclusive, while still rigorously defining exactly what a narrative is. Miller's model helps us understand exactly which components of a game come into focus when we consider them from a narrative perspective.

Miller's definition is in some ways a formal approach to narrative. Events, characters, and patterned action describe the qualities of the narrative object, rather than the experience of that object. Because *Games as Narrative Play* falls within our primary schema **PLAY**, our intention is not just to arrive at a formal understanding of narrative (*What are the elements of a story?*) but instead an experiential one (*How do the elements of a story engender a meaningful experience?*). In our schemas based on **PLAY**, our concern is with the experience of players: their internal state of mind, and the relationships they form with each other and with the dynamic system of a game. If we shift Miller's definition of narrative into an experiential framework, we can begin to discuss narrative play in familiar terms. Everything we know so far about the experiential components of games—

that they are complex sensual and psychological systems, that they create meaning through choice-making and metacommunication, that they sculpt and manipulate desire—are tools for crafting narrative experiences.

These experiences emerge from the design of events, actions, and characters. Take our analysis of Centipede, from *Games as the Play of Experience*. The taut interaction between the game's five elements—mushrooms, centipedes, spiders, scorpions, and fleas—provides a formal framework filled with the possibility of narrative play. Each type of creature interacts with the mushrooms in different ways. Accordingly, the personification of each creature's interaction, the way that it becomes a meaningful representation, is based on its designed relationships. Spiders *eat* mushrooms, for example, whereas scorpions *poison* them. When shot, the deadly centipede's segments *transform* into mushrooms, an evolutionary action that changes the state of the creature from *insect* to *landscape*. Although these interactions are formal on one level, players experience them within a narratively descriptive space. How do we design such a space? How can we design game events as narrative events? What kinds of personifications do game actions allow? Next we begin to address these questions by looking in detail at one game, through an experiential application of Miller's framework.

Thunderstorm

We first introduced the dice game Thunderstorm in *Games as Systems of Uncertainty,* where we investigated the dramatic uncertainty created through the game's formal structure. We now look at the game again, this time with an eye toward narrative play. Thunderstorm embodies a very simple narrative. Players await the approach of a thunderstorm. If they play well their houses will be safe from the storm; if not, a powerful bolt of lightning will destroy their homes. Beware the player that fails to roll a 1!

Although Thunderstorm is a game of pure chance, the design of the experience crafts narrative drama on many levels. The experience of the game's "story" is intrinsically structural, tied directly to the game *events*. The roll of the dice not only controls the rate at which a player's house is built, but simultaneously the speed at which the storm approaches. As the game progresses, players build their houses step by step. Every time a player rolls a 1, he or she skips house construction that turn, stalling the inevitable approach of the storm. Once the house is built, the drama heightens, as each time a player rolls the dice there is a chance that lightning will strike. The climactic narrative drama is enacted in that final roll, when lightning strikes, destroying the house. The finish could not be more dramatic.

Thunderstorm provides a many-layered narrative experience. Dramatic tension emerges from the varying rates at which players build their houses. At different moments in the game, some players may be "safe" from the storm (at least momentarily!), while others sit poised at the front line of its fury. These positions can change quite quickly, depending on the outcome of the dice rolls as they progress around the circle. Snapshots of the game in progress would reveal constant shifts and adjustments to which house was closest to being built—and thus destroyed.

The translation of a player's performance into a drawing of a house is a distinctly narrative component of the design that makes all of the rich story elements possible. Although the game could have players keep track of their progression in other ways (counting to six, collecting six cards, losing six pennies, etc.), none of these methods would support the story framework of the game nearly as well. By having players draw pictures of the houses that the storm will destroy, the game's design provides a context that grants narrative meaning to the uncertain outcome of the dice roll. The drawn houses *personify* the formal events of the game, in Miller's sense of "character created out of signs." Additionally, players build their houses in full view of everyone else. This use of public information helps to maintain a sense of narrative coherence through shared experience. The drama of one player's experience is ultimately linked with their ability to see how close the storm is to destroying everyone else's house.

The narrative of Thunderstorm also dovetails nicely with the game's structure of pure chance. As players roll and pass dice, they enact a fable about the folly of hubris and the inevitability of fate. As quickly as men and women might build houses—symbols of domestic civilization—nature will inevitably destroy them. Although it is satisfying to slowly build your house, it is at the same time a march toward destruction, a race in which the winners are executed at the finish line. Like the word guessing game Hangman, in which a hanging corpse is drawn line by line with each incorrect guess, completing the image is synonymous with death. The poetic irony of Thunderstorm is that the game's image isn't a negative icon of mortality as in Hangman, but a positive image of construction. In Thunderstorm, the meek player prevails, the most timid builder rewarded for his or her lack of speed, the game ending in the aftermath of the deadly storm, with only one complete or nearly complete house left standing.

The formal patterning that emerges from the core mechanic of Thunderstorm supports narrative experience on both macro - and micro-levels. The moment-to-moment *rhythms* of rolling, drawing, and passing the dice set up *patterns* of events, which are experienced as a story of an approaching storm. As the game progresses and players are eliminated, the circle closes until there is only one house left. The moment-to-moment rhythm of lightning striking individual houses is different every game, but inevitably, as the circle closes, the narrative pace quickens as fewer players remain alive. On a macro-level, the narrative pattern is one of construction and destruction, of movement and stasis. The overall result is a surprisingly rich narrative experience.

Two Structures for Narrative Play

Throughout the rest of this chapter, we extend these formal notions of game interaction into the particularities of narrative game experience. As the example of Thunderstorm makes wonderfully clear, it is the dynamic structures of games, their emergent complexity, their participatory mechanisms, their experiential rhythms and patterns, which are the key to understanding how games construct narrative experiences. To understand game narratives, it is essential to analyze game structures and see how they ramify into different forms of narrative play.

We can identify two broad structural rubrics for understanding the narrative components of a game:

- Players can experience a game narrative as a crafted story interactively told: *the characters Jak and Daxter are saving the world.*

- Players can engage with narrative as an emergent experience that happens while the game is played: *Jak and Daxter's story arises through the play of the game.*

Both of these points of view, crafted interactive story versus improvised play experience, place narrative within the context of interactivity. Specifically, these viewpoints represent two ways of understanding how a game system produces narrative. The best terms we have found for these two structural relationships between games and narrative come from a talk by Marc LeBlanc at the 1999 Game Developers Conference. According to LeBlanc, game narratives can be "embedded" or "emergent."[5]

Embedded narrative is pre-generated narrative content that exists prior to a player's interaction with the game. Designed to provide motivation for the events and actions of the game, players experience embedded narrative as a story context. The narrative of Jak and Daxter saving the world, for example, is a narrative embedded in the game system: it is experienced through player interaction but exists formally apart from it. It is the embedded narrative that gives Jak a reason for collecting Precursor Orbs and Power Cells; without the pre-generated storyline the game would feel like an abstract fetch-the-next-item quest. The embedded narrative also provides the major story arc for the game, structuring a player's interaction and movement through the game world in a meaningful way.

Embedded narrative elements tend to resemble the kinds of narrative experiences that linear media provide. In Jak and Daxter, the embedded elements are the "pre-scripted" moments and structures that are relatively fixed in the game system. Any player, for example, that begins the game for the first time will see the same introductory cinematic. The first time a player encounters the Mayor of Sandover Village, he or she will hear the same prerecorded bit of dialogue. Embedded narrative elements can take a variety of forms and be reached through a variety of means, but regardless of how they are experienced, embedded narrative elements are fixed and predetermined units of narrative content, like text on the page of a Choose-Your-Own-Adventure book.

But not all narrative in games takes the form of pre-generated, embedded content. Narrative can also be *emergent,* which means that it arises from the set of rules governing interaction with the game system. Unlike embedded narrative, emergent narrative elements arise during play from the complex system of the game, often in unexpected ways. Most moment-to-moment narrative play in a game is emergent, as player choice leads to unpredictable narrative experiences. In the section of Misty Island where Jak battles the Balloon Lurkers, the narrative experience does not consist of pre-scripted sequences of dialogue, animation, and camera movements. Instead, the game rules allow the player to hop on a Zoomer to try and defeat the Lurkers and gather resources through skillful maneuvering. The exact narrative experience of a particular game, whether it is Jak easily dispatching the Lurkers, or whether it is a series of crushing defeats that leads to an eventual victory, depends on player interaction.

Emergent narrative is possible because of the way games function as complex systems. As the name implies, emergent narrative is linked directly to our earlier explorations of emergent complexity and meaningful interaction. For example, emergent narrative arises from interactions that are both *coupled* and *context-dependent.* These two terms, which we introduced in *Games as Emergent Systems,* describe interactions between elements in a complex system. When interactions within a complex system are *coupled,* it means that the elements of the system are linked recursively. Like bees in a hive, the elements in the system act together to perform in ways that single elements cannot. A player's moment-to-moment actions as Jak are linked to all other actions taken over the course of the game. Is it time to finally explore that strange-looking island just offshore? Perhaps you should go back to the village, because Jak's health is a bit low. On the other hand, you only need a few more Orbs to unlock the next level. Do you take the risk? How will the story unfold? Because actions in a game are linked to one another, one change in the system can create another change, giving rise to narrative patterns over the entire course of the game.

Interactions in emergent narratives are also *context-dependent,* which means the changes that occur are not the same every time. Instead, the exact outcome of an interaction depends on what else is happening in the system at any given moment. The first time the player fights a Lurker, perhaps it goes badly and the player has to beat a hasty retreat. The player's overall interactive pattern might shift from bold exploration to cautious stealth, the appearance of a Lurker signaling a terrifying threat. Later on in the game, when the player is skilled and powerful, a single Lurker no longer poses a danger: running into one would be a routine or even amusing encounter. Within emergent narratives, coupled interactions produce global patterns across a system; context-dependent interactions ensure that the exact arrangement of these narrative patterns dynamically changes over time.

Both embedded and emergent game elements contain characters, events, and patterns, and so both are narrative by Miller's definition. LeBlanc is not the only game designer to make such a structural distinction and tie it to the design of game narra-

tive. In his article "Formal Abstract Design Tools," Doug Church comes to a similar set of conclusions:

> The most obvious uses of story in computer and video games can be found in adventure-game plot lines. In this game category, the story has been written in advance by designers, and players have it revealed to them through interactions with characters, objects, and the world....
>
> But story comes into play in NBA Live, too. There, the story is what happens in the game. Maybe it ends up in overtime for a last-second three-pointer by a star player who hasn't been hitting his shots; maybe it is a total blowout from the beginning and at the end the user gets to put in the benchwarmers for their moment of glory. In either case, the player's actions during play created the story.[6]

Church's two examples closely mirror LeBlanc's categories of embedded and emergent. According to Church, embedded strategies such as those found in adventure games are the "most obvious uses of story in computer and video games." They are more clearly narrative because they more closely resemble what we normally think of as a story experience. As Church puts it, these games contain "plot lines...characters, objects, and the world." But that doesn't mean that emergent narratives, such as in a sports game like NBA Live, can't be just as important in generating narrative experience. Ultimately, the unique narratives games produce come from a balance of both of these approaches.

Embedded elements are narrative structures directly authored by game designers that serve as a frame for interaction. Emergent narrative approaches emphasize the ways that players interact with a game system to produce a narrative experience unique to each player. Some games, such as the classic adventure game The Secret of Monkey Island, emphasize embedded, content-based narrative. As Church points out, the structure of an adventure game, with its fixed settings and puzzles, lends itself to embedded narrative content that a player unlocks piece by piece over time. Other games, such as The Sims, embody a more system-based design approach, in which the game rules represent a space of emergent narrative possibility that plays itself out differently every time.

Virtually every game combines embedded and emergent elements. The Secret of Monkey Island is not entirely pre-scripted, like a slide show: there are many routes to take through the game, making for a limited kind of emergent experience. The Sims, conversely, has an overall setting that resembles suburban southern California. This pre-generated, embedded narrative frame contextualizes all of the emergent events that happen during play.

A common digital game design approach that combines embedded and emergent narrative elements is a mission-based game structure in which the larger narrative frame is pre-generated but most of the moment-to-moment game outcomes are determined through emergent means. The single-player web game Spybotics: The Nightfall Incident uses an overarching cyberpunk narrative that does not change from game to game. However, as a player makes her way through the game story, traveling from node to node on the network, she uses her accumulated inventory of programs to fight "databattles," the outcomes of which are not determined in advance. The introductory animation, pre-scripted narrative, appearances of characters, and the map of the network itself are all forms of embedded narrative content. However, the way that the player chooses to make her way across the network, the hacker programs she decides to purchase, and the experience of strategically deploying them at each node, represent the emergent elements of the narrative. The total narrative experience of the game includes both embedded and emergent approaches, woven together within a single game structure.

Narrative Goals

Within narrative we order and reorder the givens of experience. We give experience a form and a meaning.
—**J. Hillis Miller**, *"Narrative"*

Embedded and emergent structures are useful ways of conceptualizing narrative structures in games. But for narrative play to be fully engaging, it is important to remember the core principles of meaningful play. In the next several sections we take a look at some of the basic elements of games, including goals, conflict, uncertainty, and core mechanics, to see how they can be put to use in the design of narrative play.

One fundamental building block of narrative game design is the *goal* of a game. Goals not only help players judge their progress through a game (how close are they to winning), but also guide players in understanding the significance of their actions within a narrative context. In Super Breakout, for example, the goal is to "break out" of the force field by destroying as many colored blocks as possible. The goal describes the nature of player interaction within a narrative context, making the interaction meaningful. The outcome of the interaction is clear on a formal level (blocks are destroyed) as well as on a narrative level (the space ship breaks through the force field!). In this example we see again how embedded narrative can provide a framework that makes the more immediate game play narratively meaningful.

In addition to the embedded narrative arc of the game, narrative play can occur on the moment-to-moment, emergent level as well. In the Hostage Rescue mode of multiplayer Counter-Strike, players compete in teams as either counter-terrorists or terrorists. Each team has complementary goals: to find and rescue the hostages or keep them from being rescued, over a series of rounds. The larger narrative arc of the game swings in tempo with the success or failure of each round, as one of the teams emerges as victor. But narrative is also experienced each moment of the game, as players make decisions regarding their interaction with teammates and opponents. Where are the hostages hidden? Why are the terrorists so unorganized? Can you count on your teammate to cover you as you sneak into enemy territory? With half your team down, will you be able to rescue enough of the hostages to beat the terrorists? Counter-Strike players constantly interact with one another through the narrative frame of counter-terrorist military operations. The collaboration and competition of the game experience, defined by the intertwined goals of each team, shape moment-to-moment player behavior and narrative experience.

Level or mission-based structures in games also provide important narrative goals for players. Completing a level means not only reaching an objective, but also passing through one episode of a larger story. As the player moves through multiple levels, the succession of completed goals creates narrative coherence. Game levels offer players access to specific areas of the narrative world, each level populated by unique events, objects, and characters that create a particular narrative tone and texture. Spybotics: The Nightfall Incident proceeds as a series of levels, in the form of network nodes that the player must defeat. The enemy programs at each level increase in difficulty, as do the abilities of the hacker programs under the player's control. More than just ramping up challenge, these new game elements enlarge the emergent narrative possibilities. As a result, the player's expanding palette of strategic actions corresponds with an expanding palette of narrative experience. Each successfully completed node rewards the player with messages and updates from the game's cast of characters; as the play unfolds, the level structure also drives the embedded cyberpunk storyline of espionage, sabotage, and betrayal.

The Sims Hot Date Expansion Pack uses both levels and goals to shape the game's narrative. Going on a date is a narrative experience composed of several smaller events. A romantic date has several distinct components:

·   *Getting ready to secure a date:* A player must prepare her Sim by making sure that the Sim has adequate Energy and

that her Sim's Motive values are at their maximum. Mood, an aggregate of all Motive scores, plays a big role in the duration of the date and the success of each interaction during a date. Because a date's overall success is entirely based upon the sum of interactions between Sims, a large number of bad interactions results in an unsuccessful date.

·   *Getting a date:* A Sim can get a date by asking one of her housemates, accosting a visitor, calling a friend or acquaintance, or by randomly meeting someone downtown. Whether a Sim accepts the proposal of a date from another Sim depends on a Relationship score, which develops through social interactions. Sims can joke, flirt, apologize, tease, and scare each other in an attempt to accomplish the goal of getting a date.

·   *Sharing one or more activities:* A date consists of a set of carefully considered interactions and events, designed by the player to maximize the Relationship score of the two Sims. A poorly designed set of events will inevitably lead to bad interactions—and a bad date. A rejected kiss at the bar, for example, immediately ends a date. Each kind of event players choose to include in their date has its own set of narrative expectations. Trying on clothes in a store, for instance, offers a very different narrative experience than a dip in the hot tub!

·   *Going home together (optional):* The ultimate end to a date is to get a Sim to come home for some shenanigans on the Love Seat or in the Love Tub. In order for this to occur, however, a player must carefully manage Energy resources as well as maintain a high Relationship score throughout the date. Achieving this goal affords clear narrative resolution.

·   *Saying goodbye:* If the date goes well, a Sim might invite a date to move in, or even to get married. With either of these outcomes, the new Sim becomes a member of the household. There is also the possibility that the date will end badly, meaning that the Sim's Relationship score has

Sims Hot Date

bottomed out. The player has some choice in defining his or her own goals for a date, but the final outcome is determined by the events and interactions that have taken place up to that point, and are emergently generated. This concluding step in the larger narrative event of the romantic date provides a snapshot of the overall experience, giving the player a sense of narrative closure.

Level or mission structures allow players to feel the details of a story while the game designer maintains control of the larger narrative experience. A game's goal, or series of goals, is part of the narrative context that makes up the game. When goals are well-designed to support narrative play, a player's interaction with the game world becomes consistently meaningful. As usual, the discernability and integration of meaningful play is critical. The elaborate multi-step process of going on a Sims date is only meaningful because of the complex system that supports and links player actions. If every date ended the same way no matter what actions the player took, there would be no reason for the player to engage deeply in the decision-making process. Because each step of the process plays a role in determining the outcome, the experience of a Sims date provides genuinely meaningful narrative play.

Conflict

Goals in a game are never easy to achieve. As players struggle toward the goal, *conflict* arises. Game conflict provides both opportunity for narrative events and a narrative context that frames the obstacles a player must overcome. Players in a game of Thunderstorm must overcome the obstacle of failing to roll a 1 in order to stave off the approaching storm. In the rhythm-action console game Um Jammer Lammy, players must overcome the obstacles of challenging rhythmic structures and hair-raising slapstick adventures to make sure Lammy makes it to her rock-n-roll gig on time. Overcoming conflict in a game is one way narrative events advance.

Because conflict presumes a struggle between opposing forces, in a game there should always be some element that works against player success, an element that acts to try and ensure the failure of the player. This role is often taken by a villain character, a competing player or team, or may be embodied in the game system as a whole. From a narrative perspective, this element motivates and contextualizes player action. It does not make much narrative sense to knock down rows of colored blocks if the behavior of those blocks has no connection to your presence in the game world. Once you identify those colored blocks as a force field designed by the forces of evil to stop your advance through the universe, you are much more motivated to enter into a conflict with them. Your action becomes meaningful within the narrative frame of the game. In traditional storytelling, the internal conflict of a character often shapes the kinds of experiences encountered by the audience. Internal conflict reveals a character's vulnerability, which is usually exploited by those who wish to see the character fail. Lex Luthor knows Superman is vulnerable to kryptonite and in love with Lois Lane. The trick to using game conflict as a narrative game design tool is to tie it closely to the formal game structure itself.

In the strategy board game Settlers of Catan, the narrative premise is that the players are competing to colonize a small island, establishing their own networks of roads, settlements, and resources. Players can trade resources with each other, and conflict quickly arises out of the tension between diplomacy and self-interest. Every trade you complete helps you, but it also helps the opponent with whom you traded. If you drive too hard a bargain, no one will trade with you, which means you won't be able to acquire the resources you need to prosper: *You need a Brick resource to build that next stretch of road and connect your settlements, but the only player willing to trade with you is about to win—what action do you take?* In Settlers of Catan, narrative conflict, social conflict, and strategic conflict are tightly intertwined. As you make strategic decisions, you are building social relationships, which themselves have narrative implications for the emerging story of the game.

The conflict of a game infuses every moment of its play. To maximize the narrative play in your game, you must pay close attention to how the conflict in your game is narrativized. When game conflict provides a narrative context for action, your players will help you tell your game's story, infusing their own actions with narrative meaning. Even in a relatively abstract game like Settlers of Catan, the conflict provides a narrative space where players can flesh out the game's story and take on narrative roles. In our own experience with the game, slang terms such as "Mountain King," "Road Baron," and "General" emerged to describe play strategies focused on controlling mountain resources, building long roads, and constructing a large army. This is transformative narrative play: a game conflict enriched by a narrative level of meaning that emerges from the social, strategic, and representational structures of the game. We are not saying that players engage with Settlers of Catan in order to role-play fictional characters. But narrative play is clearly part of the game's appeal. Without its narrative framework, designed to function in concert with the game conflict, Settlers of Catan would feel like an exercise in number shuffling.

Uncertainty

Uncertainty is another requisite quality of meaningful play. If a game is certain, if the outcome is known in advance, there is no reason to play in the first place. But uncertainty is also a narra-

tive concept, for the element of the unknown infuses a game with dramatic tension. In Thunderstorm, the narrative of the approaching storm is only complete once the storm has destroyed every house but one. If it were known in advance which player would win, there would be no real need for a narrative device. In The Drome Racing Challenge, an online multiplayer racing game, players customize racing cars and prepare a racing strategy, then select an opponent online and race. During a race, players do not directly control their cars, but instead watch their preparations play out as an Animé-style animation that depicts each moment of the race, event by event. The fact that players do not know the result of the race until the animation has played out makes viewing the race highly dramatic. Despite the fact that a player might have the utmost confidence in his or her race strategy, there is always the chance to lose.

The dramatic tension of Poker, too, gains its bite from the uncertainty of outcome. Bluffing contributes to the narrativity of the experience, heightening the potential for deceit. As players enter into the psychological space of the bluff, narrative tensions mount. *Does she really have the hand she says she has, or is she bluffing? What if she isn't bluffing? Can she still be beaten? He just made a large bet, so he must have a good hand. But he bluffed last round, and he wouldn't try that same trick twice in a row. But maybe that's what he wants me to think….* The mechanics of betting heighten the feeling of uncertainty. Players with strong hands wage higher bets against uncertain outcomes, whereas players may limit bets when the degree of uncertainty in a game feels too great. As players fold and the circle of active players shrinks, narrative tension grows. Although players may have good hands, the outcome remains uncertain until all bets are made and the cards are called. This moment can be quite dramatic, particularly when a hand has been well-played.

Even in role-playing games, which often lack a final game outcome, the uncertainty of each action, each encounter, and each adventure plays a crucial role in building narrative engagement. Experienced tabletop role-players will shun game masters with reputations for being too easy or too hard. In these cases, certain death or certain success removes the enjoyable uncertainty of the game. On the other hand, when role-players feel like they are truly uncovering mysteries and exploring strange new areas of their worlds, powerful narrative play can result. As with the use of conflict, successful use of uncertainty in a game story ties the narrative elements to the formal system of the game. Do you dare explore the dank dark cave, with its legends of horrible monsters and priceless treasures? Should you first consult the oracle at the top of the mountain for advice, risking starvation during the long journey? Do you spend your last few gold coins hiring a few extra guards to accompany you? Each of these choices involves not just dramatic narrative outcomes, but different uses of the role-players' limited resources. As players make a choice and its uncertain outcomes slowly unfold, new choices present themselves, each emerging option cloaked in its own narrative uncertainty.

Core Mechanics

Whereas uncertainty tends to affect the larger trajectory of a game's narrative arc, *core mechanics* represent the essential moment-to-moment activity of players. During a game, core mechanics create patterns of repeated behavior, the experiential building blocks of play. Designing moment-to-moment play as narrative play means paying attention to exactly what players are doing in your game, how their choices and outcomes are represented, and how these moments fit into larger narrative frames.

Recognizing games as narrative experience means considering them not just as bits of plot that are arranged and rearranged through interaction, but instead considering them as an ongoing *activity* in which a player engages with a core mechanic to make meaningful choices and explore a space of possibility. Often, interactive narratives are diagrammed as points connected to lines, with each point representing a piece of text or a segment of video that is accessed by the player.

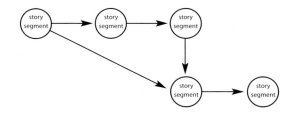

What this kind of formal approach to interactive narrative leaves out is *how* a player moves from point to point in the system. This is where the core mechanic comes into play. In designing games, you aren't simply creating content. You are creating a set of actions, a series of stylized behaviors. What are your players *actually doing* from moment to moment in a game? More importantly, how can you craft these core mechanics to most effectively embody the narrative experience you have in mind? A number of examples follow.

In the unusual virtual creature game Seaman, the player interacts with the title character Seaman by talking into a microphone that attaches to the Dreamcast controller, enacting a wonderfully conversational style of play that literally involves speaking, looking, and listening. Because the game's story casts the player as a scientist observing and interacting with a strange form of life evolving in a fishtank, these core mechanics are entirely appropriate to the narrative of the game. Even when the player is using the controller buttons to take action, the game design creates evocative mechanics of interaction. Grabbing Seaman and lifting him up out of the virtual fish tank is accomplished by a slightly awkward, single-handed button combination that creates a hand gesture very much like grabbing a fish with your forefinger and thumb. The core mechanics of Seaman not only let the player access new content, but actually force the player to *perform* the narrative of the game from moment to moment.

The default rules for Mind's Eye Theater, the live-action version of the role-playing game Vampire: The Masquerade, resolve actions by means of Rock-Paper-Scissors. Although this system is convenient for the real-world context of a LARP (where it would be awkward and time-consuming to pull out dice and scoresheets to resolve every conflict), many role-playing groups have opted for different resolution mechanics better suited to the narrative content. For example, some player groups simply translate rock, paper, scissors into more appropriate content (devil, angel, human); instead of using hand signals, they use sets of elaborately designed custom cards. Flashing an image of a devil before your opponent in order to resolve a psychic attack suits the dark Goth narrative of Vampire much more than making the schoolyard gesture of scissors. This game design solution keeps the formal system of Rock-Paper-Scissors completely intact, while modifying the experiential component of the core mechanic for dramatic narrative effect.

Narrative Space

The last several sections of this chapter have utilized fundamental game concepts, reframing them in narrative terms to shed light on the intersection of game design and storytelling. Goals, conflict, uncertainty, and the core mechanic are all general elements of games that game designers can use to craft meaningful narrative experiences. Another familiar game concept that we can understand narratively is the *space of possibility*. Game designer Warren Spector connects this concept to narrative when he states that "games create 'possibility spaces,' spaces that provide compelling problems within an overarching narrative, afford creative opportunities for dealing with these problems and then respond to player choices with meaningful consequences."[7] Spector's description of a game's "possibility space" links the embedded "overarching narrative" of a game to the emergent actions and outcomes of moment-to-moment play.

So far in this book, we have invoked the space of possibility metaphorically, to mean an abstract decision-space or a conceptual space of possible meaning. But what if we consider the space of possibility *literally*—as an actual 2D or 3D space in which a game takes place. In other words, one way to think of

the space of possibility is as an actual narrative *place*. In Berzerk, the space of the game consists of a series of connected rooms, seen from a bird's eye view. The checkerboard pattern of a Chess board mathematically slices the space of the game into discrete modules of equal dimension, whereas the elegant grid of the Go board uses the intersection of points to describe the territory of play. In Super Mario 64, the three-dimensional space of the game is composed of concealed rooms, magical trapdoors, and secret worlds that create a vast landscape of mysterious hidden places.

The spatial features of a game have a strong impact on creating the narrative space of possibility. As game scholars Henry Jenkins and Kurt Squire explain,

> Game designers use spatial elements to set the initial terms for the player's experiences. Information essential to the story is embedded in objects such as books, carved runes or weapons. Artifacts such as jewels may embody friendship or rivalries or may become magical sources of the player's power. The game space is organized so that paths through the game world guide or constrain action, making sure we encounter characters or situations critical to the narrative.[8]

Volleyball, for example, takes place within a court 60 ft x 30 ft, divided in the center by a net 8 ft high. The only objects that exist in this space are players—six to a side—and a ball. The game play emerges from the interactions made possible by the players' positions within the spatial grid. Players occupy designated spatial positions on the court which guide and constrain player action. How and when players touch the ball, for example, is a product of their positions within the grid. The net that divides the court engages narrative play as well, for it articulates the space of friend and foe, of teammate and opponent. Across this net, dramatic narratives of attack and defense occur each time a player serves the ball.

The organization of spatial features in a game is critical to the design of a game's narrative space of possibility. If you want

Case Study: A Loopy Core Mechanic

In LOOP, the player uses the mouse to draw lines and capture butterflies moving about the screen. The formal core mechanic, drawing lines around shapes, is framed as a narrative act (catching butterflies) with which players take action in the game world. In LOOP, there is a strong fit between core mechanic and game narrative. The looping action of drawing lines with a mouse metaphorically evokes the swooping gesture of catching butterflies with a net. One could imagine an abstract version of LOOP as a game without butterflies, in which the player is simply drawing lines around colored geometric shapes—but the framing of the player's action as butterfly catching adds layers of narrative meaning to the core mechanic, creating a story context that incorporates other aspects of the game as well.

Each level in LOOP gives the player a limited amount of time to catch a certain quota of butterflies, or else the game ends. LOOP communicates this time limit by the condensed representation of a single day: the rising and setting of the sun. This narrative device ties the core mechanic of the game to an episodic structure. A clock, hourglass, or even just numbers counting down could have been used to mark the passing of time, but these design solutions do not complement the narrative context of the game. Each "day," players have a chance to collect more butterflies. Once the sun sets, providing that players have managed to catch enough butterflies, the colorful insects disappear until the dawn of another day when it is time to catch some more. As the level of difficulty steadily increases, the dramatic tension is heightened. Because of the intense concentration required to col-lect as many of the increasingly agile butterflies as possible, the sun seems to set faster and faster with each passing day. It doesn't of course—it only feels that way!

Every five levels, a player has a chance to catch a special butterfly and reach a bonus level. These levels are set at nighttime and feature a rising moon as a timer instead of a setting sun. Bonus levels do not have a quota of butterflies to catch and therefore provide a more relaxed context for the core mechanic within the overall rhythm of the game. These night-time levels reframe the core mechanic in a narrative context opposite to that of the daytime levels. In this way, the narrative framing works hand in hand with the formal game structure to maximize narrative meaning from the simple core mechanic.

your players to form strong social relations, make sure to create narrative spaces that support social interaction. The spatial design of a house or restaurant in The Sims defines the type of social interactions that can occur there. If a player designs a bar that doesn't allow the bartender access to the cash register, no drinks can be served. Without the action > outcome of ordering and serving drinks, a slew of narrative interactions fail to materialize. In Black & White, the spatial features of the game world change in relation to the actions of a player, placing the consequences of player action in a narrative of moral choice. The world at the beginning of the game is an image of Edenic innocence. As a player moves through the world, taking actions and making choices, the world changes to reflect the moral nature of these choices. "Bad" choices darken and scar the world, whereas "good" choices transform it into a flowering garden. The story of good and evil is metaphorically both reflected and enacted within the spatial features of the game world. Even the way that the player moves through the world of Black & White, by "grabbing" it with the game's hand-cursor and pulling it into view, emphasizes the unusually intrinsic connection between the player and the space of Black & White.

What about a game that has no predefined physical space? Mafia is a social game of secret identities and clever bluffing in which players sit in a circle and take turns voting which among them are the secretly designated killers. There is no game board or physical materials, and playing the game does not require a specific kind of space. Yet the loose arrangement of players in a circle creates a spatial order that maximizes narrative interaction. Players must be able to see each other clearly, in order to scrutinize body language and make guesses about who might be the hidden members of the Mafia. The spatial configuration of players is critical to the system of public and private information at the center of the game. A player out of sight would be able to avoid scrutiny from the others. Instead, the democratic arrangement of players ensures that everyone playing is both observer and observed, equally culpable and suspect.

The play activity of Telephone shares a similar spatial design, but a very different set of narrative interactions. Players of Telephone sit in a tight circle (the tighter the better) in order to facilitate whispering into a neighboring player's ear. Although this formal interaction could occur in another spatial configuration (such as a line), the game would lose its essential narrative of circulation—of watching the message travel through a physical and social space that stretches from a starting point, through the bodies of the players, to arrive at its final destination in the ear of the last player. The spatial arrangement of the players in a circle, although not a formal requirement of the game, enriches the narrative quality of the play experience by teasing out the game's inherent story of the same-but-different transformation of information.

What are the implications for design? Pay careful attention to the way that your game creates and organizes space. What kind of seating arrangement does the design of your board game imply? Will players be able to hold the cards they need to keep hidden or will they have to improvise screens that limit social interaction? How do the two teams first approach each other on the field of play? Does the way your game breaks up the classroom space imply narrative ownership of territory? Does the structure of the space between two dueling card players express the magical territory where their epic battle takes place? In every game you create, consider how the design of the space weaves together formal and experiential elements to represent and facilitate the stories you want to tell.

Digital Game Spaces

Although games have been played in real-world spaces for millennia, the appearance of electronic and digital games in the last few decades have provided new kinds of game spaces: playgrounds that exist only on the screens of computer monitors and televisions. These game spaces take a multitude of forms, from blocky 2D grids to expansive 3D worlds. One useful taxonomy for describing the range of these digital spaces comes from Mark J. P. Wolf, in his essay "Space in the Video

LOOP

The patterns of behavior created through the core mechanic of LOOP support narrative play in a number of ways: by situating play within a repeating framework of a day, by linking the formal interaction of looping to the narrative context of butterfly catching, and by creating numerous levels of choice, from the number and kind of butterflies captured within a single loop to the pace at which the collecting occurs. In addition to the elements of narrative play tied to the core mechanic, there are a number of embedded narrative components as well. These include the butterfly-catching main character Ada; her procedurally generated dream poems that appear on bonus levels; and the visual motif of a book that links the act of butterfly catching to writing and storytelling. These narrative contexts add yet more meaning to the player's interaction, forming an overall system of play that results in an experience full of narrative possibility.

Game." Wolf lists eleven ways that video games operate to structure and represent space. We paraphrase these categories below, with examples from Wolf's essay:

- *Text-only space:* text adventure games such as Zork and Planetfall

- *One contained screen:* Pong, Space Invaders, Breakout

- *One screen with wraparound:* Asteroids, Pac-Man (with teleporter wraparound)

- *Scrolling on one axis:* Defender, Atari's Football arcade game

- *Scrolling on two axes:* Gauntlet, Sim City

- *Adjacent spaces displayed one room at a time:* Berzerk, Atari's Adventure

- *Scrolling with separate background layers:* Zaxxon, Double Dragon

- *Limited 3D space:* Tempest, Night Driver

- *Two spaces on one screen or two separate screens:* Spy vs. Spy, Dactyl Nightmare

- *Full 3D spaces:* Battlezone, DOOM, Tomb Raider

- *"Mapped" Spaces:* Defender, Myst (both have a separate radar or map display)[9]

Wolf's categories are not without some conceptual problems. For example, there is a fundamental difference between a "two-and-a-half" dimensional space like DOOM and a more fully 3D space like Tomb Raider (in DOOM the player can only move in two dimensions and the objects are completely flat). Additionally, some of his categories, such as separate background scrolling layers and "mapped" spaces, seem to be fuzzier designations (most of the categories he lists could also incorporate a "map" element). Wolf's typology is certainly not the only way to conceptualize digital game spaces, but his categories are useful in pointing out the wealth of forms they take.

Zork: Text-only space

```
Kitchen                                              Score: 10/5

>enter
Kitchen
You are in the kitchen of the white house. A table seems to have been used
recently for the preparation of food. A passage leads to the west and a
dark staircase can be seen leading upward. A dark chimney leads down and
to the east is a small window which is open.
On the table is an elongated brown sack, smelling of hot peppers.
A bottle is sitting on the table.
The glass bottle contains:
  A quantity of water

>drink water
You have to be holding the glass bottle first.

>
```

The structure of a digital game space always grows directly from the formal system that defines the game. However, the space that a player experiences is also a function of representation (how the space is displayed to the player) and interaction (how a player navigates through the space). These three elements—formal structure, structure of display, and interactive structure—together constitute the experience of a digital game space. All three of them need to be designed in concert to achieve proper narrative effect in your game.

For example, the feeling of zero-G drift in Asteroids is linked directly to the design of the game space. Rather than bouncing off the screen wall like a Pong ball, the player's ship moves right on through to the other side, evoking the illusion of endless movement through the darkness of space. The game's style of movement, emphasizing inertial drift and retro-rocket maneuvers, also heightens the feeling of space travel. Although the player's ship never leaves the screen, at the beginning of each wave, asteroids drift in from the edges. Once they appear, these asteroids follow the same wraparound logic as the player's ship. Other objects, such as the UFO saucers, don't ever wrap around, and simply disappear once they reach the edge of the screen. Curiously, these inconsistencies never break the game's spatial continuity. The fact that some objects remain constantly on screen (the player's ship and existing asteroids) whereas others

Asteroids: One screen with wraparound

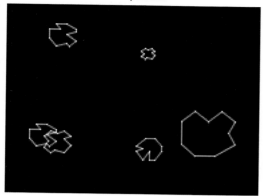

Double Dragon: Scrolling with separate background layers

Tempest: Limited 3D space

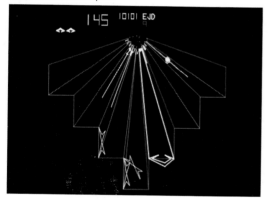

Spy vs. Spy: Two spaces on one screen

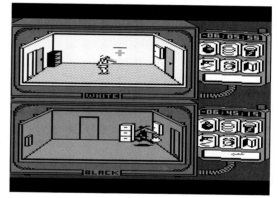

Tomb Raider: Full 3D space

Defender: "Mapped" space

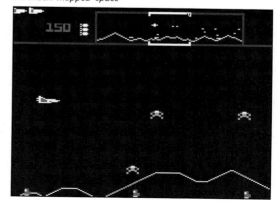

seem to drift in from parts unknown (new asteroids and UFOs), adds up to a rich and multi-layered narrative of cosmic exploration and survival. Space creates narrative in all senses of Miller's definition: space helps define the "characters" (the game objects); space is the context in which narrative events occur; and space patterns narrative experience over time for the player.

The design of a game space creates a context for narrative interaction, by structuring events in patterns of space, time, and causality. As Marsha Kinder notes in *Playing with Power in Movies, Television, and Video Games,* "Narrative creates a context for interpreting all perceptions. Narrative maps the world and its inhabitants, including one's own position within that grid."[10] The narrative play of games is always connected to an underlying grid of possibility, to goals and conflict, to uncertainty and the moment-to-moment action of the core mechanic. The space of a game is quite literally its space of play.

In a fighting game such as Tekken, the space is tightly constrained, crowding the two fighters up against each other. There is nowhere to run and nowhere to hide. All you can do is fight your opponent, an action the design of the space explicitly encourages and facilitates. In contrast, the corridors and rooms of a Quake deathmatch space create a narrative of stealthy maneuvers, mad dashes to grab power-ups, and the surprise of sudden death. Tekken has no hidden spatial information. But in Quake, walls block players from seeing each other, dark lighting makes hiding in shadows possible, and the periodically appearing power-ups create uncertainty about when and where they can be found. In both Tekken and Quake, a player's "position on the grid," as Kinder puts it, is simultaneously a location in the space of the game and a position within the space of the game narrative. The formal, represented, and interactive spaces of games are also narrative spaces, contexts for interpreting the experience of a game as a story.

When we frame experience as narrative, the events and actions of game play take on form and meaning within the game's representational universe. The dynamic properties of the space of Tekken and Quake are important in creating emergent narratives of conflict. But the spaces contain embedded narrative qualities as well. In Quake, the spaces embody the sets, props, and characters of pulp sci-fi horror. In Tekken, as with most fighting games, each arena is thematically linked to one of the game's characters. Space can therefore be used to express information about a character's persona or backstory, or to create narratives about defending one's home turf or invading an enemy's territory.

Spaces of Adventure

One of the wonderful qualities of digital game spaces is their plasticity and flexibility. The emphasis in recent years on photo-realistic, logically consistent 3D game spaces has eschewed experimental approaches to space design in favor of increasingly "realistic" ones. Yet by exploiting the flexibility of the computer medium, space can be a powerful narrative tool. For example, take the Atari 2600 game Adventure, arguably the first graphical adventure game. Let's begin by looking at the backstory of Adventure from the game manual:

> An evil magician has stolen the Enchanted Chalice and has hidden it somewhere in the Kingdom. The object of the game is to rescue the Enchanted Chalice and place it inside the Golden Castle where it belongs.

> This is no easy task, as the Evil Magician has created three Dragons to hinder you in your quest for the Golden Chalice. There is Yorgie, the Yellow Dragon, who is just plain mean; there is Grundle, the Green Dragon, who is mean and ferocious; and there is Rhindle, the Red Dragon, who is the most ferocious of all. Rhindle is also the fastest Dragon and is the most difficult to outmaneuver.

There are three castles in the Kingdom; the White Castle, the Black Castle, and the Golden Castle. Each castle has a Gate over the entrance. The Gate can be opened with the corresponding colored Key. Inside each Castle are rooms (or dungeons, depending at which Skill Level you are playing).

The Castles are separated by rooms, pathways, and labyrinths. Common to all the Skill Levels is the Blue Labyrinth through which you must find your way to the Black Castle. Skill Levels 2 and 3 have a more complicated Kingdom….[11]

This embedded narrative weaves together traditional elements of character, setting, and conflict (Evil Magician, Kingdom, and hidden treasure) with explicit descriptions of the spatial mechanics of the game (keys open gates, castles are connected by pathways and labyrinths, higher skill levels have more complex kingdoms). This introductory description even makes explicit the ways that spatial arrangements acquire narrative meaning. For example, according to the text, what is it that makes Rhindle the Red Dragon the most ferocious dragon of them all? It is his ability to move through space more quickly than the others.

Within Adventure, the player is represented as a square dot that moves through the space of the game, collecting and using objects, avoiding enemies, and navigating the kingdom in order to find the hidden chalice. As Wolf pointed out in his taxonomy of game spaces, Adventure represents space as a series of interconnected adjacent rooms, each room displayed one at a time. When a player enters a new room, the player's dot appears on a point at the edge of the screen corresponding to the entrance of the room. If the player uses an exit to leave the room, a new room fills the screen. As opposed to a more contemporary, smoothly scrolling space, Adventure's spatial scheme designates each room as a kind of theatrical tableau, a self-contained scene that focuses the dramatic action. This elegantly spare structure, imposed in part by technological limitations, nevertheless perfectly suits the mythical fairytale narrative of the game. For example, when a player enters a room with a locked castle gate, movement is severely

restricted to the lower and side borders of the screen, clearly evoking the experience of being locked out. On the other hand, when the proper key opens the gate, a simple but dramatic animation of the raising castle portcullis transforms the space of the castle from imposing barrier to inviting gateway, leading to new spaces beyond.

closed castle

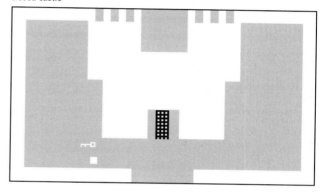

open castle

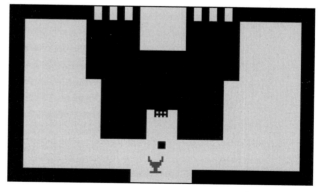

Much of Adventure's delightful use of space comes from its inconsistencies. The room one reaches inside a castle, for example, is larger than the castle appears from the outside. This illogical use of space expresses the magical nature of the game narrative and reaches true virtuosity in the construction of the game's four labyrinths. As suits the creation of a mad Evil Magician, these mazes do not follow a consistent topography. The labyrinths all exist as a series of self-contained rooms with passageways. However, entrances and exits from the rooms do not follow a consistent spatial logic but instead wrap around in erratic ways. The image to the right shows a map of the Blue Labyrinth, along with indications of the wraparound entrances and exits from each room.

The experience of navigating these mazes can be initially disconcerting, especially because some of them are darkened "catacombs," where you only see the walls in a limited area immediately surrounding your dot. It is possible in these mazes to feel completely and utterly lost—a wonderfully appropriate emergent narrative effect. Yet at the same time, the labyrinths are not gratuitously complex, containing only three, four, or five rooms. The difficulty of moving through them comes from their magical wraparound logic, not from an overabundance of navigational choices. This is a well-designed, balanced spatial challenge. The player never loses a strong sense of the overall system, and over the course of playing several games, learns to navigate the mazes with greater and greater ease.

Blue Labyrinth (expanded view)

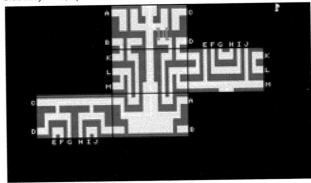

Inside the Black Castle

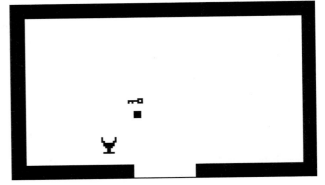

More than in most games, the formal, representational, and interactive qualities of Adventure's spaces contribute directly to the game's rich narrative experience. You finally locate the Black Key in the Catacombs and you race through a labyrinth toward the locked Black Castle. But then you come across Rhindle, the Red Dragon! Can you squeeze by Rhindle, or will you end up trapped in the narrow corridors of the maze? You can only carry one object at a time, and you dropped the Sword when you found the Black Key. With the Sword, you could slay Rhindle. But can you remember exactly where it is? You better decide quickly, because Rhindle is rapidly approaching! These emergent narratives are ensconced within the larger fairytale context of the game, and are made possible by the way that the simple yet structurally intricate space of Adventure frames and enables game action. The formal game elements become narratively meaningful within the story context that the game provides.

Narrative Descriptors

On a black screen there's nothing but white Rorschach-shaped outlines moving around, and you're to hit them, so to speak, before they hit you. Once you've figured out what "you" is. The name on the machine implies you're in a field of asteroids, not that you know what a field of asteroids is, or what it'd be like to be a being in one.— **David Sudnow,** *Pilgrim in the Microworld*

We will return presently to the narrative play of digital games. But first we must pause to identify a key storytelling element: *narrative descriptors.* Narrative descriptors are representations, which means that they are depictions of one or more aspects of the game world. Games offer players narrative descriptors on many levels. Graphics on the side of arcade cabinets depict objects or characters that will appear in the game world. Game manual text explains many aspects of a game experience, from the interactive controls to plot and backstory. Audio soundtracks help establish and embellish the narrative setting, while opening cinematics tell us what the game world looks like and why we are there. Even within game play, graphical elements and sound effects communicate the narrative identity of game objects and characters. Each type of narrative descriptor plays a different storytelling role in explicating the game universe, creating a narrative context for events and actions.

Everything in a game is potentially a kind of narrative descriptor. Thinking in terms of narrative descriptors means framing the elements inside and outside of a game as objects that communicate the story. As players, we rely on narrative description to help us make sense of the settings, events, and characters encountered. Although narrative descriptors bear some relation to the formal structure of a game, they are somewhat separable from it. The very same game can be depicted in different ways by different narrative descriptors. For example, Breakout has been narrativized in a number of ways. The original arcade game had pictures of escaping prisoners on the game cabinet, telling the story of a jailbreak. In this case, the layers of blocks on

the screen represent the walls of the prison from which the prisoner is attempting to "break out." The first Atari 2600 version of Breakout framed the narrative as a Pong-style Tennis match: the box cover featured stylish illustrations of Tennis players. The sequel Super Breakout moved into the realm of science fiction, a lone spaceship facing off against a mysterious force field.

Although the core formal structure of Breakout remained the same in each of these three variations, the framing narrative changed radically. But don't get the wrong impression: this doesn't mean that any narrative can be applied to any game. In the case of Breakout, the abstract quality of the game graphics and sound lent themselves more easily to multiple narrative interpretations. Furthermore, each of the three narrative frameworks (jailbreak, Tennis match, force field) bore a genuine relationship to the actual game play, although each narrative emphasized different aspects of the game structure and interaction.

It is interesting to note that narrative descriptors are not always effective in creating a clear context for interaction. In Super Breakout, for example, the written narrative in the game manual is actually somewhat confusing. We quoted it at the beginning of this chapter, but below is a short excerpt:

> Suddenly, without warning, there's a brilliant flash straight ahead. You check the radar screen. Nothing. Pretty soon there's another flash, and another. Next thing you know the flashes have turned into one gigantic force field of some kind and it's dead ahead. You check the radar screen, still nothing.

From a game play perspective, this narrative is strangely disconnected from player interaction. Twice in the text the "you" of the narrative checks the radar screen. What radar screen? There isn't any radar element in the game at all. And what about the flashes of light? When the game begins, there are no flashes of light, only solid rows of colored blocks and a ball. What is it suppose to mean? The narrative's insistent emphasis on the blankness of the radar screen, the fact that the force field doesn't show up on the spaceship's radar, emphasizes the light-based immateriality of the Breakout experience, still a novelty in the early era of digital gaming. Perhaps the text references the first moment of play, the instant the television set is turned on and the darkness suddenly lights up with the glowing pattern of a warming cathode ray tube. Sometimes, a narrative descriptor doesn't have to provide a logical basis for play, and can simply reference a more general narrative genre. In the case of Super Breakout, the descriptor fails to produce an accurate narrative for the impending game play, but it does tell a wonderfully meta-textual story of electrons dancing on a phosphor screen, circa 1981.

In addition to acting as a "frame" for the central game play, narrative descriptors also can appear within a game. In Thunderstorm there is little or no pre-game narrative set-up that describes player interaction. Instead, the narrative play of Thunderstorm transforms the numbers on the dice into a story of an approaching storm, during the game itself. Lines on a page become houses; dice rolls become acts of construction and destruction. Narrative descriptors work in two ways. They can act to identify objects or events inside a game: "prison," "house," "thunderstorm," "force field." They can also provide frameworks of interaction for players: "this is a game about thunderstorms;""this is a Tennis simulation." (These two uses of descriptors correspond directly with the two modes of game representation from the previous chapter—that games *can represent* and that they *are representations*.)

Let's take a close look at one game, Asteroids, to see how it integrates narrative descriptors to create a compelling game experience. The game instructions on the arcade cabinet contain the following text:

> Shoot the asteroids while avoiding collisions with them. Occasionally a flying saucer will appear and attempt to shoot you down with guided missiles. Destroy it or the missiles for more points.

What information does this narrative description contain? We can infer that:

- There are two kinds of objects in the game we will battle: asteroids and flying saucers. Both have destructive capabilities. Destruction occurs through collision, either with an asteroid or a guided missile.

- Interaction with the asteroids takes two forms: we can shoot them or we can maneuver around the asteroids to avoid contact.

- Interaction with the flying saucers involves shooting and maneuvering as well. Because the flying saucers use guided missiles, it will be more difficult to outmaneuver them.

- Flying saucers are more rare and therefore more valuable. We gain additional points by destroying them.

- Flying saucers are active enemies: they will try to destroy us. Asteroids are passive enemies: we must avoid running into them.

- The movement of the asteroids is independent of the movement of our ship, whereas the movement of the guided missiles is directly linked to it.

- The guided missiles can destroy asteroids if we position our ship behind an asteroid. The asteroid then becomes a shield for the ship.

So much information contained within such a short descriptor! But there is more. Although it is not explicitly stated that we are in a spaceship or that we are in outer space, both of these facts follow from the instructions. We know asteroids and flying saucers exist in outer space, not in the desert or the ocean. We also know that if we are able to shoot and maneuver we must be in a vehicle that allows these actions. We can conclude from the story's narrative logic that we are in a spaceship. The details about our spaceship—what it is called, what it uses for fuel, the size of the crew—don't matter. The key narrative information is that it can maneuver and shoot the enemy.

But what if a player skips over the instructions and just starts playing? Without the introductory textual description, will players know what to do? In a well-designed game like Asteroids the answer is yes, as there are many other narrative descriptors to orient the player. First, the name of the game and the hard-to-miss cabinet graphics communicate that Asteroids is a science-fiction narrative that takes place in outer space and that the white geometric outlines moving on the dark screen are *asteroids*. Second, the representation of objects in the game world provides information about what they are and what forms of interaction will take place. When the game begins, the screen is filled with many asteroids but only one arrow-shaped object, located dead center. If the central placement and unique identity of the arrow-shaped object is not enough of a clue, a player who simply starts mashing the button interface will quickly discover that he or she can directly control the arrow (but not the asteroids). It is easy to conclude that the arrow object represents the player, situated in the game world of an asteroid field.

A player unfamiliar with the game or its objectives will quickly be smashed to bits by an asteroid. This dramatic event is represented by a visual and audio explosion, as well as by the removal of one of the player's remaining ships from the corner of the screen. The act of being destroyed by an asteroid contains a wealth of information for the player, signifying that the asteroids are lethal and should be avoided. When a flying saucer suddenly appears and starts shooting at the player, it is logical to infer that it too is an enemy and therefore worthy of destruction. When a player successfully destroys a flying saucer and receives bonus points, he or she learns that flying saucers are more valuable than asteroids. Flying saucers only appear at intermittent intervals, and their rarity emphasizes their bonus point value and their extra degree of deadliness.

Each of these events is made possible by a narrative descriptor, a *representation* that helps players understand the activity of the game within a larger narrative context. In Asteroids, all of the narrative elements are both integrated and discernable, the two key qualities of meaningful play. Even without reading the instructions, players can, through interaction with the game world, experience narrative play. This is a sign of a well-designed game, one that provides a clear and compelling system of meaning. In this kind of context, play itself reveals the narrative meaning of the game world.

Every element of a game brims with narrative potential. The narrative components of a game are not just the backstory and cutscenes. *Any* representational element can be a narrative descriptor, an opportunity for you to communicate the story that you want your players to experience. In Asteroids, the game elements, the interface, and even the arcade game cabinet all play a role in the narrative. Nothing is irrelevant: every piece helps tell the story, which is greater than the sum of the parts. Is *your* game narrative as tightly and elegantly designed as Asteroids?

Worlds and Stories

Representations in games do not exist in isolation from the rest of culture. They rely on conventions drawn from narrative genres in other media. Although the playgrounds of games may offer fictive and fantastical spaces, these spaces are almost always familiar in some way to players. The deep space of Asteroids is not something any of us have experienced directly, but it is part of a genre-based universe found in the stories of science fiction writers and astrophysicists. Players can appreciate the narrative of the game even if they have never piloted a space ship in a field of asteroids, because of the familiar conventions of its representation.

In order to understand the setting of a game world, players rely on knowledge from other, similar stories. Players starting a game of Asteroids for the first time know what to do in part because they are familiar with a fictive genre describing interactions between spaceships, flying saucers, and asteroids in outer space. *(UFOs that shoot at you are enemies and must be destroyed or avoided.)* The narrative knowledge that players bring with them to games not only helps them recognize the conventions of the game universe, but also limits and constrains their actions. As game scholar Rune Klevjer writes in an analysis of Grand Theft Auto III,

> Sniping a Columbian gangster in the head in GTA III is one thing. Doing the same to, say, a little girl would not be the same (consequently, there are no children in Liberty City). The difference between these two representations is partly rooted in their respective real-world references—a mean-looking adult male versus a pretty little girl—but also linked to a specific, typified universe constructed by the game. Within this familiar fictional ready-made, the mean-looking guy turns into (through a few, stylized hints) a very familiar gangster of the most ruthless, drug-dealing kind.[12]

Grand Theft Auto III takes place within the pulp genre setting of urban gang warfare and organized crime. As a fictional universe, a set of narrative conventions stylizes this world. Shooting a gangster fits within these narrative conventions, whereas doing the same to a little girl does not. Similarly, being attacked by flying saucers in Asteroids establishes a narrative frame that wouldn't include an Appalachian mountain man firing at the player with a slingshot. In other words, the setting of a game determines the characters, events, and actions permitted within its narrative frame.

> The gangster universe [of GTA III] as a setting, and as a set-up for play, is partly founded on the formulaic stories told within it. The actions performed by the player…become meaningful within the genre-based universe as a whole. "Story" and "fictional world" are two flips of the same coin—a pre-written, typified symbolic action, defining a typical identity of the playground. Even though we can imagine a similar fictional world without one, single, overarching story framing the game play, there would at least have to be recognizable narrative elements that could give some more genre-specific substance to an otherwise vague atmosphere of urban crime. In genre fiction, description evokes implied narratives, and narration evokes implied description.[13]

Klevjer identifies two components of game narratives: *fictive worlds,* which represent narrative context, and *story events,* the actual game incidents that take place within the fictive world. There is a complex relationship between these two narrative elements, each informing and enriching the other with narrative meaning. In Asteroids, the fictive world is the genre of space-based science fiction, and the story events are the actions that happen to the player's ship and other game elements within this narrative setting. The story events of shooting, maneuvering, destruction, and survival gain narrative meaning from the larger fictive world of the game, even as they simultaneously help to define that fictive world.

It may seem like fictive worlds and story events mirror the concepts of embedded and emergent narrative structures. Actually, they are not parallel concepts. The embedded/emergent distinction identifies how narrative elements are organized in the formal structure of a game: is this narrative element pre-generated or does it emerge from play? Fictive worlds and story events reference game narrative in a very different way, on the level of a player's imaginative engagement with the game story. Both embedded and emergent elements can play a part in defining either a game's fictive world or its story events.

Klevjer's concepts provide a useful way to think about game narratives. Too often, a game's fictive world is taken for granted, a generic backdrop for scripted plot events. Game designers should more rigorously engage with the complex, interdependent relationship between the fictive world and story events. The events of the plot, the "game story," are made possible by the existence of a larger fictional world in which the story takes place. At the same time, the story events themselves help to flesh out and inform the fictive world. Designing fictive worlds means paying close attention to the narratives such worlds inspire. And vice versa. Together these two elements of game narratives create an artificial context where game experience acquires narrative meaning. Although the crazy cartoon world of Super Mario does not mirror the space of the real world, events within the universe of Super Mario faithfully follow our expectations of the kinds of things that should happen in that world. Players are not surprised or confused to come across colorful magic mushrooms, cute and menacing enemies, or gigantic green pipes. Each of these elements makes narrative sense within the specific setting of a Super Mario game. The inclusion of a photorealistically rendered dog, on the other hand, would feel out of place. Thus, narrative descriptors imply a representational logic that limits and constrains the design of the space of possibility. These limitations allow for the integration and discernability of all elements contained with the game world, a world whose setting describes the limits of its own action.

When designing a game it is critical to pay attention to the relationship between the narrative setting of the game world and the kinds of events that would occur within such a setting. If you are designing a far-future anti-gravity racing game, the narrative descriptors of characters, events, objects, and behaviors should be contained within the logical limits of this setting. Players should have a sense that the technology powering their vehicles has not yet been invented, and that the physics affecting the speed and movement of the vehicles is not something they have experienced on Earth. The design of a board game titled "Dot.Com Mania" should model the events and aesthetics of the 1990s bubble economy, not that of the Great Depression, perhaps taking visual and story cues from films like *Startup.com* and magazines like *Red Herring*. Creating game narratives means playing in the realms of culture, engaging with tropes and conventions of genres from literature, media, popular culture, entertainment, and art. Incorporating representational frameworks from relevant narratives will help you elaborate on and transform those frameworks in ways that lead to compelling (and perhaps unusual) game experiences.

This certainly doesn't mean that you can only design games that exist within established narrative genres. It is possible to create new kinds of fictive worlds or combine and re-mix conventional narrative universes in new ways. Rules are made to be broken. Perhaps it is possible to drop a photorealistic dog into a Super Mario-like game. But the resulting game narrative has to incorporate this inconsistency in a coherent way. Perhaps the game is about a real world dog that became transported into a video game (hence the different representational style). Or maybe it becomes a game with a collage aesthetic, in which *every* character has its own unique visual language.

When you are creating games with less typical narrative experiences, your design task becomes more challenging. Your players will not already be familiar with your game's fictive world. For example, what are the narrative conventions of a game about office supplies that come to life at night when the workers go home? In this case, it is up to the game designer to establish the fictive world for the player as quickly as possible, perhaps making direct or indirect reference to relevant narratives, such as *Toy Story's* inexplicably living toys, the playful tale of Pinocchio, or even the office life parody *9-to-5*. Each of these narrative contexts offers different ways to establish both the fictive world and to organize the events that happen within it.

Crafting Game Narratives

How do you create the details of a narrative that will let you achieve the fictional world and story events that you want your players to experience? There is no single magic formula, and as storytellers in every medium know, the devil is in the details. Because our focus is game design, this book does not include sections on the visual aesthetics of character design, tips for writing in-game dialogue, or other specifics of how to construct narrative descriptors. However, we can offer some general ways of thinking about the craft of game narratives. By paying careful attention to the details of your game representations, and how they bridge the formal game system and the player experience, you will be able to generate meaningful narrative play.

Consider the following text from the Wipeout XL game manual:

> Future world…
>
> A ball bounces. A pin drops. A man falls.
>
> Gravity is the glue which binds us to our planet.
>
> We are about to apply the solvent which will free our species for-
> ever.—Pierre Belmondo, Director of European AG [anti-gravity]
> Research, Nevada, April 2035

Although Wipeout XL's introductory narrative is extremely abstract, it communicates a sense of what it is going to *feel* like within this future world. The sparseness of the description, the metaphors of gravity's glue and the solvent used to "free our species forever," work to create an emotional story context. The formal qualities of the narrative description establish a particular mood and setting. If the text had been written in Middle English, the narrative context of the world would feel quite different. *How* something is said is just as important as *what* is said when you are creating narrative contexts. This text, situated within the future-stylish, techno visual context of the Wipeout XL game graphics, acquires yet more narrative meaning, even as it imbues the rest of the game with meanings of its own.

Consider the design of objects or settings. The visual and audio aesthetics of Silent Hill creates a distinctly creepy and unsettling atmosphere. The home movie-style opening sequence, set to discordant music, establishes a mood of underlying horror that is supported by the limited use of light throughout the game. Even in daylight it is foggy and difficult to see very far. When it is dark, a player's field of vision is limited to the tight radius of a single flashlight. Light operates as a narrative element, creating a dense mood and a framework for cautious interaction. Audio is also significant in creating the distinctive narrative experience of Silent Hill. Background noises such as the haunting sobs of a child in the deserted school create a larger narrative setting and work to gradually unnerve the player. The unsettling, distinctive sounds of approaching enemies,

which range from flapping winged beasts to harmless ghost babies to shuffling homicidal nurses, foreshadow their likely appearance and attack. The game uses cinematic storytelling techniques to good effect, by intrinsically linking them to the game system and player interaction: the enemies are revealed first in sound, then in visuals, then through combat interaction. Gratuitous "spooky" sound effects can quickly wear thin, but when those effects signify future game events, the player will sit up and take notice.

Narrative descriptors in games include everything from the written introduction to the opening cinematic, from the design of light and sound to the style of the game interface. These narrative elements not only pertain to plot, character, and setting, but also give players information about the types of interaction that are appropriate and how they are to behave. Together, these elements form an interlocking, complex narrative system, from which the player's narrative experience emerges. How does this experience become meaningful play? Through design choices that create discernable and integrated relationships among the parts of the system. In all of the successful examples of narrative play discussed so far, the core design values of integration and discernability still hold true. For example, the approaching enemy sound effects in Silent Hill become meaningful because they are integrated into the game system, warning the player about impending known (or unknown) monsters in a way that is consistently clear and discernable.

Games as Narrative Systems

The creation of a game narrative is really the creation of a narrative *system*. This notion unifies all of the concepts presented so far in this chapter. As a design problem, creating the narrative elements of a game is very much like creating other aspects of your game. You are crafting a system of parts, simple elements that interrelate to form a complex whole. The meanings that emerge from a system arise out of the individual relationships between elements, as well as the more global patterns that emerge across many sets of smaller relationships.

Case Study: Drome Racing as Narrative System

Even games that are not explicitly oriented toward story creation can be framed as a narrative system. The LEGO Drome Racing Challenge is a massively multiplayer game in which players create a game persona, collect and customize LEGO race cars, and then race them against each other on a variety of tracks. During a race, players do not directly control their cars but instead see how their racing strategies and car customization plays out on the constantly changing tracks. As a large-scale community game, the Drome Racing Challenge offers many modes of interaction, manifesting narrative play though a variety of means.

As a game system, the narrative of the Drome Racing Challenge emerges from the interaction of the many parts of the game. The total narrative experience of the Drome Racing Challenge does not lie in any one of these individual elements, but instead, their overall effect arises out of the system as a whole, which includes:

Pre-existing backstory. The game exists within a larger narrative world that includes comic books and the LEGO Racers toy products. This sci-fi racing fictive world, where speed-hungry drivers compete against each other in the many dangerous tracks of the Drome, provides the setting for the game, as well as the primary frame for the narrative play.

Player as protagonist. Each player constructs a driver character that represents him or her in the world of the Drome Racing Challenge. This driver is defined through a cluster of narrative descriptors: team name and colors, helmet icon, racing motto, and text phrases that the driver utters when making or accepting a racing challenge and winning or losing a race. All of these characteristics are embedded narrative content, selected by the player from pregenerated lists. Other player characteristics, such as a player's racing record, status on the leader boards, progress toward the next license rank, and particular cars and parts collected and assembled, are more modular and emergent ways of personifying the player.

Multiple goals. The Drome Racing Challenge embeds long- and short-term goals throughout the game experience and ties them directly into the narrative. Players build a collection of cars and parts, upgrade and evolve cars that they own, improve their license class, compete on the rankings boards, and interact in limited social ways with other players through the narrative world of the game.

The total narrative experience of Ms. Pac-Man arises from a myriad of components: the title of the game and its reference to the existing narrative of Pac-Man, the arcade cabinet graphics and text, the looping animated title screens, the in-game cartoons between levels, and all of the visual and audio elements of the game itself. These elements do not exist in isolation, but combine to form a narrative whole that is more than the sum of the parts. The narrative is multi-faceted, and not only establishes a cartoony fictive world and a romantic backstory for the protagonist, but also provides a narrative framework for the game play itself. The play produces intense emergent narratives of insatiably hungry consumption, strategic avoidance and survival, and dramatic turnabout where the hunted temporarily becomes the hunter. These emergent experiences exist in counterpoint to the light and colorful fictive world of the game, resulting in a richly textured narrative experience in which every element plays a part.

A game oriented more explicitly toward narrative play is Advanced Dungeons & Dragons. In D&D and other tabletop role-playing games, the game is a system for generating narrative play, a system that can help define the characters, settings, conflicts, plots, and goals of the game narrative. These designed game materials usually include a formal system that details the rules of the game, as well as a narrative world that provides the overall settings and backstory. These two components are intertwined into the larger narrative system of the game. For example, in the fantasy medieval world of D&D, rules for armored swordplay, fantastical creatures, and magical spells are included, whereas rules for computer technology are not.

Although players can purchase pre-generated D&D adventures, it is more common for a game's Dungeon Master (the player that leads each role-playing session) to create original adventures. The Dungeon Master leads the rest of the players through these homebrewed stories, each participant role-playing a single player-character. The Dungeon Master provides the rest of the narrative elements, describing each setting the players enter, role-playing allies and enemies the players encounter, and slowly revealing the dark mysteries and unexpected plot twists of the ongoing story.

Dungeons & Dragons and other similar games are quite explicit story-creation systems, designed to facilitate the structured, collaborative authorship of narrative play. Each player is a part of that system, as are the player-characters, the Dungeon Master, and the many elements of the game world. These game world components might be formally defined (*a long sword does 1–12 points of damage*), narratively defined (*the wizard hermit doesn't seem to like us*), or both (*if we can convince the wizard to enchant my long sword, it will do +2 damage*). As the players converse, roll dice, and consult the game rules, they enact pitched battles and dramatic dialogues, brokering power, knowledge, and personality as they together create meaningful narrative play. Every action taken, whether a difficult feat that requires a die roll or a clever conversational stratagem, has its place in the overall narrative system, buoyed up by the formal rules that make such actions possible. Actions simultaneously expand the ongoing story as new narrative elements are added to the series of events.

Cutscenes

*Kane sneering out from the briefing video of **Command and Conquer**. Lantern light over a wrecked inn in **Diablo II**. Bahamut blasting your foes to ashes in **Final Fantasy VII**. There is no doubt that the humble cutscene has left its mark on the memories of most gamers. But how did these beautiful scenes affect the gameplay of the titles they graced?—**Hugh Hancock**, "Better Game Design Through Cut-Scenes"*

The concepts for designing narrative play we have identified so far are relevant for all kinds of games, on and off the computer. However, there are new forms and techniques for the design of narrative play emerging specifically from digital games, and we finish this chapter by investigating a few of them. One narrative

Drome Racing Challenge

Narrative space. Initially, every player goes through a short introductory tutorial. After that, the player is free to create his or her own patterns of movement through the game. As a web-based game, the Drome Racing Challenge consists primarily of HTML web pages, designed in the high-speed future-style of the Drome. The narrative space of the game is a space of information and technology rather than a represented physical space, appropriate for the media-centric fictive world of the game.

Patterns of activity. The two core activities of the game are customizing cars and racing them on tracks. Both activities have their own dramatic structures and patterns. Car customization occurs in the "garage," a narrativized pit-stop and auto store where players acquire and manipulate car parts, attaching them to slots in their cars. In the garage, players prepare for a race, tuning and tweaking their cars for particular tracks. A common game play pattern is to run a few races, then head back to the garage to buy a new part, tweak a car, and return to the tracks to test it out. This behavioral loop becomes a narrative pattern, evoking the dedicated lifestyle of a hard-working race driver.

The race. In some respects, the race preparation is simply a prelude for the dramatic narrative moments of an actual race. Once a player readies a car and places it on a track, any other player can challenge it. The game program generates a race made up of random hazards and obstacles, takes into account both of the customized cars entered into the race, and generates a series of race events as a result. The program translates this formal information into a 2D cartoon, emergently created by software that uses the race events to structure pacing and shot structure. The animation then plays out as a Speed Racer-style, action-packed sequence of events. Abstract speed lines, informational overlays, and inset views of the drivers are combined with shots of the vehicles racing through the Drome's hazardous environments. The resulting experience references the cartoony, sci-fi style of the overall game space, generating a compelling narrative out of the linkages among descriptor aesthetics, the fictive world frame, and meaningful game outcomes.

design tool many digital games utilize is the cutscene. Although cutscenes are often described as being "out-of-game" narratives that cut into game play, this distinction is only useful if we limit the definition of game play to those moments when players take action within the game world. As we know, all kinds of narrative descriptors, from the graphics on a game box to the text in a game manual, are important in defining a game's fictive world. Rather than focusing on whether cutscenes occur in or out of game play, we want to consider the *role* of cutscenes in the overall design of narrative play.

Cutscenes take many forms, from text-based descriptions to comic-book style storyboards to real-time 3D cinematics or pre-rendered animated sequences. Sometimes these forms are mixed, as in Max Payne, which combines real-time cinematics with the visual language of a graphic novel to tell its story. Pre-scripted voice-overs or text-based captions are often combined with animated visual sequences; sound usually plays an important role in establishing a mood or atmosphere. In all of these cases, cutscenes are clearly an *embedded* narrative element—a scripted narrative sequence that is the same every time.

As storytelling devices integrated into the formal structure of the game, cutscenes contain narrative descriptors on many levels. More than other game elements, cutscenes closely resemble existing forms of narrative media: they are linear, pre-scripted, non-interactive, and story-driven. Even the term "cutscene" refers to their patently filmic nature. The ubiquity of cutscenes sometimes earns them derision from experienced game players, but in fact, cutscenes contribute to narrative play in a number of important ways. As Hugh Hancock writes in "Better Game Design Through Cut-Scenes:"

> The cutscene is there to make a game's world more real—not just by telling a story, but also by reacting to the player, by showing him the effects of his actions upon that world and thus making both the world more real and his actions more important. The cutscene

fills the role of both prequel and epilogue: showing the player what the world is like before he enters it, what needs he has to fill, what he has to work with and what he has to face, and afterwards showing what the effects of his actions upon the world were, whether good, bad or both.[13]

Although we might quibble with Hancock's use of the term "real," we agree with the spirit of his statement. Cutscenes are a way of leading players through the narrative space of a game, highlighting key moments and punctuating important events and outcomes. As a kind of narrative in miniature, cutscenes help fill out the larger narrative frame of the game, playing a crucial role in establishing the fictive world of a game's story. They can introduce story, setting, and character, particularly in the early sections of a game when players are still becoming familiar with the game world. The cutscenes in GTA III help establish the pulp gangster setting of the game. Because this is a narrative genre that often appears in filmic form, the highly cinematic cutscenes do a more efficient job of setting up these narrative conventions than the moments of game action.

Cutscenes may "cut" into player interaction, but they directly support narrative play on many levels. Cutscenes can foreshadow events to come, operate as flashbacks, or create transitions between settings. They can show players how to interact with objects and give players information about resources in the game. Consider the following uses of cutscenes, some of which come from Hancock's essay:

Surveillance or Planning Tool
Cutscenes can provide players with access to information unavailable to them during game play. As a surveillance tool, cutscenes might allow players a glimpse of another part of the game space, or provide information on the current whereabouts of a character or treasure they are seeking. As a planning tool, cutscenes can provide players with information about an event or obstacle they will soon encounter, or elaborate on the outcome of an action.

Drome Racing Challenge

Multiple narrative tellings. After a race, the race events are translated into a "race analysis." The race analysis is a spreadsheet-style summary of each race event, listing the car and track factors that determined its outcome. The exact same race events that appeared in the animation here become numbers and text, interpreted through a new set of narrative descriptors that emphasize strategic, rather than visual, play.

Drome Racing animation

Say you just completed a mission that used up most of your health resources. A cutscene shows that you are about to encounter a heavily armed opponent. What to do? Perhaps you should to return to the previous level and garner more health. Or maybe it's time to haul out that powerful limited-use weapon that you have been saving for an emergency. Because the cutscene provided you with useful information about the implications of your past actions in relation to an upcoming event, you can plan accordingly. Cutscenes create narrative scenarios that can enrich the decision-making process for players.

Game Play Catapult

Although cutscenes are often used informationally to provide players with critical data, they can also work to catapult a player into a new situation. They can add narrative drama by building suspense, or provide narrative movement from one situation to the next.

For example, imagine that you are in an adventure game and you have just solved a puzzle that rewarded you with a rope. It is an unusual reward and you are not sure what to do with it, as you are traveling through a desert: not much use for a rope here! The animated cutscene that follows shows a trapdoor at the top of the next sand dune. Just as the cutscene makes a dramatic pan from your casually strolling character to the open trapdoor, the cutscene ends and you find yourself back in active game play, falling through the trapdoor and down an abyss. Thinking quickly you use the rope to lasso a rocky overhang. Safe now, you check your surroundings and realize that you are no longer in the desert, but are hanging high above a river in the middle of a dense forest.

In this instance the cutscene not only catapulted the player into the middle of a dramatic game event, but also transported the player to another part of the game world. Cutscenes that drop players directly into the middle of

game action allow them to resolve the cutscene's mininarrative through game play. Using a cutscene in this way enhances suspense and drama by grafting the non-interactive sequence directly to player action.

Scene and Mood Setting

Many digital games consist of a series of linked levels or game spaces. Although these levels or spaces are part of a larger system, they each have their own unique identity. Cutscenes can reinforce the differences between settings and highlight what might be new and unusual about an upcoming level. In Virtua Fighter 4, for example, there are fifteen different fighting arenas. Brief cutscenes used before each bout show off the details of the environment, establishing the setting and creating a sense of place for the upcoming match.

Cutscenes can also establish mood, or reinforce the emotional arc of game events. As players move deeper into Silent Hill, the cutscenes become increasingly eerie and disturbing. In Final Fantasy IX, cutscenes reinforce the epic quality of the hero's journey through the use of dramatic animation, sound, and editing. The tongue-in-cheek dialogue of Max Payne's cutscenes lends an ironic edge to the urban noir of the game world. In each example, cutscenes establish a mood that becomes part of the game's narrative play.

Choice and Consequence

Cutscenes give game designers the power to dramatically reveal the outcomes of player choices, outcomes that can affect not only the player's character, but often the game world as well. Cutscenes can show a player's character achieving a goal, such as winning a race and receiving a gold medal, or saving a planet and being surrounded by throngs of cheering civilians. Cutscenes can also show failure outcomes, when goals are not achieved or poor choices are made: a protracted grisly death sequence, a scene of swarming enemies ravaging the game world, or a shot of the bad guy riding off with both the treasure *and* the girl. Representing the consequences of player actions in story form enriches the narrative play of the game and often makes the game world feel more alive.

Rhythm and Pacing

In James Bond 007 In Agent Under Fire, short cutscenes provide regular moments of release from intense action, allowing a player to catch his or her breath or contemplate upcoming choices. The rhythm created by the cutscenes is a way of controlling the game's overall pacing. Once the pattern has been established, players learn to expect breaks in game action, which can heighten the pace or slow it down. At the conclusion of a big battle, for instance, the pace of the game can be reduced by inserting a slow-motion cutscene of the falling enemy, or it can be sped up by immediately catapulting the player into the middle of another battle. Variation and control of cutscene pacing contributes to narrative play by emphasizing specific moments in a game. A long, slow cutscene that follows a player's solution to a particularly difficult puzzle can signify the importance of the event in the overall game experience.

Player Reward

In *Games as the Play of Pleasure,* we explored games as a series of punishments and rewards. Cutscenes are often used for both of these purposes: as a visceral punishment for failure as well as a tangible reward for achieving a game goal. As Hancock notes, "the *Final Fantasy* series' game play is often driven by this imperative, whether trying to advance through the game to see the next cutscene in the story, or trying to find the magical 'summon' spells within the game, which a lot of people have noted are primarily worth finding in order to enjoy the spectacular animations which accompany them."[14] The gorgeous

Hardcore Gamers and Cutscenes

Within communities of game developers and game players, debate rages about the value of cutscenes. Hardcore gamers have a reputation for ignoring game guides, opening cinematics, and in-game cutscenes, preferring to dive right into the action. If one purpose of these elements is to provide information about the game world and setting, what happens when players skip over this information? If these dedicated gamers have no problem stepping into the narrative space of game play despite their avoidance of cutscenes, does this mean that the information and experiences they provide is superfluous?

Many long-time gamers make the argument that narrative descriptors found in cutscenes and game manuals do not affect game play. This argument is both true and false. It is true that these forms of narrative description are not necessary for *their* play of the game. Remember that a chief function of these framing devices is to establish the game's fictive world. As hardcore gamers, these impatient players have experienced enough games to have internalized the common uses of game setting and story. Their long experience with the codes and conventions of games—with stories, settings, events, and characters—has replaced the need for an external description of these worlds.

Players who lack this experience, on the other hand, have much to gain from the information provided in backstories and opening cinematics. Even expert players in one genre of game will find narrative descriptors useful when playing a game from another genre for the first time. In a complex role-playing game, for example, the explication of the story in the game guide creates a context for the interactions to come. A player quickly learns the premise and goal of the game, the kinds of actions she can take in the game world, the characters she will meet along the way, and above all, why she is in the game world in the first place. This kind of information might not be self-evident to a gamer that plays mostly simulation games.

The lesson? Design for both types of players. Never assume that your players will carefully examine every framing narrative descriptor: be sure to make your story come alive in the actual play of the game. On the other hand, when appropriate you should feel free to embellish your core game events with opening cutscenes and other preliminary narratives that extend your fictive world for players that want a richer story experience. If you manage to hook players with your game play, they may go back and actually watch the introductory cinematic they skipped earlier to make sure they didn't miss anything important.

cinematic cutscenes in Warcraft III were designed, in part, to reward players for their investment in many hours of game play. Although using cutscenes as rewards might seem like a straightforward design idea, the experience of receiving such a gift during game play can be tremendously satisfying and motivating.

There are plenty of other ways to employ cutscenes in the design of narrative play, whether by mixing and matching the uses listed here or by finding completely different methods that are better suited for your own game. However, it is worth noting that games certainly do not have to include cutscenes. Narrative play arises from the complex interaction between numerous elements of a game system. Cutscenes represent just one of these possible elements, albeit one that is highly narrative in its own right.

Retelling Game Stories

*It's natural for players to construct a story from a game play experience, but it is not inevitable, nor is the story the game.—**Greg Costikyan**, RE:PLAY*

*Narrative has happened, or been created, while "playing" is always happening, a particular realization of the potential offered by the game, the precise shape or outcome of which is indeterminate.—**Geoff King and Tanya Krzywinska**, "Computer Games / Cinema / Interfaces"*

When does the narrative play of a game become a narrative *about* the play of the game? When is game experience retold as story? There is a difference between playing the narrative of a game and telling the story about that play experience. Up to this point in the present schema our exploration has dealt strictly with narrative play within the space of the magic circle. We examined how narrative play emerges from elements within the game world and how game designers can craft meaningful narrative contexts for their players.

But narrative play can also occur when a story is created through a recounting of a game experience. Why does this retelling occur? Below are examples of various reasons why players re-count game experiences.

To recount a particularly dramatic victory: *You should have seen it! I had just a sliver of health left, but I threw one of those elbow-backfist-spin-kick combos, followed by a triple dragon punch. I barely finished him off!*

To share a series of story events: *In a game last week our characters were attacked and we were forced into an emergency landing on an asteroid. We were rescued by the local population who fed us and took care of our injured crew. But unbeknownst to everyone, we were carrying a virus deadly to their species, spawning an epidemic. Many people died.*

To share strategic information: *I found this secret door at the beginning of the mission that let me sneak up behind the demon snipers and I was able to get through the entire level using only the chainsaw.*

To celebrate the pleasure of play: *I was running so fast I felt like I was flying!*

It is common for players to construct stories out of game play experience, creating narratives that exist separately from the actual narrative play in the game. This is a subtle point that bears repeating. Narrative play *within* game play emerges from a player's interaction with the game system. Narrative play *outside* of game play is the retelling of this experience in story form. This phenomenon of *retelling play* shouldn't seem surprising. When we see a great movie or overcome a life obstacle, there is a natural tendency to share this personal information with friends. Games can also represent powerful experiences in our lives that we want to share and relive with others, particularly other game players that will appreciate the details of play. Retelling play helps build communities of players through a common interest in the experience of a particular game.

Retelling play can take many diverse forms, such as verbally recounting a Dungeons & Dragons encounter, pantomiming a thrilling Basketball play, posting a sequence of edited Sim City screenshots online, writing fan fiction about an EverQuest adventure, watching an instant replay in a drag racing stadium, text-chatting about a Tennis match post-game, or uploading a recorded demo of a Quake deathmatch to a community website. Because retelling play is such a common phenomenon, game designers have found many strategies for fostering it. What about including an instant messaging system within your online game that allows players to comment on the action while playing? Or allowing players to review recorded game actions after the fact? Or providing functions that let players take screengrabs of your game to post online? All of these are existing devices game designers use to support re-telling play. In the next few pages, we look at strategies for designing retelling play in more detail.

The Replay

One common tool designed for retelling play is the in-game *replay* mode. Many sports games such as Tony Hawk's Pro Skater 3 or NBA Courtside offer this function, which allows players to watch a recording of their game play. Players can usually save replays, giving them a chance to review their greatest moments many times over. In NBA Courtside, for example, the Instant Replay mode affords players the opportunity to look at the action from any vantage point. A zoom function allows for a close-up look at players' faces, which can be enjoyable in a game where NBA greats such as Karl Malone have lent their faces for digitization. The Instant Replay mode also offers seamless, frame-by-frame slow-motion advancement of the game footage by interpolating between key frames in a move.

The design of the replay mode can heighten the drama of the retelling by offering players dramatic camerawork or shifting points of view. In the XBox driving game Wreckless: The Yakuza Missions, the sophisticated replays involve shifting cameras, changing filmic styles, and dramatic pacing. Players watch the

replay unfold from a variety of perspectives, as the camera quickly shifts from a wide overhead shot to a racing view from under the chassis to an extreme close-up of the car's battle-dented hood. There are quick cuts and jittery camera work, and the program simulates a constant shifting of "film stock," moving between shots that look like they were taken on 35mm film, 16mm film, a home video camera, and grainy black and white surveillance footage, with the occasional wireframe rendering thrown into the mix. The resulting narrative flavor produces a high-powered feeling of immediacy, increasing a player's connection to the "reality" of their game play. The replays become short films to watch, enjoy, and share.

The driving game Gran Turismo 3 offers several different types of replay modes, giving players multiple incentives to view their victories and defeats. The Standard replay mode follows a player's own car around the track, useful for reviewing the events of a race. Race mode skips around to any of the cars on the track, greatly increasing the narrative drama of the playback. The strategically helpful Training mode overlays a glowing line on the track to show the most efficient racing path. Video mode synchronizes the replay to any song on the game's soundtrack, from Snoop Dog to Lenny Kravitz and Jimi Hendrix, employing a variety of video effects to make the replay look like a music video. Lastly, the incredibly detailed Analyzer mode is available when there is only a single car in the race. This form of replay allows players to see telemetry data at each segment of the track, illustrating where a player hit his or her brakes, where the player should have hit them, and just what caused the player's car to go skidding into the wall.

All three of these game replay examples, NBA Courtside, Wreckless, and Gran Turismo 3, use retelling play not only to recall recent game actions, but to recast and extend them in a particular narrative light. In each case, the retelling play creates its own narrative experience appropriate for the particular game. The replays of NBA Courtside replicate the language of television sports coverage, narrativizing the context of the player's TV as if the game just played was a televised sports event. In the action game Wreckless, the replay serves to retell the play of the game not as a sports show but instead as a fast-paced sequence from an action film. The flurry of filmic styles, camera angles, and rapid-fire editing references Hong Kong action films that also inspired the game's settings, characters, and missions. Although this kind of shifting visual style would be too disconcerting to include in the real-time game play, the replay mode allows the cinematic underpinnings of Wreckless to reach full fruition. Lastly, the diverse replay options of Gran Turismo 3 suit the game very well. As a racing series known for its detailed simulation of driving physics, it is appropriate that some of the replay modes emphasize the minutiae of racing strategy (although the Video mode is always available as a lighter counterpoint). The act of replaying a game, although not formally part of the game experience proper, is still part of the overall designed interaction. These three games demonstrate how retelling play can be used to wonderful narrative effect.

Recams

Tools that support players' natural inclination to transform their experience of play into a story to re-experience and share can enhance the narrative play of a game. In addition, these tools can spawn new forms of narrative production that emerge from the game, but exist entirely apart from it. One such example is the *recam*.

Recams originated from the culture of the first-person shooter, from games such as DOOM and Quake that gave players the ability to record and save their game play. Known as "demos," these recordings quickly became a way for players to show off their gaming prowess. Rather than just watching a replay, players could edit the game footage, alter the perspective from first-person to third-person, post it and share it with others. The term "recam" refers to the ability of players to alter camera positions, angles, and motions after recording a replay. Dr. Uwe Girlich of Philosys Software was an early developer of tools to assist players in making these recam demos:

I came into serious contact with computer games via Wolfenstein 3D and later DOOM. With DOOM I could create a recording of my game play and send this demo to other people to show my ability to solve some puzzles or complete a level in a shorter time than anyone else. I became fairly famous for my DOOM demos, but besides playing, I was more interested in programming and analyzing these demo files and so (after some research) I created LMPC, the Little Movie Processing Centre.

LMPC is a decompiler/compiler. It can be used to convert a binary demo file into a simple ASCII text file (decompile). Such a text file can be edited with any editor and afterwards it can be converted back into a binary demo file (compile). It is very easy to analyze and also to alter the demo file and even to create a demo file, which is not the actual recording of someone playing the game but a purely fictional movement in the game engine.[16]

Girlich recognized players' drive to narrativize game play—even to fictionalize it. Rather than showing the match from a first-person point of view, the perspective from which the game is played, a recam allows a shift in perspective to third person. What players see onscreen in a recam varies greatly from what they see while playing the game. In a first-person shooter, the game play perspective has players staring down the barrel of a gun. Player interaction with the game space is determined by the line of sight the weapon affords. But in a recam, the point of view is literally outside of the action. There is no vantage point other than the camera itself.

Recams highlight the role of point-of-view in narrative representation. The recammed match between two of the world's top Quake players, Thresh and Billox (expertly recammed by Overman of Zarathustra Studios), for example, not only lets viewers experience the game play from a third-person perspective, but situates the viewer both literally and figuratively outside of the militarized language of Quake and other FPS games. Recamming offers a point of transition between player and spectator, opening up the line of sight to include a new kind of narrative eye.

The car racing and combat game, Driver: You Are the Wheel-man, gives players a very different kind of retelling play: the opportunity to produce their very own recam movie. First, a player plays through a game mission. Then the player can access editing tools to select camera angles, film stock, and edit together moments of the game play into a cinematic story. The retelling play translates the fragmented, moment-to-moment action of a game into a single, unified narrative event.

Narrative play of this sort can become truly transformative. Players of Driver sometimes play the game as if they were actors in a film, making driving decisions based on how dramatic the action will look in the replay. Rather than playing the game to achieve goals dictated by the game's rules, players impose their own external, narrative goals. Playing the game to achieve a cinematic retelling bypasses the usual meaning of any action > outcome unit in the game. Actions are no longer singularly linked to goals internal to game play, but grow to encompass external, representational concerns. Play is pursued for the sake of creating story.

Demos, recams, and other forms of retelling are forms of narrative play supported by one or more elements of a game's design. Created as part of a game's formal system, features such as a replay function have the potential to enhance player experience on a variety of levels. Because players have a tendency to construct stories from their game play experience and to share these stories with others, giving players tools to craft these stories strengthens social community by providing an economy of exchange. These tools also deepen player engagement, as they encourage play in new and often innovative ways. What can retelling play do for your game?

Games Within Games

We began this chapter with a tightly focused, formal definition of narrative. One by one we took note of the narrative elements of games, pulling farther and farther back until we have all but exited the game itself. There is no doubt that game replays and recams are part of the total game experience, but they dance at the border of the magic circle, somehow just outside the core game play while still very much participating in the meanings of the game.

There is certainly nothing wrong with looking at such border phenomena, or in examining aspects of games that are both inside and outside the game itself. Our **RULES** schemas focused on the inner workings of game systems, but as we move through the schemas on **PLAY**, we will increasingly find ourselves peering outside the magic circle, whether it is to look at the relationships between represented game-reality and the "real world" or to examine the social metagames that occur outside the play of individual games. Of course, by the time we reach our **CULTURE** schemas, we will have pushed through the border of the magic circle entirely, focusing more on context rather than on the structures and play internal to a game.

The next schema, *Games as the Play of Simulation,* will straddle the border of the magic circle. Building on the previous two chapters, we look at the way games represent through simulated depiction, a mode of representation that grows from the status of games as dynamic systems. Analyzing the mechanisms of simulation in one sense means dissecting the internal representational machinery of games. At the same time, it also entails a much wider focus that looks at the relationship between games and the real-world phenomena they reference, a relationship fraught with the double-meanings of metacommunication and play.

If you are reading this book in order to tell better stories with your games, don't stop at the end of this chapter. The schemas that precede and follow this one, *Games as the Play of Meaning* and *Games as the Play of Simulation,* make up a special triad:

three chapters that focus on *games as systems of representation.* Together they provide a series of structures for generating strong story experiences. And of course, they are also three ways of understanding the design of meaningful play.

Further Reading

Computer Games and Digital Cultures Conference Proceedings, Frans Mäyrä, editor

Organized by the Hypermedia Laboratory of University of Tampere, Finland, the CGDC conference focused on the academic study of computer games, from perspectives including ludology and game studies. The essays readily acknowledge the challenge of studying digital games in the academic community. Of particular interest are several essays focusing on the relationships between narrative, emergence, interactivity, and community.

> *Recommended:*
>
> "Computer Games/Cinema/Interfaces," by Geoff King and Tanya Krzywinska
>
> "In Defense of Cutscenes," by Rune Klevjer
>
> "The Open and the Closed: Games of Emergence and Games of Progression," by Jesper Juul

Cybertext: Perspectives on Ergodic Literature, by Espen J. Aarseth

Aarseth looks closely at electronic texts like hypertext fiction, text adventure games, MUDs, and MOOs. He categorizes these texts as forms of "ergodic" literature—a term borrowed from physics to describe open systems—with which the reader must interact to generate a literary sequence. Although Aarseth's argument doesn't fit cleanly within the model of narrative play we propose, his work has had a wide influence on the study of narrative and games.

> *Recommended:*
>
> Chapter 2: Paradigms and Perspectives
>
> Chapter 5: Intrigue and Discourse in the Adventure Game

GAME ON: The History and Culture of Videogames, Lucien King, editor

GAME ON is the catalog for a museum exhibition on videogames. The collection of essays covers everything from the culture of Pokémon to debates over violence in videogames. The three recommended essays each take a different point of view on games and narrative.

> *Recommended:*
>
> "The Art of Contested Spaces," by Henry Jenkins and Kurt Squire
>
> "Telefragging Monster Movies," by Katie Salen
>
> "Story as Play Space: Narrative in Games," by Celia Pearce

Hamlet on the Holodeck: The Future of Narrative in Cyber-space, by Janet Murray

Murray explores the connection between the properties and pleasures of digital media and the future of storytelling, particularly electronic fiction. In looking at interactive fiction, MUDs, MOOs, "cyberdramas," and other forms of storytelling within the digital realm, Murray discusses ideas of authorship, immersion, agency, and the aesthetics of electronic representation. The text is useful in outlining some of the basic issues connecting digital media and storytelling forms.

> *Recommended:*
>
> Chapter 3: From Additive to Expressive Form
>
> Chapter 4: Immersion
>
> Chapter 5: Agency
>
> Chapter 6: Transformation

Shared Fantasy, by Gary Alan Fine

In one of the best sociological studies of fantasy gaming groups and role-playing games available, Fine offers an in-depth analysis of RPGs as a subculture, identifying how players generate meanings and identities in social worlds. Fine's research is based on extensive observation of tabletop RPG players and offers many insights into the role of fantasy and imaginative play in the construction of social and interactive narrative fictions.

> *Recommended:*
>
> Chapter 1: FRP
>
> Chapter 2: Players
>
> Chapter 3: Collective Fantasy
>
> Chapter 6: Frames and Games

Notes

1. *RE:PLAY: Game Design + Game Culture.* Online conference. 2000. <www.eyebeam.org/replay>

2. Jesper Juul, "Games Telling Stories? A Brief Note on Games and Narratives." Gamestudies.org

3. J. Hillis Miller, "Narrative," In *Critical Terms for Literary Study,* edited by Frank Lentricchia and Thomas McLaughlin (Chicago: The University of Chicago Press, 1990), p. 77.

4. Ibid. p. 76.

5. Marc LeBlanc, presentation at the Game Developers Conference, 1999.

6. Doug Church, "Formal Abstract Design Tools." Gamasutra.com

7. Henry Jenkins and Kurt Squire, "The Art of Contested Spaces." In *GAME ON: The History and Culture of Videogames,* edited by Lucien King (London: Laurence King Publishing, 2002), p. 70.

8. Ibid. p. 65.

9. Mark J. P. Wolf, "Space in the Video Game." In *The Medium of the Video Game,* edited by Mark J. P. Wolf (Austin: University of Texas Press, 2002), p. 53–70.

10. Marsha Kinder, *Playing with Power in Movies, Television, and Video Games: From Muppet Babies to Teenage Mutant* (Los Angeles: University of California Press, 1993), p. 2.

11. Atari Inc., Adventure. *Atari Game Program Instructions* (Sunnyvale, CA: Atari, Inc., 1980), p. 2–3.

12. Rune Klevjer, "In Defense of Cut-Scenes," In *Computer Games and Digital Cultures, Conference Proceedings,* edited by Frans Mäyrä (Tampere, Finland: Tampere University Press, 2002), p. 198.

13. Ibid. p. 199.

14. Hugh Hancock, "Better Game Design Through Cut-Scenes." Gamasutra.com

15. Ibid.

16. Personal email correspondence between Dr. Uwe Girlich and Katie Salen, November, 1999.

Games as Narrative Play
SUMMARY

- The study of games and narrative is an interdisciplinary field of inquiry that has been surprisingly contentious. Game design has a specific set of concerns that sidesteps many of these debates. In considering games as **narrative play,** the primary question is not *Are games narrative?* but instead *How are games narrative?*

- J. Hillis Miller defines a narrative as possessing the following characteristics:

    - **Situation:** A series of *events* that change over time.

    - **Character:** A narrative is conveyed through a *system of representation.*

    - **Form:** Representation is constituted by *patterning* and *repetition.*

- Games elements can have embedded or emergent narrative structures:

    - **Embedded** elements are pre-generated narrative components such as video clips and scripted scenes.

    - **Emergent** narrative elements are created on-the-fly as the player interacts with the game, arising from the operation of the game system.

- Games make use of embedded and emergent elements in various balances. The narrative of a game arises out of the combination of emergent and embedded narrative components.

- **Goals** help structure narrative play by making player planning and decision outcomes narratively legible.

- **Conflict** is another characteristic of all games that can shape narrative play. Conflict between players or between players and the game system can be tied to narrative conflicts for dramatic effect.

- **Uncertainty** of game outcome is linked to dramatic uncertainty that can fuel narrative tension. In narrative play, the unknown outcome of the game (or section of the game) is synonymous with the unknown outcome of the narrative.

- The **core mechanic** of a game, when considered as a narrative activity, can create game stories by having players perform narrative acts.

- **Space** in a game plays a large role in shaping the narrative frame and experience. Represented narrative space in digital games is particularly plastic and can engender narrative play through careful design.

· A **narrative descriptor** is any component of a game that participates in the game's system of representation. Instructional text, in-game cinematics, interface elements, game objects, and other visual and audio elements are all narrative descriptors. All of these elements must be carefully crafted with narrative experience in mind in order to maximize narrative play.

· Narrative descriptors imply a representational logic that limits and constrains the design of the space of possibility. These limitations allow for the narrative integration and discernability of all elements contained within the game world.

· Narrative descriptors play two roles in a game, as fictive worlds and as story events:

  · **Fictive worlds** are the larger frames that contain the game world narrative.

  · **Story events** are the individual moments of narrative play generated as the game moves forward.

  These two elements are interrelated. Fictive worlds create the coherent narrative spaces in which story events take place and become meaningful. At the same time, story events help expand and refine the fictive world. Games maintain consistent and understandable narrative experiences when there is a good fit between these two elements.

· A game is a **narrative system** in which the narrative experience of the player arises out of the functioning of the game as a whole. As with other kinds of complex systems, the whole is more than the sum of the parts, as individual elements interact with each other to form global patterns.

· **Cutscenes** are a common storytelling technique used in digital games. They help define the fictive world of a game, as well as fulfill a number of game play functions.

· **Retelling play** is the popular phenomenon of recounting game experiences. Digital games have developed specific techniques for encouraging retelling play, including:

  · **The replay,** in which a game experience is played again for the player.

  · **Recamming,** a special kind of replay in which the player can cinematically manipulate the information contained within the replay.

Unit 3: **Play**

GAMES AS
THE PLAY OF SIMULATION

simulation
procedural representation
abstraction
numerical
stylized
case-based vs. generalized
immersive fallacy
remediation

27

*A video game usually mimics some real-life situation: rockets accelerating and moving in space, bouncing Ping-Pong balls, a kayak in river currents, the food-chain in an ecology. The game of Chess is an abstraction based on a battle between two small groups of warriors: similarly, video games imitate life. A video game is a simulation, a model, a metaphor.—**Warren Robinett,** Inventing the Adventure Game*

Introducing Simulation

Games as the Play of Simulation is our third and final schema exploring the play of representation. In *Games as the Play of Meaning,* we examined how games become meaningful through the process of signification. In *Games as Narrative Play,* we unearthed the wealth of techniques by which games tell stories. For the purposes of this schema, we hone in tightly on the mechanics of play itself, and the way representations are constructed dynamically, through interaction with a game. How, for example, does the board game Diplomacy simulate the art of negotiation? How does the paper-based game Ace of Aces dynamically represent World War I air combat? How does the digital game Deus Ex depict action and intrigue through designed algorithms and rules? The concept of *simulation* lies at the intersection of representation and dynamic systems. As simulations, games create representations, but they do so in a very particular way: through the process of play itself.

We look for answers to questions regarding games and simulations by focusing on the representational mechanics of game systems. A game creates representations in many ways, from its instruction manual text and imaginative fictive world to the visual design of its spaces and the audio design of its soundtrack. At the center of all of these depictions is the game system itself. This system generates representations from a player's interaction with the game, out of the experience and logic of play. This special class of representations, experienced as procedures, sets of behaviors, or forms of interaction, is the raw material from which simulations are constructed. We call this form of depiction *procedural representation.* A simulation-based approach to representation in games, it is the central concept of this schema.

However, procedural representation is only part of what we study in this chapter. In addition to exploring the mechanisms of procedural representation, we also investigate the relationship of those representations to the world outside the game. We know something is a simulation, in part, because we are familiar with the thing that it is simulating. Diplomacy is a polit-ical simulation because it mimics processes of negotiation that are known and familiar in the real world. Yet even though Diplomacy faithfully models the art of negotiation, its representation is still in some measure artificial, contained within the game, separate from the real world. The relationship between a game and the "reality" that it depicts is a fundamental aspect of considering games as simulations.

This is not our first mention of representation and "reality." Back in *Games as the Play of Meaning* we introduced the concept of the cognitive frame. A cognitive frame is a way of organizing or understanding the world, a framework that shapes interpretation and therefore what we take things to mean. Considering not only how a game simulates, but also what it simulates raises questions regarding the relationship between the artificial world of a game and the "real life" contexts it intersects. These questions will play an important role in our understanding of games as simulations, and will become increasingly important as we move into our primary schema on **CULTURE.**

Defining "Simulation"

A video game is an imaginary world: its inhabitants are nonexistent creatures that nevertheless the eye can see, and the hand can move. It is imaginary in the sense that there is no solid reality behind the picture. A bouncing ball may be faithfully simulated, but that moving blip of light has no real mass or elasticity. The ball's position, velocity, mass, and elasticity are just numbers stored in the computer that controls the video game; and the laws of physics that govern the ball's trajectory and its bounce are just mathematical equations stored in the computer's program.—Warren Robinett, Inventing the Adventure Game

In *Inventing the Adventure Game,* Warren Robinett, the game designer and programmer best known for the Atari 2600 game Adventure, looks at games through the lens of simulation. He is particularly interested in the way that digital games are "imaginary worlds," as he puts it, in which players experience blips of light and sound as a representation of some other real-life situation. His description of a simulated bouncing ball, in which the sensory components of position, velocity, mass, and elasticity are peeled back to reveal the underlying mechanisms of the programmed software, reminds us of the often hidden relationship between the formal structure of a game and the experience of that structure through play.

Robinett specifically addresses the way that representations in video games "mimic" real-world phenomena as diverse as bouncing balls and warring soldiers. "A video game is a simulation, a model, a metaphor," writes Robinett. What exactly does he mean? What is a simulation? How are games simulations? Is every game a simulation? What is the relationship between a simulation, a model, a metaphor, and the real-world? We tackle these thorny questions in the pages to follow. But first, let us take a moment to define the concept of simulation. The educational game reference *A Handbook of Game Design* provides a good starting point:

> A *simulation* can be defined as "an operating representation of central features of reality." This definition again identifies two central features that must both exist before an exercise can reasonably be described as a simulation. First, it must represent an *actual situation* of some sort—either a situation drawn directly from real life, or an imaginary situation that conceivably could be drawn from real life (invasion by extraterrestrial beings, for example). Second, it must be *operational,* i.e., must constitute an *on-going process*—a criterion that effectively excludes from the class of simulations static analogues such as photographs, maps, graphs, and circuit diagrams, but includes working models of all types.[1]

The authors Eddington, Addinall, and Percival identify two components that make a representation a simulation. First, a simulation *represents* something: an "actual situation," which is either a circumstance from real life or an imaginary situation

that is conceivably real. This component points out the referential qualities of a simulation: a simulation *refers* to something in the real world. It is significant that the authors use the phrase "central features of reality" rather than just "reality" when describing what a simulation represents. As we will see, a simulation cannot depict every aspect of something; it has to choose a very small subset of characteristics around which to build its representation.

The second component of the definition identifies the fact that a simulation is a very particular type of representation, what the authors call "operational." According to them, a simulation is a representation in the form of "an on-going process" instead of a static representation such as a diagram or flowchart. This component of the definition describes the *systemic* character of simulations. A simulation is a dynamic system: a set of parts that interrelate to form a whole. A simulation is therefore a *procedural* representation, one achieved through an ongoing process. In the case of games, the ongoing process is play.

Eddington, Addinall, and Percival's statement, "A simulation is an operating representation of central features of reality," offers quite an efficient little definition. In proposing our own definition, we would, however, like to make three small adjustments: first, in keeping with our system-based terminology, we replace the word "operational" with "procedural." Second, we generalize the idea of "central features" to "aspects" of reality. Third, we add quotation marks around the word *reality*. The result is the following definition of simulation:

A *simulation* is a procedural representation of aspects of "reality."

Both components of this definition, the fact that simulations represent procedurally and that they depict elements of "reality," represent surprisingly complex concepts. In the pages that follow, we look closely at these two aspects of simulations, considering each in turn.

Game and Non-Game Simulations

The general concept of a simulation is certainly not restricted to games. For example, economists and sociologists use simulations to study mathematical relationships among variables, often as a set of equations that process data. The data might be information from the U.S. Census—demographic information about income, housing, and voting patterns, for example—and the equations might spell out sets of relationships among data. Using this kind of simulation, a researcher would be able to speculate on changes in some of the variables, such as income and housing, input these changes into the simulation, and see how voting patterns would change as a result. This kind of simulation doesn't seem like much fun to "play" (it certainly is not a game), but it does fulfill the requirements of a simulation. There are real-world referents represented in the simulation (economic and political realities) and the simulation functions by processing data through a set of procedures. The process might be merely a mathematical equation, but it is a process just the same.

Economic simulations are rarely explicitly interactive. Usually, a researcher sets up data and then "runs" the simulation to process the data. However, some simulations are designed to be highly participatory, such as training simulations. These include computer-based simulations allowing airplane pilots to practice flying without leaving the ground, live role-playing simulations that allow salespeople to refine their social skills on difficult clients, underwater simulations where astronauts practice zero-G maneuvers in a swimming pool, and emergency simulations in which the residents of an apartment building hold fire drills. Each simulation takes its identity from a *real-world situation:* flying a real plane, pitching a real sale, attempting a real space walk, or escaping from a real fire. In every case, the representation the simulation creates is a process: the complex machinery and interactivity of a flight simulator, the social and conversational process of role-playing, the physical simulation of being in outer space, and the flow of bodies down stairwells and along fire escapes.

Clearly there are many simulations that are not games. But what about game simulations? In the digital game industry, there is a genre of games called simulations, or "sims" for short. Sim City, for example, is a complex depiction of the process of urban planning, city economics, and the evolution of a human community; it is a simulation game. Other game simulations depict historical processes, natural ecosystems, or military vehicles. Although sims, perhaps more than other games, explicitly fulfill both components of our definition (a procedural representation of aspects of "reality"), all games can in fact be considered simulations. Remember that a game design schema must be applicable to all games. Therefore in proposing the schema *Games as the Play of Simulation,* we are arguing that any game can be considered a simulation.

As abstract or fantastical as games may be, it is possible to see them as simulations of one kind or another. Chess and Tic-Tac-Toe, for example, can be framed as representations of territorial conflict, in which simulated units war for control of a stylized battlefield. Games that involve fantastic elements, such as Dungeons & Dragons, also simulate through their play. Detailed rules, for example, simulate the way that different weapons impact different kinds of armor. Even the spell-casting system in D&D is a simulation of sorts: it simulates an imaginative "reality,"

What About Those Quotation Marks?

Well, what about them? Why did we alter Eddington, Addinall, and Percival's definition by putting the term "reality" in quotation marks? This adjustment was necessary because the relationship between so-called "reality" and representation is complex. Is reality a fixed and known quantity, or is it something constructed by our senses, cognition, or cultural understandings? Is reality something that exists outside of representation, or is it something that is constructed by the process of representation? Should representations themselves be included as part of "reality?" We don't have the space to tackle these long-debated philosophical questions here. But we ask that over the course of this chapter, you keep in mind the fact that the "reality" that simulations depict is not a simple given. Putting quotation marks around the word is just a little punctuational string-around-the-finger to remind us of this fact.

one rooted in myth, religion, and popular culture. As the example of extraterrestrial invasion in the quote from Eddington, Addinall, and Percival illustrates, *aspects of "reality"* can refer to things outside our lived experience.

Some games, such as Tetris, present more ambiguous referents, but that does not mean that they are not a kind of simulation. Tetris simulates the way objects can fall down, stack up, and even make noises when they slide into place next to each other. In this way, Tetris is a simple simulation of the forces of gravity. Then there is the fact that falling Tetris objects are called "bricks," and these bricks form an interlocking brick wall grid. These aspects of the game point to a different kind of depiction, perhaps a simulation of construction. Tetris may not be a particularly accurate or instructive simulation of gravity or construction, but accuracy and instructiveness are not necessarily what a game simulation is about. A game simulation, as any kind of game representation, can be geometrically minimal, outrageously whimsical, or even intentionally misleading. Unlike a simulation designed for scientific research purposes, a game simulation is not beholden to a notion of representing empirical truth. Pong is not meaningful to players because it is a scientifically accurate representation of Table Tennis; it is meaningful because as a simulation it provides a context for deep and engaging play.

Meaningful Play and Simulation

How does framing a game as a simulation assist in designing meaningful play? In considering the play of simulation, we are simply re-working fundamental game design concepts established in previous chapters. Although the emphasis here is on how games create representations, fundamental principles of the design of meaningful play remain the same. Whether a simulation allows players to experience the representation of something known and familiar or fantastically imaginative, it does so through the design of meaningful play. In order to see this principle at work, we can take a close look at Ace of Aces, a game designed by history teacher Alfred Leonardi in 1980.

Ace of Aces simulates a dogfight between two World War I aircraft, using a complex formal system to represent the speed, maneuverability, visibility, weapons fire, and other aspects of two-plane air combat. The striking thing about Ace of Aces is that the game takes place not on a computer or even on a paper wargame map, but instead inside two paperback game books. Each player has his own book, and each of the more than 200 pages has an illustration of what the player sees from his or her airplane cockpit. The point-of-view illustration shows the enemy plane at a certain distance, location, and angle relative to the player's own plane. For example, if an illustration shows your opponent's plane coming towards you over your own tail, it means the other player is directly behind you!

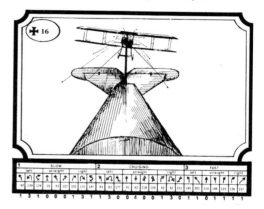

Players interact within the simulation by navigating through their book (players cannot look into each other's books) and selecting maneuvers. At the bottom of each page is a list of the possible maneuvers a player can take, with a number assigned to each. Both players select a maneuver in secret and call out the corresponding number, which determines the next page each player turns to in their book. The elegant formal system of the game is amazingly effective at simulating a dogfight between two World War I airplanes.

Does this seem hard to believe? Consider the scenario we describe: your opponent positioned directly on your tail. You choose a maneuver to slow down and perform a weaving turn to the right, in which you shift your position to the side, ending up parallel to your previous position—something like a car changing lanes. Let's say your tailing opponent thought you were going to make a run for it and made a decision to move forward at top speed—this choice would cause your opponent's plane to zoom right by your decelerating plane. When you turn to the appropriate page in your book and see the outcome of last round's maneuvers, the illustration would show your opponent's plane ahead of you and to the left; and in your opponent's book your plane would be visible behind and to the right.

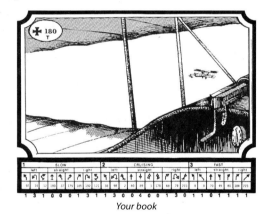

Your book

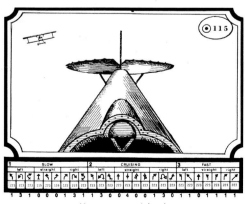

Your opponent's book

Through the use of a clever spatial model, Ace of Aces simulates aspects of World War I air combat. It does not simulate every facet of the experience (there are no rules to handle different kinds of weather and their effect on flying, for example), but it does represent important aspects of its referent. Spatial logic, tactical maneuvers, weapon jams, and even an increase in skill over several combats are all aspects of World War I air combat the game depicts. Furthermore, these representations are made possible through a dynamic system—a process based on a multifaceted mathematical model of air combat. It is through this process that Ace of Aces *simulates* a World War I dogfight.

Ace of Aces constructs this simulation by combining emergent and embedded elements. The drawings and pages themselves are fixed in print, and do not change as the game is played. In this sense, the book pages might be considered embedded narrative elements, pre-scripted narrative descriptors experienced by the player during play. However, the complexity of the underlying game rules incorporates these pages as elements within a truly emergent system. The Ace of Aces book pages are less like the pages of a Choose-Your-Own Adventure book and more like video frames from a real-time simulation display, snapshots of an ongoing battle. In creating a simulation, both emergent and embedded elements can be incorporated into the overall game. However, because of the way that simulations rely on dynamic systems, framing a game as a simulation tends to emphasize the emergent components of the game, the more purely systemic elements that interact in complex ways to generate unexpected results.

Ace of Aces not only provides a rich and coherent simulation of air-to-air combat, but also facilitates meaningful play. Because the pages of the two books contain all of the possible spatial relationships between planes (made possible by a set of rules), the players are literally navigating through the game's space of possibility, experimenting with maneuvers, taking daring risks, and psyching each other out. Each decision they make is both discernable and integrated into the larger game experience, an experience made possible by the simulation. The representational mechanics of the simulation solidly support player decisions, establishing a taut and meaningful domain of interaction. The simulation creates a space of play that exists somewhere between the two printed books, the social interaction of the players, and the battle playing itself out in their overlapping imaginations.

Ace of Aces is a fascinating example of a game simulation, not just because it provides meaningful play, but because it does so through such unexpected means. Since the game was first published, real-time flying simulations on computers have become commonplace, used both for training and entertainment purposes. But Ace of Aces manages to engage players without illusionistic 3D graphics and sophisticated force-feedback pilot controls. Playing Ace of Aces is radically different than flying a plane, yet it somehow still manages to function as a successful simulation. Simulations do not need to literally embody the material and sensual forms of the phenomena they are simulating. This is what Robinett means when he calls a game "a simulation, a model, a metaphor." As representations, simulations often represent metaphorically, meaning they can create representations in non-literal ways. Sometimes, game simulations try and replicate the actual experience of the thing they are simulating, as with VR displays that take over a player's entire field of vision. More often, however, simulations take on modes of representation that are not so literal. There is an underlying mathematical model that connects Ace of Aces to planes moving through space. But the activity of playing the game—turning pages and calling out numbers—is nothing like sitting in an actual cockpit. In fact, this metaphorical difference between the core mechanic of Ace of Aces and its simulated referent is one source of the game's pleasure.

Procedural Representation

Seen as simulations, games are dynamic systems that construct representation through play. Asteroids, for example, represents the feeling of vast space through the inertial drift of the player's ship. The game designers could have created any navigational scheme they wanted, such as a space ship that could start and stop instantly and turn on a dime even when in motion. Instead, the player must maneuver the ship retro rocket-style, taking into account acceleration and momentum. Through this designed activity, the game expressively depicts deep space. In the Lord of the Rings Board Game, the dark force of Sauron is represented as a figure on a track that moves steadily toward the players; his evil nature manifest in his terrifyingly inevitable advance as well as in the deadly ramifications of an encounter with him on the board. The board game Up the River playfully recreates the experience of a flowing river through the unusual format of its board, which is made out of horizontal strips. Each turn, a player takes the strip from the rear and places it in the front. In this way, the sailboats belonging to the players must battle the steadily flowing water current as they race to be the first to reach the dock.

In these three examples, formal and experiential elements of the game work to create a representation that emerges out of the procedures of game play. We call this form of depiction *procedural representation*. The term "procedural" is shorthand for all of the process-based ways that games can signify. A procedural representation might arise from the functioning of a computer program's AI; it might be an emergent result of players following the rules of a game; or it could be an expressive core mechanic that references a particular action outside the game.

A miniatures-based wargame is a representation of war partly because the pieces themselves resemble miniature soldiers and because the battlefield can be painted to look like a contested landscape. But these visual signs make up only one part of the game's larger representation. Wargame representation is also procedural, created through the rules of the game and player choices that the rules engender. For example, units in a wargame generally have a movement rating, representing the number of hexes or spaces through which the unit can move in a turn. In a typical wargame, a cavalry unit will have a higher movement rating than an infantry unit. This statistical difference between types of units is not only a formal distinction; it is a form of representation.

The fact that a cavalry unit moves more quickly in the game than an infantry unit is an act of signification that is fundamentally different than the visual aesthetics of the game token. Its representation is procedural, based on the unit's formal identity and its interactive capabilities within the game system. Of course, the units in wargames have many other kinds of formal statistics as well, from offensive and defensive abilities to movement strengths and weaknesses on different types of terrain. All of these formal designations are based on the simulated characteristics of various battle units. As the game is played, these formal identities become systemic relationships that constitute a dynamic, procedural representation of war.

We can consider games as procedural representations on two levels. Borrowing concepts from *Games as the Play of Meaning,* we know that games *are representations* and also that they *can represent*. The idea that games are representations means that an entire game can serve to depict something. Considering procedural representation on this macro-level, a game represents as a whole. Pong is a procedural representation of Table Tennis; Tony Hawk's Pro Skater 3 is a procedural representation of skateboarding. The notion that games *can represent* means that games contain smaller, internal depictions. This also holds true when considering the procedural aspect of game representation. We can look at the structure of a game on a micro-level and identify the procedural representations that make up the whole, such as the movement rules for cavalry and infantry wargame units.

Macro- and micro-level procedural representations can be embedded in each other. A card game that depicts social life in an eighteenth century royal court is a game that as a whole simulates a particular historical moment. But within the game, we find several micro-procedural representations. There might be one set of rules to simulate swordfight dueling and another to simulate the current political climate of the court. Of course, these micro-procedural representations are linked together within the complete system of the game that constitutes the overall simulation. The same is true of digital games, where the code that simulates light falling on 3D objects is generally separate from the code that simulates the behavior of computer opponents. Although they simulate different aspects of the game's subject matter, these components are all contained within the larger macro-system of the game simulation.

Because procedural representations emerge out of the play of a game, the player's participation is crucial in bringing the signifying procedures to life. As with all game representations, however, procedural representations also grow directly from the rules of the game, gaining meaning as players interact with them through play. Following are three examples of games that make very different use of procedural representation. In each case, the representation is brought to life through both the formal rule structure and the experience of play.

Diplomacy

The board game Diplomacy is a complex representation of World War I political negotiation. The game takes place on a map of Europe and (depending on the particular edition of the game) the tokens used by players might resemble land-based and naval military units, or they might be abstract shapes. Each player assumes the role of a European military power, vying to occupy a number of key cities and conquer the continent.

The game is played in turns. Each turn, players negotiate in public and private for a limited amount of time (usually about 10 or 15 minutes). At the end of the negotiation period, players write down and simultaneously reveal their selected actions. The outcomes of their actions that turn are contingent on the decisions of other players. For example, during a turn one player moves an army into a territory occupied by another player. Support that the invading player has garnered from other players determines the success of the invasion. If the invasion pits one attacking unit against one occupying unit, the action is unsuccessful. However, if the invading player received support from another player with a unit in an adjacent region, the attack is successful: the strength of the invasion becomes two units acting against one. These rules make advancement of your armies on the board difficult, requiring players to make alliances and coordinate their actions.

The formal game mechanics of Diplomacy result in a dramatic procedural representation of negotiated alliances, uneasy agreements, and broken peace treaties: a representation, in other words, of diplomacy itself. Only one player can ultimately emerge as victor, and it is usually just a matter of time before deceit festers and player alliances are broken, reshuffled, and reformed. Which of your allies are going to betray you—and how? In the game of Diplomacy, as in the diplomatic processes it depicts, social skills are at least as important as strategic thinking.

Diplomacy as a whole procedurally represents the subject matter of diplomacy, and it does so through a number of internal representations that combine to form the overall simulation. For example, although Diplomacy could take place on an abstract map and still maintain the same sense of diplomatic intrigue, the map is also used as a means of procedural representation. Switzerland, for instance, is a central but impassable neutral territory, mirroring its isolationist role in World War I. Each country's starting forces are a representation in miniature as well, appropriate to the time period: England has the strongest naval force but a weak army.

Diplomacy is a wonderfully engaging procedural representation of World War I political negotiation, but it only achieves status as a simulation because of careful design decisions. Procedures embodied in private player negotiations, simultaneous player action, contingent action > outcomes, the ability to support other players' actions, and procedural use of the map and tokens combine to create a complex representation of diplomacy. This representation is a product of the process of play; a representation that only gains meaning when it is experienced as a system of dynamic relationships driven by player interaction.

Vampire

Vampire is a game that relies on procedural representation as well. The game comes from the *New Games Book,* which lists the following rules:

To start, everyone closes their eyes (Vampires only roam at night) and begins to mill around. You can trust the Referee to keep you from colliding with anything but warm living flesh. However, you can't trust him to protect you from the consequences, for he is going to surreptitiously notify one of you that you are the vampire.

Like everyone else, the vampire keeps her eyes closed, but when she bumps into someone else, there's a difference. She snatches him and lets out a blood-curdling scream. He, no doubt, does the same....

If you are a victim of the vampire, you become a vampire as well. Once you've regained your composure, you too are on the prowl, seeking new victims. Now perhaps you are thinking that the game too quickly degenerates into an all-monster convention? Ah, but then you didn't know that when two vampires feast on *each other,* they transform back into bread-and-butter mortals.

Will the vampires neutralize each other before all mortals are tainted by the blood-sucking scourge? Why don't you try a little experiment and see? There's always hope, even in the midst of a blood-curdled crowd.[2]

The referent that Vampire simulates is quite different than the referent of Diplomacy. Whereas Diplomacy procedurally represents a real-world historical situation, Vampire comically evokes images of vampires ripped straight from the pages of pulp fiction. The way the game design achieves its procedural representation, however, is no less sophisticated.

Because Vampire requires no game materials (no map or game pieces), it relies entirely on the activity of the players' bodies to generate play: game representations emerge solely from the interaction between players. The initial limitation on the game, the fact that players must keep their eyes closed for the duration of play, orchestrates a certain kind of representational experience. Enclosed in darkness, the player is taken out of the ordinary world and placed in the imagined world of the vampire night, a setting whose drama is amplified by the fact that players spend the entire game stumbling through an unfamiliar space, feeling around for each other.

This tension-filled core game mechanic makes every meeting between players a surprise. There are three different ways that an encounter can play out, from two non-vampires exchanging thankful sighs of relief to a screaming vampire attack, (or double-attack, if two vampires collide). As players wander aimlessly, the sound of shrill yells map the darkness surrounding the players, transforming their invisible game world into a screamingly theatrical sonic landscape. In addition to supporting the goofy-horror flavor of the game, the sound component allows players to "see" the larger playfield, signaling areas of action. Are those bloodcurdling yells coming from somewhere safely far away? Or perhaps from RIGHT BEHIND YOU! These simple procedures (wandering around with eyes closed, meaningful chance encounters, screams erupting in the darkness) together create a coherent and distinctive vampire experience for every player in the game.

Furthermore, as with many New Games games, Vampire plays with the conventions of winning and losing. Does an individual player win at Vampire? How? Do players try to become bitten? Or do they try and remain safe? As vampires, are players seeking new victims? Or a cure for their condition, in the form of another vampire? How will the game end? With a field full of vampires or with the group purged of their vampiric tendencies? The emergent representational system of the game, in which players collide like charged particles, takes on unpredictable patterns. The fact that the game can end in one of two states heightens the drama of the experience and gives the overall game play the suspense of a thriller.

Vampire creates a representation through a number of procedures, from the game's immediate core mechanics to the long-term trajectory of play. Vampire is successful as a representation because it is squarely focused on the player experience. From the outside, Vampire looks like a silly group activity. It is only inside the game that the procedural representation works its magic.

Illuminati

We first mentioned the board game Illuminati in *Breaking the Rules.* The game design is remarkable, among other reasons, because it offers a play variant that encourages rule-breaking within certain boundaries. Although Illuminati uses many means to simulate its subject matter, we focus here on how rule-breaking itself acts to create a procedural representation.

Illuminati is based on the *Illuminatus* books of Robert Anton Wilson, and the subculture of conspiracy theory associated with them. Players in Illuminati assume the roles of shadowy power brokers that manipulate world events and political structures to their own devious ends. There are groups that players can control and link in the game, from the FBI to Trekkies to the entire state of California. Each of these elements is represented in non-procedural ways (through illustrations and text descriptions), as well as in more procedural ways (each group is represented through a set of attributes, making California, for example, a much more lucrative group to control than the Trekkies).

When players use the rule-breaking variant, a completely different kind of representational experience results. The premise of the game requires players to twist existing social structures and institutions to the mysterious—and often ridiculous—ends of the Illuminati. A player might arrange things, for example, so that Trekkies control the FBI, and the FBI in turn controls California. Therefore, the idea of reworking existing power structures to devious effect is already an important part of the overall representation of the game. But by breaking the rules, players take the act of manipulation one step further. The game rules themselves become a representation of the staid rules of society, which the players, as shadowy power brokers, subvert. The action of breaking the rules is itself a procedure, representing the way players turn the game world upside-down in order to undo existing power structures and the well-laid plans of other players.

This kind of game play takes players right to the edge of the magic circle, as they engage in an experience that actively plays with the destruction of the game's authority. This is precisely why it is such a powerful representational device, because breaking the rules allows players to play with genuine power. The authority of the rules, the social contract of a game, the safety and trust of play, all become radically undermined, as the game flirts with its own destruction. Can you imagine a better way to represent the topsy-turvy world of the Illuminati?

Represented Conflict

We are beginning to understand how procedural representations work to simulate phenomena through dynamic depictions. But there is a question that precedes a discussion of how games create such representations. It is the question of what phenomena a dynamic system can depict. Can a game designer pick anything to simulate, or are there inherent limitations? Are there certain things that games are predisposed to simulate, certain subjects that lend themselves naturally to games? Game designer Warren Robinett seems to think that just about anything might be simulated:

> Many provocatively complex phenomena await interpretation …trains and other vehicles which move cargo through spaces, kayaks in swirling river currents, planets orbiting their stars, competing creatures in evolving ecologies, visible melodies smeared upon harmonic wallpaper, looping programs in throbbing execution, and human thought darting across a tangled network of knowledge….

> The real world offers a vast set of phenomena to simulate—animals behaving, plants growing, structures buckling, traffic jamming, snowflakes forming. Any process is a candidate. Every verb in the dictionary suggests an idea.[3]

Since Robinett originally penned this challenge, games have been designed to simulate some of the phenomena he describes: Sim Life attempted to simulate evolving ecologies of creatures; the shareware game Bridge Builder simulates structures buckling under the weight of a train. However, many of the phenomena on his list are still waiting to find themselves in games. As Robinett points out, "every verb in the dictionary suggests an idea" for a simulation. Why then, do games seem to focus on a narrow range of processes to simulate? Why do we see the same genres of games over and over: fighting, racing, war, sports, and so on? Of course, economic and business concerns greatly influence game content. But is there something else, something deeper about the underlying structure of games that determines the kinds of processes they can and cannot depict?

Our definition of a game describes them as *systems in which players engage in an artificial conflict, defined by rules, that results in a quantifiable outcome.* The part of the definition relevant to our present discussion of simulation and representation is *conflict.* Games are contests of power: they are systems of conflict. Conflict is not only a product of the game's rules, but of its system of representation as well. Every game, on some level, dynamically represents conflict. The elements of a game—the players, the pieces, the rules—all have a role in generating the representation. The insight that games represent conflict through a dynamic process might help to explain the prevalence of certain content in games: perhaps some forms of conflict are simply easier to model than others. At the same time, understanding the kinds of conflict that games most often depict also helps us to strategize new kinds of subjects for games to simulate.

What are the forms of conflict we find dynamically represented in games? If the game has a strong narrative component, the conflict is easy to spot. The Lord of the Rings Board Game clearly simulates the struggle of the players, as the Fellowship hobbits, to reach Mount Doom at Mordor and destroy the One Ring. But in many games, it is more difficult to pin down the simulated conflict. What is the conflict in Baseball, Checkers, or Jeopardy? The key to comprehending the form of conflict simulated by a game is to figure out what is being contested. In what kind of arena is the conflict being held? Over what is the conflict being waged? How is the progress of the conflict measured? What aspects of the conflict are dynamically represented?

In order to answer these questions we distill the range of game conflict into three general categories: *territorial conflict, economic conflict,* and *conflict over knowledge.* These three categories are neither discrete nor mutually exclusive: many games incorporate two or all three of them at once within their design. Rather than a strict typology, they are instead conceptual frames for looking at the kinds of conflict that games can dynamically represent. Next, we explore each of these three categories in more detail.

Conflict Over Territory

Conflict over territory is perhaps the most intuitive of the three categories. Board games such as Chess, in which pieces are moved on a limited playing field, are a common game of this sort. In games of territorial conflict, players strategically position their units to capture enemies and gain ground. Conflicts of this kind are abstract representations of war: the pieces depict military units, and the play area dynamically represents the territory over which the battle is waged.

Go is another good example of a game focused on capturing territory. As players lay down their stones, their primary goal is to surround areas of the playfield to secure the captured space. At the end of the game, each player receives a point for each grid intersection secured (plus a point for each captured enemy piece). The game originated as a military simulation—in feudal Japan, Go was considered a martial art. As a territorial conflict, Go is a strikingly elegant representation.

There are many other games that simulate the process of territorial conflict. Tic-Tac-Toe is a simple territorial conflict where players attempt to strategically occupy territory in a pattern that will lead to victory. Ball-based sports such as Football and Soccer entail moving a team or a special marker across a stretch of terrain into the opponent's end zone or goal: the enemy invaded. Tabletop games such as Warhammer offer incredibly complex representations of warfare dynamically enacted, with dozens of different kinds of units, large detailed maps, and thick rulebooks controlling the particulars of interaction. The U.S. military uses even more complex war games as training exercises, in which hundreds or even thousands of troops play vast games of laser tag in real and simulated environments.

Economic Conflict

Economic conflict is another common form of conflict in games. Within simulations of economic conflict, it is not terrain that is contested, but a unit of value. The word "economic" does not necessarily refer to money, but to any collection of pieces, parts, points, cards, or other items that form a system through which the conflict takes place. In a pinball game, you are trying to rack up a high score. In Magic: The Gathering, you are trying to reduce your opponent's life to zero. In these game economies, the rules give each unit a value, and progress through the game is measured according to the values assigned by this economy.

An economy in a game is generally a *limited economy*. This means that the units that make up the economy are finite, and usually the players know the composition of the economy. In Poker, it is crucial that all players understand the limited economy of a deck of playing cards. Knowledge about which cards appear in the deck allows them to understand which hands are more difficult to build. Four-of-a-kind is harder to build than a pair; a straight flush harder still. The other economy of Poker—the betting money—might or might not be a limited economy. Each player might start with the same amount of chips, in which case all players know the parameters of the chip economy. If players can use money in their pockets or other valuables for betting, the players don't know the full extent of the economy—although the economy is ultimately limited by the capital each player possesses outside the magic circle. On the other hand, if players are not betting "real money" but are instead playing for fun using an endless supply of chips, the normally limited betting economy becomes unlimited.

Because economic conflict is generally reducible to numbers and points, and games are intrinsically mathematical, we can frame almost any game in this way. For example, a race game, in which players roll a die and move a marker down a track, might at first seem to be a territorial conflict.

However, the same game could also be played by throwing dice and adding up the points that players receive each turn, making the game more of an economic conflict. Since the two games would have similar constituative rules, the operational rules would help determine what kind of conflict the game represents. Yet some games combine categories: Is Quake a territorial conflict or an economic one? It is clearly a hybrid. The play takes place within the representation of a space, in which relative position at each moment is quite important. However, much of the game consists of managing economies of resources such as health, armor, ammo, weapons, and kills.

Even the strongly territorial games of Chess and Go can be seen as procedural representations of economic conflict. In Chess, the pieces represent an economy, and the use-value of each piece is derived from the total set of relationships on the board. Of course, one unit—the King—has a special value, which determines the winner of the game. Similarly, at the end of a game of Go, territory is translated into points, and as with the race game example, Go could be interpreted as an economy—of contested points. Remember that the three kinds of conflict are not hard and fast categories; they are merely frames we use to understand the kinds of conflict that games traditionally simulate.

Conflict Over Knowledge

Conflict over knowledge offers a different model for understanding the way games simulate conflict. In Trivial Pursuit, for example, it is true that pieces move about on the spatial territory of a board. It is also true that the players acquire a set of colored plastic pieces within an economy of parts in order to win the game. But these ways of framing Trivial Pursuit seem to leave out the key component of the game conflict: the process of asking and answering trivia questions.

In Trivial Pursuit, as with many other games in which information itself forms the arena of conflict, the contested "terrain" of the game is *knowledge*. Game shows such as Hollywood Squares, computer trivia games such as You Don't Know Jack, and even games about translation of information from one form to another such as Charades, can all be understood as games in which the conflict is one of knowledge. Conflicts over knowledge are inherently cultural, because the game conflict itself engages with a cultural space that lies outside the game. In a game of conflict over knowledge, the outcome of a game action is dependent on whether or not the player knows the right answer to a question of some kind. This is quite different than representation of territorial or economic conflict: the process being simulated is the conflict of acquiring and sharing cultural knowledge. Games designed with factual knowledge as part of the system of conflict cross over the border of the magic circle, creating a game contingent on information brought into the game from external sources.

Games represent conflict as acquisition of and contestation over territory, economy, and knowledge. These three rather abstract categories don't tell us exactly *what* games are capable of simulating, but describe the general sorts of processes that games *most often* simulate. Identifying these three categories also helps explain why we see the same kinds of conflict being modeled over and over in games. For example, why is it that video games often seem to focus on simulating military conflict: fighting, shooting, and conquering? Or that so many games overflow with collectable item economies: magic coins, money, or other precious objects? Like it or not, the tendency toward military and economic representation in games has a long history, directly linked to the processes of territorial and economic conflict intrinsic to most games.

There is a relatively clear line of descent, for example, from Go and Chess to Kriegspiel, wargaming miniatures, and role-playing games, and from these non-digital games to today's RPGs,

FPSs, and RTSs (*role-playing games, first-person shooters,* and *real-time strategy games*). A tremendous amount of design thinking regarding wargaming, military simulation, and other forms of territorial conflict has accumulated over the centuries. Simulating the difference between mounted units and infantry units; between melee and ranged weapons; between attacks that spread damage and attacks that penetrate; between size and maneuverability, strength and speed, and so on, have become well-worn design problems of game representation over the years. In this sense, today's highly detailed military games are the inheritors of millennia of design thinking.

Happily, this long history in no way limits what it is possible to simulate in games, even when it comes to forms of conflict. An important question for today's game designer is: What other kinds of conflict can games simulate? For example, what about Robinett's wish list? How could a game be designed to simulate social conflict, psychological conflict, or interpersonal conflict? These are truly tough design challenges. As we will see in the following pages, part of the challenge lies in the fact that simulations require radical simplification and stylization. Sid Meier's Civilization series are wonderful strategy games that tackle the Herculean task of simulating cultural development. But because cultural knowledge in the game is necessarily stylized into abstract units ("Do you trade *Monotheism* for *Iron Working*?") the game never comes close to representing the subtlety of its subject matter.

The history of games contains many robust examples for simulating military and economic conflict. A design lexicon for simulating social or cultural conflict may take generations to develop. Of course, these unsolved challenges are part of what makes game design as a field so remarkable. Despite the fact that games are a truly ancient phenomenon, there are still countless avenues for representational innovation—as long as you are ready to question long-standing assumptions about what games are and what they can be.

Procedural Characters

Conflict is an abstract, elemental way of thinking about the kinds of processes that games simulate. But it is not the only way to frame games as simulations. What about simulation and storytelling? Any of the game narratives discussed in the previous chapter could be thought of as a simulation, providing it was represented through a dynamic process. Combining narrative and simulation is a powerful way of thinking about games as a representational medium, because it forces a truly experiential approach to participating with a story. As Reiner Knizia wrote in his earlier essay for this book, his hope for the Lord of the Rings Board Game was that it would "not just re-tell Tolkien's plot, but more importantly it would make the players feel the emotional circumstances of the story."

Following are four examples of just one part of the storytelling equation, the element of *character*. The four examples each examine a very different strategy for procedurally creating narrative experience via character (here we are using a general concept of "character" that refers to a fictional persona contained within a game representation). Some of the examples are characters under the direct control of a player, whereas others remain outside of player control. In all cases, rules and interaction are used to procedurally construct a character, while also weaving the character into the larger fabric of the game representation.

Zelda: Link's Awakening

In this adventure game for the Game Boy, players control a character named Link, moving him about the fictional world of the game, exploring new spaces, acquiring objects, and defeating enemies. The game is rich with characters—in addition to Link, many personalities populate the world of the game, including a witch character that players encounter early in the game.

The character of the witch signifies the idea of "witch" in many different ways. The character looks like a witch (she wears a tall pointed hat), sits next to a cauldron, cackles as she talks, and possesses other stereotypical trappings of a cartoon witch. In addition to these non-procedural representations, depiction of the witch occurs procedurally as well: the witch character has a number of systemic qualities that allow her to signify in ways that a non-procedural character could not.

For example, like many characters encountered in Zelda: Link's Awakening, the witch's character lives in her own house. Most houses are found in villages, where many of them are clumped together. As a result, they are easy to locate. But the witch's house lies deep in the heart of a dangerous wood. In order to reach it, the player must overcome obstacles as he or she searches through the maze-like forest. Not only is the witch represented in the space of the game as living a life isolated from the villagers, but her very separation from society makes her character more difficult to find. Both of these attributes (isolated and dangerous to visit) are very "witchy" characteristics. In the game, these characteristics are a function of the position of the witch's house relative to other elements on the game-grid of the imaginary world: they are procedural, growing from the formal characteristics of the game and the player's own game interactions.

When a player reaches the witch, she informs Link (via on-screen text) to bring her a mushroom. If the player goes back out into the forest, collects a mushroom, and then brings it back to the witch, she will take the mushroom, stir her cauldron, and produce a magical powder for the player. The witch enacts a procedure that transforms the mushroom, changing its properties within the game. As a liminal character living outside the bounds of society, the witch has the ability to convert natural objects to useful technologies. This kind of procedural characteristic is common in adventure games *(take object A to character X and receive object B)*. Yet in the case of the witch, it works very well to depict her character. The procedural elements constituting her representation (her location in the world, her ability to convert objects) are truly witch-like and serve to create an effective and memorable character.

One last note of clarification: imagine a witch character in a book similar to the witch in Zelda: Link's Awakening. The book's story would describe how the witch lives in the woods, makes magical potions, and so on. What would be the difference between the two witches? Aren't they basically the same character? Perhaps, but the form of their representation is radically different. Although both witches might have the same "literary" characteristics, the witch in the book would not possess these traits as procedural qualities, which are triggered as part of an activity of meaningful play. In fact, the witch in the story is exactly the kind of witch that the game witch references. Actively exploiting the witch's witch-like qualities, not just by reading about them but also by *playing with them,* is what makes her representation so powerful to experience in the context of the game.

Virtua Fighter 4
The fighting game Virtua Fighter 4 integrates procedural representation into the narrative play of the game by tying the formal characteristics of the fighting characters to their appearance, personality, and embedded backstory. Every character is designed with explicit strengths and weaknesses, which are procedurally represented through character attributes. For example, Pai Chan has incredible speed but lacks power and hard-hitting moves. Kage-Maru has complex combinations and special moves, but they take time to execute, leaving him vulnerable to attacks from his opponent. Jeffry McWild has great power, but is large and heavy, and therefore less agile. Each character's strengths are countered by logical weaknesses, adding up to a fighting "personality" that plays itself out during each match.

In a well-designed fighting game these procedural representations have strong ties to the fictive world and narrative of the game. How a character fights is usually an external representation of internal qualities, and fighting styles are mirrored in the narrative histories provided for each character, as well as more mundane information such as height and weight, profession, gender, and country of birth. All of these non-procedural narrative descriptors may seem superficial to the game play, but they help create an integrated character in which procedural and non-procedural elements are brought together in a character representation that players experience on many levels.

For example, Virtua Fighter 4's Pai Chan is an action film star whose hobby is dancing. She is small and light and favors a fighting style that uses combos and quick reverses. Her father, Lau, bested her in a previous tournament, and in VF4 Pai is determined to defeat him and prove herself a worthy successor to her father's legacy. Each component of this narrative offers players insight into the strengths and weaknesses of the character. Pai Chan's background as an action hero and dancer make her quick and agile. Her preferred style of fighting favors rapid combinations that often leave her defenseless if her attacks are blocked. Because of her intense desire to defeat her father, Pai Chan is driven by emotion, not logic. As a result, her fighting style is visceral and immediate. She reacts quickly, but rarely plans for the long fight.

This character sketch not only describes Pai Chan herself, but also the playing style that her procedural characteristics engender. By "playing" Pai Chan in a match, the player participates in her representation, bringing her procedural characteristics to life. The play becomes a meaningful representation because of the well-designed synergy between her formal characteristics, appearance, backstory, and emergent personality. This kind of richly layered simulation is a fantastic example of the unique ways that games signify through an integrated suite of representational mechanisms.

Deus Ex

Deus Ex is a role-playing game designed for both computer and console platforms. A strong feature of the game is the computer-generated characters, which respond to game events in surprisingly subtle and expressive ways. These characters follow a series of AI algorithms that determine how they behave in any given situation. In *Swords and Circuitry,* Hallford and Hallford reprint a section of the Deus Ex design document that outlines how different character types act in certain circumstances. This fascinating document reveals the designed mechanisms by which the game's characters are procedurally represented. Here is a brief excerpt from the document :

Civilian:

·   Does not harm civilians

·   Ignores unidentified sounds

·   Aware of alarms

·   Issues warning before attacking

·   Flees when wounded below X% (where X is high)

·   Tends to protect self

·   Ground-based movement, normal

Thug:

·   No concern for safety of civilians

·   Investigates unidentified sounds

·   Aware of alarms

·   Attacks without warning

·   Flees when wounded below X% (where X is low)

·   Ground-based movement, normal

Military:

·   Does not harm civilians

·   Investigates unidentified sounds (if possible without abandoning post)

·   Aware of alarms

·   Issues warning before attacking

·   Never flees when wounded

·   Ground-based movement, fast [4]

These character descriptions are quite high level—they do not formally specify exactly how each character will behave. For example, the speed of each character is only defined as "normal" and "fast" rather than numerically. However, as an abstract character sketch, these descriptions offer a snapshot of the sort of design decisions the game's designers made as they developed the characters' behaviors. Compare the thug character and the military character. Whereas the more cowardly thug will flee when his health is low, the brave military character will never abandon his post and will fight it out to the bitter end. The unscrupulous thug will attack without warning, but the honorable military character will issue a warning before attacking. In this way, the programmed characteristics of the characters take on a simulated personality, becoming expressive by virtue of their procedural differences. By adding different types of characters defined along a number of parameters, an entire cast of procedurally generated actors could be developed.

To appreciate the sophistication of these strategies for representation, compare the Deus Ex characters to the witch in Zelda. The witch behavior is fairly simple and wholly predictable (if: receive mushroom, then: create powder). In contrast, several Deus Ex characters encountering each other in the game create a scene rife with emergent drama.

Imagine, for example, the following situation: A thug approaches a civilian. The civilian (who *ignores unidentified sounds*) pays no heed to the footsteps of the approaching thug, who begins to mercilessly beat the civilian (*attacks without warning; no concern for safety of civilians*). After the thug strikes a single blow, the civilian starts to flee (*flees when wounded below X%, where X is high*), pursued by the thug (both characters move at *normal* speed). The pair of them run by a military character who takes notice of them (*investigates unidentified sounds*) and takes up the chase herself, quickly catching up to them (moving at *fast* speed). The military character ignores the civilian but catches up to the thug and begins to issue a warning… How will the scene play out? Does the thug pause when warned, giving the civilian time to flee? Do the military character and the thug battle to the finish? Or does the entire scene disperse as characters each go their separate ways?

This sequence of actions is not pre-scripted, but instead emerges from the simulated behaviors of the characters. Each character has a very distinct personality. Of course each character also has a different visual appearance, style of movement, tone of voice, and so on. These non-procedural traits are certainly important to their overall representation. But it is through the procedural representation of the characters, representation emerging from behavioral characteristics, that they take on active roles in the dramatic events of the game.

Blob

Procedurally represented characters are not exclusive to the domain of digital games. Our final example of a procedural character comes from a non-digital game, a New Games tag variant called Blob.

If you're addicted to late-night TV monster movies, here's a sure way to kick the habit and break out into the light of day…

The Blob begins innocently enough as a mere individual playing a game of tag. As soon as she catches someone, she joins hands with him. Now he's part of the Blob too, and they both set out, hand-in-hand, in search of victims. Everyone the Blob catches (only the outside hand on either end of the Blob can snatch at players) joins hands with it and becomes part of the lengthening protoplasmic chain. And thus the insidious Blob keeps growing.

Unlike your run-of-the-mill, mad scientist-created Blobs, this one is not content to merely ooze along, seeking its prey. It gallops around the field, cornering stray runners and forcing them to join up….

Moreover (horrors), the Blob can split itself into parts and, with its superior communal intelligence, organize raiding parties on the lone few who have managed to escape. The thrilling climax occurs when there's only one player left to put up a heroic last-ditch stand on behalf of humanity. But alas, there is no defense against the Blob, and humanity succumbs. (If that seems unfair, well, that's the plot.)

The moral of our story could well be, "You become what you fear." If you have the heart to destroy humanity again, you can have the last person caught start the Blob for the next game.[5]

The game of Blob is centrally focused on the procedural representation of a single character: the Blob. The form that the character takes, a mass of moving bodies, is quite different than the characters in Zelda: Link's Awakening, Virtua Fighter 4, and Deus Ex, which are experienced as visual images and audio. Yet, like these characters, the Blob is generated out of a set of representational procedures.

The Blob parodies a B-grade movie monster: a humongous, horrifying, pudding-like creature. The rules of the game cleverly bring this character to life through a set of behavioral procedures for representation. The fact that the rest of the players try to avoid the Blob immediately creates an environment of fear. The slow-moving Blob scatters players before it, lumbering through the playfield. The touch of the Blob is deadly, and when a player is brushed by one of the edges of the Blob, that player is ingested and incorporated into the body of the character.

As the Blob grows, it tends to move more slowly while covering a wider area; it can also fragment and recombine in a very protoplasmic way. The size of the Blob is an inverse function of the number of players running loose around the playfield. The dwindling non-Blob players become a community of hard-nosed survivors. *Oh no! Don't tell me it got Sharyn too!* At the game's climax, the Blob symbolically ingests the entire world, becoming synonymous with the group of players as they reach a competitively and cooperatively achieved endpoint. The game's narrative may only have one ending, but as the rules point out, there is a moral to the story.

Just as the witch in Zelda: Link's Awakening was represented through procedures that created distinctively "witchy" characteristics, the character of the Blob possesses procedural character traits (fearful, steadily growing, ingests players, fragments and recombines, inevitably wins) that are exceedingly Blob-like. An elegantly designed game persona, the Blob generates a character through exceptionally effective procedural means—and completely without digital technology!

Designing Simulations

Procedural representations clearly can provide meaningful play for game players. But designing simulations is challenging. Once you decide what it is you want your game to simulate, how do you put the pieces together to arrive at the kind of simulation that you want? A simulation, as a representational process, is more than a series of independent procedures producing a result. A simulation arises from the operation of a system in which every element contributes in an integrated way to the larger representation.

Designing the mechanisms of that system presents many challenging decisions for a game designer. In *Inventing the Adventure Game,* Warren Robinett outlines some of the key design issues involved in creating a simulation:

> Given a phenomena to simulate, the problem is to decide what are its parts, how these parts can be represented with numerical values, and what the relationships are that let these parts affect one another….
>
> Making a simulation is a process of abstracting—of selecting which entities and which properties from a complex real phenomena to use in the simulation program. For example, to simulate a bouncing ball, the ball's position is important but its melting point probably isn't. Any model has limitations, and is not a complete representation of reality.[6]

In these few sentences, Robinett makes a number of very important points about the design of simulations, including:

- *Simulations are abstractions.* The real or imagined phenomenon you want to depict in your game is most likely overflowing with layers of detail. But as with all forms of representational media, you will never be able to fully represent every facet of your subject. Thus your simulated representation, as Robinett points out, is an abstraction. Chess is a highly abstracted representation of war. Sim City is a very stylized version of government and city planning. D&D even abstracts people—into the characteristics of Strength, Intelligence, Wisdom, Dexterity, Constitution, and Charisma. A simulation does not attempt to simulate every aspect of its referent, but instead focuses on those elements necessary to the game. Virtua Fighter 4 simulates the fighting capabilities of its characters: it does not simulate their biological immune systems or taste in classical music, since these are not relevant to the play of the game. Being able to select which components of your subject to ignore and which to retain and abstract is an absolutely critical game design skill.

- *Simulations are systems.* A simulation is a whole made up of smaller, interrelated parts. As with any complex system, meaning emerges from the interaction of the parts. Brainstorming a list of attributes or effects that you want to include in a simulation is not enough. You must conceive of a system that incorporates them all. You might want a fighting game that can simulate the difference between a fast but weak character and a slow but strong character. But what does "fast," "slow," "strong," and "weak" *mean* in your system? How do they interrelate? How do these attributes affect the decisions and outcomes a player makes? All games are systems, but when we frame them as simulations, the systemic aspect of the game is harnessed directly for representational effect.

- *Simulations are numerical.* Not only are simulations abstracted, systemic representations, but they are also reducible to a formal, numerical structure. We know this already about games: at some level games are composed of rules, and at their most formal level, all rules are logical, mathematical, constitutive rules. The six D&D statistics listed previously are represented in the game as numerical digits between three and eighteen. Complex physics simulations in computer games are based on mathematical modeling. The behavior of artificial characters, whether on a Magic: The Gathering card or inside Deus Ex, can be reduced to their formal identity. The fact that simulations must reduce their subjects to formal, numerical values is exactly why it is so challenging to procedurally depict social, psychological, and other experientially complex phenomena in a game.

- *Simulations are limited.* Because simulations are numerical abstractions, they are intrinsically limited. As Robinett points out, "every model has its limitations and is not a complete representation of reality." We emphasize this aspect of simulations because of prevalent ideas in the computer game industry that more complex simulations

automatically guarantee meaningful play. In fact, on a digital platform even a supposedly "realistic" simulation only depicts a tiny slice of any real world or imagined phenomenon. But this doesn't mean that simulations can't provide meaningful play. The inventive shareware game Bridge Builder simulates its subject, but it chooses a very narrow aspect of bridge building—the engineering challenges of the support structure. This design leaves out thousands of other possible characteristics that might be simulated, from the aesthetics of the building materials to the effect of the bridge construction on the surrounding ecosystem. But that's OK. The game turns the intrinsically limited nature of simulation into an asset, by focusing player activity on a fun and educational aspect of building bridges.

Design involves choice: to create a simulation, you need to decide what to simulate and how. Every choice you make as a game designer opens some possibilities and closes others. What is meaningful in the context of a particular simulation? Is it meaningful to blow wind into the face of the player as she is piloting a hang glider? Is it meaningful to provide a full-body harness in which the player can lie as she interacts with the simulation? Is it meaningful to simulate the insurance and legal procedures by which a player purchases or rents a hang glider? Pilotwings for the Nintendo Entertainment System, a popular game simulation of hang gliding, includes none of these features.

In digital games, much of this decision-making process involves the scope and depth of a simulation. If a racing game is composed of a single car on a single track, it can be extremely detailed. It might include a complex set of physics models, simulations of the internal suspension of the car, or wear on tire treads as they are used over time. Given the same design resources, the addition of more cars and more tracks means that fewer characteristics can be simulated in an equally detailed way. If even more elements are added—such as cars that can transform into jets and fly around the track—the focus of the simulation shifts once more. If a character can get out of the vehicle, walk around, and interact with other people, that casts the net even wider and the "depth" of the simulation decreases accordingly.

In designing a simulation, you must decide exactly what kinds of procedural representations you want to provide for players. In a fighting game series such as Tekken, a detailed (if fancifully cinematic) fighting simulation, the characters don't also get into cars and drive around a track. On the other hand, in an ambitiously open-ended game such as Shenmue, a player's character can have simple conversations with many other characters in the environment, examine, carry, and utilize a wide array of objects, and explore a large detailed space. As a result of the range of activities simulated, the fighting system in Shenmue is much more stylized and limited in scope than that of Tekken.

Why is it that games can't simulate everything with a high degree of detail? Why can't a game simulation be both wide *and* deep? There are several reasons. Limited development resources require that game designers decide where those resources will be spent. But the limitations of time and budget are not the only things affecting the scope of simulations. There are game design factors as well. Meaningful play stems from the ability of players to make meaningful choices from a limited set of knowable options. If a player has trouble recognizing everything that is being simulated, an understanding of knowable options decreases.

In an essay by game designer Harvey Smith on simulation and games,[7] he uses the fictional example of a vehicle-based game with terrain simulation so exacting that the geometry of a player-driven truck can get stuck on a tiny bump on the ground. In this case, the designer chose the wrong element of the game to simulate in detail. Smith's example also points out the problem of thinking that a simulation is anything but an abstraction. The "reality" of a game is determined by the mean-

ings it creates within the magic circle. The terrain simulation in Smith's fictional example might be based on scientifically accurate mathematical models, but the only thing the player will experience is the frustrating, "unrealistic" experience of being unable to drive on what looks like relatively smooth terrain.

The proper scope of detail for a simulation is largely determined by expectations set by the broader context of the game. In Gran Turismo, a game that deeply simulates real-world car physics, players come to expect a finely grained driving experience. However, driving is clearly the focus of the game. No player expects to exit their car, wander up into the stands, and interact with spectators. A game such as Shenmue, on the other hand, has been criticized for disappointing players. If players can interact with many different kinds of objects in the game, why can they enter only some of the buildings and not others? Player expectations are raised to unrealistic levels: the implied breadth of the simulation is far greater than what the game actually delivers.

Given that simulations are abstract and limited, as a game designer you must choose your battles wisely. The elements you select to depict through the procedural representation of a simulation determine the experiential focus of your game. Another of Harvey Smith's thought experiments is to take a typical driving game and give it additional depth by having computer opponents take note of their fuel consumption and try to drive directly behind other cars, strategically using wind shear to conserve fuel. He contrasts this to a driving game with emotional simulation, in which one of the computer opponents might drive recklessly during a race because he had just ended a relationship with a girlfriend.[8]

Whereas Smith prefers the fuel consumption adjustment to the driving game, we find both of the game ideas equally interesting. Each of the two scenarios points to a very different game experience. Both driving games—one a hardcore strategic sim and the other a romance set on a race course—would require simulating different kinds of phenomena. These procedural representations would be part of the larger game system and would determine what the game could represent and what the player would experience. You most likely wouldn't want both the fuel consumption simulation and the romance simulation in the same game. Why? Because each pull the space of possibility and the focus of the play in opposite directions. The fuel consumption feature implies an entire system of detailed car simulation mechanics that would be the central focus of the game. The heartbroken driver implies a game system that would focus on simulating dating, emotions, and stylized romance. As you craft representations in your game system, you simultaneously create the meanings that players will experience.

The key is to remember that just because a simulation is limited in scope doesn't mean that it is impoverished in what it can provide players. The abstract play of Go contains an infinite number of strategic options. The fine-grained driving focus of Gran Turismo supports meaningful exploration because the simulation rewards players for learning about and taking advantage of its subtleties. And the broad-but-shallow world simulation of Shenmue lets players focus on the rich narrative surface of the world without getting tripped up in interactive complexities that would not be appropriate to the game. The creation of a simulation is the creation of a space of possibility. By defining the exact nature of your game's simulation, you are sculpting the shape of your game's meaningful play.

Learning from Wargames

Working within the intrinsic limitations of simulations is one of the key challenges of game design. What are you going to simulate in your game? How are you going to abstract it? Which features of the phenomena will you include and which will you ignore? How deep and how broad can your simulation be? How do you tie each aspect of your simulation to the larger player experience? To understand these kinds of design decisions more fully, we look in detail at a particular genre of game, the historical wargame.

Historical wargames are complex strategy games that use cardboard chits or metal figures on a map to simulate a battle. We have already noted that game simulations are not universally beholden to "realism" or "accuracy." But historical wargaming is a genre of game design where both realism and accuracy are important. Historical wargame designers base their troop composition, map layouts, and game rules on historical research, a numerical approach to military history that wargame designer James Dunnigan calls "analytic history." In the game design subdiscipline of historical wargaming, part of the design ethos is that a game accurately simulates historical circumstances.

History, in a very general sense, represents a fixed series of events. But a historical wargame is a *game,* which means that uncertainty, risk, and unpredictable outcomes play a role. What a historical wargame really simulates are the starting conditions of a conflict. The way that the conflict plays out is what makes the game interesting as a game experience. Will history repeat itself? Was the historical outcome inevitable? How much can masterful strategy affect the outcome? These are all questions that wargame designers and players seek to answer through the creation and play of their games. The meaningful play of a historical wargame derives not only from the strategic complexities of military decision making, but also from the fidelity of the game to its historical referent.

As we know, a simulation can never contain every possible aspect of the phenomena being simulated. Historical wargaming has been wrestling with this challenge for at least a century, making it a wonderful case study for the design of simulations. We have already touched on one aspect of wargame design, the abstraction of unit characteristics. The pieces in a war-game are far more complex than in a game like Chess. When a wargame unit "attacks" an enemy piece, the outcome of the simulated combat is not simply to remove the attacked unit (as in Chess); instead, a variety of factors determine the outcome. Resolving an attack might involve some or all of the following:

- offensive strength of the attacking unit

- defensive strength of the defending unit

- whether or not either unit has already been wounded in battle

- terrain that might give advantages and disadvantages to either unit

- nearby units that can lend support

- the nearby presence or absence of a General or other leader

- the morale of a unit or of its team

- a random dice roll (to simulate the uncertainty of actual combat)

Generally, players tally these factors and consult an appropriate table that lists the outcome of the encounter. The complexity of the simulation doesn't end there, however, because the result of an attack can also take a variety of forms, including:

- one or both units is eliminated

- one or both units is reduced in strength

- one or both units is forced to retreat

- one unit displaces the other's position

A rich procedural representation emerges out of the factors going into and coming out of an encounter between wargame units. By tweaking the formal characteristics of units and the overall resolution system of a game, game designers can arrive at highly specific procedural representations of a historical battle. Depending on the particular game, the simulation might be a World War II tank division encountering enemy infantry, or a troop of horse-mounted archers fighting a phalanx of spearmen in the ancient Middle East.

Wargames are incredibly detailed. At the same time, everything about the representation of units in a wargame is highly stylized: a simple cardboard chit or metal figure "stands in" for a military unit, with each piece representing a whole group of soldiers or vehicles that move as a single block; the straightline or grid-based movement of the units; the reduction of combat to simple numerical factors; a single human player directing the entire battle from a birds-eye view. These are only a few examples of the many ways historical wargames radically abstract their subject matter. However, if you accept these limitations, if you take on the conventions of the game genre, within them there is room for endless play, both for the player exploring permutations of history and for the game designer constructing the systems that make the historical simulation possible.

The Field of Battle

In addition to characteristics of the units and the rules for their interaction, the design of the field of play presents its own challenges. A historical wargame has to function as both a playable game and an accurate simulation of history, two concerns that can often be at odds with each other. Wargame designer James Dunnigan writes about some of the design concerns in creating a game map:

> There are two primary things to keep in mind when examining a geographical game map. First, it often has a grid, most often a hexagonal grid, superimposed over it…. The second point is that in most historical situations, only very large ("gross") terrain features have any significant effect on operations. Thus, a great deal of detail on a map will often get in the way of providing an accurate simulation. The designer usually feels obliged to justify all of this detail. Often the gamer will be equally expectant that all of this detail be put to some use or otherwise why bother him with it. There is an unspoken assumption that only that which is essential is displayed. It is normally considered a bad design if information is included in the game that does not contribute to one's understanding of what is going on.[9]

The real world is infinitely rich, and cartographers—including game map-makers—are faced with the representational challenge of simplifying geography in a way that is meaningful for the intended use of the map. In a map for a historical wargame, designers must decide what to include and what to leave out, how to abstract and structure the information to fit in the larger game system. As Dunnigan puts it, too much detail in the terrain can get in the way of a player's understanding; only "gross" terrain features have a real impact on military operations. Abstraction emphasizes the features critical to understanding the terrain, while minimizing the "noise" created by less important elements.

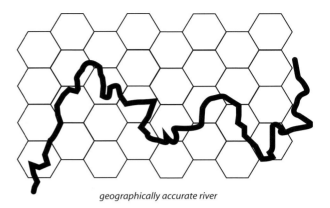

geographically accurate river

The grid of the map is one important consideration. Units in a grid-based wargame move only within the hexagons or squares superimposed on the map. Because of this, there is a very specific relationship between the grid and the terrain. The game designer not only needs to select the relevant terrain features, but also decides how those features fit into the grid. Because terrain can affect movement, simply laying a grid over topographically correct terrain creates formal ambiguity. For example, in a particular game, units might not be able to cross rivers. If a river flows through the middle of a map hex, does it mean that players can enter the hex but not exit out the other side, or that they cannot enter the hex in the first place? A common solution in wargame map design is to stylize the shape of rivers so that they are located only on the edges of hexes. This solution makes the movement-blocking role of rivers in the game completely clear. Designing the terrain to accommodate the game grid lessens the geographic accuracy of the map: there are no naturally occurring rivers that can be plotted exactly along a hexagonal grid. But for game design purposes, abstraction that eliminates formal ambiguity is essential.

Questions about rivers and wargame map design do not end there. If one purpose of a historical wargame is fidelity to the real battlefield, which rivers should be included? When does a tributary or stream become too small to be indicated on the

map? Which rivers should have an impact on the play of the game? As Dunnigan points out, if something is prominent on the map, a player will expect it to impact game play: a visible feature that does not contribute to the functioning of the rules is bad design.

In designing a wargame map, in deciding which features to include and how to represent them within the larger simulation, you are doing more than just creating a map. You are constructing a space of meaning. If your game simulates combat between individual soldiers, the terrain elements you include make a representational statement about which type of terrain affects a certain kind of combat. The *meaning* of a wargame map arises not just from its geographic or pictorial features: the meaning derives from the role the map plays in the larger game experience. The formal qualities of the map make certain player actions possible, actions that constitute the ongoing moments of game play.

Not all wargames use a grid. Some miniatures games measure unit movement in inches, and in some digital wargames, unit movement is free-form and highly granular. In these cases, the principles of abstraction and meaningful play still hold. Are the map elements communicating their meaning to the player? Do they affect game play in ways that make sense within the

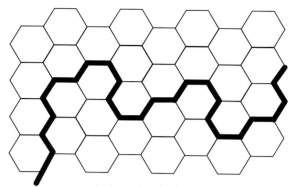

hexagonally stylized river

larger system of the game? Is the simulation creating a coherent representation? Are the outcomes of the player's choices meaningful? As play unfolds moment by moment, the total experience of the game emerges. In this way, the play of simulation brings us back to the most fundamental questions of game design.

Simulation in Context

Historical wargaming provides a terrific context for better understanding issues of representation and simulation because the premise of the genre is that a game accurately depicts a real-world historical referent. Most kinds of games do not have such an orthodox view of how accurately they simulate "reality." However, a related set of issues has increasingly come to prominence within digital games. Exactly how does a computer or video game procedurally represents its subject? At stake are the same core concerns we explored in historical wargames: how it is that a game simulation can create meaningful play.

The steadily increasing power of computer technology to simulate and manage complex systems has opened up new possibilities for game design in the digital realm. Incredibly detailed simulations of light, sound, physics, agent behavior, and other phenomena are becoming commonplace within games. Many

recent writings from digital game designers focus on this feature of digital media and suggest strategies for game designers to use in their work. Let's compare three such examples:

- In *Swords & Circuitry*, Hallford and Hallford discuss simulation design in games using the example of a grenade destroying a door. One approach to simulating this effect would be to specify the relationship between each grenade and each door in the game. In this case, every possible instance of a grenade effect in the game would have to be explicitly spelled out in the program. In contrast, in a more flexible system, grenades would belong to a general category of objects that cause damage, and doors would belong to a general category of objects that break when they receive damage. Hallford and Hallford strongly prefer this latter approach to simulation design.[10]

- In *Game Design: Theory and Practice,* Richard Rouse III discusses a related set of ideas through the example of a dungeon puzzle, in which players open a secret door by dropping objects on a pressure plate trigger. One design approach would be to hard-code relationships between every object and the pressure plate, so that objects defined as "heavy" trigger the plate. Rouse advocates the creation of a generalized weight system instead, in which every object in the game has a numeric weight rating; if the weight value of the objects on the pressure plate reaches a certain number, the plate is triggered.[11]

- In "The Future of Game Design," Harvey Smith shows a similar preference in an example involving bird behavior. Bird behavior could be modeled so that when a player moves within a certain radius of a simulated bird, the bird flies into the air. However, Smith would rather see a more detailed simulation in which the bird's behavior could be triggered by the perception of light, sound, motion, or other modeled stimuli that would be more tightly integrated into the system of the game as a whole.[12]

All three of these examples make a similar point: there is a difference between a simple, *case-based* structure for a simulation and a more complex *generalized* structure that relies on integrated, systemic relationships. Although both approaches create procedural representations, the authors show a clear preference for one approach over the other. In their work, they cite a number of reasons why a generalized strategy is better for designing simulations:

·   *It decreases work time:* When a game system is large, generalized systems allow for much more flexible design. In the grenade example, specifying every possible interaction between every possible weapon and every possible object in the game would be a major programming task. Making adjustments to these relationships once they are established (such as reverse-engineering metal doors to be immune to grenade damage) means going back into the code and modifying every affected instance. By creating classes of objects as Hallford and Hallford suggest, categories of objects can be moved in and out of different effect classes, so that game designers can quickly try out different combinations of relationships in the game.

·   *It increases emergence:* More flexible game simulations lead to a greater degree of emergence in the game as a whole. In Smith's example, having a more detailed behavioral simulation for the birds creates more varied roles for the birds to play in the game. If the birds react to sound and not just to proximity, a game moment in which gunshots ring out and the flock of birds dramatically takes to the sky becomes possible. This is not necessarily something designed directly into the game, but it is an emergent effect of the simple rules governing bird behavior. With more detailed simulations, the space of possibility is enlarged and complexified.

·   *It increases play options:* More generalized simulation systems give players more choices and more ways to solve problems. In Rouse's example of the dungeon pressure

plate, a player that had no object to drop might create a magical snowstorm that created enough weight on the floor to affect the plate. Idiosyncratic play styles are encouraged, rewarding players for exploring the increased space of possibility. This leads to more distinct styles of play and more avenues for meaning. If a group of Smith's birds were present in a deathmatch game, for example, a smart player might strategically position himself, fire a shot to scatter the flock, and then use the motion of the birds as visual cover for an assault on the enemy.

A Balanced Approach

Hallford and Hallford, Rouse, and Smith strongly advocate the use of generalized simulation design techniques as opposed to a case-based approach. But is it really possible to integrate every aspect of a game within a generalized system? One eloquent thinker on this topic is game designer Marc LeBlanc:

> By "simulation" I mean game systems that are rich, many-faceted analog models, whereas by "emulation" I mean coarse, case-based game systems. An example of "simulation" might be the physics system in a shooter or the damage model in an RPG. The rules of the system create a space for exploration, allow for emergent complexity, and so forth. An example of "emulation" might be, in either game, a button that opens a door. There is no physical simulation of the electro-mechanical process of opening the door. It's just a single rule: "if button pushed, then door opens." The button is more of a semantic object than a physical object; in some sense it exists only on a functional level. Emulation is the smoke-and-mirror approach.[13]

LeBlanc brings to light a point we made at the start of this chapter: *simulations can be embedded.* Even though an entire game can be considered as a single representation, it is important to be able to identify the smaller procedural representations that make up the larger whole. Although LeBlanc shares a preference for generalized simulation design strategies, he takes a measured approach and ultimately suggests a balance of case-based and generalized techniques. No game can rely entirely on rich, open-ended, emergent simulation. Nor should it. To demonstrate this balancing act, LeBlanc takes an example from a title he helped create, the computer game Thief, in which players can use water to put out a torch:

> This is an emulated game system; there's a single rule that says water puts out fire 100 percent of the time. There's no simulation; no chance of using too little water and just getting steam, and no chance of drowning the torch so that it can never be relit. However, the other systems that interact with that system are simulations; you typically douse a torch by tossing a "water balloon" at it, the motion of which is physically simulated. The way the light from the torch affects your vision, and more relevantly, the vision of the opponents you want to stay hidden from, is also simulated.[14]

(Remember that LeBlanc is using his own terminology—for example, he is using the term "simulation" to mean a *generalized* design approach, which is only one part of what we identify as the larger issue of simulation in games.)

LeBlanc's example contains intersecting systems of representation, some case-based and some generalized. In Thief, water puts out fire 100 percent of the time. Rather than a complex physics simulation with a variety of possible results, there is a predictable and consistent outcome: water extinguishes fire. But this case-based approach interacts with more complex structures. Tossing a water balloon at the torch involves the generalized simulation of motion; the diminished visibility from the extinguished torch results from a generalized simulation of light. The whole of the game representation emerges from the complex relationships of these parts.

In fact, most games use an approach that combines case-based and generalized representations. The Deux Ex characters of thug, civilian, and military agent were designed with generalized heuristics that produce emergent behavior. But other characters in the game were designed with simple, case-based behavior, such as a character that activates a cinematic cutscene when encountered. Even simple board games such as Candyland combine a generalized movement system with a number of case-based special spaces on which players can land.

If Rouse, Smith, and Hallford and Hallford are correct, if a generalized approach saves time, increases emergence, and provides players with richer play, why would a digital game designer (or any game designer) use a case-based approach for structuring a procedural representation? One answer is that a truly generalized system could easily become overly complex to implement and might not save work time in the end. Another answer is that although case-based approaches can sometimes become simple and flatfooted, the opposite danger is true of generalized strategies. Taken too far, generalized simulation design can become fuzzy and ambiguous. If you are playing a game and you see a group of birds that suddenly takes to the air for no reason, their behavior will seem random and meaningless. It might be that their behavior is simulated in such detail that their internal clocks told them it was time to leave the scene and migrate south for the winter. Unfortunately, the accuracy of the simulation would be lost on the player, who has no way of knowing how the meaning of the birds' actions fit into the larger game experience.

Neither case-based nor generalized design strategies guarantee a successful game experience. The goal of game design is the creation of meaningful play, which should guide the selection of representational strategies in a game. In the example of the Zelda witch, a compelling character was created out of a central case-based procedure: if the player brings a mushroom to the witch, she will turn it into magic powder. This procedural representation was well-integrated into the other more generalized representational strategies of the game (the witch's hut is isolated, difficult to find, and dangerous to reach; mushrooms are hidden in the forest; magic powder has special effects in the game). Thus the meaning of the witch gained its power from the total game context in which it was experienced.

The fact that rich meanings can emerge from a representational context not based on software complexities offers an important insight into game design and simulation. As we've mentioned, games currently suffer from a narrow range of simulated subject matter. Although there are important historical reasons for the prevalence of military and economic conflict in games, other forms of conflict, such as social, cultural, or emotional conflict, can and should be represented as well. Some presume that an increase in technological complexity will make such representations possible. For example, a widely published quote from an executive at a major console manufacturer not too long ago looked forward to the day when the faces of game characters could represent emotion. According to the executive, on that day, games would become a mature and sophisticated form of cultural production. Clearly, media such as literature, theater, and comics have been capable of sophisticated representation for centuries without relying on high-resolution animation. Furthermore, even within the history of animation, many animated tears have already rolled down numerous animated cheeks. That fact alone is no guarantee that the story was meaningful to its viewers. In the case of computer games, although animated elements do play a part, the systemic and interactive qualities of the form have to be taken into account when envisioning future directions for the medium.

The procedural representation of new kinds of game content is within our grasp, but new content can only be discovered by paying attention to the fundamental principles of game design and meaningful play. Game designers need to cultivate a deeper understanding of the form in which they work. This is especially true in considering games as simulations. More than just choosing a representational design strategy, there is a complex interplay between a simulation and its simulated subject. It is to this relationship that our attention now turns.

The Value of Reality

We have come to a turning point in this chapter. Up to now, our primary focus in considering the play of simulation has been on how simulations operate: the mechanisms that generate procedural representation, the abstraction necessary when game designers simulate a particular subject, the selection of case-based and generalized strategies for structuring simulations. But there is a very different aspect of simulations for us to consider. Recall our definition: *a simulation is a procedural representation of aspects of "reality."* So far, our emphasis has been on the procedural component of simulations. But now we turn to the equally important and immensely complicated set of questions regarding simulations and "reality."

What is the relationship between the simulated content of a game and its real-world or imagined referent? At the 1998 Game Developers Conference, game designer Steve Jackson shared a fascinating anecdote about creating a driving combat computer game based on his classic paper game Car Wars. Using real-world physics and car data, the development team created an unusually detailed driving simulation that incorporated minute details of driving physics and a detailed simulation of the car engine. They also created a track based precisely on the geometry of an existing speedway. But when they test-drove their simulated car, using a steering wheel and pedal interface, they weren't able to reach the top speeds of the car on which the simulation was based. One day a professional race car driver visited the company. He sat down at the game prototype and immediately drove the simulated car around the track at breakneck speed, completing it close to the real-world speed record.

The simulation was so "accurate" that it required expert manipulation in order to resemble the real-world phenomena it had been designed to replicate. What's the lesson? Don't forget the player. The designers of the game had assumed that simulation design meant only formally recreating a mathematical model of the car and the track. In fact, a game simulation not only includes the formal mechanisms of the system, but also the ways that those mechanisms engender and permit player action. The rules never solely determine the play of a game. The rules are always set into motion within an experiential context that includes particular players with their own levels of desire, skill, and expectation. The Car Wars designers had created a certain space of possibility with their design, but it took the right kind of player to navigate that space in the way it was meant to be explored.

The Car Wars anecdote reminds us that questions regarding the "reality" of a representation are never as simple as they seem at first glance. Was the car simulation "accurate"? Or was it only accurate in the hands of a professional race car driver? Is sitting in front of a computer monitor anything like driving a car? Would the race car driver have been able to reach top speeds playing with a standard console controller? Does the fact that the experience was "only a game" impact the answers to these questions?

When players interact with a simulation, they are never playing with the real thing. If they were, it couldn't be called a "simulation." At the same time, a simulation does reference its depicted subject through images, sound, and procedures. But how do these representations relate to their referents? In language, we know that the letters C-O-W don't resemble a cow in any way. But a photograph of a cow does bear some similarity to our own perception of a cow in the real world. How do games relate to their depicted subject matter? To answer these important questions, we return to the concept of metacommunication.

Framing the Simulation

*Children know that they are manipulating their thoughts about reality, not reality itself; and they know that their play self is not the same as their everyday self.—**Brian Sutton-Smith,** The Ambiguity of Play*

In **Games as the Play of Meaning,** we introduced Gregory Bateson's concept of metacommunication, the unique form of communication that takes place in the context of play. To use

Bateson's own example, when a dog nips another dog, the nip signals two things. On the one hand, the nip signifies a bite; it is a stand-in for the action of a real bite. On the other hand, the nip signifies just the opposite of a bite: it signals the fact that the two dogs are playing and not actually fighting. This kind of metacommunication—communication about communication—is present not just in informal play but in games as well. It is a significant part of the complex mechanisms games use to construct meanings for their players.

Why is the concept of metacommunication so important, especially in the context of simulation? Metacommunication makes it clear that to play a game is to take part in a kind of double-consciousness. Game actions refer to actions in the real world, but because they are taking place in a game, they are simultaneously quite separate and distinct from the real world actions they reference. A kiss in Spin the Bottle or a frag in a Quake deathmatch refer to kissing and killing, but at the same time are actions that communicate *I'm not kissing or killing you. I'm just playing.* The magic circle is the space within which such paradoxical signals become meaningful.

In "A Theory of Play and Fantasy," Bateson uses the following diagram to illustrate the paradoxical state of mind embodied in play:[15]

> All statements within this frame are untrue.
>
> I love you.
>
> I hate you.

This schematic is a riff on Epimenides' Paradox, also known as the Liar Paradox. The Liar Paradox is the philosophical problem of someone asserting "I am lying." If the speaker *is* a liar, then he is telling the truth, and vice versa: the liar's statement is a logical paradox. In the diagram, the first sentence, *All statements within this frame are untrue,* echoes this classical logic problem. But significantly, it locates the statement within a *frame,* a limited context within which the paradoxical sentence asserts its meaning.

For Bateson the frame is a psychological and philosophical construct that delimits the peculiar space of play. For game designers, Bateson's frame offers another way of understanding the magic circle of a game. It is a boundary that makes the paradoxical meanings of play possible. At the same time, the frame is only sustained by virtue of the continued metacommunicative assertions of play. In Bateson's illustration, the frame enables the statement's meaning, even as the frame's own meaning comes directly from the statement itself.

The magic circle is both a prerequisite and an effect of play. It is a robust context for the exhilarating experiences of game play. But it is similarly fragile, and vanishes quickly when a game ends. Bateson's diagram is a schematic of the cognitive frame of play, a visual retelling of the state of mind of a player in the midst of a play context. As a way of understanding what happens when a player enters into the magic circle and plays with a game simulation, it is a subtle and powerful illustration.

What about the other two statements, *I love you* and *I hate you*? These statements are also part of the paradoxical meanings captured within the frame. The two sentences address a larger point Bateson makes about set theory, and whether some or all of the statements within the frame could be considered true or untrue. For our present purposes, we will sidestep his larger argument to make a point of our own. Bateson could have included any two contradictory sentences in the frame. But he chose emotional statements about love and hate, statements seemingly addressed to someone else outside the frame.

These two little sentences, signals of pure emotion, remind us that the questions of play and meaning, of metacommunication and paradox, are not just abstract philosophical chatter. In understanding how games construct meaning, we are address-ing the deeply felt ways that players engage with games and the emotional and social realities games reflect and construct. The metacommunicative state of mind is deeply intertwined with the unique pleasures and experiences of play.

The Immersive Fallacy

*All forms of entertainment strive to create **suspension of disbelief,** a state in which the player's mind forgets that it is being subjected to entertainment and instead accepts what it perceives as reality.— **François Dominic Laramée,** "Immersion"*

We will return to Bateson's ideas about metacommunication and meaning in just a moment. But for now, let's bring the discussion back to the play of simulation, specifically the relationship between a game and the "reality" upon which it is based. The preceding quote is from a book on game design, appearing in an essay on "Immersion." Game designer and programmer François Dominic Laramée argues for a particular relationship between a game player and a game, between the player's state of mind and the perceived reality of the experience. He asserts that a game should strive to create an experience in which the player forgets that he or she is experiencing designed entertainment and instead believes that playing the game is experiencing reality firsthand. In fact, Laramée states that "all forms of entertainment" function in this way. This is a point of view very much at odds with our own.

We don't mean to unfairly single out Laramée. His ideas about how a player experiences the "reality" of a game are extremely common in the digital game industry, the game press, and even in the public at large. Game designer Frank Lantz has called these kinds of ideas about immersion "widely held but seldom examined" beliefs.[16] We wholeheartedly agree, and in the pages that follow we refute these beliefs, referring to them as the *immersive fallacy.* The immersive fallacy is the idea that the pleasure of a media experience lies in its ability to sensually transport the participant into an illusory, simulated reality.

According to the immersive fallacy, this reality is so complete that ideally the frame falls away so that the player truly believes that he or she is part of an imaginary world.

Although the immersive fallacy has taken hold in many fields, it is particularly prevalent in the digital game industry. Common within the discourse of the immersive fallacy is the idea that entertainment technology is inevitably leading to the development of more and more powerful systems of simulation. These technologies will be able to create fully illusionistic experiences that are indistinguishable from the real world. In an online discussion about the future of gaming, game designer Warren Spector speculated on this topic:

> Is the Star Trek Holodeck an inevitable end result of games as simulacra? The history of media (mass and otherwise) seems pretty clearly a march toward ever more faithful approximations of reality —from the development of the illusion of perspective in paintings to photography to moving pictures to color moving pictures with sound to color moving pictures with sound beamed directly into your home via television to today's immersive reality games like Quake and System Shock. Is this progression inevitable and will it continue or have we reached the end of the line, realism-wise?[17]

To be fair, Spector self-consciously exaggerated his views in order to spark discussion. But in the debate that followed, it was clear that many participants take for granted the propositions that Spector articulated.

Spector's selective history of entertainment technologies offers one reading of the development of media. But there are others. History rarely provides such a linear progression, and in regard to immersion, cultural developments tend to be cyclical. As theorist Marie-Laure Ryan puts it, "The history of Western art has seen the rise and fall of immersive ideals."[18] According to Ryan, immersion as a representational goal has gone through a number of stylistic cycles over the centuries. In the last several decades, she asserts, immersion has in fact become less promi-

nent and respected in fields like art and literature. Ryan may be correct in regard to larger cultural movements, but within the digital game industry, belief in the immersive fallacy remains alive and well.

Metacommunicative Media

The immersive fallacy is symptomatic of contradictory ideas about technology. On one hand, there is a technological fetishism that sees the evolutionary development of new technology as the saving grace of experience design. On the other hand, there is a desire to erase the technology, to make it invisible so that all frames around the experience fall away and disappear. Nowhere are these contradictory ideals more clearly expressed than in the concept of the holodeck, a fictional technology that first appeared in the television show *Star Trek: The Next Generation*. The holodeck is the dream of the immersive fallacy, a room in which matter and energy are manipulated to create a simulated environment of sight, sound, touch, smell, and taste that is a representation completely indistinguishable from lived reality.

What is wrong with this picture, and how does it relate to games? On one level, the immersive fallacy actually does make intuitive sense. When we play a game, we feel engaged and engrossed, and play seems to take on its own "reality." This is all certainly true. But the way that a game achieves these effects does not happen in the manner the immersive fallacy implies. A game player does become engrossed in the game, yes. But it is an engagement that occurs *through play itself*. As we know, play is a process of metacommunication, a double-consciousness in which the player is well aware of the artificiality of the play situation.

During the same online conversation in which Spector posted his intentionally provocative question, film studies scholar Elena Gorfinkel responded:

Immersion is not a property of a game or media text but is an effect that a text produces. What I mean is that immersion is an experience that happens between a game and its player, and is not something intrinsic to the aesthetics of a game. The confusion in this conversation has emerged because representational strategies are conflated with the effect of immersion. Immersion itself is not tied to a replication or mimesis of reality. For example, one can get immersed in Tetris. Therefore, immersion into game play seems at least as important as immersion into a game's representational space. It seems that these components need to be separated to do justice and better understand how immersion, as a category of experience and perception, works.[19]

Gorfinkel makes a number of critical points. First, with her example of Tetris she points out that there are plenty of examples of games in which "immersion" is not tied to a sensory replication of reality. In fact, there are countless examples of art and entertainment media, from techno music to comic books to expressionist painting, which are clearly not premised on a simple suspension of disbelief. As Gorfinkel states, mistaken ideas about immersion can be framed as confusion between the intrinsic qualities of a media object and the effects that object produces. Gorfinkel argues that to understand the subtleties of "immersion," we need to look not just at the attributes of games (such as how detailed the graphics are), but at the way games function in relation to the experience of the player.

In the case of play, we know that metacommunication is always in operation. A teen kissing another teen in Spin the Bottle or a Gran Turismo player driving a virtual race car each understands that their play references other realities. But the very thing that makes their activity *play* is that they also know they are participating within a constructed reality, and are consciously taking on the artificial meanings of the magic circle. It is possible to say that the players of a game are "immersed"—immersed in *meaning*. To play a game is to take part in a complex interplay of meaning. But this kind of immersion is quite different from the sensory transport promised by the immersive fallacy.

Remediating Games

In some sense, the layered, metacommunicative state of play is similar to our experience of all media. In their book *Remediation*, theorists Jay David Bolter and Richard Grusin analyze the mechanisms by which media function, arguing that media operate according to a double logic. On one hand, media participate in what Bolter and Grusin call *immediacy*, the ability to authentically reproduce the world and create an alternative reality. At the same time, media also remind their audiences that they are constructed and artificial, a characteristic that Bolter and Grusin call *hypermediacy*.

> Like other media since the Renaissance—in particular, perspective painting, photography, film, and television—new digital media oscillate between immediacy and hypermediacy, between transparency and opacity. Although each medium promises to reform its predecessors by offering a more immediate or authentic experience, the promise of reform inevitably leads us to become aware of the medium as a medium. Thus, immediacy leads to hypermediacy.[20]

For example, as Bolter and Grusin point out, a web cam promises immediacy though authentic, real-time access to another part of the world. But the fact that users have to view the web cam on a computer, in an operating system, in a browser, on a web page, inside an interface, reminds them that they are not transparently experiencing the locale where the web cam exists, but are instead interacting with a highly artificial media construct. The main argument made by Bolter and Grusin is that all media combine these two processes into what they term *remediation*, an experience of media in which immediacy and hypermediacy co-exist.

We can also analyze games within this model. The double consciousness of play finds a strong parallel in the process of remediation, which mixes transparent immediacy with a hypermediated awareness of the constructed nature of play. In Cops and Robbers, players willingly take on the theatrical roles of criminals and police, even as they infuse those playful representations with meaning through their actions. In a first-person shooter such as Halo, part of the experience is the sensual vertigo of navigating a coherent, imaginary 3D space. But playing the game also involves an awareness of the game interface, the strategic use of the frame-breaking options, the use of text-based chat, fluctuating server speeds, and the sharing of tips with friends in the larger social context of play. These frame-related aspects of the Halo experience remind the player that the game is a constructed, hypermediated experience.

The value of Bolter and Grusin's model is that it doesn't do away with illusionistic immersion, but includes it as one element within a more complex process. There is no doubt that the immediacy of sensory engagement is part of the pleasure of playing a game, particularly digital games with detailed representations that respond in real-time to player action. The immersive fallacy grossly overemphasizes these forms of pleasure, and in so doing, misrepresents the diverse palette of experiences games offer.

The Character of Character

The danger of the immersive fallacy is that it misrepresents how play functions—and game design can suffer as a result. If game designers fail to recognize the way games create meaning for players—as something separate from, but connected to the real world—they will have difficulty creating truly meaningful play. To highlight these complexities, we now take a detailed look at just one aspect of a game's representation, *character*, to see how an understanding of metacommunication can impact the game design process.

We have already looked at character once in this schema, examining the way that procedural representations construct fictional personas in Zelda: Link's Awakening, Virtua Fighter 4, Deus Ex, and The Blob. Now we'll take aim at the other part of the simulation equation, pointing out the way that character representation relates to the "reality" outside the game. Two key questions arise: How does the player relate to a character in a game? And how can this relationship be understood in terms of the "reality" of the represented world? Just to keep things focused, we will limit our analysis to protagonist characters that a player directly controls, such as Mario in Super Mario World or Pai Chan in Virtual Fighter 4.

The immersive fallacy would assert that a player has an "immersive" relationship with the character, that to play the character is to *become* the character. In the immersive fallacy's ideal game, the player would identify completely with the character, the game's frame would drop away, and the player would lose him or herself totally within the game character.

These ideas have some validity, but they represent only one element of a much larger and more complicated process. A player's relationship to a game character he or she directly controls is not a simple matter of direct identification. Instead, a player relates to a game character through the double-consciousness of play. A protagonist character is a persona through which a player exerts him or herself into an imaginary world; this relationship can be intense and emotionally "immersive." However, at the very same time, the character is a tool, a puppet, an object for the player to manipulate according to the rules of the game. In this sense, the player is fully aware of the character as an artificial construct.

This double-consciousness is what makes character-based game play such a rich and multi-layered experience. In playing the role of Cloud in Final Fantasy VII, the player has a portal into the complex narrative world of the game. Through Cloud, the player encounters the settings, characters, and events of the game world; many players report a strong emotional attachment to their digital counterpart. At the same time, Final Fantasy VII is a complex role-playing game. The play experience occurs by watching cutscenes, navigating Cloud and his comrades though virtual spaces, managing a detailed inventory of weapons, items, and magic, taking part in constant strategic battles, and engaging with the game's intricate spreadsheet-like interface. Through these diverse activities, the performance of play acknowledges and celebrates its own hypermediated construction.

The psychologist Gary Alan Fine, in his excellent book *Shared Fantasies,* offers a model for understanding the complex relationship between player and character. *Shared Fantasies* is an ethnographic study of tabletop role-playing game communities. Borrowing from psychologist Erving Goffman's theories of Frame Analysis, Fine identifies three "levels of meaning" within which the player/character game experience takes place:

> First, gaming, like all activity, is grounded in the "primary framework," the commonsense understandings that *people* have of the real world. This is action without laminations. It is a framework that does not depend on other frameworks but on the ultimate reality of events.

> Second, players must deal with the game context; they are *players* whose actions are governed by a complicated set of rules and constraints. They manipulate their characters, having knowledge of the structure of the game, and having approximately the same knowledge that other players have.

> Finally, this gaming world is keyed in that the players not only manipulate characters; they *are* characters. The *character* identity is separate from the *player* identity.[21]

This three-fold framing of player consciousness—as a *character* in a simulated world, as a *player* in a game, and as a *person* in a larger social setting—elegantly sketches out the experience of play. The *player* and *character* frames both take place within the magic circle, whereas the *person* frame gains its primary meaning from the cultural context outside the immediate space of play. Fine makes the important point that movement among these frames is fluid and constant, and that it is possible to switch between them several times in the course of a single verbal statement or game action.

In digital games, the same multi-layered phenomena occurs. Imagine a player, holding a joystick-like controller, looking at a glass screen. The player is deeply engrossed in a game activity, sweating and anxious, focused completely on the space in front of him, leaning his body in synch with the visceral rhythms of the game, smiling and grimacing as he battles opponents and his actions play out in the world on the other side of the glass. What game is he playing? Try on both of these answers for size:

He is playing Tomb Raider. Our hypothetical player is looking at a television screen and manipulating a console controller. In one sense, our player immerses himself in the game's narrative world, taking on the identity of Lara Croft with her requisite strengths and weaknesses (*I feel lost… I can't believe I survived that trap!*). Simultaneously, he views her exaggerated anatomy from behind, pushing buttons and manipulating her like a puppet on his quest to find power-ups, overcome obstacles, and unlock doors to reach the next level (*What was that cheat code again? This cutscene sucks.*). He is both *character* and *player.* In addition, the larger social and cultural context in which he plays constitutes Fine's category of the player as *person.* Maybe he is trying to impress a friend with his skillful play. Or perhaps he is taking mental notes for a lecture he is going to give at an academic conference. In any case, the player is always present as a person connected to and situated in the real world.

He is competing in Comedy Central's BattleBots. In this case, the player's character is a battling, remote-controlled robot moving about the real world, the pane of glass not a television screen but a large sheet of plexi that protects the players and audience from flying scraps of metal. The BattleBots player is immersed in his activity too, and like the Tomb Raider player he is always aware that his actions are governed by the rules of the game. During game play, he might switch between the *character/player/person* frames many times, moving between emotional identification with his robot character (*Ouch! I just got slammed!*) and his role as player in the game contest (*Let's see if I can get my bot out of the corner*). He might even break the frame of player to wave to a friend in the crowd or to offer a sound bite to the television host.

Fine's three-layer model is an extension of the double-consciousness of play. Players always know that they are playing, and in that knowledge are free to move among the roles of person, player, and character. Players of a game freely embrace the flexibility of this movement, coming in and out of moments of immersion, breaking the player and character frames, yet all the while maintaining the magic circle.

This model applies even when players are not directly controlling a game protagonist. In any game, players move constantly between cognitive frames, shifting from a deep immersion with the game's representation to a deep engagement with the game's strategic mechanisms to an acknowledgement of the space outside the magic circle. Devotees of the immersive fallacy tend to see this hybrid consciousness as a regrettable state of affairs that will only evolve to its true state of pure immersion when the technology arrives. Play tells us otherwise. The many-layered state of mind that occurs during play is something to be celebrated, not repressed—it is responsible for some of the unique pleasures that emerge from a game.

Hacking the Holodeck

The questions surrounding games as simulations are always more complex than they first appear. [22] There is no simple relationship between player and character, or player and game, or game and outside world. This is one reason why the immersive fallacy continues to colonize most design thinking about the future of games and the role of technology in creating compelling experiences: it is simply an easier position to take.

But the immersive fallacy is more than an idea. It is also a stumbling block to advances in game design, as it represents an overly romantic and antiquated model for how media operate. As long as game designers are caught up in a desire for the technology of the holodeck, they lack the vision to appreciate the potential for game innovation today. What if game designers focused their efforts on actively playing with the double-consciousness of play, rather than pining for immersion?

Imagine the kinds of games that could result: games that encourage players to constantly shift the frame of the game, questioning what is inside or outside the game; games that play with the lamination between player and character, pushing and pulling against the connection through inventive forms of narrative play; games that emphasize metagaming, or that connect the magic circle so closely with external contexts that the game appears synchronous with everyday life. Innovation is only bound by a failure to see the fundamental principles of play.

A common complaint among game developers is that games are not recognized as a significant form of culture, and that they lack a diverse mass audience. Instead, games seem to be relegated to the backwaters of culture. A sea change in cultural status will only occur when game designers acquire a more sophisticated understanding of how their media operates. Robust forms of contemporary pop culture are not premised on naïve ideas of immersion. Just take a look at the explicit self-consciousness of hip-hop, fashion, and Animé. These forms of popular culture have a deep understanding of the way media cultivates immersion while making explicit the mechanisms through which the representation is experienced.

This, of course, brings us back to simulation. Even though simulations are premised on the notion of fidelity to their referent, the very fact that they are dynamic systems means they allow for the exploration of alternate permutations. Simulations allow players to explore a space of representational possibility through the very act of play. Certainly there are a great many game designers driven by a desire to tell stories and provide narrative worlds for players. Framing games as simulations, as dynamic systems of procedural representation, unlocks the potential of games as a powerful representational and narrative medium. But games have only just scratched at the surface. Questions remain: What can games represent? How can games engage players through meaningful play? And how can games challenge, critique, and contribute to the world outside the magic circle?

Further Reading

Narrative as Virtual Reality: Immersion and Interactivity in Literature and Electronic Media, by Marie-Laure Ryan

An eloquent articulation of the relationships between literary theory, hypertext, and VR, *Narrative as Virtual Reality* focuses on what Ryan sees as the competing interests of immersion and interactivity. Although Ryan's sophisticated approach elevates her above the usual pitfalls of the immersive fallacy, she is an apologist for immersion, and her discussions of interactive design suffers as a result. That said, for the topics that this thick volume covers, it is essential reading.

> *Recommended:*
> Part II: The Poetics of Immersion
> Part III: The Poetics of Interactivity

Remediation: Understanding New Media, by Jay David Bolter and Richard Grusin

Bolter and Grusin introduce the concept of remediation, the process in which new media forms define themselves by borrowing from and refashioning old media. This process also works in reverse: older media forms borrow from new media forms, such as television remediating the windowed world of computing. The book's most useful concepts for game designers are *immediacy,* and *hypermediacy,* which refer to the way media forms can both authentically reproduce the world while simultaneously reminding the audience that the reproduction is both constructed and artificial.

> *Recommended:*
> Introduction: The Double Logic of Remediation
> Chapter 1: Immediacy, Hypermediacy, and Remediation
> Chapter 2: Mediation and Remediation
> Chapter 4: Computer Games

Shared Fantasy, by Gary Alan Fine *(see page 417)*

> *Recommended:*
> Chapter 1: FRP
> Chapter 2: Players
> Chapter 3: Collective Fantasy
> Chapter 6: Frames and Games

"A Theory of Play and Fantasy" by Gregory Bateson *(see page 373)*

Notes

1. Henry Eddington, Eric Addinall, and Fred Percival, *A Handbook of Game Design* (London: Kogan Page Limited, 1982), p. 10.
2. Andrew Fluegelman and Shoshana Tembeck, *The New Games Book* (New York: Doubleday, 1976), p. 109.
3. Warren Robinett, *Inventing the Adventure Game,* unpublished manuscript.
4. Neal Hallford with Jana Hallford, *Swords and Circuitry: A Designer's Guide to Computer Role-Playing Games* (Roseville, CA: Prima Publishing, 2001), p. 175.
5. Fluegelman and Tembeck, *The New Games Book*, p. 107.
6. Robinett, *Inventing the Adventure Game.*
7. Harvey Smith, "The Future of Game Design," <www.gamasutra.com>.
8. Ibid.
9. James F. Dunnigan, *Wargames Handbook, Third Edition: How to Play and Design Commercial and Professional Wargames* (San Jose: Writers Club Press, 2000), p. 109.
10. Hallford and Hallford, *Swords and Circuitry,* p. 170–171
11. Richard Rouse III, *Game Design: Theory and Practice* (Plano, TX: Wordware Publishing, 2001), p. 122-123.
12. Harvey Smith, "The Future of Game Design"
13. RE:PLAY: Game Design + Game Culture. Online conference, 2000 <www.eyebeam.org>.
14. Ibid.
15. Gregory Bateson, "A Theory of Play and Fantasy" in *Steps to an Ecology of Mind* (Chicago: University of Chicago Press, 1972), p. 184.
16. Frank Lantz, *Hacking the Holodeck,* unpublished manuscript.
17. RE:PLAY: Game Design + Game Culture. Online conference, 2000.
18. Marie-Laure Ryan, *Narrative as Virtual Reality: Immersion and Interactivity in Literature and Electronic Media* (Baltimore: John Hopkins University Press, 2000), p. 2.
19. RE:PLAY: Game Design + Game Culture. Online conference, 2000.
20. Jay David Bolter and Richard Grusin, *Remediation: Understanding New Media* (Cambridge: MIT Press, 1999), p. 16.
21. Gary Alan Fine, *Shared Fantasies* (Chicago: University of Chicago Press, 1983), p. 186.
22. Frank Lantz, *Hacking the Holodeck,* unpublished manuscript.

Games as the Play of Simulation
SUMMARY

- A *simulation is a procedural representation of aspects of "reality."* Simulations represent procedurally and they have a special relationship to the "reality" that they represent.

- There are many kinds of simulations that are not games. However, all games can be understood as simulations, even very abstract games or games that simulate phenomena not found in the real world.

- Game simulations usually operate metaphorically: they do not literally recreate a representation of their subject matter. The difference between a game simulation and its referent can be a source of pleasure for players.

- A **procedural representation** is a process-based, dynamic form of depiction. Procedural representation is how simulations *simulate* their subject matter. These forms of representation emerge from the combination of the formal system of a game and the interaction of a player with the game.

- An entire game can be considered a procedural representation of a particular subject. In addition, games include smaller procedural representations that make up the larger depiction.

- The subject matter of game representations is linked to the kinds of conflict that a game can represent. Games typically represent **territorial conflict, economic conflict,** or **conflict over knowledge.** Most games combine two or all three of these categories. It is possible to represent other forms of conflict as well.

- Simulations are a powerful way of thinking about narrative because procedural representation is an approach to storytelling that directly emphasizes the player's experience.

- Simulations are **abstract, numerical, limited,** and **systemic.** A simulation cannot be both broad and deep. Because designing a simulation means radically reducing the simulation's subject matter, a game designer must carefully select which aspects of a phenomenon to depict and how to embody them within the system of the game.

- Simulations, especially in digital games, can be structured according to a **case-based** logic, in which relationships between every element of a system are specified in advance, or a more **generalized** logic in which system elements share a set of general attributes. Generalized structures can save work time and lead to more emergent games where players have greater options for action. However, a balance between the two kinds of structures is usually necessary in any given game.

- The phenomenon of **metacommunication** implies that game players are aware of the frame of a game and that a player's state of mind embodies a kind of double-consciousness that both accepts and refutes that frame.

- The **immersive fallacy** is the belief that the pleasure of a media experience is the ability of that experience to sensually transport a player into an illusory reality. Although the immersive fallacy is prevalent in the digital game industry, it does not take into account the metacommunicative nature of play.

- Media theorists Bolter and Grusin argue that all media operate through the process of **remediation.** The two opposing elements of remediation are **immediacy,** which promises true and authentic representation, and **hypermediacy,** which emphasizes the constructed nature of media representation.

- Psychologist Gary Allen Fine identifies three layers of game player consciousness: direct identification with the game *character,* engagement with the game procedures as a *player,* and existence in larger social contexts as a *person.*

GAMES AS SOCIAL PLAY

play community
player roles
emergent social systems
bounded and unbounded communities
safety and trust
ideal vs. real rules
transformative social play
gaming the game
forbidden play
metagaming

28

We are beginning to create a play community—not a forever community with a fixed code, but a temporary community with a code we make up as we go along, a community that we can continue creating anywhere, any time we find the people who want to create it with us.—**Bernard DeKoven,** *"Creating the Play Community"*

Introducing Social Play

The last few chapters have been a little bit lonely. In looking at experience, pleasure, and systems of representation, we emphasized an individual player's relationship to a game. It is, of course, important to consider each player as an individual: game designers need to make sure that every player who enters a game ends up having a meaningful experience, regardless of who else is playing. However, with this schema on *Games as Social Play,* we focus not just on the relationship between an individual player and a game, but also on the social experiences that occur when more than one player participates in the same game. The emphasis in the last few decades on single-player computer and video games is something of an anomaly in the eons-old history of gaming. While there are notable exceptions, such as solitaire card games, by and large over the centuries games have been valued as social experiences, as a way for people to relate to each other, as a way for people to *play* together. The fact that digital games are swinging back to favoring multiplayer experiences is not a new trend by any means: it is merely games returning to their roots as social play.

As players mingle with each other inside the magic circle, their social interactions highlight important aspects of a game's design. Meaningful play can be framed as a social phenomena. Understanding how social play becomes meaningful, manifest both as interactions occurring within an individual game, and as interactions across larger play communities, is the focus of this chapter.

This is not the first time we have discussed the interaction between players in a game. In *Games as Game Theory Systems,* for example, we explored the decision-making process of rational players within very specialized kinds of games. Even within the incredibly narrow constraints of game theory, the consideration of two-player strategies transformed simple choices into remarkably complex game problems. Now as we consider player interaction within the full gamut of social play, things get very tricky indeed.

Social Relations

When we frame a game as social play, we consider the relationships between elements in the game system to be social relationships. The word "social" refers broadly to player interaction, and occurs on two levels. The first level of social interaction occurs *within* the magic circle, as a product of the formal system of a game. For example, in a game of Tag players assume social roles of "It" (the chaser) or "not It" (the chased). These social interactions are *internally* derived, as they emerge from the game's rules. The second level of social interaction is derived *externally*—social roles brought into the game from outside the magic circle. Pre-existing friendships and rivalries that affect in-game strategic choices, for example, are externally derived elements of social play.

Whether internally or externally derived, social relationships between players are modified by every action taken in the game. Social roles playfully shift and transform as the game proceeds. (You may be "It," but not for long if you are quick!) Navigating, manipulating, and transforming these relationships is one way that players achieve meaningful play in the social realm. Furthermore, the social play that occurs between players is a function of the way the game operates as a system of meaning. Playing games generates meanings for players, which reproduce and challenge codes of social interaction. The kinds of meaning generated as players relate to one another within and through a game is at the center of our exploration of games as social play.

In earlier chapters, we established the idea that games are symbolic systems of meaning. Extending this idea through social play, we can consider a game as a symbolic system players use to communicate with each other. For example, two players can sit down and play Tic-Tac-Toe even if they don't share the same native tongue, because they both know the "language" of the game. This is communication via game play, in which a game becomes a context for stylized communication, mediated through social interaction. The rules of a game determine the communication that takes place, limiting what players can do and say to each other. Marking Xs and Os on empty grid squares is how Tic-Tac-Toe players "speak" to each other in the language of the game.

External contexts always already affect communication via game play as well. Compared to other facets of play, the influence of factors brought to the game from external contexts is particularly strong when considering the social play of a game. Strategic and athletic skills, for example, generally evolve as a player becomes more familiar with the internal workings of a game. Social interaction skills, in contrast, build directly on human experience. Therefore, existing relationships of trust and distrust, friendship and enmity can have a tremendous impact on the way that a game is played from a social point of view.

Because the forms of social interaction that occur *within* a game have strong connections to forms of social interaction *outside* the game, it will be impossible to consider social play without straying just a bit into the realm of culture. For this reason, **Games as Social Play** has a somewhat ethnographic character: understanding games as social play requires a great deal of careful observation. These initial forays to the edge of the magic circle and beyond will help set the stage for the **CULTURE** chapters to follow.

Player Roles

From a social play point of view, when a player enters into the system of a game, that player is given a role to play. By "role" we don't mean that a player becomes a character in a story. Rather, we mean that each player has a role in the social network of a game. Within this system of social relationships there are a wide variety of roles that players can assume, from arch-enemy to team leader to partner-in-crime. Roles are not fixed and may change many times within the course of a game. For example, in a three-player competitive game with one winner, at any moment during play one player might play the role of fast friend, bitter enemy, cloying annoyance, feared power, or grudg-

Clarifying "Community"

The term "community" has gained status as a game industry buzzword in recent years, referencing the groups of players that can form inside and around multiplayer games. Although a group of players using their virtual avatars in an online game such as Everquest does indeed represent a game community, it represents only one very particular instance.

When we use the term *community* in the context of social play we are referencing something much more elemental and varied. As DeKoven indicates in the quote that opened this chapter, a play community occurs any time a group of players gets together to play a game. The community may last for years or decades, or only come into being for a single afternoon. A community could be created by a highly formalized professional car race, or by two friends sitting down to play Checkers. Play communities can persist across more than one instance of the same game or across the play of many different games over time. Communities can arise around a single game, a series of games, or a larger game context, ranging from two players having a quick match of Dance Dance Revolution in the mall arcade, to several thousand players competing every four years in the Olympics.

Every month, gameLab hosts a group of NYC-area game developers to play board games. These monthly gatherings create a social play community on at least three levels. First, each individual game forms a play community, which arises when the game begins and ends when the game concludes. Second, each evening get-together—in which a player is likely to play a handful of different games—also represents a play community, comprised of the people that attended the event. Third, it is also possible to consider a number of gatherings over months or years as a play community, even though the players that attend and the games that are played differ from evening to evening.

The exact scale at which you might conceptualize the notion of a play community depends on the game design problem you are trying to solve. If your intention is to have players take part in a game only once or twice in isolation, then you will most likely focus on the play community that exists within the magic circle of an individual game. The more cohesion you want to create between plays of your game (sequels and expansions, a website that expands the narrative of the game, a fan club, etc.) the wider your social design focus will need to be.

ingly temporary ally to the other players. As the game proceeds and the balance of power shifts, these roles change and fluctuate, reaching an endpoint in which one player assumes the role of winner. Games are complex emergent systems. The relationships between objects in the system—between players—is in a constant state of redefinition.

For example, imagine a different kind of game in which players work together to attain a common goal: in this case, players take on the social role of comrades who must use teamwork to play well together. What if there was a single enemy hidden among the group of friends? Suddenly, the relationships between players take on a completely different tone, and the game is infused with an air of deceit. The role Richard Hatch assumed as the self-proclaimed leader of "the alliance" in the first season of the television series *Survivor* created a sharp divide among the three other members of the group, culminating in feelings of bitterness and betrayal. Although the alliance was originally conceived as a collaborative game strategy, the emergence of one of its members as a cutthroat competitor forced a re-evaluation of social (and strategic) roles within the game. Clearly, the social roles that a game provides exert a tremendous influence on the overall experience of play.

The chart to the right presents a list of social play roles from Brian Sutton-Smith's "A Syntax for Play and Games" in *Child's Play,* a book he edited with R.E. Herron.[1] Each of the roles Sutton-Smith identifies represents *internally* derived social interactions. In other words, they are roles created by the formal system of a game. Sutton-Smith's category "motive of play" is an abstraction of the game's core mechanic. Each "motive" refers to a general kind of interaction between players.

Although the opposition of an actor and a counteractor is not the only way to frame social game play, it is one way of calling attention to the quality of conflict intrinsic to games. In Sutton-Smith's model, the roles of *actor* and *counteractor* are both

Role of Actor	Motive of Play	Role of Counteractor
To overtake	Race	To stay ahead
To catch, tackle, tag	Chase	To outdistance, dodge, or elude
To overcome a barrier, enter a guarded area, overpower a defense; to injure psychologically or otherwise	Attack	To defend an area or a person, to ward off, to be on guard
To take person, symbol	Capture	To avoid being taken
To tease, taunt, lure; to mistake or unsuccessfully attack	Harassment	To see through, to move suddenly and punish an attacker, to bide time
To find by chance or clue (object, person)	Search	To hide, to cover or mislead, to feign
To spring prisoner; to be savior	Rescue	To be jailer, to guard against escape
To tempt another forbidden action	Seduction	To resist, to have self-control

Social play roles

equally important in constructing the experience of play. The actual play activity is a function of the two player roles. The activity of Chase, for example, occurs when one player (the chaser) attempts to catch another player (the chased), who in turn attempts to elude the chaser. If the chased player decided not to run anymore, to give up the role of eluding the chaser, the chase play would end (possibly turning into a different kind of activity, such as the attack play of informal wrestling, or the seduction play of stealing a kiss).

Social roles are crucial, because play emerges directly from the relationships between players. From a social play perspective, *Survivor* was a compelling example of the power of social roles. Debates raged about which contestant was the better person;

the fact remains that Richard was the better *player,* as he recognized that he could manipulate social relations within the game to strategic ends. (And of course, this observation won him a million bucks.) The example of *Survivor* gets to the heart of this chapter: when we frame a game as social play, the social relationships constitute the entire experience of the game. Even in a very simple game like Chutes and Ladders, players are still enacting a race, in which each player is trying to stay ahead of, or catch up to, the other players.

Sutton-Smith's model is quite useful in understanding play as a function of player roles. It provides a wonderful way to analyze the existing social play in your game, as well as provides ideas for new social play experiences. In thinking about how you might apply Sutton-Smith's model to your game, consider the following:

· **Not just two players.** Although Sutton-Smith's model is based on a relationship between two players (an actor and a counteractor), these roles don't have to be played by just one player each. Game roles are rarely so simple and singular. In Hide-and-Seek (where the core activity is the search), the player that is "It" plays the role of actor while all of the other players are the hiding counteractor.

· **Many activities.** As with other kinds of play, a player can assume a range of social roles in the course of a single game. In Capture the Flag, almost every one of the activities listed on the chart takes place at one point or another, with any individual player playing both actor and counteractor at different moments in the game.

· **More than one activity at once.** Beyond switching roles, a player might inhabit more than one role simultaneously. Imagine a pair of Hide-and-Seek players hiding together. As they bide their time they playfully try to get the other to laugh and reveal the hiding place. The laughing game is a daring example of seduction, in which players tempt and

resist a forbidden action. The hiding players are thus playing several roles simultaneously (hiders, seducers, and the seduced).

· **Not just human players.** Both roles don't have to be taken on by human players. A runner might be trying to beat her own best time in a race, in which case her previous time serves as the opponent. In the single-player arcade game Robotron, the program provides different game elements that must be avoided (indestructible enemies), destroyed (shootable enemies) and rescued (humans).

· **Different activities at different levels.** Different social game activities can be applied to the same game depending on how the game is framed. Although Robotron can be described in terms of chase, attack, capture, and rescue, it is also possible to frame an entire game of Robotron as a race, in which a player tries to beat a previous high score.

Sutton-Smith's list of social play roles is quite extensive, but it is certainly not exhaustive. The essay "Hearts, Clubs, Diamonds, Spades: Players Who Suit MUDs," by MUD designer Richard Bartle, considers another typology of social play roles. In opposition to Sutton-Smith's model, Bartle's roles are *externally* derived, coming from outside the magic circle. Sutton-Smith derived his model from a study of children's playground games, and Bartle similarly focuses on one kind of game: text-based online MUDs. Bartle finds that within MUDs there are four types of roles, or playing styles: *Achievers, Explorers, Socializers,* and *Killers.* Although many individual players assume hybrid roles, according to Bartle one is generally dominant. Bartle associates each role with a playing card suit. In his account of the categories below, he desribes how each player role regards the other three styles of play:

> *Achievers* [diamonds] regard points-gathering and rising in levels as their main goal, and all is ultimately subservient to this. Exploration is necessary only to find new sources of treasure, or improved ways of wringing points from it. Socializing is a relaxing method of dis-

covering what other players know about the business of accumulating points, so that their knowledge can be applied to the task of gaining riches. Killing is only necessary to eliminate rivals or people who get in the way, or to gain vast amounts of points (if points are awarded for killing other players).

Explorers [spades] delight in having the game expose its internal machinations to them. They try progressively esoteric actions in wild, out-of-the-way places, looking for interesting features (i.e., bugs) and figuring out how things work. Scoring points may be necessary to enter some next phase of exploration, but it's tedious, and anyone with half a brain can do it. Killing is quicker, and might be a constructive exercise in its own right.... Socializing can be informative as a source of new ideas to try out.... The real fun comes only from discovery, and making the most complete set of maps in existence.

Socializers [hearts] are interested in people, and what they have to say. The game is merely a backdrop, a common ground where things happen to players. Some exploration may be necessary so as to understand what everyone else is talking about, and points-scoring could be required to gain access to neat communicative spells available only to higher levels (as well as to obtain a certain status in the community). Killing, however, is something only ever to be excused if it's a futile, impulsive act of revenge, perpetrated upon someone who has caused intolerable pain to a dear friend. The only ultimately fulfilling thing is...getting to know people, to understand them, and to form beautiful, lasting relationships.

Killers [clubs] get their kicks from imposing themselves on others. [Killers] attack other players with a view to killing off their personae. ...The more massive the distress caused, the greater the killer's joy at having caused it. Normal points-scoring is usually required...and exploration of a kind is necessary to discover new and ingenious ways to kill people. Even socializing is sometimes worthwhile beyond taunting a recent victim, for example in finding out someone's playing habits, or discussing tactics with fellow killers. They're

all just means to an end, though; only in the knowledge that a real person, somewhere, is very upset by what you've just done, yet can themselves do nothing about it, is there any true adrenaline-shooting, juicy fun.[2]

Whether a player is an achiever, explorer, killer, socializer, or some combination, interaction depends in large part on the kind of social identity the player assumes within the game world. Although socializers are the only group described as overtly "social," all four roles represent not just styles of play, but more specifically, styles of social play. Achievers compete with other achievers for power; killers annoy other players with their mischief; explorers trade and covet information; and socializers, of course, spend their time in conversation. Each type of player role gains its identity through negotiation of the social framework of the larger play community.

One primary difference between the player roles Bartle identifies and the model Sutton-Smith offers is that Bartle is looking less at the social core mechanics of the game, and more at higher-level social roles that players can assume. Being a socializer, for example, is a role that emerges from a collection of activities and priorities, in which typing chat statements to other players and visting spaces of the game world devoted to social interaction are of primary importance. The role of socializer, is a kind of macro-role, emerging from a cluster of related activities and interactions.

Three Emergent Social Games

In *Games Emergent Systems,* we established that meaningful play in a game requires a complex, emergent system. The same is true for social play: social interaction in games is closely tied to the concept of emergence. When we frame a game as a social system, it literally begins to burst with emergent social play. From the emergent bluffing of Poker, to the competitive camaraderie of Gauntlet, to the collaborative storytelling of a large-scale LARP, social play results in a variety of emergent experiences. Think about Bartle's four categories of players. The remarkable thing about these wildly varying player types is that all of them can occur *within the same game*. If the space of possibility of a game is large enough, players will find ways to create their own roles and styles of play.

Next we take a close look at three different games that exemplify emergent social play. Each game is remarkably simple, stylizing player interaction through a limited set of behaviors—yet the social roles and activities that arise from the games is remarkably emergent.

Little Max

The first game example seems quite formal on the surface. It is a dice-bluffing game that has a number of variations; we will use the rules from the traditional game Little Max described in Reiner Knizia's *Dice Games Properly Explained*. Not only is Little Max a simple and elegant version of a dice-bluffing game, but a game rich in social play. Here are the rules, paraphrased from Knizia's description:

You will need two dice and a cup. The object of the game is to remain in the game by making the other players believe what you say about your dice roll. The last remaining player in the game wins.

Play moves clockwise around the table in turns. The first player shakes the dice under the cup and then peeks at the result so that no other player can see. Then he claims any result he wishes and passes the cup to the next player. When you receive the cup, you have two options:

> *Accept:* If you accept the claim, you don't look at the dice but instead shake the cup, peek at the result, make your new claim and pass the cup. Your claim must be a higher total than the previous player's claim.

> *Challenge:* You can challenge and lift the cup. If the dice show a result lower than the claim, the player that made the false claim is out of the game and you start a new round by shaking the dice. You can claim any result on the dice you want.

However, if the dice show a combination that is at least as high as the claim, you are out of the game. The next player starts a new round.

Following are the ranking of dice results:

- *A Little Max*, when one die shows a 1 and the other shows a 2, is the highest result in the game and must always be challenged when it is called.

- *Pairs* are the next highest results, with a pair of 6s the highest pair and a pair of 1s the lowest. Below pairs are *figures*, any other two numbers.

- *Figures* are declared with the highest number in front (so a 4 and a 2 beats a 4 and a 1). A 6 and a 5 is the highest figure and a 3 and a 1 is the lowest.

Play continues until only one player is left. Note that a player may decide not to look at his roll and simply claim a result. He doesn't even have to reroll the dice if he wants, in which case he passes the cup unseen with a higher claim.[3]

Along with his description, Knizia includes a chart listing the percentage chance for being able to make each potential die result. This resource is useful for players who are going to play strictly by the numbers. But as Knizia explains in his analysis of the game, there is far more going on in Little Max than mere number-crunching:

The Psychology, or How to be a Duck

Besides keeping a firm Poker face, Little Max is about making the right choice when the dice are handed to you.

Your decision to challenge depends on your chances to better the current claim, but also on your evaluation of the previous player's chances to produce his claim. . . .

The chances of beating a 6-1 or better are exactly 50%. In theory you should challenge the claim if the previous player had to beat 6-1 or better, because the odds are in your favor.

Practical play turns out to be different. Challenges happen less frequently as most players tend to duck and hope that the evil will pass over them. If you can assume that the next player will follow this trend and not challenge you, why should you take any risks? Ducking among ducks is the best strategy.

When you bend the truth, be careful not to squeeze the next player too much or he might find himself forced to challenge you. On the other hand, just going one step higher with your result looks implausible. The more you exceed your old claim the more you appear to speak the truth, because nobody expects you to go that far over the top. A contradiction! What about calling out the next possible result even when you produced something higher?

Body language and trembling nerves usually prevail over logical analysis. You will soon find yourself desperately searching for a good combination to claim while staring in disbelief at your incredibly low dice. Mumbling something like "five-six" obviously indicates that your mind is distracted. Could it be fear?…

There is the marvelous anecdote of a game of Little Max where one of the dice actually got lost during play and the game continued for several rounds because everyone was terrified of being caught out. What a feeling, if you claim "Two fives" with only one die under the cup.[4]

At first glance, the game seems to be a formal affair about number guessing and pushing your luck with the roll of a pair of dice. However, as Knizia makes clear, Little Max is really a game of psychology and social play. Even though it seems like the game takes place as a series of isolated claims between two players, the decision to challenge or not to challenge has far-reaching implications. It is safer to "duck" and accept a claim that comes to you; as soon as you do, however, you are going to have to immediately turn around and present a claim to someone else. Having just played the role of the guesser, you are now going to have to assume the role of the bluffer.

Furthermore, as a bluffer you always present a claim that is less likely to be true than the previous one, because you have to claim a higher result each turn. In Little Max, bluffing is at the center of the game. In Poker, you can *choose* to bluff or not to bluff. But in Little Max, circumstances can *force* you to bluff if your roll is too low. As if that were not enough, the rest of the players also come into play. How trustworthy are you? You can keep on ducking, of course, but eventually the cup will come back to you. How ridiculous will your claim have to be by then? The result of this tightly interlocking set of play roles is a game of deeply engaging social play. Even though Little Max is an abstract game of numbers and probability, the logical play of the game quickly becomes a desperate, nervous experience of deceptive bluffing. Such simple rules, generating such emergent social play!

Mafia

The social play of Little Max emerges from a tight fit between the game's formal structure and its changing play roles. Mafia is a game that strips down the formal structure even further, creating play activities that are almost entirely social. As with Little Max, although the rules of Mafia are simple, the social play is incredibly deep. There are a great many variations on Mafia, and below we outline one simple version we enjoy:

Mafia is a game for approximately 8–10 players, although it can be played with more or fewer participants. It works best when all of the players are sitting around a table and can see each other. At the beginning of the game, three of the players are secretly given roles. This is usually accomplished by passing out a pre-sorted and shuffled set of playing cards, one card for each player. The set includes one heart, two spades, and the rest of the cards are diamonds.

The player that receives the heart is moderator and is out of the game. The moderator serves as referee and runs the game. The moderator collects the cards at the start of the game—they are not used again. The two players that received spades are the members of the mafia. Their objective is to eliminate all of the other players in the game. The rest of the players are villagers. Their task is to eliminate the mafia.

A turn consists of two parts, night and day, beginning with the night portion of the turn. The moderator instructs all players to close their eyes. Then the moderator tells the mafia to open their eyes. Through silent gesture, they indicate to the moderator who they want to kill. The moderator then has the two designated mafia players close their eyes.

The moderator announces the dawn and all of the players open their eyes, as the moderator declares the name of the player that the mafia killed during the night. That player play-acts a horrible death and is out of the game. All of the remaining players begin a debate about who is in the mafia. After 5–10 minutes of discussion, the moderator calls for a vote. The player receiving the most votes is killed by an uprising of the villagers and is out of the game. A moderator can call for a re-vote if there is a tie, or can end the day without an uprising if there is a true deadlock. Then the moderator instructs everyone to close their eyes as night falls once more and the mafia select another victim.

The game continues until the two mafia players have been eliminated, or until there are only mafia players left and the moderator announces the end of the game. If one member of the mafia is eliminated by an uprising, the game continues (but the villagers are *not* informed that there is only one mafia member left). Players that are out of the game are not permitted to talk or give hints of any kind. Note that because of voting mechanics, the moderator can end the game as a mafia victory when there are equal numbers of mafia and villagers.

If you've never played Mafia, the rules might seem perplexing. As long as the mafia do not noisily gesture as they select a victim, the rest of the villagers have little logical basis for making their decisions about who is a suspected member of the mafia.

In the case of Little Max, bluffing and guesswork are based on the formal framework of a progressively increasing probability of a bluff. In Mafia, on the other hand, the decision of the villagers is based entirely on hunches and social guesswork. The hidden information around which the game revolves in Little Max is the numbers on the dice. The hidden information of Mafia is the allocation of the player roles themselves. Who *are* the mafia? How many of them are left? The mafia players aren't just playing a role, they are playing a double role, strategically eliminating villagers during the night while playing at being villagers during the day.

The drama of the game, in which the circle of victims grows smaller and smaller, heightens the tension and makes for a remarkably subtle social experience. How will each villager make his or her guess? Has one player been too talkative? Or too quiet? What is *she* hiding? How innocent is *he*? Are those two exchanging glances? Just what motivated the mafia last night? Did they get rid of the villager that suspected one of them last turn? Or are they using double-psychology to get the villagers to kill one of their own? Suspense builds as the villagers are whittled away one by one, the mafia and the villagers both edging closer to winning, but also closer to elimination. Each player represents a point within a complex social space, each point mapped to the other points in delicate and puzzling ways. None of the villagers can fully trust anyone. Although the mafia players can work together, they have to keep their partnership a secret. The game of Mafia is truly a tangled knot of social play. Mafia also plays wonderfully with the magic circle. Once a player has been eliminated, that player steps halfway out of the magic circle, finally learning the information they had been seeking, but forced by the rules they are still observing to remain silent as the engaging drama unfolds.

Stand Up

We complete our trio of examples with another game that seems extremely simple on the surface: it contains no hidden information, all players have the same role, and there is only one thing they can do. The game is called Stand Up, and it comes from the *New Games Book:*

Sit on the ground, back-to-back with your partner, knees bent and elbows linked. Now simply stand up together. With a bit of cooperation and a little practice, this shouldn't be too hard.

By the time you've got this mastered, you'll probably have drawn an interested spectator. Have her join you on the ground, and all three try to stand up. This feat should take you just long enough to attract another onlooker. Have him join you. Four people standing up together might be a genuine accomplishment.

By this time you should realize that there's more struggling, stumbling, and giggling each time you add another person. But this very fact assures you of an endless supply of fascinated spectators, ready to join up to help you get off the ground.[5]

Believe it or not, Stand Up is in fact a game, a cooperative game in which the players win together when they accomplish the task of standing up. Yes, it is incredibly minimal, but it is also rich in social play. The core mechanic of Stand Up is not only athletically engaging for the entire body, but also extremely social. Even when only two players take part in the game, they are challenged to work in concert as they struggle to move from one stable state (sitting) to another (standing), by making their way together through an interstitial state of great unbalance.

As they play together, the fact that the players are facing away from each other means that their primary method of communication comes from their bodies. You can talk to the other player if you like, but you don't have time to make complex statements once you begin to stand up. The awkward interlocking of your elbows not only limits your movements, but ties these movements closely to those of your partner. You are, in a sense, creating a single body the two of you together must control. Although this kind of interaction may not seem "social," social relationships between players can take many forms, including physical interaction. There clearly is a great deal of meaningful social play in Stand Up.

The more people that are added to the game, the more emergent the group behavior becomes, and the more challenging it is to win. The more individuals that play, the more bodies there are to join into a single collective organism; the more moving parts added to this unstable system, the more difficult the collaboration becomes. As a system of rewards and punishments, the increasing challenge is leavened by the sense of accomplishment that the group feels when they achieve the goal together. This leads to what is perhaps the most fascinating aspect of the design of Stand Up. As the description indicates, the game itself represents a simple repeatable activity that makes for an entertaining public spectacle. This means that the play of Stand Up itself can act as a lure to bring more players into the game. Stand Up offers a great example of social play in action. Many games advocated by the New Games Movement are specifically intended to recruit new players from the immediate environment, while also providing an experience of meaningful play. Stand Up is an example of such a game, designed to build and grow a play community as part of the play itself. We find it to be a truly remarkable game design.

Bounded Communities

Earlier in this chapter we introduced the concept of the play community, a term borrowed from Bernard DeKoven's book, *The Well-Played Game*. We like his terminology and use the idea of a play community in the spirit of DeKoven, even though our use of the term does not exactly coincide with his. For our purposes, a play community is a group of players engaged in play. This play may occur within the space of an individual game or across a series of games.

It may seem like play communities are social phenomena that spring up mysteriously and autonomously around a game. However, game designers can have an impact on the play communities generated by their games. It is therefore important to understand what a play community is and how it works. A play community arises out of the operation of a game. It is a function of the rules of the game, the personalities of the players, the interactions between players, and the larger social context in which the game takes place.

Play communities emerge from play. Although some play communities become quite official, such as professional sports teams, most play communities are informal, temporary affairs. A play community is not usually like a housing development, requiring extensive advance planning and preparation before it can be properly inhabited. Instead, a play community is often more like a conversation, in which the improvisational act of communication itself creates the conversational context. This emergence of a social play context is not unlike that of the magic circle, which also arises spontaneously and is experienced temporally. The social boundaries of a play community are tied to the boundaries of its game or games.

There is a paradoxical relationship between a game and the play community it generates. In a sense, the play community is an effect of the game, an emergent property of the game system. At the same time, the game has no life apart from the play that activates it, and is dependent on the play community for its sustenance. One would simply not exist without the other.

To understand the beauty of this paradox, we can revisit systems theory and the concept of closed and open systems. A closed system has no exchange with its outside environment, while an open system does have some kind of exchange. As **RULES,** games are closed systems, as **CULTURE,** games are open systems, but as **PLAY,** we can frame games as either closed or open systems, depending on which aspects of the experience we highlight. As artificial social systems with their own special rules of meaning, games are closed systems of play. But as transformative systems that affect and are affected by what the players bring into the game, the play of a game is an open system.

Similarly, a play community can be framed as bounded or not bounded by the magic circle of a single game. A *bounded* play community is a closed system: it arises from the social play that takes place strictly within the space of an individual game. When we frame a play community in this way, it exists only within the time and space defined by the magic circle. However, we can also frame a play community to include more than one instance of a game. With this framing, we are considering a group of players across a number of games or across a number of sessions of play. These communities are not contained within an individual game and are *not bounded*. A play community that is not bounded is an open system. Both framings are useful, and in the sections that follow we look at each, focusing first on bounded play communities.

Contract for Artifice

Within the bounded play community of a game, the community arises with the onset of the game and disappears when the game is finished. A bounded play community is more synonymous with an individual game, and the rules of the game have a great influence on the nature and experience of the play community. In other words, a bounded play community is more *artificial* than an unbounded one, because it has less traffic with contexts outside the magic circle. This social contract for artifice affects the meaning of social relationships within the limited context of the game.

In order to understand how the social system of a game can be considered artificial, we turn to the work of the psychologist Jean Piaget. Much of Piaget's work focused on the cognitive development of children; his research had a tremendous impact on theories of the mind in the twentieth century. For our purposes, the most applicable of Piaget's works is his book *The Moral Judgment of the Child,* in which he details some of his research on child development. Working with children from a particular region of Switzerland, Piaget systematically studied the process by which young children acquire the ability to understand game rules. He did so in order to draw a correlation between the process of understanding game rule structures and the process of understanding moral structures. From this work, Piaget drew conclusions about a child's social and psychological development as a whole, tracking the child's entry into the moral realm through an understanding of the social contract engendered by the rules of play. Although we won't be detailing Piaget's experiments or the complex stages of a child's psychological development, he makes a number of important insights relevant to a discussion of social play and game design.

One of the assumptions shaping *The Moral Judgment of the Child* is that the rules of a game are fundamentally different than larger social rules shaping social convention, such as the cultural and legal rules that guide moral and ethical behavior. The difference lies precisely in the artificiality of a game's rule-system, as Piaget makes clear:

> All morality consists in a system of rules, and the essence of all morality is to be sought for in the respect which the individual acquires for these rules.
>
> Now, most of the moral rules which the child learns to respect he receives from adults, which means that he receives them after they have been fully elaborated, and often elaborated, not in relation to him and as they are needed, but once and for all and through an uninterrupted succession of earlier adult generations.

> In the case of the very simplest social games, on the contrary, we are in the presence of rules which have been elaborated by the children alone…the rules of the game of marbles are handed down, just like so-called moral realities, from one generation to another, and are preserved solely by the respect that is felt for them by individuals. The sole difference is that the relations in this case are only those that exist between children.[6] [our emphasis]

Although Piaget is referring specifically to traditional children's folk games such as Marbles, we can glean a larger point from his premise. "Rules of society," such as moral guidelines, permeate our lived social experience and affect all of our interactions with others. A person might need money to get on the subway, but by and large, observance of society's rules (for whatever mix of personal, cultural, and legal reasons) keep subway riders from taking that money by force from a stranger. These kinds of behavioral rules and guidelines are one way of understanding social identity within society.

Rules of games, on the other hand, are quite different. We know that games operate only within the time and space of the magic circle. Only when a game of Chess is in play do players covet the King and avoid the illegality of moving pawns backward on the board. Outside a game, players do not feel compelled to "capture" a king piece, or otherwise structure their behavior according to the rules of Chess. Conversely, within bounded play communities, game behavior is not entirely constrained by life outside of the game. As Huizinga states (or perhaps overstates), "Inside the circle of the game, the laws and customs of ordinary life no longer count."[7]

This is why Piaget can use children's games as a special, isolated case of social rules: because the rules are, in fact, generated without concern for larger social institutions. The rules emerge from the context of the games themselves, the play of children, rather than from culture at large. As Piaget notes, *"We are in the presence of rules which have been elaborated by the children alone."* Piaget's marvelous insight into the autonomy of children's folk games is true to some extent of all games. Even in the case of commercial games designed by adults for adults, there is a sense in which the games create their own private social sphere. Although it is true that there is plenty of interplay between game rules and societal rules, such as a game designed to propagate a certain ideology or make use of existing social content, the bounded play communities games create exist in an artificial space marked off in some way from society at large.

As a result of this isolation, the bounded play community of a game implies a kind of social contract. This contract consists of rules that determine how players interact with each other in the game, as well as the meanings and values that the players give life through play. Sustaining the contract to the end of a game requires players to maintain the integrity of the magic circle. Rule-breakers can damage this fragile frame. A cheating player will test the limits of the social contract and possibly disrupt it. A spoil sport is likely to destroy the social contract entirely.

A social contract, a commitment to a shared set of behaviors and values, is a social frame for understanding what it means to enter into the magic circle. For example, a game is a space of conflict with an uncertain outcome. In other spheres of our lives, most of us would not willingly enter into a conflict, especially one with a real risk of loss. The social contract of a game acts as a kind of psychological buffer against uncertainty, protecting players from the risk inherent in game play. There are many elements to this social contract, such as the level playing field of conflict we discussed in *Games as Systems of Conflict.* There are also distinctly interpersonal aspects of the social contract of a game as well. DeKoven describes two of these, safety and trust, in *The Well-Played Game:*

Safety

The safer we feel in the game we're playing, the more willing we are to play it. But, for this experience of safety, we can't rely solely on the game. We must also be able to believe that we are safe with each other.

Trust

We need…some guarantee, somewhere, that no matter what happens in our pursuit of the well-played game, we will not be risking more than we are prepared to risk. Even though I'm aware that I might die as a result of trying to climb this mountain with you, I can accept that as part of the game. On the other hand, when I discover that you're cutting my rope so that you can get to the top first, I find myself much less willing to play.[8]

Safety and trust are two elements that are part of the social contract of a game. Generally, players must feel a sense of safety and trust to be comfortable enough to enter into the social space of a game. The concepts of safety and trust are, in many ways, more a function of a player's existing relationships and attitudes than something a game guarantees. As DeKoven states, players "can't rely solely on the game" for trust. They must rely on each other. Having a sense of trust allows players to enter into the game in the first place. What is trust? It is a shared sense of understanding, not just of the knowledge of the rules of a particular game, but of the way all games are played, including the rules of etiquette that allow you to trust that other players won't become cheaters, spoil sports, or bullies.

Once again we have a paradox. The game itself is an artificial social space that players enter, yet the "rules" by which players come to know a sense of trust belong to the world outside the game, to the realm of shared social and cultural values. What connects the values of the game and the values of the real world? The answer is a concept we introduced many chapters ago: the implicit rules of a game.

Knowing the Rules

*When children play together, in the street or the back lot, they too establish a play community. When someone gets hurt, the game stops. When there's a little kid around, you watch out for him, you play softer when you're near him, you give the kid a break. At all times there is an acceptance of a shared responsibility for the safety of those with whom you play.—**Bernard DeKoven,** The Well-Played Game*

In **Rules on Three Levels,** we identified three layers of game rules: the underlying *constitutive rules* of a game, the *operational rules* that directly guide player action, and the *implicit rules* of proper game behavior, such as etiquette. The examples DeKoven gives in the passage above, that a game stops when someone gets hurt or that play is softened when little kids join a game, are implicit rules, unspoken guidelines for how to play.

The implicit rules of a game bridge the paradoxical relationship between the artificial space of the game and the social context in which the game is played. The fact that both players in a game of Tic-Tac-Toe know that each will take a reasonable amount of time on their turn is part of the social trust that enables players to sit down and play together. So is the assumption that players will not cheat or become spoil sports. All are examples of implicit rules. Similarly, the implicit rules that DeKoven identifies facilitate the social play of a neighborhood backlot play community. The implicit rule of stopping the game when someone gets hurt has an *intrinsic* effect (the game pauses temporarily) only because of an *extrinsic* social rule (help people that are injured).

Considering the role of implicit rules in social play, questions arise. By what process do implicit rules come into being? How do players come to know these rules? How do they affect play? For answers, we turn again to Piaget's *The Moral Judgment of the Child.* Piaget outlines distinct stages through which children progress as they learn the rules of Marbles. In paraphrasing Piaget's more complex formulations, we divide the acquisition of game rules into three stages:

During the first stage, beginning around age 5, the child does not yet understand there are fixed rules to the game. Children of this age will play Marbles in an improvisational way, possessing a vague notion of rules but not yet understanding the idea of fixed rules.

In the second stage, around ages 8 to 10, the child comes to know that there are rules, and will regard these rules with a near religious reverence. The rules are felt to have their own implicit authority, which cannot be questioned.

The third and final stage generally begins after age 10. Here the child comes to realize that the rules of a game are dependent on a social contract and can be changed if all of the players agree to do so. This final stage is essentially how adults view the rules of games.[9]

Our interest is in the transition into the third and final stage, when a child's consciousness of the rules undergoes a complete transformation. Rather than believing that rules are absolutely fixed, children begin to see rules as the outcome of a free decision reached through respectful mutual consent. Piaget sums up this transformation elegantly:

He no longer relies, as do the littlest ones, upon an all-wise tradition. He no longer thinks that everything has been arranged for the best in the past and that the only way of avoiding trouble is by religiously respecting the established order. He believes in the value of experiment in so far as it is sanctioned by collective opinion.[10]

Piaget's model for the acquisition of rules sheds light on a number of issues relating to social play. When a child acquires an understanding of a game's rules, he or she also develops an understanding of the social contract of a game. Like adults, children at this stage of development are able to see rules as structures that describe how players are to relate to one another within the game, both formally and socially. They are also able to recognize that the game world is a flexible world that can be altered collectively. This is an important part of recognizing the existence of a play community.

Additionally, Piaget's developmental model has a loose correlation to the way an adult player comes to know a game. When a player is initially brought into the magic circle of a game, a player is often not yet familiar with its specific rules. Instead, a player has a vague sense of the game's operation, similar to a child in Stage one of Piaget's model. When a player is learning to play a game, the mechanisms of a game seem fixed and the player's attention is focused on learning how to play, like a child in Stage two. The more that a player plays a game the more she sees the game as a system open to manipulation (albeit one whose binding authority must be respected). When the player gets stuck in the middle of a computer adventure game, for example, she might purchase a strategy guide or go online to find a walkthrough guide. Later in her play experience, she might download a hack, design her own level, or start a fan web page. The play patterns of an experienced player demonstrate an understanding of the game as something that is amenable to change. In a very approximate sense, the progress of a player into a game or the general culture of games recapitulates Piaget's model of a child coming to understand the concept of game rules.

Transformative Social Play

Whether describing the way a child comes to know the rules of Marbles or the way an adult gradually enters into a game's fan community, the rules of a game are experienced and transformed through social play. In **Defining Play,** we identified transformative play as an instance of play when free movement within the more rigid structure of a game actually changes the game structure itself. We can also consider transformative play from a social play point of view, a phenomenon we call *transformative social play.*

In transformative social play, players use the game context to transform social relationships. They actively engage with the rule system of a game, manipulating it in order to shift, extend, or subvert their relations with other players. Transformative social play forces us to reevaluate a formal understanding of rules as fixed, unambiguous, and omnipotently authoritative. In any kind of transformative play, game structures come into question and are re-shaped by player action. In transformative *social* play, the mechanisms and effects of these transformations occur on a social level.

How does transformative social play work? Borrowing some useful terms from folklorist Kenneth Goldstein, let's begin by making a basic distinction between "ideal" and "real" rules.[11] *Ideal rules* refer to the "official" regulations of a game, the rules written in a player's guide to Zelda or printed on the inside cover of a game of Candyland. *Real rules,* on the other hand, are the codes and conventions held by a play community. Real rules are a consensus of how the game *ought* to be played.

As sociologist Frank E. Manning notes in *The World of Play,* "Real rules embody the players' ludic values and social relations while ideal rules have a legal, but not social, validity."[12] This distinction between ideal and real rules has less to do with the *interpretation* of rules (whether or not players of Pictionary may use hand gestures to encourage potential guesses, for example) and more to do with the *elaboration* of the rules of the game by players. Young kids playing Basketball, for example, might elaborate on the rule of "no double-dribbling" and transform it into "no double-dribbling unless you can't help it." This movement from the ideal, or legal rule, to the real, or popular rule, offers insight into the social values held by a community of players.

Ideal and Real Foursquare

In the early 1980s, sociologist Linda Hughes (then a graduate student at the University of Pennsylvania) spent three years observing children playing the game of Foursquare on a playground in the suburbs of Philadelphia. Her interest was in understanding how children elaborate rules to support existing social relations. Hughes focused specifically on the difference between the "basic" (or ideal) rules of a game and the rules that were defined as the "real rules" by players. The basic rules of Four-square require that players:

1. Hit a ball that lands in your square to another square.

2. Let the ball bounce once, but only once, in your square.

3. Don't hit a ball that lands in another square.[13]

The real rules of the games, however, describe a much more complex set of interactions. A list of in-game calls documented by Hughes reveals a rich language of social play *(see Figure 1)*. Calls include such shots as Babies, Bops, or Spins, as well as types of play, such as Nice or Friends, which describe the quality and social tone of player interaction. The real rules matter a great deal to players, for they transform the formal structure to support existing social relations. Players often dismissed the basic rules as "just things you had to do"—they were not included among the list of "real rules" reported by the children. As Hughes notes, "Players were far more interested in the rules they generated and controlled, and that they could use to introduce excitement, variety, strategy, and fun into the game."[14] This elaboration of basic, ideal rules into a complex set of real rules is transformative social play. It is not that the basic rules of the game undergo a radical change; rather, they are experienced within a social context that decreases their value in favor of a socially-biased ruleset over which players have more control.

In "Beyond the Rules of the Game: Why Are Rooie Rules Nice?" Hughes presents a case study of a specific Foursquare ruleset developed by the children she observed. Foursquare offered fertile ground for such a study because a ruleset is called by an individual player (the "king") before each round of play. "Such calls can be used for a wide variety of purposes, including increasing game excitement, adjusting the level of difficulty, and assisting or scapegoating other players."[17] These rulesets prescribe and prohibit certain actions while setting a general tone for a particular round of play. A call of "Rooie Rules," for example—a ruleset named after a girl named Rooie who was one of the regular players on the playground at the time

1–2–3–4	Fish	No Outs	Time Out
AC/DC	Friends	Mandy-slams	Times
Babies	Front Spins	One-handed	Tough Rules
Baby Bottles	Frontsies	Part-Rules Poison	Trades
Baby Stuff	Goody Rules	Purpose Duckfeet	Tricks
Backsides	Half Slams	Purpose Stuff	Untimes
Backspins	Half Wings	Randi Rules	Volley Round
Bishops	Holding	Ready	The World
Bops	Interference	Regular Ball	Volleys
Chances	Kayo Stuff	Regular Rules	Volley Regular
Comebacks	Knee Balls	Regular Spins	Saves
Country & City	Lines	Regular Square	Saving Places
Donna Rules	Low Ball	Regular Volley	Secrets
Double Taps	Main Rules	Rough Slams	Slams
Duckfeet	Mean Stuff	Rough Square	Slow Ball
Fair Ball	Medium Ball	Spins	Smitty Rules
Fair Square	Mini-slams	Takeovers	Special Rules
Fakes	My Rules	Taps	Wings
Fancy	Nice Ball	Teenie boppers	
Fancy Day	Nice Slams	Three Square	
Fast Ball	Nice Square	Time In	

Figure 1: The "Real Rules" of Foursquare[15]

Many of the social concerns of this play community are apparent in their terminology. Terms such as "mean," "nice," "friends," and "purpose," for example, are extensively used to label game "moves."

Hughes' research was conducted—meant that players were to play "nice." Rooie Rules included the following: "no holding" (the ball must be hit, not caught and thrown); "no slams" (bounces high over a player's head); no "duckfeet" (being hit on the legs); "spins" are allowed; and so on. "Rooie Rules" operated as short-hand for a long list of individual calls.

Among the community of players Hughes observed, the call of "Rooie Rules" created a general framework for player interaction. This framework rested upon shared social standards for fairness, perceived intentionality (did a player illegally hold the ball "on purpose," or accidentally), and appropriate demeanor within the group (playing "nice"). Yet interestingly enough, despite the fact that everyone was able to play by Rooie Rules, no player, including Rooie, was able to supply a complete list of the real rules this call encompassed. According to Hughes, "What allows the game to proceed with such apparent ambiguity concerning the precise rules of the game is the tacit understanding that Rooie Rules are 'nice,' and 'nice' is perhaps the paramount concern among these players. It is far more important to understand 'nice' play than to understand the rules."[16] The community of players used the term "nice" to refer to a rather complex matrix of social rights and obligations. The real rules of the game referred to a standard of social behavior, a standard which players had to accept and uphold if they were to remain a part of the game.

When Players Won't Be "Nice"

In the cutthroat social ecosystem of the playground, games are often contexts for asserting and challenging social power. In the following extended excerpt from Hughes' research, Four-square becomes an arena of conflict for boy players and girl players. The tension between the ideal and real rules comes to the fore, with both sides brokering social authority to define the game in a particular way.

As might be predicted among boys and girls of this age, the boys almost immediately drove the girls crazy by very overtly using "rough stuff" ("slams" and "wings") to get the girls out of the game. This does not mean the girls were also not using such moves. What enraged them was the boys' failure to disguise "purpose stuff" in the kinds of "I couldn't help it" performances demanded by "nice" play. The boys would, for example, call, "Rough square. Getting out on serves," and then slam the ball high over one of the girls' heads on the serve.

Totally outraged, the girls would counter, when one of their number was "king," with a call of "Rooie Rules." But, as we might expect, calling "nice" rules had little effect. The boys blatantly continued to "slam" and "wing" the ball past them. Since the girls were still bound by their "nice" rules, which prohibited direct confrontation over such actions, there was little they could do. As play proceeded, however, the girls gradually abandoned some of the trappings of "nice" play. They began handling violations quite differently. The following are excerpts from field notes. We begin with three girls and one boy on the court.

Angie (the "king") [the player that makes the call]: "Rooie Rules. Rooie Rules."

Angie pauses, looks around, and then walks over to the players waiting in line to get into the game.

Angie (to Rooie, who is waiting in line): "Rooie, tell them your rules."

As Angie returns to her square, she glares rather pointedly at Andy, the boy who just entered the game, while Rooie lists her rules.

(It should be noted that another understanding among these gamers is that players are only responsible for violating a rule they know about. Only if they know, and then violate, a rule can they be denied a takeover of the last round. This attempt to list very explicitly the rules in effect is highly unusual. It functions as a kind of warning to the offending players.)

A little later, Cindy (who is now "king") calls: "Rooie Rules."

But Andy continues to "wing" and "slam" the ball consistently. After several such hits, Rooie, who is waiting in line, walks over to Andy's square.

Rooie (to Andy): "You're out! Wings are out!"

Cindy steps forward to back Rooie up.

Cindy (to Andy): "I called Rooie Rules and there's no wings! You're out!"

As Andy leaves the court he mumbles something about being a "fish."

The term "fish" refers to a scapegoated player. In over six months of observing this game, this was the first time the author had observed anyone being called out for "wings." The exchange above is a very significant departure from the usual patterns of play. Andy is well aware of this. He knows he's been had.

The girls' revenge was short-lived, however. In reacting to the boys' refusal to play "nice" by becoming more explicit in their calls of the rules, and by applying direct sanctions for violations, the girls began digging themselves into a rather deep hole. They expanded a call of "Rooie Rules," for example, to "Rooie rules. No slams. No wings. No rough stuff." They tried explicitly to prohibit each of the boys' offending actions. Naturally, the boys could always find actions the girls had not specifically prohibited. One particularly exasperated "king" recognized the problem when she tagged her call of the rules with, "And nothing you guys do!" Of course, on the other side, the girls could not completely avoid violating their own rules, now differently defined. The boys were not only too happy to point this out.[18]

The Foursquare players are not just playing Foursquare. They are playing *with the rules of Foursquare*, strategically bending and tweaking the real rules to their advantage. Significantly, the goal of each group is not just to win, but to play the game in a

way that embodies the proper spirit of play, to play the game in a way that expresses their social being. These players are not merely playing a game; they are gaming the game itself, manipulating real rules within the boundaries established by the ideal rules and the larger social context in which they are playing. Framing play as *gaming the game* echoes some of the play styles we visited in **Breaking the Rules**—and it also foreshadows many of the phenomena to come in **CULTURE.**

Rooie Rules offers an excellent example of transformative play within the social realm. Like Piaget's study of children and the rules of Marbles, Hughes exposes the underlying social mechanisms that direct the actions and motivations of a play community. Clearly, the *experience* of play must be understood as a highly complex system of interaction that is influenced by formal, social, and cultural factors. These factors shape the play of a game in wonderful and often unexpected ways.

Forbidden Play

There is an exception to every rule. Our prior discussions of implicit social rules have assumed that etiquette and proper behavior are the same both inside and outside of a game. After all, it is only when a player feels the safety and trust of a familiar social framework that he or she will be comfortable entering into the magic circle. However, there can also be strong differences between the implicit rules of society and the implicit rules of a game—between the rules for what is permitted in each context. Games create social contexts in which, very often, behaviors take place that would be strictly forbidden in society at large. In a game, you can plot treachery against your friends and backstab them when they least expect it. You can engage in representations of criminal behavior. Or you can put on padded gloves and try to knock another person unconscious.

Games permit and often encourage normally taboo behavior, or *forbidden play*. Games throughout history and across the world have subverted norms of social behavior. Perhaps this should come as no surprise. Inside the artificial context of the magic circle, games not only create meaning, but they *play* with meaning as well. The social contract of a game ensures that play spaces are "safe" spaces in which risks have fewer consequences than in the outside world. In "The Kissing Games of Adolescents of Ohio," Brian Sutton-Smith investigated kissing games played by high school and college students in 1959, and the complex social interplay they engendered. About the forbidden play of these games, Sutton-Smith writes:

> [A kissing game] allows for the expression of given impulses but at the same time safeguards players by putting limits on the way in which those impulses can be expressed. That is, the game allows the player to grow along the lines that he desires, but it safeguards him against the danger of risking too much. The game is essentially an adventure of a nonhazardous kind.[19]

Forbidden play, like all play, is "free within the limits set by the rules."[20] Recall the runner at the starting line we analyzed in *Games as the Play of Pleasure.* The runner wants to spring forward, but the pleasurable restriction of waiting for the starting gun heightens the pleasure of the play. In forbidden play, the sense of pleasurable restriction continues through the entire play experience, the player always in danger of overstepping the social boundaries of play, jumping the gun, and breaking the magic circle.

The difference, of course, is that forbidden play embodies behaviors not normally permitted between players. Forbidden play both sanctions and restricts social play in the complex dance of desire that Sutton-Smith outlines in the quote above. Kissing games stretch the implicit rules of play just enough to accommodate the kissing behaviors of the game, but never quite going far enough to threaten a complete breakdown of the social order. These games simultaneously challenge and reinforce the rules of society.

On this page and the next, we quote descriptions and provide our own commentary on several games Sutton-Smith describes in his essay.[22] Each game offers a fascinating example of how games mold and shape desire and social relations by sanctioning and forbidding particular play actions.

The Card Game: The players go round in a circle, and take turns to pick a card from a pack. Having picked a card they then pick a person of the opposite sex. If they pick a spade they slap the person they have chosen on the back. If a club, they shake hands. If a diamond it is a public kiss. If a heart, a private kiss.

The forbidden play: This game operates as a system for determining the form of social interaction that a pair of players will have. Chance plays a very important role in this game, as it does in most kissing games. The players get to choose who they wish to have as a partner, but the cards determine the exact action. Thus the shuffled deck takes responsibility for the actual kissing, relieving players of that socially onerous yet libidinally desirable task.

Draw and Kiss: All the player's names are placed in a dish. All the players place their hands in together and draw a name. They must kiss the name drawn out as well as be kissed by the person who has drawn their name. As soon as they have kissed and been kissed they may run to take their place in a line of chairs. There is one chair short, and the person who is left over must kiss everyone.

The forbidden play: Draw and Kiss is a structural inversion of The Card Game. The form of interaction is fixed (kissing) but chance determines who kisses whom. The fact that there is an overall "loser" in this game is fascinating. What is the implied social message? Is the slowest player the one that was most prudish and hesitant or the most indulgent? Is being kissed by everyone else a punishment or an inverted reward?

Endurance Kissing: It is essentially a comic endurance test, in which a couple sees how long they can hold a kiss without breathing. A watch is used. The bystanders laugh at the competitors. It is done usually only with one's steady date. On a double date the losers might be expected to buy a Coke for the winners.

The forbidden play: In Endurance Kissing, we find an unusually agônistic forbidden play competition instead of a chance-based activity. The taboo activity—kissing—is made even more sexually indulgent by extending its length. At the same time, the normally intimate act is transformed into a performance of skill, which sanctions the activity as a contest, disguising its sexual nature. The wagering of a soda emphasizes the competitive nature of the activity.

Flashlight: Couples sit around the edge of a dark room. One person sits in the center with a flashlight. If he flashes it onto a couple that is not kissing, then he joins the opposite sex member of that couple, and the other member takes his place in the center with the flashlight…. In short it was normal in this game to be kissing, not normal to be caught unembraced.

The forbidden play: In Flashlight, there is a truly complex interplay with the taboo of kissing. The game provides opportunity for physical contact, while also offering a defense against the possibility of intimacy. The fact that players are hiding in the dark as they smooch makes it clear that kissing is something that is not a public activity. At the same time, the entire premise of the game is that another player spends his time "checking" to see if players are kissing. This moderator heightens the forbidden aspect by monitoring the action, while also punishing players who are not taking part. The game also acts as a sorting mechanism: if you don't like your partner enough to kiss him or her, you become the monitor, looking for a non-kissing couple with a partner that suits you.

Pass the Orange: This is usually played as a relay. The orange is placed under the chin and then the next player, a member of the opposite sex, endeavors to get it under his chin without the use of his hands. Or it may be played with the members of each sex alternating around in a circle…. In a number of reports the couple must kiss if they drop the orange while passing it from one chin to the next. In one, they kiss if they pass it on successfully.

The forbidden play: Like Endurance Kissing, Pass the Orange permits physical contact in public, by framing the game as a competitive activity. The kissing component of the game can act as either a reward or punishment for dropping the orange, depending on the game variant used. This ambiguity makes it clear that the elements of taboo, desire, and sexual contact can be configured in a myriad of arrangements within the social play space of the game.

Spin the Bottle: All versions have the traditional circle of players with one player in the center spinning the bottle…. Generally, the center player must kiss the peripheral player pointed out by the bottle. Usually the kissing is done in public, but the couple may go off and do it in private. If it points to a player of the same sex that player may go into the center, or it may be spun again, or the person to the right may be kissed…. There is much report of pretending to avoid the bottle, and of cheating so that it ended up pointing toward the pretty or the handsome and not towards the unattractive.

The forbidden play: Spin the Bottle remains the classic game of adolescent kissing. It offers a flexible structure that allows for both public and private smooching, while also providing a defense against the responsibility of choice. As with the eenie-meenie-miney-moe "counting out" games we discussed in *Games as Systems of Uncertainty* and *Breaking the Rules,* the role of chance in Spin the Bottle is clearly manipulated as part of the play of the game.

The social play of kissing games is highly structured, allowing players to experience normally taboo behavior within restricted contexts. Games such as Pass the Orange and Endurance Kissing guarantee gratification of certain desires (physical contact), while placing limitations on excess. As Sutton-Smith notes, "One may enjoy a kissing relationship, but be protected from a more total and intimate commitment. The uncertainty of what "might" happen is removed by the structure of the game."[21]

Forbidden play entails a shift in the implicit rules of a game. Playing in a sportsmanlike manner usually means adhering to the etiquette of proper behavior that exists outside the game. Implicit rules embody more general social values. It isn't proper to cheat in a game, in the same way that it isn't proper to cheat on your spouse. But by permitting improper behavior within defined limits, the operational rules of forbidden play trump the implicit rules of society. Thus when a player engages in forbidden play, he isn't only rebelling against the general rules of game play, he is also rebelling against larger social rules as well. If that were not the case, forbidden play would not have the transgressive quality of being *forbidden*. Like the Rooie Rules Foursquare players, people engaged in forbidden play don't just play games, but play with social structures. The Foursquare players gamed the system of rules. Forbidden play participants game the tension between desire and the limits of the socially permissable.

Forbidden play can appear in commercially designed games as well as in folk games, and it doesn't have to involve sexual play. Dressing and acting like a fictional character in a LARP, for example, is a kind of behavior that only happens within the sanctioned space of a game. So is the ruthless mob mentality of SiSSYFiGHT 2000 or the physical melee of full-contact martial arts tournaments and Rugby matches. In all of these examples, forbidden play bridges social relations inside and outside the game's boundaries. Without the "proper" social contexts that exist outside the game, the playful expression of hidden desires, nutty behavior, or normally criminal actions would not gain status as pleasing and transgressive; forbidden play would just be plain old play. At the same time, the game's magic circle protects those within the game from sanction. The game itself maintains this paradoxical tension with the real world: the forbidden play occurs only because of the artificiality of the game, even while it gains intensity as it both challenges and satisfies real-world desires.

Metagame: the Larger Social Context

Throughout this schema, we have investigated many kinds of play communities, from the elemental social roles of actor and counteractor to the complex social tangles of forbidden play. Each offered a different instance of the interplay between the game and the outside world, between social interactions on both sides of the magic circle. We finish this chapter by presenting a powerful concept, one that can help us make sense of the relationship between the artificiality of game play and genuine social reality. This concept is the *metagame*. The Latin root "meta" means *between, with, after, behind, over,* or *about*. Thus metagame means "the game beyond the game" and refers to the aspects of game play that derive not from the rules of the game, but from interplay with surrounding contexts.

Metagaming refers to the relationship between the game and outside elements, including everything from player attitudes and play styles to social reputations and social contexts in which the game is played. Post-game locker room conversations about the match are metagame interactions. Memorizing words in the Scrabble dictionary is a metagame activity, the honing of in-game skills. The typical playing strategies of a particular Go master are metagame information, useful if you are playing against him in a tournament next week. In all cases, the metagame refers to the way a game engages with factors permeating the space beyond the edges of the magic circle.

Game players use the term "metagame" in several different ways. For example, in live-action role-playing games, "metagaming" is when a player gains an advantage by using information that his or her character would not possess—and it is generally considered cheating. Some forms of metagaming, such as trash-talking to distract your opponent in a Racquetball match, fall into the category of unsportsmanlike behavior. Still other kinds of metagaming, such as painting and preparing wargaming figures, are thought of as valuable pursuits. These various uses of the term essentially all refer to the same thing: activities that link the game to outside contexts.

A Metagame Model

In an essay titled "Metagames," written for *Horsemen of the Apocalypse: Essays on Roleplaying,* game designer Richard Garfield presents a useful model for thinking about metagames. In it, he defines metagame as the way in which "a game interfaces outside of itself."[23] Under the rubric of this broad definition, Garfield includes a wide array of social play phenomena. He divides manifestations of the metagame into four categories:

1. What a player brings *to* a game

2. What a player takes away *from* a game

3. What happens *between* games

4. What happens *during* a game other than the game itself[24]

On the next few pages, we outline each of these categories in turn, using some of the examples that Garfield himself presents.

To: What a Player Brings to a Game

Players always bring something to a game, sometimes in tangible form and sometimes not. For example, a deck taken to a game of Magic: The Gathering or a bat carried to a Baseball game are physical components a player might bring. The study of certain openings in Chess or the ability to memorize cards in Hearts are examples of intangible, mental resources. A player usually has some level of choice in what to bring to a game, though some resources are mandatory: no Soccer ball, no Soccer game. Garfield notes that the selection of resources for a game is a process that players often enjoy. In minatures wargaming such as Warhammer, players spend many hours prior to a game designing their armies, both aesthetically and strategically.

Garfield organizes what players bring to a game into four categories. *Game Resources* refers to necessary game components, such as a deck of cards, a pair of dice, a Tennis racket, Baseball bat, or even physical reflexes. *Strategic Preparation or Training* includes studying an opponent's playing style or memorizing levels. *Peripheral Game Resources* refers to optional elements like game guides, cheats, and knowledge of play patterns. These resources are often created and shared among a game community, either through "official" channels or unofficial ones, such as fan sites. *Player Reputation* is the final category of what players bring to a game, and is often not voluntary. Are you known to bluff, open up the board early, or take advantage of weaker players?

From: What a Player Takes Away from a Game

Players always take something away from a game. It is not uncommon, for example, to play a game for some kind of *stakes.* Winning a stakes game might mean taking away something quantitative, like prize money or standings in a formal competition, or the stakes might be something less tangible, like gloating rights or social status among a group of players. Sometimes, a player takes something away after just a single game. Other times, victory might emerge from a series of games: *best two out of three.* Large-scale tournaments can span weeks or months. The seriousness with which players take a game is affected by how much the current game affects another game, particularly within a ladder structure or other organized contest. This aspect of the metagame can have a strong postive or negative influence on player attitude and performance.

Players also take things away from a game unrelated to the stakes, such as the *experience* of the game itself. A player's experience might serve to validate or contradict their beliefs about an opponent or about the game as a whole, thereby influencing future games. Crafting play experience into a tale, a player can also take away the story of the game: the way victory was seized from the jaws of defeat (or vice versa), spectacularly good or bad moves, the bizarre occurrences that happened during the course of play. *I can't believe I pitched a perfect game!* As we discussed in *Games as Narrative Play,* some games, such as a driving game with replay capability, make this *retelling play* an explicit part of the game. Of course, players can also take away *resources* for future games, whether it is the knowledge about how the game works or a collectible card won as the stakes of the game.

Between: What Happens Between Games

The space between games is filled with a rich palette of metagame activities that can add value to the core play experience. For many players, the activities that take place between games can be as important as what happens during a game. Players commonly reflect on strategy, training, or planning for the next game. *I have got to play more aggressively next time.* Planning what to bring to the next game, whether that involves assembling a new deck for Yu-Gi-Oh, buying a new Tennis racket, or planning a new Go strategy, are all important between-game activities. But not everything that happens between games is a solitary pursuit, and between-game metagaming can include players communicating with each other about what happened last game or players spreading stories and building reputations.

Additionally, not all between-game metagaming is strategic. Decorating a skateboard with stickers between X Games competitions, or reading historical accounts of a battle about to be enacted in a miniatures wargame is also part of the metagame. Both of these activities occur between games and add to the meaning of the play experience, but neither is usually done primarily in order to win.

During: What Happens During a Game Other than the Game Itself

This category of the metagame is quite diverse, and refers to the influence of real life on a game in play. There are many factors external to the magic circle that enter into the experience of play, factors that are always present and often quite powerful. Among the ways that the metagame occurs during play are social factors such as competition and camaraderie, or the physical environment of play such as good lighting or a noisy atmosphere. Trash talking, playing "head games," and exploiting player reputations all affect the metagame as well. If you are playing Table Tennis and are trying to distract your opponent with a steady stream of vociferous insults, you are playing a metagame against him. This kind of metagaming behavior may turn into unsportsmanlike behavior, violating implicit rules of play. It is then up to the social community of players to either endorse or censor the metagame behavior.

Garfield's categories of To, From, Between, and During illuminate the diverse possibilities of the metagame. In his essay, Garfield uses these categories to discuss the metagame of Magic: The Gathering, a game he designed early in his career. Its wildly popular success is due in large part to the innovative way in which Garfield actively incorporated metagame play into the game design itself. Even the game's subtitle, "The Gathering," references the game as a collection of parts that pass in and out of the magic circle. The comments that follow regarding the game are taken from a talk Garfield gave at the 2000 Game Developers Conference:

> *To:* Magic was distinctive in that each player brings half of the cards for the game. Choosing game resources to bring is a large part of the appeal to many players, and it can occupy as much time as the actual play of the game. This is such an important part of the game that there are players who specialize in it, known not as Magic players but as deck constructors and analysts.

> *From:* A traditional way to play Magic is for ante, in which each player randomly selects a card from her deck before play and sets it aside before the game starts. The winning player wins both cards.

Magic is often played in formal tournament settings as well, in which official standings or cash prizes can result from play.

Between: Between games of Magic, there is much circulation of game resources and information. Players trade cards, share strategies, and take part in rich player communities.

During: Reputation is important in all kids of Magic play. While some people simply strive to be victorious as often as possible, others are driven to win with unusual strategies, or in order to prove that particular combinations of cards are viable.[25]

Designing the Metagame

Magic's rich metagame emerges from a handful of key game design decisions. The essential structure of the game is that players create their own collections of cards and bring them to a game. Because preparation is a necessary part of play, players quickly understand that the planning metagame of Magic goes hand in hand with the game's face-to-face dueling.

The rules of play revolve around a simple turn structure. The complexity of Magic doesn't come from these core rules but instead from the many special cases that the thousands of different cards make possible. Magic is what game designer Greg Costikyan calls an "exceptions game," a game that contains many variants on a simple set of standard rules.[26] For example, Magic contains a simple set of rules to resolve creature attacks, but individual cards detail many special kinds of creatures, such as walls, which can only defend, or flying creatures, which can bypass any non-flying defending creatures. These "exceptions" lead to new creature-combinations, such as flying walls, which can intercept flying creatures, but can only defend. This kind of classificatory complexity, combined with variability in creature "stats" (casting cost, attack rating, defense rating, color type), plus numerous other "special case" abilities, makes for thousands of different kinds of possible creatures. And creatures are only one of several types of Magic cards!

The modular, specialized nature of Magic cards ensures that part of the metagame is exploring the range of cards, card combinations, deck constructions, and play strategies. As game pieces, the cards are portable and collectible and lend themselves naturally to trading and wagering. On innumerable levels, Magic: The Gathering facilitates and encourages metagaming play. That is one of the reasons why, more than ten years after its release, it still continues to engage players.

To guarantee a game's long-term success, the designer must take the metagame into account. As game designer François Dominic Laramée writes, "Metagaming can drastically increase a game's life span. I remember an online adventure game where players stayed on for months after solving the mystery, serving as 'elders' and giving clues to newbies."[27] Without a metagame, a play experience will provide its own short-lived intrinsic pleasures, but will not affect meaningful play in contexts outside the game.

Designing meaningful social play, usually means designing a meaningful metagame. But how? As we have noted in earlier chapters, game design is a second-order design problem. Game designers only directly design rules; the play experience is an emergent, indirect outcome of the rules. In a similar sense, social play, and the metagame in particular, are only indirectly linked to formal game design. In fact, most of any given game's metagame is beyond the reach of the game designer, for it emerges from play communities and their larger social worlds.

Yet careful game design can contribute to the emergence of a rich metagame. In many online games, web community features such as chat systems transform play via the metagame by allowing players to establish and nurture in-game social relations that gain life outside of game play. For example, the online gaming group *homemakers* spends hours online playing Hearts and Bridge while devoting most of their attention to chatting with friends. Players who make friends playing Hearts with *homemakers* will value the game not only for the formal play experience it provides, but also for the social community developed as part of the metagame. The strength of this community, like that of Magic, largely derives from the designed context in which it makes it meanings. Although the metagame can only be indirectly designed, it is up to you to encourage the experiences you want for your players, both within and around the games you design. Richard Garfield might not have designed a particular player's style of Magic trash-talking, but he helped provide the play context in which it is put to use.

Too often, game designers get caught up in the intricacies of design and production, losing sense of the larger social contexts where their game will be played. What will players bring to and from your game? How will they metagame between and during play sessions? What structures can you provide that will encourage the right kind of metagame? Will it be narrative worlds that open up imaginative metagame play? Deep formal structures that reward players for boning up on strategy before a game? Physical economies that encourage social trading and playing for stakes? Tools that let players create their own play communities? There are endless game design approaches.

One key: remember to *observe* your players. As you go through the iterative design process, pay attention to how your players interact before games, after games, between games. Ask them how they'd play if you let them take your game home. *Let* them take your game home—and see what happens. It is true that you can't directly design the metagame. But by understanding that you are always already designing within and for social contexts, you can do your best to cultivate rich metagaming play.

The Limits of Social Play

The metagame and social play bring us to the brink of the magic circle and beyond. In our **RULES**-based explorations of games, we kept our understanding of game systems firmly closed. In **PLAY,** things shifted. We sometimes viewed games as enclosed, internally driven systems of experience, at other times as systems that interact with the world at large. Nowhere has this double-framing been as evident as in our discussion of social play. Whether it is bounded and unbounded play communities or the ideal and real rules of games, social play is at once contingent on the formal structures of rules, while also very much a product of larger social contexts.

What are those larger social contexts? They are, of course, the cultures of games. Every Magic duelist, every *homemaker* card shark, every Spin The Bottle kisser doesn't merely exist in a play community, but is part of myriad cultural contexts, from spheres of nationality and ethnicity to ideologies and political beliefs. It is to those contexts we now turn, to the cultures in which games are played. In doing so we leave behind the sometimes open, sometimes closed territory of **PLAY** to take up instead the wonderfully open-ended landscape of games as **CULTURE.**

Further Reading

"Beyond the Rules of the Game: Why are Rooie Rules Nice?" by Linda A. Hughes

An excellent case study of children playing Foursquare and the differences they hold between ideal rules and "real" rules. "Real" rules refer to the actual rules children make use of, rather than the rules they are *supposed* use. Hughes' study reveals the close connection between games and the social contexts in which they are played, and helps to identify how social relationships between players dramatically impact the enactment of a formal systems of rules.

Notes

Children's Folklore: A Source Book, Brian Sutton-Smith, Jay Mechling, Thomas W. Johnson, and Felicia R. McMahon, eds.

A collection of essays from fields as far ranging as American studies, folklore, anthropology, psychology, sociology, and education, focusing on interactions among children at play. The essays include case studies, historical surveys, and methodological treatises on the study of play and children. Several of the essays offer excellent explorations of the interactions that emerge from the context of play, and offer insight into different forms of pleasure and social play engendered by games.

Recommended:

"Overview: Methods in Children's Folklore," Brian Sutton-Smith

"Double Dutch and Double Cameras," Ann Richman Beresin

"Urban Schoolyard," Ann Richman Beresin

"Children's Games and Gaming," Linda A. Hughes

"Hearts, Clubs, Diamonds, Spades: Players Who Suit MUDs," by Richard Bartle <http://www.mud.co.uk/richard/hcds.htm>

In this online essay, Bartle creates a taxonomy outlining four approaches to playing MUDs. Different player types interact with each other and with the game world in different ways toward radically distinct ends, and Bartle outlines how to build and manage communities to encourage particular player types. His essay is useful in considering the kinds of social interactions and play styles games encourage, especially in online multiplayer games.

The Moral Judgment of the Child, by Jean Piaget

Piaget's study of "the rules of the game" of Marbles draws a parallel between the cognitive development that allows children to play and understand games and the moral development by which children learn to distinguish right and wrong. Piaget focuses on the qualities of rules handed down from one group of children to another, and tracks the changing attitudes of children toward the authority of these rules.

Recommended:

The Rules of the Game, chapters 1–6

1. Brian Sutton-Smith, "A Syntax for Play and Games" In *Child's Play,* Brian Sutton-Smith and R.E. Herron (New York: John Wiley and Sons, 1971), p. 304.

2. Richard Bartle, "Hearts, Clubs, Diamonds, Spades: Players Who Suit MUDs." <http://www.mud.co.uk/richard/hcds.htm>.

3. Reiner Knizia, *Dice Games Properly Explained* (Tadworth, Surrey: Right Way Books, 1992), p. 197–8.

4. Ibid., p. 198–99.

5. Andrew Fluegelman and Shoshana Tembeck, *The New Games Book* (New York: Doubleday, 1976), p. 65.

6. Jean Piaget, *The Moral Judgment of the Child* (New York: Free Press, 1997), p. 13–14.

7. Johann Huizinga, *Homo Ludens: A Study of the Play Element in Culture* (Boston: Beacon Press, 1955), p. 12.

8. Bernard DeKoven, *The Well-Played Game* (New York: Doubleday, 1978), p. 16–17.

9. Piaget, *The Moral Judgment of the Child*, p. 28.

10. Ibid., p65.

11. Kenneth Goldstein, "Strategies in Counting Out" In *The Study of Games,* edited by Elliott Avedon and Brian Sutton-Smith (New York: John Wiley & Sons, 1971), p. 172–177.

12. Frank E. Manning, *The World of Play.* Proceedings of the 7th Annual Meeting of The Association of the Anthropological Study of Play (New York: Leisure Press, 1983), p. 19.

13. Linda Hughes, "Children's Games and Gaming." In *Children's Folklore: A Source Book,* edited by Brian Sutton-Smith, Jay Mechling, Thomas W. Johnson, and Felicia R. McMahon (Logan: Utah State University Press, 1999), p. 100.

14. Ibid., p. 100.

15. Ibid., p. 100.

16. Linda Hughes, "Beyond the Rules of the Game: Why are Rooie Rules Nice?" In *The World of Play,* edited by Frank E. Manning.

17. Ibid., p. 192.

18. Ibid., p. 192–194.

19. Brian Sutton-Smith, "The Kissing Games of Adolescents of Ohio." In *The Study of Games,* edited by Elliott Avedon and Brian Sutton-Smith (New York: John Wiley and Sons, 1971), p. 213.

20. Roger Caillois, *Man, Play, and Games* (London: Thames and Hudson, 1962), p. 8.

21. Sutton-Smith, "The Kissing Games of Adolescents of Ohio," p. 213–216.

22. Ibid., p. 213.

23. Richard Garfield, "Metagames." In *Horsemen of the Apocalypse: Essays on Roleplaying* (London: Jolly Roger Games, 2000), p. 16.

24. Ibid., p. 17.

25. <http://www.gdconf.com/archives/proceedings/2000/ >

26. Greg Costikyan, "Don't be a Vidiot: What Computer Game Designers can Learn from Non-Electronic Games." Speech given at the 1998 Game Developer's Conference. Archived at: <www.costik.com/vidiot.hmtl>.

27. <http://www.gignews.com/fdl_mainstreamdesign.htm>.

Games as Social Play **SUMMARY**

- When games are framed as **Social Play** the relationships between elements in the game system are considered to be social relationships.

- **Social play interactions** may emerge in two different ways:

  - Interactions *internally* derived emerge from the functioning of game rules.

  - Interactions *externally* derived come from outside the magic circle.

- A social **play community** occurs anytime a group of players get together to play a game. Play communities can arise around:

  - a single game

  - a game event or series of games

  - a larger game context

- **Player roles** refer to the kinds of social relationships that exist between players in a game. Roles are not fixed and may change several times within the course of a game.

- **Sutton-Smith's model** for player roles includes an actor, a counteractor, and an overall "motive" or format for play. For example, if the motive is *capture,* the actor's role is *to take,* while the role of the counteractor is to *avoid being taken.*

- **Bartle's model** of player roles divides online MUD players into four categories:

  - *Achievers:* Players that seek to advance in experience and power.

  - *Explorers:* Players that want to explore the remote spaces of the world.

  - *Socializers:* Players that place a premium on direct social interaction.

  - *Killers:* "Antisocial" players that seek to harm and frustrate others.

- Games are **emergent social systems** in which simple play behaviors and social interactions can result in incredibly complicated experiences of play.

- A **bounded** play community is a closed system: it arises from the social play that takes place strictly within the space of an individual game. A play community that is **not bounded** is an open system, as there is an exchange between the game and its environment. Whether or not a play community is bounded or not bounded often depends on how it is framed.

- The bounded play community of a game results in a form of **social contract.** The social contract:

- emerges from the rules stylizing the ways that players interact with each other in the game

- consists of the meanings and values which the players give life through play

- ensures that play spaces are "safe" spaces where players can take risks with fewer consequences than in the real world

- **Safety** and **trust** are two elements of the social contract of the game. They are also requisite psychological qualities that players must feel in order to be comfortable enough to enter into the social space of the game.

- **Piaget** argues that when a child acquires an understanding of a game's rules, he is also developing an understanding of the social contract of a game. As children develop, they learn to see rules as flexible structures that can be altered through collective consensus.

- In **transformative social play** players extend, transform, and manipulate existing social relationships through play itself.

- Players make a distinction between "ideal" and "real" rules. **Ideal rules** refer to the "official" regulations of a game. **Real rules** are the codes and conventions held by a community of players. Real rules reflect a consensus of how the game ought to be played.

- Players often broker social power by asserting competing sets of real rules. This is the phenomena of **gaming the game,** when players don't merely play within the game, but play with interpretations of rules and propose their own play variants.

- Games permit and often encourage normally taboo behavior, the phenomenon of **forbidden play.** Forbidden play rebels against both the implicit rules of game play and against larger social values. The rules of a game both permit and put limits on forbidden play.

- **Metagaming** refers to the relationship of a game to elements outside of the game. Garfield's model of the metagame includes four categories:

  - What a player brings **to** a game

  - What a player takes **from** a game

  - What happens **between** games

  - What happens **during** a game other than the game itself

Sneak
A game for 3 or more players

Introduction

How well do you know your friends? In Sneak, you'll find that out, as well as how creative—and deceitful—they can be.

Half the players are Sporks, and the rest are Foons. But one of you is the Sneak, and can masquerade as either Spork or Foon. Can you figure out who's the Sneak as you perform the challenges you are given?

Rules

Goal

Earn the most points by successfully guessing who the Sneak is, and by fooling other players into guessing incorrectly. You'll draw your conclusions based on how players react to written or acted "challenges."

Materials

- Challenges (found on p. 506–587 in this book, the **CULTURE** primary schema)

- Counters (beans, pennies, paper clips, etc.)

- Lots of index cards or slips of blank paper

- Pens or pencils

Setting up

This game is for 4 or more players. Each player gets 4 counters, something to write with, and a number of index cards.

Assigning Camps

Each player is a Spork, a Foon, or the Sneak. These aren't teams, but indicate your game identity, called your "camp." Everyone's looking out for themselves in this game.

Slips of paper or index cards are put into a hat: one slip reads "Sneak" and the rest read either "Spork" or "Foon." Each camp's name appears on half the cards. If there are an even number of players, one camp will have an extra player—which camp this is should be made clear at the start, so everyone knows how many Sporks and Foons there are.

Each player draws a card. This is the player's camp card and is kept secret. If players are directed by a challenge to switch camps, they will update this card to reflect their new camp. This card is only revealed to all players at the end of a match after everyone votes on who they think is the Sneak.

Turns

Play moves clockwise, starting with the player who owns the hat. For his or her turn, each player can: 1) Select a challenge for the group to perform or 2) Purchase information or 3) Call for a vote.

A **round** is over when everyone's had one turn. A **match** is over when a vote occurs. Three matches make a complete game of Sneak.

Drawing Challenges

The player flips to a random page in the **CULTURE** schema of this book with a challenge printed in the gutter space of the page. The challenge is chosen before reading—no peeking! Some challenges are private, marked "Write," and others, marked "Act," are public.

The player reads the challenge aloud. The challenges contain instructions for the players, either for one camp or for everyone. After the instructions are read, all players perform the challenge. The Sneak (being sneaky) can follow either the Spork or Foon instruction, unless the challenge tells him or her to act like a specific camp.

Types of Challenges

Write challenges—doodle, answer a question—are written on cards, one challenge per card, and are kept hidden from other players.

Act challenges—take or give counters, perform a charade—are ones everyone can see.

If the selected challenge directs players to **switch camps,** then each Spork and Foon crosses out their previous camp name on the camp card and writes down their new camp name, keeping the card hidden. The Sneak remains the Sneak.

If the selected challenge is to show another player one of your *Write* cards and there haven't been any *Write* challenges yet in the match, the current player should flip to a new challenge. If the selected challenge has already been performed that round, the player should flip to a new challenge.

Purchasing Information

Instead of choosing a challenge from the book, a player can buy a look at one of any player's *Write* challenge cards. The purchaser names the card by challenge, such as "Show me your astronaut/alien card." The player who's been targeted must show the card: no refusing the buyer.

For **one** counter, the card is shown to all players. For **two** counters, the card is shown only to the player who bought the information. Counters go to the player whose information was purchased.

Calling for a Vote

Any player can call for a vote during his or her turn. There's a scoring bonus (explained below) if the player calls for a vote and guesses correctly, and a scoring penalty if he or she calls for a vote and guesses wrong.

The Sneak can call for a vote just like any other player, but gets no penalty or bonus points.

Force Vote

If after three rounds (everyone has taken three turns each) no one has called for a vote, a mandatory Force Vote occurs and the match is over.

Voting

A vote—whether called for by a player or a Force Vote—ends the match. All players vote secretly on whom the Sneak is, writing their guesses on their camp cards. The Sneak writes "I'm the Sneak!"

When the vote is complete, all players hold up their camp cards, making the results public, then everyone marks their scores.

Scoring

Sporks and Foons

- Player who correctly guessed the Sneak: +5 points

- Player guessed wrong: –1 point

- Player wasn't the Sneak but was named by another player: +1 for each player incorrectly named as the Sneak

The Sneak

- –1 point for each player who guessed correctly

- +3 points for each player who guessed wrong

Vote bonus and penalty

- Player called for a vote and guessed correctly: +3 points (in addition to correct-guess points, for +8 total)

- Player called for a vote and guessed wrong: –2 points (in addition to wrong-guess points, for –3 total)

If the Sneak is the person who called for a vote or a Force Vote ended the round, no one gets the bonus or penalty.

Hoarders beware: the number of counters you have left doesn't affect your score.

Next matches

Players start fresh each match. New camp cards are written and put into the hat, and players start over with 4 counters. A player can be the Sneak more than once.

During the Game

Players may NOT take written notes. Observe and remember…

The camp card can help remind players of their camp, should anyone get confused. Players can consult this card as often as they need to during the game.

This game is a chance to get to know each other better—and also play head games. Players are welcome to share and discuss their answers and strategies throughout the game.

Play continues around the table until a player calls for a vote, or until a Force Vote is required.

Winning

At the end of 3 matches, the player with the most points wins.

Kira Snyder

Kira Snyder designs for There, Inc. and has written extensively for stage, screen, and interactive media. Before joining There she was the Game Designer and Lead Writer on Majestic at Electronic Arts, and prior to that developed ZDTV's online community. She has worked in story, game, and virtual world design at Microsoft, Purple Moon, and in a wide range of independent projects, from a 3D sci-fi adventure to text MUDs to an RPG drama for women. Kira holds an Honors B.A. in Drama from Stanford and a Masters from NYU's Interactive Telecommunications Program.

DESIGN DIARY

Kira Snyder

Sneak

Initial idea

Social deception game. 3 or more players. Players are blindly assigned to one of two groups, one player is a double agent. Turn-based play. Players flip a coin, and turn to a page in the book (e.g. heads=even, tails=odd). In the header or footer are two simple tasks, which the group performs according to their assignation. Double agent can do either. Tasks can be public (e.g. A's raise right hand, B's raise left) or private (A's write down a number 1–10, B's a number 10–20). Game mechanics allow you to buy peeks at private information. At the end of a round, players guess the identity of the double agent. Points awarded for correct guesses, etc. Players all reassigned for next round, play continues. Player with the most points at end of X rounds wins.

Initial Notes

Cloak and Dagger

- Teams, Cloaks and Daggers, one double agent.

- At beginning of game, slips are put into a hat, one Double Agent, the rest are Cloaks and Daggers, as even as can be devised (not a problem if there's one more of one type).

- Something for counters—coins, beans, slips of paper. Each player gets 3 of these.

- Turns: flip coin, go to odd or even page in book. Read task, e.g. Cloaks write down a number 1–10, Daggers write a number 10–20. Double agent can do either.

- Some tasks private, some public. E.g. raise right hand, left hand. Change seats. Give beans.

- Instead of task you can exchange slips with another player, viewing their entire list.

- "Pay off" player—one bean for peek at last entry.

- After everyone's had a turn (10 tasks?), people write down who they think the double agent is.

- Get 5 points for correct guess, Double Agent loses 1 point for each correct guess. 1 point per bean as well.

- Then everyone's reassigned, new Double Agent, new round.

- At the end of 3 rounds, person with the most points wins.

- Header or footer space required on a number of pages.

I plan to hold three playtests over the course of 5 weeks, allowing time in between to gather feedback and iterate the rules.

Drafted and revised rules and list of missions. Some missions are clear-cut, meaning that you can tell by what someone wrote what faction they belong to. Others are more slippery and open to interpretation, allowing all players to be sneaky (thereby causing other players to guess wrong and lose points), not just the sneak. I'm finding the actions are tending to be more playful—drawings or personal information—than spyish, as the name Cloak and Dagger might suggest. Players may well want a way to share more of this info with the group. Also included some missions that make everyone switch faction.

50 missions total

· 6 are switch-faction

· 15 are public (5 are public to one person only)

· 35 are private

Cloak and Dagger
Rules for Playtest 1

Materials
Missions
Coin
Counters (beans, pennies, paper clips, etc.)
Index cards and pencils

Setting up
Each player gets 3 counters.

The numbered missions are placed into Even and Odd piles (mimicking the book layout). This is so the missions can be discarded, for purposes of testing.

Assigning Factions
Slips of paper with faction names are put into a hat. There is one Double Agent slip, the rest read either Cloak or Dagger, as evenly distributed as can be for the number of players (it's fine if the factions are uneven by 1). Players write their faction, or Double Agent, on their first index card and place it face down in front of them.

Turns

Play moves clockwise from some randomly chosen first player. For his or her turn, each player can either assign a mission or purchase information.

Assigning Missions

The player flips a coin. If the coin is heads, the player chooses a mission at random from the Even pile. If the coin is tails, the player chooses a mission at random from the Odd pile. The mission should be chosen before reading—no peeking.

The player then reads the mission aloud. The missions contain instructions to the players, either by faction or to all players. After they've been read, all players perform the mission, be it public or private. Private missions should be written such that other players cannot see. The Double Agent can perform either Cloak or Dagger missions.

Once the mission has been performed, it is placed onto a discard pile and removed from play.

Purchasing Information

Instead of assigning a mission, the player can buy a look at any one player's most recent private mission entry with one counter. This counter goes to the player whose information is being looked at. Only the player who bought the information can see it.

Scoring

At the end of a round (after each player has had two turns), all players vote secretly on who the Double Agent is.

- Correct guess: +5 points

- Incorrect guess: –1 point

- Double Agent: –1 point for each correct guess, +3 points for each incorrect guess

- Players also get +1 point for each counter they still have

Next rounds

Players start fresh each round, drawing new slips from the hat and starting over with 3 counters. A player can be the Double Agent more than once.

Winning

At the end of 3 rounds, player with the most points wins.

Notes from Playtest 1

5 players. Went well. Game was fun. Got some great feedback on what didn't work, and what people liked as well as ideas for refining the rules.

- Rather than have a round comprise X turns, try having play continue until someone calls for a vote. If you call for the vote and guess wrong, you lose points.

- Drawings: info about yourself was fun. People indeed wanted more opportunities to make this public. For next test I added 5 more public actions, where players state answers aloud or act them out.

- Cloak and Dagger not really working as a name. Something lighter and more representative of the playful nature of the actions would probably work better. For next test, will go with "Sneak" as the game title and Spork and Foon as the camp names.

- Need some mechanism to keep the double agent from just following one faction. The Double Agent in one round just allied with one camp. For next test, added a rule that the Sneak can't act in accord with one camp throughout.

- Some missions didn't quite cut it. Revised them to get rid of ones that were boring or didn't work in testing.

- Number of counters and the scoring system seemed to work fine.

- Didn't seem too easy to guess double agent, especially in the second round when everyone had the hang of things.

55 actions total

- 6 are switch-camp

- 20 are public

- 5 are public to one person only

- 35 are private

Sneak
Rules for Playtest 2

Goal

Be the player to earn the most points by successfully guessing who the Sneak is and fooling other players into guessing incorrectly.

Materials
Actions
Coin
Counters (beans, pennies, paper clips, etc.)
Index cards and pens or pencils

Setting up
Each player gets 3 counters.

The numbered Actions are placed into Even and Odd piles (mimicking the book layout). This is so the actions can be discarded, for purposes of testing.

Assigning Camps

Slips of paper with camp names are put into a hat. There is one Sneak slip, the rest read either Spork or Foon, as evenly distributed as can be for the number of players (it's fine if the camps are uneven by 1) Players write their camp, or "Sneak," on an index card and set it aside, face down.

Turns

Play moves clockwise from some randomly chosen first player. For his or her turn, each player can: 1) Draw an action for the group to perform or 2) Purchase information or 3) Call for a vote.

Drawing Actions

The player flips a coin. If the coin is heads, the player chooses an action at random from the Even pile. If the coin is tails, the player chooses an action at random from the Odd pile. The action should be chosen before reading—no peeking.

The player then reads the actions aloud. The actions contain instructions to the players, either by camp or to all players. After they've been read, all players perform the action, be it public or private. Private actions should be written such that other players cannot see. The Sneak can perform either Spork or Foon actions, unless they are directed to perform the action of a specific camp.

If the action is to switch camps, then each player's card with their new camp should join the original camp card, out of regular game play (i.e. these cards are not viewable as private entries).

If the action is a public one requiring the use of a private action and there hasn't been one yet the player should discard that action and draw a new one.

Once the action has been performed, it is placed onto a discard pile and removed from play.

Purchasing Information

Instead of assigning an action, the player can buy a look at any one player's most recent private action entry with one counter. This counter goes to the player whose information is being looked at. Only the player who bought the information can see it.

Calling for a Vote

If a player has an idea of who the Sneak is, he or she can call for a vote.

Play continues around the group until a vote is called for.

Scoring

When a vote is called for, all players vote secretly on whom the Sneak is. When everyone has voted, all players hold up their camp card, making the results public, then play is scored.

· Correct guess: +5 points

· Incorrect guess: –1 point

· Sneak: –1 point for each correct guess, +3 points for each incorrect guess

· Called for a vote and guessed wrong: –5 points

· Players also get +1 point for each counter they still have.

Next rounds

Players start fresh each round, drawing new slips from the hat and starting over with 3 counters. A player can be the Sneak more than once.

Winning

At the end of 3 rounds, the player with the most points wins.

Notes from Playtest 2

4 players. Refinements seemed to work, and the balance of public to private info was closer to what players wanted. Getting there…

· Calling for a vote basically worked but people seemed to need a stronger incentive to make the call. Will add a bonus for calling and being right, to try to balance out the penalty for calling and being wrong.

· There's no real need for coin flip when choosing an action. Will change rules to have players just pick an action at random.

· Still need to address keeping the Sneak from just aligning with one camp. "Because it's a rule" just didn't seem strong enough. Will revise some actions to require Sneak to align with specific camp.

- People still wanted more public actions. Will try out expanding the purchasing-info option—for 2 counters, private view. For 1 counter, public, meaning all players see the entry. Increase number of counters to 5.

- Camp card. Just for housekeeping—one card that contains all your camp assignations.

- Will change rules to allow choice about which private entry to view. With the limitation of latest/first, many got buried.

- We hit a lot of switch-camps. Will trim down to 4.

- Maybe not quite enough actions for full game? Unused pile seemed a little thin. Added 11 more: 4 public, 7 private.

65 actions total

- 4 are switch-camp

- 8 require the Sneak to follow a particular camp

- 25 are public

- 6 are public to one person only

- 40 are private

Notes from Playtest 3

6 players. The new buying-info mechanism was successful, and the balance of public and private actions felt right finally. Players had fun, and reported that the difficulty of guessing the Sneak not too hard or too easy.

- Number of counters seemed a little high this time. Will change to 4 in final version.

- Will remove counters from scoring. Although no one did this, it would seem to promote an alternate strategy aside from actually playing the game: hoarding counters and guessing the Sneak's identity randomly, since you only lose 1 point that way.

- Added one action for an even number, thinking that would be more helpful for the book layout.

Final count

66 actions total

4 are switch-camp

8 require the Sneak to follow a particular camp

26 are public

7 are public to one person only

40 are private

Thanks to all my playtesters: Michael Becker, Lisa Clark, Zack Ford, Roy Gatchalian, Margaret Foley-Mauvais, Eileen McMahon and George Rivello.

Notes from Eric and Katie's playtesting

Helpful feedback came in from playtesting with a different group, organized by Eric and Katie. Based on their comments, I made some further changes.

- The rules were clarified in spots, and I added a "During the Game" section for general game play rules.

- Actions are now labeled "Write" and "Act" to make clear which are private and which are public.

- A player who was not the Sneak but who got another player's vote gets a point for each person who named him or her.

- Players still were hesitant to call for a vote, leading to rounds that dragged on a bit. I reduced the penalty for calling for a vote then guessing wrong by 1 point, and added a Force Vote, which occurs after 3 trips around the table if no one's called for a vote by then. Interestingly, this was the mechanism in the first iteration of the rules, before the option to call for a vote during a turn. Seems that both the voluntary and mandatory votes are needed to keep the pace moving and the stakes high.

I sent the updated rules to several friends for a cold read (thanks, Jennie Sharf, Allen Blue, and Greg Gibson!), and further revised them based on that feedback.

- Added an Introduction section to briefly describe the game.

- Renamed "actions" to "challenges." A more interesting word, and less confusing now that "Act" is a challenge type.

- Cleared up the turn/round/match confusion and other sections that were a bit vague.

- Gave the whole shebang a polish to give the rules more personality and make them less dry.

Unit 4: CULTURE

Defining Culture

Games as Cultural Rhetoric

Games as Open Culture

Games as Cultural Resistance

Games as Cultural Environment

...media never functions in a vacuum. Playing a game in an arcade is a very different experience than playing it in one's own home or as part of a military training exercise. Media consumption gains its meaning through association with a range of other activities that constitute our everyday life.—**Henry Jenkins,** *"Lessons from Littleton: What Congress Doesn't Want to Hear About Youth and Media"*

No game is an island.

Games are always played somewhere, by someone, for some reason or another. They exist, in other words, in a *context*, a surrounding cultural milieu. The magic circle is an environment for play, the space in which the rules take on special meaning. But the magic circle itself exists within an environment, the greater sphere of culture at large. In the following chapters, we continue our outward movement from the heart of the magic circle, beyond **RULES** and **PLAY,** into the vast and colorful expanse of **CULTURE.**

Unit 3: **Culture**

DEFINING CULTURE

culture
context
reflecting culture
transforming culture
cultural text

29

1. There must be a ball: it should be large.

   (This in prescient expectation of Connie Hawkins and Julius Erving, whose hands would reinvent basketball as profoundly as Jimi Hendrix's hands reinvented rock-and-roll.)

2. There shall be no running with the ball.

   (Thus mitigating the privileges of owning portable property. Extended ownership of the ball is a virtue in football. Possession of the ball in basketball is never ownership; it is always temporary and contingent upon your doing something else with it.)

3. No man on either team shall be restricted from getting the ball at any time that it is in play.

   (Thus eliminating the job specialization that exists in football, by whose rules only those players in "skill positions" may touch the ball. The rest just help. In basketball there are skills peculiar to each position, but everyone must run, jump, catch, shoot, pass, and defend.)

4. Both teams are to occupy the same area, yet there is to be no personal contact. *(Thus no rigorous territoriality, nor any rewards for violently invading your opponent's territory unless you score. The model for football is the drama of adjacent nations at war. The model for basketball is the polyglot choreography of urban sidewalks.)*

5. The goal shall be horizontal and elevated. *(The most Jeffersonian principle of all: Labor must be matched by aspiration. To score, you must work your way down court, but you must also elevate! Ad astra.)*—**James Naismith's Guiding Principles of Basket-Ball, 1891,** (With commentary by Dave Hickey, in *Air Guitar*)

Introducing Culture

Why would cultural critic Dave Hickey compare a rule about the size of a basketball to the hands of players such as Connie Hawkins and Julius Erving? What does he mean by suggesting the model for Basketball is the "polyglot choreography of urban sidewalks," or that the elevated hoop is Jeffersonian in principle? Hickey's comments on James Naismith's *Guiding Principles of Basket-Ball* differs from the formal and experiential focus of **RULES** and **PLAY.** His interest is not primarily in the formal structure of the game, nor in what players experience as they play. Analyzing the original rules of the game of Basketball, Hickey's interest is situated not inside the game, but elsewhere: in the cultural spaces within which the game is embedded.

Much of our emphasis so far has been on the space *inside* the magic circle of a game. Occasionally, in our explorations of **RULES** and **PLAY,** we ventured to the border of the magic circle and took tentative steps just beyond it. We considered, for example, how breaking the rules can turn players into designers, and how social relations in the real world impact social relations within the space of play. But what if we continued pushing outwards, into the space beyond the boundaries of games? What would we find? The context of the game, of course. We know from systems theory that every system has an environment. But what contexts constitute the environment of a game? How do cultural contexts affect representation and game play? How do games, in turn, affect cultural contexts? These questions are the focus of our final set of game design schemas, contextual frameworks that usher game design into the richly textured realm of **CULTURE.**

Write | **ALL PLAYERS:** Switch camp. Spork is now Foon and vice versa. Sneak remains the Sneak. Write the name of your new camp on your camp card.

The schemas contained within **CULTURE** move beyond rules and play to map relationships between the magic circle and culture at large. In "The Heresy of Zone Defense," Hickey is writing *not* about the rules of Basketball, but the cultural contexts these rules represent and reinvent. Stated simply, games are culture. Chutes and Ladders is not just a children's playtime activity, but a cultural document with a rich history, designed to express a religious doctrine of a particular time and place. The Sims is not merely a simulation of suburbia, but a representation of cultural interaction that relies on an ideological reality located beyond the scope of actual game play. The Olympics are not just a series of sporting events, but a complex context in which global politics infuse the play of the games on many levels. All games are part of culture. Just as any game can be framed in terms of their formal or experiential qualities, they can also be framed according to their status as cultural objects.

Unlike the schemas in **RULES** and **PLAY**, cultural game design schemas do *not* directly derive from the internal, intrinsic qualities of games; rather, they come from the relationship between games and the larger contexts in which they are played. These contexts might be ideological, practical, political, or even physical. In all cases, the contexts exist separately from the games themselves: the inner-city abandoned lot exists whether stickball is played there or not. Because our focus is not on the formal qualities of a game or its experiential effects, there are many ways to approach cultural analysis. In this sense, the cultural schemas we offer represent only a sampling of ways to frame the relationship between game design and culture. This is true also of the schemas presented in **RULES** and **PLAY**, but it is especially pronounced here. Culture is inimitably open-ended, and we have no doubt that new perspectives will emerge to enrich and extend the concepts we introduce.

Culture: A Framework

Games are designed objects that engage culture on several levels. As systems of representation they *reflect* culture, depicting images of gender (think of Barbie Fashion Designer, Duke Nukem', or Tomb Raider), as well as portrayals of race and class (Street Fighter II, State of Emergency, or Dope Wars). In this case, the cultural dimensions of a game are part of the game itself, reflecting values and ideologies of surrounding contexts. As interactive systems, on the other hand, games offer players forms of participation that extend the boundaries of play *beyond* the edges of the magic circle. From player-produced objects like skins, mods, or game patches, to role-playing games in which players explore and alter their personal identity, games have the potential to *transform* culture. These cultural transformations emerge from the game, to take on a life of their own outside the framework of game play.

This ability of games to affect the contexts in which they are played represents a cultural instance of *transformative play*. As we noted in **Defining Play**, transformative play occurs when the free movement of play alters the more rigid structures in which it takes place. A mod that feminizes the gothic fictive world of DOOM by littering the space with objects from the Animé Sailor Moon is an example of transformative play. A Soccer match played between two rival nations that leads to international disputes or cultural alliances is also transformative play. So is the design of a game patch that fills the bitmapped spaces of Tempest with hooded members of the Ku Klux Klan. Each of these instances of transformative play occurs on formal and experiential levels. However, a significant feature of these examples is the way they reference, influence, and alter cultural contexts beyond the formal limits of the game.

These two ways of understanding games as culture, *reflection* and *transformation*, are not both universal to all games. We do believe that all games *reflect* culture to some degree, as they are objects produced and played within culture at large. But not all games manifest transformative cultural play to actually *transform* culture. Only certain games transgress the magic circle in such a way as to have a genuine effect on the cultural contexts in which they are created and played. Arriving at an understanding of how games can reflect and transform culture is the focus of this chapter. How can game designers explore the cultural dimensions of games in concert with their formal and experiential qualities? What are game design's reflective and transformative capabilities? How exactly are games culture? A point of view game designers rarely address, the connection between games and cultural contexts acknowledges the game designer's role in shaping the very cultures we inhabit.

Cultural Structures: A List

From a game design perspective, it is crucial to understand the kinds of cultural structures your games engage. Does your game enact a set of past attitudes and beliefs, as with historical or quasi-historical sims such as Civilization, Age of Empires, or Settlers of Catan? Does your game engage the style and behavior of a subculture, as with the youth-oriented snowboarding content of SSX Tricky and Cool Boarders? Does your game challenge cultural stereotypes in the fashion of Parappa the Rapper by offering alternative or hybrid forms of character representation? Since all games can be considered culture, any game you create will have cultural qualities. Yet it is not enough to merely point out that games and culture can affect one another. Instead, we need to look closely at the specific kinds of relationships that occur between them.

How do games and culture relate? Let's begin by interrogating the key term of this primary schema. The word "culture" commonly refers to all of the knowledge and values shared by a society or group, and often is used to refer collectively to a society and its way of life. It was Edward Tylor, the nineteenth-century British anthropologist, who originally proposed the contemporary definition of culture as "socially patterned human thought and behavior."[1] But because culture is such a complex and open-ended concept, there are plenty of other definitions from which we can choose. For example, consider this open-ended list of "culture" definitions compiled by anthropologist John H. Bodley, based on the work of Tylor:

Topical: Culture consists of everything on a list of topics, or categories, such as social organization, religion, or economy.

Historical: Culture is social heritage, or tradition, that is passed on to future generations.

Behavioral: Culture is shared, learned human behavior, a way of life.

Normative: Culture is ideals, values, or rules for living.

Functional: Culture is the way humans solve problems of adapting to the environment or living together.

Mental: Culture is a complex of ideas, or learned habits, that inhibit impulses and distinguish people from animals.

Structural: Culture consists of patterned and interrelated ideas, symbols, or behaviors.

Symbolic: Culture is based on arbitrarily assigned meanings that are shared by a society.[2]

Each element in this list offers a possible definition for "culture." Although the listings seem diverse in perspective, every one directly or indirectly involves the same three basic components: what people think, what they do, and the material products they produce. None of these definitions of culture is correct or incorrect. In fact, unlike many of our other key terms, we will not propose a single definition for the concept of culture. There are so many ways to study and understand "culture" that a solitary definition would too sharply limit the concept.

For the purposes of game design, we understand "culture" to refer to what exists outside the magic circle of a game, the environment or context within which a game takes place. This broad formulation of culture, as a context for game rules and player experience, can itself be framed in many ways, such as the list of definitions above. The cultural context of a game might be its historical context; or the set of ideological values that it reflects and transforms; or the way the game fits into the lifestyle of its players. Culture is a diverse and flexible concept.

Act | All players state your answers aloud. SPORK: Name someone you looked up to when you were a child. FOON: Name someone you look up to now.

Grappling with questions of culture and game design is therefore quite difficult. Whenever you consider the cultural aspects of a game, you need to define exactly what you consider culture to be.

This does not mean, however, that all cultural readings of games are equally useful. For a game designer, the goal of a cultural game analysis stays true to the core pursuit of this book: the design of meaningful play. Investigating the cultural identity of a game is simply another way for game designers to generate successful play experiences. Conceived as a system of shared ideas, values, and behaviors negotiated and transformed over time, culture can play a powerful role in shaping the meaning of a game. Understanding which systems of meaning make up the context in which your game is to be played is critical to the design of meaningful play. It is through play itself that layers of meaning emerge and accumulate to shape the play experience, inside as well as outside the magic circle.

Cultural Meanings: A Few Examples

Although many facets of a play experience depend on relationships established by a game's formal and experiential structures, there are other important qualities that achieve resonance by way of culture. The "meaning" of a game of Dominos played on a hot summer night on a Brooklyn street corner, for example, gains richness from a whole slew of contextual factors: the hot, sultry air that provides a perfect acoustical buffer to the slapping ivory tiles; the loose and easy postures of the four Puerto Rican-American men gathered around the makeshift card table; the well-known story of the grand champion who is said to have never lost a match but who now sits poised to lose. Each of these contextual factors plays a role in qualifying just what the game *means* at any particular moment.

From Dominos and DigDug to Pong and Pachinko, any game admits to many different levels of meaningful play. More than just rules and play, all games involve a series of cultural structures against and within which the play of the game occurs.

From the social hierarchies of fan participation to the architectural spaces where games take place, what is "at play" in culture directly affects the game experience. Consider the following passage from Stefan Fatsis' book *Word Freak,* in which he points out some of the cultural structures at play in and around the game of Scrabble:

> Rosie O'Donnell regularly talks about her Scrabble addiction. Higher brows love it, too. In a bit about mythical Florida tourist traps, Garrison Keillor lists the international Scrabble Hall of Fame. Charles Bukowski's poem "pulled down shade" ends with the lines: "this fucking / Scotch is / great. / let's play / Scrabble. Vladimir Nabokov, in his novel *Ada,* describes an old Russian game said to be a forerunner of Scrabble. The game is a cultural Zelig: a mockable emblem of Eisenhower-era family values, a stand-in for geekiness, a pastime so decidedly unhip that it's hip.[3]

Pop cultural artifact or highbrow pastime? Emblem of geekiness or symbol of the tragically hip? Scrabble is all of these things and more, when considered from a cultural perspective. Scrabble appears in so many cultural contexts and interacts with culture in so many ways that appreciating every aspect of Scrabble's cultural play would be an impossible task.

Any game that establishes a strong presence in culture immediately engages with innumerable cultural structures. Take Basketball, for example. With what contexts outside of the magic circle does the game connect? We could consider the roles of players, coaches, referees, cheerleaders, or fans, each of whom affects the cultural identity and experience of the game. There is the physical context of the arena to consider, as well as the roles of the vendors, technicians, ticket scalpers, and mascots. What about the context of the media, including television and radio announcers, newspapers, satellite broadcasting, and Pay-Per-View TV? Or the economics that make the game possible, from ticket and licensed t-shirts sales to the negotiation of player salaries? Then there are the professional organizations that regulate and administrate the game. For fans or players of the game, Basketball can also be a context for establishing social status, group affiliation, cultural identity, or access to a college education. Every one of these elements contributes to the overall cultural significance of the game. Whether players and spectators realize it or not, when they play or watch a game they are taking part in generating, embodying, and transforming these cultural meanings. These meanings are not fixed, but are always in some way "at play" within existing cultural structures.

As we know from earlier chapters, play is free movement within more rigid structures. Recognizing just what cultural structures can be brought into the cultural play of a game is a powerful design strategy. Grand Theft Auto III, for example, plays with the mythos of urban criminal culture and gangster cinema; Jet Grind Radio offers a stylish sci-fi exposition on graffiti and skate cultures. Silent Hill II, on the other hand, looks to the genres of horror and film noir for its cultural play. This kind of play can pair the more rigid forces of cultural convention with the loose and poetic qualities of human participation. As we play a game like Jet Grind Radio or GTA III, we are not just playing with the game rules: we are also playing with the rules and conventions of culture that the games reflect and transform.

Cultural Texts: Trafficking in Signs

In previous game design schemas, we explored the ways in which games, as both formal and experiential systems, have the capacity to represent. In the game of Mafia, for example, an assassin's silent hand gesture represents "kill!" and the act of closing one's eyes at nightfall marks a player as a "villager." These acts of representation take place within the artificial space of the game world, and although the representation may serve to simulate something in the real world, it only gains its primary value within the space of meaning created by the game itself. We framed games as being able *to represent* phenomena internally, as well as *being representations* as a whole.

Mafia internally represents Mafiosi, villagers, day and night, and death. As a whole, it is a stylized representation of a village struggling against hidden, shadowy mafia figures.

But what happens if we shift our perspective from looking at the capacity of games *to represent* or *as representations*, to games as forms of *cultural representation?* Such a shift requires us to regard the game from the outside, to consider ways we might read games as cultural objects in their own right, as objects that *reflect* their cultural contexts. When we view games in this way, we regard them as *cultural texts.*

As game designers, we can consider games as cultural texts in order to demonstrate how *design* contributes to their meaning. What in the design of Capcom's Mega Man, for example, fully embodies "boy culture" and its ethos? How do games designed by the New Games Movement represent community-based, socially utopian ideals? Game design can be used to represent cultural ideas and phenomena existing beyond the space of the game. Take Ms. Pac-man, for instance. From a perspective *internal* to the game, what does Ms. Pac-Man represent? We might say that she represents a dot-munching, ghost-busting avatar, or we might refer to the in-game backstory that tells the tale of Pac-Man and Ms. Pac-Man meeting and falling in love. But if we consider Ms. Pac-man from a cultural point of view *external* to the game, our reading of the character changes dramatically. We might see Ms. Pac-Man as a powerful and positive feminist icon, a superior successor to the original Pac-Man. Or we might view her as a very unfeminist symbol, a derivative character that equates lipstick and a hair bow with the female gender. We might see Ms. Pac-Man as a new kind of video game "celebrity"; as an ever-hungry symbol of capitalist consumption; or the marker of a historical moment when Japanese pop transformed global electronic culture. This process of *interpreting* games as symbolic objects, as cultural texts that reflect their contexts, is one way of understanding games as culture.

Write | SPORK: Write the name of a European country. FOON: Write the name of an Asian country.

Framing games as cultural texts brings an additional perspective to our interrogation of the term *culture*. Anthropologist Clifford Geertz writes that "Man is an animal suspended in webs of significance he himself has spun....I take culture to be those webs, and the analysis of it to be therefore not an experimental science in search of law but an interpretive one in search of meaning."[4] Geertz compares the methods of an anthropologist analyzing culture to those of a literary critic analyzing a text: "Sorting out the structures of signification... and determining their social ground and import.... Doing ethnography is like trying to read (in the sense of 'construct a reading of') a manuscript."[5]

This concept of "reading culture" comes from the social sciences, and in particular, from the discipline of cultural anthropology and its more recent cousin cultural studies. The practice of reading culture refers to the potential of objects, processes, and phenomena (such as subcultures) to be "read" as stories or narratives. These stories might tell the tale of political relations, as in the case of a game such as Diplomacy, or of ethics and morality, as in a game such as Black & White. The status of a cultural text can even be applied to the formal materials of games. Consider the design of a deck of cards. Popularized in Europe during the fourteenth and fifteenth centuries, the four suits represent the four classes of medieval society: spades, the nobility; hearts, the clergy; diamonds, the merchants; and clubs, the peasants.[6] A deck of cards can thus be "read" as a representation of society at a particular point in history.

It is one of the tasks of social scientists and humanists to read these cultural texts and formulate frameworks that help game designers develop strategies for creating and analyzing games. Clifford Geertz's famous essay "Deep Play: Notes on the Balinese Cockfight," for example, richly describes how a culture is an ensemble of texts, of which games are an important part. Media scholar Henry Jenkins' work with video games and fan culture has led him to testify on Capitol Hill about the effects of media violence, countering many popular assumptions shaping current legislation. The work of designers and educators Amy Bruckman and Amy Jo Kim on MUDs and MOOs has given game developers new frameworks within which to consider the creation of online communities. Brenda Laurel's work, especially her recent book *The Utopian Entrepreneur,* continually challenges us to question our cultural assumptions about how we "read" computer games and other facets of computer culture. Although not all this research is written from a design perspective, it can offer tremendous insight into how the "meaning" of a game arises from the intersection of its formal, experiential, and cultural features. Being cognizant of how critics and scholars read game culture is part of being a game designer. If you can better understand your own game as a cultural text, you will be better equipped to design powerful experiences for players in whatever context they encounter your game.

Redefinition: Locating Design

Just as there are endless ways to read games as culture, there are innumerable perspectives from which to understand the concept of culture itself. We conclude with a final framing of culture that brings our focus squarely back to design. Design historian Richard Buchanan defines culture as "an activity of ordering, disordering, and reordering in the search for understanding and for values which guide action."[7] Buchanan's definition challenges and de-centers many common sense notions of design and culture. As he puts it, the fate of design "does not lie entirely within the framework of design culture or in the hands of a few gifted individuals. It lies within the framework of culture as a whole."[8] The activity of "ordering, disordering, and reordering" suggests that the practice of design is, above all, a cultural one.

Many game designers eschew cultural approaches to their work, preferring craft-centric methods that repress the existence of games within larger cultural contexts. You might or might not choose to recognize that as a game designer you are a producer of culture. You may choose to rely on the cultural conventions set by others, conventions that are at best obstacles to innovation and insight and at worst destructive ideologies tied to racism, sexism, and xenophobia.

Regardless of your approach, the status of games as culture is not something to be negotiated or debated. They are indisputably cultural. As a game designer, it is your responsibility to acknowledge this fact and make use of it in your design process. The recognition that you are designing in the context of culture can become a powerful game design asset. It can lead to new audiences for your games, new kinds of game content, new forms of mischief and subversion, and new ways for people to play. If your aim is to design truly meaningful play for your players, your games should be effective on every possible level. Creating culturally meaningful play, the focus of the four schemas to follow, is as important as rules or play in the successful execution of game design.

Notes

1. John H. Bodley, *Cultural Anthropology: Tribes, States, and the Global System* (New York: McGraw-Hill Higher Education, 1994), p. 171–72

2. Ibid., p. 172.

3. Stefan Fatsis, *Word Freak: Heartbreak, Triumph, Genius, and Obsession in the World of Competitive Scrabble Players* (Boston: Houghton Mifflin, 2001), p. 4.

4. Clifford Geertz, "Emphasizing Interpretation." In *The Interpretation of Cultures* (New York: Basic Books, 1977), p. 4–5.

5. Ibid., p. 5.

6. E.M. Avedon and Brian Sutton Smith, *The Study of Games* (New York: Wiley, 1971), p. 240.

7. Richard Buchanan, "Branzi's Dilemma: Design in Contemporary Culture." In *Design: Pleasure or Responsibility?* eds. P. Takhokallio and S. Vihma (Helsinki: University of Art and Design Helsinki, 1995), p. 10.

8. Ibid., p. 10.

Write | SPORK: Draw a fruit. FOON: Draw a vegetable.

Defining Culture SUMMARY

- Considering games as culture entails moving beyond the borders of the magic circle to consider how games interact with contexts that lie outside the actual rules and play of the game itself.

- Unlike formal or experiential schemas, culture-based contextual schemas are not directly tied to the internal, intrinsic qualities of games. There are any number of ways that games can be regarded as culture.

- All games **reflect** culture, reproducing aspects of their cultural contexts. Some games also **transform** culture, acting on their cultural contexts to affect genuine change.

- A game transforming its cultural context is a cultural instance of **transformative play.** In this case, the cultural "free play" of the game is altering the more rigid cultural contexts in which the game is taking place.

- There are many definitions of **culture.** Most of them directly or indirectly involve what people think, what they do, and the material products they produce. For our purposes, culture is what exists outside the magic circle, the context within which game play occurs.

- In addition to understanding that games *can represent* and that games *are representations,* we can frame games as *cultural representations,* reflecting the meanings of the contexts where they are produced and played.

- Understanding the meanings that make up the context in which your game is played is critical to designing meaningful play.

- When we consider a game as a cultural representation, we are considering the game as a **cultural text.** This means making an interpretative reading of a game, similar to analyses performed in cultural anthropology or cultural studies.

Unit 4 | Culture

GAMES AS CULTURAL RHETORIC

ideology
cultural rhetorics
social contexts for cultural learning
rhetorics of play
transformative cultural play
the New Games Movement

30

The World Cup, which begins on Friday in Japan and in South Korea, will be watched by billions. The spread of satellite dishes has taken the world's best teams to the farthest-flung places. People in Shenyang or Khartoum, who have no idea that Manchester is a town in England, now support Manchester United. A statue of the team's star, David Beckham, adorns a Buddhist temple in Bangkok. Osama bin Laden, if he is alive, will presumably be among those billions sitting in front of the television, and all of them, with the exception of most Americans, will appreciate the roiling political context in which the game is so often played.—**Simon Kuper,** *"The World's Game Is Not Just a Game"*

Introducing Cultural Rhetoric

Soccer fans do love their game. Although Soccer enthusiasts around the world have a passion for the game itself, there is no doubt that the meaningful play of Soccer also includes a diversity of symbolic functions. From the national and neighborhood team cultures to the reputations of players on (and off!) the field, Soccer is infused with values brought into the frame of the game from beyond the edges of the magic circle. Sometimes these values go beyond leisure fandom to acquire genuine political resonance. As sports columnist Simon Kuper notes, "Soccer is distinguished by its political malleability…. It gets presidents elected or thrown out, and it defines the way people think, for good or ill, about their countries."[1] At other times, the game's values resonate on a social level. In the U.S., for example, Soccer is seen as a sport that is female and child-friendly: the U.S. is the only country in which the women's national Soccer team is better known than the men's. Soccer in the U.S. is seen less as a professional sport and more as a family pastime: the ubiquitous term "Soccer mom" testifies to the integration of Soccer into suburban American life.

Soccer, like all games, embodies cultural meaning. In the last chapter, we introduced the idea that the structures of a game are reflections of the culture in which it is played. As play scholar Brian Sutton-Smith writes, "One might ask two Olympic runners how much of their thought while racing is given to the moves within the race, how much to the gold medals that might follow it, and how much to the glory of the country they represent…. All of which is to say that the play and the game are played partly for their own sake and partly for the values attributed to them within the ideologies that are their context."[2] As objects produced and played within culture at large, all games reflect their cultural contexts to some degree. In this chapter, we dig more deeply into this premise, focusing specifically on the way that games reflect *cultural values*. We explore how the internal structures of a game—rules, forms of interaction, material forms—mirror external ideological contexts.

Another way of saying games reflect cultural values is that *games are social contexts for cultural learning*. This means that games are one place where the values of a society are embodied and passed on. Although games clearly do reflect cultural values and ideologies, they do not merely play a passive role. Games also help to instill or fortify a culture's value system. Seeing games as social contexts for cultural learning acknowledges how games replicate, reproduce, and sometimes transform cultural beliefs and principles. This way of looking at games—as ideological systems—forms the basis of this first contextual game design schema, *Games as Cultural Rhetoric.*

Games reflect the values of the society and culture in which they are played because they are part of the fabric of that society itself. For example, the capitalist rhetoric of the American Dream infuses many American games. State lotteries are marketed with tag lines like, "Anyone can be a millionaire." The TV game show *Who Wants to be a Millionaire?* (adapted from the British version) glibly celebrates the pursuit of wealth in the rhetorical question that makes up its title. The question is not *if* you want to become rich, or *what* the ramifications might be, but merely *who* will be given the chance. These games encapsulate the paradox of American identity and its accompanying ideologies of wealth. They speak to the clash between a rugged, pioneering individualism and a desperate desire for shortcuts to success and submission to fate.

In historical games, as much as in contemporary ones, cultural ideologies permeate the magic circle to impact rules and play. The rules governing movement and interaction in the game of Chaturanga, an ancient forbearer of Chess, reflect the values and social hierarchies of the Indian military of the fifth century. According to historical sources, the unknown inventor of the game used the armies of India as his design model. The pieces of Chaturanga include the king, the minister, the elephant (which later became the bishop in Europe), the horse (knight), the chariot (rook) and the foot soldier (pawn).[3] Over time, as the game spread from country to country, modifications were made to the design of the game pieces to reflect the particular strengths of national armies. The introduction of these new pieces (such as the queen and the bishop) were not merely superficial changes, but impacted the formal structure of the game and the player experience as well.

What is Rhetoric?

We are analyzing cultural values and ideologies, but the schema is called *Games as Cultural Rhetoric.* What does that term mean? We take the word "rhetoric" from Brian Sutton-Smith's remarkable treatise *The Ambiguity of Play,* a wide-ranging, interdisciplinary investigation of the cultural ideologies surrounding play. Sutton-Smith writes, "The word rhetoric is used here in its modern sense, as being a persuasive discourse, or an implicit narrative, wittingly or unwittingly adopted by members of a particular affiliation to persuade others of the veracity or worthwhileness of their beliefs."[4] Rhetoric, in other words, is a method of discussion or expression that contains underlying values or beliefs, a method that attempts to persuade others that it is correct. Rhetoric can be heavy-handed and obvious or can be subtle and nearly invisible, and can take a multitude of forms. Rhetoric can manifest in the words and discourse of a philosophy (the "language" of Catholicism or Marxism), in clothes and insignia worn by members of a group (the fashion that identified members of the '60s counterculture movement), or in more general behavior (the spitting and gratuitous rudeness that were part of Punk). In each example, cultural rhetoric is a language of expression embodying and propagating particular values and beliefs.

Applied to games, the organizing principle of cultural rhetoric reveals how games represent broad patterns of ideological value. The design of a game, in other words, is a representation of ideas and values of a particular time and place. For example, historical research on the children's games of African-American slaves has revealed that combative activities and player elimi-

nation were strikingly absent. The rules and play interactions of the games were a reflection of an oppressed culture's need for solidarity and collaboration. The games of Israeli Kibbutz children also demonstrate "a strong expression of cooperation and egalitarianism, with a preference for as few overprivileged or underprivileged participants as possible," reflecting the communal philosophies of the Kibbutz lifestyle.[5] In each of these examples, the formal and experiential structures of games echo and reinforce external cultural rhetorics.

What is the relevance of cultural rhetoric to game design? Creating games is also creating culture, and therefore beliefs, ideologies, and values present within culture will always be a part of a game, intended or not. For example, what are the winning conditions of your game? Amass the most resources? Destroy the enemy's units? Arrive at a balance of powers? Each of these victory conditions implies a particular set of values, fleshed out through the game rules, materials, and experiences of play.

Although cultural rhetoric will always be intrinsically present in a game, it also can be actively incorporated into a game design. For example, the Mad Magazine Game takes a typical board game winning condition (accumulating the most money) and turns it on its head: the actual way to win the Mad Magazine Game is to *lose* all of your money. This simple formal reversal has a strong impact on the cultural rhetoric of the game. Parodying a Monopoly-style winner-take-all game, the Mad Magazine Game calls attention to conventional ideologies of greed and economic power. Just like *Mad Magazine* itself, the game pokes fun at American institutions and values.

Whether a game's cultural rhetoric is unconsciously implicit (Monopoly's capitalistic ideology) or consciously playful (The Mad Magazine Game's satiric reversal), it involves the play of cultural values. As we discussed in *Defining Culture,* our concept of play as *free movement within a more rigid structure* can occur on a cultural level. Games put culture "at play," not just reflecting culture, but shifting between and among existing cultural structures—sometimes transforming them as a result. It is not entirely clear whether The Mad Magazine Game ultimately undermines or reinforces the capitalistic rhetoric it parodies. But the fact that it plays with such ideas at all reveals the presumptions of more rigid structures involving economics, competitive conflict, and even game design. By highlighting the rigid structures it puts "at play," a game can shed light on the operations of culture as a whole.

Seven Rhetorics of Play

Games embody cultural rhetorics. But what specific ideologies do they represent? In *The Ambiguity of Play,* Brian Sutton-Smith does more than simply introduce the general idea of cultural rhetoric. Sutton-Smith identifies seven different "rhetorics of play," large-scale value-systems that have historically informed and defined the concept of play. These rhetorics—*progress, fate, power, identity, the imaginary, the self,* and *the frivolous*—are part of broad symbolic systems (political, religious, social, and educational) that help construct cultural meanings. They are seven ways that the concept of play has traditionally been brokered by culture. As rhetorics, these seven categories are persuasive discourses, invisibly embedded in our day-to-day lives and conceptions of play, taken for granted until they are challenged by a competing rhetoric.[6]

Although we can't summarize Sutton-Smith's complex ideas and do them justice, we can outline the key concepts of his seven rhetorics. In the chart to the right we describe the way each rhetoric uses, interprets, and justifies the concept of "play." In addition, the chart also lists the types of games and play with which the rhetoric is usually associated, as well as whether or not Sutton-Smith locates the origin of the rhetoric in ancient or contemporary times.

Sutton-Smith's work investigates play in general and therefore includes ludic activities that are not games. However, his ideas are still quite valuable to game designers. Games can embody any of the seven rhetorics, and Sutton-Smith's framework can help identify ideological presumptions in your games or help you chart new courses for the cultural rhetoric you want your game to express.

For example, according to Sutton-Smith, the dominant rhetoric in our culture is *play as progress.* By and large, play is seen as an activity for children, and a play experience is valuable because it helps children evolve into better adults cognitively, socially, ethically, or otherwise. Some of the current controversies about computer and video games stem directly from the fact that they do not fit neatly into the idea of *play as progress.* It is possible, for example, to see video games as part of an ideology of *power,* in which values of conflict are celebrated through play, as with professional sports; but equating video game play with sports (an adult pastime) would threaten the *play as progress* idea that games are for children. Similarly, video games could be seen as a form of *play as the imaginary,* in which video game play is a form of creative cultural production; however, this connection ties games to art, threatening conventional distinctions between high art and popular culture.

Sutton-Smith's rhetorics of play are not descriptive terms that identify what play *actually is.* Instead, his categories identify how games and play embody ideological values and how specific forms and uses of play perpetuate and justify these values. Rhetorics conflict and compete within the ecosystem of culture. A museum exhibit that included video games might spark a clash of rhetorics: perhaps the curator uses *play as the imaginary* to justify the creative value of video games, offending outraged adherents of *play as progress* that see no cultural value in games that merely entertain.

Just as one rhetoric can include many games, a single game can embody more than one rhetoric. As complex objects, games can contain many different, and sometimes contradictory, cultural rhetorics in their design and use. The lottery is based on an ancient game form that embodies *play as fate;* at the same time,

Act | SPORK: Raise your right hand. FOON: Raise your left hand.

in contemporary culture it can be a way for players to share a sense of *play as identity* (the office workers gather during happy hour to Pick Five, sharing a communal desire to win big and finally tell off the boss.) The parodic inversion of the Mad Magazine Game is premised on the idea of *play as frivolous,* even while its very reference to Monopoly-style games invokes the rhetoric of *play as power.*

Brian-Sutton Smith's Seven Rhetorics of Play

Play as Progress	Play is a way of turning children into adults. Play is valuable because it educates and develops the cognitive capacities of human or animal youth.	All forms of children's play and animal play	Contemporary origin
Play as Fate	Human lives and play are controlled by fate in the form of destiny, gods, atoms, neurons, or luck, but not by free will.	Gambling and games of chance	Ancient origin
Play as Power	Play is a form of conflict and a way to fortify the status of those who control the play or are its heroes.	Sports, athletics, and contests	Ancient origin
Play as Identity	Play is a means of confirming, maintaining, or advancing the identity of a community of players.	Traditional and community celebrations and festivals	Ancient origin
Play as the Imaginary	The essence of play is imagination, flexibility, and creativity. Play is synonymous with innovation.	Playful improvisation in art, literature and other forms of culture	Contemporary origin
Play as Rhetoric of the Self	Play exists to evolve the self, by providing intrinsic experiences of pleasure, relaxation, and escape, either through play itself or through the aesthetic satisfaction of play performances.	Solitary play activities like hobbies and high-risk play like rock climbing	Contemporary origin
Play as Frivolity	Play is oppositional, parodic and sometimes revolutionary; this rhetoric is opposed to a "work ethic" view of play as a useless activity.	The activities of the idle or the foolish, and the historical multi-cultural roles of the Trickster and the Fool	Ancient origin

Two Examples

The challenge of recognizing cultural rhetoric is that ideologies often pass unnoticed in our own actions and behaviors. Luckily, because of their intrinsically playful and artificial nature, games present particularly ripe contexts for highlighting the operation of cultural rhetoric at work. Following are two detailed examples to help us better understand how games can embody rhetoric through design.

The Landlord's Game

The Landlord's Game, designed by Lizzie Magie in 1904, is the precursor to the popular contemporary board game Monopoly, and was designed with very clear rhetorical intentions in mind. The Landlord's Game was created as a fun-filled vehicle for teaching the evils of land monopoly. Magie was a young Quaker woman living in Virginia, and an ardent follower of economist Henry George. George was the originator of the single tax movement, which held that the economic rent of land and the unearned increase in land values profited a few individuals rather than the majority of the people, whose very existence produced the land values. He therefore advocated a single tax on land alone to meet all the costs of government, a policy that would erode the power of monopolies to suppress competition, and therefore equalize opportunity.[7] Magie designed The Landlord's Game for educational play: as a way to explain George's political theories in terms that the average citizen could understand.

In the decades that followed the release of The Landlord's Game, Parker Brothers released a series of titles that were clearly derivative, including Easy Money and, of course, Monopoly. The formal structures of the games bear a striking resemblance. Magie's game board included rental properties such as "Poverty Place" (land rent $50), "Easy Street" (land rent $100) and "Lord Blueblood's Estate" ("no trespassing: go to jail"); there are banks, a poorhouse, and railroads and utilities such as the "Soakum Lighting System" ($50 fine) and the "PDQ Railroad" (fare $100); there is also, of course, the well-known "Jail" space. Unlike Monopoly, however, properties in The Landlord's Game were for rent only, and could not be purchased and released.

Despite the strong similarity between The Landlord's Game and Monopoly, there are distinct (and wonderfully incongruous) differences in the rhetorics each evokes. While the play rhetorics of *progress* and *power* apply to both games, The Landlord's Game was distinctly anti-capitalist in its conception. The game's conflict was not premised on property acquisition and the accumulation of monopolies, but instead on an unraveling of the prevailing land system. Because properties in the game could only be rented, there was no opportunity for domination by a greedy land baron or developer. Monopoly, on the other hand, championed the rise of the land baron and the art of speculation. Players were encouraged to exploit the financial weaknesses of other players to become the wealthiest monopolist, a conception of power in direct opposition to that explored within Magie's original design.

This difference in ideology is clearly evident in the way each game describes itself. The rules for Lizzie Magie's game read:

> The object of this game is not only to afford amusement to players, but to illustrate to them how, under the present or prevailing system to land tenure, the landlord has an advantage over other enterprisers, and also how the single tax would discourage speculation.

The introduction to Parker Brothers' Monopoly reads:

> The idea of the game is to buy and rent or sell property so profitably that one becomes the wealthiest player and eventually monopolist…. The game is one of shrewd and amusing trading and excitement.

Write | SPORK: Write the name of a month that has a Y in its name. FOON: Write the name of a month that has an R in its name.

The Landlord's Game

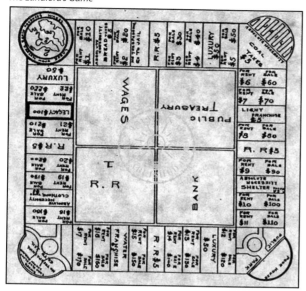

As the direct progenitor of Monopoly, it is ironic that Magie's game became a parody of exactly what it intended to critique. What began as an earnest attempt to educate the masses about the ills of land monopoly was transformed by Parker Brothers into a rhetorical tool for capitalism itself. Thus, although the two games share many formal elements, their designs embody radically different ideologies. These cultural rhetorics are expressed through the language of the written rules, naming conventions of game properties, and the rules and victory conditions. Through the experience of their play and the distribution of the games in culture, their opposing rhetorics were propagated in competition with each other. (For better or worse, we know who won that game!)

Vampire: The Masquerade

Vampire: The Masquerade illustrates another instance of game design and cultural rhetoric. Unlike The Landlord's Game, Vampire: The Masquerade was not designed with

political, pedagogical intentions. Nevertheless, cultural rhetoric was an important part of the thinking behind the game.

The design of Vampire: The Masquerade draws directly on existing subcultures to create meaningful play. As opposed to the swords-and-sorcery or science fiction narratives of most popular role-playing games, Vampire: The Masquerade is designed to appeal to a Goth sensibility. Its vampiric political storylines resemble Ann Rice novels, and game play emphasizes atmosphere and mood rather than combat. Compared to the typical role-playing game, its rules are approachably minimal. As a result of these features, when the game was first introduced it found an audience not merely among existing gamers, but among people who had never role-played before.[8] Players of the game, in many cases already immersed in the Goth subculture, brought their own systems of meaning to the game as they entered the space of play. At the same time, the game itself became a way to propagate Goth subculture and extend it to an audience of game players that might not normally have an affinity for black clothing, heavy eyeliner, and the occult. Cultural rhetorics entered into the game from the outside > in, even as the game itself became a bastion of Goth/gamer culture, extending its hybrid rhetorics from the inside > out.

Vampire: The Masquerade exhibits the cultural rhetoric of *play as identity*: the play of the game separates its players from the rest of society, creating a space that catalyzes their unique sense of community identity. The game embodies other cultural rhetorics as well, such as the alter-ego role-playing that implicitly advocates *play as the imaginary*—or even *play as frivolous,* since the underground, subcultural status of Goth celebrates a visible opposition to more dominant cultures and styles. Although Vampire: The Masquerade was in part a product of an existing ideology and culture, it is important to note that the designers of the game recognized the untapped Goth gaming audience by designing the game to directly incorporate the subculture. The simplicity of the formal system made the game inviting to novice gamers, while the overall design encouraged role-playing, storytelling, and knowledge of vampire lore over strategic deployment of rules. This design approach effectively allowed the *already existing* attitudes and ideologies of players to shine through and contribute to the play and culture of the game.

The success of Vampire: The Masquerade has changed the culture of gaming. Admittedly, there was already some overlap between role-playing subcultures and Goth sub-cultures, but Vampire: The Masquerade managed to mix these two audiences in the context of actual game play. The game made role-playing "cool" (at least in some cir-cles), highlighting the fact that cultural rhetorics them-selves are often a form of currency in culture at large. The transition from geek to Goth stretched the frame of role-playing across the space of the hip and cool, broadening the game genre's reach and establishing a new approach to role-playing game design.

In each of the two examples—The Landlord's Game and Vamp-ire: The Masquerade—games act as social contexts that allow exploration of certain values and attitudes. Furthermore, in both cases the cultural rhetoric of the game was something consciously incorporated by the designers. There is a long-standing lament among digital game designers that the general public does not consider games an important form of media culture. One answer to this complaint is that game designers need to be more rigorous in how they conceive of their games as *culture*. Recognizing that all games contain and endorse par-ticular cultural rhetorics is a good first step. But if we want to stretch people's conceptions of games into spaces beyond gaming subcultures, into spaces occupied by art, literature and film—or politics, punk rock, and the academy—then designers need to be much smarter in how they incorporate cultural rhetorics in the actual design of their games.

Rhetorics of Gender

By now it should be clear: when framed as cultural rhetoric, games are systems of representation imbued with cultural beliefs and values. Designers must recognize how cultural rhetorics operate within their games and design accordingly. What ideologies are you reflecting, replicating, and promoting in your game? Do you want your game to faithfully depict a par-ticular set of beliefs? Or would you rather question, reverse, or undermine them? Can you incorporate cultural rhetoric into the very experience of your game, encouraging your players to actually play with cultural codes?

The challenge of designing with cultural rhetorics in mind is the sheer complexity by which culture operates. We can artificially isolate cultural rhetoric in a game, such as the way that Vampire: The Masquerade reflects and informs Goth subculture, but the subculture itself and its interaction with the game are tremen-dously subtle. To highlight the challenges of using rhetorics within games, we focus for the next few pages on an important debate involving the cultural rhetoric of gender. Our goal is not to draw definitive conclusions about how gender operates in games, but instead to demonstrate the complexity of the issues raised when we frame games as expressions of cultural rhetoric.

Investigating the cultural rhetorics of gender means examin-ing the ways that games reflect, reinforce, question, or subvert cultural ideas about the categories of masculine and feminine, male and female, transgender and other concepts related to gendered identity. Saying that games can interact with ideolo-gies of gender presupposes that gendered cultural codes exist within society at large. This is indeed the case. There is a long history of thinkers, from Virginia Woolf to Judith Butler, who have commented on the ways gender is socially constructed and performed in culture, including the role that media repre-sentations play in this construction. More recently, writers like Brenda Laurel, Justine Cassell, Henry Jenkins, and other scholars have examined the representation of gender within digital games. A concern for games and gender extends to game designers as well. A game design movement (loosely called *Girl*

Write | ALL PLAYERS: Switch camp. Spork is now Foon and vice versa. Sneak remains the Sneak. Write the name of your new camp on your camp card.

Games) was spawned in the early 1990s by designers and scholars interested in questioning and reinventing assumptions about gender and games.

Rather than summarize these theoretical and ethnographic investigations, material that is well covered elsewhere (see *Further Reading*), we instead explore a few ways that game design intersects with cultural rhetorics of gender. Our intention is to demonstrate the complexities by which any particular cultural rhetoric operates in games. We selected the rhetoric of gender because of the history of the debate within gaming. There are certainly innumerable other cultural rhetorics we could have chosen as well, from the representation of race and ethnicity to narratives of colonialism and imperialism.

Boy Games

One writer that has commented extensively on gender in games is media scholar Henry Jenkins. In his essay "Complete Freedom of Movement: Video Games as Gendered Play Spaces," Jenkins explores the ideology of boy's play spaces described in children's literature, as a way of characterizing contemporary forms of representation in digital games. He argues that the conventions of the nineteenth and early twentieth century boy's adventure story have affected the kinds of representation we see in current video games. Platform scrolling games such as Capcom's Mega Man and Nintendo's Super Mario Brothers, according to Jenkins, utilize the iconography of adventure stories. These games allow players to struggle against obstacles, explore fantastic lands, fight menacing enemies, and even die (only to be reborn at the beginning of the level). Above all else these games exhibit thrilling, non-stop action.

In Jenkins' account, the games' levels and worlds follow the set-piece structure of adventure stories, in which all elements are streamlined down to their essential features. The plots and characters are reduced to familiar genre archetypes, defined primarily through their capacity for action. Similarly, the game

settings follow the pulp model of the "adventure island," a staple of boy's books and games. The island represents "an isolated world far removed from domestic space or adult supervision, an untamed world for people who refuse to bow before the pressures of the civilizing process, a never-never-land where you seek your fortune."[9] Many video games clearly embody features of the adventure island narrative as described by Jenkins, and therefore reflect established rhetorics of "boy culture."

Significantly, the cultural rhetoric of gender is not restricted to the visual design of the games Jenkins cites. Although it is true that the games share the graphic trappings of comic books, cartoons, and other forms of traditional boy's culture, the gendered rhetoric of these games is embedded in their systemic and interactive dimensions as well. As Jenkins writes, "Each screen overflows with dangers; each landscape is riddled with pitfalls and booby traps. One screen may require you to leap from precipice to precipice, barely missing falling into the deep chasms below. Another may require you to swing by vines across the treetops, or spelunk through an underground passageway, all the while fighting it out with the alien hordes."[10] The action-oriented, stimulus-based interactivity of the game is part of the cultural rhetoric of the boy's adventure archetype. Whether the designers intended to or not, they were reproducing an established rhetoric of gender in the design of the game itself.

Jenkins' work offers a great example of how cultural rhetorics can impact game design. The imaginary spaces to which boys find themselves attracted are not just neutral places of play: they are specifically gendered spaces that invite boys in and keep girls out. The kinds of games Jenkins mentions reflect gendered leisure preferences (thrilling non-stop action; settings outside domestic spaces) even as they perpetuate them, echoing earlier genres of boy's culture that operated in similar ways. Although the games may be new, the rhetoric they embody has been passed down from an earlier era.

Flipping the Gender Bit

The games Jenkins wrote about in his essay are primarily console or PC games from the late 1980s and early 1990s. Since that time, graphics resolution in digital games has become more complex—and along with it, the rhetoric of game gender representation. An important case in point is Lara Croft, the star of the popular Tomb Raider series. Although the Tomb Raider games are 3D rather than 2D like the games Jenkins studied, they and other over-the-shoulder action-adventure games are direct descendents of "boy's game" platform scrollers like Mega Man and Super Mario Bros. The obstacle-avoiding, power-up-snatching, fight-and-explore-a-series-of-levels game play is remarkably similar, despite graphical differences.

Because games of this type typically feature male characters, as a female lead Lara Croft is in some ways an intervention into the cultural rhetoric of gender. Or is she? "At the time we created Tomb Raider, I don't think there had ever been a good game with a heroine," remarks Toby Gard, the game designer credited as Lara's creator. "Most women in games before Lara wore thigh-high boots and thongs."[11] Originally conceived as a cross between riot grrrl icon Tank Girl and British pop star Neneh Cherry, Lara developed into a buxom female version of Indiana Jones. The end result, according to Gard, was "an empowered woman…. Not a smutty sex object, but an inaccessible, gun-toting bitch."[12]

Gard is correct in one sense. Prior to Tomb Raider, there were few female characters that played active roles in a game. Previous characters such as Smurfette in Smurf Rescue and Princess Toadstool in Super Mario were merely damsels in distress, helpless females waiting to be rescued at the end of the final level. These characters are synonymous with the end of the game, acting as passive objects of desire, the carrot held out to entice the player to finish. This remote and powerless female is an archetype that fits neatly into the traditionally gendered space of a young boy's world. The female is structurally acknowledged as a source of desire, but she is not generally present during play, and certainly does nothing so threatening as usurp the leading role from the male protagonist.

Tomb Raider offers an alternative game role for players. Lara Croft is a gun-toting action hero, a powerful character that can kick ass as well as any male avatar. But does Lara Croft rise to the level of the "empowered woman" Gard describes? There were any number of ways that a female character might have been visualized, and the character of Lara represents some very specific design choices. Her impractical cut-off shorts and skintight tank top emphasize her waspy waist and enormous breasts. It is true that Lara is not as scantily clad as many other female game characters (such as the whip-wielding dominatrixes of Bad Dudes), but she is hardly the model for an "empowered woman." Lara is a kind of action slut, an adolescent boy's idea of a woman, a digital pin-up girl. This role is literally played out in the many provocative full-page images of Lara published throughout the gaming press since the first Tomb Raider game was released. Lara herself was a trend setter: scores of similar female game protagonists have followed in her wake.

How does Lara play into ideologies of gender present within culture at large? Which values does she reinforce and which values does she call into question? As a powerful and playable avatar, Lara challenges the passive role usually accorded female game characters. In fact, a disproportionately high number of women have been consumers of the Tomb Raider games. But as an overtly sexualized representation, she replicates and exaggerates images of women found in other media, images often seen as objectifying and disempowering.

The rhetoric of gender is complicated even further when we consider that the representation of Lara is composed both visually and interactively. Beyond her "looks," how does a player's interaction with Lara reinforce a rhetoric of gender? We know from our discussion of the immersive fallacy in *Games as*

Act | ALL PLAYERS: Show the person on your left your most recent *Write* card.

Lara Croft

Smurfette

Princess Toadstool

Lara Croft

the Play of Simulation that players' relationships to game characters are never simple. When a player plays a game, he or she is never merely "immersed" within a representation; through the process of metacommunication, the player is aware of the constructed nature of the character within the larger system of the game. A game avatar is simultaneously both subject and object: on one hand a mask to be worn, and on the other a tool to view and manipulate. Lara Croft plays out this double role to its paradoxical conclusion. In one sense, a Tomb Raider player is the spectator of a grossly sexist female image, even as the same player interactively takes on an empowering female role.

Unpacking the complex cultural rhetorics of gender in Tomb Raider, fundamental ambiguities remain. Is Lara a feminist icon or a sexist object? Does she challenge gender stereotypes or reinforce them? Perhaps we can never ultimately resolve these questions. When we consider representations of female characters in other games, similar double-meanings appear:

- *Ms. Pac-Man* is arguably the first game avatar gendered female. Although she is cute, she certainly wasn't given a curvaceous "womanly" figure. Rather, she is nothing more than a feminized version of Pac-Man, designed as if lipstick and a bow were equivalent to being female. Pac-Man, the male gerund, is the presumed neutral identity. Ms. Pac-Man is the marked, special case.

- *Female Fighting Game Characters* also offer active female roles for players to take on. But by and large, these characters suffer from the same hyperfeminization as Lara Croft, even joining her in game magazine pin-ups and posters. The marketing of contemporary fighting games (touting features such as a "breast jiggle" option) emphasize the sexist stereotypes these characters embody.

- *Samus Aran,* the heroine of the popular Metroid series, is a female character that in the original Metroid game doesn't reveal her gender until the end, when she removes her high-tech helmet. This clever design decision reveals the rhetorical presumptions players make about game character gender—many gamers recall with relish their shock when the hero of Metroid was unmasked as a heroine. But why is it only at the end of the game that Samus Aran can "come out" as a woman? Would the play of the game, or the interest of the players, be any different if the protagonist were male?

- *SiSSYFiGHT 2000* features unusual female characters that are neither passive Princess Toadstools nor sexist action sluts. They are bratty schoolgirls, equal parts cute and ugly, designed consciously as a playful intervention into existing cultural rhetorics of gendered game representation. Despite these feminist intentions, the bratty girls of the game have been criticized as portraying negative images of women, perpetuating stereotypes of catty, gossipy female behavior.

The politics of gender representation in media has been endlessly debated within the academy, the press, and culture at large. The recent visibility of female protagonists in games has only fueled these discussions. The question is, where do you stand? Any design decision you make regarding the representation of gender in your game will be connected to one form of rhetoric or another. There is no single "correct" rhetoric that your game should embody. However, be aware of the rhetorics that your game reflects and perpetuates. The cultural dimensions of games are exceedingly complex; your game should recognize this complexity and do it justice within its design.

Transforming Spaces

Do not despair! It's true that cultural rhetorics are complicated, but that does not mean they cannot be successfully incorporated into a game design. In fact, it is possible for games to take the concept of cultural rhetoric by the horns, not only representing and challenging ideologies, but also changing them. Most of our examples so far in this chapter have focused on the

Samus Aran: Metroid

Vanessa: Virtua Fighter 4

Chun Li: Street Fighter

Ms. Pac-Man

Nina: Tekken 3

Ling: Tekken 2

SiSSYFiGHT 2000

Ivy: Soul Calibur 2

way that the space of meaning *internal* to the magic circle reflects cultural rhetorics *external* to the game. Both The Landlord's Game and Monopoly reflect existing ideas about power and economics and were designed to express these ideas. But games have the ability not only to reflect but to transform cultural values. When this happens, *external* contexts are shaped by ideologies *internal* to a game. We have already mentioned that the cultural play of a game is free movement within more rigid cultural structures. But when game play alters and shifts those cultural structures, the play becomes truly *transformative:* the rigid structures out of which play emerges are themselves reshaped through the very act of play.

A wonderful example of transformative play as a game design practice is the New Games Movement, which utilized play to comment on and experiment with new conceptions of culture and community. An outgrowth of 1960s San Francisco counterculture, the New Games Movement believed that the kinds of games people play and the ways they play them are of major significance to society. "Sports represent a key joint in any society," George Leonard writes in *The New Games Book,* "How we play the game may turn out to be more important than we imagine, for it signifies nothing less than our way of being in the world."[13] The New Games Movement was less about the design of individual games and more about the development of an ethos intended to alter the way people interacted with one another. Its goal was to transform culture by creating opportunities for people to play collaboratively.

Play hard. Play fair. Nobody hurt. These three core principles order the design (and play) of any New Games game. The movement organized festival-like "Tournaments" that brought people together to play cooperatively, erasing (if only for a brief time) barriers of race, age, sex, size, ability, socioeconomic background, and creed. Values of freedom and the creation of community through game play were woven into a utopian

rhetoric that advocated new forms of player empowerment. As Bernard DeKoven notes in *The Well-Played Game,* "No matter what game we create, no matter how well we are able to play it, it is our game, and we can change it when we need to.... This is an incredible freedom, a freedom that does more than any game can, a freedom with which we nurture the play community. The search for the well-played game is what holds the community together. But the freedom to change the game is what gives the community its power."[14] This powerful, poetic rhetoric conflates the act of changing an individual game with changing the larger "game" of society—a premise at the heart of the New Games Movement.

Earthball, a classic New Games design, clearly embodies the movement's rhetoric. Created in 1966 by Stewart Brand for a public event sponsored by the War Resisters League at San Francisco State College, Earthball involved a huge inflatable ball painted with continents, oceans, and swirling clouds, guided by opposing teams. The game had a single rule, which Brand explained in the following way: "There are two kinds of people in the world: those who want to push the Earth over a row of flags at that end of the field, and those that want to push it over the fence at the other end. Go to it."[15] Intended as a way of formalizing player interaction and victory conditions, when the game was first played these simple rules created a space of possibility with a surprising ideological outcome:

> People charged the ball from both sides, pushing and cheering. Slowly it began to move, first toward one end, then back to the other. The game got hotter. There was plenty of competition, but something more interesting was happening. Whenever the ball approached a goal, players from the winning side would defect to lend a hand to the losers.... That first Earthball game went on for an hour without a score. The players had been competing, but not to win. Their unspoken and accepted agreement had been to play, as long and hard as possible.[16]

Write | SPORK: Draw a tree. FOON: Draw a flower.

Although the game was premised as a competition between two teams, the play that emerged was radically cooperative (in the sense of *player cooperation* defined in **Games as Systems of Conflict**). The emergence of collaborative play from a formal structure designed to support competitive interaction demonstrates the power of the New Games Movement rhetoric. The game may have looked competitive on the surface (two teams facing opposite goal lines), but the players enacted cultural rhetorics that valued collaboration and play-for-play's sake. These philosophies emerged from within the game to transform the game, turning traditional competitive play into something else entirely.

Later New Games games explored game structures that more explicitly embodied the cultural rhetorics of the movement. For example, the game of Catch the Dragon's Tail (first mentioned in **Games as Systems of Conflict**), has a definite winning condition and goal, but certain players (in the dragon's middle) are not clearly on one team or the other. The New Game titled Vampire (analyzed in **Games as the Play of Simulation,** not to be confused with the LARP game Vampire: The Masquerade) also plays with competition, collaboration, and victory conditions. The game can end with the players either all turned into vampires or all cured of their vampirism; in both cases the initially heterogeneous group resolves to a state of homogenous equality.

Was the New Games Movement a success? Did it manage to transform society in the way that its founders intended? Yes and no. Although the New Games Movement has waned in recent decades, it asserted tremendous influence on physical education in the United States. If you played with a giant rubber Earthball or a parachute in your elementary school gym class, you can thank the New Games Movement, which helped transform the traditionally sports-based curriculum of phys ed into a more play-centric, cooperative learning experience.

Much of the success of the New Games Movement emerged because of its relationships with other forms of counterculture.

New Games "Tournaments," for example, mixed the communality of a peace protest with the cultural nihilism of an art happening. There is no doubt that in many ways the New Games Movement and its game designs emerged out of a particular cultural milieu. But the uniquely transformative agenda of the movement is truly inspiring. Playing with the codes and conventions of gaming and social interaction, the New Games Movement sought to create positive social change through play. It did so not by creating games with explicit political content, but by designing play experiences that intrinsically embodied its utopian ideals. Is there room for a similar movement in present-day game design? The New Games Movement was a function of its historical moment, and could not be revived in precisely the same form today. But the notion that game designers could take on transformative rhetorics, unleashing them in culture as a mighty revolution of play, is by no means unrealistic. It did happen; it can happen again.

Battling Toys

By now it should be clear that we can connect games' artificial spaces of meaning to the values and ideologies of the world at large in countless ways. Each of the examples we explored within this chapter shares a common premise: games are part of culture. Whether they reflect or transform notions of economic class, subcultural style, gender identity, or utopian community, games exemplify ideas about the ways things are, or even the way we would like them to be.

This chapter concludes by exploring the reflection and transformation of cultural rhetoric in the context of a particular game design. Toys is a game for two players Eric created in collaboration with school children during a residency at the Bellevue Museum of Art in Seattle in 2000. The design mimics the battling character structure of a game like Pokémon, feeding on the rich social codes created by children for their toys—one plays the game by inhabiting, interpreting, and disputing these codes.

To begin the game, each player selects three character toys from a large collection of action figures scavenged from Seattle flea markets; the figures then "fight" with each other one by one. The battles between toys are waged via modular sentences, randomly constructed from a set of 44 cards. These statements, such as *"The female toy beats the unwanted toy,"* or *"The American toy beats the expensive toy,"* determine the outcome of conflict. Once the sentence has been dealt, it is up to the players to resolve the battle between the pair of toys by interpreting the statement and coming to an agreement on which toy it identifies as the victor.

Toys: A social game for two players.

Setup:

· Each player selects 3 toys to create his or her toy collection.

· Shuffle the game cards and deal 2 to each player. Keep these cards hidden.

· Place the rest of the cards face-down in a pile.

Object:
The goal of the game is to defeat your opponent's toy collection.

Game play:
First, each player selects one toy to fight. Deal two cards from the deck face-up and place onto the dotted line rectangles printed on the gameboard. The result will be a statement like, *"The naked toy beats the violent toy."*

Both players must then decide the result of the match based on the best application of the statement to the two toys. If the players cannot agree, deal two new cards to create a new statement. At any point in the game, players can use the two cards they were dealt to change the statement on the board.

After a match the loser selects a new toy from his or her collection to face the winning toy. If you defeat all three of your opponent's toys, you win.

Conflict is an intrinsic part of every game. As we outlined in **Games as the Play of Simulation,** game conflict is typically a territorial military conflict, a numerical economic conflict, or a conflict over fixed units of knowledge. The design of Toys, however, presents an alternative model. Although it superficially resembles a fighting game, in actuality, it is a game of *cultural* conflict. Battles between toys pit cultural feature against cultural feature (expensive, popular, American, female) and are resolved through an explicit ranking of these features within a shared system of meaning. The resolution of each match rests in the negotiation of the toys' symbolic value. In order to reach the conclusion that a Transformer toy is more masculine than a Big Bird figure, for example, players must agree that the value of one toy exceeds that of the other when it comes to relative maleness. What makes the collaborative element of Toys so compelling is that players work together not only to meet a set of victory conditions (this toy beats that toy) but also to navigate a rich playground of cultural signs. The game complexifies this negotiation by using not just one comparative term but two *(the American toy beats the expensive toy)* and by allowing players to intervene twice during a game to strategically change the linguistic equation.

The statements generated in Toys contain a high degree of strategic and cultural ambiguity; resolving this ambiguity is the point of the play. Although there are many games that reward players for cultural knowledge (such as Trivial Pursuit), these games generally provide correct answers to game questions. Toys does not provide the right or wrong answer to the resolution of a match; the game instead relies on the players' authority in determining the answer. In most games, players are expected to act in their own self-interest. But Toys turns the conventional authority structure of a game inside-out: instead of relying on the rules of the game to resolve the conflict each turn, players must resolve the battles through a potentially heated negotiation.

In developing and testing the game with school children, Eric found to his surprise that two players would virtually never both gratuitously claim victory, but almost always reached rapid mutual agreement on which toy won a conflict. In effect, the game revealed that the kinds of meanings circulated in children's play culture are shared, and through their shared value, they acquire the status of fact—a fact that overrides even a player's desire to win. A game about the negotiation of complex social and cultural systems, Toys illustrates how symbolic codes of race, class, gender, and aesthetics circulate within culture at large. Throughout the game, the signifiers of a toy's cultural status are used as the basis for both conflict and resolution. Knowing which toy is "stronger," "faster," or more "popular" than the other not only makes the game possible but fun as well. The Swamp Thing versus My Little Pony: *The ridiculous toy beats the naked toy.* Who wins?

As Toys playfully demonstrates, games are *social contexts for cultural learning.* Games always reflect the cultural rhetorics of the spaces in which they were designed or played; some games can even transform the ideologies of their contexts. The real game design challenge is to engage with cultural rhetoric on more than just a superficial level. Rather than merely applying a veneer of political content or cultural narrative to your game, how can you embed your questioning or refashioning of cultural rhetoric into the actual play itself? These are truly difficult design problems. But for game designers seeking to create meaningful play on not just a formal or experiential level, for game designers that want to explore play and innovation in culture itself, **Games as Cultural Rhetoric** is an indispensable design tool.

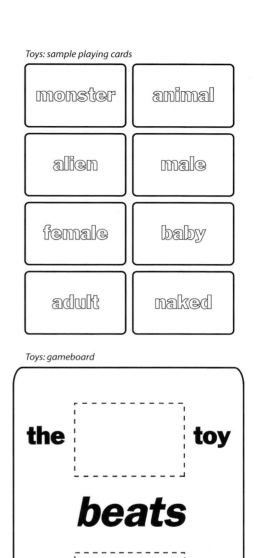

Toys: sample playing cards

Toys: gameboard

Further Reading

Air Guitar, by Dave Hickey

The essay "The Heresy of Zone Defense" is cultural critic Dave Hickey's love letter to the game of Basketball, couched as a critical essay on the democracy of rules. A funny and moving piece on the joys of rule-breaking and the artistry of Dr. J, the text makes clear the connection between games, culture, and the often hidden ideologies that the rules of a game express and exploit.

> *Recommended:*
> "The Heresy of Zone Defense"

The Ambiguity of Play, by Brian Sutton-Smith

Brian Sutton-Smith has made monumental contributions to the study of play. This work is in some ways a summation of his decades of study, a skeleton key to his interdisciplinary investigations of play and games in culture. In the book, Sutton-Smith outlines seven primary "rhetorics" or ideologies framing play and explores how each rhetoric offers a different understanding of how and why we play.

> *Recommended:*
> Chapter 1: Play and Ambiguity
> Chapters 2–11 focus on the seven rhetorics of play

From Barbie to Mortal Kombat: Gender and Computer Games, Justine Cassell and Henry Jenkins, eds.

A collection of essays focusing on connections between girls and computer games and the kinds of cultural and gender identities evoked by such connections. Much of the discussion is based on the early research of the Girl Games movement, which argued that girls have play patterns and interests different from those of boys. The ideology of this movement has itself come under attack, represented by the book's final essay, recommended below.

> *Recommended:*
> Chapter 1: Chess for Girls? Feminism and Computer Games
> Chapter 12: "Complete Freedom of Movement": Video Games as Gendered Play Spaces
> Chapter 14: Voices from the Combat Zone: Game Grrlz Talk Back

The Interpretation of Cultures, by Clifford Geertz

In the classic essay "Deep Play: Notes on the Balinese Cockfight," anthropologist Clifford Geertz argues that the function of rituals such as games is interpretive. Games are a culture's reading of its own experience, a story that people tell themselves about themselves. In understanding how games can operate as forms of cultural rhetoric it is useful to think about them in regard to the kinds of stories games tell about the cultures in which they are played.

> *Recommended:*
> "Deep Play: Notes on the Balinese Cockfight"

Testimony Before the U.S. Senate Commerce Committee, May 4, 1999, by Henry Jenkins

<http://brownback.senate.gov/FinishedDocs/MediaViolence/99050 4jen.pdf>

Jenkins is the Director of the Comparative Media Studies Program at MIT. In May 1999, he was invited to speak in front of the U.S. Senate committee on the effects of video games and violence. Jenkins makes a compelling argument against links between medium and behavior, debunking many of the myths commonly touted in the media. According to Jenkins, media and violence have a complex relationship that cannot be reduced to singular arguments.

Act | SPORK: Exchange writing utensils with another player of your choosing. FOON: Do nothing.

Notes

1. Simon Kuper, "The World's Game Is Not Just A Game," *The New York Times Sunday Magazine,* May 26, 2002.

2. Brian Sutton-Smith, *The Ambiguity of Play* (Boston: Harvard University Press, 2001), p. 77.

3. E.M. Avedon and Brian Sutton Smith, editors, *The Study of Games* (New York: Wiley, 1971), p. 274.

4. Sutton-Smith, *The Ambiguity of Play,* p. 8.

5. Nwokah and Ikekeonwu, "Nigerian and American Children's Games," in *The Study of Play, Vol 1. Diversions and Divergences in Fields of Play.* Margaret C. Duncan, Garry Chick, and Alan Aycock, eds. (New York: Ablex/Greenwood Publishing Company, 1998), p. 61.

6. Sutton-Smith, *The Ambiguity of Play,* p. 7–17.

7. Burton H. Wolfe, "The Monopolization of Monopoly: The Story of Lizzie Magie," *The San Francisco Bay Guardian,* 1976.

8. Greg Costikyan, RE:PLAY: Game Design + Game Culture. Online conference, <2000.www.eyebeam.org.replay>.

9. Henry Jenkins, "Complete Freedom of Movement: Video Games as Gendered Play Spaces." In *From Barbie to Mortal Kombat: Gender and Computer Games,* edited by Justine Cassell and Henry Jenkins (Cambridge: MIT Press, 1998), p. 279.

10. Ibid., p. 280.

11. Katie Salen, "Lock, Stock, and Barrel: Sexing the Digital Siren. In *Sex Appeal: The Art of Allure in Graphic and Advertising Design,* edited by Steven Heller (New York: Allworth Press, 2000), p. 148.

12. Ibid., p. 149.

13. Andrew Fluegelman and Shoshana Tembeck, *The New Games Book* (New York: Doubleday, 1976), p. 10.

14. Bernard DeKoven, *The Well-Played Game* (New York: Doubleday, 1978), p. 68.

15. Fluegelman and Tembeck, *The New Games Book,* p. 9.

16. Ibid.

Games as Cultural Rhetoric SUMMARY

- **Games are social contexts for cultural learning.** This means that games have an ideological dimension: they are one context through which society passes on its values.

- **Rhetoric** is a persuasive discourse or implicit cultural narrative. It is a set of connected ideas used to convince others of the truthfulness of one's own beliefs.

- All games **reflect** the rhetoric of the cultural context in which they are designed or played. This is true of both historical and contemporary games.

- Cultural rhetorics can be an unconscious aspect of a game's ideology or they can be consciously designed into a game. When game designers allow cultural rhetorics to enter into the play of a game, they are creating an instance of free play within more rigid cultural structures.

- Brian Sutton-Smith identifies seven **rhetorics of play.** Four rhetorics stem from ancient ideologies—**fate, power, identity,** and **the frivolous.** Three rhetorics have more contemporary origins: **progress, the imaginary,** and **the self.** The prevalent rhetoric of contemporary Western culture is *play as progress:* the notion that play is for children and that it is valuable because it helps them properly evolve into adults.

- Cultural rhetorics, such as the representation of gender in games, are exceedingly complex. Such rhetorics do not always resolve into a single ideological interpretation. For example, although the game character of Lara Croft challenges rhetorics of boy-based play in some respects, in other respects the character follows rigid gender stereotypes.

- Sometimes the cultural rhetorics of a game can change the cultural structures in which they exist. This is the phenomenon of **transformative cultural play.**

- **The New Games Movement** is an example of a game design ideology that consciously sought to transform cultural rhetorics through specific forms of community and play design.

Act | All players state your answers aloud. SPORK: Name a food you currently hate. FOON: Name a food you hated as a kid. *Sneak acts like a Spork.*

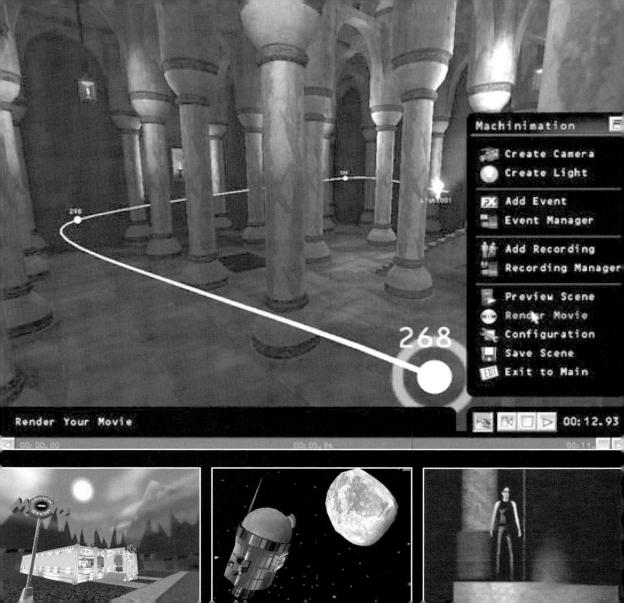

Unit 4 | Culture

GAMES AS OPEN CULTURE

transformative cultural play
player-as-producer
open source
metagaming
non-hierarchical
accessible
non-guided
emergent
game systems
machinima

31

I think one of the changes of our consciousness of how things come into being, of how things are made and how they work...is the change from an engineering paradigm, which is to say a design paradigm, to a biological paradigm, which is a cultural and evolutionary one. In lots and lots of areas now, people say, How do you create the conditions at the bottom to allow the growth of the things you want to happen?
—Brian Eno

Machinimation | Fountainhead Entertainment | **Hardly Workin'** | ILL Clan | **Rendezvous** | Peter Rasmussen | **Matrix: 4 x 1: Subway** | Strange Company |

Icehouse | Looney Labs

Introducing Open Culture

In 2001 at the Institute for Contemporary Art in London, musician Brian Eno gave a lecture linking his compositional process to John Conway's Game of Life. The "game" of Life, something we first encountered in *Games as Emergent Systems,* creates unexpected patterns of events out of a very simple set of rules. Working along similar lines, Eno generates unexpected musical compositions from the interactions of simple algorithms. In his comments, Eno identified the design challenge of generative music as the difficulty of writing the rules for his system: "How do you create the conditions at the bottom to allow the growth of the things you want to happen?" The designer of an emergent system is never directly designing actual behavior or outcomes. Instead, he or she can only design the formal structures that then go on to produce patterns of events. A game designer faces a similar challenge, designing rules directly but only indirectly creating play. Because games are emergent, it is not possible to fully anticipate how a given set of rules will play out in a particular play experience.

These concepts should be familiar by now. In *Games as Emergent Systems,* we saw how the coupled and context-dependent formal operations of a game give rise to unexpected complexity. In our **PLAY** schemas, we investigated this phenomenon further: exploring how the emergent same-but-different quality of a game seduces players into repeat play; or how a simple social game like Mafia can produce emergent social play; or how emergent (as opposed to embedded) narrative game structures produce unexpected story outcomes. But what about **CULTURE?** What would it mean to frame games as culturally emergent systems, where the complex play produced by the game occurs not just on a formal or experiential level, but on a cultural level as well? We know from our chapter on *Systems* that games can be considered either open or closed systems. Closed systems do not permit exchange between the game and its environment; open systems do. When a game is considered as an open culture system, the space of possibility is expanded to include contexts outside the magic circle. The exchange of meaning between a game and its surrounding cultural context can change and transform both the game and its environment.

This schema, *Games as Open Culture,* stems from two propositions: that the emergent, open-ended play of a game can occur on a cultural level; and that as an open system, games exchange meaning with their surrounding contexts. *Games as Open Culture* builds on the insights of our previous **CULTURE** chapters, while expanding them considerably. This schema also brings us back more concretely into the realm of design. Framing games as open culture reminds us that even as culture, games are systems composed of designed elements that interact to produce emergent cultural effects. A game designed as open culture allows players in some way to access the game structure and directly change its meanings. But what is the extent of this change? *How deep* is the exchange of meanings between the game and its context? Is the game system affected on an aesthetic level, as when the skins of game avatars are customized by players? Is the game system affected on the level of experience, as in a custom mod that adds new interactive possibilities? Or are the game rules themselves changed, at the level of code? How does each of these transformative effects change the cultural meaning of the game?

Inventing Jenny

What is an open culture game? Let's start with an example. After the launch of massively multiplayer online role-playing game Ultima Online, the open-ended nature of the game play immediately gave rise to a rich ecosystem of play styles. Ultima Online's skill systems support an impressive array of preset player professions, ranging from Archery to Blacksmithing to Wild Animal Taming. Yet no sooner was the game up and running than one particularly enterprising player introduced a new line of work, which took advantage of the game's emergent properties. Side-stepping the designed system of player professions in the game, the player began operating two characters, one named Jenny and the other Pimp Daddy. Through these characters, the age-old profession of prostitution was introduced as a new revenue stream into the UO universe. Together the characters solicited johns, arranged meetings, and collected payment for services rendered. Although players' avatars could not actually engage in sex within the game structure, the implied narrative of the interaction was enough to generate a steady flow of customers for Jenny and her entrepreneurial boss.

This player behavior was truly emergent. It was not designed directly into the game, but was made possible by the designed formal structures allowing players to name and customize characters, move about the game space, give and receive money, and chat and interact with each other. The new kind of play facilitated by Jenny and Pimp Daddy was deeply cultural, as the characters mixed the medieval fantasy world of Ultima Online with contemporary pulp fantasy (note the blacksploitation-style name "Pimp Daddy"). The playful act reinvented the idea of a "profession" in the game world and gave new meanings to the exchange and use of money. It also took sexual interaction beyond racy text chatting by adding a more meaningful structure of narrative and interaction (arranging a meeting, finding a secluded space, exchanging capital). These emergent cultural effects were made possible by a game design that offered players modular social expression through a set of very simple interactions.

When game designers frame games as open systems and take into account the potential for emergent cultural effects, games can be specifically crafted to produce unexpected forms of play. But the emergent play can also extend beyond the borders of the game itself. Designing for open cultural play can increase the permeability of the magic circle, so that a transformative exchange of meaning occurs at multiple levels. *Games as Open Culture* implies a game design model in which the structure of a game offers players explicit creative agency.

Players are encouraged to add to, delete from, or altogether alter the experience of play through manipulation of the game's system. We call this the *player-as-producer paradigm,* a design strategy linked to the creation of culturally transformative play.

Player-as-Producer

Designing a game means creating a set of very specific conditions. These conditions prescribe relationships both internal and external to the game space, and determine not only what the game system is, but also by implication what the game has the potential to become. Designs for open system games include conditions that let players affect the games as *producers* —of new game worlds, stories, and characters. Open system games, in other words, are designed to be manipulated and modified by the people who purchase and play them. The design of The Sims, for example, includes features that allow players to download objects for their houses, create their own skins and consumable goods, or download game patches that offer variations on game play. Player-designers have gone even further, creating graphics and sound patches that give characters the ability to talk in new ways. Each of these points of entry allows players to make choices about how deeply they will intervene into the system of The Sims.

Player-oriented design tools can give rise to a whole ecology of fan culture. Will Wright, lead designer of The Sims, has described this social system as a pyramid. At the top (with the fewest number of participants) are players that make game creation tools, like a 3D graphics tool that lets players model new character bodies. The next tier contains players that use the design tools to make game objects, such as new character bodies with animal-inspired anatomy. These objects are disseminated by players in the next tier, webmasters that host Sims websites. At the bottom of the pyramid (highest in number of participants) are the players that make use of these objects in their game.

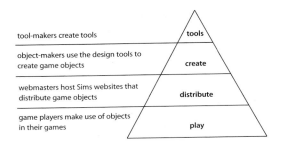

tool-makers create tools — **tools**

object-makers use the design tools to create game objects — **create**

webmasters host Sims websites that distribute game objects — **distribute**

game players make use of objects in their games — **play**

The design of The Sims facilitates the development of these groups at every level. Rather than a closed, airtight system, The Sims is structured as modular code, designed for expansion and manipulation by players. However, flexible code is not enough: you need to communicate to your audience the possibility of player-as-producer intervention and carefully foster the kind of player community that is appropriate to your game. Several months before The Sims launched, Maxis released an initial set of design tools. These tools were quickly taken up, shared across the community of players, and prodigiously utilized—before the game ever hit stores. Writer J.C. Herz notes, "At this point, more than 90 percent of The Sims' content is produced by the player population…. This is a completely bottom-up, distributed, self-organizing process."[1] Although it is certainly true that the growth of The Sims community was fostered by an existing base of Maxis game fans, the immense player-producer community of The Sims only came about through careful community design.

When players become producers, their activities as players fall outside the magic circle and largely take place in spaces external to the game. These activities are a form of metagaming, a play phenomenon described in *Games as Social Play.* In metagaming, players engage with the game and each other through activities and interactions outside the confines of explicit game play. The player-as-producer paradigm exaggerates these metagaming tendencies to create more radical forms of open play. When the player becomes a producer, metagaming elements take on a life of their own, expanding beyond activities that merely comment on the play of the game to become pursuits that literally transform the structure of the game.

There is no single best method for integrating the player-as-producer paradigm into a game design. Game forms are radically varied and so are the ways that game designers can encourage players to become producers. Game tools to create new game assets might ship with the game, as with the role-playing game Neverwinter Nights. Level design tools can be made freely available within a designed online community, as with the puzzle game BLiX. Extra blank cards for players to fill out can be part of a game deck, as in the narrative card game Once Upon a Tale. Code for a digital game can be made available to the public, as with DOOM. Or the very premise of the game can be based on active player creation, as with tabletop role-playing games that require one player (the "Game Master") to invent the adventures for play.

When game players become game producers, emergence is multiplied: in addition to the unexpected forms of play that occur inside a game, player-producers create entirely new contexts for play, which in turn generate whole new play experiences. As we noted in *Games as Emergent Systems,* one of the sweetest pleasures as a game designer is seeing your game played in ways that you did not anticipate. Casting the player in the role of a producer can multiply this pleasure many times over; seeing your players constructing brand new worlds to share across a community of players is incredibly exciting. There is something deeply satisfying about creating a game that allows players to participate as designers in their own right.

Meaningful Production

The key to creating emergent player-as-producer play is the same as in other aspects of games. Designing successful play is designing *meaningful play,* where the game system supports the choices players take by making them *discernable* to the player and *integrating* them into the larger system of the game. In the case of games as open culture, the scope of meaningful play extends to include the cultural contexts outside the magic circle of the game.

One example of successful open play stems from a particular designed feature of The Sims—the Family Album. According to the game's creators, the Family Album was intended to let players take snapshots of particular moments in their Sims' lives and add the photos to a family album, which they could design and curate. Interestingly enough, the Family Album ended up becoming a tool for the creation of fictive stories that often had nothing to do with actual game events. As originally envisioned, players could take screenshots during play that would record the current state of a game in progress. In this way, the Family Album could document the day-to-day activity of a player's Sims. Yet many players took this basic functionality and transformed it into an alternate form of play, using the feature to craft *stories* that took on a variety of forms. Sometimes these stories borrow from popular culture (such as the story of a Sim appearing on the television show *Big Brother*). Other narratives are informed by players' real-life experiences (the story of a struggling alcoholic mother). Still other stories parody the game world itself through meta-Sims narratives (such as the tale of the "KTS" family's war with Maxis, the company that developed The Sims.). The Sims Family Album feature is a wonderful instance of the player-as-producer paradigm, generating play that both *reflects* and *transforms* the game world.

The Family Album feature facilitates meaningful play on many levels. As a game play recording device, it adds a layer of meaning to the standard play of the game. As in other forms of *retelling play* (a concept we first introduced in **Games as Narrative**

Excerpts from The Metamora Family: User ID: dnknt98

Magoria, unsure of the words Elanora spoke, began to prepare for the events that were to come.

As darkness arose, and spirits wandered Magoria spoke of the evil deeds that she was ready to carry out. Magoria approched her family and spoke: "This All Hallows Eve, the moon wiil be full and the time has come to complete The Passage of the Dead."

Charlie, unsure of what was being spoken, asked, "What is this evil you speak of Magoria?"

"I know, I know we are going to summon the demon of Guton," Wenticia screamed.

"Yes that is correct, we shall begin to sacrifice the youth and in return be granted Eternal life." Magoria turned and placed a hand on the grave of Elanora, saying, "This is our family's destiny; we will prevail."

Excerpts from Gingerbread: User ID: GoodHumor

1

2

Welcome to the home of George and Ginny Gingerbread! After being on the run most of their lives, this couple has just purchased a home that seems to have been made just for them.

A soft blanket of snow covers the ground on this cold day in the month of December. George and Ginny, former college track stars, dream of opening a brand new Gourmet Bakery in Simville. But for now, are looking forward to celebrating Christmas in their new home…that is, if they last that long.

Like most fleeing edibles, George and Ginny are tormented by the possibility of becoming someone's next meal. Ginny, longing for some normalcy in her life, is hoping to meet new friends and finally settle down in a neighborhood where she and her husband can relax. George, on the other hand, is consumed with the danger of winding up as part of somebody's holiday buffet. It is with some trepidation that Ginny announces,

"George, I have decided to throw a house warming party to get to know our new neighbors."

George is not too keen on this idea until he realizes this would be a golden opportunity to scope out potential enemies, you know, those that might find his curly que hairdo just a little too appetizing. Actually, he worries more for Ginny. She tends to be too trusting. Her kind nature has unfortunately gotten the couple in more than a few mixes…er…fixes. The upside to this is that all this "escaping" has kept the two in prime physical condition.

Gingerbread (shown here) and ***The Metamora Family*** (previous page) are Sims Family Albums created by players and posted for review at the Sims Exchange, www.thesims.ea.com

Write | ALL PLAYERS: Switch camp. Spork is now Foon and vice versa. Sneak remains the Sneak. Write the name of your new camp on your camp card.

3

…George insists that he and Ginny sleep in the guest room on the first floor. This way he will be ready for anything that might pop up…a burglary, a fire, a gingernapping…whatever. He worries about Ginny because he loves her so. George has a bad feeling about this Newbie character and plans to keep one frosted eye on him.

4

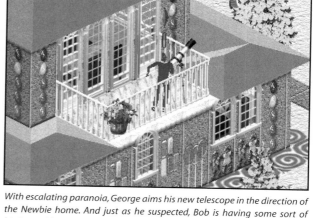

With escalating paranoia, George aims his new telescope in the direction of the Newbie home. And just as he suspected, Bob is having some sort of kitchen table meeting with one of Simville's senior citizens, Joy Holiday.

"OK," sighs George, "That makes Joy suspect #4. Geez, you can't trust anyone these days."

5

…A roaring fire seems to calm George, taking him back to his roots. He wishes that just once, he and Ginny could exist in a world free of ginger-bread groupies.

With Ginny asleep upstairs, George consumes cup after cup of Expresso in an effort to stay awake as long as possible…just in case.

He is aware that Joy Holiday is lurking outside the window, in cahoots with Bob, of course. George already informed Joy that he and Ginny have no desire to be storefront props for her stupid Bakery. These humans!!!

But George is playing it cool. He does not want Joy to know he is on to her. He's not worried, though. She'll get hers too.

6

George notices Bob Newbie spending way too much time at the house with Ginny. And just the other day, he noticed Bob hand Ginny a slip of paper. What was THAT all about? And, to make matters worse, George is not imag-ining that Frankie still wants to claim the gingerbread home as his own, preferably not including its present inhabitants. George decides surveil-lance cameras, alarms, and telescopes alone won't due. Extra precautions are needed. He heads over to the shed out back…

Play), the play itself is retold and recast for the player, as game choices are given a new context for appreciation. As Sims players creatively explored the possibilities of the Family Album feature, it shifted from a documentary tool to a creative tool. Players quickly began to make adjustments to the way they played the game, in order to compose the exact "shots" they wanted for their storyboard-like narratives. Strategies for successful game play, such as keeping game characters happy, were superceded by strategies for positioning objects and characters in a scene. Because Sims characters move about on their own, it can be quite challenging to compose a multi-character shot.

The Family Album feature also generated a new context, just outside the game, where players could create and share meaning online. Family Album photos became ways to trade play strategies, game experiences, and (most commonly) to create original stories. The out-of-game web context supported the creation of these meanings, and the community of players became a rich social context where the story albums could be appreciated and shared.

The Family Album feature was the result of deliberate design decisions on the part of The Sims' creators. Its simple functionality was then taken up by players and used in delightfully unexpected ways. Moreover, other player-as-producer aspects of The Sims, such as players' ability to create new character models, worked in concert with the Family Album to multiply meaningful play. For example, player-artists created Sims that looked like Star Wars characters. These characters were distributed online by community managers and could be used to play a Star Wars themed version of The Sims. But the characters could also be used by player-storytellers in conjunction with the Family Album feature to tell stories set in the Star Wars universe. All of this open play was possible because the game was designed as a system open to manipulation, encouraging players to produce new forms of culture as part of their play.

What is it about games, particularly digital games that make them such fertile ground for player participation? One answer is that games are intrinsically systemic, and systems can be designed to be open. As we know from earlier chapters, systems are composed of interrelated elements with specific attributes and relationships, situated within an environment. Within a system, there are multiple opportunities for intervention on the part of the player. In an open game system like The Sims, a player might change the *attributes* of an object in the system, designing a skin for a character, or change one of the system's *elements* by designing a new object and adding it to the game world, such as putting a player-created toaster in a Sim's kitchen. This new element might then change the *relationship* between elements in the system: the toaster transforms what Sim characters can do in the kitchen. A player might also intervene on the level of the game's *environment,* by making a fan site that distributes game objects or by creating a Sims Family Album. In every case, the system of the game accommodates the changes by absorbing them and transforming itself accordingly.

Player-as-producer artifacts not only reflect the meanings and values of the games from which they arise, but also contribute to the meaning and value of the cultural contexts in which the games exist. Some forms of player production move from inside the game outward (inside > out), such as when the Family Album is used to extract a retelling story out of game play. Other forms can move from outside the game inward (outside > in), such as when a player-generated character model is downloaded for use in the game. In both cases, the permeability of the magic circle feeds innovation, resulting in rich systems of cultural production and new forms of creative expression.

Open Source Games

The play of open systems concerns more than player experience: there are ideological dimensions as well. To explore some of the values underlying open culture, we will take a brief detour through the phenomenon of open source software.

Write | SPORK: Write the name of a color. FOON: Write a person's last name.

Open source has two important features: first, code is written as an open system that can be improved and modified by a community of designers rather than by a single development team; and second, open source software is freely shared among users and its source code made available. The model of open source software development is a non-game instance of the player-as-producer paradigm, a precursor to the open play of many contemporary digital games.

Open source software had its beginnings in the 1960s with the sale of the first large-scale computers by IBM and other manufacturers. These computers came with "free" software that let users *share* and *modify* the source code. This open source model was soon replaced by proprietary software as an industry standard; it would not find a voice again until the early 1990s. As Jesus M. Gonzalez notes regarding the history of open source software, "In the late 1960s, the situation changed after the 'unbundling' of IBM software, and in the mid-1970s it was usual to find proprietary software, in the sense that users were not allowed to redistribute it, that source code was not available, and that users could not modify the programs."[2]

Although open source software continued its development during the 1970s and 1980s within relatively small, isolated communities, it wasn't until the early 1990s that the programming community underwent larger changes. According to Gonzalez, one of the most important events was the public release of the first versions of the Linux kernel (the core code elements of the Linux operating system) by Linus Torvalds, a Finnish computer science student. Torvalds made the code for the Linux kernel available to programmers around the world, encouraging them to collaborate on refining and expanding its code. Torvalds believed that an open system approach to software design involving the participation of user-programmers was the most effective way to develop the kernel. He knew that the people who took up his offer to play with and modify the code could push the software beyond what he could accom-

plish on his own. The fact that many people were working with the source code simultaneously allowed for a form of creative redundancy: when several programmers would find the same bug, or make the same modification, the strengths and weaknesses of the software as a whole became much clearer.

There is a strong connection between Torvalds's model and the emergent play of games as open culture. Open game systems, like open source software, are designed to be evolutionary, not static, and to be expressed in multiple forms. Players operate as a community of developers, transforming elements of the game system, playtesting them, sharing them with other players, and submitting them for further modification. This free play is not obligatory, of course: players of an "open source" game can modify it if they wish, but are not forced to do so. The spirit of open source accommodates many levels of participation, from players who like the game as it is to those who want to transform it completely.

When users or players manipulate a structure and distribute modifications to other interested parties, they participate in an economy of exchange open to all. This open source approach has the characteristics of being *non-hierarchical, openly accessible, non-guided,* and *emergent.* These four principles are the cornerstone of open source software, but also happen to describe open culture games as well. According to the open source model, open source users have the freedom to:

- Use the software as they wish, for whatever they wish, on as many computers as they wish, in any technically appropriate situation.

- Have the software at their disposal to fit it to their needs. Of course, this includes improving it, fixing its bugs, augmenting its functionality, and studying its operation.

- Redistribute the software to other users, who could themselves use it according to their own needs.

- Users of a piece of software must have access to its source code.[3]

Now reread these principles, replacing "software" with "game" and "user" with "player." It is striking how smoothly the concepts of open source software transfer to games as open culture. In the case studies that follow, we explore these principles in the context of two games, one non-digital (Icehouse), and one digital (Elemental). Even though open source emerged from computer science, its ideas can be applied to games both on and off the computer. All that is required is the design of an open system and a community of players intent on participating.

Game Systems

Within the domain of non-digital games, a special class of games is known as *game systems*. A game system is a set of components that function together across multiple games. The most commonly used game system is a standard deck of playing cards. It has 52 components (the cards) that can be used together to play thousands of games, from Go Fish to Strip Poker. The tiles of a Mah Jongg set comprise a game system used in several different games, as do a bat and a ball. A game system is akin to a computer's operating system. A single OS can run many different kinds of software, just a like a game system can "run" many different sets of rules. The open-ended and variable qualities of game systems make them truly fascinating instances of game design.

Game systems, intentionally designed to be "open," stand in contrast to "closed" games that lack the opportunity for modification by players. Closed games contain a single set of rules and rely on components that can only be used for that game. The specialized equipment of a game such as Golf makes it a very closed game. There are few popular variations on Golf for the simple reason that the relationship between ball, club, and golf course are quite specific; there is relatively little room for reinvention.

Unlike a closed game, a game system exemplifies all four qualities of open source software. A game system is non-hierarchical, openly accessible, non-guided, and emergent. Like open source

code, game systems provide players with the "source code" (the game's components and perhaps a sample ruleset or two) and encourage players to modify them in whatever way they wish, in as many ways as they wish (usually by inventing new games to be played with the system). Players can then redistribute the rules to others, who play or modify the new games according to their needs and interests.

One highly expressive example of a non-digital game system is the Icehouse Set, designed by Andy Looney and John Cooper. The components of an Icehouse Set are stackable, colored plastic pyramids, in three sizes (small, medium, and large). There are five pyramids of each size, and a four-player set of Icehouse therefore contains 60 pyramids, fifteen for each player. The original game for the Icehouse Set (called "Icehouse") is an unusual strategy game played in real-time without turns. Players simultaneously position their colored pyramids in a central area one by one, stacking and pointing their pyramids to attack and defend. Icehouse play is fast-paced, highly strategic, and quite unique.[5]

The Icehouse Set has led to the invention of a great many delightful and unconventional games, including Zarcana and Gnostica, both played on a board made of Tarot cards; Chess-like variants such as Martian Chess and Pikeman; a computer sim called RAMbots; a building game known as Thin Ice; and a deep-space epic about good and evil called Homeworlds. To get a sense of the incredible range of games designed for the Icehouse Set, we summarize a few of the games in a bit more detail:

> *Volcano* is a clever, puzzle-like game in which players move "caps" around the tops of volcanoes, triggering eruptions that cause colored streams of lava to flow out across the playing field. The object of the game is to capture as many pieces as possible, with bonus points awarded for special combinations. Each player attempts to accumulate the highest score and then bring the game to a close before

Write | SPORK: Write the name of one of your current favorite TV shows. FOON: Write the name of a TV show you liked a lot as a kid.

another player has a chance to steal the lead away. Multi-player Volcano supports any number of players, though between two and six is best. It can also be played by a single player as a solitaire challenge.

Zarcana is a game of war, journeys, growth, life, and death. Icehouse pieces are your minions, spreading out across a world composed of tarot cards. You move your minions across the board, trying to occupy valuable cards. The board can change, grow and shrink, so players must be prepared to defend their holdings, invade enemy territory, and colonize new lands. Each player also has a hand of cards, drawn from the tarot deck. Every card has a unique power, and you can make use of the cards you occupy on the board in addition to the cards in your hand. The goal is to occupy the most valuable set of cards on the board at the end of the game.

Zendo is a game of inductive logic, in which one player, the Master, creates a rule that the rest of the players, as Students, try and figure out by building and studying configurations of Icehouse pieces. The first student to correctly guess the rule wins. What is the hidden rule? Does it have to do with relative color? Size? Number? Pattern? Or maybe it is based on something outside the magic circle…. Beguilingly simple, Zendo rewards cleverness and creativity on the part of both Students and Masters.[6]

The challenge of designing a game system is finding a balance between specificity and flexibility. The formal and material attributes of the game system components lend themselves to particular kinds of game rules and play experiences. The game system must have a very specific identity—compare the specificity of suit and rank of a deck of playing cards to a set of blank white index cards. At the same time, if the components are too specific, as with Golf, the game system will lack the flexibility to produce novel games. Flexibility often comes down to the details of physical form: playing cards can be shuffled, dealt, hid-

Zendo

den, displayed, stacked, spread, and even tossed across a room. A Golf club is designed for a much more limited function.

The pyramids of the Icehouse Set are a great example of a well-designed game system. They can be physically configured in any number of ways: stacked on top of each other, aimed at each other like arrows, organized into patterns, or distributed randomly—different Icehouse games take different advantage of these material affordances. The number of pieces and distribution among the three sizes and four colors also determines the formal relationships and logical groupings that can be expressed by the organization of pieces. The Icehouse Set components elegantly embody a flexible yet expressive set of potential formal and experiential relationships.

Game system design is a kind of meta-game design. A game system designer designs the structure within which other game designers will create games. The "rules" of the system are the physical qualities of the game system components; the "play" that takes place is game design itself, resulting in sets of rules that make use of the game system. This kind of process requires that the game system designer give up a significant degree of control, as other player-designers decide how the game system will be used in actual games. But this loss of control is ultimately what is so satisfying about designing game systems: as a platform for player-driven creativity, a game system is a catalyst for truly transformative and emergent play.

Escape from the Dungeon

As we have mentioned, game systems are like open source "operating systems." Player-designers interact with data and write their own software, creating programs (rulesets) that manipulate or transform the organization of game system data. New games result, which can then be manipulated and transformed again. The operating system of the Icehouse Set is nothing more than the collection of 60 colored pyramids and the mathematical and physical rules structuring their space of possibility. A simple and elegant OS kernel, the Icehouse Set is nonetheless capable of a huge variety of expression.

Perhaps not surprisingly, game systems find a natural home when we turn our attention to digital games. Starcraft, Pac-Man, EverQuest, Pong: each is a game, and each is a piece of software (literally). Digital games have always had a naturally affinity with an open source software model: the very first computer game, Spacewar!, was an open source game whose code underwent modification and distribution by players from the moment of its conception. Without open source thinking, Spacewar! might never have come into being. Digital games have always been ready candidates for an open source paradigm; it is within digital games, in fact, that the model of player-as-producer has found the most significant and transformative voices to date.

One such voice is Elemental, a player-produced mod for the fantasy role-playing game Dungeon Siege, created by Gas Powered Games. Elemental is what is known as a "total conversion" mod: rather than simply inventing a new character skin, game level, or in-game object, the mod transforms Dungeon Siege into a completely different game. The result is a game that utilizes elements of Dungeon Siege's core game system within a radically altered context of expression. As Zendo to Icehouse, Elemental recasts Dungeon Siege within an altogether different space of play.

The possibility for a mod such as Elemental only exists because of software developers that work from an open source model. Gas Powered Games recognized open source as an ideology that could effectively enhance and extend the life of their games. As a result, they released Dungeon Siege with a robust suite of editing and game development tools that players could use to modify the game in an infinite variety of ways. The proprietary Siege Editor, for example, gives players the freedom to rework nearly every aspect of the game, making Dungeon Siege not only a game, but also a role-playing platform for those who want to create their own characters, spells, and dungeons—or even entire worlds. Players can publish these user-created files to the web, making them available for anyone to download and explore or play as a multiplayer game.[7]

Team Elemental, the development team of (mostly amateur) programmers, artists, game designers, level designers, GUI and concept artists living and working in various countries across the globe, took these tools and began to mod. Impressed by the robust Dungeon Siege engine, they quickly realized that the limits of what could be done with the game lay only in their imaginations. They decided to depart from the Tolkienesque world of the original game to invent something with a radically different setting, storyline, and game play mechanic. The resulting experience of play would be very different than what the original game offered. Affectionately described as "biblepunk" (players are former slaves seeking retribution in the ancient city of Jericho), it remains to be seen if the Dungeon Siege community will embrace the new world by modding it in turn.

One of the unique features of Elemental's creation was the collaborative environment nurtured by Dungeon Siege's developers. Although many open source games make their code available for modification by players, and often provide toolsets to help them do so, Gas Powered Games assumed an active role in assisting Team Elemental. Programmers coding the mod worked in direct contact with engineers from the original game, who offered hints and advice for working with the intricacies of the code. Clearly, Gas Powered Games embraced the player-as-producer paradigm in constructing

Act | ALL PLAYERS: Show the person on your right your most recent *Write* card.

Dungeon Seige editor

and nurturing an active player community. As Chris Taylor, president and game designer of Gas Powered Games, noted in an interview, the drive to support the mod community came out of their experience with a previous game:

> Most of this drive comes from our experience working on Total Annihilation. We learned that a great community could propel a game to new levels of fun and turn it into more than anyone thought it could be. We found this idea to be very exciting, and in many ways, feel it is the way of the future. Imagine, people all over the world working together on teams to create fantastic new adventures, stories, characters. The possibilities are endless, and this is just the beginning![8]

Taylor's investment in supporting player community and creativity has clearly paid off. Elemental is just one example how far players will go when a game's design invests in them a desire to extend and reinvent play by playing with the rules of the game. The culturally transformative play that emerges from player production feeds back into the open source model out of which the game developed, growing the possibilities of the community's space of play exponentially.

Both Icehouse and Dungeon Siege exhibit three essential qualities of open source games: the games are open systems that can be *modified* by a community of players, rather than a single developer; the games are freely *shared* among players and developers; and the *source code* is made available. In the case of Dungeon Siege, not just the source code, but also development tools were made available to players, increasing the ease and depth of possible modifications.

Telefragging Monster Movies

Sometimes, the player-as-producer paradigm takes the modification of a game so far that the invented activity no longer resembles the play of the game at all. Such is the case with machinima, a player-as-producer open culture phenomenon we first mentioned in **Games as Narrative Play** that evolved out of first-person shooter games. FPS games such as Quake and DOOM were some of the first to offer an open source editor to players, which allowed them to design and program their own maps (environments), skins (character avatars), weapons, and tools for game play. This pioneering approach, a direct outgrowth of open source software culture, offered players unprecedented power to modify game play by altering the forms and spaces of interaction.

DOOM set the standard for open culture digital gaming, but its high-resolution prodigy, Quake, took everything to a higher level. Players (or groups of players known as clans) wrote Quake code modifications and posted them online for other enthusiasts to download and use. Almost instantly, an economy of Quake cultural production was born. This economy pushed the

edge of technical innovation, fueled as it was by hardcore gamers' desire to explore the absolute limits of the technology. How far could the code be pushed before the system was transformed? Witness the birth of the Quake movie.

Almost as soon as Quake was released in 1996, gamers began to try and play through its levels as fast as possible and to share recordings of their feats with others, competing to beat each others' times. This type of competition, known as speedrunning, was established in the early days of DOOM, a game that like Quake gave players the ability to record and save their game play. Although these demos were clearly a form of retelling play, they soon took on a very different role. Like The Sims Family Album feature, players began to use the recording function to tell stories. Rather than creating narratives in a graphic novel form, as with The Sims, FPS players embraced the real-time editing capabilities of the robust 3D game engines upon which their games were based. It was only a matter of time before someone made the leap to film.

According to Quake lore, in August 1996, a clan known as The Rangers conceived the idea to record a demo that would exploit the built-in moviemaking capabilities of the game's software. Rather than restrict their demo recording to play within the game, The Rangers would use Quake as a filmmaking tool. This decision transformed the game space into a virtual movie set, complete with lights, camera, and action—lots of action. The Rangers used their characters as virtual actors and recorded their movements on a deathmatch map; typed text messages represented speech. As short and simple as their first effort appears to us today, "Diary of a Camper" established the filmic genre machinima, which has spawned hundreds of movies to date. Creatively responding to the affordances of the game system, Quake players not only transformed the play of the game, but took an open source model and applied it to the production of new forms of culture.

Part theater, part film, part computer game, machinima represents the kind of wild exchanges that result from thoroughly

Scourge Done Slick, 1998 | Quake Done Quick

Devil's Covenant, 1998 | Clan Phantasm

Father Frags Best, 1999 | Phil Rice aka Overman

Anachronox, 2001 | Jake Hughes, Director

transformative play. The cultural play of machinima crosses formal, experiential, and contextual levels, as players playfully repurpose the original structures of the game. The formal structure of the game code gave shape to a new form of storytelling, born from the culture of the first-person shooter.

Stylized forms of both public and private expression, Quake movies embody alternative trajectories for creative output. Players in the culture of machinima may assume a range of roles: map builders, coders, skinners, actors, model makers—or perhaps a distributor for the completed films. Web sites such as machinima.com, the Quake Movie Library, Planetquake's Cineplex, and Zarathustra Studios support movie production by offering tools, tutorials, movie reviews, and most important of all, free downloads of the movies themselves.

Quake movies and other forms of machinima offer a unique space of culturally transformative play: machinima producers deconstruct the game in order to play with it. Instead of accepting the rules, they challenge and modify them. This creative practice is a form of rule-breaking, one occurring at the deep level of code. By bending and modifying the game's formal structure, players affect their experience with the game by remolding its play into something that only barely resembles its former shape.

Circle Back

The model of games as open culture offers players rich opportunities to participate in larger systems of cultural production. The design artifacts left in the wake of such production—from open game systems to Family Album stories to machinima—permeate the magic circle from two directions. First, the artifacts feed the game from the outside *in:*

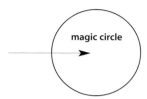

in other words, many instances of player production occur within the frame of the game itself. Whether new costumes designed by players for a LARP or new skins designed for Half-Life or Quake, the elements are absorbed *into* the magic circle, where they are made meaningful through the play of the game.

At the same time, player-created artifacts can also feed the game from the inside *out,* bringing meaning to the game through their circulation within culture.

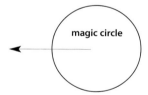

The Family Album stories of The Sims, for example, affect the popular value of the game through personal revelation within a community context. The stories crafted by players speak of cultures in transition and offer a glimpse into the psyche of a social milieu. In gaining a life beyond the borders of the game space from which they were born, artifacts like Family Album stories create feedback loops of their own, formulating new cultural territories to be explored and eventually, transformed in turn. This movement from *reflection* to *transformation* is another case of culturally transformative play.

Framing games as open culture is just one way of looking at the potential of games to act as open systems. Most games engage cultural contexts in a very open way. Games are embedded in lifestyles, media, ideologies, histories, and a range of social contexts. As designers, we must identify and invent design strategies that encourage forms of exchange between players, their games, and culture. Game designs that give players the tools to act as creative producers within open game systems is one such strategy, a rich model for a collaborative design practice between designer and community, between game and player.

As we know from our studies of emergence, the play of games produces unexpected results. Seeing your game create play experiences, player artifacts, and emergent cultural effects you could not have anticipated is a special pleasure reserved for game designers. So make sure your games have the potential to surprise you, by creating moments of open play for your audience. This doesn't mean you have to create a radically player-centric game every time: remember that the design of open culture exists along a sliding scale, from wholly internal activities such as finding new game strategies to the production of new game elements to the transformative potential of games to affect a larger culture. Rising to this design challenge means deciding what forms of open culture you want to facilitate in your game and what kinds of meaningful play you would like to see emerge. Above all, trust your players. Empower and engage their communities. And design for open culture. Who knows—you just might end up inspiring beautiful new ways to play.

Write | **SPORK:** Draw a train. **FOON:** Draw a plane.

Further Reading

Game On: The History and Culture of Videogames, Lucien King, ed.
(see page 426)

> *Recommended:*
> "Gaming the System: Multi-player Worlds Online," J. C. Herz
> "Pokémon as Japanese Culture?" Masuyama

"Game Systems: Part I, II, III," by Ron Hale-Evans <www.thegamesjournal.com/articles/GameSystems1.shtml>

In this three-part series, game designer Ron Hale-Evans explores the concept of a game system: a set of components (like a deck of cards) that function together to form a variety of different games. His investigation includes a range of lesser-known and fascinating game systems. Although Hale-Evans focuses on paper-based games, his discussion has relevance for an exploration of the mod culture of digital games.

Textual Poachers: Television Fans and Participatory Culture, by Henry Jenkins

In his study of media fan culture, Jenkins represents media fans within a player-as-producer paradigm: actively constructing their own objects and meanings from borrowed materials. Jenkins' study is of particular relevance to the culture of hacks, mods, and cheats emerging from open source games.

> *Recommended:*
> Chapter 1: "Get a Life!": Fans, Poachers, and Nomads
> Chapter 5: Scribbling in the Margins
> Chapter 7: "Layers of Meaning": Fan Music Videos and the Poetics of Poaching

Notes

1. J. C. Herz, "Gaming the System: Multi-player Worlds Online." In *Game On: The History and Culture of Video Games,* edited by Lucien King (London: Laurence Ling Publishing, 2002), p. 91.

2. Jesus M. Gonzalez, "A Brief History of Open Source Software." <http://eu.conecta.it/paper/brief_history_open_source.html>.

3. Ibid.

4. Ron Hale-Evans, "Game Systems: Part 1." <www.thegamesjournal.com/articles/GameSystems1.shtml>

5. Ibid.

6. The Official Icehouse Homepage, <www.wunderland.com/ice-house/Default.html>

7. <http://dungeonseige.com>

8. Tricia "Kazi Wren" Harris, "Mod World: Part 12." *Gamespy.com.* August 22, 2002. <www.gamespy.com/modworld/august02/modworld12/>.

Games as Open Culture
SUMMARY

- The schema *Games as Open Culture* is based on two premises: first, as open systems, play occurs on the level of culture; second, games exchange meaning with their surrounding contexts.

- **Transformative cultural play** occurs when the open system quality of a game leads to an exchange between the meanings of a game and culture at large, changing the context of the game.

- The **player-as-producer paradigm** is a design approach and social phenomenon in which players are given the opportunity to act as creative producers within the system of the game, modifying it on formal, experiential, or cultural levels.

- When players become producers, their activities are a form of **metagaming,** as they interact with the game outside the bounds of the magic circle.

- Player-producers have the potential to create entirely new contexts for play, an emergent property of games as open culture. These new contexts themselves can encourage new play experiences, creating instances of transformative play.

- **Open source** is a software development model with two important features that support user-centered production: first, code is written as an open system available for modification and exchange by a community of designers; second, the source code is always available and freely shared.

- The qualities of open culture games are similar to the fundamental features of open source software. They are: **non-hierarchical, openly accessible, non-guided,** and **emergent.**

- Player-produced modifications can occur in one of two ways: production occurring within the magic circle moving outward (inside > out), or production taking place within culture that moves inward to affect the game (outside > in).

- **Game systems** are sets of components that can be used to play different games. Game systems can be digital (an open source game engine) or non-digital (a set of physical game materials).

- **Machinima** are animated movies created with game engine technology.

Act | **SPORK:** Do nothing. **FOON:** Exchange writing utensils with a player of your choosing.

GAMES AS CULTURAL RESISTANCE

culturally transformative play
friction as resistance
game modifications
DIY gaming
alteration
juxtaposition
reinvention

32

*So, you've just hopped onto the playground after scouting the homeroom for an open game. There are five other girls in the room, two of whom are noticeably silent. The game begins. Without warning, a tease from the two girls suddenly takes out half your points! The next round, one of their tattles nearly wipes you out! The two silent girls remain **without a scratch**—literally. By the end of the very short game, the two completely silent girls stand victorious over the broken bodies of everyone else in the room—**and not a word was spoken between the two of them!** How'd they do it?*

You might be the victim of a pair of cheaters…

*Regardless of whether you win or lose, you have an obligation to let the rest of the SiSSYFiGHT community know about the cheaters.—**www.sissyfightnews.com***

Introducing Cultural Resistance

In *Games as Open Culture,* we looked at *what* forms of player-production can occur in games and *where* those forms of production are situated relative to the magic circle. But we still have questions to answer: *How* are forms of player-production designed and *why* do they occur? How, for example, do communities of cheaters and vigilantes arise within the SiSSYFiGHT 2000 online community? Why do they appear at all and what is their significance for the play of the game?

In this schema, *Games as Cultural Resistance,* we carry forward many of the themes and concepts from the previous chapter, including player-production, transformative cultural play, and the exchange of meaning between a game and its context. In doing so, however, our focus narrows considerably. *Games as Cultural Resistance* highlights design interventions that call specific attention to the borders of the magic circle through acts of creative resistance.

What exactly do we mean by "resistance?" We see the concept of resistance through a broad rubric of *friction,* a more general notion than the usual understanding of "resistance" as political opposition. Resistance can sometimes be political, but it can take other forms as well. When two phenomena come into conflictual contact with one another, friction, or resistance, results. In this chapter, we look at the friction that can occur between games and their cultural contexts, when one acts to resist the other. The term "friction" may make this process sound negative, but the resistance that results can affect play in deeply meaningful ways. For example, we can use the concept of friction to reframe the relationship between rules and play. In *Defining Play,* we identified play as *free movement within a more rigid structure.* Considering a game as resistance or friction, free-wheeling play rubs up against rigid structures of rules, producing tension. The exact quality of this tension determines the specific play experience of a game.

Framed as this kind of resistance, "free play" is always already transformative. Play never merely resides in a system of rules, but through an ongoing process of friction, affects change in the system. The friction of water flowing against rock and earth over time will alter the more rigid structure of a riverbed. Similarly, when we frame a game as a system of resistance, the very play of the game is intrinsically transformative. This transformation not only takes place on the level of rules but on cultural levels as well, as the resistance creates tensions between the magic circle and the contexts surrounding the game.

In the previous chapter, we introduced Jenny and Pimp Daddy as characters who emerged out of an act of transformative play. From the perspective of cultural resistance, the pair gain resonance not only within the formal constructs of the Ultima Online game world, but also as a strategy of resistance against received cultural assumptions about what constitutes a "proper" profession in the game. In effect, the friction created through the addition of an "unsanctioned" profession called attention to invisible moral biases in the game. The bias was tinged, perhaps, with a *play as progress* cultural rhetoric that sought to repress forms of transgressive sexual play. Yet one has to wonder whether the emergent play of Jenny and Pimp Daddy itself produced further instances of friction. For example, a feminist critique against Jenny's status as a female sexual object might have sprung up in the game, leading to anti-prostitution protests, or perhaps an all-male gigolo service. Resistance in a game often leads to more resistance, creating multi-layered systems of cultural play.

Key to this example is the fact that the "profession" of prostitution in Ultima Online emerged as a property of player interaction. Jenny and her pimp were created as in-game characters; the resulting transformative play grew from an understanding of the roles such characters would play in the real world. Prostitution in Ultima Online emerged from the formal and narrative structures of the game as they came into conflict with real-world narrative expectations. The whole result, as with all complex systems, was more than the sum of the parts, an instance of play that modified the game, even as it transformed the attitudes and assumptions of the game community.

DIY Gaming

Of punk music, rock critic Greil Marcus writes, "The Sex Pistols made a breach in the pop milieu, in the screen of received cultural assumptions governing what one expected to hear and how one expected to respond."[1] Decades later, the same cultural sensibility would resurface in a game called DOOM. As the game that introduced the world to the open sourcing of games and consequently, the art of the mod, DOOM's infiltration of popular culture was a truly emergent phenomenon. As we learned last chapter in a discussion of DOOM's direct descendent Quake, the open system methodology DOOM introduced and Quake embraced had a tremendous impact on both the design and culture of games to follow.

The link we're making between punk rock and DOOM is not an aesthetic one; DOOM's horror-movie pulp kitsch is quite different than punk's noisy anti-aesthetic style. Instead, the similarity between the two is an aggressive embrace of a do-it-yourself (or "DIY") mentality. In punk, DIY was manifest in a belief that control of the tools of production could be wrested from the dominant culture and used to create an alternate version of reality. Playing in a punk band meant picking up a guitar and making noise; making a 'zine simply required access to scissors, ink, and a photocopy machine. Years later this spirit was carried forward into the design of DOOM, where the DIY attitude was embodied in the way players were given access to the game's development tools. DOOM shared punk's desire to remove distinctions between player and producer, between historically rigid categories drawn along participatory lines. Thus, the "free play" of DOOM's source code, still undergoing manipulation by players today (more than ten years after its release), made a breach in long-held assumptions about how one could, and should, interact with a game.

Additionally, the hacker culture and open source methodologies embraced by DOOM find a close parallel in punk's willful annihilation of economic and social hierarchies. Encouraging amateur programmers to come up with their own spin on the ground-breaking first-person shooter had the dual effect of dramatically increasing DOOM's longevity (people played player-designed levels long after they had tired of the original set) and dramatically increasing sales (people had a reason to buy the game long after it would otherwise have been considered unthinkably ancient).[2] A strong DIY mentality has, in one form or another, been an important part of digital gaming's development ever since.

Resistant Strategies

Designed strategies of resistance in a game, whether created by players or designers, are called game *modifications,* or *mods.* Modifications can be officially sanctioned, such as a developer-distributed modification that enhances game play or fixes a bug, or they can be "unofficial," such as unsanctioned game levels, designed and distributed by players. Typically, player-produced modifications are not designed to "mend" an error in the game but are specifically developed to alter game play in some way.[3] Modifications call attention to the borders of the magic circle by creating friction between existing and alternative versions of the game. This is especially true when we consider the larger social contexts for which game modifications are designed, disseminated, and put to use. Game modifications are inherently transformative—they do, after all, literally change the game. The friction they create connects game to context, player-as-producer to player-as-consumer, designer to user, fan to developer, programmer to hacker. In blurring these categories, game modifications enact cultural resistance in a variety of contexts.

Not every act of game resistance is explicitly political. Remember that our use of the term "resistance" refers generally to any act of play that creates friction with more rigid structures. Resistance can be a highly useful model for game designers, particularly if you want your game to engage culture along critical lines. There are many examples of design interventions that modify games to create a dialogue with larger institutional forces. In his study of game patches, Erkki Huhtamo notes that these strategies include modifications motivated by ideological concerns, an urge to re-assert the role of the player as a co-cre-ator, or the subversion of prevailing race, class, or gender rela-tions.[4] Like the borrowed safety pins or swastikas of punk, game modifications have the potential to mutate and resist traditional symbolic codes, creating a critical view from within familiar contexts.

Whether political or not, game modifications can act as forms of resistance, affecting the meaning, experience, and cultural identity of a game. In the next several pages, we look at a range of different game modifications, broadly grouped according to design method. We have divided the modifications into exam-ples of *alteration, juxtaposition,* and *reinvention,* each category representing a different strategy for achieving resistance in a game:

· Strategies of *alteration* make changes to existing game structures.

· Strategies of *juxtaposition* combine unexpected elements within a game space.

· Strategies of *reinvention* rework entire game structures on deeper levels.

Although these three methods overlap, as a whole they provide a conceptual model for understanding existing forms of game resistance, as well as planning new ones.

Strategies of Alteration

Alterations are game modifications that rework existing forms of representation or interaction. Game patches such as the Fighter Chicken patch for DOOM or the Gumby Doll patch for Marathon Infinity, for example, alter traditional forms of cultural representation by substituting standard game characters with player-produced ones. Replacing traditionally "macho" soldier images with silly or absurd characters, "Fighter Chicken" and "Gumby Doll" reframe stereotyped depictions of the male hero-ic ideal. The friction that results from this play between the new representations and those supported by traditional codes chal-lenges assumptions about what, and who, games represent.

SOD

Dirk Paesmans and Joan Heemskerk, artists known by the joint name Jodi, transform game systems through formal-ist reductions of game code. Their patch for Castle Wolfenstein, a modification called SOD, strips the 3D shooter of all color and depth. Basic geometric forms such as squares, circles, and triangles replace the game's original visual components—the castle walls, guards, and weapons. Rather than replacing character sprites with alternate character images, Jodi designs resistance by completely emptying the game of figurative representa-tion. The resulting game space is rendered as simple geo-metric blocks and lines and players are forced to consider how the game engine creates a meaningful space through illusions of depth, movement, and object behavior. Although the graphics code has been altered, the sound-track remains untouched, resulting in screaming triangles and barking, rotating squares that confront the player. Through several layers of absurdist juxtapositions, SOD's overt but expressively enigmatic alterations create new connections between abstraction and representation, flatness and depth, sound and form.

Sailor Moon Wad

Humor and parody can inform a strategy of alteration as well. The Sailor Moon Wad, developed by the SOS Doom Team in support of the Save Our Sailors (SOS) campaign, "aims at keeping Sailor Moon on the air in North America."[5] Drawing directly on the lexicon of Japanese Animé in the construction of its heroine Priss, the wad (a nickname for DOOM level files based on the filename extension) alters the gothic architecture of DOOM by littering the space with objects from the world of Sailor Moon: cupcakes, slices of chocolate cake, hearts, roses, bunny suitcases, and messenger bees. Here the implicit masculinity of DOOM is playfully called into question through the addition of an entire system of feminized artifacts.

Write | ALL PLAYERS: Switch camp. Spork is now Foon and vice versa. Sneak remains the Sneak. Write the name of your new camp on your camp card.

SOD

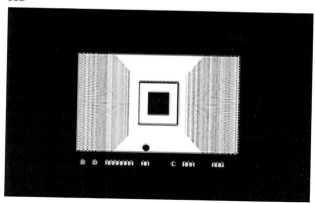

Sailor Moon Wad

SimCopter Hack

Whereas the previous two examples involved modifications by resistors who did not design the original game, sometimes the game developers themselves can use alteration as a strategy of resistance. SimCopter Hack was was the result of a collaboration between the art collective rtmark and a programmer actually working on the computer game SimCopter. While the game was still in development, the programmer (an rtmark member) substituted what rtmark has since termed "boy bimbos" for the game's token bikini-clad females, "infecting the game's traditional heterosexual gaze with homoerotic undertones."[6]

In SimCopter Hack, the play of resistance occurs across several levels. Like Fighter Chicken, Gumby Doll, and the Sailor Moon wad, SimCopter Hack created friction around systems of cultural representation, particularly along gender lines. Additionally, SimCopter Hack created tension within the marketplace. According to rtmark sources, the game may have sold as many as 80,000 copies before the modification was discovered.[7] Maxis, the company that developed the game, surely viewed the modification as an act of economic sabotage, albeit one that had only been intended to rouse critical debate.

Strategies of Juxtaposition

A second strategy of designed cultural friction, *juxtaposition*, achieves resistance by placing unexpected elements together in the same space. It is a strategy that has long been used as a form of resistance by those interested in achieving critical conflict. From the artist Marcel Duchamp's inclusion of a urinal in the Armory Show of 1917 to designer Jamie Reid's pairing of a safety pin and British royalty on the 1977 album cover of the Sex Pistol's *God Save the Queen,* juxtaposition is an established means for "talking back" to culture. A special form of game alteration, in the examples of juxtaposition that follow, resistant meanings emerge through the expressive pairing of unlikely elements.

Frag Queens

Many of the early female skins designed for Quake evolved out of a strategy of juxtaposition enforced by the limitations of the software. The original version of Quake included only male 3D geometry for designing new skins. Players interested in playing female characters ended up with female skins mapped onto the standard male muscular figure. The juxtaposition between "feminine" attributes (hair, clothing, facial features) and the "male" base figure resulted in what came to be known as "frag queens." The female skinners of a Quake clan known as the Psycho Men Slayers embraced this limitation by mixing and matching elements to create frag queens of ambiguous gender. Not quite male, not quite female, but undoubtedly tough, the newly minted avatars challenged traditional notions of gender, introducing into gamer culture highly transgressive forms of identity.

Blacklash

A game designed by the London-based activist group Mongrel, Blacklash juxtaposes racial politics and arcade nostalgia in a racial re-versioning of the arcade game Tempest. Building upon the game's existing shoot-or-be-shot structure, Blacklash transforms the aliens of the original game into comic book renditions of hooded Ku Klux Klan members and uniformed British police officers. Described by Mongrel as "a wake-up call for young black youth under threat by ignorance and racist fools,"[8] Blacklash references the retro styling of the arcade classic as a means of calling attention to outdated acts of racial prejudice. A conceptual game modification, Blacklash creates resistance between the formal and experiential components of the game. The use of Tempest's rule structure as the basis for Blacklash's political commentary encourages players to make a connection between feelings of nostalgia for a beloved game and patterns of institutional racism, patterns that players experience formally through the play of the game.

Frag Queens

Los Disneys

Los Disneys, a game patch for Marathon Infinity by Jason Huddy, rearticulates the genre of the first-person shooter though the creation of a game level that mimics Disney's Magic Kingdom. The patch transforms the theme park into a post-apocalyptic playground, replete with surveillance camera-toting tourists and clusters of pleasure-seeking children. Los Disneys creates friction between the simulated actions of the game and the external events those actions mirror. Players can shoot any number of oversized Disney characters (including Mickey, Donald, and Goofy) wandering the grounds and are also at liberty to blast their way through lengthy lines of children and their parents waiting for rides. The interactivity and aesthetics of Los Disneys subverts accepted conventions of the first-person shooter by reforming them into critical caricatures. The substitution of aliens with guns by tourists with surveillance cameras, for example, offers a softer, more insidious experience of game attack and conflict. Los Disneys' "play" on the play of violence in games is an articulate and humorous strategy of resistance.

Blacklash

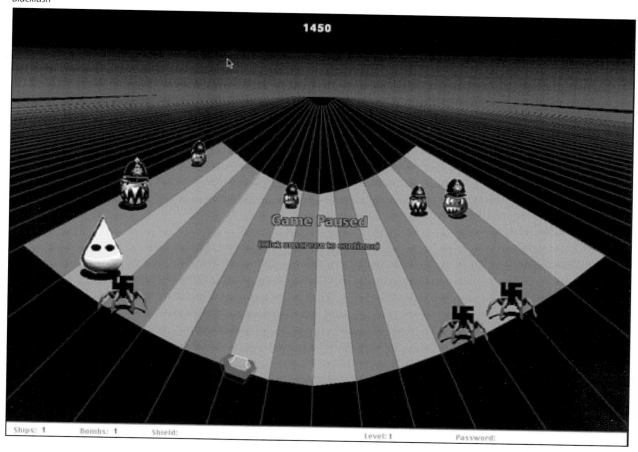

Strategies of Reinvention

Our third strategy of resistance—*reinvention*—overlaps with the categories of alteration and juxtaposition, while offering some distinct critical affordances of its own. Like the two previous strategies, reinvention affects form and context through a change in the game's representational or interactive structures. But strategies of reinvention go deeper, modifying the core structures of a game, reshaping them from the inside out. Of the three categories we outline, strategies of reinvention are perhaps the most radical form of cultural resistance through transformative play.

Universal Square

In artist Uri Tzaig's Universal Square, two Soccer teams (one composed of Jewish Israelis, the other Arab Israelis) were invited to take part in a televised Soccer match. Held in Lod, Israel in 1996, the game was played according to the standard rules of Soccer, except for a simple modification: Tzaig redesigned the game so that it was played with not one ball, but two at the same time.

This elegant design act created resistance in several ways. The game could not be played in a "normal" fashion: players had to invent new forms of interaction that took into account the loss of a single, unifying object around which all of the game activity was centered. Similarly, the behavior of spectators was transformed as well. With the addition of a second ball came the loss of the customary angle of vision (the eyes of all spectators focused on a single ball). Photos of the crowd show them looking in many different directions, rather than the typical, singular focus of a sports spectator audience.[9]

Tzaig's transformation of the game of Soccer is effective for several reasons. His successful dispersion of the crowd's normally unified point of view creates a critical commentary around ideas of cultural spectatorship. Adding a second ball made the game quite difficult to play, forcing a new level of collaborative play among the players from both teams. Tzaig's design reinvention dislocated the centralized power structures in the game, a particularly poignant decision in Tzaig's cultural context. The doubled Soccer game became a representation of the chaotic, decentered, and multi-layered cultural conflicts of the Middle East. At the same time, the redesign offered a model for how such a complex conflict could be contained and resolved through new forms of interaction. In this powerful work, an elegant formal design choice takes on culturally transformative significance.

Counter-Strike
A tremendously popular modification of Half-Life, Counter-Strike, is an excellent example of how the player-as-producer paradigm can reinvent a game. More than just a mod, Counter-Strike transformed the original game on numerous levels, creating a game experience wholly its own.

Unlike many mods that simply tweak the game's look and feel, the design of Counter-Strike shifted the representational plane entirely, stripping away the sci-fi narrative of Half-Life and replacing it with an engaging naturalism. In a review of Counter-Strike, game critic Justin Hall notes, "Counter-Strike exists only in the world prepared for it by the war in Vietnam and *COPS*, where game-players grew up seeing footage of real men with real guns storming into houses and buildings and fields. Television made that veracity attractive. Minh Le [the mod's designer] made it interactive."[10] In casting the game as a terrorist/counter-terrorist conflict, Counter-Strike created rich, team-oriented game play. The resistance between typically fantastic first-person shooters and the real-world setting of Counter-Strike was heightened by the intensified social reality of the game experience.

Counter-Strike's resistant strategies include economic reinvention as well. The mod evolved out of collaboration between small groups of shareware developers and later became a commercial product sold in stores. Winning several major awards at the 2001 Game Developers' Conference, including the Rookie Studio Award and the Game Spotlight Award, Counter-Strike's movement from the noncommercial culture of shareware to the commercial marketplace offers reinvention as a model for independent game development.

Alteration, juxtaposition, and reinvention offer methods to design or redesign games along cultural lines, aggressively engaging symbolic spaces beyond their borders. Whether the approaches taken are more formal in nature, as in the case of SOD, or politically driven, as in Blacklash, the cultural dimensions of these acts call attention to the typically invisible magic circle. When a game enacts cultural resistance, the seamless transition between the space *inside* and *outside* the game is interrupted; players are made aware of aspects of the game which usually pass unnoticed. Allowing players to experience this kind of transformative play increases options for play: when critical consciousness is enriched, play too becomes richer.

Act | All players state your answers aloud. SPORK: Name something you were afraid of when you were a kid. FOON: Name something you're afraid of now.

Write | SPORK: Write what you did on your first date. FOON: Write what you did on your most recent date.

Additional Lines of Resistance

At the very beginning of his book *Homo Ludens,* philosopher and historian Johann Huizinga makes the profound assertion that, "In play there is always something 'at play.'"[11] Games always already play, an activity that explores and expands structures, stretching and re-forming them. In this sense, games are particularly well-suited for modification by players, for the creation of friction between fixed structures and mobile interventions. The concept of games as cultural resistance grows naturally out of what we already know about play.

Because a game by its very nature has room for the movement of free play, it is always possible for players to drive a wedge into the system, bending and transforming it into a new shape. In *Games as Systems of Uncertainty* and *Breaking the Rules,* we looked at how children subvert the ritual of counting-out through a number of subtle and devious strategies, from adding an extra "eenie-meenie-minee-moe" to switching places in the counting-out circle in order to avoid becoming "It." This kind of game "modification" is certainly different from the examples discussed in this schema, yet there are important similarities. In all cases, players "play" with the structure of the game itself. They are creating meaning by recognizing Huizinga's insight: in play, there is always something *at play*.

We have commented in several chapters on the importance of players and fans to a game's larger cultural identity. Fans play an important role in maintaining the game and keeping it alive in culture, but they can also take on roles of resistance as well. Our next example offers a scenario where two groups of players, acting within and without the magic circle, bend the "shape" of the game system in two competing ways.

Friction on the Playground

The sidebar text on this page and the next is excerpted from sissyfightnews.com, a fan site devoted to the game SiSSYFiGHT 2000. The text is a manifesto against cheating; it details how to identify and combat rule-breaking in the game, and is directed toward resisting those who would bend the system too far out

of shape by conspiring to cheat. There are competing ideologies in the game (resist the game through cheating; resist cheating by policing the cheaters) and the manifesto therefore represents an act of double-resistance. On one hand, cheating exists as a form of friction against the authority of the game, resisting the public chat that is a key game play element. On the other hand, there is resistance to this resistance, a vigilante group working to raise the consciousness of the community and eliminate cheating. These double-movements become part of the larger culture of the game.

from sissyfightnews.com

How do you know a cheater when you see one? Let's use a working definition. You can identify cheaters as:

> Two or more allied characters who perform extremely coordinated attacks in succession, with little or no communication within the SiSSYFiGHT word bubbles.

Let's take this apart piece by piece, to clarify. The important thing to remember is that *all* of these elements *together* must be present to identify cheaters—otherwise, you might just be dealing with a perfectly legit team.

Two or more allied characters: The first sign of cheaters is that they never attack each other. Usually cheaters will work in pairs, although there are some who actually try to coordinate more. *Please remember* that there's nothing wrong with having allies or teams alone! One of the main points of the game is to build up alliances.

Who perform extremely coordinated attacks: Coordinated attacks are a result of good strategy and communication. In a two-person team, these combination moves can be mapped out like this:

If Character X performs this:	Then Character Y performs this:
tease	tease
grab	scratch *or* lick lolly
tattle	cower *or* lick lolly
scratch	scratch

Again, *please remember* that if any two players perform these actions, that does not necessarily make them cheaters…yet. Up to this point, we're still talking about fair gaming and good strategy.

In succession: This is the point where we *start* to draw the line between honest players and cheaters. If you see two characters performing several coordinated attacks in a row, something is up.

With little or no communication within the SiSSYFiGHT word bubbles: This is the kicker, right here. The big giveaway to pairs or groups of cheaters is that they *never communicate their moves* in the SiSSYFiGHT window. This provides them with a distinct and unfair advantage over honest players, because there are no signals (either direct or indirect) for other players to attempt to read. Note, sometimes cheaters will actually talk smack in their word balloons, but they will never actually give any indication to each other as to what their next moves will be.

There are two ways to cheat in SiSSYFiGHT: external communication and multiple sessions.

Cheaters who use external communication basically resort to some form of telegraphing their moves to each other by any means *outside* of the SiSSYFiGHT window itself. This most often takes its form in either AOL Instant Messaging or ICQ, but may also include phone conversation or two people sissyfighting at adjacent workstations in a computer lab. Cheaters who use this method are so insecure in their strategic impotence, they would rather subvert the integrity of the game than use what few brain cells they have left. If you're ever beaten by one of these external communicators, you can rest assured that in real life, they're probably overweight drooling idiots who still live with their parents and can't actually make any *real* friends.

Cheaters who use multiple sessions are even sadder creatures on the social pecking order. This kind of cheater is a *single person* who runs SiSSYFiGHT from one workstation in two or more separate browsers. These people are so socially inept that the mere thought of actually communicating and working with someone else sends them into panicked spasms. They've never kissed anyone, and spend a lot of time breaking into password-protected porn sites. Rest assured that if you're ever beaten by someone coordinated enough to run multiple sessions, they've probably also developed the enviable talent of typing one-handed. (Oh, NOW you get it.)

Breaking the Rules was a RULES schema—a formal way of understanding a game. What is rule-breaking in the context of CULTURE, particularly in a schema on cultural resistance? The broken rules identified in the SiSSYFiGHT manifesto are implicit rules, the violation of which most often represents unsportsmanlike conduct. But the emotional force with which this manifesto was written implies that something deeper is at work. Indeed, because of complaints about cheating, the game's developer Word.com, posted a "code of ethics" on the game website which explicitly defined and banned cheating. As a result, the ability to chat in private was recategorized as a true rule infraction: private chat became an operational rule breach. So-called cheaters bending the rules led to this structural transformation, a process in which cheating players, vigilante players, and game designers all took part.

In the complex case of the SiSSYFiGHT cheating manifesto, factors both internal and external to the game drove resistance. The alleged cheating represents a form of resistance that seeks to undermine the experience of play in undesirable ways, transgressing the magic circle from within. When this violation came to the attention of a few astute and passionate players, a strategy of retaliation was formalized, an act of resistance that came from outside the magic circle. The resulting solution is both elegant and inspiring: as a cultural artifact created and disseminated by players of the game, the manifesto represents a wonderful example of player-production; as a strategy of resistance, it demonstrates that meaningful play can be brought into the game from contexts beyond its permeable edges. And in this instance, the story had a happy ending: the designers intervened, reaching the entire community of players through the game's official website, revising the rules of the game and raising the consciousness of the player community as a whole.

Write | SPORK: Draw something you'd see at a circus. FOON: Draw something you'd see at a rodeo. *Sneak acts like a Spork.

Write | **SPORK:** Draw something you'd find at a school. **FOON:** Draw something you'd find in a back yard.

Resist!

The resistant strategies taken by independent game designers such as the Counter-Strike team, dedicated players such as the Sissyfightnews crew, and game artists such as Uri Tzaig suggest how games can be designed or redesigned from a cultural perspective to support transformative play. Whether the approaches taken are formal, aesthetic, or politically inspired, the cultural dimensions of these acts of resistance shape ideology and interaction. If game designers were to embrace strategies of resistance more often, the potential for games to affect culture in significant ways would surely increase.

Remember: games intrinsically support and encourage the movement of free play. It is always possible for players to throw a monkey wrench into the system, bending it into a new shape. Game designers must consider how this process can be enhanced or interrupted, modified or transformed, either by players or by the design of the game itself. The Sissyfightnews manifesto, for instance, turned the practice of resistance into a cautionary tale, tightening the borders of the magic circle just enough to remind players that the game, too, could bite back.

Games clearly derive meaning from the contexts within which they are played. Consideration of these contexts enables game designers to see potential lines of cultural engagement. The open dissemination of the DOOM source code, for example, was visionary in its recognition of a hacker mentality already present in communities of gamers. Given the right tools, players will transgress the magic circle in pursuit of alternate forms of expression. These transgressions can shape and reshape the game so that the values of the "real" world are made explicit within the artificiality of the game, values that might be reinforced, questioned, inverted, or subverted through play.

What if game designers considered the possibility of working with this natural desire of players to bend the shape of the game? In massively multiplayer games such as EverQuest or Ultima Online, vast resources are spent trying to root out and punish cheating. But other scenarios are possible. What if players were allowed to police each other, as a form of game play? Or what if players were encouraged to cheat? Or given the source code and let loose in the field of play? Clearly we would have a very different kind of game, perhaps a game that would radically reinvent the potential for culturally transformative play. The possibilities are out there. But until you begin to resist the conventions of game design, we will never find out just how fun they are to play. Fight the establishment! Down with the old rules! Vive la resistance!

Further Reading

Cracking the Maze: Game Plug-ins and Patches as Hacker Art, Anne-Marie Schleiner, curator

<http://switch.sjsu.edu/CrackingtheMaze/>

In 1999, Anne-Marie Schleiner curated an online exhibition of game patches, mods, and game plug-ins. Most of the game modifications were produced by artists, and many had socio-political agendas. The online archive has visual examples of a range of artist-produced patches, downloads of the patches, and several good introductory essays on issues of cultural representation in games and the practice of tactical media intervention.

Game Girl Advance, <www.gamegirladvance.com>

The Game Girl Advance website is a journalistic website addressing the culture of digital games. Resisting content of standard commercial game sites, Game Girl Advance features short essays on topics such as the gender politics of gaming conferences or how games personally impact the lives of players. Although there are many grassroots alternative game news sites on the web, Game Girl Advance distinguishes itself with smart writing that is both culturally critical and industry-savvy.

Subculture: The Meaning of Style, by Dick Hebdige

Hebdige investigates subcultures as systems of meaning, particularly subcultures like Punk and the Teddy Boys, that resist larger cultural institutions. These systems, like games, create their own boundaries within which forms, behaviors, and actions gain meaning separate from, but connected to the real world. He explores style as a system of communication, a stylized, symbolic, and interactive language borne from the "rules" of the system. Although Hebdige is speaking from a Marxist, structuralist, and semiotic perspective, his approach is quite applicable to the study of games.

> *Recommended:*
> Introduction: Subculture and Style
> Chapter 1: From Culture to Hegemony
> Chapter 7: Style as Intentional Communication
> Chapter 8: Style as Homology

Textual Poachers: Television Fans and Participatory Culture, by Henry Jenkins *(see page 553)*

> *Recommended:*
> Chapter 5: Scribbling in the Margins
> Chapter 7: "Layers of Meaning": Fan Music Videos and the Poetics of Poaching

Notes

1. Greil Marcus, *Lipstick Traces: A Secret History of the Twentieth Century* (Cambridge: Harvard University Press, 1989), p. 3.

2. "Brave New Worlds: A Special Issue on Video Games," *Feed Magazine.*

3. Erkki Huhtamo, "Game Patch: the Son of Scratch?" In *Cracking the Maze,* curated by Anne-Marie Schleiner. July 16, 1999. <switch.sjsu.edu/CrackingtheMaze>.

4. Ibid.

5. Anne-Marie Schleiner, "Game Plug-ins and Patches as Hacker Art." *Cracking the Maze.* July 16, 1999. <switch.sjsu.edu/CrackingtheMaze>.

6. Ibid.

7. Ibid.

8. Ibid.

9. Janet Abrams, "Other Victories." In *If/Then,* edited by Janet Abrams. (Amsterdam: Netherlands Design Institute, 1999), p. 245.

10. "Brave New Worlds: A Special Issue on Video Games," *Feed Magazine.*

11. Johann Huizinga, *Homo Ludens: A Study of the Play Element in Culture* (Boston: Beacon Press, 1955), p. 1.

Act | **ALL PLAYERS:** Choose one player and show him or her a *Write* card of your choice.

Games as Cultural Resistance
SUMMARY

- *Games as Cultural Resistance* explores the tension between games and their cultural contexts. The focus of the schema is exclusively on culturally transformative play.

- Resistance is the **friction** that occurs when two phenomena come into conflictual contact. Framed as resistance, the free movement of play has intrinsic friction with the systems of rules that seek to contain it. Through this process of resistance, the normally invisible edges of the magic circle become visible.

- A **DIY** or Do-It-Yourself approach to cultural resistance appears in **modifications,** designed strategies of resistance in a game. Game modifications or *mods* can be "official" utilitarian changes enacted by game designers, or "unofficial" projects created and distributed by players.

- Game modifications fall into three overlapping categories: alteration, juxtaposition, and reinvention.

  - **Alterations** change the representational or interactive structures of a game. *Examples: SOD, Sailor Moon Wad, SimCopter Hack*

  - **Juxtapositions** place unlikely elements together in the same game space. *Examples: Frag Queens, Blacklash, Los Disneys*

  - **Reinventions** more radically redesign the structure of a game. *Examples: Universal Square, Counter-Strike*

- Resistance flows naturally from the intrinsic qualities of games. The free play of a game already involves the friction of movement within a rigid structure. For this reason, games are rich with possibilities for players or designers to intervene with strategies of resistance.

GAMES AS CULTURAL ENVIRONMENT

*THIS IS NOT A GAME—**A.I.: Artificial Intelligence** movie trailer*

blurring of boundaries
etiquette
ethos
convention
context
artificial status

33

Raise the Red Flag

A game is a system in which players engage in an artificial conflict, defined by rules, that results in a quantifiable outcome.

With that single sentence, many, many pages ago, we offered a definiton of games. Since then, we have proceeded on the assumption that this formulation does, in fact, accurately describe what games are and how they operate. However, our final schema, *Games as Cultural Environment,* may force us to re-evaluate our definition.

The definition is rooted in the formal properties of games. In general, during our long march across the varied territory of game design schemas, it has served us well. But in the course of exploring games within a cultural context, one element of the definition doesn't seem to do justice to the complexities of the phenomenon. It is not the idea that games are systems, nor that they have rules and outcomes, nor that through games players engage in a conflict. The element of the definition that seems increasingly suspect is the idea that games are *artificial,* that they are removed from ordinary life.

How are games artificial? Even though we frame games as open culture systems, they remain systems with defined elements and attributes. The way that games operate as systems implies some kind of separation from the rest of culture. The meanings that games produce, while intertwined with larger cultural meanings, still acquire their distinct identity as game meanings because they emerge out of the system of relations made possible by the game itself. This system of relations is not something that naturally occurs out in the world. If games weren't *artificial* in some way, they wouldn't be *designed.* Instead, they would be some kind of "natural" phenomena bopping about the cultural ether.

But the wider our cultural frame grows in defining games as culture, the more their artificiality begins to unravel. As culture, games are open systems. They are not isolated from their environment, but are intrinsically part of it, participating in the ebb and flow of ideas and values that make up a larger cultural set-

ting. Framed contextually, the magic circle is not an impermeable curtain but is instead a border that can be crossed. Cultural elements from outside the circle enter in and have an impact on the game; simultaneously, cultural meanings ripple outward from the game to interact with numerous cultural contexts. Given all of this play at and across the border, given the fact that games are not separate from but are part of culture, what would happen if we questioned the artificiality of games? What if a schema specifically sought to frame games as systems completely synchronous with their surroundings?

Introducing Cultural Environment

This is the premise of *Games as Cultural Environment,* a chapter engaged with the question of the "reality" of games, a schema that interrogates the relationship between the artificial world of games and the "real life" contexts that they intersect. Rather than calling attention to the borders of the magic circle, as we did in earlier **CULTURE** schemas, here we look at games in which the boundary is so completely erased that it is difficult to distinguish the space of play from ordinary life. These kinds of games have a number of curious characteristics. They create a heightened overlap between the artificial space of the game and the physical spaces and lifestyles of their players. They blur the distinction between players and non-players, sometimes involuntarily roping in unsuspecting participants. Perhaps most importantly, these sorts of games raise fundamental questions about the artificiality of games and their relationship to real life.

The most familiar examples of games that bleed over into their cultural environment are designs such as Assassin (also known as Killer), made popular on college campuses in the 1970s and 1980s, a game in which players stalked, hunted, and evaded each other with dart guns over days or weeks of real time. Game play took place not in a special, isolated game space, but in and among the activities of daily life. Recent digital games have adopted similar design strategies, such as Majestic, a large-scale experimental game by Electronic Arts that took place through fictitious web sites, faxes, and telephone voicemail. When a player's phone rang in the middle of the night it might be a call from the pizza delivery service—or from a character in the game whispering a secret code. Other games, such as the cell phone game Botfighters, tracks the physical location of players at all times and lets them challenge one another to unexpected duels. This chapter will focus on these kinds of games: play activities that overtly become part of their cultural environment. The idea that a game can become so co-extensive with its context that it blurs the borders that facilitate its own artificiality is a rarely taken but powerful approach to game design. And as we will see, it has important implications for the design of all games.

Considering games as cultural environments raises a number of questions. How does the play of a game change when the difference between the "inside" and the "outside" of the game is ambiguous? How permeable is the boundary between the real world and the artificial world of the game? Are only certain games capable of blurring these boundaries, or does it happen to some extent in all games? To answer these questions, we revisit many of the fundamental elements of games. More so than in any other schema, we make generous use of terms and concepts introduced in chapters leading up to this one. Part of the reason for doing so is that these concepts genuinely inform an analysis of games as cultural environments. However, our hidden agenda is to use these game analyses as an informal review of material covered previously. The review is not meant to be comprehensive, but it does demonstrate how a framework of related ideas, connected through the concept of meaningful play, is necessary for a truly sophisticated and integrated understanding of game design.

Back to Basics

A game creates a special place of play. Following Huizinga, these spaces define the game's *magic circle,* a "temporary world within the ordinary world, dedicated to the performance of an act apart."[1] It is within the magic circle that the authority

of the rules hold sway. If you are visiting a casino equipment store, you might give a Roulette wheel a test spin to see if it is in working order, but you would neither gain nor lose money as a result of the spin. On the other hand, if you are playing a game of Roulette and your chips are on the table, the outcome of the spin will have a real impact on the quantity of your betting chips. Only when a player has entered into the magic circle of a game do game rules imbue game actions with meaning and consequence.

The rules of a game define its formal essence. Each game is composed of three kinds of rules: constitutive, operational, and implicit. *Constitutive rules* are the logical, mathematical structures that gird the formal system of a game. *Operational rules* are the practical "rules of play" that direct player action. *Implicit rules* are the "unwritten rules" of play that players bring to every game, rules that are usually unstated in the official "rules of play," making implicit rules something that players have to infer or intuit.

Implicit rules arise via cultural custom, tradition, and player experience. They directly link the formal and cultural aspects of a game, creating a bridge between the forms of authority that exist inside and outside of a game's space of play. The operation of implicit rules is usually invisible and incredibly subtle. Stephen Sniderman, in his essay "Unwritten Rules," looks closely at what players must know and do in order to play even the simplest game. Among other requirements, they must:

> Consciously understand and follow the *etiquette* of the game—i.e., the unwritten but sometimes stated traditions associated with the game that do not necessarily affect the play itself (e.g., appropriateness of talking, gloating, taunting, celebrating, stalling, replaying a point, giving advice to your opponent or teammates, letting players take back moves, etc.).

> Intuitively understand and follow the *ethos* of that particular game—i.e., the unwritten and rarely expressed assumptions about how to interpret and enforce the "written" rules (e.g., palming in

basketball; the strike zone in American and National leagues; the footfault in tennis).

Intuitively understand and follow the *conventions* of playing any game according to the culture of the participants—i.e., the unwritten and generally unstatable customs related to playing, competing, winning/losing, etc. (e.g. taking the game with the appropriate seriousness, knowing what takes priority over winning and over playing, not faking injury or personal obligation to avoid losing; playing "hard" regardless of the score; not claiming that previous points didn't "count").

Intuitively understand and respond to the "real-life" *context* in which the game is being played—i.e. the social, cultural, economic, political, and moral consequences of the result (e.g., whether someone's livelihood or self-esteem depends on the outcome).[2]

A player's intuitive understanding of implicit rules is strikingly sophisticated. The constitutive and operational rules of a game might define its formal essence, but etiquette, ethos, convention, and context are equally important in facilitating a game's play. These four categories are forms of cultural knowledge that permit the magic circle to come into being. Without them, players might be able to understand and even follow rules, but the social frameworks allowing the artificial conflict of a game to take place would break down. If you were invited to join in a game but were concerned that your opponent might take the game too seriously and injure you, or take advantage of superior knowledge of the rules, or just give up in the middle if he or she was losing, it is highly unlikely that you would choose to play at all. The mechanisms that guide the operation of implicit rules are a crucial part of any game's play. Implicit rules take place simultaneously on the level of rules and on the level of culture, linking these two disparate dimensions of games in a distinctly powerful way.

From a player's point of view, acceptance of the implicit rules (as well as the operational rules) of a game is only made possible

by the *lusory attitude*. A concept borrowed from philosopher Bernard Suits, the lusory attitude is the state of mind whereby game players consciously take on the challenges and obstacles of a game in order to experience the play of the game itself. Accepting the artificial authority of the magic circle, submitting behavior to the constraints of rules in order to experience the free movement of play, is a paradoxical state of mind. This state of mind is manifest in the lusory attitude.

In previous chapters, we considered the lusory attitude primarily in relationship to the formal rules of a game. But taking on the lusory attitude doesn't just mean accepting the limitations of the operational rules. It also entails following implicit rules. Playing a game means submitting to the authority of the magic circle, which includes the cultural conventions expressed through implicit rules. In this sense, the magic circle of a game extends beyond any individual game to include culture as a whole. To play a game, any game, is not just to play within the rules of that particular game, but within the rules of a larger cultural context that define what it means to play at all.

Consider the case of Japanese Sumo wrestling. As the national sport of Japan, Sumo wrestling is more than mere sport; it is seen as the epitome of Japanese honor and ethos. The sport has spiritual ties to Shinto, the Japanese religion, and is linked to politics as well. According to Brian Sutton-Smith, Japanese emperors over the centuries have sometimes been selected to rule through a Sumo contest.[3] To take part in a Sumo competition requires much more than simply adhering to the formal rules of the game. Engaging with the play of Sumo wrestling only truly occurs when a player takes on the etiquette, ethos, context, and conventions of the game as well.

Shall We Play a Game?

Upon first glance it might seem that only highly unconventional games like Assassin, Majestic, and Botfighters genuinely blur the boundaries of the magic circle. However, implicit rules, the lusory attitude, and the magic circle operate in such a way

Act | SPORK: Stick out your tongue. FOON: Put your thumbs in your ears and waggle your fingers.

that we can consider any game, at least in part, as a cultural environment. By the end of this schema we will return to this important proposition. Before doing so, however, we will explore these concepts through particular examples, by looking at games designed to explicitly blur the boundaries of the magic circle.

Our first example focuses on a game reportedly designed and operated by Microsoft as a viral marketing campaign for the film *A.I.: Artificial Intelligence*. The web-based game, known by its players informally as "The Beast," "The A.I. Game," or just "A.I.," had participants from all over the world collaboratively deciphering cryptic puzzles and clues across a range of media. The game began with an enigmatic credit at the end of the preview trailer for the film. Savvy viewers picked up on a mysterious listing for "Jeanine Salla, Sentient Machine Therapist" and a set of mysterious symbols. When viewers (now players) entered the name "Jeanine Salla" into an Internet search engine, they began a Wonderland-style journey through a series of linked websites. The sites blended real-world information and information from the fictive world of A.I.'s backstory, which concerned a dramatic struggle between humans and robots capable of human emotion.

Over the course of several months leading up to the film's premiere, thousands of players took part in the game. Many expressed profound reactions to the distortion of the boundaries between game, film, life, and reality. As one player wrote in an essay on cloudmakers.org, the most active community site developed by players of the game, "Here we are, every one of us excited at blurring the lines between story and reality. The game promises to become not just entertainment, but our lives. But where in the story is there room for the too-mundane matters of our actual lives that must be attended?"[4] While players were intrigued by and often obsessed with the game, there was a clear sense of uneasiness about the truth of what was actually going on. The ambiguity surrounding the game's

status (was it a game, a puzzle, a story, an evil marketing ploy?) made the experience of play oddly compelling. Another player noted,

> On the morning of the premiere, we'll know the plot, subplot, conflict, climax and dialogue down to the last poignant pause. Surely the PMs [Puppet Masters, the game's developers] know this; they also know that most of us will go anyway, to experience it for ourselves. So something undiscovered still remains—the heart of this (and whatever that implies).[5]

Puzzles in the game had players reading *Göedel, Escher, Bach*, translating from German, Japanese, and an obscure language called Kannada, decrypting Morse and Enigma code, and performing a range of operations on sound and image files downloaded and swapped between players.[6] Sometimes players received actual phone calls from unnamed parties to attend real-world events. At one "anti-robot" rally, for example, attendees solved puzzles and phoned the answers to players at rallies being held simultaneously in other cities. At every moment, A.I. played with the boundaries between the game's magic circle and the cultural spaces outside of it. The play experience of most games can be framed as a closed system, in which the play of the game is in some respects bounded by the magic circle. But because the space of play in A.I. was ambiguous, it operated as an open system, defying implicit assumptions about the scope of the space of possibility. As a result, A.I. mixed freely with its environment at a very deep level. Players were clearly affected by the play such an approach afforded.

Although there is much to be said about this game from a marketing perspective, our interest lies elsewhere—in how its play became meaningful, even as it erased and redefined traditional boundaries separating fact from fiction. From a game design perspective, what elements of the game contributed to its status as real-world interloper? Listed next are some of A.I.'s salient design features, incorporating commentary from player Daragh Sankey's online analysis of the game.[7]

Web-based

Although the format of web-based games is not new, A.I. made wonderful use of the web's unique properties. The story was built from an amalgamation of distributed sites. A core mechanic of the game play involved searching and surfing the web, making the Internet fundamental to the game's structure.

Fictional game content disguised as reality

All of the information contained in the numerous sites created for the game was fabricated. There were not, however, any pages that announced, "This is a work of fiction." In fact, many of the websites could easily have been misconstrued as real, such as www.rational-hatter.com. This representational strategy helped reinforce the illusion that the game was part of the real world, rather than part of an artificial game world.

Decentralized content

Unlike most web-based games, A.I. had no single gateway or homepage. Content was spread across many websites, allowing for numerous points of entry. However, the distributed complexity of the game demanded a need for a central information hub. As an emergent effect of player behavior, the website www.cloudmakers.org was quickly adopted as the game's primary player-created portal.

Game events occurred outside the web

Although the bulk of the game was located on the web, the most dramatic events seemed to occur offline. Email, faxes, and phones all played a part in the game. For example, the *A.I.* trailer included an encoded phone number, which when called, played a mysterious voice message from "mother." Players were able to enter characters' passwords into fictional voicemail accounts and uncover new information. Game associated A.I.s even called players at home. Most dramatic, however, were three real-life "rallies" held by the "Anti-Robot Militia" (www.unite-and-resist.org) in New York, Chicago, and Los Angeles. Players were given

a date and address, and attended what turned out to be clever theatre pieces. The rallies included puzzles that required real-time collaboration between players at the events and those at home in front of their computers.

Episodic content

Game content was updated weekly, as elements were added, modified, and taken away. Emails were sent out to players; increasingly, sites attached to the game were "hacked" by rampant A.I.s. With its complex, ongoing narrative, the disadvantage of A.I.'s episodic release was that players who joined the game later had a hard time catching up. The advantage was a heightened sense of urgency, because the game couldn't ever be put on pause. As a narrative structure, the episodic release was a natural fit for a web-based game, because most real sites do change over time. Additionally, because the game led chronologically to the launch of the film, it made sense that it built to a single climax.

Distributed problem-solving

Many of the puzzles in the game were extremely difficult to solve (some of them remain unsolved today). For example, messages were hidden in the html source code of certain web pages. Anyone could uncover this information, but since the game had so many websites, solitary players could not possibly get it all. It is safe to say that an isolated individual could never have played the entire game from start to finish. Thus, fan sites served as a meeting ground for game players, who collaborated by sharing new developments and puzzle answers, organizing and sharing problem-solving tasks. This was a bold design decision, because in designing a game it is generally better to err on the side of simplicity and ease rather than complexity. However, with A.I. the risk paid off—the design encouraged players to interact socially, and the collaborative play heightened the satisfaction each time a puzzle was solved.

Write | SPORK: Write the name of a movie that makes you sad. FOON: Write the name of a movie that makes you laugh. *Sneak acts like a Spork.

Interaction between authors and players

Players presumed from the moment the game began that there was a set story arc to the game, which would end in the release of the film. The weekly updates generally involved puzzles that players had to solve before they could access new story content. Many players speculated that because the size and effectiveness of the groups solving the puzzles was an unpredictable variable, the design of new puzzles by the authors of the game was based on past player performance. For example, if a puzzle turned out to be much too hard for the players, the authors were forced to find an alternative means to provide the story update that the solution to the unsolved puzzle would have granted. If the authors did not seek out alternate forms of dissemination, there was a risk of the story never being completed.

Line blurred between players and game designers

It is worth noting that the game's creators deliberately blurred the lines between themselves and the players. In a few cases, game pages linked to fan pages without breaking the dissimulation. Jeanine Salla's essay on "Multiperson Social Problem-Solving Arrays Considered as a Form of 'Artificial Intelligence'" linked to the cloudmakers page (www.cloudmakers.org); the Center for Robotic Freedom (www.inourimage.org) urged players to help fight for A.I. rights by visiting the spherewatch page (www.spherewatch.net), another fan site. In fact, one player noted that the easiest way for game authors to control the story delivery would have been for them to surreptitiously join the ranks of the fans, posting solutions to puzzles when they saw that the real players were having trouble.

Each of these design decisions contributed in distinct ways to blur the boundaries between the space of the game and everyday life. All of the elements we listed share one thing in common: careful attention to the creation of meaningful play. The web-based aspect of the game, for example, took good advantage of the medium. Players were rewarded for careful web searches and source code sleuthing with meaningful outcomes. Similarly, the social play of the game, from the collaborative puzzles to the real-world gatherings, were also forms of meaningful play engendered by specific game design choices. Even the fine line separating fact from fiction—a line made all the more porous by the game's distributed, improvisational format—was only possible through successful design. Each of these game elements—use of the web, collaborative social play, fiction disguised as fact—take advantage of the game as a cultural environment, intentionally blurring the boundaries of the magic circle. The many play dimensions of A.I., from its play with pleasure to its social and narrative play, all intentionally "play" with the border between the game and the surrounding world that it infiltrates, infests, and inhabits.

A.I. takes the idea of game as cultural environment to extremes. But in one sense, all game experiences involve playing with the distinction between the game world and the rest of the world. Gregory Bateson's concept of *metacommunication,* first introduced in ***Games as the Play of Meaning,*** reminds us that to play a game is not an act of naïve immersion, but an act of constant communication about the act of play itself. A dog that nips another dog signifies a bite through its action, but also communicates the idea that the bite is not a real bite; the dog is not actually attacking, but is instead just playing.

All games engender this quality of double-consciousness, but A.I. took it to new heights. Part of the brilliance of the game's design is that it incorporated metacommunication itself as a form of play. By blurring the boundaries of the magic circle as a key design choice, it made new forms of boundary-crossing possible, intensifying the pleasure of metacommunication. As players moved through the designed structures of the game, at every moment tensions between belief and skepticism, between playing a game and playing real life, moved the game forward and created compelling forms of play.

The Invisible Playground

From the electronically mediated spaces of A.I. we turn to another game that emphasizes the play of its cultural environment: the LARP, or live-action role-playing game. LARPs also blur the boundaries between the inside and outside of a game, but do so through very different means. Live-Action Role-Playing Games are direct descendents of tabletop role-playing games such as Dungeons & Dragons. As in tabletop RPGs, LARP players take on the persona of fictional characters, defined through formal game statistics as well as through narrative backstory and an invented personality.

Live-Action Role-Playing Games, however, do not take place around a table. Instead, LARPs occur in real physical spaces, as players walk about and interact with each other, dramatically acting out their characters' actions in real-time. Although LARPs do have Game Masters that plan and referee the sessions, as well as rules that handle combat and other complex player actions, most LARP activity consists of social interaction, as players converse "in character" to make plans, pursue narrative threads, and scheme against each other. Live-Action Role-Playing Games can take place in outdoor or indoor settings, in private or public spaces. The location in which the LARP takes place, as well as the dress and interaction of the players, depends largely on the narrative setting of the LARP. A Medieval-themed LARP might occur in a wilderness environment or a Renaissance Fair. A futuristic LARP might take place in a series of convention hall rooms or in the house of one of the players.

Nick Fortugno, a game designer and LARP Game Master, ran a LARP for many years in New York City based on Vampire: The Masquerade. His game, set in present day NYC, met regularly in public spaces that ranged from Washington Square Park to Grand Central Station. The players all took the role of vampires, ancient and powerful creatures that live secretly among humans. In typical Vampire: The Masquerade games, emphasis is not on physical confrontation or on players hunting humans for blood. Instead, the interest of the game comes from baroque power struggles waged between the aristocratic vampire clans. Fortugno's LARP, titled Seasons of Darkness, was designed along these lines, and was a game of dense social politics and intricate storytelling. Seasons of Darkness successfully engaged with its cultural environment in a variety of ways.

Public Spaces

Although many LARPs take place exclusively in isolated settings, most Seasons of Darkness sessions were held in public urban spaces. Through this design decision, Fortugno (and Tami Meyers, the game's administrator) created a game that intrinsically blurred the boundaries of the magic circle. In most games, even real-world physical games, the play takes place in a field, on a court, or someplace set aside specifically for the game. Seasons of Darkness did not use an artificially designed space, but instead appropriated existing ones. The players integrated their "found" context into the game play in many ways. A balcony overlooking the World Trade Center's Winter Garden, for example, might be used to heighten dramatic effect for a player delivering a speech to other players below; the same balcony might also be used strategically, as a vantage point for spying.

The game-space of Seasons of Darkness was congruent not just with the material setting but also with the cultural environment of New York City. Media, signage, and unknowing passersby were all fodder for the game. A character on the run might duck into a throng of commuters, camouflaging herself among the passing crowds in an attempt to evade her pursuers. Or two players might be inspired by a clothing store window display to have a conversation about current fads in "human" culture. This use of public space as the space of the game greatly increased options for narrative play. As we first introduced in *Interactivity,* a game's *space of possibility* is the event-space of all possible game actions that might occur in the course of play. The space of possibility even in a closed magic circle can be quite large. But chance events and a constant flow of people and culture through a session of Seasons of Darkness made the game's space of possibility truly infinite. The game was played nowhere and everywhere at once, as players continually improvised and invented new ways to engage with their environment.

Real-World Interaction

As with most LARPs, Seasons of Darkness players played their game by moving, speaking, and gesturing "in character." In contrast to most games, in which game actions are stylized, artificial gestures (move a plastic token to a new space on the board when it is your turn; pass the ball to certain players in certain ways), Seasons of Darkness players made use of naturalized behaviors. In Freeze Tag, touching another player on the arm has formal ramifications for play. But in a LARP, touching another player on the arm usually has the same communicative meaning it does in everyday life: perhaps it is a gesture of empathy, or a silent request for the recipient to stop speaking. This is a significant departure from more typical games. The blurring and erasure of the magic circle takes place not only in terms of the game's setting, but also on the level of the player's interactions. The core mechanics of a game are basic game actions or set of actions that players repeat over and over as they play. In the case of Seasons of Darkness, the game's *core mechanics* overlapped with the behaviors of everyday life. Gestures, speech, dramatic skills: these tools for social interaction were part of the cultural environment each player brought to the game. Although social communication occurs in most games, in Seasons of Darkness these activities were themselves core game actions.

This is not to say that the game didn't have its own set of stylized play actions; it certainly did. Combat and the use of supernatural powers required stylized behavior, which Fortungno designed as part of the game. It might be the case, for example, that a tap on the arm did not denote an innocent communicative speech-gesture, but instead sig-

naled the use of a magical action. In Seasons of Darkness, a player that had used a special power to turn invisible crossed his or her arms. This gesture signified invisibility, and other players had to act as if the invisible player was not present.

There is an important distinction to make here. Although it is true that a LARP blurs the border of the magic circle, the boundary is nowhere close to being completely eradicated. Despite its lamination with the actions and events of daily life, the game remains capable of generating its own meanings. The meaning of the crossed-arm gesture is artificial, *not* a part of our everyday lexicon of interaction. Yet this is entirely consistent with what we already know about games. As we discussed in **Games as the Play of Simulation,** the metacommunicative aspect of player consciousness creates what folklorist Gary Allen Fine calls "layers of meaning" in which game character, game player, and real-world context exist together within a web of interconnected cognitive frameworks.

Emergent Storytelling

Whereas some LARPs rely on pregenerated storylines and tightly scripted events, the narrative of Seasons of Darkness was a largely *emergent system.* Fortugno encouraged *bottom-up* instead of *top-down* narratives: many of the most significant story events were *player-produced:* the result of characters scheming and plotting against one another. Each session was a complex system, with the characters bumping into each other like narrative particles. Every interaction between characters built on previous ones, adding up to larger patterns of narrative behavior. In managing these patterns from session to session, Fortugno had to balance *emergent* with *embedded* narrative elements. The unexpected, emergent qualities of the game kept it moving in lively, unpredictable directions. But over the course of the years that the game was played, Fortugno also developed elaborately embedded plots that were only fully realized during the game's final climax.

Emergence takes place within a context, the *environment* of the system. In Seasons of Darkness, narrative contexts were established out of the complex backstory of the game, which was derived from a host of sources: vampire lore and legend; the mythos of the published game rules; a fictional history of NYC vampires that Fortugno had written; established events of previous game sessions; consistent character personalities and their allegiances and enmities; and the public setting and other elements of the cultural environment. Any conversation or interaction between characters took place within a rich narrative context brimming with story potential.

Meta-Narratives

Playing a game in a public space has its challenges, especially when the players are pretending to be vampires. Large groups of players, milling about for hours late at night, could attract unwanted attention from police and security guards. Part of the play of the game included negotiating the friction between the real-world settings and the unusual way that players inhabited them. But remarkably enough, this very negotiation was a site of meaningful play.

In the narrative universe of the game, vampires live in secret, pretending to be human (thus the "masquerade" of Vampire: The Masquerade). The most severe crime a vampire can commit is to leak information to human society about the existence of vampires. For this reason, players speaking about matters of vampire clan politics or supernatural occult powers lower their voices when non-players walk nearby. Players manifest the in-game narrative of secrecy by pretending that passersby need to be kept in the dark about the sinister truth. At the same time, players maintain another form of secret information: the fact that they are playing a game. The secret meanings of the game, like the fact that a player with crossed arms is "invisible," remain unknown to the general public.

There is a beautiful double logic to the way these game elements play out. Just as vampires in the fictional game-world keep their existence to themselves, players of the game secret away the very presence of the magic circle. *Games as Systems of Information* explored the ways that games manipulate public and private information in order to drive meaningful play. In Seasons of Darkness, the game itself was a kind of private information, kept hidden from the public. This approach is in contrast to most games, where both players and spectators acknowledge the presence of the magic circle, and the distinction between players and non-players is immediately evident. The special information that Seasons of Darkness players have about the existence of the game is more than the formal information about its rules: it is cultural information, information that defines the *play community* and binds it together.

The private knowledge that players have about the game acts to exemplify the narrative itself. Players' imaginative existence as non-human vampires is heightened by the secret status they hold within the public cultural environment where the game takes place. Private knowledge about the game functions as a form of *procedural representation,* a concept we introduced in *Games as the Play of Simulation,* in which signification arises from a dynamic process. A crowd of hapless tourists parts to reveal the menacing black-clad figure of an enemy vampire striding confidently toward you: this is a powerful moment of procedural narrative that could only happen in a LARP. But unlike most forms of procedural representation, where the closed set of rules and game interactions generate a depiction, here representation arises by layering the game onto the real world. The blurring of the game with its cultural environment is itself an act of representation.

Current Events

The Seasons of Darkness game was set in the real world, in the present day. As a result, political events occurring locally, nationally, and globally could be incorporated into the game narrative. For example, in the game narrative, Rudolph Giuliani, the mayor of New York City for the duration of game, was a mind-controlled stooge of one of the more powerful players. As the Game Master, Fortugno had free reign to tie real-world events to the narrative play of the game; he freely encouraged players to do so as well. When fashion designer Gianni Versace was murdered, the clan of vampires that influence and guide human art and culture played their characters in full mourning for the entire game session following the news. Building on this creative game action, Fortugno decided to make the death a vampiric assassination with larger political implications.

In this way, Seasons of Darkness was a system of *open culture,* exchanging meaning with its cultural context and transforming that meaning into game-specific narratives with integrated outcomes affecting future play. Fortugno encouraged a *player-as-producer paradigm,* encouraging players to modify and transform the game's meaning through independent acts of creation. Although Fortugno always had final approval of a player's appropriation of a real-world event, the shared context of the game and its storyline meant that he very rarely had to exercise censuring authority. The significance of player-production in Seasons of Darkness lies in the fact that players were not simply inventing an isolated game object such as a Quake skin or a work of fan fiction. Their act of creation consisted of locating an event in the real world and stretching the game narrative to accommodate it. In Seasons of Darkness, the cultural environment of current events was the raw material for player-production.

Each of these design elements, acting in concert, created an extremely meaningful experience, supporting a play community of several dozen players for more than five years. Each game element was the result of careful game design choices. The danger and difficulty of designing a game as fully integrated into its cultural environment as Seasons of Darkness is that the game can run away with itself. Because of its intentional play with the boundaries of the magic circle, the game has the potential to blend too well into its environment. If it becomes too ambiguous, the shared *safety and trust* that allows a play community to persist can disappear.

Acknowledging this danger, Fortugno kept the game design tightly constrained in many respects. Treating the published game as an open system, he re-wrote the rules, streamlining the formal game mechanics so players could focus on role-playing and storytelling. Although the game existed in public spaces, there were always constraints on where players could travel and what they could do during a game. The time of a game session was also clearly marked: every session began and ended with a Peter Pan-inspired ritual in which Fortugno blew imaginary pixie dust and pink smoke over the players. Even in a game with such permeable borders, the time and space of the magic circle remained unambiguously demarcated.

As we have noted many times, game design is a *second-order design process.* Game designers create play experiences, but only indirectly, by creating rules and structures which then give rise to play. As a game designer, Fortugno skillfully manipulated the game's formal structures and their relationships to cultural contexts, balancing tight constraint with an open-ended integration into the game's cultural environment. The result was the passionate and refined play of Seasons of Darkness.

Ideological Environment

For a third and final case study, we look at Suspicion, an unpublished card game designed for an office environment, to be played over a week of real time. Eric created Suspicion while working at a game development company in New York City in the mid-1990s and organized two full playtests of the game. As with A.I. and *Seasons of Darkness*, the game's design makes explicit use of its surrounding cultural environment. But it also engages in a form of cultural resistance not found in the other two case studies.

Each game of *Suspicion* began with an invitation. Everyone in the company received an email explaining that a game would take place the following week; if they wanted to play, they needed to send a reply. Players were instructed not to disclose to other employees whether or not they had decided to play. In a company of about a hundred, each game involved approximately 20 players. The following week, when the game began, players were given the game rules and a small collection of cards.

One of these cards contained the player's identity. Each player in the conspiracy-themed game belonged to two groups, a sect and an institution. A player might, for example, belong to the Sect of the Turquoise Gear and the Institution of the State. Every player's pair of group affiliations was unique, so no two players belonged to the exact same pair of groups. Each player also began the game with six Stash Cards. Each Stash Card had the color and insignia of one of the groups in the game. The goal of the game was to locate other players in your groups and work with them to acquire Stash Cards with the color and insignia of the group you shared. The first Sect and the first Institution that came to the referee (Eric) with all of their members and a certain number of Stash Cards corresponding to the group won the game. To help players find each other, each group was given a code word or code gesture to help identify other players in that group.

In order to acquire Stash Cards, a player had to use Accusation Cards to formally accuse another player of being in a group. If your accusation was correct, you could use any of your Stash Cards to "attack" the accused, an attack that played out as a simple dueling card game. If your accusation was incorrect, the target could take a Stash Card from you. Players could also freely trade cards with each other, but usually did so only with other members of their groups. The general trajectory of the game started with players figuring out who was and was not playing, next using code words and gestures to identify others in their groups, and eventually sharing knowledge and Stash Cards within a group in order to strategically attack other players. The play of *Suspicion* engaged with its cultural environment in a variety of ways.

Lived Conflict

As with *Seasons of Darkness*, *Suspicion* took place in a physical space not designed for the artificial play of a game: an office environment. Unlike the LARP, the game space was not a public space that players visited for a limited time. It was the place where they worked, including their offices, lunchrooms, and conference rooms. The game's cultural environment was a space players already knew intimately. For this reason, the game truly colonized its environment. The workspace became synonymous with the magic circle; the time and place of the workday became the time and place of the game. There were a few formal restrictions on where the game could be played (a scheduled meeting with an outside client was out of bounds), but otherwise, when a player arrived at work, he or she had to be ready to attack or be attacked. All games embody a *conflict*, and tension arises in a game as players struggle to resolve the conflict. One of the roles that the magic circle plays is to contain game conflict rather than allowing it to spill out into ordinary life. As with *Assassin*, in *Suspicion* there was no escape from the game conflict; the play of the game had to be integrated into the rest of one's life.

Act | **SPORK:** Take one counter from the player to your left. If he or she has no counters, take one from the player to his or her left. **FOON:** Take one counter from any player you choose. *Sneak acts like a Foon.*

Interventions

Because Suspicion operated in and among ordinary work activities, the play of the game took over and transformed the workplace. For example, in Suspicion each group has a code word or code gesture that it can use to identify other members of the same group. This communicative game mechanic leads to strangely strategic conversations. Each player attempts to reveal his own code word or gesture to find allies, but does so in a very surreptitious manner, so that another group won't notice and acquire the information.

As a result of this mechanic, players became very self-conscious about how they interacted with one another. The game added a new layer of meaning to every in-office speech-act, turning it into a complex action that could be used to identify allies or to foil rivals. As we explored in **Games as the Play of Meaning,** part of the play of any game is *making sense* of its meanings and representations. By invading and appropriating ordinary communication, Suspicion brings this sense-making aspect of games center stage. Is the person you're talking to about a work task playing the game? Are they trying to tell you something? Have you unintentionally let your code word slip? The sense of altered consciousness was so pervasive that even workers not playing the game joined in, pretending that they too, had a secret identity. From the player reports that followed each playtest, it was clear that these extra layers of meaning were somewhat uncomfortable to inhabit, but nevertheless intensely pleasurable as play.

In **Defining Play,** we established that *play* is free movement within a more rigid structure. When the rigid structures themselves change as a result of play's movement, the result is *transformative play*. Through the play of Suspicion, the social spaces of work were altered. Even when players were not talking about the game, the distrust and self-consciousness of Suspicion inflected their interactions.

Shaking It Up

Suspicion was designed to undercut the existing power relationships at work. In any company, an institutional structure defines control and authority: who makes the decisions, who is paid more, who is the boss of whom. When Suspicion players are randomly assigned to sects and institutions at the start of the game, the makeup of these groups has nothing to do with the existing departmental, spatial, economic, or authoritative relationships among players. Suspicion reshuffled and thereby transformed these power relations, changing in some way each player's relationships to the other participants.

The structure of player identity in Suspicion (each player is assigned a unique combination of group allegiances), ensures that you cannot completely trust anyone else. You might have found the members of your Sect, but each of them belongs to a different Institution that is opposed to your own. One of your Sect members might suggest that you pool your Stash Cards with his, so that your Sect's valuable cards are more properly protected—but he might simply be planning to selfishly use the cards for his Institution. This sense of constant uncertainty and distrust created a tense game atmosphere. The game rewarded deception and play involved much trickery and backstabbing. Not only were existing power relationships undermined, but they were never given the chance to settle into a stable hierarchy. Suspicion revealed some of the *cultural rhetorics,* or ideologies, that help constitute the workplace. But because the game transformed power relationships, it also served as a site of *cultural resistance.* By undermining the company's existing patterns of authority, it highlighted the typically invisible ways that power usually operated.

Games sometimes exhibit *forbidden play,* forms of non-game interaction not permitted in ordinary life. In Suspicion, a worker might drop in on his boss, accuse her of being an enemy, and attack her mercilessly with his Stash

Cards. By recasting company authority as a tangled web of deception, relationships among company workers were radically transformed. Through its play, Suspicion operated as a cultural critique. It succeeded only because of the way it blurred the edges of the magic circle. A softball game at a company picnic might act temporarily to reframe company authority, but it is not taking place *in* the participants' actual workplace. The subversive potential for cultural resistance in Suspicion emerges directly from its literal appropriation of the cultural environment.

As with our other examples, Suspicion achieves its distinctive play through specific design decisions. Of the three games, Suspicion in some ways plays most radically with its cultural context. Seasons of Darkness, as a role-playing game, did not involve explicit competition between players. A.I. was a huge project, but its puzzle structure, in which the game designers held the solutions, kept the structures of authority clear. Through the contextual ambiguities that it created, Suspicion was truly culturally transgressive.

In a typical game, the magic circle acts to contain inter-player conflict. Suspicion was not only designed to create mistrust and deception, but had players acting against each other in their usual place of work. The magic circle enframed the office; there was no escape from other players after the game if things went wrong. During the climax of the second game, one player made an offer to pay another cash for her Stash Cards. The exchange of money never took place, but its mere possibility caused intense emotions to erupt. The game was in danger of imploding, leading the designer to implement a rule outlawing the use of real-world money in the game.

This anecdote points out the power and challenge of designing games as cultural environments. As a transformative political statement about the power of the corporate workplace, Suspicion was a success, seducing players with its genuinely pleasurable game play even while the game play itself engaged in a cultural critique of the players' work context. At the same

time, the mischievous resistance of the game was balanced by the need for a sense of responsibility toward the players. Cultural environments are always home to someone and even a game that embodies a radical critique needs to maintain a spirit of fair play to those it impacts.

Game Design Fundamentals

Games as Cultural Environment is the final schema in *Rules of Play*. In some ways, this chapter has brought us full circle. In the course of analyzing A.I., Seasons of Darkness, and Suspicion, we revisited many of the concepts that form the conceptual basis of the book as a whole. Below is a partial list of the game design concepts mentioned in this schema, in the order that they appear and the chapters where they were first introduced:

definition of games	*Defining Games*
magic circle	*The Magic Circle*
three kinds of rules	*Rules on Three Levels*
lusory attitude	*The Magic Circle*
open and closed systems	*Systems*
metacommunication	*Games as the Play of Meaning*
space of possibility	*Interactivity*
core mechanics	*Games as the Play of Experience*
emergent system	*Games as Emergent Systems*
embedded narratives	*Games as Narrative Play*
emergent narratives	*Games as Narrative Play*
system environment	*Systems*
the play community	*Games as Social Play*
public and private information	*Games as Systems of Information*
procedural representation	*Games as the Play of Simulation*
open culture	*Games as Open Culture*
player-as-producer paradigm	*Games as Open Culture*
safety and trust	*Games as Social Play*
second-order design	*Games as the Play of Experience*
conflict	*Games as Systems of Conflict*
making sense of meaning	*Games as the Play of Meaning*
free play	transformative play	*Defining Play*
cultural rhetorics	*Games as Cultural Rhetoric*
cultural resistance	*Games as Cultural Resistance*
forbidden play	*Games as Social Play*

There are many concepts we didn't mention in the course of these analyses. But a comprehensive overview was not the intention of our review. Our purpose was to demonstrate how a suite of fundamental game design concepts work together to build a full understanding of the operation of a complex game. Comprehending a game requires more than simply selecting a schema and applying it in isolation to a game design problem. The intricate operation of a game can only be fully appreciated when you take a multifaceted approach, combining many points of view, strategically constructing your analysis in order to solve the problem at hand. In this chapter, we were specifically looking at games as cultural environments. But in order to do so, it was necessary to make extensive use of ideas from the **RULES, PLAY,** and **CULTURE** of games.

The Artificial Question

We now return to the question posed at the beginning of this chapter. The premise of the schema asserts that games can be framed as cultural environments, as phenomena that co-exist with real-world contexts. If this framing is carried to its logical extreme, the magic circle disappears altogether, and the game becomes synonymous with its surroundings. If this is the case, even for some games, this schema would force a fundamental reevaluation of our basic assumptions about what games are and how they function.

In the course of this chapter, we took a detailed look at three games that explicitly blurred the boundaries of the magic circle. In very different ways, A.I., Seasons of Darkness, and Suspicion played with their cultural environments, effacing the boundaries of the magic circle to a more extreme degree than more conventional games. Yet in each case, although the magic circle blurred, shifted, and blended in with its environment, it still in some way remained intact. In A.I., the players never forgot that the game was really a promotion for a Hollywood film. In Seasons of Darkness, the game sessions took place within strictly delimited physical and temporal boundaries. And in Suspicion,

play boundaries, such as the restriction on using money, nudged the game in the direction of being a closed, rather than a more open system. In these three games, the magic circle never entirely vanished. If it had, we probably would not be able to call them games.

So the magic circle did not disappear after all. But each game, in its own way, played with its possible disappearance. The rigid structure among which the play of the games took place was in fact the conventions of games themselves. A game framed as a cultural environment plays with the very definition of what a game is. But some part of that defining game structure remains intact, even as it is transformed through play. A game that plays with the possibility of its own existence offers game designers potentially rich approaches. As a design strategy, understanding a game as a cultural environment can create entirely new forms of game experiences.

Designing a game as a cultural environment is also an effective way to mount a powerful cultural critique. During the twentieth century, most forms of art and entertainment have engaged critically with their cultural contexts, from Marcel Duchamp's readymades to Hip-Hop's sampled tracks. As a new century dawns, it is time for games to recognize their role within larger cultural environments, in order to celebrate their complex relationships with the rest of culture.

Yet the question of the artificiality of games remains. If we are calling for a more culture-centric approach to games, why would we still maintain the idea that they are artificial? Don't cultural framings of games—framings that acknowledge their status as open systems—call the artificiality of games into question? If games are not separate from the rest of culture, are they still really artificial? Yes. Calling games artificial does not mean that they are wholly distinct from culture. No matter how integrated into culture games might be, there will always be some aspect of a game's operation that relies on its own system, rather than that of culture, to create meanings for players.

For example, Scrabble makes use of language, letters, and words borrowed from its cultural environment, but that does not mean it can't also designate its own set of meanings as well. The letter "Q" and the letter "E" both appear on this page. But in the context of reading this book, the Q is not worth more points than the letter E. In fact, neither one of them is worth any points. Only in the highly specialized context of a Scrabble game do we assign Scrabble points to letters. Scrabble is certainly not a wholly artificial system. But neither does it disappear entirely into its cultural environment. However we frame it, Scrabble will always maintain its artificial status in some measure. That is simply part of what makes it a game.

Final Framings

One last note about the importance of game design fundamentals. There is a widespread impulse among those who study games to want to leapfrog over the basics, immediately break all of the rules, violate the magic circle, turn players into designers, and radically reinvent the phenomenon of games. This is not an inherently bad instinct for game designers or game scholars to possess. As the games studied in this schema demonstrate, blurring the magic circle to question the fundamental properties of games can lead to new kinds of play experiences. However, radical innovation and the design of meaningful play can only be accomplished by paying attention to the fundamental design principles that apply to all games. Even when you dissect or design breakthrough games that bend, break, and transform traditional gaming structures, the fundamentals of game design remain. For every A.I., Seasons of Darkness, or Suspicion, there are hundreds or thousands of unsuccessful game designs: online/real-world scavenger hunts that never found an audience, LARPs that fizzled out before they got off the ground, and game experiments that were just no fun at all to play.

Games as Cultural Environments takes us to the edge of the void: it lets us consider a game that undermines its own existence by creating the means for its erasure. It is ironic perhaps that the abstraction and complexity of this phenomenon was best deciphered by a return to the game design fundamentals, to the core language of meaningful play, to the concepts that constitute the *Rules of Play*.

Further Reading

The Fantasy Role-Playing Game: A New Performing Art, by Daniel Mackay

This book is about role-playing as a performance art. Of particular interest to game designers is the discussion of the performance aesthetics and collaborative narrative creation of role-playing games, including relationship of players in the game to social and cultural structures.

> **Recommended:**
>
> Introduction: The Role-Playing Game: Defined, Described, and Systematized
>
> From Part One: A New Category of Popular Entertainments and a New Kind of Sandbox: Playing in Imaginary Entertainment Environments
>
> From Part Four: The Theater of Events: Narrative as Aesthetic Object

www.cloudmakers.org

Cloudmakers.org was founded as a discussion group for the web game centered around the film *A.I.: Artificial Intelligence*. The site houses an archive of the game, including an approximate reproduction of the game from July 23, 2001, the day before the game was officially "solved," as well as essays and editorials written by players, links to media coverage, and a moderated discussion board. It is an excellent document of the play of a game from the perspective of a community of its players.

Write | SPORK: Name a costume you wore on Halloween (or another occasion) when you were a kid. FOON: Name a costume you wore on Halloween (or another occasion) as an adult.

Notes

1. Johann Huizinga, *Homo Ludens: A Study of the Play Element in Culture* (Boston: Beacon Press, 1955), p. 10.

2. Stephen Sniderman, "Unwritten Rules." <www.gamepuzzles.com/tlog/tlog2.htm>.

3. Brian Sutton Smith, *The Ambiguity of Play* (London: Harvard University Press, 1997), p. 77.

4. Andrea Phillips, "Deep Water." 26th July 2001. Cloudmakers.org

5. Maria Bonasia, "MetaMystery." 30th May 2001. Cloudmakers.org

6. Daniel Sieberg, "Reality Blurs, Hype Builds with Web 'A.I.' Game." May 2001. CNN.com

7. Daragh Sankey, "A.I. Game." Joystick101.org

Games as Cultural Environment SUMMARY

- The schema *Games as Cultural Environment* explores the following aspects of games:

  - Blurring the spaces inside and outside the magic circle

  - Ambiguity between players and non-players

  - Overlap between game and real life

- It is only within the magic circle that the authority of formal rules holds sway; at the same time, the implicit rules of games are based not in the magic circle, but within culture at large.

- **Etiquette, ethos, convention,** and **context** are among the forms that implicit rules can take. As manifestations of cultural authority, they link the artificiality of games to the real-world contexts they inhabit.

- The lusory attitude applies not just to the formal rules of a game, but to the implicit rules as well. When a player submits to the authority of a game, he or she is accepting its formal as well as its cultural authority. In this sense, the magic circle of a game extends to embrace larger cultural domains.

- A.I., Seasons of Darkness, and Suspicion are all games that explicitly operate as cultural environments. In each case, meaningful play arises because careful game design maintains the magic circle in some way.

- Considered as a cultural environment, a game plays with the possible erasure of the magic circle and therefore plays with the possibility of its own existence. However, some semblance of the magic circle always remains.

- The premise that the boundaries of the magic circle can be blurred or erased calls into question whether or not games can be considered **artificial.** Games are always in some way artificial and capable of producing internal game meanings, even when they are framed as culture; games are artificial because they are *designed*.

Caribbean Star
A game for 2 players

Overview

Welcome aboard the Caribbean Star, Caribe Cruise Lines' most luxurious cruise ship. It's chock to the gills with newlyweds and nearlydeads who have ventured to the Caribbean to float into the Panama Canal, buy knickknacks in Jamaican straw markets, and drink Piña Coladas from the source. And you have been brought here to entertain them. You and your opponent are magicians with, more or less, the same act. The Caribe Line's Miami office accidentally booked both of you on the same ship, and now you've got exactly one week to prove who's the better magician.

Rules

Equipment

You need a deck of playing cards, a score pad, and a pencil.

How to Begin

First, determine which player will be Red, and which will be Black. Each player "owns" one color of cards. There is no difference between the two colors. Next, shuffle the deck and deal a hand of five cards to each player. Turns will be simultaneous, so there is no need to determine who goes first.

On Each Turn

Both players choose one card from their hand and play it face down. After both cards are played, turn them over to reveal each player's action for the turn. After all actions have been resolved, both players draw a card.

Card Functions

Each card has a unique function, described below. Although they are played at the same time, cards always take effect from lowest to highest. Deuces are low, and Kings are high. (Aces are played differently, as explained later). If both cards are the same rank, then suit determines the order. Clubs are first, followed by Diamonds, Hearts, and Spades (alphabetical order).

> *Magic Tricks, 10–K*
>
> Tens and face cards are Magic Tricks. When you play a Magic Trick, it means you are practicing it for your next performance. If you play your opponent's color, he practices that trick. When you play a Magic Trick in your color, put it in your "Practice" pile, which is a set of cards face up on the table in front of you, spread out so that every card in the pile is visible. If you play a Magic Trick in your opponent's color, you put that card in your opponent's Practice pile.

Point Values and Times

A perfect show is 15 minutes long. Face cards add 5 minutes to your show. Jacks are worth 2 points, Queens are worth 4 points, and Kings are worth 6 points. Tens add 10 minutes to your show, and are worth 10 points.

Showtimes, 7:00pm and 9:00pm

Sevens and Nines are Showtimes. When you play a Showtime in your own color, you will perform your act, which means you discard your Practice pile and convert it into points. If you play a Showtime in your opponent's color, they perform their act. Obviously, you want to convert your own Practice pile when it is worth maximum points, and convert your opponent's pile when it is worthless. The exact scoring of the Practice pile is described later. After you perform, all the cards from your Practice pile and the Showtime card go into the discard pile.

Dinner Buffet, 8:00pm

Eights are Dinner Buffet cards. When you play an Eight in your color, you may perform (i.e., discard) one of the Magic Tricks in your Practice pile for half its value. For example, if you use an Eight to convert a King, you would score 3 points. You don't have to use your Dinner Buffet. You might play an Eight and then, seeing what your opponent has played, decide to ignore the buffet. Whether you use it or not, the Eight is discarded. If you play an opponent's Eight, he may convert one of his Magic Tricks or he may ignore it. You can't force your opponent to perform at the Dinner Buffet.

Rehearsal, 6:00pm

Sixes are Rehearsal cards. You can "rehearse" your act before performing it and double its final value. When you play a Six in your color, you add it to your Practice pile. If you play a Six in your opponent's color, it goes into his Practice pile. If you have two Sixes in your Practice pile, your show will be worth quadruple points!

Afternoon Nap, 5:00pm

Fives are "Afternoon Nap" cards. When you play a Five of any color, you will swap hands with your opponent. Discard the Five after you swap hands.

Mistakes, 2 through 4

Twos through Fours are Mistakes. These are a little like Magic Tricks but they are worth negative points. If you play a Mistake of your own color it will go into your Practice pile. If you play a Mistake of your opponent's color, it will go into his Practice pile. Mistakes don't always hurt you: if you perform a show composed entirely of Mistakes, it's called a "Comedy Act" and is worth nothing—which is better than negative points!

How to Score Your Shows

Now that we've described all the possible contents of a Practice pile (Magic Tricks, Rehearsals, and Mistakes) here is how to score the show.

First, evaluate the Magic Tricks by the length of the show. The perfect show is 15 minutes long. Face Cards add 5 minutes each and Tens add 10 minutes. If your show is the perfect length, you will score full value for all your Magic Tricks. If you run long or short by 5 minutes, you must cut the value of your biggest Trick (or one of your biggest Tricks, if you have two big Tricks of the same size) by half. If you run short or long by 10 minutes, you must cut all your Tricks by half. If you run 30 minutes or longer, you get no points at all for your Magic Tricks. However, if you run 0 minutes (you have no Magic Tricks at all) you are doing a Comedy Show, which is scored differently.

Second, subtract the values of your Mistakes. Twos are worth –2, Threes are worth –3, and Fours are worth –4. Mistakes do not add time to your act, and you always score full value for these cards unless you are doing a Comedy Show. Mistakes can easily result in a negative value for your show.

Last, apply the Rehearsal cards. If you have a Six in your Practice pile, double the value. If you have two Sixes, you double it twice.

Comedy Show

If your act has no Magic Tricks in it, it is always worth exactly 0 points. This is true regardless of the number of Mistakes and Rehearsals in your pile.

An Example of Scoring a Show

A Practice Pile has the following cards in it: King, King, Ten, Six, Four, Three, Two. The Show is 5 minutes too long (5 + 5 + 10 = 20), so the highest Magic Trick, the Ten, will be worth only half value. The base value of the show is therefore 6 + 6 + 5, or 17 points. The Mistakes are worth 4 + 3 + 2, or 9. These are deducted from 17, leaving 8 points. Finally, the show is doubled, making for a final value of 16 points.

Stop Cards, the Aces

Aces are not played like other cards. They are not color-specific and they always work for the player who uses them. You can play an Ace from your hand to cancel the effect of any other card immediately before it is resolved. In other words, once the cards are revealed, and just before executing a particular card, either player may use an Ace to stop that card from happening. When you play the Ace, you pick up the card you canceled and put it in your hand. You also discard the Ace. You cannot use one Ace to cancel another.

An Example of Playing an Ace

Red has played a Red Five, and Black has played a Red Ten. Black holds an Ace. Before the Five swaps both players' hands, Black has the opportunity to play his Ace, but he chooses not to. The Five is discarded, and the players swap hands. Now Red holds the Ace, and he can play it to cancel the Red Ten. He discards the Ace, and puts the Red Ten into his hand. (Red has canceled the Ten because it would have made his act too long. He plans to use the Ten in his next act.)

Ending the Turn

At the end of the turn, each player draws one card. Once there are no more cards to draw, players still continue to play cards until their hands are empty, or until one player can no longer play cards because he holds nothing but Aces.

Ending the Game

The game ends when both players' hands are empty, or when one player holds nothing but Aces. At this point, each player gets one "Farewell Show" in which he scores the cards remaining in his Practice pile. The Farewell Show is not optional: you can lose a lot of points in this show if you're not careful. After the farewell show, the player with the most points wins.

Scoring a Show

1. Add up the minutes in the Show and score your Magic Tricks:

   · If the show is 15 minutes long, Magic Tricks score their full value.

   · If the show is long or short by 5 minutes, the biggest Magic Trick value is cut in half.

   · If the show is long or short by 10 minutes, the value of all tricks are cut in half.

   · If the show is 30 minutes or longer, you get no points for your Magic Tricks.

2. Add up any Mistakes and subtract them from the Magic Trick total.

3. Double your points for each Rehearsal in the pile.

If you have no Magic Tricks in your show it is a Comedy Act and is worth zero points.

Magic Tricks

Card	Minutes	Points
King	5	6
Queen	5	4
Jack	5	2
10	10	10

Mistakes

Card	Points
Two	−2
Three	−3
Four	−4

Other Cards

Card	Function
Five	Afternoon Nap: *Swap hands with the other player*
Six	Rehearsal: *Doubles value of a Show*
Seven & Nine	Showtimes: *Score and discard your Practice pile*
Eight	Dinner Buffet: *Discard one Magic Trick from your practice pile for half its value (optional)*

Caribbean Star

Stage 1: General Constraints

Usually when I create a new game, all the notes, variations, and failed attempts wind up in the garbage. This article chronicles the development of a new card game, including all the decisions and dead ends involved.

June 18, 2001

My wife and I are cruising to Alaska aboard the Norwegian Sky, on our first full day at sea. A vacation seems like a good environment for creating this new game. Considering that the only available playtester is my wife Carol, I think I'll write a two-player game.

I have no means to make custom components, even custom cards (which I usually use for inventing new games) so I'm going to write this game with the "bare essentials." Those materials include: two packs of playing cards, several 6-sided dice including ten dice in each of two colors, and one each of 4, 8, 10, 12, and 20-sided dice. I also have four Pawns, one Poker Chip, blank paper, pens, and pencils. Certainly this is enough material to develop a new two-player game.

Whereas some game designers prefer to create a game mechanic first and then adapt that mechanic to an appropriate theme, I prefer to start with a theme wherever possible. This gives me more creative ideas when trying to invent the game mechanics, and it makes for a game whose mechanics seem better to suit the theme. When a storyline gets added after the game is designed, you can really tell, especially when a play that seems reasonable in the storyline is not allowed in the game. When I invent a game for sale I must consider the marketability of the theme, but I'm not so constrained here, because this will be a free game. In this case, I can come up with a very basic premise and move forward, rather than agonizing too much over the story.

I have an extensive list of "good ideas" that I have compiled over many years. I usually go to this list when choosing a new game design project for Cheapass Games. A good game idea should not only be entertaining, it should also provide the basis of a good system. Some good jokes make terrible games.

Here is a short brainstorm of possible themes for my game, inspired by my vacation:

- Bellhops angling for tips.

- Cruise directors booking acts for their ships.

- Passengers collecting raffle tickets.

- Travel Agents booking trips.

Let's examine the game possibilities of each of these storylines. You will notice that in each story I name a type of character (the players) and some sort of competitive activity (the game).

Bellhops Angling for Tips: Who are the players in the Bellhop game, and what is their goal? Are they the bellhops, competing with one another for the best tip? Are they the hotel guests, trying to tip as little as possible while still getting their bags? Or, if this is a two-player game, can we create an imbalanced game in which one player is the Bellhop, the other is the Guest, and each has his own objective?

These aren't the only options. In a game involving bellhops and bags, there's nothing that says the players can't be the bags. Maybe the Bags have a game objective that's almost completely unrelated to the goals of the Bellhops and the Customers. For instance, maybe they get satisfaction from being moved around. Or from staying packed as long as possible. Or even from sitting in the dark. Perhaps the players manage the hotel. Perhaps they manage hotel chains. This could go on forever. But let's move on to our next scenario.

Cruise Directors Booking Acts: Who are the players in this game? Are they cruise directors working on multiple ships? Are they multiple acts working on a single ship? Are they trying to get a job, or keep the job they have?

If we wanted to use the Cruise Director scenario, but think further outside the box, where would we go? The players might be passengers trying to get the most entertainment on a one-week cruise; they might be land-based talent agents trying to make the most money booking the best acts on the longest cruises. They might be jokes trying to propagate through the acts of Cruise Ship comedians, whose acts are really basically all the same.

Passengers Collecting Raffle Tickets: On our cruise ship, a variety of activities earn you a raffle ticket. The players in this scenario would probably be Passengers, and there would be a whole game of collecting tickets followed by a raffle at the end. This isn't the only way to present this story, though. The players could represent the cruise staff whose job is to give out the raffle tickets. The story could revolve around fixing the raffle, or stealing tickets from other players. Or there could be several raffles, and this could be a game about trading tickets in one raffle for tickets in another.

Travel Agents Booking Cruises: In this game, players would probably try to make the most money by booking the best trips at the most competitive prices. If you charge more money for a trip, you will make more when you sell it, but you might not sell as many. If you were a travel agent in this game, you might be trying to make the most money at the end of the game. Or, you might be trying to make the most people happy, with the money being less important. Or you could be trying to book the most trips to a particular destination to win a trip there yourself, and so on.

Racing Games vs. Fighting Games

Most games can be sorted into two categories, based on their scoring system: racing games and fighting games. The distinction makes the most sense with multiplayer games, because in a two-player game the two types are essentially interchangeable. In a racing game, players are trying to get the most points, and can't directly interfere with other players. Scrabble is a good example of a racing game. Everyone acquires points, and the object is to have the highest score at the end. Golf is actually this type of game also. Even though the object is to score the least, the players are still collecting their own points with no influence on the scores of the others.

In fighting games, the object is to take away the other player's points, or to do him as much damage as possible. Chess is a fighting game, with both players bent on capturing their opponent's pieces, especially the King. Hearts is also a fighting game, though the scoring is inverted. In Hearts, points are bad for you, and when one player breaks 100 points, the player with the fewest points wins. This is functionally equivalent to starting everyone with 100 points, and deducting from that score until someone reaches zero. The difference between Hearts and Golf is that in Hearts your actions affect your opponents' scores.

The salient difference between racing and fighting games is that fighting games make great two-player games, but aren't always good with more than two players. When you can decide whom to hit, the game becomes political, and often the most strategic move is to hurt the player who's closest to being eliminated. That player can be driven out of the game early, and will have to sit out the rest of the game.

The last two scenarios, the Raffle Ticket and Travel Agent games, seem like racing games. So are some versions of the first scenario, the Bellhop game. These might be good multiplayer games. But because I'm interested in writing a two-player game, I'm inclined to look first at the game that allows me to do damage to my opponent. This looks like a good argument for Scenario 2, the Cruise Directors and Acts. Let's look again at the story of acts trying not to get thrown off cruise ships.

First Rules Draft

When I have a half-baked game idea, I will usually just start writing down the rules. This helps me work out some of the more mundane aspects of the game, such as the mechanics of card drawing, piece moving, turn sequence, and so on. If I haven't settled on game mechanics by this point, the exercise of writing a rulebook tends to force me into something. I can always change it later, but I need something to change. Here is the first draft of the rules for our new card game, with notes in italic explaining what's going on in my head.

Caribbean Star

A Card Game for Two Players

Almost every cruise line has a "Star," such as the Star Princess and the Regent Star, which are both ships I've worked on. Before I became a game publisher, I was a professional juggler for about seven years, so I have a bit of experience with this subject. I like the idea of calling the game "Caribbean Star" because it has a double meaning, with "Star" referring to the performers.

For our story, imagine a cruise ship on which the cruise director has accidentally hired too many acts. Player One is the ventriloquist, Player Two is the magician. One of these two acts is superfluous, and will have to go home at the end of the week. It will depend on how well each player performs his act, and his other shipboard duties. And of course, interfering with your opponent will be the key to winning.

> *I'm currently thinking of this as a card game, played with a standard deck. The Magician's cards are the black ones; the Ventriloquist's cards are the red ones. After one pass through the deck, the player who has given more good performances while destroying his opponent's credibility wins, and keeps his job on the Caribbean Star.*

Equipment: You need a deck of playing cards.

Story: Welcome aboard the Caribbean Star, Caribe Cruise Lines' most luxurious cruise ship. It's chock to the gills with newlyweds and nearlydeads who have ventured to the Caribbean to see the Panama Canal and drink Piña Coladas from the source. And you are here to entertain them.

You and your opponent are performers aboard the Caribbean Star, two acts doing the work of one. The line has accidentally booked both a Magician and a Ventriloquist on the same boat, and…

At this point, I'm already thinking it's funnier if you are just two magicians, rather than a magician and a ventriloquist. Writing the intro from scratch like this always gives me good insight into the main joke of the game.

The Caribe line has accidentally booked two magicians on the same ship, and you've got exactly one week to prove that you're better than the other guy. You both have the same bag of tricks, so it's up to your cunning and skill to get your opponent thrown off the boat before he does the same to you. Happy sailing!

The idea that you have only a week ties in with my plan to make this game end after one pass through the deck. Incorporating a time limit and a sense of urgency on this contest should make it more fun. At this point in the first pass of the rules, I really have no other mechanics in mind other than the idea that one player will "own" the red cards, while the other player owns the black cards.

Dividing ownership of the cards makes the same cards do different things for each player, which in turn leads to more variety in the games. Because this is a two-player game, it's easy to divide the deck fairly. When I see a chance like this, I jump at it!

How to Begin: Shuffle the deck and determine randomly which player will be the Red Magician, and which player will be Black. After shuffling, deal a hand of five cards to each player. Determine randomly who will go first.

After writing "determine randomly who goes first," I'm starting to think of the card functions, and also wondering if I can make this game a simultaneous-play game rather than a turn-based game. A game this simple can sometimes be significantly better for the player who goes first, or second, depending on the mechanics. Simultaneous play solves this problem, but presents some others. Let's try simultaneous play.

After shuffling, deal a hand of five cards to each player. Turns will be simultaneous.

On each turn: Players choose one card from their hand and play it face down on the table. This card will determine their action for the round.

Card functions: Each card has a unique function, as described below. Both players have the same bag of tricks, but the order in which you play them can make a big difference. Also, each player "owns" half of the deck. Playing your own cards has a different effect than playing the same cards for your opponent.

This section is not really very clear, but it is mostly there to help me remember what I'm thinking. It will probably be trimmed up or removed in the final rules.

Card precedence: Although they are played at the same time, cards always take effect in order from lowest to highest. Aces are low, and Kings are high. Furthermore, the order of suits from lowest to highest is: Clubs, Diamonds, Hearts, Spades (alphabetical order).

> *You can tell I haven't figured out what Aces do yet; in the final draft Aces don't figure into the play order at all. The general purpose of giving each card a priority is so that resolving the simultaneous play is always easy. It also allows me to fine-tune the functions of each card based on the order it falls in the series.*

Face cards: Face cards are "rehearsal" cards. When you play a face card, you are practicing tricks for your next performance. Each player will have a maximum of four performances during the game, and the point value of those performances determines your score.

When you play a face card, set it aside in your Practice pile, a set of face up face cards that denote your set for the next show. A perfect set is 30 minutes, which means three cards. If scored for full value, a Jack is worth 2 points, a Queen is worth 4, and a King is worth 6 points.

> *I have picked the values of 2, 4, and 6 because I'm planning to make rules that sometimes cut these values in half. This means that for simplicity's sake I want them to be even numbers. At this point, I'm working with the idea that a perfect show is three cards, and running longer or shorter than that will penalize you.*

If you play a rehearsal card that is not your color, you put it in your opponent's Practice pile instead of your own.

> *Here is why the perfect show length is the critical mechanic: If you play a Rehearsal card for your opponent, you will be able to lengthen his show beyond the perfect length. So, if he's practiced a three-card show but can't convert it to points until you make it longer, he'll suffer a penalty. This makes the same cards better or worse at different points in the game, which is a great way to get a complex game out of a simple set of cards.*

Tens: Tens are Big Tricks. They count as two cards when measuring the length of a show, and are worth 10 points when scored for full value.

Nine and Seven are Showtimes: If you play a Showtime, you discard your Practice Pile and convert it to points. Conversion of the Practice Pile works as follows:

> *Now I'm formalizing the show-length penalties I was thinking about when I wrote the Rehearsal cards.*

If you have three cards (Tens count as two) you get full value for your entire act. If you run long or short, you lose points. If you have two or four cards, score half points for your largest card. If you have one or five cards, score half points for your entire act. If you have no cards or more than five, you score no points when you play a Showtime.

If you play a Showtime for your opponent, he must perform his act right now. This is true even if he just performed, and even if he has no cards in his Practice Pile.

Eight: Dinner Buffet. You can do an additional show at a dinner buffet. When you play an Eight, you can perform (discard) one of the cards in your Practice pile for half value. You don't have to, however. You might play an Eight and then, seeing what your opponent has played, decide to skip the buffet. If you play an opponent's Eight, he may convert one of his Practice cards or he may do nothing about it.

> *Eights are added to give you the opportunity to fine-tune your show if it is running long.*

Six: Rehearsal. You can "rehearse" your act before you perform, and double its value. When you play a Six, add it to your Practice pile. You will score double points the next time you play a Showtime. If you have two Sixes in your Practice Pile, the show will be worth quadruple points.

> *This is a language problem: I'm unknowingly using "rehearsal" to describe both the Face Cards and Tens, and the Sixes. This is fixed in the final draft.*

Five: Afternoon Nap: When you play a Five you must discard your hand and draw four new cards. If you play your opponent's Five, he must do the same.

> *Fives will be the spoiler cards. I want people to be able to discard their hands in order to clear out cards that are especially bad for them. The aspect of killing your opponent's hand turns out to be unbalanced, and I will later revise the function of the Fives.*

Four through Two: These cards are mistakes. They are like practice cards but they are worth negative points, 4 through 2 respectively. If you play a mistake of your own color it will go into your Practice Pile. If you play a card of your opponent's color, it will go into his. The negative points are doubled by Sixes but are not halved by going long or short. They do not count as cards for the length of your act, and you cannot perform them to get rid of them at the dinner buffet.

> *The exact order of resolving points, negative points, and doublers, needs some work here. But this is a first pass. It becomes evident on playing this game that this math, while critical to the game, needs to be presented in the simplest possible manner. In general, when*

math gets too hard in a game it doesn't just slow down the execution of the game. It also makes forecasting, or strategic play, much harder. So good math needs to be obvious and transparent. The show-length penalty is pretty important here, so I'm not going to let it go. But I will, as I said, try to make it easy to understand.

Aces (Cancel Cards): Aces are not played face down like other cards. They are not color-specific and they always belong to the player who plays them. You can play an Ace from your hand to cancel the effect of any other card immediately before it goes off. When you play an Ace, you draw a card to replace it.

At the end of your turn, draw one card, or however many it takes to get your hand up to five. When there are no cards left to draw, the cruise is over and the player with the most points wins.

There, that's the first pass on the rules. Now I'll write up a cheat sheet and play the game.

Playtest Notes

I was lucky enough to have Carol on hand while working on this rules draft, so we immediately played a few rounds and determined the following:

Card Functions: In general the cards work well and are easy to remember. Because many of the card functions are based loosely on times of day, and others are grouped pretty logically, the whole set seems to make sense. One should easily be able to play this game without a cheat sheet.

Scoring: The order in which scoring functions are carried out isn't really clear in the first pass, so we decided to define more exactly how you score a show:

First, you count the Face Cards and Tens. If you think of a perfect show as 30 minutes, then Jacks through Kings are 10 minutes each, and Tens are 20 minutes. Based on the length of the show, you apply your scoring penalty (if any) by halving the appropriate cards. Next, add the negative cards at full value. Last, apply the doublers. So if a show contains a Jack, King, and Ten, as well as a Four and a Six, then it's long by 10 minutes, which means chopping the Ten. The cards sum to 13, minus 4 is 9, doubled is 18. *Don't let this confuse you if you've read the final draft: I later cut all the showtimes in half to make Tens last 10 minutes.*

Score Tracking: It's possible to track your score by the way you stack your tricks, but it's probably much cleaner to use a score pad and write down each show as you finish it. That will also make it more obvious who is winning, of which I'm a big fan.

Endgame: It's a little unsatisfying to finish with cards left in your hand, so I want players to play out their hands. I'm not sure what to do in the case where one player has more cards, such as when exactly one Ace is left to play. This problem is solved later.

Spoiler Cards: Fives have been changed to swap the players' hands, not discard them. If you play a Five, players swap hands. The reason for this is that otherwise the deck is burned far too quickly. I don't like being able to avoid playing the really bad cards by discarding them. But most of all, I don't like the effect of saving up a really good hand only to have it burned down by a Five.

The Comedy Show: We decided to add one completely new rule, based on the abject frustration of being hit with a big show that's all mistakes. This rule is called the Comedy Show. If your Practice pile contains nothing but mistakes, you can clear it with a Showtime for 0 points. This is a great way to get rid of a bunch of mistakes.

The timing rules are very useful in this instance. If you have a Comedy Show and you play a Showtime, you can be sure that your opponent can't add a trick to it. This is because the Showtimes happen before the tricks. The best your opponent can do is play an Ace to foil your Showtime, but this is significantly more expensive to him.

All in all, this game worked fairly well with a few tweaks. It's definitely good enough to pursue, because it was fun to play and we found ourselves wanting to play again. Now we'll play it a few more times with these revisions, and see if any more refinements are required.

Final Revisions: Friday June 22, 2001

We played more of this game and learned that aggressive play is critical. I like this aspect. Because every card will be played sooner or later, deciding when to play your cards is the key. We made one more change. Because Aces screwed up the card drawing pattern by causing one player to discard more than one card in the same turn, we decided that instead of discarding the card they stopped, Aces scoop that card into your hand instead. This means that there will always be the same number of rounds in the game, and that all the cards will eventually get played.

One change I'm considering after a rather lackluster couple of endgames is to introduce a "farewell show" rule. Whatever is left in your Practice pile at the end of the game is scored like a normal show. This means every show card eventually gets scored as well.

After three days of playtesting and revision, and a second rules edit some weeks later, I arrived at the final version of the game. You'll notice I changed some terminology and numbers to make the game easier to explain. Most obviously, I've made the perfect show 15 minutes long so that Tens can be 10 minutes long. This deviates pretty strongly from real life (A magician would actually be doing 45 to 60 minutes, but verisimilitude of that degree isn't really necessary in this simple of a game). I also finally noticed that I was using "rehearsal" to mean two different things, so I changed the term for point cards to "Magic Tricks."

Caribbean Star was designed by James Ernest, playtested by Carol Monahan. If you enjoyed Caribbean Star, James encourages you to try more of his free games online at www.cheap-ass.com.

James Ernest

James Ernest is the president and lead designer for Cheapass Games, a small but prolific game company in Seattle, Washington. His award-winning titles include Kill Doctor Lucky, Give Me the Brain, BRAWL, and Button Men. Ernest is known for his quirky humor and innovative game mechanics, and he writes about 30 new games every year.

ADDITIONAL READING AND RESOURCES

Although suggested readings accompany most of this book's chapters, here we list a number of more general references that didn't fit neatly into any particular chapter. These additional readings and resources range from academic websites to visual histories of digital gaming. Obviously, there are innumerable websites and books that we had to leave off of this short list, but our hope is that these sources and the others we list throughout this book can be starting points for your own research investigations.

Computer Game Graphics, by Liz Faber and State Design
Originally published under the title *Re:Play* in the U.K., *Computer Game Graphics* showcases the art and visual culture of computer games. The book's strong visual design lends itself to the subject matter, with many of the spreads functioning as essays in picture form. The writing takes a backseat to the presentation of graphics, and the primary value of the book is in its documentation of the games' visual design.

Digital Games Research Association (DiGRA)
At the time of this book's publication, this fledgling academic organization was still getting off the ground. However, DiGRA promises to be the first professional association devoted to the interdisciplinary study of digital games. Its members range from play historians and media theorists to design educators and game developers. The association's website can be found at: <www.digra.org>.

Electronic Plastic, by Jaro Gielens, Büro Destruct, Uwe Schütte
Electronic Plastic is a visual survey of over 400 old-school computer games, including portable handhelds and cocktail table arcade games. The book offers a terrific overview of the visual design of games from the 1970s and 1980s, including retro-typography, period branding and packaging, and colorful cast plastic cases.

The 400 Rules Project

Located at <http://www.theinspiracy.com/400_project.htm>, The 400 Rules Project is a collaborative game design project headed by veteran computer game designers Noah Falstein and Hal Barwood. Inspired by a talk Barwood gave at the 2001 Game Developers Conference, Falstein has continued the project through a column in *Game Developer Magazine*. The premise of the 400 Rules Project is that there are a limited number of "rules," or design guidelines, that apply to all games, and the goal of the project is to uncover them. While quite formal in scope, the Project represents a wonderfully collaborative game design initiative.

International Game Developers Association

This professional organization serves the digital game development industry. The website, located at <www.igda.org>, is rich with resources for the aspiring and established game developer, from listings of local IGDA chapters to regular columns on a variety of subjects to extensive educational resources.

Joystick Nation: How Video Games Ate Our Quarters, Won Our Hearts, and Rewired Our Minds, by J.C. Herz

Written in 1997, *Joystick Nation* was one of the first comprehensive, popular reports on the cultural phenomenon of video games. A straightforward journalistic account, the book offers a good overview of the pop culture flavor of games and traces some of the factors affecting the rise of video games as a cultural form.

Ludology.org

This website, maintained by game theorist Gonzalo Frasca, is one of the better clearinghouses for events and issues related to the academic study of games. It includes extensive lists of game studies blogs, conferences and calls for papers, and supports a healthy discussion community.

Phoenix: The Fall and Rise of Videogames, by Leonard Herman

Phoenix takes a detailed look at the history of home videogame consoles. The emphasis is technological and the focus is not on games, but on the design of the consoles themselves. While the reading can be dense, the book offers an important overview of the history of the console industry and is an invaluable reference work.

Sirlin.net

An endearingly quirky website, www.sirlin.net is the work of David Sirlin, a former mathematician and sometime game designer. The site contains a large number of short articles about game design, most of them taking a formal approach to understanding phenomena like rule design, narrative, and competition. While there are many homegrown game design sites on the web, Serlin.net contains a surprising amount of thoughtful commentary and analysis.

Supercade: A Visual History of the Videogame Age 1971–1984, by Van Burnham

Supercade is both a visual history and a technological timeline of videogame development during one of the industry's most important periods. The book offers informative summaries of almost every videogame produced between 1971–1984, along with well-researched documentation of the games' visual design.

Trigger Happy: Videogames and the Entertainment Revolution, by Steven Poole

Trigger Happy posits that games are a cultural form to be reckoned with, not only because of their growing economic dominance within the entertainment industry, but because of their status as an art form. Poole examines games from a variety of perspectives, and applies a literary, philosophical, and semiotic analysis to them. He also traces the development of the form from early 8-bit games into the complex technological and cultural systems they are today.

> *Recommended:*
> Chapter 3. Unreal Cities
> Chapter 8. The Player of Games

CONCLUSION

Once you know where you can go and where it's worth going, getting there's no sweat. Just caring and nerves.—**David Sudnow**, *Pilgrim in the Microworld*

Caring and nerves. That's what it took to complete this book.

Certainly a big part of our process was learning how to see: seeing where we were coming from, where we were going, and how to move forward. Like a devilishly intricate puzzle, each step resolved another piece of the pattern, even while opening up whole new vistas to navigate. Everything, we found, hinged on seeing the hinges, and the patterns in the pattern. When we learned to see them we realized they had been there all along, waiting patiently to be discovered.

Having built the system, played it through, and exited out the other side, we find ourselves transformed. We spent so many months (years even) inside the system, playing with it, resisting it, at times breaking it. It was easy to forget that we too were being played, resisted, and at times, broken. (But this is not as bad as it sounds.) And to be honest, the transformation caught us by surprise. Although this book grew out of our experiences teaching game design, designing games, and—especially—playing them, it was not until we began writing that our endeavor found a soul. This soul is filled to bursting with the joy of play: filled with kids dueling Magic on a Brooklyn stoop, a lone runner sweating along a blistering cross country track, a pair of grandmothers trading Canasta tricks for hard cash, a LAN party up past 4 a.m. playing just one more round of Quake. The soul is colored by the passion of game designers who spend untold hours tuning a game to make play by the alchemy of rules, by level designers who invent fabulous new worlds of possibility for us to inhabit, by programmers who build game engines so elegant even the code appears pleased. It is in this soul of play that we discovered ourselves.

What we discovered is no big secret, as it is written on nearly every page. Game designers create meaningful play. Truly meaningful play. The kind that players talk about years after the match has ended, the kind that rallies loyal fans and wakes us up in the middle of the night longing to play again, the kind of play that teaches us what it *means* to play. And perhaps the deepest meaning for play to effect is its ability to transform. Transformative play is a moment of transcendence, in which those structures we took for granted suddenly find themselves cast as players. Grammar tells a joke. The ballroom floor gets up to dance. The rigid Rule become supple and limber and jumps into the arms of Play. Transformative play can metamorphosize the players of a game, the culture of which the game is a part, even the game itself. As the authors of this book, we were also taken hold by transformative play, altered by the hinges and patterns uncovered. It is our hope that you too have been transformed by your experience with these pages, by an ancient and sublime body of knowledge, by the newness of the questions raised, by the beautiful nature of play.

Which really brings us back to caring and nerves. What will it take to alter the face of game design? At what moment will the system be transformed by the play of designers working within it? Do you care enough to take the risk? Do you? This is an important moment, for the field is poised for change and the outcome is uncertain. We honestly don't know what kind of change a transformation might bring. But we nevertheless are unapologetic activists for a radical transformation in game design.

We know what constitutes a game; we know how they work, why they matter, and the kinds of experiences they are capable of producing. But we have barely tested the limits of what they have the potential to become. It is our challenge to you to test those limits, to find your own game design soul, and to muster all of the caring and nerves you've got to transform and discover what it means to play.

Finally: Special thanks to the teachers and students we have had the pleasure and honor of being challenged by in the course of our own evolution as students of the game. And to each other…the end, at last.

Thanks for a great game.

Shall we play again?

Appendix

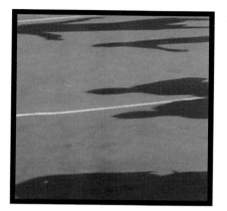

bibliography
list of games cited
index

BIBLIOGRAPHY

Aarseth, Espen J. *Cybertext: Perspectives on Ergodic Literature*. Baltimore: John Hopkins University Press, 1997.

Abrams, Janet. "Other Victories." In *If/Then*, ed. Janet Abrams. Amsterdam: Netherlands Design Institute, 1999, p. 245–47.

Abt, Clark C. *Serious Games*. New York: Viking Press, 1970.

Alexander, Christopher. *Notes on the Synthesis of Form*. Cambridge, MA: Harvard University Press, 1964.

Ambasz, Emilio. *Emilio Ambasz: The Poetics of the Pragmatic*. New York: Rizzoli International Publications, 1988.

Apter, Michael J. "A Structural-Phenomenology of Play." In *Adult Play: A Reversal Theory Approach*, ed. J. H. Kerr and Michael J. Apter. Amsterdam: Swets and Zeitlinger, 1991, p. 192–201.

Atari, Inc., Super Breakout. Atari Game Program Instructions. Sunnyvale, CA: Atari, Inc., 1981 (archived at <www.atariage.com>).

Avedon, E. M. "The Structural Elements of Games." In *The Study of Games*, ed. E.M. Avedon and Brian Sutton-Smith. New York: John Wiley, 1971, p. 419–426.

Avedon, E.M., and Brian Sutton-Smith. *The Study of Games*. New York: John Wiley, 1971.

Bak, Per. *How Nature Works: The Science of Self Organized Criticality*. New York: Copernicus Books, 1996.

Bartle, Richard. "Hearts, Clubs, Diamonds, Spades: Players Who Suit MUDs." <http:// www.mud.co.uk/richard/hcds.htm>.

Barwood, Hal and Noah Falstein. The 400 Rules Project. http://www.theinspiracy.com/400_project.htm.

Bates, Bob, and Andre LaMothe, eds. *Game Design: The Art and Business of Creating Games*. Boston: Premier Press, 2001.

Bateson, Gregory. "A Theory of Play and Fantasy." In *Steps to an Ecology of Mind*. Chicago: The University of Chicago Press, 1972, p. 191–222.

Beach Frank A. "Current Concepts of Play in Animals." In *Child's Play*, ed. R.E. Herron and Brian Sutton-Smith. New York: John Wiley, 1971, p. 196–211.

Berman, Joshua, and Amy Bruckman. "The Turing Game: Exploring Identity in an Online Environment." *Convergence* 7(3): 83–102, 2001.

Bodley, John H. *Cultural Anthropology: Tribes, States, and the Global System.* New York: McGraw-Hill Higher Education, 1994.

Bolter, Jay David, and Richard Grusin. *Remediation: Understanding New Media.* Boston: MIT Press, 1999.

Bonasia, Maria. "MetaMystery," May 30, 2001, <www.cloudmakers.org>.

Boria, Eric, Paul Breidenbach, and Talmadge Wright. "Player Talk and the Social Mediation of Virtual Violence." Unpublished paper, 2002.

Buchanan, Richard. "Wicked Problems in Design Thinking." In *The Idea of Design: A Design Issues Reader,* ed. Victor Margolin and Richard Buchanan. Cambridge, MA: MIT Press, 1995, p. 3–20.

Buchanan, Richard. "Branzi's Dilemma: Design in Contemporary Culture." In *Design: Pleasure or Responsibility?* ed. P. Takhokallio and S. Vihma. Helsinki: University of Art and Design Helsinki, 1995, p. 15–27.

Burnham, Van. *Supercade: A Visual History of the Videogame Age 1971–1984.* Cambridge, MA: MIT Press, 2001.

Caillois, Roger. *Man, Play, and Games.* London: Thames and Hudson, 1962.

Cameron, Andy. "Dissimulations: Illusions of Interactivity." *MFJ* No. 28: Spring, 1995. <http://infotyte.rmit.edu.au/rebecca/html/dissimulations.html>.

Campbell, Jeremy. *Grammatical Man: Information, Entropy, Language, and Life.* New York: Simon and Schuster, 1982.

Carroll, Lewis. *Alice's Adventures in Wonderland and Through the Looking Glass.* New York: Signet Classic, 2000.

Cassell, Justine, and Henry Jenkins, eds. *From Barbie to Mortal Kombat: Gender and Computer Games.* Cambridge, MA: MIT Press, 1998.

Casti, John. *Complexification: Explaining a Paradoxical World Through the Science of Surprise.* New York: HarperCollins Publishers, 1994.

Chandler, Daniel. *Semiotics for Beginners.* <www.aber.ac.uk/~dgc/semiotic.html>.

Church, Doug. "Formal Abstract Design Tools," <www.gamasutra.com>.

Cloudmakers.org. <www.cloudmakers.org>.

Cohen, Scott. *Zap: The Rise and Fall of Atari.* Philadelphia, PA: Xlibris Corporation, 1964.

Costikyan, Greg. "Don't be a Vidiot: What Computer Game Designers Can Learn from Non-Electronic Games." Speech given at the 1998 Game Developer's Conference (archived at <www.costik.com/vidiot.hmtl>).

Costikyan, Greg. "I Have No Words and I Must Design." In *Interactive Fantasy #2* <www.geocities.com/SiliconValley/Bay/2535/nowords.html>.

Cowen, George, and David Pines. *Complexity: Metaphors, Models and Reality.* Santa Fe: Addison Wesley Longman, 1994.

Crawford, Chris. *The Art of Computer Game Design.* <www.vancouver.wsu.edu/fac/peabody/ game-book/Coverpage.html>.

Crawford, Chris. *The Art of Interactive Design: A Euphorious and Illuminating Guide to Building Successful Software.* San Francisco: No Starch Press, 2002.

Crawford, Chris. *Understanding Interactivity.* San Francisco: No Starch Press, 2002.

Csikszentmihalyi, Mihaly. *Flow: The Psychology of Optimal Experience.* New York: HarperCollins Publishers, 1991.

Davis, Morton D. *Game Theory: A Nontechnical Introduction.* Mineola: Dover Publications, 1970.

DeKoven, Bernard. "Creating the Play Community." In *The New Games Book,* ed. Andrew Fluegelman and Shoshana Tembeck. New York: Doubleday, 1976, p. 41–42.

DeKoven, Bernard. *The Well-Played Game.* New York: Doubleday, 1978.

de Saussure, Ferdinand. *Course in General Linguistics.* London: Peter Owen, 1960.

Dilnot, Clive. *The Science of Uncertainty: The Potential Contribution of Design Knowledge.* Proceedings of the Ohio Conference, Doctoral Education in Design. Pittsburgh School of Design, Carnegie Mellon University, October 9, 1998.

Dunnigan, James F. *Wargames Handbook: How to Play and Design Commercial and Professional Wargames,* 3rd ed. San Jose: Writers Club Press, 2000.

Edwards, Paul N. *The Closed World.* Cambridge, MA: MIT Press, 1996.

Ekeland, Ivar. *The Broken Dice: And Other Mathematical Tales of Chance.* Chicago: University of Chicago Press, 1993.

Ellington, Henry, Eric Addinall, and Fred Percival. *A Handbook of Game Design.* London: Kogan Page Limited, 1982.

Epstein, Richard. *The Theory of Gambling and Statistical Logic.* San Diego: Academic Press, 1977.

Faber, Liz. *Computer Game Graphics.* New York: Watson-Guptill Publications, 1998.

Fatsis, Stefan. *Word Freak: Heartbreak, Triumph, Genius, and Obsession in the World of Competitive Scrabble Players.* Boston: Houghton Mifflin, 2001.

Feed Magazine. "Brave New Worlds: A Special Issue on Video Games." <www.feedmag.com>.

Findeli, Alain. "Moholy-Nagy's Design Pedagogy in Chicago, 1937–46." In *The Idea of Design: A Design Issues Reader,* ed. by Victor Margolin, and Richard Buchanan, Cambridge, MA: MIT Press, 1995, p. 29–38.

Fine, Gary Alan. *Shared Fantasy.* Chicago: University of Chicago, 1983.

Fluegelman, Andrew, and Shoshana Tembeck. *The New Games Book.* New York: Doubleday, 1976.

Frasca, Gonzalo. Ludology.org. <www.ludology.org>.

Gamasutra.com. *The Art and Science of Making Games.* <www.gamasutra.com>.

Gamestudies.org. The International Journal of Computer Game Research, eds. Espen Aarseth, Markku Eskelinen, Marie-Laure Ryan, Susana Tosca.

Garfield, Richard. "Metagames," In *Horsemen of the Apocalypse: Essays on Roleplaying,* ed. Jim Dietz. Sigel, IL: Jolly Rogers Games, 2000, p. 16–22.

Geertz, Clifford. *The Interpretation of Cultures.* New York: Basic Books, 1977.

Gielens, Jaro. *Electronic Plastic*. Berlin: Die Gestalten Verlag, 2000.

Game Girl Advance. <www.gamegirladvance.com>.

Gleitman, Henry. *Psychology*, 2nd ed. New York: W.W. Norton & Company, Inc., 1986.

Goldstein, Kenneth. "Strategies in Counting Out." In *The Study of Games*, ed. Elliott Avedon and Brian Sutton-Smith. New York: John Wiley & Sons Inc., 1971, p. 172–77.

Gonzalez, Jesus M. "A Brief History of Open Source Software." <http://eu.conecta.it/paper/ brief_history_open_source.html>.

Gygax, Gary. *Advanced Dungeons and Dragons Players Handbook*. Lake Geneva: TRS Hobbies, 1978.

Hale-Evans, Ron. "Game Systems Part 1." <www.thegamesjournal.com/articles/Game Systems1.shtml>.

Hall, Justin. "Brave New Worlds: A Special Issue on Video Games." *Feed Magazine*. <www.feedmag.com>.

Hallford, Neal and Jana Hallford. *Swords and Circuitry: A Designer's Guide to Computer Role Playing Games*. Boston: Premier Press, Incorporated, 2001.

Hancock, Hugh. "Better Game Design Through Cut-Scenes." Gamasutra.com. <www.gamasutra.com>.

Hans, James S. *Play of the World*. Boston: University of Massachusetts Press, 1981.

Harris, Tricia "Kazi Wren." "Mod World." In *Gamespy.com*, August 22, 2002. <http://www.gamespy.com/modworld/August02/modworld12/>.

Hayles, Katherine. *How We Became Post-Human*. Chicago: University of Chicago Press, 1999.

Hebdige, Dick. *Subculture: The Meaning of Style*. London: Methuen & Co., Ltd., 1988.

Herman, Leonard. *Phoenix: The Fall and Rise of Videogames*. Springfield, NJ: Rolenta Press, 1994.

Herron, R. E. "A Syntax for Play and Games." In *Child's Play,* ed. Brian Sutton-Smith and R. E. Herron. New York: John Wiley and Sons, 1971, p. 298–307.

Heskett, John. *Industrial Design.* New York: Oxford University Press, 1980.

Herz, J. C. "Gaming the System: Multi-player Worlds Online," In *Game On: The History and Culture of Video Games,* ed. Lucien King. London: Laurence King Publishing Ltd., 2002, p. 86–97.

Herz, J. C. *Joystick Nation: How Videogames Ate Our Quarters, Won Our Hearts, and Rewired Our Minds.* New York: Little, Brown & Company, 1997.

Heskett, John. *Industrial Design.* New York: Oxford University Press, 1980.

Hickey, Dave. *Air Guitar: Essays on Art and Democracy.* San Francisco: Foundation for Advanced Critical Studies, Incorporated, 1997.

Holland, John. *Emergence.* Reading: Helix Books, 1998.

Hughes, Linda. "Beyond the Rules of the Game: Why Are Rooie Rules Nice?" In *The World of Play,* ed. Frank E. Manning. Proceedings of the 7th Annual Meeting of the Association of the Anthropological Study of Play. New York: Leisure Press, 1983, p. 188–199.

Hughes, Linda. "Children's Games and Gaming." In *Children's Folklore: A Source Book.* ed. Brian Sutton-Smith, Jay Mechling, Thomas W. Johnson, and Felicia R. McMahon. Logan, UT: Utah State University Press, 1999, p. 93–120.

Huhtamo, Eric. "Game Patch: the Son of Scratch?" In *Cracking the Maze.* Curator Anne-Marie Schleiner. July 16, 1999. <www.switch.sjsu.edu/CrackingtheMaze>.

Huizinga, Johann. *Homo Ludens: A Study of the Play Element in Culture.* Boston: Beacon Press, 1955.

Ikekeonwu and Nwokah. "Nigerian and American Children's Games." In *The Study of Play, Vol 1. Diversions and Divergences in Fields of Play,* ed. Margaret C. Duncan, Garry Chick, and Alan Aycock. New York: Ablex/Greenwood Publishing Company, 1998, p. 61–75.

International Game Developers Association, <www.igda.org>.

Jenkins, Henry. "Complete Freedom of Movement: Video Games as Gendered Play Spaces." In *From Barbie to Mortal Kombat: Gender and Computer Games*, ed. Justine Cassell and Henry Jenkins. Cambridge, MA: MIT Press, 1998, p. 262–297.

Jenkins, Henry. "Testimony Before the U.S. Senate Commerce Committee, May 4, 1999." <www.senate.gov/~commerce/hearings/0504jen.pdf>.

Jenkins, Henry. *Textual Poachers: Television Fans and Participatory Culture*. New York: Routledge, 1992.

Jenkins, Henry and Kurt Squire. "The Art of Contested Spaces." In *Game On: The History and Culture of Video Games*, ed. Lucien King. London: Laurence King Publishing Ltd., 2002, p. 64–75.

Johnson, Steven. *Emergence: The Connected Lives of Ants, Brains, Cities, and Software*. New York: Scribner, 2001.

Jonas, Wolfgang. "On the Foundations of a 'Science of the Artificial.'" Breman, Germany: Hochschule fur Kunst und Design Halle, 1999. <http://home.snafu.de/jonasw/JONAS4-49.html>.

Juul, Jesper. "Games Telling Stories? A Brief Note on Games and Narratives." Gamestudies.org. <www.gamestudies.org>.

Kim, Scott. "What is a Puzzle?" <www.scottkim.com/articles.html>.

Kinder, Marsha. *Playing with Power in Movies, Television, and Video Games: From Muppet Babies to Teenage Mutant Ninja Turtles*. Los Angeles: University of California Press, 1993.

King, Geogg and Tanya Krzywinska. "Computer Games | Cinema | Interfaces." In *Computer Games and Digital Cultures, Conference Proceedings*, ed. Frans Mäyrä. Tampere, Finland: Tampere University Press, 2002, 89–107.

King, Lucien, ed. *Game On: The History and Culture of Video Games*. London: Laurence King Publishing Ltd., 2002.

Klevjer, Rune. "In Defense of Cut-Scenes." In *Computer Games and Digital Cultures, Conference Proceedings*, ed. Frans Mäyrä. Tampere, Finland: Tampere University Press, 2002, p. 191–2002.

Knizia, Reiner. *Dice Games Properly Explained*. Tadworth, Surrey: Elliot Right Way Books, 2001.

Krippendorff, Klaus. "On the Essential Contexts of Artifacts or On the Proposition that 'Design is Making Sense (of Things).'" In *The Idea of Design: A Design Issues Reader*, ed. Victor Margolin and Richard Buchanan. Cambridge, MA: MIT Press, 1995, p.156–86.

Kuper, Simon. "The World's Game Is Not Just A Game." In *The New York Times* Sunday Magazine, May 26, 2002.

Langton, Christopher. *Artificial Life: An Overview*. Cambridge, MA: MIT Press, 1995.

Laramée, François Dominic, ed. *Game Design Perspectives*. Hingham, MA: Charles River Media, 2002.

Lantz, Frank and Eric Zimmerman. "Rules, Play, and Culture: Checkmate!" *Merge Magazine*, 1999, p. 41–43.

Laurel, Brenda. *Computers as Theater*. Reading, MA: Addison-Wesley Publishing Company, 1993.

LeBlanc, Marc. "Feedback Systems and the Dramatic Structure of Competition." Game Developers Conference, 1999.

Littlejohn, Stephen. *Theories of Human Communication*, 3rd ed. Belmont, CA: Wadsworth Publishing Company, 1989.

Lupton, Ellen and J. Abbott Miller "Laws of the Letter." In *Design, Writing, Research: Writing on Graphic Design*. New York: Princeton Architectural Press, 1996.

Mackay, Daniel. *The Fantasy Role-Playing Game: A New Performing Art*. London: McFarland & Company, Inc., 2001.

Manning, Frank E., ed. *The World of Play*. Proceedings of the 7th Annual Meeting of the Association of the Anthropological Study of Play. New York: Leisure Press, 1983.

Marcus, Greil. *Lipstick Traces: A Secret History of the Twentieth Century*. Cambridge: Harvard University Press, 1989.

Manovich, Lev. *The Language of New Media*. Cambridge: MIT Press, 2001.

Martin, Ben. "The Schema." In *Complexity: Metaphors, Models, and Reality,* ed. George Cowan and David Pines. Santa Fe: Addison Wesley Longman, 1994, p. 263–286.

Mäyrä, Frans. ed. *Computer Games and Digital Cultures Conference Proceedings.* Tampere, Finland: Tampere University Press, 2002.

Miller, J. Hillis. "Narrative." In *Critical Terms for Literary Study,* ed. Frank Lentricchia and Thomas McLaughlin. Chicago: The University of Chicago Press, 1990, p. 66–79.

Morganstern, Oscar, and John Von Neumann. *Theory of Games and Economic Behavior.* Princeton: Princeton University Press, 1944.

Murray, Janet. *Hamlet on the Holodeck.* New York: The Free Press, 1997.

Norman, Donald. *The Design of Everyday Things.* New York: Doubleday, 1988.

Nwokah and Ikekeonwu. "Nigerian and American Children's Games." In *The Study of Play Vol. 1. Diversions and Divergences in Fields of Play,* ed. Margaret C. Duncan, Gary Chick, and Alan Aycock. New York: Ablex/Greenwood Publishing Company, 1998, p147–153.

Parlett, David. *The Oxford Dictionary of Card Games.* Oxford: Oxford University Press, 1992.

Parlett, David. *The Oxford History of Board Games.* Oxford: Oxford University Press, 1999.

Pearce, Celia. *The Interactive Book: A Guide to the Interactive Revolution.* Toronto: Macmillan Technical Publishing/New Riders, 1997.

Peirce, Charles Saunders. *Charles S. Peirce: Selected Writings,* ed. P. O. Wiener. New York: Dover, 1958.

Peterson, Ivars. *The Jungles of Randomness: A Mathematical Safari.* New York: John Wiley, 1997.

Phillips, Andrea. "Deep Water." 26th July 2001. Cloudmakers.org. <www.cloudmakers.org>.

Piaget, Jean. *The Moral Judgment of the Child.* New York: Free Press, 1997.

Poole, Steven. *Trigger Happy: Videogames and the Entertainment Revolution.* New York: Arcade Publishing, 2000.

Poundstone, William. *Prisoner's Dilemma.* New York: Doubleday, 1992.

Prensky, Marc. *Digital Game-Based Learning.* New York: McGraw-Hill, 2001.

Reider, Norman. "Chess, Oedipus, and the Mater Dolorosa." In *The Study of Games,* ed. E.M. Avedon and Brian Sutton-Smith. New York: John Wiley, 1971, p. 440–464.

Resnick, Mitchell. *Turtles, Termites, and Traffic Jams.* Cambridge: MIT Press, 1997.

Robinett, Warren. *Inventing the Adventure Game.* Unpublished manuscript.

Rollings, Andrew and Dave Morris. *Game Architecture and Design.* Scottsdale, AZ: Coriolis Group, 1999.

Rouse, Richard III. *Game Design: Theory and Practice.* Plano, TX: Wordware Publishing, 2001.

Rumelhart, David E. and Andrew Ortony. "The Representation of Knowledge in Memory." In *Schooling and the Acquisition of Knowledge,* ed. R. C. Anderson, R. J. Spiro, and W. E. Montague. Hillsdale, N.J.: Erlbaum, 1977, p. 99–135.

Ryan, Marie-Laure. *Narrative as Virtual Reality: Immersion and Interactivity in Literature and Electronic Media.* Baltimore: John Hopkins University Press, 2000.

Salen, Katie. "Lock, Stock, and Barrel: Sexing the Digital Siren," In *Sex Appeal: The Art of Allure in Graphic and Advertising Design,* ed. Steven Heller. New York: Allworth Press, 2000, p. 148–51.

Salen, Katie. "Telefragging Monster Movies." In *Game On: The History and Culture of Video Games,* ed. Lucien King. London: Laurence Ling Publishing Ltd., 2002, p. 98–111.

Sankey, Daragh. "A.I. Game," 2001. Joystick101.org. <www.joystick.org>.

Schell, Jesse, and Joe Schochet. "Designing Interactive Theme Park Rides: Lessons From Disney's Battle for the Buccaneer Gold." <www.gamasutra.com/features/20010706/ schell_01.htm>.

Schleiner, Anne-Marie. "Game Plug-ins and Patches as Hacker Art." *Cracking the Maze.* July 16, 1999. <switch.sjsu.edu/CrackingtheMaze>.

Schmittberger, R. Wayne. *New Rules for Classic Games.* New York: John Wiley, 1992.

Schon, Donald. *The Reflective Practitioner: How Professionals Think in Action.* New York: Basic Books, 1983.

Shannon, Claude and Weaver, Warren. *Mathematical Theory of Communication.* Champaign: University of Illinois Press, 1963.

Sieberg, Daniel. "Reality Blurs, Hype Builds with Web 'A.I.' Game." May 2001, CNN.com.

Simon, Herbert. *The Sciences of the Artificial.* Cambridge, MA: MIT Press, 1968.

Sirlin, David. Sirlin.net. <www.sirlin.net>.

Smith, Harvey. "The Future of Game Design." <www.gamasutra.com>.

Sniderman, Stephen. "Unwritten Rules." <www.gamepuzzles.com/tlog/tlog2.htm>.

Stewart, Susan. *Nonsense. Aspects of Intertextuality in Folklore and Literature.* Baltimore: The John Hopkins University Press, 1978.

Sudnow, David. *Pilgrim in the Microworld.* New York: Warner Books, 1983.

Suits, Bernard. *Grasshopper: Games, Life, and Utopia.* Boston: David R. Godine, 1990.

Sutton-Smith, Brian. *The Ambiguity of Play.* Boston: Harvard University Press, 2001.

Sutton-Smith, Brian. "Boundaries." In *Child's Play*, ed. Brian Sutton-Smith and R. E. Herron. Malabar, FL: Warrior Books, 1971, p. 173–92.

Sutton-Smith, Brian, Jay Mechling, Thomas W. Johnson, and Felicia R. McMahon, eds. *Children's Folklore: A Source Book*. Logan, UT: Utah State University Press, 1999.

Sutton-Smith, Brian. "The Kissing Games of Adolescents of Ohio." In *The Study of Games,* ed. Elliott Avedon and Brian Sutton-Smith. New York: John Wiley and Sons, Inc., 1971, p.213–16.

Sutton-Smith, Brian. *Toys as Culture.* New York: Gardner Press, Incorporated, 1986.

Thompson, J. Mark. "Defining the Abstract." <http://www.flash.net/~markthom/html/game_thoughts.html>.

Underwood, Mick. CCMS.
<http://www.cultsock.ndirect.co.uk/MUHome/cshtml/semiomean/semio1.html>.

Von Bertalanffy, Ludwig. *General Systems Theory Foundations.* New York: George Braziller, 1968.

Von Neumann, John and Oscar Morganstern. *Theory of Games and Economic Behavior.* Princeton: Princeton University Press, 1944.

Vygotsky, L. S. "Play and Its Role in the Mental Development of the Child." In *Play and Its Role in Evolution and Development,* ed. J. S. Bruner, A. Jolly, and K. Sylva. New York: Penguin, 1976, p. 548–63.

Wolf, Mark J.P. "Space in the Video Game." In *The Medium of the Video Game,* Austin: University of Texas Press, 2002, p. 53–70.

Wolfe, Burton H. "The Monopolization of Monopoly: The Story of Lizzie Magie." In *The San Francisco Bay Guardian,* 1976.

LIST OF GAMES CITED

The following index contains all of the games mentioned in *Rules of Play*. Each game is listed alphabetically by title, including date of release, medium in which it is played, and developer or designer of the game.

A great many of the games we cite do not have an identifiable author or group of authors—or the exact origin of the game is in dispute by game historians. In these cases, the game is listed as "Traditional" and the approximate dates of origin are indicated, if known. Oftentimes, such games have rich historical evolutions, such as the board game Chutes and Ladders, which has striking similarities to games played in ancient Egypt, as well as to traditional games from India, Nepal, and Tibet. In these cases, we chose as the date of origin the first historical instance of a game that is recognizably similar to the game we cite. (In the case of Chutes and Ladders, for example, we use the date 1892: this is the publication date of F.H. Ayre's Snakes and Ladders, a game virtually identical to present-day Chutes and Ladders).

In deference to the typically collaborative process of game creation, individual designers are listed as the creator of a game only when a single designer or pair of designers created the entire game by themselves, or when a single designer is commercially credited with sole authorship, as is the case with many contemporary board games.

We often cite more than one version of a digital game that was produced in a series, such as Virtua Fighter and Virtual Fighter 4. In these cases, we list the game as a series but include only the date and creator of the first game in the series. Also, when important versions of a game appear in more than one medium (such as an arcade game that later became a console game), we list all of the relevant forms, with the original medium listed first.

In organizing the games by medium, we opted for very "broad stroke" categories, such as "Arcade game" or "Physical game." Some of the categories do overlap, but we grouped the games into clusters that seemed most conceptually useful for the sake of comparison. Our intention here is not to provide a detailed accounting or taxonomy of these games, but instead to give a general indication of the rich range of games that we mention and analyze in the course of our investigations. If you are inclined to research any of these games further, a list of references used in putting together the information in this index is included at the end.

Arcade game: Games in this category are digital games played on dedicated machines that only play a single game. This includes typical arcade games like Pac-Man and Space Invaders as well as location-based entertainment games like the Disneyworld attraction Battle for the Buccaneer Gold.

Board game: In addition to games like Chess and Go—games that are literally played on a board—we include in this category games played on some kind of board-like structure, such as Battleship and Connect Four.

Book-based game: The book-based flying simulation Ace of Aces didn't fit into any other category, so we gave it its own. Other book-based games do exist, but are not mentioned in *Rules of Play*.

Card game: Some games in this category, such as Poker and Bridge, use a standard set of playing cards. Others, such as Magic: The Gathering, use specialized cards designed specifically for one game.

Computer game: This group includes games designed to be played on personal computers, from the venerable PDP-1 to present-day Macintosh and Windows machines. These games are played primarily on a single machine by a single player.

Console game: These games are played on game console machines that attach to a television, ranging from the Atari 2600 to today's Xbox, GameCube, and Playstation2.

Dice game: Games in this group are played primarily or exclusively with dice. They include gambling games like Craps and traditional family games like Pig and Yatzee. Additionally, we included the game of Roulette in this category, as it is a game based entirely on chance.

Handheld game: This category includes games played on a portable digital device such as a Game Boy or Palm Pilot. Electronic handheld devices that only play a single game, such as P.O.X., are also grouped here.

Icehouse game: Icehouse is a game system that uses colored plastic pyramids as the pieces for a great many different games. There were enough Icehouse games mentioned in *Rules of Play* that we included it as its own category.

Mobile game: Games in this group are played primarily by using a cell phone, whether single-player or multiplayer.

Online game: This is a special type of digital game that emphasizes web-based social interaction as the primary form of play. Included in this category are trans-media games like Majestic that take place over the Internet, through fax machines, and over the telephone.

Physical game: This category includes games like Tag or Marbles in which the play of the game primarily involves physical movement and interaction. These games are less regulated than games included in the category Sport.

Puzzle: As described in *Defining Games,* puzzles are games with a single correct answer or set of answers. Puzzles can take a wide variety of forms, but the ones we cite are single-player games that use simple materials such as pencil and paper.

Role-playing game: These games are highly narrative experiences where the primary form of play involves players taking on imaginative personas. The classic Dungeons & Dragons is the prototypical example of this category of game. Live-action role-playing games such as Vampire: The Masquerade are also included here.

Social game: Social games are games in which the play consists primarily of social interaction between participants. Typically, these games have little or no material components, and include party games as diverse as Charades, Mafia, and Spin the Bottle.

Sport: The games in this category are physical games that are typically played as an organized, regulated sport—usually with very specialized equipment in a special space set aside for the game. In some cases, games listed as Sports can also constitute a leisure activity, such as Skiing.

Television game show: These games exist as televised experiences, and include shows like *Survivor, Jeopardy,* and *Who Wants to be a Millionaire.*

Tile game: Games in this group are played with some form of modular tiles, and include games like Dominoes and Mah Jongg.

1000 Blank White Cards
Nathan McQuillen, 1994
Social game

20 Questions
Traditional
Social game

A.I.
Puppet Masters / Microsoft, 2001
Online game

Ace of Aces
Alfred Leonardi, 1980
Book-based game

Advanced Dungeons & Dragons
(see Dungeons & Dragons)

Adventure
Will Crowther and Don Woods, 1975
Computer game

Adventure
Warren Robinett, 1980
Console game

Age of Empires
Ensemble Studios, 1997
Computer game

Alleyway
Nintendo, 1989
Handheld game

Arm Wresting
Traditional
Physical game

Assassin
Traditional, 1966
Role-playing game

Asteroids
Atari, 1979
Arcade game; Console game

Atari Football
Atari, 1978
Arcade game

Bad Dudes
Data East, 1988
Arcade game

Backgammon
Traditional, circa 1600
Board game

Barbie Fashion Designer
Mattel, 1996
Computer game

Baseball
Abner Doubleday, circa 1839
Sport

Basketball
James Naismith, 1891
Sport

Battle for the Buccaneer Gold
Disney, 2001
Arcade game

Battlebots
Comedy Central, 1998
Sport / Television game show

Battleship
Milton Bradley, 1967
Board game

Battlezone
Atari, 1980
Arcade game

Bejeweled
Popcap Games, 2001
Online game

Berzerk
Stern, 1980
Arcade game

Billiards
Traditional, circa 1500
Sport

Black & White
Lionhead Studios, 2001
Computer game; Console game

Blackjack
Traditional, circa 1750
Card game

Blob
New Games Movement, circa 1976
Physical game

Botfighers
It's Alive, 2001
Mobile game

Bowling
Traditional, circa 1880
Sport

Breakout (series)
Atari, 1976
Arcade game; Console game

Boxing
Traditional
Sport

Bridge
Traditional, circa 1885
Card game

Bridge-Builder
Alex Austin, 2000
Computer game

Bughouse
Traditional, circa 1965
Board game

Bust-A-Groove
Square Enix, 1998
Console game; Arcade game

Canasta
Traditional, circa 1945
Card game

Candyland
Milton Bradley, 1949
Board game

Can't Stop
Sid Sackson, 1980
Dice game

Capture the Flag
Traditional
Physical game

Car Wars (series)
Chad Irby and Steve Jackson, 1982
Board game

The Card Game
Traditional
Social game

Castle Wolfenstein
Muse, 1981
Computer game

Catch the Dragon's Tail
New Games Movement, circa 1976
Physical game

Centipede
Atari, 1980
Arcade game

Charades
Traditional
Social game

Chaturanga
Traditional, circa 650
Board game

Checkers
Traditional, circa 1500
Board game

Chess
Traditional, circa 850
Board game

Chinese Checkers
Ravensburger, 1892
Board game

Chutes and Ladders
F. H. Ayres, 1892
Board game

Civilization (series)
MicroProse, 1991
Computer game; Console game

Command and Conquer
Westwood Studios, 1995
Computer game

Cool Boarders (series)
Sony, 1996
Console game

Cops and Robbers
Traditional
Physical game

Cosmic Wimpout
CQ Incorporated, circa 1975
Dice game

Counter-Strike
The Counter-Strike Team, 2000
Computer game

Craps
Circa 1700
Dice game

Crash Bandicoot
Naughty Dog, 1996
Console game

Cricket
Traditional, 1700
Sport

Croquet
Traditional, circa 1830
Sport

Dactyl Nightmare
Virtuality, 1993
Arcade game

Dance Dance Revolution
Konami, 1998
Arcade game; Console game

Defender
Williams, 1980
Arcade game

Deus Ex
Ion Storm, 2000
Computer game; Console game

Diablo (series)
Blizzard Entertainment, 1996
Computer game

Dig-Dug
Namco, 1982
Arcade game

Diplomacy
Allan Calhammer, 1959
Board game

Dodge Ball
Traditional
Physical game

Dominoes
Traditional, circa 1850
Tile game

Donkey Kong
Nintendo, 1981
Arcade game

Don't Wake Daddy
Parker Brothers, 1992
Board game

DOOM
id Software, 1993
Computer game

Dope Wars (originally Drug Wars)
John Dell
Computer game; Handheld game

Double Dragon
Taito, 1986
Arcade game

Draw and Kiss
Traditional, circa 1959
Social game

Driver: You are the Wheelman
Reflections, 1999
Console game

Drome Racing Challenge
gameLab, 2002
Online game

Duke Nuke 'Em 3D (series)
3D Realms, 1996
Computer game; Console game

Dungeon Siege
Gas Powered Games, 2002
Computer game

Dungeons & Dragons (series)
Dave Arneson & Gary Gygax, 1973
Role-playing game

Earthball
New Games Movement, circa 1976
Physical Game

Easy Money
Milton Bradley, circa 1955
Board game

Elemental
Team Elemental, unpublished
Computer game

Enchanted Forest
Michel Matsechoss and Alex Randolph, 1992
Board game

Endurance Kissing
Traditional, circa 1959
Social game

Euchre
Traditional, circa 1860
Card game

EverQuest
Verant Interactive, 1999
Online game

Fencing
Traditional, circa 1670
Sport

Final Fantasy (series)
Square Enix, 1990
Console game

Flashlight
Traditional, circa 1959
Social game

FLUID
gameLab, 2002
Computer game

Flux
Andrew Looney, 1997
Card game

Football
Walter Camp, 1879
Sport

Foursquare
Traditional
Sport

The Game of Life
John Conway, 1970
Puzzle; Computer game

Gauntlet (series)
Atari, 1985
Arcade game; Console game

Gearheads
R/GA Interactive, 1996
Computer game

Gin
Traditional, circa 1920
Card game

Go
Traditional, circa 2000 BCE
Board game

Go Fish
Traditional, circa 1585
Card game

Golf
Traditional, circa 1450
Sport

Gnostica
John Cooper, 2001
Icehouse game

Gran Turismo (series)
Ployphony Digital, 1998
Console game

Grand Theft Auto III (series)
Rockstar North, 2001
Console game

GURPS: Generic Universal Role-Playing System
Steve Jackson, circa 1986
Role-playing game system

Gymnastics
Traditional, 1896
Sport

Half-Life
Valve Software, 1998
Computer game; Console game

Hearts
Traditional, circa 1880
Card game

Hex
Piet Hein, 1942
Board game

Hide-And-Seek
Traditional
Physical game

Hollywood Squares
NBC, 1965
Television game show

House of the Dead
Sega, 1997
Arcade game; Console game

Ice Hockey
Traditional, circa 1850
Sport

Icehouse
Andrew Looney and John Cooper, 1991
Icehouse game

Illuminati
Steve Jackson, 1982
Board game

Jak & Daxter
Naughty Dog, 2001
Console game

James Bond 007 In Agent Under Fire
Electronic Arts, 2001
Console game

Jeopardy
NBC, 1964
Television game show

Jet Grind Radio
Smilebit, 2000
Console game

Joust
Williams, 1982
Arcade game

Junkbot (series)
gameLab, 2001
Computer game

Kick the Can
Traditional
Physical game

Killer *(see Assassin)*

Kriegspiel
Lt. von Reisswitz, 1824
Board game

The L Game
Edward DeBono, circa 1974
Board game

The Landlord's Game
Lizzie Magie, 1904
Board game

Little Max
Traditional
Dice game

LOOP
gameLab, 2002
Computer game

Lord of the Rings Board Game
Reiner Knizia, 2000
Board game

Mad Magazine Game
Parker Brothers, 1979
Board game

Mafia
Traditional
Social game

Magic: The Gathering
Richard Garfield, 1993
Card game

Mah Jongg
Traditional, circa 1880
Tile game

Majestic
Electronic Arts, 2001
Online game

Mancala
Traditional, circa 3000 BCE
Board game

Marathon (series)
Bungie Software, 1994
Computer game

Marbles
Traditional, circa 100 BCE
Physical game

Mario Bros. (series)
Nintendo, 1983
Arcade game; Console game; Handheld game

Martian Backgammon
Andrew Looney, 1997
Icehouse game

Mastermind
Invicta, 1972
Board game

Max Payne
3D Realms, 2001
Computer game; Console game

Mega Man (series)
Capcom, 1987
Console game; Handheld game

Memory
Traditional
Card game

Metal Gear Solid (series)
KCEJ, 1998
Console game

Metroid (series)
Nintendo, 1985
Console game

Milles Bournes
Parker Brothers, 1954
Card game

Missile Command
Atari, 1980
Arcade game; Console game

Monopoly
Charles B. Darrow, 1933
Board game

Mortal Kombat (series)
Midway, 1992
Arcade game; Console game

Mother May I?
Traditional
Physical game

Mousetrap
Ideal, 1963
Board game

Ms. Pac-Man
Namco, 1982
Arcade game; Console game

Musical Chairs
Traditional
Physical game

Myst
Cyan, 1993
Computer game

Myth: The Fallen Lords
Bungie Software, 1997
Computer game

NBA Courtside (series)
Left Field Productions, 1998
Console game

NBA Live (series)
Electronic Arts, 1995
Console game; Computer game

NeoPets
NeoPets Inc, 1999
Online game

Netrunner
Wizards of the Coast, 1995
Card game

Neverwinter Nights
Bioware, 2002
Computer game; Online game

Night Driver
Atari, 1976
Arcade game

Oddworld (series)
Oddworld Inhabitants, 1997
Console game; Computer game

Olympic Decathlon
Traditional, 1896
Sport

Once Upon a Time
Richard Lambert, Andrew Rilstone, and
 James Wallis, 1993
Card game

Othello
Lewis Waterman, 1888
Board game

P.O.X.
Hasbro, 2001
Handheld game

Pac-Man
Namco, 1980
Arcade game; Console game

Parappa the Rapper
Interlink, 1997
Console game

Pass the Orange
Traditional, circa 1959
Social game

Pick-Up Sticks
Traditional
Physical game

Pictionary
Rob Angel, 1986
Board game

Pig
Traditional
Dice Game

Pilotwings
Nintendo, 1990
Console game

Ping Pong (see Table Tennis)

Pinochle
Traditional, circa 1900
Card game

Planetfall
Steve Meretsky / Infocom, 1983
Computer game

Pokémon
Nintendo, 1998
Handheld game; Console game; Card game

Poker
Traditional, circa 1820
Card game

Pong
Atari, 1972
Arcade game; Console game; Computer game

Populous: The Beginning
Take-Two Interactive, 1998
Computer game

Powerstone (series)
Capcom, 1999
Console game

Quake (series)
id Software, 1996
Computer game; Online game; Console game

Racquetball
Joe Sobek, 1949
Sport

RAMbots
Kory Heath, 2001
Icehouse game

Risk
Albert Lamorisse, 1959
Board game

Robotron 2084
Williams, 1982
Arcade game

Rock-Paper-Scissors
Traditional
Physical game

Roulette
Traditional, circa 1900
Dice game

Rugby
Traditional, circa 1800
Sport

Scrabble
Alfred M. Butts, 1948
Board game

Seaman
Vivarium, 2000
Console game

Secret of Monkey Island (series)
LucasArts, 1990
Computer game

Settlers of Catan
Klaus Teuber, 1995
Board game

Shenmue (series)
Sega, 2000
Console game

Silent Hill (series)
Konami, 1999
Console game

Sim City (series)
Maxis, 1989
Computer game

Sim Copter
Maxis, 1996
Computer game

SimLife
Maxis, 1992
Computer game

Simon Says
Traditional
Social game

The Sims (series)
Maxis, 2000
Computer game; Console game

SiSSYFiGHT 2000
Word.com, 2000
Online game

Skiing
Traditional, circa 1880
Sport

Soccer
Traditional, circa 1850
Sport

Softball
Traditional, circa 1930
Sport

Solitaire (many variations)
Traditional, circa 1600
Card game

Space Invaders
Taito 1978
Arcade games

Spacewar!
Steve Russell, 1962
Computer game

Spin the Bottle
Traditional
Social game

Spy Vs. Spy (series)
Kemko, 1986
Computer game; Console game

Spybot: The Nightfall Incident
gameLab, 2002
Computer game

SSX (series)
Electronic Arts, 2000
Console game

Stand Up
New Games Movement, circa 1976
Physical game

Starcraft
Blizzard Entertainment, 1998
Computer game

State of Emergency
VIS Entertainment, 2002
Console game

Stay Alive
Milton Bradley, 1971
Board game

Stealth Chess
Dice Corp, 1997
Board game

Stratego
Milton Bradley, 1961
Board game

Street Fighter (series)
Capcom, 1987
Arcade game; Console game

Sumo Wrestling
Traditional, circa 712
Sport

Super Breakout *(see Breakout)*

Super Mario *(see Mario Bros.)*

Super Monkey Ball (series)
Amusement Vision, 2001
GameCube

Survivor
CBS, 2000
Television game show

Suspicion
Eric Zimmerman, 1995
Card game

System Shock (series)
Looking Glass Studios, 1994
Computer game; Console game

Table Tennis
J. Jaques & Son, circa 1890
Sport

Tag
Traditional
Physical game

Tanktics
Chris Crawford, 1978
Computer game

Tekken
Namco, 1995
Arcade game; Console game

Telephone
Traditional
Social game

Tempest
Atari, 1981
Arcade game

Tennis
Walter Wingfield, 1873
Sport

Tetris
Alexy Pajnitov, circa 1986
Computer game; Handheld game; Console game

Thief (series)
Looking Glass Studios, 1998
Computer game

Thin Ice
Jacob Davenport, circa 2001
Icehouse game

Thunderstorm
Traditional
Dice game

Tiddlywinks
Joseph Assheton Fincher, 1888
Physical game

Time Crisis
Namco, 1996
Arcade game; Console game

Tomb Raider (series)
Core Design, 1996
Console game; Computer game

Tony Hawk Pro Skater (series)
Neversoft Entertainment, 1999
Console game

Total Annihilation
Cavedog Entertainment, 1997
Computer game

Toys
Eric Zimmerman, 2000
Social game

Trivial Pursuit
Chris Haney and Scott Abbot, 1981
Board game

Twister
Charles Foley and Neil Rabens, 1966
Physical game

Ultima (series)
Richard Garriot / Origin, 1980
Computer game; Online game

Um Jammer Lammy
Sony, 1999
Console game

Universal Square
Uri Tzaig, 1996
Sport

Uno
Merle Robbins, 1971
Card game

Unreal (series)
Epic Megagames, 1998
Computer game; Console game

Up the River
Manfred Ludwig, 1988
Board game

Vampire
New Games Movement, circa 1976
Physical game

Vampire: The Masquerade
White Wolf, 1992
Role-playing game

Verbal Tennis
Traditional
Social game

Virtua Fighter (series)
Sega, 1993
Arcade game; Console game

Volcano
Kristin Looney, 2002
Icehouse game

Volleyball
William G. Morgan, 1895
Sport

War
Traditional
Card game

Warcraft: Orcs and Humans (series)
Blizzard Entertainment, 1994
Computer game

Warhammer (series)
Games Workshop, 1983
Board game

Who Wants to be a Millionaire
Celador, 1998
Television game show

Wipeout (series)
Psygnosis, 1996
Console game

Wolfenstein 3D
id Software, 1992
Computer game

Wreckless: The Yakuzi Missions
Bunkasha Games, 2002
Console game

Yatzee
Milton Bradley, 1956
Dice game

You Don't Know Jack (series)
Jellyvision, 1995
Computer game; Online game

Zarcana
John Cooper, 2001
Icehouse game

Zaxxon
Sega, 1982
Arcade game

Zelda (series)
Nintendo, 1987
Console game; Handheld game

Zendo
Kory Heath, 2001
Icehouse game

Zork (series)
Marc Blank & Dave Lebling / Infocom, 1980
Computer game

Research References

<http://www.about.com>.

<http://www.atariage.com>.

<http://boardgamegeek.com>.

<http://chessvariants.com>.

<http://www.classicgaming.com >.

<http://www.coinop.com>.

<http://www.classicgaming.com>.

<http://encarta.msn.com>.

<http://www.gamecabinet.com>.

<http://www.gamers.com>.

<http://www.gamefaq.com>.

<http://www.gamespot.com>.

Kent, Stephen L.. *The Ultimate History of Video Games* (Roseville, CA: Prima Publishing, 2001)

<http://www.looneylabs.com>.

<http://www.mobygames.com>.

Parlett, David. *The Oxford Dictionary of Card Games* (New York: Oxford University Press, 1992).

Parlett, David. *The Oxford History of Board Games* (New York: Oxford University Press, 1999).

Scarpone, Desi. *Board Games* (Atglen, PA: Schiffer Publishing, 1995).

INDEX

Father: ...*The point is that the purpose of these conversations is to discover the "rules." It's like life—a game whose purpose is to discover the rules, which rules are always changing and undiscoverable.*

Daughter: *But I don't call that a* game, *Daddy.*

—**Gregory Bateson,** *Steps to an Ecology of Mind*